Koren Talmud Bavli

THE NOÉ EDITION

BAVA BATRA

Steinsaltz Center

KOREN

תלמוד בבלי

KOREN TALMUD BAVLI

THE NOÉ EDITION

בבא בתרא

BAVA BATRA

Daf 61a through Daf 73a

COMMENTARY BY

Rabbi Adin Even-Israel Steinsaltz

EDITOR-IN-CHIEF

Rabbi Dr Tzvi Hersh Weinreb

SENIOR CONTENT EDITOR

Rabbi Dr Shalom Z Berger

EXECUTIVE EDITOR

Rabbi Joshua Schreier

•

STEINSALTZ CENTER

KOREN PUBLISHERS JERUSALEM

Supported by the Matanel Foundation

Koren Talmud Bavli, The Noe Edition
Vol. 23c: Tractate Bava Batra, Daf 61a through Daf 73a
Paperback, ISBN, 978-965-7766-10-1

First Hebrew/English paperback edition, 2021

Koren Publishers Jerusalem Ltd.
PO Box 4044, Jerusalem 91040, ISRAEL
PO Box 8531, New Milford, CT 06776, USA
www.korenpub.com

Steinsaltz Center

Steinsaltz Center is the parent organization of institutions established by Rabbi Adin Even-Israel Steinsaltz

PO Box 45187, Jerusalem 91450 ISRAEL
Telephone: +972 2 646 0900, Fax +972 2 624 9454
www.steinsaltz-center.org

הִנֵּה יָמִים בָּאִים, נְאֻם אֲדֹנָי יֱהוִה, וְהִשְׁלַחְתִּי רָעָב בָּאָרֶץ,
לֹא־רָעָב לַלֶּחֶם וְלֹא־צָמָא לַמַּיִם, כִּי אִם־לִשְׁמֹעַ אֵת דִּבְרֵי יהוה.

Behold, days are coming – says the Lord God – I will send a hunger to the land, not a hunger for bread nor a thirst for water, but to hear the words of the Lord. (AMOS 8:11)

The Noé edition of the Koren Talmud Bavli
with the commentary of Rabbi Adin Even-Israel Steinsaltz
is dedicated to all those who open its covers
to quench their thirst for Jewish Knowledge,
in our generation of Torah renaissance.

This beautiful edition is for the young, the aged,
the novice and the savant alike,
as it unites the depth of Torah knowledge
with the best of academic scholarship.

Within its exquisite and vibrant pages,
words become worlds.

It will claim its place in the library of classics,
in the bookcases of the Beit Midrash,
the classrooms of our schools,
and in the offices of professionals and business people
who carve out precious time to grapple with its timeless wisdom.

For the Student and the Scholar

DEDICATED BY LEO AND SUE NOÉ

Steinsaltz Center

Executive Director, Steinsaltz Center

Rabbi Meni Even-Israel

Managing Editor

Rabbi Jason Rappoport

Senior Content Editor

Rabbi Dr. Shalom Z. Berger

Editors

Rabbi Dr. Joshua Amaru, *Coordinating Editor*
Rabbi Yehoshua Duker, *Final Editor*
Rabbi Avishai Magence, *Content Curator*
Yedidya Naveh, *Content Curator*
Tal Avrahami
Menucha Chwat
Rabbi Adin Krohn
Betzalel Philip Edwards
Rabbi Yonatan Shai Freedman
Raphael Friedman
Rabbi Ayal Geffon
Rabbi Uri Goldstein
Nechama Greenberg
Rabbi Tzvi Chaim Kaye
Rabbi Yonatan Kohn
Catriel Lev
Elisha Loewenstern
Adina Luber
Rabbi Simcha Mirvis
Rabbi Jonathan Mishkin
Rabbi David Sedley
Avi Steinhart
Rabbi David Strauss
Rabbi Yitzchak Twersky

Copy Editors

Aliza Israel, *Coordinator*
Ita Olesker
Debbie Ismailoff
Shira Finson
Ilana Sobel
Deena Nataf
Eliana Kurlantzick Yorav
Erica Hirsch Edvi
Nava Wieder
Sara Henna Dahan
Shalom Dinerstein

Language Consultants

Dr. Stephanie E. Binder, *Greek & Latin*
Rabbi Yaakov Hoffman, *Arabic*
Dr. Shai Secunda, *Persian*
Shira Shmidman, *Aramaic*

KOREN

Design & Typesetting

Dena Landowne Bailey, *Typesetting*
Tani Bayer, *Jacket Design*
Raphaël Freeman, *Design & Typography*

Images

Eliahu Misgav, *Illustration & Image Acquisition*
Daniel Gdalevich, *Illustration & Image Acquisition*

Introduction by the Publisher

The Talmud has sustained and inspired Jews for thousands of years. Throughout Jewish history, an elite cadre of scholars has absorbed its learning and passed it on to succeeding generations. The Talmud has been the fundamental text of our people.

Beginning in the 1960s, Rabbi Adin Even-Israel Steinsaltz שליט״א created a revolution in the history of Talmud study. His translation of the Talmud, first into modern Hebrew and then into other languages, as well the practical learning aids he added to the text, have enabled millions of people around the world to access and master the complexity and context of the world of Talmud.

It is thus a privilege to present the *Koren Talmud Bavli*, an English translation of the talmudic text with the brilliant elucidation of Rabbi Steinsaltz. The depth and breadth of his knowledge are unique in our time. His rootedness in the tradition and his reach into the world beyond it are inspirational.

Working with Rabbi Steinsaltz on this remarkable project has been not only an honor, but a great pleasure. Never shy to express an opinion, with wisdom and humor, Rabbi Steinsaltz sparkles in conversation, demonstrating his knowledge (both sacred and worldly), sharing his wide-ranging interests, and, above all, radiating his passion. I am grateful for the unique opportunity to work closely with him, and I wish him many more years of writing and teaching.

Our intentions in publishing this new edition of the Talmud are threefold. First, we seek to fully clarify the talmudic page to the reader – textually, intellectually, and graphically. Second, we seek to utilize today's most sophisticated technologies, both in print and electronic formats, to provide the reader with a comprehensive set of study tools. And third, we seek to help readers advance in their process of Talmud study.

To achieve these goals, the *Koren Talmud Bavli* is unique in a number of ways:

- The classic *tzurat hadaf* of Vilna, used by scholars since the 1800s, has been reset for great clarity, and opens from the Hebrew "front" of the book. Full *nikkud* has been added to both the talmudic text and Rashi's commentary, allowing for a more fluent reading with the correct pronunciation; the commentaries of *Tosafot* have been punctuated. Upon the advice of many English-speaking teachers of Talmud, we have separated these core pages from the translation, thereby enabling the advanced student to approach the text without the distraction of the translation. This also reduces the number of volumes in the set. At the bottom of each *daf*, there is a reference to the corresponding English pages. In addition, the Vilna edition was read against other manuscripts and older print editions, so that texts which had been removed by non-Jewish censors have been restored to their rightful place.
- The English translation, which starts on the English "front" of the book, reproduces the *menukad* Talmud text alongside the English translation (in bold) and commentary and explanation (in a lighter font). The Hebrew and Aramaic text is presented in logical paragraphs. This allows for a fluent reading of the text for the non-Hebrew or non-Aramaic reader. It also allows for the Hebrew reader to refer easily to the text alongside. Where the original text features dialogue or poetry, the English text is laid out in a manner appropriate to the genre. Each page refers to the relevant *daf*.

- Critical contextual tools surround the text and translation: personality notes, providing short biographies of the Sages; language notes, explaining foreign terms borrowed from Greek, Latin, Persian, or Arabic; and background notes, giving information essential to the understanding of the text, including history, geography, botany, archaeology, zoology, astronomy, and aspects of daily life in the talmudic era.
- Halakhic summaries provide references to the authoritative legal decisions made over the centuries by the rabbis. They explain the reasons behind each halakhic decision as well as the ruling's close connection to the Talmud and its various interpreters.
- Photographs, drawings, and other illustrations have been added throughout the text – in full color in the Standard and Electronic editions, and in black and white in the Daf Yomi edition – to visually elucidate the text.

This is not an exhaustive list of features of this edition, it merely presents an overview for the English-speaking reader who may not be familiar with the "total approach" to Talmud pioneered by Rabbi Steinsaltz.

Several professionals have helped bring this vast collaborative project to fruition. My many colleagues are noted on the Acknowledgments page, and the leadership of this project has been exceptional.

RABBI MENACHEM EVEN-ISRAEL, DIRECTOR OF THE STEINSALTZ CENTER, was the driving force behind this enterprise. With enthusiasm and energy, he formed the happy alliance with Koren and established close relationships among all involved in the work.

RABBI DR. TZVI HERSH WEINREB שליט״א, EDITOR-IN-CHIEF, brought to this project his profound knowledge of Torah, intellectual literacy of Talmud, and erudition of Western literature. It is to him that the text owes its very high standard, both in form and content, and the logical manner in which the beauty of the Talmud is presented.

RABBI JOSHUA SCHREIER, EXECUTIVE EDITOR, assembled an outstanding group of scholars, translators, editors, and proofreaders, whose standards and discipline enabled this project to proceed in a timely and highly professional manner.

RABBI MEIR HANEGBI, EDITOR OF THE HEBREW EDITION OF THE STEINSALTZ TALMUD, lent his invaluable assistance throughout the work process, supervising the reproduction of the Vilna pages.

RAPHAËL FREEMAN, EXECUTIVE EDITOR OF KOREN, created this Talmud's unique typographic design which, true to the Koren approach, is both elegant and user friendly.

It has been an enriching experience for all of us at Koren Publishers Jerusalem to work with the Steinsaltz Center to develop and produce the *Koren Talmud Bavli*. We pray that this publication will be a source of great learning and, ultimately, greater *avodat Hashem* for all Jews.

Matthew Miller, Publisher
Koren Publishers Jerusalem
Jerusalem 5772

Contents

For the vocalized Vilna Shas layout, please open as a Hebrew book.

Introduction to **Perek IV**

This chapter discusses the interpretation of sales agreements and contracts relating to various types of landed properties.

When a buyer and seller draw up a detailed agreement defining all the particulars of a transaction, it is clear what exactly is being sold and what is not. Since this is a monetary matter, the parties are entitled to introduce stipulations and conditions as they wish.

The chapter examines sales that are formulated in general terms, and it discusses how to interpret the wording of general sales agreements for the sale of different types of real estate.

As the Gemara phrases it, the central question is as follows: When one sells property, does he sell it generously or sparingly? In other words, should a sales agreement be interpreted in a way that expands the rights of the buyer or in a manner that restricts them as much as possible? This issue gives rise to secondary questions, e.g., whether there is a difference with regard to this matter in the case of a sale and in the case of a gift, and whether land that was consecrated using general wording is treated in yet another manner.

Many questions arise with regard to the details of these issues. Some of the questions relate to the limits of what is being sold. When one sells a house, does the sale include rooms that open into the house? When one sells a field but fails to define its boundaries in their entirety, what is included in the sale? What rights, if any, does the buyer have to the land underneath the property he purchases or the airspace above it?

Another topic of discussion relates to the items found in the property being sold. When one sells a house, are all or only some of its accompaniments included in the sale? Does the sale include the furniture and other items located in the house at that time? With regard to the sale of buildings that serve a particular purpose, such as an olive press or a bathhouse, which accompaniments are considered an integral part of the building and are therefore included in the sale, and which are not? Does the sale of a courtyard include all of the houses and the accompaniments in that courtyard? With regard to the sale of a field or a vineyard, does the sale include the utensils and equipment needed to cultivate it? Does such a sale also include any buildings or trees located in the field or vineyard?

This chapter's primary concern is the detailed clarification of these issues.

מתני׳ הַמּוֹכֵר אֶת הַבַּיִת – לֹא מָכַר יָצִיעַ, וְאַף עַל פִּי שֶׁהִיא פְּתוּחָה לְתוֹכוֹ; וְלֹא אֶת הַחֶדֶר שֶׁלִּפְנִים הֵימֶנּוּ; וְלֹא אֶת הַגַּג בִּזְמַן שֶׁיֵּשׁ לוֹ מַעֲקֶה גָּבוֹהַּ עֲשָׂרָה טְפָחִים; רַבִּי יְהוּדָה אוֹמֵר: אִם יֵשׁ לוֹ צוּרַת פֶּתַח, אַף עַל פִּי שֶׁאֵינוֹ גָּבוֹהַּ עֲשָׂרָה טְפָחִים – אֵינוֹ מָכוּר.

MISHNA One **who sells a house** without specifying what is included in the sale **has not sold the gallery,**[H] an extension built above or alongside the main building, **and** this is so **even if** the gallery is attached to the house and **opens into it. Nor** has he sold **the room**[HN] **behind** the house, even if it is accessible only from inside the house. He has **also not** sold **the roof**[H] **when it has a parapet**[N] **ten handbreadths high,** as such a roof is considered a separate entity and is therefore not included in the sale of the house. **Rabbi Yehuda says: If** the parapet **has the form of a doorway,**[N] that is, if it consists of two upright posts with a beam crossing over them, then **even if** the parapet **is not ten handbreadths high,** the roof **is not sold** together with the house, unless it is specifically included in the sale.

גמ׳ מַאי יָצִיעַ? הָכָא תַּרְגִּימוּ: אַפְּתָא. רַב יוֹסֵף אָמַר: בִּדְקָא חֲלִילָה. לְמַאן דְּאָמַר אַפְּתָא לָא מִזְדַּבְנָא, כָּל שֶׁכֵּן בִּדְקָא חֲלִילָה לָא מִזְדַּבְנָא; לְמַאן דְּאָמַר בִּדְקָא חֲלִילָה, אֲבָל אַפְּתָא מִזְדַּבְנָא.

GEMARA What is a gallery? Here in Babylonia **they interpreted** this as referring to **an attic** [***apta***].[LN] **Rav Yosef said:** It means **a windowed structure** [***bidka ḥalila***][N] attached to the main building. The Gemara notes that **according to the one who says** that **an attic is not sold** together with a house, **all the more so is a windowed structure** attached to the house **not sold** together with a house, as it is certainly considered a separate entity and not part of the main building. But **according to the one who says** that a gallery is **a windowed structure** attached to the house, it is only such a structure that is not included in the sale of the house, **but an attic is sold** together with a house.

תָּאנֵי רַב יוֹסֵף, שָׁלֹשׁ שֵׁמוֹת יֵשׁ לוֹ: יָצִיעַ, צֶלַע, תָּא; יָצִיעַ – דִּכְתִיב: ״הַיָּצִיעַ הַתַּחְתֹּנָה חָמֵשׁ בָּאַמָּה רָחְבָּהּ״. צֶלַע – דִּכְתִיב: ״וְהַצְּלָעוֹת צֵלָע אֶל צֵלָע שָׁלֹשׁ וּשְׁלֹשִׁים פְּעָמִים״. תָּא – דִּכְתִיב: ״וְהַתָּא קָנֶה אֶחָד אֹרֶךְ וְקָנֶה אֶחָד רֹחַב וּבֵין הַתָּאִים חָמֵשׁ אַמּוֹת״. וְאִי בָּעֵית אֵימָא, מֵהָכָא: כּוֹתֶל הַהֵיכָל שֵׁשׁ, וְהַתָּא שֵׁשׁ, כּוֹתֶל הַתָּא חָמֵשׁ.

Rav Yosef taught: A small structure attached to a building **has three names** in the Bible: **Gallery** [***yatzia***], **side chamber** [***tzela***], and **cell** [***ta***]. Such a structure is called **a gallery, as it is written: "The bottommost gallery** [***hayyatzia***] **was five cubits wide"** (I Kings 6:6). It is also called **a side chamber, as it is written: "And the side chambers** [***vehatzelaot***] **were one over another, thirty-three times"** (Ezekiel 41:6). Additionally, it is called **a cell, as it is written: "And the cell** [***vehata***] **was one reed long, and one reed wide; and the space between the cells was five cubits"** (Ezekiel 40:7). **And if you wish, say** instead that it can be seen that a small structure attached to a building is called a cell **from here,** as was taught in the mishna (*Middot* 4:7): **The wall of the Sanctuary** was **six** cubits wide, **and the cell** [***vehata***] in back of it was **six** cubits wide, and **the wall of the cell** was **five** cubits wide.

HALAKHA

One who sells a house without specifying what is included in the sale has not sold the gallery – הַמּוֹכֵר אֶת הַבַּיִת לֹא מָכַר יָצִיעַ: One who sells a house has not sold the gallery built around the house if it is more than four cubits wide, even if it is accessible only via the house (*Sma*). But if it is less than four cubits wide it is part of the house and is included in the sale, even if it is not accessible via the house (Rema, citing *Tur*). This is in accordance with Rav Yosef's interpretation of a gallery and the opinion of Mar Zutra. Similarly, an attic that is built on top of a house and opens into it, even if it measures four cubits, is part of the house (Rambam *Sefer Kinyan*, *Hilkhot Mekhira* 25:1; *Shulḥan Arukh*, *Ḥoshen Mishpat* 214:1).

Nor has he sold the room – וְלֹא אֶת הַחֶדֶר: One who sells a house has not sold the room behind it, even if it is accessible only via the house (*Kesef Mishne*, citing Rashbam). The Rosh and Ramban say that if it is less than four cubits wide it is part of the house (Rambam *Sefer Kinyan*, *Hilkhot Mekhira* 25:2; *Shulḥan Arukh*, *Ḥoshen Mishpat* 214:2).

Also not the roof – וְלֹא אֶת הַגַּג: When one sells a house, if the roof is four cubits wide and it has a parapet ten handbreadths high, he has not sold the roof (Rambam *Sefer Kinyan*, *Hilkhot Mekhira* 25:2; *Shulḥan Arukh*, *Ḥoshen Mishpat* 214:2).

LANGUAGE

Attic [*apta*] – אַפְּתָא: The source of this word is unclear. Some trace it to the Greek word ὕψος, *hupsos*, meaning high or uppermost. This supports the explanation offered by several commentaries that *apta* means attic. Others maintain that it is an Aramaic word derived from the Assyrian phrase: *Beit ipti*, meaning: A room attached to a house.

NOTES

Nor has he sold the room – וְלֹא אֶת הַחֶדֶר: Even if it is accessible only from inside the house, it is still considered a separate entity. According to Rabbeinu Gershom, this room is not used as full-time living quarters, but only for storage or sleeping. Other early commentaries understand that, unlike a gallery, this room is not structurally part of the house; rather, it stands on its own behind the house (Rabbeinu Yona; Ritva).

When it has a parapet – שֶׁיֵּשׁ לוֹ מַעֲקֶה: This is so because a roof that has a parapet is put to use, and it is therefore considered a separate entity. Additionally, since the roof is surrounded by a significant parapet, it is deemed a significant place in itself. The Ritva understands that, according to the Jerusalem Talmud, the reference here is to a roof that is covered and enclosed by partitions.

If the parapet has the form of a doorway – אִם יֵשׁ לוֹ צוּרַת פֶּתַח: The Ramah interprets this as a roof with a parapet on three of its sides, and a doorway on its fourth side.

An attic – אַפְּתָא: Most commentaries interpret this word to mean some sort of attic, based, among other indications, upon its use above (60a). Others explain that it is referring to an ordinary room that is especially tall (Rabbeinu Ḥananel, citing one of the *ge'onim*; Rabbeinu Gershom). Some suggest that it means a small structure built upon projections inside the house or over the entrance to the house (Ri Migash). The Rif and others interpret it as an upper story built on the roof, which can be accessed only via the house. Rabbeinu Barukh explains that it is a low structure inside the house, while the Rashbam describes it as a low structure built outside, adjacent to the wall of the house.

Windowed structure [*bidka ḥalila*] – בִּדְקָא חֲלִילָה: The Rif interprets this as a room built within the outer wall of the house. There were structures with walls that were fashioned of two partitions (see *Middot* 4:3–7), so that a small room could be contained between the inner and outer partition. He also suggests that it is a structure built around its outer wall. Rabbeinu Barukh describes it as a room protruding from the house's external wall. Similarly, Rabbeinu Gershom explains it as a corridor built in front of the house. The Rashbam also interprets it as a low structure alongside the house, but adds that it has many windows. Each of these explanations assumes a different meaning for the word *ḥalila*.

NOTES

When it has an area of at least four by four cubits – דְּהָוֵי אַרְבַּע אַמּוֹת: The Rashbam explains, as does the Jerusalem Talmud, that since the gallery is a significant place of four by four cubits, the seller does not include it in the sale of his house. According to the Rambam, four cubits in width suffices to make the place significant. In the Jerusalem Talmud, Rabbi Ḥiyya bar Abba states that the gallery must be covered and enclosed with partitions (see Ritva). The Ramban holds that the same is true for a room that is behind the house, but the Rashba disputes this.

Gallery – יָצִיעַ: The Rashbam understands that people use a gallery in a manner similar to the way they use a house. This is true even if it is a windowed structure, as it is used as a place to rest (*Nimmukei Yosef*). This is not the case with regard to a room behind the house, which is used solely for storage. Other early commentaries understand that a gallery is structurally part of the house and does not stand on its own separate land, whereas a room behind the house is built as a separate structure on its own land (Rabbeinu Barukh; Rabbeinu Yona).

BACKGROUND

Cistern [*dut*] – דּוּת: This word appears in ancient Aramaic, Arabic, and in other sources in the form of *ḥadut*. It refers to a place built for gathering water or produce. A pit and a cistern serve the same purpose, but a pit is dug into the ground or rock, whereas a cistern is a stone structure built above the ground.

אֲמַר מָר זוּטְרָא: וְהוּא דְּהָוֵי אַרְבַּע אַמּוֹת.

§ Relating to the mishna's statement that a gallery is not included in the sale of a house, **Mar Zutra said: And that** is the *halakha* only **when** the gallery **has** an area of at least **four** by four **cubits.**[N]

אֲמַר לֵיהּ רָבִינָא לְמָר זוּטְרָא: לְדִידָךְ, דְּאָמְרַתְּ עַד דְּהָוֵי אַרְבַּע אַמּוֹת, אֶלָּא מֵעַתָּה, גַּבֵּי בּוֹר דִּתְנַן: לֹא אֶת הַבּוֹר וְלֹא אֶת הַדּוּת, אַף עַל פִּי שֶׁכָּתַב לוֹ ״עוּמְקָא וְרוּמָא״, הָכִי נַמֵי אִי הָווּ אַרְבַּע אַמּוֹת – אִין, אִי לָא – לָא?

Ravina said to Mar Zutra: According to your opinion, **that you say** a gallery is not excluded from the sale of a house **unless it is** at least **four** by four **cubits** in size, there is a difficulty. As **if that is so,** then **with regard to** the exclusion of **a pit** or a cistern from the sale of a house, **about which we learned** in a mishna (64a): One who sells a house has sold **neither the pit nor the cistern,**[B] **even if he writes for** the buyer in the bill of sale that he is selling **him the depth and the height** of the house; **so too,** should we say that only **if they have** an area of at least **four** by four **cubits, yes,** they are excluded from the sale of the house, but **if not, no,** they are not excluded? This is difficult, as a pit is not four cubits wide, and consequently, it would never be excluded.

הָכִי הָשְׁתָּא?! הָתָם הָא תַּשְׁמִישְׁתָּא לְחוּד וְהָא תַּשְׁמִישְׁתָּא לְחוּד, הָכָא אִידֵי וְאִידֵי חֲדָא תַּשְׁמִישְׁתָּא הִיא, אִי הָוֵי אַרְבַּע אַמּוֹת – חָשִׁיב, וְאִי לָא – לָא חָשִׁיב.

Mar Zutra responded: **How can** these cases **be compared? There,** in that mishna, **this,** the excavations, have **a discrete use,** to store water, and they cannot possibly be used as living quarters, **and that,** the house, has **a discrete use,** to serve as living quarters, and so they are considered separate entities even if the excavation is not four cubits wide. But **here,** in the case of a gallery, both **this,** the gallery, **and that,** the house, **have the same use,** and so if the gallery **is** at least **four** by four **cubits** it is deemed **significant** and considered a separate entity, **but if** it is **not** four by four cubits, it is **not** deemed **significant** in its own right, but simply another part of the house.

״וְלֹא אֶת הַחֶדֶר שֶׁלְּפָנִים הֵימֶנּוּ״. הַשְׁתָּא יָצִיעַ לָא מִיזְדַּבַּן, חֶדֶר מִיבַּעְיָא?!

The mishna teaches that one who sells a house without specifying what is included in the sale has not sold the gallery, **nor** has he sold **the room behind** the house, even if it is accessible only **from it.** The Gemara asks: **Now** that the mishna taught that **a gallery**[N] **is not sold** along with the house, **is it necessary** to teach that **a room** behind the house is not included in such a sale?

Perek **IV**
Daf **61** Amud **b**

לָא צְרִיכָא, דְּאַף עַל גַּב דִּמְצַר לֵיהּ מִצְרֵי אַבְרָאֵי;

No, this ruling is **necessary** to teach that the room behind the house is excluded from the sale of the house **even if** the seller **delineated**[H] **the boundaries** of the house **for** the buyer in the bill of sale by listing places **outside**[N] the room, e.g., noting the houses that border the property being sold. Even though this might suggest that the room is included in the sale, the mishna teaches that it is not.

HALAKHA

Even if the seller delineated – אַף עַל גַּב דִּמְצַר לֵיהּ: One who sells a house has not sold the room behind the house even if he delineated the boundaries of the house in the bill of sale by listing places that are outside the room, and even if he wrote: And I have not withheld anything for myself in this sale (*Tur*), as a room is not called a house. Some (*Nimmukei Yosef*) maintain that if he wrote: And I have not withheld anything for myself in this sale, the room is included in the sale (Rambam *Sefer Kinyan*, *Hilkhot Mekhira* 25:2; *Shulḥan Arukh*, *Ḥoshen Mishpat* 214:2, and in the comment of Rema).

NOTES

Delineated the boundaries for him outside – מְצַר לֵיהּ מִצְרֵי אַבְרָאֵי: This means that the seller describes the boundaries of the house he is selling by noting the houses or courtyards upon which it borders. This account encompasses the entire external structure of the house, including the room that is located behind the house. Nevertheless, since the room is distinguished from the house in the way that it is used (Rashbam), or with regard to the land upon which it stands, it is assumed that the seller did not mean to include it in the sale, but simply delineated the boundaries in a broad manner.

כְּדְרַב נַחְמָן, דְּאָמַר רַב נַחְמָן אָמַר רַבָּה בַּר אֲבוּהּ: הַמּוֹכֵר בַּיִת לַחֲבֵירוֹ בְּבִירָה גְּדוֹלָה, אַף עַל פִּי שֶׁמָּצַר לוֹ מְצָרִים הַחִיצוֹנִים – מְצָרִים הִרְחִיב לוֹ.

This is **in accordance with** the opinion **of Rav Naḥman, as Rav Naḥman says that Rabba bar Avuh says:** With regard to one **who sells a residence to another in a large building** [*bira*][NHL] containing several residences, **even if he delineates for him the external boundaries** of the large building, he did not sell him the entire building, but rather **he enlarged** upon **the boundaries for him.**[N] That is, the seller did not mean to delineate the precise borders of what he was selling; rather, he delineated the boundaries in a broad manner, giving the general location of the specific residence subject to the transaction.

הֵיכִי דָמֵי? אִילֵימָא דְּקָרוּ לֵיהּ לְבַיִת בַּיִת, וְלְבִירָה בִּירָה – פְּשִׁיטָא, בַּיִת זַבֵּין לֵיהּ, בִּירָה לָא זַבֵּין לֵיהּ! אֶלָּא דְּלְבִירָה נַמִּי קָרוּ לָהּ בַּיִת – כּוּלֵּיהּ זַבֵּין לֵיהּ!

With regard to Rav Naḥman's statement, the Gemara inquires: **What are the circumstances** of the case? **If we say** that this is referring to a place **where they call a residence a residence, and a building a building,** and they always differentiate between the two terms, it is **obvious** that he did not intend to sell him the entire building but merely enlarged upon the boundaries for him, as **he sold him a residence** and **did not sell him a large building. Rather,** explain that this is referring to a place **where they also call a building a residence.** But in that case, why not say that the seller **sold him the entire** building, since he delineated the external boundaries of the large building?

לָא צְרִיכָא, דְּרוּבָּא קָרוּ לֵיהּ לְבַיִת בַּיִת, לְבִירָה בִּירָה, וְאִיכָּא נַמִּי דְּלְבִירָה קָרוּ לֵיהּ בַּיִת. מַהוּ דְּתֵימָא כּוּלֵּיהּ זַבֵּין לֵיהּ, קָא מַשְׁמַע לַן, מִדַּהֲוָה לֵיהּ לְמִכְתַּב "וְלָא שַׁיְּירִית בִּזְבִינַי אִלֵּין כְּלוּם" וְלָא כְּתַב, שְׁמַע מִינַּהּ: שִׁיּוּרֵי שַׁיֵּיר.

The Gemara answers: **No,** Rav Naḥman's ruling is **necessary** in a place **where most** of the people **call a residence a residence,** and **a building** they call **a building, but there are also** some people **who call a building a residence. Lest you say** that since the seller delineated the building's external boundaries, this indicates that he meant to **sell him the entire** building, Rav Naḥman **teaches us** that this is not so. **As,** if the seller intended to sell him the entire building, **he would have written** in the bill of sale: **And I have not withheld anything** for myself **in this sale, but** if **he did not write** this clause, **conclude from it** that the seller **withheld** something for himself and did not mean to sell everything located within the delineated boundaries.

וְאָמַר רַב נַחְמָן אָמַר רַבָּה בַּר אֲבוּהּ: הַמּוֹכֵר שָׂדֶה לַחֲבֵירוֹ בְּבִקְעָה גְּדוֹלָה, אַף עַל פִּי שֶׁמָּצַר לוֹ מְצָרִים הַחִיצוֹנִים – מְצָרִים הִרְחִיב לוֹ.

And in a similar fashion, **Rav Naḥman says** that **Rabba bar Avuh says:** With regard to one **who sells a field to another in a large expanse of fields,**[H] **even if he delineates for him the external boundaries** of the large expanse of fields he did not sell him the entire expanse of fields; rather, **he enlarged** upon **the boundaries for him.** That is, the seller did not mean to delineate the precise borders of what was being sold; rather, he delineated the boundaries in a broad manner, giving the general location of the particular field he was selling.

הֵיכִי דָמֵי? אִילֵימָא דְּקָרוּ לֵיהּ לְשָׂדֶה שָׂדֶה, וְלְבִקְעָה בִּקְעָה – פְּשִׁיטָא, שָׂדֶה זַבֵּין לֵיהּ, בִּקְעָה לָא זַבֵּין לֵיהּ! וְאֶלָּא דְּלְבִקְעָה נַמִּי קָרוּ לָהּ שָׂדֶה – כּוּלָּהּ זַבֵּין לֵיהּ!

The Gemara inquires: **What are the circumstances** of the case? **If we say** that this is referring to a place **where they call a field a field, and an expanse of fields an expanse of fields,** and always differentiate between the two terms, it is **obvious** the he did not intend to sell him the entire expanse of fields, as **he sold him a field** and **did not sell him an expanse of fields. Rather,** explain that this is referring to a place **where they also call an expanse of fields a field.** But in that case, why not say that the seller **sold him the entire** expanse of fields, since he delineated the external boundaries of the expanse of fields?

לָא צְרִיכָא, דְּאִיכָּא דְּלְשָׂדֶה קָרוּ לֵיהּ שָׂדֶה, וּלְבִקְעָה – בִּקְעָה, וְאִיכָּא נַמִּי דְּלְבִקְעָה קָרוּ לָהּ שָׂדֶה, מַהוּ דְּתֵימָא כּוּלֵּיהּ זַבֵּין לֵיהּ, קָא מַשְׁמַע לַן, מִדַּהֲוָה לֵיהּ לְמִכְתַּב לֵיהּ "לָא שַׁיְּירִית בִּזְבִינַי אִלֵּין קֳדָמַי כְּלוּם" וְלָא כְּתַב לֵיהּ, שְׁמַע מִינַּהּ: שִׁיּוּרֵי שַׁיֵּיר.

The Gemara answers: **No,** Rav Naḥman's ruling is **necessary** in a place **where there are** some people **who call a field a field, and an expanse of fields** they call **an expanse of fields, but there are also** some people **who call an expanse of fields a field. Lest you say** that since the seller delineated the expanse's external boundaries, this indicates that he meant to **sell him the entire** expanse, Rav Naḥman **teaches us** that this is not so. **As,** if the seller intended to sell him the entire expanse, **he would have written for him** in the bill of sale: And **I have not withheld anything for myself in this sale, but** since **he did not write** this clause **for him, conclude from it** that the seller **withheld** something for himself and did not mean to sell everything located within the delineated boundaries.

NOTES

Large building – בִּירָה גְּדוֹלָה: The Rashbam explains that this large building is a central structure, like a grand entrance hall, which leads to the various residences that open from it. Rabbeinu Gershom describes it as a large structure, such as a building containing many different residences (see 6b). Rabbeinu Barukh writes that the reference here is to a large building or palace that contains various units, e.g., storerooms, washrooms, and the like.

Has enlarged upon the boundaries for him – מְצָרִים הִרְחִיב לוֹ: Recording a property's boundaries in a deed of sale can be understood in two ways. It can be understood as a record of the precise boundaries of the property being sold. This is particularly important when there is no clear boundary between the property being sold and the adjacent property. Alternatively, it can be understood as a sort of address, through which the identity of the property can be established. When understood in this manner, the address might not be defined in a precise manner; rather, the property is identified as being located within a general area. This is somewhat similar to noting a street name and building number in our time, without recording the precise apartment. Rav Naḥman established the criteria for determining in which sense the boundaries of a property are being delineated. When the seller inserts the clause: I have not withheld anything for myself in this sale, he is recording the precise boundaries of the property, but when he omits this clause, he is simply giving an address-type definition of the property, without specifying its exact boundaries.

HALAKHA

One who sells a residence to another in a large building – הַמּוֹכֵר בַּיִת לַחֲבֵירוֹ בְּבִירָה גְּדוֹלָה: One who sells a residence in a large building, even if he delineates for the buyer the external boundaries of the large building, and even if some of the people in that place refer to a large building as a residence, has, nevertheless, sold only the residence. The large building referred to here is one used not for living quarters, but only to access the smaller houses attached to it, and the seller stood in one of those houses and said to the buyer: I am selling you this residence (*Tur*). Had the seller intended to sell the entire building, he would have written in the bill of sale: I have not withheld anything for myself in this sale. If most of the people in that place use the term residence for the entire building, the seller acquires the entire building (*Sma*). If no one in that place uses the term residence for a building, the buyer acquires only the residence in any case. The Rema adds that in a place where everyone uses the term residence for the entire building, and reference to an individual residence must be made in an explicit manner, the seller acquires the entire building even if its external boundaries were not delineated (Rambam *Sefer Kinyan*, *Hilkhot Mekhira* 21:17; *Shulḥan Arukh*, *Ḥoshen Mishpat* 214:7).

One who sells a field to another in a large expanse of fields – הַמּוֹכֵר שָׂדֶה לַחֲבֵירוֹ בְּבִקְעָה גְּדוֹלָה: If one owned an expanse of fields, each field having defined boundaries, and the owner stood in one field and said to another: I am selling you a field (*Sma*), he has sold him only that field. This is so even if he delineated the boundaries of the entire expanse of fields, and there are some people who use the term field for the entire expanse. If most of the people in that area use the term field for the entire expanse of fields, or if the seller explicitly writes: I have not withheld anything for myself in this sale, the buyer acquires the entire expanse of fields (*Sma*). According to the Rema, he also acquires the entire expanse if the fields have no boundaries differentiating between them (Rambam *Sefer Kinyan*, *Hilkhot Mekhira* 21:17; *Shulḥan Arukh*, *Ḥoshen Mishpat* 218:22).

LANGUAGE

Building [*bira*] – בִּירָה: This word has a parallel in Assyrian meaning fortress. In biblical and rabbinic Hebrew, it has several interconnected meanings. Here the word means large building.

וּצְרִיכָא, דְּאִי אַשְׁמְעִינַן בַּיִת – מִשּׁוּם דְּהָא תַּשְׁמִישְׁתָּא לְחוּד וְהָא תַּשְׁמִישְׁתָּא לְחוּד, אֲבָל בִּקְעָה דְּכוּלַּהּ חֲדָא תַּשְׁמִישְׁתָּא הִיא – אֵימָא כּוּלַּהּ זַבֵּין לֵיהּ;

The Gemara notes: **And** it was **necessary** for Rav Naḥman to teach the *halakha* in both cases, even though the two rulings appear to be the same. **As had he taught us** the *halakha* only in the case of the **residence**, that he did not sell him the entire building even if he delineated the building's external boundaries, I might have said that this is **due to** the fact **that this,** the residence, has **a discrete use,** separate from that of the rest of the building, **and that,** the building, has **a discrete use. But** as for **an expanse of fields, all of which has a single use,** since it can be sown with grain in its entirety, **say** that the seller **sold him the entire** expanse.

וְאִי אַשְׁמְעִינַן בִּקְעָה – מִשּׁוּם דְּלָא הֲוָה לֵיהּ לְמִימְצַר לֵיהּ, אֲבָל בַּיִת דַּהֲוָה לֵיהּ לְמִימְצַר לֵיהּ וְלָא מְצַר לֵיהּ – כּוּלֵּיהּ זַבֵּין לֵיהּ, צְרִיכָא.

And had Rav Naḥman **taught us** the *halakha* only in the case of **an expanse of fields,** that he did not sell him the entire expanse even if he delineated its external boundaries, I might have said that this is **due to** the fact **that** the seller **had no way to delineate** the particular field's boundaries, since all of the fields are similar, and they all belong to the seller. **But** as for **a residence, with regard to which** the seller **had** a way **to delineate** its borders, through the use of descriptive terms that would isolate it from the rest of the building, **but he did not delineate** them, I might say that **he sold him the entire** building. Therefore, it was **necessary** to mention both cases explicitly.

כְּמַאן אָזְלָא הָא דְּאָמַר רַב מָרִי בְּרֵיהּ דְּבַת שְׁמוּאֵל (בַּר שֵׁילַת) מִשְּׁמֵיהּ דְּאַבָּיֵי: הַאי מַאן דְּמְזַבֵּין לֵיהּ מִידֵּי לְחַבְרֵיהּ, צָרִיךְ לְמִכְתַּב לֵיהּ ״לָא שַׁיְירִית בִּזְבִינַי אִלֵּין קַדְמַי כְּלוּם״, כְּמַאן? כְּרַב נַחְמָן אָמַר רַבָּה בַּר אֲבוּהּ.

The Gemara asks: **In accordance with whose** opinion **is that which Rav Mari, son of the daughter of Shmuel,**[P] **said in the name of Abaye: One who sells something to another must write for him**[H] in the bill of sale: **I have not withheld anything for myself in this sale. In accordance with whose** opinion is that? It is **in accordance with** the opinion of **Rav Naḥman,** who says that **Rabba bar Avuh says** that even when the seller delineates the boundaries of what he is selling, he does not necessarily mean to sell everything included within those boundaries. Inserting this clause in the bill of sale removes uncertainties that could lead to conflict.

הַהוּא דַּאֲמַר לֵיהּ לְחַבְרֵיהּ: ״אַרְעָא דְּבֵי חִיָּיא מְזַבֵּנְנָא לָךְ״, הֲוַאי לֵיהּ תַּרְתֵּי אַרְעָתָא דַּהֲוָה מִתְקַרְיָין ״דְּבֵי חִיָּיא״. אָמַר רַב אָשֵׁי: חֲדָא אֲמַר לֵיהּ, תַּרְתֵּי לָא אֲמַר לֵיהּ.

The Gemara relates: There was **a certain** man **who said to another: I am selling you land of the house of Ḥiyya,**[H] but **there were two** plots of **land that were called** that **of the house of Ḥiyya,** and the Sages deliberated as to whether both were included in this sale or only one. **Rav Ashi said: He said to him** that he was selling him **one** plot of land,[N] and **he did not say to him** that he was selling him **two** plots of land, as he employed a singular term. Therefore, only one is included in the sale.

וְאִי אֲמַר לֵיהּ ״אַרְעָתָא״ סְתָמָא – מִיעוּט אַרְעָתָא שְׁתַּיִם. וְאִי אֲמַר לֵיהּ ״כׇּל אַרְעָתָא״ – כׇּל אַרְעָתָא דְּאִית לֵיהּ, לְבַר מִבּוּסְתָּנֵי וּפַרְדֵּיסֵי. וְאִי אֲמַר לֵיהּ ״זִיהֲרָא״ – אֲפִילּוּ בֵּי בּוּסְתָּנֵי וּפַרְדֵּיסֵי, לְבַר מִבָּתֵּי וְעַבְדֵי.

And if he said to him: I am selling you **fields, without specifying** how many,[H] **the minimum** number of fields that would justify being called **fields** in the plural is **two,** and therefore the seller has to give the buyer only two of his fields, even if he owns many fields. **And if he said to him:** I am selling you **all** of my **fields,** what he means is that he is selling him **all the fields that he owns, excluding** his **orchards** [*bustanei*][L] **and vineyards. And if he said to him:** I am selling you my **landed property,**[N] what he means is that he is selling him **even** his **orchards and vineyards,** but **excluding** his **houses and** Canaanite **slaves.**

HALAKHA

One who sells…must write for him – הַאי מַאן דִּמְזַבֵּין לֵיהּ...צָרִיךְ לְמִכְתַּב לֵיהּ: One who sells land to another must write for him in the bill of sale: I have not withheld anything for myself in this sale, in order to preclude claims that are liable to arise in the future (Rambam *Sefer Kinyan, Hilkhot Mekhira* 24:14; *Shulḥan Arukh, Ḥoshen Mishpat* 216:2).

I am selling you land of the house of Ḥiyya – אַרְעָא דְּבֵי חִיָּיא מְזַבֵּנְנָא לָךְ: If one says to another: I am selling you the field of the house of Ḥiyya, and he owns two fields called by that name, he has sold him only the less valuable of the two (Rambam *Sefer Kinyan, Hilkhot Mekhira* 21:20; *Shulḥan Arukh, Ḥoshen Mishpat* 218:23).

And if he said to him, I am selling you fields without specifying – וְאִי אֲמַר לֵיהּ אַרְעָתָא סְתָמָא: If one says to another: I am selling you fields, he has sold him only two fields, since the minimum number of fields that justify use of the plural is two. If he said: I am selling you all of my fields, he has sold him all of his fields, but not his gardens and orchards. If he said: I am selling you all of my land, he has sold him his gardens and orchards as well (*Tur*, citing Rabbeinu Yona). Similarly, if he said: I am selling you my property, he has sold him his gardens and orchards as well, but not his houses or Canaanite slaves. But if he said: I am selling you all of my property, he has sold him all of his property, even houses, Canaanite slaves, and movable property known to be his, including the phylacteries on his head. The *Tur* writes, citing Rabbeinu Yona, that if he said: I am selling you my property, without the word all, everything is included in the sale. But if he said: I am selling you so-and-so's property, even if he includes the word all, the movable property is not included, because movable property is not identified by the owner's name (Rambam *Sefer Kinyan, Hilkhot Mekhira* 21:18; *Shulḥan Arukh, Ḥoshen Mishpat* 218:24, and in the comment of Rema).

NOTES

He said to him he was selling him one plot of land – חֲדָא אֲמַר לֵיהּ: In this case the buyer receives only one plot of land, and if the two plots are not equal in quality and value, he receives the less valuable of the two, in accordance with the principle that he who holds the document is at a disadvantage (Rashbam).

Landed property [*zihara*] – זִיהֲרָא: The Rashbam explains the word *zihara* as a general term for all landed property. The Ramah understands that this word is referring to any land that yields produce, including grains that are sown each year and fruit that grows on trees. In a similar fashion, the Meiri explains that it means cultivated land. The Rambam, as well as the Rif, have a version of the text that reads: My properties [*nekhasai*], followed by: All my properties [*kol nekhasai*], in the next clause, which includes also houses, Canaanite slaves, and movable property.

LANGUAGE

Orchards [*bustanei*] – בּוּסְתָּנֵי: From the Middle Iranian bōstan, a compound composed of the words bōy, meaning fragrant, and stan, meaning place. It refers to a garden or orchard.

PERSONALITIES

Rav Mari, son of the daughter of Shmuel – רַב מָרִי בְּרֵיהּ דְּבַת שְׁמוּאֵל: This is a fourth-generation Babylonian *amora*, Rav Mari, the son of Raḥel, who was the daughter of the *amora* Shmuel. His unconventional appellation is explained by the history of Shmuel's family. The daughters of the *amora* Shmuel were taken into captivity. One of them, Raḥel, was captured by a gentile soldier, who later converted and married her. He became known as Issur Giyora, that is, Issur the Convert, and he served as a confidant of the prominent Jewish leaders of the generation in Babylonia.

Even though his father had already converted before he was born, Rav Mari is generally mentioned without a patronymic because his mother came from a very prestigious family. There are several instances in the Talmud where Sages are called by the names of their famous mothers who hail from distinguished families, even when their father's identity would cast no aspersion on their lineage. Rav Mari was apparently wealthy and engaged in commerce. He was also a significant Torah scholar and was appointed to a lofty position in the court in Babylonia. Rav Mari had three sons, all of whom were Torah scholars: Rav Aḥa Sava, Mar Zutra, and Rava bar Rav Mari.

וְאִי אֲמַר לֵיהּ ״נִכְסַי״ – אֲפִילּוּ בָּתֵּי וְעַבְדֵי.

And if he said to him: I am selling you my **property,** it means that he is selling him **even** his **houses and** his Canaanite **slaves.**

מָצַר לוֹ מֶצֶר אֶחָד אָרוֹךְ וּמֶצֶר אֶחָד קָצָר – אֲמַר רַב: לֹא קָנָה אֶלָּא כְּנֶגֶד הַקָּצָר.

§ The Gemara continues its examination of the concept of delineating boundaries in a wide manner, and considers the following case: If in the bill of sale the seller **delineated one boundary line** on one side of the field **long, and the other boundary line** on the opposite side of the field he delineated **short, Rav said:** The buyer **acquires only** a width of land **corresponding to the short** border, as it is assumed that the short boundary line delineates the actual size of the field that was sold to him, while the long boundary line was merely intended to point to the field under discussion. That is to say, the seller delineated the boundaries in a broad manner, but did not intend to include everything found within those boundaries in the sale.

אֲמַרוּ לֵיהּ רַב כָּהֲנָא וְרַב אַסִּי לְרַב: וְיִקְנֶה כְּנֶגֶד רֹאשׁ תּוֹר! שָׁתֵיק רַב.

Rav Kahana and Rav Asi said to Rav: But let him also **acquire the triangular plot** [*rosh tor*][HL] bounded by the diagonal line connecting the end of the short border and the end of the long border. **Rav was silent** and did not respond.

וּמוֹדֶה רַב, הֵיכָא דְּאִיכָּא מֶצֶר רְאוּבֵן וְשִׁמְעוֹן מֵחַד גִּיסָא וּמֶצֶר לֵוִי וִיהוּדָה מֵחַד גִּיסָא, מִדַּהֲוָה לֵיהּ לְמִכְתַּב לֵיהּ דִּרְאוּבֵן כְּנֶגֶד לֵוִי וּדְשִׁמְעוֹן כְּנֶגֶד יְהוּדָה, וְלָא כְּתַב לֵיהּ, שְׁמַע מִינָּהּ: כְּנֶגֶד רֹאשׁ תּוֹר הוּא דַּאֲמַר לֵיהּ.

And Rav concedes that **where there is a boundary line** defined by the fields **of Reuven and Shimon on one side** of the field being sold, **and a boundary line** defined by the fields **of Levi and Yehuda on the other side,** and in the bill of sale the seller describes the field being sold as bordered by the fields of Reuven and Shimon on one side but mentions only the field of Levi on the other side, **since** had he intended to sell only half the field **he should have written for** the buyer in the bill of sale that the field is bordered by the field **of Reuven** on the one side, which is **opposite** that **of Levi**[N] on the other, **or** by the field **of Shimon** on the one side, which is **opposite** that **of Yehuda** on the other, **but he did not write** that **for him,** one can **conclude from it that he is telling him** that he is selling him not only the area between the fields of Reuven and Levi, but also **the triangular plot** bounded by the diagonal line connecting the end of Shimon's field to the end of Levi's field.

מֶצֶר רְאוּבֵן מִזְרָח וּמַעֲרָב, וּמֶצֶר שִׁמְעוֹן צָפוֹן וְדָרוֹם – צָרִיךְ לְמִכְתַּב לֵיהּ: מֶצֶר רְאוּבֵן רוּחִין תְּרֵין, וּמֶצֶר שִׁמְעוֹן רוּחִין תְּרֵין.

The Gemara continues: If the field being sold is **bounded by** the fields of **Reuven** on **the east and the west,**[H] **and** it is **bounded by** the fields of **Shimon** on **the north and the south,** it is not enough to designate the field for the buyer as the field between the fields of Reuven and Shimon, but **it is necessary to write for him** in the bill of sale that the field is **bounded by** the fields of **Reuven** on **two sides, and** it is **bounded by** the fields of **Shimon** on **two sides.** Otherwise, all that the buyer acquires is a triangular plot bounded by one of Reuven's fields and one of Shimon's fields, and the boundary is the diagonal line connecting the end of Reuven's field to the end of Shimon's field.

אִיבַּעְיָא לְהוּ: סִיֵּים לוֹ אֶת הַקְּרָנוֹת, מַהוּ? כְּמִין גַּאם, מַהוּ?

A dilemma was raised before the Sages: **If** the seller **defined for** the buyer only **the corners** of the field being sold, **what is** the *halakha*? Does this mean that he is selling him only the corners of the field or the entire field marked by those corners? A second dilemma was also raised: If he defined the boundaries of the field in a shape **resembling** the Greek letter **gamma** [*gam*],[HL] or the English letter L, noting the boundaries on two adjacent sides that meet at a right angle, **what is** the *halakha*? Does this mean that he is selling him the entire field, or only the triangular plot marked by those boundaries and the diagonal line running from the end of one to the end of the other?

NOTES

That of Reuven opposite that of Levi – דִּרְאוּבֵן כְּנֶגֶד לֵוִי: The *Bah* explains that two versions of the text are combined here, and in practice, a single expression would have sufficed; either that the field is bordered by the field of Reuven on the one side opposite that of Levi on the other, or by that of Shimon on the one side opposite that of Yehuda on the other (see Rashbam).

HALAKHA

But let him acquire the triangular plot – וְיִקְנֶה כְּנֶגֶד רֹאשׁ תּוֹר: If the seller delineated one boundary line shorter than the opposite one, and the fields adjoining the longer boundary line all belonged to a single individual, the buyer acquires only a rectangular portion of the field corresponding to the short border. If the fields along the longer boundary line belong to two different people, the buyer also acquires the triangular plot bounded by a diagonal line connecting the end of the short border to the end of the long border. This is in accordance with the opinion of Rav. The Rema adds that some hold that even if the fields adjoining the longer boundary line all belong to the same person, the buyer acquires the triangular plot of land marked by the diagonal boundary line (*Tur*, citing Rosh; Rabbeinu Yona), in accordance with the opinion of Rav Kahana and Rav Asi (Rambam *Sefer Kinyan*, *Hilkhot Mekhira* 21:13; *Shulḥan Arukh*, *Ḥoshen Mishpat* 219:3).

If the field is bounded by the fields of Reuven on the east and the west, etc. – מֶצֶר רְאוּבֵן מִזְרָח וּמַעֲרָב וכו׳: One who sells a field bounded by the fields of Reuven on the east and the west, and by the fields of Shimon on the north and the south must write explicitly in the bill of sale: The field is bounded by the fields of Reuven on two sides and by the fields of Shimon on two sides (Rambam *Sefer Kinyan*, *Hilkhot Mekhira* 21:14; *Shulḥan Arukh*, *Ḥoshen Mishpat* 219:5).

If he defined only the corners…in a shape resembling the Greek letter gamma – סִיֵּים לוֹ אֶת הַקְּרָנוֹת...כְּמִין גַּאם: If one sells a field to another and defines only the corners of the property without describing the boundaries themselves; or if he does not describe the entire length of the boundaries, but defines only two diametrically opposed corners, e.g., the northeast and southwest corners, depicting them in the shape of the Greek letter gamma or the English letter L (Rashbam; *Haggahot Maimoniyyot*; *Kesef Mishne*; *Sma*; Gra), the buyer acquires only those portions of the field defined for him by the seller, or additional land at the discretion of the judges, as these dilemmas remain unresolved in the Gemara (Rambam *Sefer Kinyan*, *Hilkhot Mekhira* 21:16; *Shulḥan Arukh*, *Ḥoshen Mishpat* 219:4).

LANGUAGE

Triangular plot [*rosh tor*] – רֹאשׁ תּוֹר: Some interpret this phrase as deriving from the Aramaic word for ox, *tor*, as an ox's head is triangular in shape. Others maintain that it derives from the verse: "We will make you tiaras [*torei*] of gold" (Song of Songs 1:11), where the word *tor* refers to a triangular piece of jewelry (Rambam's Commentary on the Mishna).

Gamma [*gam*] – גַּאם: From the Greek letter gamma, Γ, the third letter of the Greek alphabet. Therefore, the Sages used this term in reference to a right angle.

בְּסֵירוּגִין מַהוּ? תֵּיקוּ.

A third dilemma was also raised before the Sages: If the seller defined the boundaries of the property he is selling **in an alternating** fashion,[HN] mentioning only some of the fields bordering each side of the field being sold, while omitting others, **what is** the *halakha*? No resolution was found for these questions, and these dilemmas **shall stand** unresolved.

מָצַר לוֹ מֶצֶר רִאשׁוֹן וּמֶצֶר שֵׁנִי וּמֶצֶר שְׁלִישִׁי, וּמֶצֶר רְבִיעִי לֹא מָצַר לוֹ – אָמַר רַב: קָנָה הַכֹּל חוּץ מִמֶּצֶר רְבִיעִי. וּשְׁמוּאֵל אָמַר: אֲפִילּוּ מֶצֶר רְבִיעִי. וְרַב אַסִי אָמַר: לֹא קָנָה אֶלָּא תֶּלֶם אֶחָד עַל פְּנֵי כּוּלָּהּ;

§ The Gemara raises a similar dilemma. If, in the bill of sale, the seller **delineated for** the buyer the field's **first boundary,** its **second boundary, and** its **third boundary,**[H] **but he did not delineate** its **fourth boundary** at all,[N] **Rav says:** The buyer **acquires the entire** field, **except for** the one furrow along which **the fourth boundary** runs, which is usually differentiated in some way from the field itself. **And Shmuel says:** The buyer acquires **even** the furrow along which **the fourth boundary** runs. **And Rav Asi says: He acquires only** the width of **one furrow**[N] **along the entire** perimeter of the three boundaries specified by the seller.

סָבַר לַהּ כְּרַב, דַּאֲמַר: שִׁיּוּרֵי שַׁיֵּיר, וּמִדְּשַׁיֵּיר בְּמֶצֶר – שַׁיֵּיר נַמִי בְּכוּלְּהִי.

The Gemara explains Rav Asi's opinion: He **holds in accordance with** the opinion of **Rav, who said** that by failing to delineate the fourth boundary, the seller **withheld** some part of the field, i.e., one furrow, for himself. But Rav Asi takes this further **and** says that **since he withheld** some part of the field for himself **at the** fourth **boundary, he withheld also** some portion **of the entire** field, and therefore the buyer acquires only that which is adjacent to the specified boundaries.

אָמַר רָבָא, הִלְכְתָא: קָנָה הַכֹּל חוּץ מִמֶּצֶר רְבִיעִי. וְלָא אֲמָרַן אֶלָּא דְּלָא מִבְלַע, אֲבָל מִבְלַע – קָנָה.

Rava said: The *halakha* is that the buyer **acquires the entire** field **except for** the one furrow along which **the fourth boundary** runs, in accordance with the opinion of Rav. **And we said** this **only** in a case **where** the fourth boundary **is not included**[N] within the space between two adjacent boundaries, but rather juts out beyond them. **But** when **it is included** within the space delineated by the other boundaries, the buyer **acquires** it as well.

HALAKHA

In an alternating fashion – בְּסֵירוּגִין: If one who sells a field to another mentions only some of the fields bordering each side of the field being sold, the buyer acquires only the portion specifically mentioned to him by the seller, and this is subject to the discretion of the judges. In any event, he receives no less than an area that suffices to sow nine *kav* of seed (Rambam *Sefer Kinyan*, *Hilkhot Mekhira* 21:16; *Shulḥan Arukh*, *Ḥoshen Mishpat* 219:4).

If the seller delineated for the buyer the field's first boundary, its second boundary, and its third boundary – מָצַר לוֹ מֶצֶר רִאשׁוֹן וּמֶצֶר שֵׁנִי וּמֶצֶר שְׁלִישִׁי: If one sells a field to another, specifying only three of its boundaries, and its fourth boundary is included within the area defined by the adjacent boundaries, there is no row of trees on it, and it is not an area fit for sowing nine *kav* of seed, the buyer acquires the land up to the fourth boundary as well. If the fourth boundary is not included within the area defined by the adjacent boundaries, there is a row of trees on it, or it is an area fit for sowing nine *kav*, the buyer does not acquire the land adjacent to it. If it is included within the area defined by the adjacent borders, and there is a row of trees on it or it is an area fit for sowing nine *kav*; or if it is not included within that area but also is without a row of trees, and it is not fit for sowing nine *kav*, such a case is decided according to the discretion of its judges, who issue a ruling based upon their assessment of the situation (Rambam *Sefer Kinyan*, *Hilkhot Mekhira* 21:15; *Shulḥan Arukh*, *Ḥoshen Mishpat* 219:2, and *Shakh* and *Beur HaGra* there).

NOTES

In an alternating fashion – בְּסֵירוּגִין: The Rashbam explains that the field being sold was bounded on each side by two fields belonging to different neighbors, and the seller specified the name of only one neighbor on each side. Perhaps in doing so he wished merely to designate the boundaries of the field, and he intended to sell the entire property. Alternatively, he may have intended to sell only those areas adjacent to the neighboring fields specifically mentioned. Others understand that there were five fields bordering each side of the field being sold, and the seller omitted the names of the owners of the second and fourth fields on each side. According to this, the seller may have intended to sell only the strip of land adjacent to each of the specified fields (Rabbeinu Barukh; Ramah).

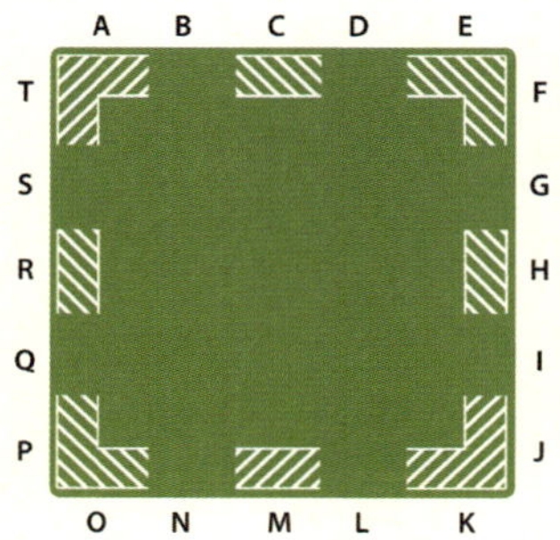

But he did not delineate its fourth boundary at all – וּמֶצֶר רְבִיעִי לֹא מָצַר לוֹ: The Rid and the Rosh write that if the seller delineated only two opposite borders, e.g., the borders on the east and the west, all agree that the buyer acquires the entire field, since the scope of the sale has been clearly defined. Uncertainty arises only when just one of the four borders has been omitted.

One furrow – תֶּלֶם אֶחָד: This means that since the field was not defined on all sides, the buyer acquires only a strip of land adjacent to each of the three specified borders, i.e., the shaded area in the image.

Above: Land acquired by the buyer

Left: Opinion of Rabbeinu Barukh and Ramah

Where it is not included – דְּלָא מִבְלַע: The Rashbam and the majority of the early commentaries explain that an included boundary is one that is entirely contained within the area defined by the two adjacent boundaries, and therefore, it may be assumed that it was not excluded from the sale of the field. Consequently, a boundary that is not included is referring to a case where the two adjacent boundaries delineate the area sold, but they do not encompass the boundary itself. Others explain an included boundary as one whose structure and form indicate that it is part of the field, while a boundary that is not included is one different in nature from the field itself, e.g., it is on a different level than the field, either above or below it, even if it is entirely contained within the area delineated by the adjacent boundaries (Rabbeinu Gershom).

וְכִי לָא מִבְלַע נַמִּי – לָא אֲמָרַן אֶלָּא דְּאִיכָּא עֲלֵיהּ רִיכְבָּא דְּדִיקְלָא וְהָוֵי תִּשְׁעַת קַבִּין, אֲבָל לֵיכָּא עֲלֵיהּ רִיכְבָּא דְּדִיקְלָא, וְלָא הָוֵי תִּשְׁעַת קַבִּין – קָנָה. מִכְּלָל דְּכִי מוּבְלָע, אַף עַל גַּב דְּאִיכָּא עֲלֵיהּ רִיכְבָּא דְּדִיקְלָא וְהָוֵי תִּשְׁעַת קַבִּין – קָנָה.

Rava adds: **And even when it is not included** in that space, **we said** that the buyer does not acquire it **only** in a case **where there is a row of trees on it, or it is** an area fit for sowing **nine *kav*[N]** of seed. **But** where **there is no row of trees on it, and it is not** an area fit for sowing **nine *kav*** of seed, the buyer **acquires** it along with the rest of the field. **By inference** one derives from here **that when** the fourth border **is included** within the space delineated by the two adjacent boundaries, **even if there is a row of trees on it and it is** an area fit for sowing **nine *kav***, the buyer **acquires** it.

אִיכָּא דְּאָמְרִי: אֲמַר רָבָא, הִלְכְתָא: קָנָה הַכֹּל, וַאֲפִילּוּ מֶצֶר רְבִיעִי. וְלָא אֲמָרַן אֶלָּא דְּמִבְלַע, אֲבָל לָא מִבְלַע – לָא קָנֵי.

There are those who **say** that Rava's ruling and the conclusion drawn from it are as follows: **Rava said: The *halakha*** is that the buyer **acquires the entire** field, and he acquires **even** the furrow along which **the fourth boundary** runs, in accordance with the opinion of Shmuel. **And we said** this **only** in a case **where** the fourth boundary **is included** within the space delineated by the two adjacent boundaries. **But** when **it is not included** within those boundaries, the buyer **does not acquire** it.

וְכִי מִבְלַע נַמִּי – לָא אֲמָרַן אֶלָּא דְּלֵיכָּא עֲלֵיהּ רִיכְבָּא דְּדִיקְלָא, וְלָא הָוֵי תִּשְׁעַת קַבִּין, אֲבָל אִיכָּא עֲלֵיהּ רִיכְבָּא דְּדִיקְלָא וְהָוֵי תִּשְׁעַת קַבִּין – לָא קָנָה. מִכְּלַל דְּכִי לָא מוּבְלָע, אַף עַל גַּב דְּלֵיכָּא עֲלֵיהּ רִיכְבָּא דְּדִיקְלָא, וְלָא הָוֵי תִּשְׁעַת קַבִּין – לָא קָנֵי.

Rava adds: **And even when it is included** within the adjoining boundaries, **we said** that the buyer acquires it **only** in a case **where there is no row of trees on it, and it is not** an area fit for sowing **nine *kav*** of seed. **But** where **there is a row of trees on it, or it is** an area fit for sowing **nine *kav*** of seed, the buyer **does not acquire** it. **By inference** one derives from here **that when** the fourth boundary **is not included** within the two adjacent boundaries, **even if there is no row of trees on it and it is not** an area fit for sowing **nine *kav*** of seed, the buyer **does not acquire** it.

שָׁמְעִינַן מִתַּרְוַיְיהוּ לִישָּׁנֵי דְּרָבָא, דְּבִשְׂדֶה לָא שַׁיֵּיר וְלָא מִידֵּי. וְשָׁמְעִינַן נַמִּי, דְּהֵיכָא דְּמִבְלַע, וְלֵיכָּא עֲלֵיהּ רִיכְבָּא דְּדִיקְלָא, וְלָא הָוֵי תִּשְׁעַת קַבִּין – קָנָה; לָא מִבְלַע, וְאִיכָּא עֲלֵיהּ רִיכְבָּא דְּדִיקְלָא, וְהָוֵי תִּשְׁעַת קַבִּין – לָא קָנָה;

We conclude according to both versions of the statement **of Rava that** even if the seller withheld something for himself along the fourth boundary, **he did not withhold anything at all in the field** itself. **And we also conclude** according to both versions **that where** the fourth boundary **is included** within the space defined by the two adjacent boundaries, **and there is no row of trees on it and it is not** an area fit for sowing **nine *kav*** of seed, the buyer **acquires** it. And furthermore, we conclude according to both versions that if the fourth boundary **is not included** within the two adjacent boundaries, **and there is a row of trees on it, or it is** an area fit for sowing **nine *kav*** of seed, the buyer **does not acquire** it.

מִבְלַע וְאִיכָּא עֲלֵיהּ, לָא מִבְלַע וְלֵיכָּא עֲלֵיהּ – אִתְּמַר לָהּ לְהַאי גִּיסָא וְאִתְּמַר לָהּ לְהַאי גִּיסָא, שׁוּדָא דְּדַיָּינֵי.

If the fourth boundary **is included** within the two adjacent boundaries, **and there is** a row of trees **on it** or it is fit for sowing nine *kav* of seed, or if the fourth boundary **is not included** within the two adjacent boundaries, **and there is no** row of trees **on it** nor is it fit for sowing nine *kav*, the ruling in these cases **was stated in this direction,** that the land adjacent to the fourth boundary is acquired by the buyer, **and it was stated in that direction,** that this land is not acquired by the buyer, depending upon which version of Rava's statement is accepted. Since there is no clear ruling in these cases, the decision is left to **the discretion of the judges,**[N] who must rule in accordance with what appears to them to be the intention of the seller.

אֲמַר רַבָּה: "פַּלְגָא דְּאִית לִי בְּאַרְעָא" – פַּלְגָא, "פַּלְגָא בְּאַרְעָא דְּאִית לִי" – רִיבְעָא. אֲמַר לֵיהּ אַבַּיֵּי: מַאי שְׁנָא הָכִי וּמַאי שְׁנָא הָכִי? אִישְׁתִּיק.

§ **Rabba said:** If one owns a field in partnership with another, and he says to a third person: I am selling you **the half that I have in this land,**[H] he means to sell him **half** of that field, i.e., his entire share. If he says to the buyer: I am selling you **half of the land that I have,** he means to sell him **one-quarter** of that field, i.e., half of his share. **Abaye said to him: What is different** about **this** wording **and what is different** about **that** wording, that you rule differently in the two cases? Rabba **was silent,** offering no reply.

NOTES

Nine *kav* – תִּשְׁעַת קַבִּין: This is the smallest area that can be called a field. It is explained earlier in this tractate (11a) that the co-owners of a field cannot compel one another to divide their jointly owned field between them unless it is at least the size of area fit for sowing nine *kav* of seed, which is the equivalent of about 900 sq m.

The discretion [*shuda*] of the judges – שׁוּדָא דְּדַיָּינֵי: The Aramaic word *shuda* derives from a root meaning to cast or throw. In the context of a court decision it means discretion, which is like casting one's opinion in a certain direction, indicating that the judges should assess the seller's intentions and rule according to that assessment (Rashbam). This means evaluating whether the seller was favorably inclined toward the buyer, or whether there are other indications that he sold the property in a generous manner (Rabbeinu Gershom); or judging how much land was included in the sale by the price paid (Rabbeinu Yona). Even though some commentaries generally interpret following the discretion of the judges as allowing the judges to make a completely arbitrary decision (see 35a), here, since the uncertainty relates to the meaning of the words used in the transaction and not the substance of the claims, all agree that the judges should simply assess the seller's intentions (Rabbeinu Yona).

HALAKHA

The half that I have in this land – פַּלְגָא דְּאִית לִי בְּאַרְעָא: If one owned half of a field and said to another: I am selling you the half that I have in the field, the buyer acquires the entire half belonging to the seller. If the seller said: I am selling you half of the field that I have, the buyer acquires only one-quarter of the field, which is half of what the seller owns (Rambam *Sefer Kinyan*, *Hilkhot Mekhira* 21:23; *Shulḥan Arukh*, *Ḥoshen Mishpat* 218:21).

אֲמַר אַבַּיֵי: אֲנָא סְבַרִי, מִדְּאִישְׁתִּיק קַבּוּלֵי קַבְּלָהּ; וְלָא הִיא, חֲזֵינָא הָנְהוּ שְׁטָרֵי דְּנָפְקִי מִבֵּי מָר, וּכְתִיב בְּהוּ הָכִי: "פַּלְגָא דְּאִית לִי בְּאַרְעָא" – פַּלְגָא, "פַּלְגָא בְּאַרְעָא דְּאִית לִי" – רִיבְעָא.

Abaye said: I had assumed that since he was silent, he must have **accepted** my opinion and retracted his statement; **but** that **is not so.** As on another occasion **I saw certain bills** of sale[N] **that issued from my Master's house,** that is, they were issued under the auspices of my master Rabba, **in which it was written: The half that I have in this land,** and it was clear from another clause in the bill that **half** of the field was being sold. And there was another bill of sale in which it was written: **Half of the land that I have,** and it was clear from another clause in the bill that **one-quarter** of the field was being sold.

וְאָמַר רַבָּה: "מְצַר אַרְעָא דְּמִינָּהּ פַּלְגָא" – פַּלְגָא, "מְצַר אַרְעָא דְּמִינָּהּ פְּסִיקָא" – תִּשְׁעָה קַבִּין.

And Rabba also **said:** If one sold land to another and delineated boundaries on three sides of the field, and with regard to the fourth side he wrote in the bill of sale: **The boundary** of the field is **the land through which** the field **is halved,** he has sold him **half** of the field. If he writes with regard to the fourth boundary: **The boundary** of the field is **the land from which** a plot **can be set apart,** he has sold him only an area fit for sowing **nine *kav*** of seed, as that is the minimum size of a plot of land defined as a field.

אֲמַר לֵיהּ אַבַּיֵי: מַאי שְׁנָא הָכִי וּמַאי שְׁנָא הָכִי? אִישְׁתִּיק. סְבוּר מִינָּהּ: אִידִי וְאִידִי פַּלְגָא.

Abaye said to him: What is different about **this** wording, **and what is different** about **that** wording, that you rule differently in the two cases? Rabba **was silent,** and did not respond. The Sages **understood from this** silence that Abaye understood that Rabba retracted his ruling and conceded that in both **this** case **and that** case, the buyer acquires **half** of the field.

NOTES

I saw certain bills of sale – חֲזֵינָא הָנְהוּ שְׁטָרֵי: He saw bills of sale from Rabba's court that recorded the testimony of witnesses that the seller said: I am selling the half that I have in this land, and the conclusion of the document was that the seller sold his entire portion, which was half of the field (Rashbam). *Tosafot* explain that he saw that Rabba's court would transfer ownership of the seller's entire portion to the buyer when he used this wording. The Ran writes that Abaye saw that when the seller used these words, the court would instruct the witnesses to record in the document that he is selling half of the field, from which he deduced that the witnesses need not always follow the exact wording of the claimant as long as they record the essence of what they saw and heard in a clear manner.

וְלָא הִיא, דַּאֲמַר רַב יֵימָר בַּר שֶׁלֶמְיָה: לְדִידִי מִפָּרְשָׁא לִי מִינֵּיהּ דְּאַבַּיֵי: בֵּין "מְצַר אַרְעָא דְּמִינָּהּ פַּלְגָא" וּבֵין "מְצַר אַרְעָא דְּמִינָּהּ פְּסִיקָא", אִי אֲמַר לֵיהּ "אִלֵּין מַצְרָנָהָא" – פַּלְגָא, לָא אֲמַר לֵיהּ "אִלֵּין מַצְרָנָהָא" – תִּשְׁעָה קַבִּין.

But that is not so, as Rav Yeimar bar Shelemya said: The matter **was explained to me by Abaye,** as follows: **Whether** the seller writes with regard to the fourth boundary: **The boundary** of the field is **the land through which** the field **is halved,**[H] **or** he writes: **The boundary** of the field is **the land through which** a plot **can be set apart, if he said to the buyer: These are its boundaries,**[N] he has sold him **half** of the field. But if **he did not say to the buyer: These are its boundaries,** he has sold him only an area fit for sowing **nine *kav*** of seed.

פְּשִׁיטָא, אֲמַר "יַחֲלוֹק פְּלוֹנִי בִּנְכָסַי" – פַּלְגָא, "תְּנוּ חֵלֶק לִפְלוֹנִי בִּנְכָסַי", מַאי?

§ The Gemara raises a question about a similar case: **It is obvious** that if one **said: So-and-so should share in my property,** he means to give him **half** of the property. If he said: **Give so-and-so a portion**[N] **of my property,**[H] **what is the *halakha*?** What portion of the property must he give him?

HALAKHA

The boundary is the land through which the field is halved – מְצַר אַרְעָא דְּמִינָּהּ פַּלְגָא: In a case where one sells the western portion of his field but withholds the eastern portion for himself, and he designates the boundary of the area he is selling on the west side, but as for the boundary on the east side he writes: The boundary is the land through which the field is halved, or: The boundary is the land through which a plot can be detached, then if he writes explicitly: These are its boundaries, the buyer acquires one-half of the field. If he does not write this explicitly, the buyer acquires only an area fit for sowing nine *kav* of seed (Rambam *Sefer Kinyan*, *Hilkhot Mekhira* 21:23; *Shulḥan Arukh*, *Ḥoshen Mishpat* 219:6).

So-and-so should share in my property…give so-and-so a portion of my property – יַחֲלוֹק פְּלוֹנִי בִּנְכָסַי...תְּנוּ חֵלֶק לִפְלוֹנִי בִּנְכָסַי: If a person on his deathbed says: So-and-so should share in my property, the recipient receives half of his property. If he says: Give so-and-so a portion of my property, the recipient receives one-sixteenth of his property, the smallest measure mentioned in the *baraita*. According to some (*Tur*, citing Rosh), these rulings apply even to a healthy donor. Others say that the recipient is given one-quarter of the donor's property (Rav Hai Gaon; Ra'avad), in accordance with the opinion of Sumakhos. Yet others (*Tur*, citing Rabbeinu Yitzḥak) say that the recipient is given only a minimal portion, as the *halakha* does not follow Sumakhos and, therefore, the burden of proof rests upon the claimant (Rambam *Sefer Kinyan*, *Hilkhot Zekhiya UMattana* 11:7; *Shulḥan Arukh*, *Ḥoshen Mishpat* 253:24, 25, and in the comment of Rema).

NOTES

These are its boundaries – אִלֵּין מַצְרָנָהָא: The Rashbam understands that when the seller delineates the borders and adds: And these are its boundaries, this additional phrase indicates that he wishes to give more, and therefore, the buyer receives half of the field. If he does not add such a phrase, the buyer receives only a minimal portion, fit for sowing nine *kav*. The Rid, like Rabbeinu Barukh, has a version of the text which reads: If the seller designates its boundaries, he has sold him half of the field, but if he does not designate its boundaries, he has sold him only an area fit for sowing nine *kav* of seed. The Rid explains that this means that if he designates boundaries that delineate half of the field, it is clear that he is selling half of the field, but if he does not do so, he means to sell only a small portion.

Most commentaries understand that this case does not involve additional wording or special boundary designation. They explain that if the seller records the boundaries of the field, this indicates that he is delineating the entire field so that half of it can be given to the buyer. If he does not record the boundaries, it is assumed that he is selling only a small portion of the field, and therefore recording the boundaries is unnecessary, as the size of the field is irrelevant (Ri Migash; Rabbeinu Gershom; Rambam).

Give so-and-so a portion – תְּנוּ חֵלֶק: The Rashbam notes that the *Tosefta* (*Bava Batra* 7:16) states that if one says: Give so-and-so a portion of my property, he receives a portion equal to that of the owner's sons. He offers several explanations for the different opinion adopted here: Either the owner has no sons, or the owner said: Give a portion of my property to my sons and the remainder to so-and-so, or perhaps the Sages here did not know of that *baraita*, or they knew of the *baraita* but assumed that the *halakha* is not in accordance with it. Some explain that here the Gemara is not dealing with a person on his deathbed dividing up his property, but with a healthy person giving a gift (Rosh).

Rabbeinu Ḥananel maintains that the Gemara here is discussing a person giving a gift, in which case there is no way to assess how much he wishes to give. But if one uses this wording when selling a portion of his field, the purchase price indicates how much of the field is sold. While some early commentaries contest this opinion, it appears to be the accepted ruling.

אָמַר רָבִינָא בַּר קִיסִי: תָּא שְׁמַע, דְּתַנְיָא: הָאוֹמֵר ״תְּנוּ חֵלֶק לִפְלוֹנִי בְּבוֹר״ – סוּמָכוֹס אוֹמֵר: אֵין פָּחוֹת מֵרְבִיעַ, ״לְחָבִית״ – אֵין פָּחוֹת מִשְּׁמִינִית, ״לִקְדֵרָה״ – אֵין פָּחוֹת מִשְּׁנֵים עָשָׂר, ״לְטָפִיחַ״ – אֵין פָּחוֹת מִשִּׁשָּׁה עָשָׂר.

Ravina bar Kisi said: Come and **hear** a proof concerning the *halakha* in this case, **as it is taught** in a *baraita*: With regard to **one who says: Give so-and-so a portion of** my **cistern**[NH] for his water needs, **Sumakhos says:** He must give him **not less than one-quarter** of the water in the cistern. If he qualifies his words and says: Give so-and-so a portion of my cistern's water **for** his **barrel,** he must give him **not less than one-eighth** of the water. If he says: Give him a portion **for** his **pot,** he must give him **not less than one-twelfth** of the water. And if he says: Give him **for** his **cup,**[B] he must give him **not less than one-sixteenth** of the water. In any event, this *baraita* indicates that the unqualified phrase: Give so-and-so a portion, should be understood to mean: Give him one-quarter.

תָּנוּ רַבָּנַן: בֶּן לֵוִי שֶׁמָּכַר שָׂדֶה לְיִשְׂרָאֵל, וְאָמַר לוֹ ״עַל מְנָת שֶׁמַּעֲשֵׂר רִאשׁוֹן שֶׁלִּי״ – מַעֲשֵׂר רִאשׁוֹן שֶׁלּוֹ; וְאִם אָמַר ״לִי וּלְבָנַיי״, מֵת – יִתֵּן לְבָנָיו;

The Gemara now considers another case in which the seller withholds something for himself in a sale. **The Sages taught** in a *baraita*: With regard to **a Levite**[N] **who sold a field to an Israelite**[H] **and said to him:** I am selling you this field **on the condition that the first tithe**[B] from the produce growing in the field, which must be given to a Levite, is **mine,** and it will be given to me every year and not to any other Levite, **the first tithe is his. And if he said:** I am selling you the field on the condition that the tithe will be given **to me and to my sons,** then if **he dies,** the buyer **must give** the tithe **to his sons.**

וְאִם אָמַר לוֹ ״כׇּל זְמַן שֶׁהַשָּׂדֶה זוֹ בְּיָדְךָ״, מְכָרָהּ וְחָזַר וּלְקָחָהּ – אֵין לוֹ עָלָיו כְּלוּם.

But if the seller **said to** the buyer: This stipulation will remain in force **as long as this field is in your possession,** then if the buyer **sold it and** afterward **bought it** back **again,** the seller **has no** claim **on him.** Since the field left the buyer's possession in the interim, the seller no longer has a claim to the tithe.

אַמַּאי? אֵין אָדָם מַקְנֶה דָּבָר שֶׁלֹּא בָּא לָעוֹלָם! כֵּיוָן דַּאֲמַר לֵיהּ ״עַל מְנָת שֶׁמַּעֲשֵׂר רִאשׁוֹן שֶׁלִּי״, שִׁיּוּרֵי שַׁיְּירֵיהּ לִמְקוֹם מַעֲשֵׂר.

The Gemara challenges the *halakha* taught in the *baraita*: **Why** should the seller ever have a right to the tithe after he has sold the field? After all, **a person cannot transfer ownership of an object that has not yet come into the world.**[H] How, then, can the seller acquire a portion of the produce that does not yet exist? The Gemara answers that **since** the seller **said to** the buyer: I am selling you this field **on the condition that the first tithe is mine,** it is as if **he withheld the site** where the **tithe** is grown for himself when he sold the field, and that site already exists.

אָמַר רֵישׁ לָקִישׁ, זֹאת אוֹמֶרֶת: הַמּוֹכֵר בַּיִת לַחֲבֵירוֹ, וְאָמַר לוֹ ״עַל מְנָת שֶׁדְּיוֹטָא הָעֶלְיוֹנָה שֶׁלִּי״ – דְּיוֹטָא הָעֶלְיוֹנָה שֶׁלּוֹ.

Reish Lakish said: That is to say that with regard to one **who sells a house to another and says to him:** I am selling you this house **on the condition that the upper story** [*deyota*][NL] **is mine, the upper story is his.**

NOTES

Give so-and-so a portion of my cistern – תְּנוּ חֵלֶק לִפְלוֹנִי בְּבוֹר: The Rashbam and many early commentaries understand that the reference here is to a water cistern; that is, the owner is transferring the right to draw water to another. Rabbeinu Ḥananel writes, citing Rav Hai Gaon, that the Gemara is discussing a pit used for storing wine. While the Rashbam rejects this opinion, the Rambam rules in accordance with it.

Levite – בֶּן לֵוִי: The Rashbam writes that the option to withhold the right to the first tithe applies not only to a Levite, but to anyone who sells a field. This right allows the seller to choose the Levite who is to receive the tithe each year. The reason the Gemara mentions a Levite is that if he is the seller, he has a personal interest in withholding the right to the first tithe, as he can take it for himself.

The upper story [*deyota*] – דְּיוֹטָא הָעֶלְיוֹנָה: The Rashbam explains that *deyota* here refers to a roof with a parapet ten handbreadths high, which constitutes a second story and which, by *halakha*, is not included in the sale of the house. Therefore, the owner's stipulation with regard to it cannot be intended to preserve his right to the roof but must grant him additional rights. Rabbeinu Tam and the Ramban, among others, understand the word *deyota* to mean a row. The reference here is to the upper row of stones of the house's walls, protruding somewhat above the level of the roof. The owner reserves for himself the right to place items on that row of stones even though they may place an added burden on the structure of the house. The Rid combines parts of each interpretation and explains that this *deyota* is a story that has not yet been built. The Ramah, in a totally different fashion, says that the *deyota* is a small attic that is included in the sale of the house.

LANGUAGE

Story [*deyota*] – דְּיוֹטָא: From the Greek δίαιτα, *diaita*, which means residence, and, by extension, upper story or attic of a house.

BACKGROUND

Cup – טָפִיחַ: The cup mentioned here is a round earthenware vessel with an attached cover. It was used for various purposes, including storage of assorted items and rinsing one's hands.

First tithe – מַעֲשֵׂר רִאשׁוֹן: After *teruma*, the portion of the crop given to the priests, is separated, one-tenth of the remaining produce is given to the Levites. This produce is called first tithe. The owner is permitted to give first tithe to any Levite he chooses. A Levite who receives first tithe is required to set aside one-tenth of this tithe as *teruma* of the tithe and give it to a priest. The remaining first tithe, after the Levite set aside the *teruma* of the tithe, remains the Levite's property. It has no sanctity and may be eaten by anyone. Produce from which first tithe was not set aside has the legal status of untithed produce and may not be eaten. Since not everyone was conscientious about setting aside first tithe, the Sages instituted that one must separate this tithe from doubtfully tithed produce as well. In that case it is not given to a Levite.

HALAKHA

Give so-and-so a portion of my cistern – תְּנוּ חֵלֶק לִפְלוֹנִי בְּבוֹר: If a person on his deathbed says: Give so-and-so a portion of my wine pit, the recipient receives one-quarter of the wine in the pit. If he says: Give him a portion for his barrel, the recipient receives one-eighth. If he says: Give him for his pot, he receives one-twelfth. If he says: Give him for his cup, he receives one-sixteenth. The *Tur* cites the opinion of Rabbeinu Yitzḥak of Dampierre and the Rosh that the recipient is given only a minimal portion, as the *baraita* was taught in accordance with the opinion of Sumakhos, while the *halakha* follows the Sages. The Rema (citing Rabbeinu Ḥananel) adds that all this applies only to a gift, but in the case of a sale the buyer's portion is determined in accordance with the purchase price (Rambam *Sefer Kinyan*, *Hilkhot Zekhiya UMattana* 11:8; *Shulḥan Arukh*, *Ḥoshen Mishpat* 253:25, and in the comment of Rema).

A Levite who sold a field to an Israelite, etc. – בֶּן לֵוִי שֶׁמָּכַר שָׂדֶה לְיִשְׂרָאֵל וכו׳: If a priest sells a field to an Israelite, stipulating that the tithes will continue to be his forever, those tithes are his, as if he withheld that portion of the field on which the tithes grow. Mahari Kurkus states that this applies also if the seller is a Levite or an Israelite. If the seller dies, his sons do not inherit the right to those tithes unless he stipulates that the sale is on condition that the tithes be given to him or his sons, in which case his sons do receive the tithes in the event of his death. If the seller stipulates that the sale is on condition that the tithes be given to him as long as the field is in the buyer's possession, then if the buyer sells the field, he no longer receives the tithes, even if the buyer later repurchases it (Rambam *Sefer Zera'im*, *Hilkhot Ma'aser* 6:19).

An object that has not yet come into the world – דָּבָר שֶׁלֹּא בָּא לָעוֹלָם: One cannot transfer ownership of an object that has not yet come into the world, e.g., the future produce of a field. If he makes such a transaction, he can renege on it, even after the object has come into the world. Just as one cannot transfer ownership of an object that has not yet come into the world, so too one cannot withhold something that has not yet come into the world. Therefore, if one sells a field to another and withholds the produce of the coming years for someone else, the produce is not withheld for him. Nevertheless, if he withholds the produce for himself, it is his; it is as if he withheld for himself the site upon which that produce will grow, as in the case of the Levite mentioned in the Gemara (Rambam *Sefer Kinyan*, *Hilkhot Mekhira* 22:1; *Shulḥan Arukh*, *Ḥoshen Mishpat* 209:4, 7).

לְמַאי הִלְכְתָא? רַב זְבִיד אָמַר: שֶׁאִם רָצָה לְהוֹצִיא בָּהּ זִיזִין – מוֹצִיא; רַב פַּפָּא אָמַר: שֶׁאִם רָצָה לִבְנוֹת עֲלִיָּיה עַל גַּבָּהּ – בּוֹנֶה.

With regard to what *halakha*[H] did Reish Lakish say this? In any case the upper story is his, as when he sold the house, it was only the lower story that he sold to the buyer. **Rav Zevid says:** He said this to teach the *halakha* **that if** the seller **wishes to extend** from the upper story **projections**[N] over the courtyard, which was included in the sale, **he may extend** them. **Rav Pappa says:** He said this to teach the *halakha* **that if** this upper story collapses and the seller **wishes to build an upper story on top of it** to replace it, **he may build** it.

בִּשְׁלָמָא לְרַב זְבִיד, הַיְינוּ דְּקָתָנֵי ״זֹאת אוֹמֶרֶת״, אֶלָּא לְרַב פַּפָּא מַאי ״זֹאת אוֹמֶרֶת״? קַשְׁיָא.

The Gemara asks: **Granted, according to Rav Zevid,**[N] **this** explanation is consistent with **that which** Reish Lakish **teaches,** which begins with: **That is to say.** As according to Rav Zevid, Reish Lakish infers from the ruling of the *baraita* about tithes that even though the seller of the house did not explicitly withhold anything for himself, the court interprets his use of his superfluous stipulation as an indication that he wished to withhold for himself the space over the courtyard for the projections. **But** according **to Rav Pappa, what** did Reish Lakish mean when he said his statement that begins with the phrase: **That is to say?** The seller's right to rebuild the upper story after it collapses is not derived from the superfluous stipulation that he attached to the transaction, and it is not inferred from the *baraita.* The Gemara concludes: Indeed, Rav Pappa's interpretation is **difficult,** as it does not account for the wording of Reish Lakish's statement.

HALAKHA

With regard to what *halakha* – לְמַאי הִלְכְתָא: If a house is sold on the condition that the upper story [*deyota*] will remain in the seller's possession, it remains his. An upper *deyota* is explained either as a roof with a ten-handbreadth-high parapet (Rashbam), or the uppermost row of stones protruding somewhat above the walls of a house, upon which people would often build an additional story (*Rabbeinu Tam*). In such a case, even if the buyer acquired the courtyard, the seller may still build projections from the *deyota* over the courtyard, and if the *deyota* collapses he may rebuild it or even build something similar on top of it, and according to Ra'avad he may even build a totally new structure. This is in accordance with Rav Zevid's opinion, which is accepted later in the tractate (148b), and also encompasses Rav Pappa's opinion (*Maggid Mishne*; Gra). The Rema writes that the same principle applies if the seller stipulates that some other part of the house, e.g., a pit or a cistern, will remain in his possession (Rambam *Sefer Kinyan*, *Hilkhot Mekhira* 24:16; *Shulḥan Arukh*, *Ḥoshen Mishpat* 212:3, 214:8).

NOTES

That if he wishes to extend projections – שֶׁאִם רָצָה לְהוֹצִיא בָּהּ זִיזִין: The Rashbam explains, in accordance with the conclusion of the continuing discussion, that the seller reserves for himself the right to build projections from the upper story over the courtyard, which was also sold to the buyer. Many early commentaries disagree with this explanation, as the Gemara does not state that the buyer bought the courtyard as well, and therefore it must have remained in the seller's possession, obviating the need for him to reserve for himself the right to use its airspace. Rabbeinu Yona, who agrees with the Rashbam, explains that presumably the courtyard was sold along with the house, as that is the usual occurrence. The other early commentaries raise additional difficulties with including the courtyard in the sale. Some explain that the seller reserves for himself the right to build projections from this upper story in order to build an additional story, even though these projections constitute an increased burden for the house itself (see *Tosafot*). Others suggest that the seller reserves for himself the right to build such projections and build a balcony upon them, even though this will block the light and darken the ground floor (Rid).

Granted, according to Rav Zevid – בִּשְׁלָמָא לְרַב זְבִיד: According to Rav Zevid's explanation, the seller's superfluous phrase withholds for himself an area in the courtyard that he sold, just as was said with regard to the *baraita*, that with the seller's superfluous phrase, he withholds for himself the site of the tithe. But according to Rav Pappa's explanation, there would be no need for Reish Lakish's statement, as the seller's superfluous phrase simply reserves the additional right to rebuild the upper story, and attaining additional rights through a superfluous phrase is already taught in a mishna (Rashbam). The Ri Migash understands the question in an almost opposite way. He assumes that Rav Pappa holds that the seller's superfluous phrase grants him the right to build another story above the house after he sells it, even if the house itself has collapsed, not just the right to rebuild an existing upper story. The Gemara therefore asks: According to Rav Zevid, just as the seller withholding tithes does not retain actual ownership of the land, but only a right to receive the tithes, so too, the seller of a house does not withhold actual ownership, but only the rights to the upper story for the sake of supporting projections. According to Rav Pappa, by contrast, the seller retains absolute ownership of the airspace above the house, which is not parallel to withholding tithes in the *baraita*.

אָמַר רַב דִּימִי מִנְּהַרְדְּעָא: הַאי מַאן דְּמַזַּבֵּין לֵיהּ בֵּיתָא לְחַבְרֵיהּ, אַף עַל גַּב דִּכְתַב לֵיהּ ״עוּמְקָא וְרוּמָא״, צָרִיךְ לְמִכְתַּב לֵיהּ: ״קְנֵי לָךְ מִתְּהוֹם אַרְעָא וְעַד רוּם רְקִיעָא״; מַאי טַעְמָא? דְּעוּמְקָא וְרוּמָא בִּסְתָמָא לָא קָנֵי, אַהֲנֵי ״עוּמְקָא וְרוּמָא״ לְמִיקְנָא עוּמְקָא וְרוּמָא, וְאַהֲנֵי ״מִתְּהוֹם אַרְעָא וְעַד רוּם רְקִיעָא״ לְמִיקְנָא בּוֹר וְדוּת וּמְחִילּוֹת.

§ The Gemara discusses what is included in the wordings of various contracts. **Rav Dimi from Neharde'a said:** Concerning **this one who sells a house to another** and wants the sale to include the entire property, **even if he writes for** the buyer in the bill of sale: I am selling you **the depth and the height**[H] of the house, he **must** also **write for him:**[N] **Acquire for yourself** the property **from the depth of the earth up to the height of the sky. What is the reason** for this addition? The reason **is that** the buyer **does not acquire the depth and the height** of the property **without** explicit **specification,**[N] and therefore, unless the matter has been explicitly stipulated, the buyer may not dig under the house or build above it. The words: **The depth and the height, effect the acquisition of the depth and the height** of the house for the buyer, allowing him to dig below or build above the house. **And the** additional phrase: **From the depth of the earth up to the height of the sky, effects**[N] **the acquisition of the pit and the cistern and the tunnels**[B] associated with the house.

לֵימָא מְסַיַּיע לֵיהּ: וְלֹא אֶת הַבּוֹר וְלֹא אֶת הַדּוּת אַף עַל פִּי שֶׁכָּתַב לוֹ ״עוּמְקָא וְרוּמָא״; וְאִי סָלְקָא דַּעְתָּךְ בִּסְתָמָא קָנֵי עוּמְקָא וְרוּמָא, לִיהֲנֵי ״עוּמְקָא וְרוּמָא״ לְמִיקְנָא בּוֹר וְדוּת וּמְחִילּוֹת! דְּלָא כְּתַב לֵיהּ.

The Gemara proposes: **Let us say** that the mishna (64a) **supports** Rav Dimi's opinion: One who sells a house has sold **neither the pit nor the cistern, even if he writes for** the buyer in the bill of sale that he is selling **him the depth and the height** of the house. **As if it enters your mind** to say that the buyer **acquires the depth and the height** of the house even **without** the **specification** that the depth and the height of the house are included in the sale, **let** the phrase **the depth and the height effect the acquisition of the pit and the cistern and the tunnels,** as he attached an additional stipulation to the transaction. The Gemara rejects this opinion: The mishna is referring to a case **where** the seller **did not write** these words **for him.**

וְהָא ״אַף עַל פִּי שֶׁכָּתַב לוֹ״ קָתָנֵי! הָכִי קָאָמַר: אַף עַל פִּי שֶׁלֹּא כָּתַב לוֹ – כְּמִי שֶׁכָּתַב דָּמֵי, לְמִיקְנָא עוּמְקָא וְרוּמָא; לְמִיקְנָא בּוֹר וְדוּת וּמְחִילּוֹת, אִי כְּתַב לֵיהּ ״עוּמְקָא וְרוּמָא״ – קָנֵי, וְאִי לָא כְּתַב – לָא קָנֵי.

The Gemara asks: **But** this line of reasoning is difficult, as the mishna explicitly **teaches** that the pit and the cistern are not sold **even if** the seller **writes for** the buyer that he is selling **him** the depth and the height of the house. The Gemara answers that **this** is what the mishna **is saying: Even though** the seller **did not write** these words **for him** in the bill of sale, **for** the purpose **of acquiring the depth and the height** of the house, **it is considered as if he wrote** them, as it is assumed that they were omitted by accident. By contrast, **for** the purpose **of acquiring the pit and the cistern and the tunnels, if** the seller explicitly **wrote for him** the words **the depth and the height,** the buyer **acquires** them, **but if he did not write** that phrase in the bill of sale, the buyer **does not acquire** them. No proof can be derived from this mishna.

תָּא שְׁמַע: וְלֹא אֶת הַגַּג בִּזְמַן שֶׁיֵּשׁ לוֹ מַעֲקֶה גָּבוֹהַּ עֲשָׂרָה טְפָחִים;

§ The Gemara now considers a different mishna. **Come** and **hear** what was taught in the mishna (61a): One who sells his house without explicitly stating what is included in the sale has **not** sold **the roof** along with the house **when it has a parapet ten handbreadths high,** as such a roof is considered a separate entity and is not included in the sale of the house.

NOTES

He must also write for him – צָרִיךְ לְמִכְתַּב לֵיהּ: The early commentaries disagree whether the seller must write for the buyer both phrases or only the second one. Those who say he must write both phrases maintain that it is the excess of superfluous phrases that secure the rights for the buyer, and therefore, both phrases must be written to guarantee those rights (Rid; Rashbam). Those who say that he need write only that the buyer should acquire for himself from the depth of the earth up to the height of the sky understand that the buyer acquires the additional rights because of the inclusive nature of this formulation (Rabbeinu Ḥananel; *Ge'onim*; see Rabbeinu Yona and Rashba).

He does not acquire the depth and the height without specification – עוּמְקָא וְרוּמָא בִּסְתָמָא לָא קָנֵי: This means that the buyer cannot dig beneath the house or build another story above it (Rashbam). The seller is permitted to do so, but in practice, the buyer can prevent this if the digging or building will damage the structural integrity of the house. Some hold that the seller is also barred from building or digging. According to this, the practical difference between the buyer and the seller is that if the buyer digs or builds, whatever was added belongs to the seller (Ri Migash).

And from the depth of the earth…effects – וְאַהֲנֵי מִתְּהוֹם אַרְעָא: This is because the phrase: The depth and the height, relates to use of the ground floor or the roof or the house itself, but it does not relate to an existing pit or cistern, nor does it refer to a roof with a ten-handbreadth-high parapet, all of which are significant in and of themselves (Ri Migash). The phrase: From the depths of the earth up to the height of the sky, does transfer ownership of those items. According to the Rashbam, the phrase the depth and the height suffices to transfer the ownership of a roof with a ten-handbreadth-high parapet, since a roof falls into the same category as a house, but it does not transfer the ownership of a pit or a cistern, which are used differently than the rest of the house. This is why the Gemara does not include the roof in the list of items requiring the phrase from the depths of the earth up to the height of the sky (Ramban).

BACKGROUND

Tunnels – מְחִילּוֹת: People used to dig cellars beneath their houses, which were structurally not part of those houses. They served as hideouts in times of danger or as storage rooms to conceal valuable items.

HALAKHA

The depth and the height – עוּמְקָא וְרוּמָא: If one sells a house to another and does not write: I am selling you the depth and the height of the house, the buyer acquires only the house itself. This includes the roof, provided that it is not four cubits wide and does not have a parapet ten handbreadths in height (Rema). The buyer may not dig beneath the house nor build above it, while the seller may do so as long as this will not damage or overburden the walls of the house. Others say that the seller may not dig beneath the house lest he damage it, but if the buyer digs pits or the like under the house, they belong to the seller (*Tur*, citing Ri Migash). If the seller writes: I am selling you the depth and the height of the house, the buyer acquires the airspace above the house and the ground below it, enabling him to build above the house and to dig beneath it. He does not acquire any existing structure in the ground or above the top of the house, nor does he acquire a roof having a ten-handbreadth-high parapet and a width of four cubits (Rema, citing Ramban). If the seller adds: Acquire for yourself from the depth of the earth up to the height of the sky, the buyer acquires the pits beneath the ground, the structures above the house, and also the roof, even if it has a ten-handbreadth-high parapet and is four cubits wide (Rema, citing Ramban). If the seller adds that phrase, he need not write: I am selling you the depth and the height of the house (Rambam *Sefer Kinyan, Hilkhot Mekhira* 24:15; *Shulḥan Arukh, Ḥoshen Mishpat* 214:3–4, and in the comment of Rema).

וְאִי סָלְקָא דַּעְתָּךְ בִּסְתָמָא קָנֵי עוּמְקָא וְרוּמָא, כִּי גָּבוֹהַּ עֲשָׂרָה טְפָחִים מַאי הָוֵי? כֵּיוָן דְּגָבוֹהַּ עֲשָׂרָה טְפָחִים – חָשִׁיב.

And if it enters your mind to say that when a house is sold **without specification,** the buyer **acquires the depth and the height** of the house, then even **when** it has a parapet **ten handbreadths high, what of it?**[N] Why shouldn't the buyer acquire the roof? The Gemara answers: **Since** the parapet **is ten handbreadths high,**[N] the roof **is significant** in its own right, and therefore, unless it is specifically included in the sale, the buyer does not acquire such a roof along with the house.

אֲמַר לֵיהּ רָבִינָא לְרַב אָשֵׁי, תָּא שְׁמַע: דְּאָמַר רֵישׁ לָקִישׁ, זֹאת אוֹמֶרֶת: הַמּוֹכֵר בַּיִת לַחֲבֵירוֹ, וְאָמַר לוֹ ״עַל מְנָת שֶׁדְּיוֹטָא הָעֶלְיוֹנָה שֶׁלִּי״ – דְּיוֹטָא הָעֶלְיוֹנָה שֶׁלּוֹ; וְאָמְרִינַן, לְמַאי הִלְכְתָא? רַב זְבִיד אָמַר: שֶׁאִם רָצָה לְהוֹצִיא בָּהּ זִיזִין – מוֹצִיא. רַב פָּפָּא אָמַר: שֶׁאִם רָצָה לִבְנוֹת עֲלִיָּיה עַל גַּבָּהּ – בּוֹנֶה;

Ravina said to Rav Ashi: Come and **hear** another proof, **as Reish Lakish says: That is to say** that with regard to one **who sells a house to another and says to him:** I am selling you this house **on the condition that the upper story is mine, the upper story is his. And** in the Gemara's examination of Reish Lakish's statement, **we said: With regard to what** ***halakha*** did Reish Lakish say this? In any case the upper story is his, as when he sold the house it was only the lower story that he sold to the buyer. **Rav Zevid says:** He said this to teach the *halakha* **that if** the seller **wishes to extend from** the upper story **projections** over the courtyard, which was included in the sale, **he may extend** them. **Rav Pappa says:** He said this to teach the *halakha* **that if** this upper story collapses and the seller **wishes to build an upper story on top of it** to replace it, **he may build** it.

וְאִי סָלְקָא דַּעְתָּךְ בִּסְתָמָא לָא קָנֵי, לָמָּה לִי ״עַל מְנָת״? אַהֲנֵי לֵיהּ ״עַל מְנָת״, דְּאִי נָפֵיל הָדַר בָּנֵי לָהּ.

And if it enters your mind to say that when a house is sold **without specification,** the buyer **does not acquire** the depth and the height of a house, Rav Pappa's statement is puzzling. As **why do I** need the seller to stipulate that he is selling the house **on the condition**[N] that the upper story is his when in any event the space above the house remains in the seller's possession? The Gemara answers: Stipulating that he is selling the house **on the condition** that the upper story is his **benefits him** in **that if** the upper story **collapses, he** may **rebuild it.** Without this stipulation the seller could not rebuild it, even if the sale did not include the depth and the height of the house.

מתני׳ לֹא אֶת הַבּוֹר וְלֹא אֶת הַדּוּת, אַף עַל פִּי שֶׁכָּתַב לוֹ עוּמְקָא וְרוּמָא. וְצָרִיךְ לִיקַּח לוֹ דֶּרֶךְ, דִּבְרֵי רַבִּי עֲקִיבָא; וַחֲכָמִים אוֹמְרִים: אֵינוֹ צָרִיךְ לִיקַּח לוֹ דֶּרֶךְ.

MISHNA One who sells a house without specification has sold **neither the pit**[N] **nor the cistern** [*dut*],[LH] **even if he writes for** the buyer in the bill of sale that he is selling **him the depth and the height** of the house, as anything that is not part of the house, like pits and cisterns, must be explicitly mentioned in the contract or else they remain in the seller's possession. **And** therefore the seller **must purchase for himself a path**[NH] through the buyer's domain to reach whatever remains his, because he has sold the area of the house along with the house itself, and he no longer has permission to walk there. This is **the statement of Rabbi Akiva. And the Rabbis say:** The seller **need not purchase for himself a path** through the buyer's domain, as this is certainly included in what he has withheld for himself from the sale.

NOTES

When it is ten handbreadths high, what of it – כִּי גָּבוֹהַּ עֲשָׂרָה טְפָחִים מַאי הָוֵי: The difficulty is that if the buyer acquires all of the airspace above a house even when it is sold without specification, what difference should it make whether the roof has a parapet ten handbreadths in height, or even no parapet at all? Since there is no roof above it, it is not an upper story that is excluded from the sale of the house, and it should simply be considered part of the airspace above the house (Rid). Several early commentaries had different versions of the text, according to which the proof offered here contradicts the opinion of Rav Dimi.

Since it is ten handbreadths high – כֵּיוָן דְּגָבוֹהַּ עֲשָׂרָה טְפָחִים: Because of its height the roof is treated as a separate building unit, like a gallery or an internal room, which is not considered part of the house. The Rashbam and *Tosafot* understand that even though the buyer does not acquire the roof, he may use the roof and even build above the roof. The other early commentaries disagree.

Why do I need to stipulate on the condition – לָמָּה לִי עַל מְנָת: This difficulty is raised only according to Rav Pappa's explanation, which grants the seller the right to build above the upper story, but not according to Rav Zevid's explanation (Rashbam; Ramban).

Neither the pit – לֹא אֶת הַבּוֹר: The pit and the cistern are not actually within the house, but rather underneath it, or above it, according to one interpretation of the Rambam mentioned in a later note; furthermore, they have different uses and distinct names. Therefore, they are not considered an integral part of the house that should be sold along with it.

And he must purchase for himself a path – וְצָרִיךְ לִיקַּח לוֹ דֶּרֶךְ: Even though the pit is his, he has sold the entire house and has no right to use it to access the pit. Therefore, he must purchase for himself a path to the pit, or appease the buyer in some other way, so that the buyer will allow him to access the pit on a regular basis.

LANGUAGE

Cistern [*dut*] – דּוּת: This word is found in Syriac in the form *ḥadut*, and that form sometimes appears in the writings of the Sages. Though its source has not been fully clarified, the term refers to a pit faced with masonry on the inside.

HALAKHA

Neither the pit nor the cistern – לֹא אֶת הַבּוֹר וְלֹא אֶת הַדּוּת: One who sells a house to another has sold neither the pit nor the cistern, even if they are not four cubits wide (*Sma*) and even if he writes in the bill of sale that he is selling the depth and the height of the house. This is the *halakha* even if he writes: I have not withheld anything in this sale (Rema, citing *Tur*), although some dispute this (Rema, citing Ran). If the seller writes in the bill of sale: Acquire for yourself from the depth of the earth up to the height of the sky, the buyer acquires even the underground pits and cisterns (Rambam *Sefer Kinyan, Hilkhot Mekhira* 24:15, 25:2; *Shulḥan Arukh, Ḥoshen Mishpat* 214:2–3, 11, and in the comment of Rema).

Purchase for himself a path – לִיקַּח לוֹ דֶּרֶךְ: One who sells a house but reserves for himself its pit by not writing in the bill of sale: Acquire for yourself from the depth of the earth up to the height of the sky, must purchase for himself a path to the pit from the buyer. If he states explicitly: I am selling you the house apart from the pit within it, he need not purchase for himself a path to the pit, in accordance with the opinion of Rabbi Akiva (Rambam *Sefer Kinyan, Hilkhot Mekhira* 25:3; *Shulḥan Arukh, Ḥoshen Mishpat* 214:2).

וּמוֹדֶה רַבִּי עֲקִיבָא, בִּזְמַן שֶׁאָמַר לוֹ "חוּץ מֵאֵלּוּ" – שֶׁאֵין צָרִיךְ לִיקַּח דֶּרֶךְ.

And Rabbi Akiva concedes that when the seller says to the buyer in the bill of sale: I am selling you this house apart from the pit and the cistern, he need not purchase for himself a path through the buyer's domain. Since the seller unnecessarily emphasized that the pit and the cistern are not included in the sale, he presumably intended to reserve for himself the right of access to them.

מְכָרָן לְאַחֵר – רַבִּי עֲקִיבָא אוֹמֵר: אֵינוֹ צָרִיךְ לִיקַּח לוֹ דֶּרֶךְ, וַחֲכָמִים אוֹמְרִים: צָרִיךְ לִיקַּח לוֹ דֶּרֶךְ.

If the seller kept the house, but sold the pit and the cistern to another,[HN] Rabbi Akiva says: The buyer need not purchase for himself a path through the seller's domain to reach what he has bought. But the Rabbis say: He must purchase for himself a path through the seller's domain.

גמ׳ יָתֵיב רָבִינָא וְקָא קַשְׁיָא לֵיהּ: הַיְינוּ בּוֹר הַיְינוּ דּוּת! אֲמַר לֵיהּ רָבָא תּוֹסְפָאָה לְרָבִינָא: תָּא שְׁמַע, דְּתַנְיָא: אֶחָד הַבּוֹר וְאֶחָד הַדּוּת בַּקַּרְקַע, אֶלָּא שֶׁהַבּוֹר בַּחֲפִירָה וְהַדּוּת בְּבִנְיָן. יָתֵיב רַב אַשִׁי וְקָא קַשְׁיָא לֵיהּ: הַיְינוּ בּוֹר הַיְינוּ דּוּת! אֲמַר לֵיהּ מָר קַשִּׁישָׁא בְּרֵיהּ דְּרַב חִסְדָּא לְרַב אַשִׁי: תָּא שְׁמַע, דְּתַנְיָא: אֶחָד הַבּוֹר וְאֶחָד הַדּוּת בַּקַּרְקַע, אֶלָּא שֶׁהַבּוֹר בַּחֲפִירָה וְהַדּוּת בְּבִנְיָן.

GEMARA

It is related that Ravina once sat and examined the matter and posed a difficulty: A pit is the same as a cistern.[N] Why, then, was it necessary to mention both of them? Rava Tosfa'a said to Ravina: Come and hear a solution to this question, as it is taught in a *baraita*: Both a pit and a cistern are dug out in the ground; the difference is only that a pit is constructed through digging alone, while a cistern is subsequently finished on the inside by building[N] masonry walls. It is similarly related that Rav Ashi once sat and posed a difficulty: A pit is the same as a cistern. Mar Kashisha, son of Rav Ḥisda, said to Rav Ashi: Come and hear a solution to this question, as it is taught in a *baraita*: Both a pit and a cistern are dug in the ground, the difference is only that a pit is constructed through digging alone, while a cistern is subsequently finished on the inside by building masonry walls.

"וְצָרִיךְ לִיקַּח לוֹ דֶּרֶךְ, דִּבְרֵי רַבִּי עֲקִיבָא; וַחֲכָמִים אוֹמְרִים: אֵינוֹ צָרִיךְ" וכו׳. מַאי לָאו בְּהָא קָא מִפַּלְגִי,

§ The mishna teaches: And the seller must purchase for himself a path through the buyer's domain; this is the statement of Rabbi Akiva. And the Rabbis say: The seller need not purchase such a path. What, is it not about this issue, which will immediately be explained, that Rabbi Akiva and the Rabbis disagree?

HALAKHA

If he sold them to another – מְכָרָן לְאַחֵר: If one sells a pit within his house to another, the buyer need not purchase for himself a path from the seller to access his pit; rather, he can simply enter the seller's house to use his pit. If there is another way to access his pit, the buyer may not access it via the seller's house (Rema, citing Rivash). This is in accordance with the opinion of Rabbi Akiva (Rambam *Sefer Kinyan, Hilkhot Mekhira* 25:3; *Shulḥan Arukh, Ḥoshen Mishpat* 214:2).

NOTES

If he sold them to another – מְכָרָן לְאַחֵר: This is not a continuation of the previous case, but rather a separate case in which a homeowner sells his pit to another. Rabbi Akiva says that in such a case, in addition to the pit the buyer also acquires access to the pit he bought. In his Commentary on the Mishna, the Rambam cites an additional interpretation that this is a case where the homeowner sells his house to one person and the pit to another. Rabbi Akiva Eiger notes that this contradicts the discussion of this mishna on 65a.

A pit is the same as a cistern – הַיְינוּ בּוֹר הַיְינוּ דּוּת: The Rashbam explains that since both a pit and a cistern are dug in the ground and both are intended for storing water, or on occasion other things, there appears to be no significant difference between them, and there is therefore no reason for mentioning both of them (see Rambam).

While a cistern is finished by building masonry – וְהַדּוּת בְּבִנְיָן: According to most commentaries, both a pit and a cistern are dug in the ground, as explained previously, but the cistern is dug in loose or soft ground, requiring the construction of masonry walls to strengthen and seal it. In his Commentary on the Mishna, the Rambam writes that a cistern is built above ground but has the same function as a pit. Some understand the Rambam as referring to a cistern built on a roof.

דְּרַבִּי עֲקִיבָא סָבַר: מוֹכֵר בְּעַיִן יָפָה מוֹכֵר, וְרַבָּנַן סָבְרִי: מוֹכֵר בְּעַיִן רָעָה מוֹכֵר. וּדְקָאָמַר נַמִי בְּעָלְמָא: רַבִּי עֲקִיבָא לְטַעֲמֵיהּ, דְּאָמַר מוֹכֵר בְּעַיִן יָפָה מוֹכֵר – מֵהָכָא.

As Rabbi Akiva holds that one who sells, sells generously,[N] so that whatever is not explicitly excluded from the sale is assumed to be sold, while the Rabbis hold that one who sells, sells sparingly, so that whatever is not explicitly included in the sale is assumed to be unsold. And perhaps that which is also stated generally: Rabbi Akiva conforms to his standard line of reasoning, as he says that one who sells, sells generously, is derived from here.

מִמַּאי? דִּלְמָא רַבִּי עֲקִיבָא סָבַר: אֵין אָדָם רוֹצֶה שֶׁיִּתֵּן מְעוֹתָיו וְיִדְרְסוּהוּ אֲחֵרִים, וְרַבָּנַן סָבְרִי: אֵין אָדָם רוֹצֶה שֶׁיִּטּוֹל מָעוֹת וְיִפְרַח בָּאֲוִיר!

The Gemara rejects this opinion and asks: From where do you arrive at such a conclusion? Perhaps Rabbi Akiva and the Rabbis do not disagree whether, in principle, a person who sells, sells generously or sparingly, but rather their disagreement is limited to this specific case. As Rabbi Akiva holds that a person does not want to spend his money on the purchase of a house and then have others tread upon his property,[N] and therefore he says that the seller must purchase for himself a path through the buyer's domain to reach his pit. And the Rabbis hold that a person does not want to receive money for the sale of his house and then have to fly through the air[N] in order to reach his pit, and therefore they say that the seller presumably withheld for himself a path to his pit.

וְאֶלָּא מִסֵּיפָא: מְכָרָן לְאַחֵר – רַבִּי עֲקִיבָא אוֹמֵר: אֵינוֹ צָרִיךְ לִיקַּח לוֹ דֶּרֶךְ, וַחֲכָמִים אוֹמְרִים: צָרִיךְ.

Rather, the proof is from the last clause of the mishna, which states: If the seller kept the house but sold the pit and the cistern to another, Rabbi Akiva says: The buyer need not purchase for himself a path through the seller's domain. But the Rabbis say: He must purchase for himself a path through the seller's domain. The *tanna'im* seem to disagree as to whether a person who sells, sells generously or sparingly.

NOTES

Sells generously – בְּעַיִן יָפָה מוֹכֵר: Rabbi Akiva holds to the principle that one who sells, sells generously, with regard to all aspects of selling (Rashbam). This means that it is assumed that the seller does not withhold for himself any rights to the object he is selling. Moreover, when he sells something, he agrees to transfer ownership not only of the items that the sale agreement requires him to transfer, but also items that relate to the sale but are not mentioned explicitly. Rabbi Akiva applies this principle even in circumstances where it constricts the seller by leaving him without any rights, e.g., without a way to access his own property.

And others tread upon his property – וְיִדְרְסוּהוּ אֲחֵרִים: This means that a buyer wishes to protect his privacy, and therefore would not ordinarily want anyone else to be entitled to pass through his domain once he has bought the property. The Rashbam explains that while this privilege actually depends upon the seller's intention at the time of the sale, with regard to whether or not he means to sell access to the property he excludes from the sale, the buyer's wishes are the foundation of the understandings with regard to the sale, and that therefore falls upon the seller to state explicitly if he wishes to retain access to his property.

And fly through the air – וְיִפְרַח בָּאֲוִיר: One is not prepared to sell his house in such a way that he will be prevented from accessing his own property; therefore, it must be assumed that he did not intend to forgo this privilege.

דִּלְמָא בְּהַאי פְּלִיגִי, דְּרַבִּי עֲקִיבָא סָבַר: בָּתַר דַּעְתָּא דְּלוֹקֵחַ אָזְלִינַן, וְרַבָּנַן סָבְרִי: בָּתַר דַּעְתָּא דְּמוֹכֵר אָזְלִינַן!

The Gemara rejects this proof as well: **Perhaps they disagree about** the following: **Rabbi Akiva holds** that **we follow the intention of the buyer,** as we assume that he would not have bought the pit if he would have to fly through the air to get there. **And the Rabbis hold** that **we follow the intention of the seller,** as presumably he would not have sold the pit if the buyer had the right to tread upon the seller's property to reach it.

אֶלָּא מֵהָא: לֹא אֶת הַבּוֹר וְלֹא אֶת הַגַּת וְלֹא אֶת הַשּׁוֹבָךְ, בֵּין חֲרֵבִין בֵּין יְשׁוּבִין; וְצָרִיךְ לִיקַּח לוֹ דֶּרֶךְ, דִּבְרֵי רַבִּי עֲקִיבָא, וַחֲכָמִים אוֹמְרִים: אֵינוֹ צָרִיךְ;

Rather, the proof that these *tanna'im* disagree whether one who sells sells generously or sparingly is **from this** mishna (71a), which teaches: One who sells a field, even if he states that he is selling everything in it to the buyer, has sold **neither the cistern, nor the winepress,**[B] **nor the dovecote,**[B] **whether** it is **abandoned or utilized,** as these items are not part of the field itself. **And** the seller **must purchase** for himself **a path** through the buyer's domain to reach whatever remains his. This is **the statement of Rabbi Akiva. And the Rabbis say:** The seller **need not** purchase a path through the buyer's domain.

הָא תּוּ לָמָּה לִי? אֶלָּא לָאו הָא קָא מַשְׁמַע לַן, דְּרַבִּי עֲקִיבָא סָבַר: מוֹכֵר בְּעַיִן יָפָה מוֹכֵר, וְרַבָּנַן סָבְרִי: מוֹכֵר בְּעַיִן רָעָה מוֹכֵר.

The Gemara explains the proof: **Why do I need this** ruling **as well,** seeing that this case involving the sale of a field appears to be identical to that involving the sale of a house? **Rather, is it not teaching us that Rabbi Akiva holds** that **one who sells, sells generously,** and therefore the seller must purchase for himself a path to his property, **while the Rabbis hold** that **one who sells, sells sparingly,** and therefore the purchase of such a path is not necessary?

וְדִלְמָא אַשְׁמוּעִינַן בַּיִת, וְקָא מַשְׁמַע לַן שָׂדֶה. וּצְרִיכָא; דְּאִי אַשְׁמוּעִינַן בַּיִת – מִשּׁוּם דִּבְעֵי צְנִיעוּתָא, אֲבָל שָׂדֶה – אֵימָא לָא;

The Gemara rejects this opinion: **Perhaps** the first mishna **taught us** this dispute with regard to **a house, and** the later mishna **teaches us** this dispute with regard to **a field. And** while this may seem redundant, both rulings are **necessary,**[N] **as had** the mishna **taught us** this *halakha* only with regard to **a house,** I would have said that the buyer is particular about people passing through his house, **because he desires privacy**[N] there. And it is for this reason that Rabbi Akiva says that in the absence of an explicit stipulation, the seller must purchase for himself a path to the pit. **But** in the case of **a field,** which is exposed to all, **say** that the buyer is **not** concerned about privacy.

וְאִי אַשְׁמוּעִינַן שָׂדֶה – מִשּׁוּם דְּקָשֵׁי לֵיהּ דַּוְושָׁא, אֲבָל בַּיִת – אֵימָא לָא!

And, conversely, **had** the mishna **taught us** this *halakha* only with regard to **a field,** I would have said that the buyer is particular about people passing through his field, **because treading** upon the field **is detrimental to it.**[N] And it is for this reason that Rabbi Akiva says that the seller must purchase for himself a path to the pit. **But** in the case of **a house,** which is not adversely affected by treading through it, **say** that the buyer is **not** opposed to the seller passing through.

אֶלָּא מִסֵּיפָא: מְכָרָן לְאַחֵר – רַבִּי עֲקִיבָא אוֹמֵר: אֵינוֹ צָרִיךְ לִיקַּח לוֹ דֶּרֶךְ, וַחֲכָמִים אוֹמְרִים: צָרִיךְ;

Rather, the proof that Rabbi Akiva and the Rabbis disagree whether one who sells, sells generously or sparingly is **from the latter clause** of that mishna (71a), which teaches: But if the seller kept the field but **sold** the cistern and winepress **to another** person, **Rabbi Akiva says:** The buyer **need not purchase for himself a path** through the seller's domain to reach what he has bought, since a seller sells generously. **But the Rabbis say: He must** purchase for himself a path through the seller's domain.

הָא תּוּ לָמָּה לִי? הַיְינוּ הַךְ! אֶלָּא לָאו הָא קָא מַשְׁמַע לַן, דְּרַבִּי עֲקִיבָא סָבַר: מוֹכֵר בְּעַיִן יָפָה מוֹכֵר, וְרַבָּנַן סָבְרִי: מוֹכֵר בְּעַיִן רָעָה מוֹכֵר, שְׁמַע מִינַּהּ.

The Gemara explains the proof: **Why do I also** need **this,** seeing as **this** case involving the sale of a pit or a winepress in a field **is** identical to **that** involving the sale of a pit or a cistern in a house? **Rather, is it not teaching us**[N] **that Rabbi Akiva holds** that **one who sells, sells generously,**[H] **while the Rabbis hold** that **one who sells, sells sparingly?** The Gemara affirms: **Conclude from** the latter clauses of these *mishnayot* that this is so.

אִיתְּמַר, רַב הוּנָא אָמַר רַב:

It was stated that the *amora'im* disagree about how the *halakha* should be decided with regard to this issue. **Rav Huna says** that **Rav says:**

BACKGROUND

Winepress – גַּת:

Winepress excavated at Migdal HaEmek, Israel

Dovecote – שׁוֹבָךְ:

View of the inside of a dovecote

NOTES

And both are necessary – וּצְרִיכָא: This argument is made according to the opinion of Rabbi Akiva, but it is also true, in inverse fashion, according to the opinion of the Rabbis. Had the mishna taught this *halakha* only with regard to a house, one might have said that the Rabbis permitted the seller to pass through it, because treading through it is not detrimental to the house, but in the case of a field they might agree with Rabbi Akiva. And, conversely, had the mishna taught this *halakha* only with regard to a field, one might have said that in the case of a house, where the buyer's privacy is affected, even the Rabbis might not allow the seller access (Rashbam; Ritva).

He desires privacy – בָּעֵי צְנִיעוּתָא: A house is a private place by its very nature, and one does things there that he does not want the public to see. Therefore, there is an especially strong reason to say that one who buys a house does not want anyone else to have the right to pass through it.

Treading is detrimental to it – קָשֵׁי לֵיהּ דַּוְושָׁא: Walking through a field and treading upon the freshly plowed or planted areas, in and of itself, can damage the crops, but this is not true in the case of a house, where no direct damage results from simply passing through it. Since there are various considerations that apply differently to a house than to a field, both examples are necessary, as if only one was given, it might be assumed that in the other instance all would agree (Rashbam).

Rather, is it not teaching us – אֶלָּא לָאו הָא קָא מַשְׁמַע לַן: This clause in the mishna is superfluous. If it teaches that Rabbi Akiva and the Rabbis disagree as to whether we follow the intentions of the buyer or of the seller, that was already taught by the parallel clause in the previous mishna; and if it teaches that their dispute applies both to a house and to a field, that was taught in the previous clause of this mishna. Clearly, then, this clause comes to teach that the disagreement between Rabbi Akiva and the Rabbis is not limited to a specific case, but rather it is a general dispute about whether a seller sells generously, with ramifications for a number of different matters.

HALAKHA

One who sells, sells generously – מוֹכֵר בְּעַיִן יָפָה מוֹכֵר: Anyone who sells, sells generously, and he does not withhold for himself any more than what he explicitly excludes from the sale. Therefore, even if, when selling a house, one withholds the pit within it for himself, he is, nevertheless, required to purchase a path from the buyer to access the pit, in accordance with the opinion of Rabbi Akiva (Rambam *Sefer Kinyan*, *Hilkhot Mekhira* 24:12, 25:3; *Shulḥan Arukh*, *Ḥoshen Mishpat* 154:28, 155:25, 216:4, and in the comments of Rema).

הֲלָכָה כְּדִבְרֵי חֲכָמִים, וְרַב יִרְמְיָה בַּר אַבָּא אָמַר שְׁמוּאֵל: הֲלָכָה כְּרַבִּי עֲקִיבָא. אֲמַר לֵיהּ רַב יִרְמְיָה בַּר אַבָּא לְרַב הוּנָא: וְהָא זִמְנִין סַגִּיאִין אֲמַרִיתָהּ קַמֵּיהּ דְּרַב הִלְכְתָא כְּרַבִּי עֲקִיבָא, וְלָא אֲמַר לִי וְלָא מִידֵּי! אֲמַר לֵיהּ: הֵיכִי תָּנֵיתָהּ? אֲמַר לֵיהּ: אִיפְּכָא תָּנֵינָא. מִשּׁוּם הָכִי לָא אֲמַר לָךְ וְלָא מִידֵּי.

The *halakha* is in accordance with the statement of the Rabbis, while Rav Yirmeya bar Abba[P] **says that Shmuel says: The *halakha* is in accordance with** the opinion of **Rabbi Akiva. Rav Yirmeya bar Abba said to Rav Huna:**[P] **But many times I said before Rav** that **the *halakha*** is **in accordance with** the opinion of **Rabbi Akiva, and never did he say anything to me,** which indicates that he holds that the *halakha* is in accordance with the opinion of Rabbi Akiva and not that of the Rabbis. Rav Huna **said to him: How did you teach** the mishna before Rav? Rav Yirmeya bar Abba **said to him: I taught** it with **the opposite** attributions, that is to say, the opinion that is attributed in the mishna to Rabbi Akiva, I would teach in the name of the Rabbis. Rav Huna said to him: **Due to that** reason, **he never said anything to you,** as Rav agreed with the version that you attributed to Rabbi Akiva.

אֲמַר לֵיהּ רָבִינָא לְרַב אַשִׁי: לֵימָא אָזְדוּ לְטַעֲמַיְיהוּ,

With regard to the opinions of Rav and Shmuel, **Ravina said to Rav Ashi: Shall we say** that Rav and Shmuel, in their opinions stated with regard to this matter, each **follow their** general lines of **reasoning,** as they appear to have disagreed about this same issue in another context as well?

דְּאָמַר רַב נַחְמָן אָמַר שְׁמוּאֵל: הָאַחִין שֶׁחָלְקוּ – אֵין לָהֶן לֹא דֶּרֶךְ זֶה עַל זֶה, וְלֹא סוּלָּמוֹת זֶה עַל זֶה, וְלֹא חַלּוֹנוֹת זֶה עַל זֶה, וְלֹא אַמַּת הַמַּיִם זֶה עַל זֶה,

As Rav Naḥman says that **Shmuel says:** With regard to **brothers who divided**[NH] their father's estate between them, **they do not have** a right of **way against each other,** i.e., to walk through the other's property to reach his own, even though this is how the place was used in their father's lifetime; **nor** do they have the right of **ladders against each other,** i.e., the right to set up a ladder in the other's property in order to get to his own; **nor** do they have the right of **windows against each other,** i.e., the right to prevent the other from building a wall facing his windows; **nor** do they have the right of **a water channel against each other,** i.e., the right to pass a water channel through the other's property.

וְהִזָּהֲרוּ בָּהֶן שֶׁהֲלָכוֹת קְבוּעוֹת הֵן; וְרַב אָמַר: יֵשׁ לָהֶן?

Rav Naḥman continues: **And be careful with these** rulings, **since they are established *halakhot*. And Rav says: They do** retain all of these privileges. Consequently, Rav and Shmuel appear to be following their general lines of reasoning here, as Shmuel holds that when the brothers, who are like sellers, divide their father's estate, they transfer property to each other generously without retaining privileges in each other's property, while Rav holds that they transfer the property sparingly.

צְרִיכָא, דְּאִי אַשְׁמוּעִינַן בְּהַהִיא – בְּהַהִיא קָאָמַר רַב, מִשּׁוּם דְּאָמַר לֵיהּ: בָּעֵינָא לְמֵידַר בֵּיהּ כִּי הֵיכִי דְּדָרוּ בֵּיהּ אֲבָהָתַי; תֵּדַע, דִּכְתִיב: ״תַּחַת אֲבֹתֶיךָ יִהְיוּ בָנֶיךָ״; אֲבָל בְּהָא – אֵימָא מוֹדֵי לֵיהּ לִשְׁמוּאֵל.

The Gemara comments: Nevertheless, it was **necessary** to teach this disagreement in both cases, as the *halakha* in the one case cannot be derived from the *halakha* in the other. **As had we been taught** this dispute only **in that** case, of the brothers who divided their father's estate, I would have said that only **in that** case **does Rav say** that they retain all of the earlier privileges, **because** one brother can **say to the** other: **I wish to live in** this house **just as my ancestors,** who had all of those privileges, **lived in it. Know** that there is substance to this claim, **as it is written: "Instead of your fathers shall be your sons"** (Psalms 45:17). **But in this** case of an ordinary house sale, **say that he concedes to Shmuel** that a seller sells generously.

PERSONALITIES

Rav Yirmeya bar Abba – רַב יִרְמְיָה בַּר אַבָּא: A first and second generation Babylonian *amora*, Rav Yirmeya bar Abba was one of the first Sages to study under Rav after Rav's arrival in Babylonia. As Rav Yirmeya bar Abba was already a scholar in his own right, he came to Rav primarily to learn the Torah of Eretz Yisrael. Rav Yirmeya bar Abba is among the most prominent promulgators of Rav's statements, and many Sages from both Babylonia and Eretz Yisrael studied with him. His son, son-in-law, and daughter's son were all Sages as well.

Rav Huna – רַב הוּנָא: One of the great second-generation Babylonian *amora'im*, Rav Huna was most closely associated with his teacher, Rav. Rav Huna descended from the house of the Exilarchs. Despite his aristocratic lineage, he lived in abject poverty for many years. Later in life, he became wealthy and lived comfortably, and he distributed his wealth for the public good. Rav Huna was the greatest of Rav's students, to the extent that Shmuel, Rav's colleague, used to treat him deferentially and direct questions to him. After Rav's death, Rav Huna became the head of the yeshiva of Sura and filled that position for about forty years. His prominence in Torah and his loftiness of character helped make the yeshiva of Sura the preeminent center of Torah for many centuries. Because of Rav Huna's extensive Torah knowledge, the *halakha* is almost always ruled in accordance with his opinion in disputes with all of his colleagues and contemporaries. The only exception was in civil law, where the rulings were in accordance with the opinion of Rav Naḥman. Rav Huna had many students, some of whom studied exclusively with him; moreover, Rav's younger students remained to study with Rav Huna, his disciple, after his death. Rav Huna's son, Rabba bar Rav Huna, was one of the greatest Sages of the following generation.

NOTES

Brothers who divided – הָאַחִין שֶׁחָלְקוּ: The Gemara's opinion here is that brothers who have divided their father's estate between them are like buyers. That is to say, it is as if each of them sold part of his inheritance to his brother, and it is not as if each of them, by virtue of his right of inheritance simply clarified which portion had been designated for him from the outset.

HALAKHA

Brothers who divided – הָאַחִין שֶׁחָלְקוּ: Brothers who divided their father's estate between them are each considered as if they had purchased their share from the other. Therefore, they do not have a right of way, a right of ladders, a right of windows, or a right of a water channel against each other, as once they have divided the inheritance, none retain any rights in the portions of the others; the *halakha* is in accordance with the opinion of Shmuel, who says that one who sells, sells generously. With regard to windows, some hold that one may build a wall facing the other's window but he may not demand that the other brother seal his windows, while others hold that he may even demand that the other brother seal his windows (Rambam *Sefer Kinyan, Hilkhot Shekhenim* 2:12; *Shulḥan Arukh, Ḥoshen Mishpat* 154:27 and in the comment of Rema, 173:3).

NOTES

They do not have a right of way against each other – **אֵין לָהֶן דֶּרֶךְ זֶה עַל זֶה**: This applies even according to the opinion of the Rabbis that one who sells, sells sparingly, as that principle applies only when the seller retains something for himself. Here, he withdraws from the property completely, and therefore, he transfers the same privileges to one property owner as he does to the other (Rashbam; Rid). According to the opinion of Rabbi Akiva, if at the outset the seller sold only the inner residence, the buyer would immediately acquire the privilege to exit through the outer one (Ri Migash).

וְאִי אִיתְּמַר בְּהָא – בְּהַךְ קָאָמַר שְׁמוּאֵל, אֲבָל בְּהָא – אֵימָא מוֹדֵי לֵיהּ לְרַב, צְרִיכָא.

And if the dispute **was stated** only **in this** case of an ordinary house sale, I would have said that only **in this** case **does Shmuel say** that a seller sells generously and does not withhold a path for himself, **but in that** case, of the brothers who divided their father's estate, **say that he concedes to Rav** that the desire to live there just as his ancestors did supersedes the seller's general tendency to sell generously. Therefore, it was **necessary** to teach this dispute in both cases.

אֲמַר לֵיהּ רַב נַחְמָן לְרַב הוּנָא: הִלְכְתָא כְּוָותִין אוֹ הִלְכְתָא כְּוָותַיְיכוּ? אֲמַר לֵיהּ: הִלְכְתָא כְּוָותַיְיכוּ, דְּמִקָּרְבִיתוּ לְבָבָא דְּרֵישׁ גָּלוּתָא דִּשְׁכִיחִי דַּיָּינֵי.

As for the ruling itself, **Rav Naḥman**, who was a disciple of Shmuel, **said to Rav Huna: Is the *halakha* in accordance with our opinion, or is the *halakha* in accordance with your opinion?** Rav Huna **said to him: The *halakha* is in accordance with your opinion, as you are near the gate of the Exilarch,**[B] **where the judges are** frequently **found,** and therefore you are more proficient in monetary law.

אִיתְּמַר: שְׁנֵי בָתִּים זֶה לִפְנִים מִזֶּה, שְׁנֵיהֶם בְּמֶכֶר, שְׁנֵיהֶם בְּמַתָּנָה – אֵין לָהֶן דֶּרֶךְ זֶה עַל זֶה, כׇּל שֶׁכֵּן חִיצוֹן בְּמַתָּנָה וּפְנִימִי בְּמֶכֶר.

§ **It was stated:** If there are **two residences, one** situated **behind the other,**[H] and the owner transferred ownership of the **two of them,** each one to a different person, **by means of a sale,** or if he transferred ownership of the **two of them,** each to a different person, **as a gift, they do not have** a right of **way against each other.** That is, the one who acquired the inner residence may not pass through the outer residence, since each of them received equal privileges from the previous owner. And **all the more so** is this the *halakha* **if the outer** residence was transferred **by means of a gift, and the inner** residence was transferred **by means of a sale,** as it may be assumed that a gift is made in a more generous manner than is a sale.

חִיצוֹן בְּמֶכֶר וּפְנִימִי בְּמַתָּנָה – סְבוּר מִינָּהּ: אֵין לָהֶן דֶּרֶךְ זֶה עַל זֶה;

As for the case where the **outer** residence was transferred **by means of a sale, and the inner** residence was transferred **by means of a gift,** some Sages at first **understood from here** that **they do not have a** right of **way against each other,**[N] that is, that the recipient of the inner residence may not pass through the outer residence.

וְלָא הִיא, מִי לָא תְּנַן: בַּמֶּה דְבָרִים אֲמוּרִים – בְּמוֹכֵר, אֲבָל בְּנוֹתֵן מַתָּנָה נוֹתֵן אֶת כּוּלָּן? אַלְמָא, מַאן דְּיָהֵיב מַתָּנָה – בְּעַיִן יָפָה יָהֵיב, הָכָא נַמִי מַאן דְּיָהֵיב מַתָּנָה – בְּעַיִן יָפָה יָהֵיב.

But that **is not so,** as **didn't we learn** in a mishna (71a): **In what** case **is this statement,** that these items are excluded, **said?** It is said **with regard to one who sells** a field, **but with regard to one who gives** it away **as a gift,** it is assumed that **he gives all of it,** including everything found in the field. **Apparently, one who gives** property **as a gift gives** it more **generously** than does one who sells it, as gifts are generally given to friends to whom one wishes to transfer as many privileges as possible. **Here too, then, one who gives** property **as a gift gives** it more **generously** than does one who sells it, and so the recipient of the inner residence acquires a right of way through the outer apartment.

BACKGROUND

Exilarch – **רֵישׁ גָּלוּתָא**: The Exilarch, who descended from the house of David, was recognized by the Jews as the heir to the scepter of Judah and entrusted with broad official powers. He served as the leader of the Jews of the Persian Empire and as their representative before the authorities, who regarded him as a scion of a royal dynasty. He enjoyed a lofty position within the Persian court, and there were periods during which he was even considered third in the royal hierarchy. The Exilarch was responsible for the collection of a major portion of the taxes paid by the Jewish community, and he was authorized to appoint leaders and judges who could impose corporal, and sometimes even capital, punishment.

Adjacent to the Exilarch's home was a special rabbinical court appointed by him to deal with monetary and property matters. He had the authority to make certain appointments within the Jewish community throughout the empire, although he appears to have made these appointments in consultation with the heads of the great academies. The Talmud refers to the Exilarchs by the honorific title Mar before or after their name. The Exilarchs were devoted to the Torah, and some were significant scholars in their own right.

HALAKHA

Two residences, one behind the other – **שְׁנֵי בָתִּים זֶה לִפְנִים מִזֶּה**: If one simultaneously transfers the ownership of two residences, which are situated one behind the other, each to a different person, whether both as gifts or both via a sale, the new owners do not have a right of way against each other, as he gives or sells to each of them generously in an equal measure (*Sma*). Therefore, the owner of the inner residence must persuade the owner of the outer one to allow him access to his property. All the more so is this true if the prior owner gave the outer residence as a gift while selling the inner one. If the prior owner gave the inner residence as a gift and sold the outer one, the recipient of the inner residence is automatically granted access through the outer one, as one who gives a gift gives it more generously than does one who makes a sale. This is the *halakha* only when the two transactions occurred simultaneously, but if the prior owner transferred ownership of the inner residence before transferring ownership of the outer one, the owner of the inner residence is granted access through the outer one even after it has been transferred to its new owner. Conversely, if the outer residence was transferred first, the owner of the inner residence is not granted access through the outer one (Rambam *Sefer Kinyan*, *Hilkhot Mekhira* 25:4; *Shulḥan Arukh*, *Ḥoshen Mishpat* 214:9–10).

מתני׳ הַמּוֹכֵר אֶת הַבַּיִת – מָכַר אֶת הַדֶּלֶת אֲבָל לֹא אֶת הַמַּפְתֵּחַ, מָכַר אֶת הַמַּכְתֶּשֶׁת קְבוּעָה אֲבָל לֹא אֶת הַמִּיטַּלְטֶלֶת, מָכַר אֶת הָאִיצְטְרוֹבִיל אֲבָל לֹא אֶת הַקֶּלֶת, וְלֹא אֶת הַתַּנּוּר וְלֹא אֶת הַכִּירַיִם. בִּזְמַן שֶׁאָמַר לוֹ: ״הוּא וְכָל מַה שֶּׁבְּתוֹכוֹ״ –

MISHNA One who sells a house[H] **has,** as part of the sale, **sold** also **the door, but not the key.**[N] **He has sold the mortar that is fixed** in the ground, **but not the portable** one. **He has sold the** immovable **lower millstone** [***ha'itzterobil***],[LN] **but not the** portable **upper stone** [***hakelet***],[LNB] the funnel into which one pours the grain to be ground. **And** he has sold **neither the oven**[NB] **nor the double stove,** as they are deemed movable. **When** the seller **says to** the buyer: I am selling you **it, and everything that is in it,**

LANGUAGE

Lower millstone [*itzterobil*] – אִיצְטְרוֹבִיל: From the Greek στρόβιλος, *strobilos*, which means a rounded or circular object. The shape of this part of the mill is understood as similar to the shape of a pinecone, which is also called *itzterobil*.

Upper stone [*kelet*] – קֶלֶת: Apparently from the Greek κάλαθος, *kalathos*, which means basket, this word is used elsewhere to mean a woman's basket. Here too, it is referring to a receptacle. Some suggest that the Greek word derives from a Semitic language, perhaps an abridged version of the word *kala'at*, a wicker basket.

HALAKHA

One who sells a house – הַמּוֹכֵר אֶת הַבַּיִת: When one sells a house, all of the stationary objects that are part of the house are included in the sale. This includes the door, the door bolt attached to the wall, the lock installed in the door, the stationary lower millstone, and the stationary boards at the entrance that are attached with clay. If they are attached with pegs, some say that they are not considered stationary (Rema). The seller has also sold the oven, the double stove, and the millstone, all of which are stationary, but he has not sold the key, even if it is set in the door, nor the portable mortar, nor the vessel into which the flour falls after milling, nor the window frames, nor the pieces of wood that are stationed beneath the legs of a bed. If the seller specified at the time of the sale that he is selling the house and all that it contains, then everything is included (Rambam *Sefer Kinyan*, *Hilkhot Mekhira* 25:5; *Shulḥan Arukh*, *Ḥoshen Mishpat* 214:11).

NOTES

But not the key – אֲבָל לֹא אֶת הַמַּפְתֵּחַ: Since it is portable and not an integral part of the house, the key is not included in the sale of the house. The Ra'avad notes that even though the key is constantly in the door, it is designated for supplementary protection of the house and therefore not sold along with the house. By contrast, the door, even though it swings on its hinges and may even be removed at times, is considered part of the walls of the house and is therefore included in the sale.

The lower millstone – הָאִיצְטְרוֹבִיל: While all the commentaries agree that this is the more stationary part of the mill, opinions vary as to its precise definition (see also 20b). Some of the *ge'onim* describe it as the lower millstone (Rav Hai Gaon), while certain early commentaries, including Rashbam, understand that it is the base upon which the millstone rests. According to the Rambam in his Commentary on the Mishna, it is made from wood. The diverse opinions depend in part upon the version of the text of the mishna that is accepted, and especially upon whether a millstone is mentioned later in the mishna, after the double stove, as it is in some versions of the text.

The upper stone – הַקֶּלֶת: This term as well is subject to various interpretations: The upper millstone (Rav Hai Gaon), the funnel through which the grain is poured into the mill (Rashbam), the enclosure around the millstone to prevent dispersal of the flour after the grinding (Rambam's Commentary on the Mishna), or the receptacle used to collect the flour as it exits the millstone (Rambam, *Mishne Torah*).

And he has sold neither the oven – וְלֹא אֶת הַתַּנּוּר: At first glance this seems to be referring to an oven or double stove that is not attached to the ground. There are, however, alternative versions of the text, such as in the Jerusalem Talmud, which indicate that these items are sold along with the house, suggesting that they are attached to the ground. Some explain that, regardless of the version, the mishna is referring to an oven or double stove that is attached to the ground with clay, and that the different versions disagree about whether such a connection is considered attachment with respect to monetary matters, as it is easily removable (*Tosafot*, citing Rabbi Shimshon of Saens).

BACKGROUND

Lower millstone [*itzterobil*] and upper stone [*kelet*] – אִיצְטְרוֹבִיל וְקֶלֶת: This type of mill was composed of the *itzterobil*, a cone-shaped stationary bed stone, which protruded upward into the *kelet*, a hollow, hourglass-shaped runner stone. The grain would be poured into the *kelet* and funneled through the top half to its midpoint, below which it would be trapped and ground between the two stones. Poles were inserted into the *kelet*, by means of which people or donkeys would rotate the heavy stone to grind the grain between it and the stationary *itzterobil*.

In the image on the right, only the bottom of the *itzterobil* is visible, since most of it is covered by the *kelet*.

Oven – תַּנּוּר: Many ovens in the talmudic period were made of clay. Wood was burned inside the oven until it turned to ash. The ash was then swept away to make room for dough that had been rolled out flat and was then stuck to the walls or base of the heated oven.

Roman mill

BACKGROUND

Mortar – מַכְתֶּשֶׁת: During the periods of the Mishna and the Talmud, extensive use was made of mortars, both to prepare grain for grinding and to crush various types of legumes. Since they were designed for a great deal of work with a large volume of produce, the mortars were relatively large, although there were also smaller mortars for grinding seasonings and spices. Sometimes, for the sake of convenience, the mortar was attached to the ground with mud, clay, or some other adhesive substance, and sometimes rocks imbedded in the ground were hollowed out and turned into mortars.

הֲרֵי כּוּלָּן מְכוּרִין.

all these components **are sold** as part of the sale of the house.

גמ׳ לֵימָא, מַתְנִיתִין דְּלָא כְּרַבִּי מֵאִיר, דְּאִי רַבִּי מֵאִיר, הָא אָמַר: מָכַר אֶת הַכֶּרֶם – מָכַר תַּשְׁמִישֵׁי כֶּרֶם!

GEMARA

The Gemara suggests: **Let us say that the mishna**[N] that distinguishes between different types of household items **is not in accordance with** the opinion of **Rabbi Meir. As if** it is in accordance with the opinion of **Rabbi Meir, doesn't he say** in a *baraita* (78b): **If one sold a vineyard, he has sold** all of **the utensils of the vineyard,**[N] including the movable ones? The same should be true for the sale of a house.

אֲפִילּוּ תֵּימָא רַבִּי מֵאִיר, הָתָם קְבִיעַ, הָכָא לָא קְבִיעַ. וְהָא מַפְתֵּחַ דּוּמְיָא דְּדֶלֶת קָתָנֵי, מַה דֶּלֶת דִּקְבִיעָא, אַף מַפְתֵּחַ דִּקְבִיעַ! אֶלָּא מְחַוַּורְתָּא, מַתְנִיתִין דְּלָא כְּרַבִּי מֵאִיר.

The Gemara answers: **You** may **even say** that the mishna was taught in accordance with the opinion of **Rabbi Meir,** as a distinction can be made between the two cases. **There,** in the case of a vineyard, the reference is to utensils that are **fixed**[N] in the vineyard and never removed from it, and therefore they are included in the sale, while **here,** in the case of a house, the mishna is referring to utensils that are **not fixed** in the house, and therefore they are not part of the sale. The Gemara objects: **But doesn't** the mishna **teach** the *halakha* governing **a key in similar fashion to** the *halakha* governing **the door,** indicating that **just as a door** is **fixed** in the house, **so too, a key is fixed**[N] in the house? **Rather, it is clear** that **the mishna is not in accordance with** the opinion **of Rabbi Meir.**

תָּנוּ רַבָּנַן: הַמּוֹכֵר אֶת הַבַּיִת – מָכַר אֶת הַדֶּלֶת וְאֶת הַנֶּגֶר וְאֶת הַמַּנְעוּל, אֲבָל לֹא אֶת הַמַּפְתֵּחַ. מָכַר אֶת הַמַּכְתֶּשֶׁת הַחֲקוּקָה, אֲבָל לֹא אֶת הַקְּבוּעָה. מָכַר הָאִיצְטְרוֹבִיל, אֲבָל לֹא אֶת הַקֶּלֶת, לֹא אֶת הַתַּנּוּר וְלֹא אֶת הַכִּירַיִם וְלֹא אֶת הָרֵיחַיִם; רַבִּי אֱלִיעֶזֶר אוֹמֵר: כָּל הַמְחוּבָּר לַקַּרְקַע הֲרֵי הוּא כַּקַּרְקַע;

The Sages taught in a *baraita* (*Tosefta* 3:1): One **who sells a house has sold the door and the door bolt and the lock, but** he has **not** sold **the key. He has sold the mortar**[B] **that was hollowed out** of the ground[N] **but not** the mortar **that was fixed** to the ground after its construction. **He has sold the** immovable **lower millstone but not the** portable **upper stone.** And he has sold **neither the oven, nor the double stove, nor the hand mill. Rabbi Eliezer says:** The principle is that **any** item **attached to the ground is** considered **like the ground** and included in the sale.

בִּזְמַן שֶׁאָמַר לוֹ ״הוּא וְכָל מַה שֶּׁבְּתוֹכוֹ״ – הֲרֵי כּוּלָּן מְכוּרִין; בֵּין כָּךְ וּבֵין כָּךְ, לֹא מָכַר לֹא אֶת הַבּוֹר וְלֹא אֶת הַדּוּת וְלֹא אֶת הַיָּצִיעַ.

When the seller **says to** the buyer: I am selling you **it and everything that is in it, all these** components **are sold** along with the house. **Both in this case and in that case he did not sell the pit or the cistern or the gallery,** as they are considered separate entities that are not at all part of the house.

NOTES

Let us say that the mishna – לֵימָא מַתְנִיתִין: The Rashbam interprets the suggestion as relating to the mishna's distinction between a stationary mortar and one that is portable. *Tosafot* and other early commentaries explain that the question is based upon the mishna's statement that a key, even though it is one of the standard utensils in a house, is not sold along with the house.

The utensils of the vineyard – תַּשְׁמִישֵׁי כֶּרֶם: This refers to the posts used to support the grapevines, as explained later (69a) and in the commentaries. According to Rabbi Meir, once these posts have been readied for this purpose, even if they have not yet been set in their designated places, they are included in the sale.

There the reference is to utensils that are fixed – הָתָם קְבִיעַ: The vineyard's utensils, even though they are not attached to the ground, are stationed there permanently and never removed, and therefore they are included in the sale (Rid). Others understand that unlike a key, the vineyard's utensils are actually attached to the ground, and therefore they are sold along with the vineyard (Rabbeinu Gershom).

So too a key is fixed – אַף מַפְתֵּחַ דִּקְבִיעַ: Rabbeinu Gershom and the Rashbam explain that the key is set in the door and never removed from it. Several of the early commentaries accept the explanation of the Ri Migash and say that initially the Gemara assumed that the key in question was not specific to this door, but fit many other doors as well; but in the end it concludes that the key was designed specifically for this door, and therefore it is considered stationary because it cannot be used for another door. Alternatively, the Ri Migash suggests that initially the Gemara assumed that this is a key for a portable lock, but it later concludes that it is a key for a stationary lock installed in the door, and so its usefulness is limited to this house.

The mortar that was hollowed out of the ground – הַמַּכְתֶּשֶׁת הַחֲקוּקָה: The reference here is to a rock in the ground that was shaped into a utensil, and it was left in its place in the ground and used as a mortar, whereas a fixed mortar is one that was attached to the ground after its construction. Rabbeinu Yitzhak of Dampierre explains that a fixed mortar is one that was attached to the ground and will not be moved again, whether it was formed into a mortar before it was attached to the ground or only afterward. In any case, Rav Hai Gaon notes that this *baraita* disagrees with the mishna, which states explicitly that a fixed mortar is included in the sale of a house. The Rashbam maintains that the mishna follows the opinion of Rabbi Eliezer. In the Jerusalem Talmud, however, the mishna is explained in accordance with the first *tanna* of the *baraita*.

תָּנוּ רַבָּנַן: צִינּוֹר שֶׁחֲקָקוֹ וּלְבַסּוֹף קְבָעוֹ – פּוֹסֵל אֶת הַמִּקְוֶה, קְבָעוֹ וּלְבַסּוֹף חֲקָקוֹ – אֵינוֹ פּוֹסֵל אֶת הַמִּקְוֶה. מַנִּי? לָא רַבִּי אֱלִיעֶזֶר וְלָא רַבָּנַן.

§ **The Sages taught** in a *baraita*: **A duct**[B] **that one hollowed out**[HN] **and afterward attached** to the ground or to a building **invalidates a ritual bath**[N] through the water it channels to the bath. The water in a ritual bath must be gathered directly from rain or a stream, not drawn with vessels. If one hollowed out a log and used it to channel water into the bath, this is considered drawn water, as he used a vessel. By contrast, if **one attached it** first **and afterward hollowed it out, it does not invalidate the ritual bath.** Before the log was hollowed out, it was already attached to and considered part of the ground, and therefore the act of hollowing it out does not turn it into a vessel. The Gemara asks: **Whose** opinion is this? It appears to be **neither** the opinion of **Rabbi Eliezer, nor** that of **the Rabbis.**

הֵי רַבִּי אֱלִיעֶזֶר? אִילֵימָא רַבִּי אֱלִיעֶזֶר דְּבַיִת, דִּלְמָא הַיְינוּ טַעְמָא, דְּרַבִּי אֱלִיעֶזֶר סָבַר: מוֹכֵר בְּעַיִן יָפָה מוֹכֵר, וְרַבָּנַן סָבְרִי: מוֹכֵר בְּעַיִן רָעָה מוֹכֵר!

The Gemara clarifies the question: To **which** opinion of **Rabbi Eliezer** is this referring? **If we say** it is referring to the opinion of **Rabbi Eliezer** in the aforementioned *baraita* **with regard to** the sale of **a house,** that any item attached to the ground is considered part of the house and is sold along with it, there is a difficulty. As **perhaps this is the reasoning** employed in the dispute with regard to the sale of a house, **that Rabbi Eliezer holds** that **one who sells, sells generously**[N] anything that is attached to the ground, **while the Rabbis hold** that **one who sells, sells sparingly,** selling only utensils that serve an intrinsic function in the house and nothing else, even if they are attached to the ground. But this teaches us nothing about the opinions of Rabbi Eliezer and the Rabbis with respect to a ritual bath.

וְאֶלָּא רַבִּי אֱלִיעֶזֶר דִּכְוֶורֶת דְּבוֹרִים. דִּתְנַן: כַּוֶּורֶת דְּבוֹרִים – רַבִּי אֱלִיעֶזֶר אוֹמֵר: הֲרֵי הִיא כְּקַרְקַע, וְכוֹתְבִין עָלֶיהָ פְּרוֹזְבּוֹל,

But rather, the reference must be to the opinion of **Rabbi Eliezer concerning a beehive. As we learned** in a mishna (*Shevi'it* 10:7): With regard to **a beehive** attached to the ground by clay, **Rabbi Eliezer says: It is like land,**[N] **and** therefore **one may write a document that prevents the Sabbatical Year from canceling an outstanding debt** [***prosbol***] based **upon it.** Such a document cannot be written unless the borrower owns some land, and a beehive is considered like land for this purpose.

HALAKHA

A duct that one hollowed out – צִינּוֹר שֶׁחֲקָקוֹ: If one hollowed out a wooden pipe and created a receptacle within it, e.g., an area that can catch dirt or stones, and afterward he fixed it to the ground, all the water flowing through it into a ritual bath is considered drawn water. If that ritual bath then lacks a majority of water that was not drawn (*Shakh*), it is invalidated. If the pipe is of earthenware, the receptacle invalidates the bath only if it holds one-quarter of a *log*. If he first fixed the wooden pipe to the ground, and afterward he hollowed it out and created a receptacle within it, the water flowing through it is not considered drawn water, and it does not invalidate the ritual bath (Rambam *Sefer Tahara, Hilkhot Mikvaot* 6:6; *Shulḥan Arukh, Yoreh De'a* 201:36).

NOTES

A duct that one hollowed out – צִינּוֹר שֶׁחֲקָקוֹ: The Rashbam explains that the reference here is to an ordinary duct made of wood or stone that is open at both ends. Since it was fashioned into a vessel before it was attached to the ground, it retains its status as a vessel even afterward. Most commentaries maintain that a pipe that is open at both ends, or even one that is open at only one end, is in any event not considered a vessel that invalidates the water flowing through it by giving it the status of drawn water. They explain that the pipe here has a small receptacle hollowed into it to catch dirt and pebbles and prevent them from flowing along with the water, and it is because of this receptacle that it is considered a vessel (Ramban; Rashba; Rid).

Invalidates a ritual bath – פּוֹסֵל אֶת הַמִּקְוֶה: According to accepted tradition, a ritual bath effects purification only if its waters are collected naturally, but not if they are drawn by human hands. Therefore, any water reaching a ritual bath via a vessel is considered water drawn through human agency, which invalidates the ritual bath.

One who sells, sells generously – מוֹכֵר בְּעַיִן יָפָה מוֹכֵר: Rabbi Eliezer holds that the seller will not bother to remove an item that is attached to the ground, and unless he explicitly states otherwise, it is assumed that the seller intends for such an item to remain in its place for the buyer. By contrast, the Rabbis hold that whatever is not an integral part of the house itself is not included in the sale, and since the seller is not generous with the buyer, he keeps whatever he can.

It is like land – הֲרֵי הִיא כְּקַרְקַע: A beehive is acquired in the same way that land is acquired, i.e., through money, a document, or taking possession of it, and it is not acquired through pulling, as one would acquire movable property (*Tosafot*). Similarly, a beehive is like land with respect to oaths mandated by Torah law, as when one admits to part of a claim, just as an oath is not taken to counter a claim with regard to land, so too, an oath is not taken to counter a claim with regard to a beehive.

BACKGROUND

Duct – צִינּוֹר: Some of the pipes referred to in talmudic literature are like modern-day pipes, hollow cylinders through which liquids flow. Others were open on top and similar to a gutter. Such pipes were produced by carving a deep groove in some solid material, such as wood, for the liquid to flow through. This explains how a pipe could be affixed to the ground before being hollowed out. According to *Tosafot*, the pipe referred to in the *baraita* had an additional indentation at some point, carved deeper than the bottom surface of the groove, for catching pebbles and other debris, so that they would not flow further along with the liquid.

וְאֵינָהּ מְקַבֶּלֶת טוּמְאָה בִּמְקוֹמָהּ, וְהָרוֹדֶה מִמֶּנָּה בְּשַׁבָּת – חַיָּיב חַטָּאת;

And such a beehive **is not susceptible to ritual impurity** as long as it is fixed **in its place.**[N] **And one who removes** honey **from it on Shabbat**[N] **is liable** to bring **a sin-offering,** as he is likened to one who harvests produce attached to the ground.

וַחֲכָמִים אוֹמְרִים: אֵינָהּ כְּקַרְקַע, וְאֵין כּוֹתְבִין עָלֶיהָ פְּרוֹזְבּוּל, וּמְקַבֶּלֶת טוּמְאָה בִּמְקוֹמָהּ, וְהָרוֹדֶה מִמֶּנָּה בְּשַׁבָּת – פָּטוּר.

But the Rabbis say: Such a beehive **is not like land,**[H] **and** therefore **one may not write a** ***prosbol*** based **upon it, and it is susceptible to ritual impurity** even when it is fixed **in its place, and one who removes** honey **from it on Shabbat**[H] **is exempt** from bringing a sin-offering. This mishna suggests that Rabbi Eliezer holds that a vessel that was affixed to the ground is considered like land for all purposes. This contradicts the *baraita* that states that if one hollowed out a pipe and then affixed it to the ground, it is still considered a vessel, and water flowing through it is considered drawn water that invalidates a ritual bath. This indicates that the *baraita* was not taught in accordance with the opinion of Rabbi Eliezer.

הָתָם כִּדְאָמַר רַבִּי אֶלְעָזָר טַעְמָא, דְּאָמַר רַבִּי אֶלְעָזָר: מַאי טַעְמָא דְּרַבִּי אֱלִיעֶזֶר? דִּכְתִיב: ״וַיִּטְבֹּל אוֹתָהּ בְּיַעְרַת הַדְּבָשׁ״,

The Gemara rejects this opinion, stating that **there,** in the mishna, Rabbi Eliezer treats the beehive like land for **the reason that Rabbi Elazar stated,** and not because he holds that all vessels that are affixed to the ground are considered like land. **As Rabbi Elazar stated: What is the reasoning for** the statement **of Rabbi Eliezer** with regard to one who removes honey from a beehive? His rationale is **as it is written:** "And he put forth the end of the rod that was in his hand **and dipped it in the honeycomb** [*ya'arat hadevash*]" (I Samuel 14:27).

מָה יַעַר – הַתּוֹלֵשׁ מִמֶּנּוּ בְּשַׁבָּת חַיָּיב חַטָּאת, אַף דְּבַשׁ – הָרוֹדֶה מִמֶּנּוּ בְּשַׁבָּת חַיָּיב חַטָּאת!

Rabbi Eliezer understands that since the Hebrew words used here for honeycomb can also mean honey forest, the verse comes to teach that **just as** with regard to **a forest,**[N] **one who picks** anything from a tree **on Shabbat is liable** to bring **a sin-offering, so too,** with regard to a beehive containing **honey, one who removes** honey **from it on Shabbat is liable** to bring **a sin-offering,** as the beehive is treated like land. Consequently, Rabbi Eliezer relies here on a special derivation, which does not necessarily apply to other vessels. Therefore, nothing can be learned from this about Rabbi Eliezer's opinion with regard to the pipe in the *baraita*.

אֶלָּא רַבִּי אֱלִיעֶזֶר דְּדַף, דִּתְנַן: דַּף שֶׁל נַחְתּוֹמִין שֶׁקְּבָעוֹ בְּכוֹתֶל – רַבִּי אֱלִיעֶזֶר מְטַהֵר, וַחֲכָמִים מְטַמְּאִין;

Rather, the reference with regard to the hollowed-out duct must be to the opinion of **Rabbi Eliezer concerning** a baker's **board** on which he kneads the dough, **as we learned** in a mishna (*Kelim* 15:2): With regard to **a baker's board** [***daf shel naḥtomin***][NL] **that was affixed to the wall,**[H] **Rabbi Eliezer renders** it **not susceptible to ritual impurity, while the Rabbis render** it **susceptible to ritual impurity.** This seems to indicate that, according to Rabbi Eliezer, anything that is affixed to the ground or to something else that is affixed to the ground is treated like land, and therefore it cannot become ritually impure.

NOTES

It is not susceptible to ritual impurity in its place – אֵינָהּ מְקַבֶּלֶת טוּמְאָה בִּמְקוֹמָהּ: According to this explanation, the beehive ceases to be susceptible to ritual impurity when it becomes attached to the ground. Though it was initially a vessel, once it is attached to the ground it has the status of land, which is not susceptible to ritual impurity (Rashbam). The phrase: In its place, means that it has this status as long as it is attached to the ground (Ritva).

One who removes honey from it on Shabbat – הָרוֹדֶה מִמֶּנָּה בְּשַׁבָּת: According to this explanation, one who removes honey from a beehive is considered to be detaching something from the place where it grew. Since a beehive that is attached to the ground is considered like the ground, when one removes the honey from it, it is as if he were detaching it from the ground. This is considered prohibited labor on Shabbat, a subcategory of the primary category of harvesting. One who does so unintentionally on Shabbat is liable to bring a sin-offering.

Just as with regard to a forest – מָה יַעַר: According to this explanation, there is no general *halakha* here concerning vessels attached to the ground, but rather, this *halakha* applies specifically to a beehive. Since the verse likens honey to a forest, one who removes honey from a beehive on Shabbat is treated like one who detaches something from the ground in a forest (Rashbam). The analogy between honey and forest applies to all aspects of *halakha* relating to them, and not just removing honey from a beehive on Shabbat. Therefore, a beehive is considered attached to the ground like the trees of a forest with respect to all *halakhot* governing land (Ri Migash). The early commentaries disagree about whether this *halakha* applies to any beehive, even one that is not attached to ground, or only to a beehive that is actually attached to the ground.

Baker's board – דַּף שֶׁל נַחְתּוֹמִין: Most commentaries explain that this is a wooden board on which the dough was kneaded or on which the loaves were arranged for baking (Rabbeinu Gershom). Others suggest that this was a board on which the baked loaves were set on display for sale (Rashbam). In the case in the Gemara, the baker's board was prepared for its purpose and then fixed to a wall. Since it was prepared for its purpose by human hands, it is a vessel, but, having no receptacle, it falls into the category of flat wooden vessels.

LANGUAGE

Baker's board [*daf shel naḥtomin*] – דַּף שֶׁל נַחְתּוֹמִין: The word *naḥtom* is mentioned in the Mishna and is used as a designation for a professional baker who sells bread to the public. This word is borrowed from the Aramaic, which, in turn, derived it from the Acadian word *nuhatimmu*, which means a baker of bread.

This baker's board is generally understood as a wooden board on which one kneads and rolls out the dough. According to the Rashbam, the reference here is to a board that is attached to the wall at an angle to display the loaves for sale. In either case, this wooden board is completely flat and lacks a receptacle.

HALAKHA

It is not like land – אֵינָהּ כְּקַרְקַע: By Torah law, oaths are not imposed to counter claims with regard to landed property or produce that is still attached to the ground and requires its nourishment. As for a movable item that was affixed to the ground, such as a beehive, some say that it is not like landed property and therefore an oath can be imposed with regard to it (*Tur*, citing *Sefer HaIttur*), as the *halakha* is in accordance with the opinion of the Rabbis, as opposed to that of Rabbi Eliezer. Others (Mordekhai; Rabbeinu Ḥananel; Gra) rule that in this matter, anything attached to the ground is considered like landed property (*Tur, Ḥoshen Mishpat* 95; *Shulḥan Arukh, Ḥoshen Mishpat* 95:1, and in the comment of Rema).

One who removes honey from it on Shabbat – הָרוֹדֶה מִמֶּנָּה בְּשַׁבָּת: Removing honey from a beehive on Shabbat is prohibited, as it is similar to the prohibited labor of detaching. The Rema limits this to cases where the honey is stuck to the walls of the beehive; but if, before Shabbat, the honeycombs were detached, or if they were broken and the honey flows freely within the beehive, the honey may be removed on Shabbat. This is in accordance with the opinion of the Rabbis that the prohibition against removing honey from a beehive is a rabbinic decree (Rambam *Sefer Zemanim, Hilkhot Shabbat* 21:6; *Shulḥan Arukh, Oraḥ Ḥayyim* 321:13).

A baker's board that was affixed to the wall – דַּף שֶׁל נַחְתּוֹמִין שֶׁקְּבָעוֹ בְּכוֹתֶל: A metal baker's board, whether it has or it lacks a receptacle, and even if it is fixed to a wall, is considered a vessel and not land, and therefore it is susceptible to ritual impurity. This is in accordance with the opinion of the Rabbis as interpreted by Rabbi Yosei ben Rabbi Ḥanina (Rambam *Sefer Tahara, Hilkhot Kelim* 11:24).

מַנִּי? אִי רַבִּי אֱלִיעֶזֶר – אֲפִילּוּ חֲקָקוֹ וּלְבַסּוֹף קְבָעוֹ, אִי רַבָּנַן – אֲפִילּוּ קְבָעוֹ וּלְבַסּוֹף חֲקָקוֹ נַמִי!

Having concluded that this is the dispute between Rabbi Eliezer and the Rabbis that was referred to previously, the Gemara repeats the question raised earlier about the ruling in the *baraita* with regard to a duct: **Whose** opinion is it? It appears to be neither that of Rabbi Eliezer nor that of the Rabbis. As **if** it is the opinion of **Rabbi Eliezer,** then **even if one hollowed out** a duct **and afterward he fixed it** to the ground, water flowing through it should not be considered drawn water that invalidates a ritual bath, as according to Rabbi Eliezer, a baker's board that was first a vessel, but then became fixed in a wall, is treated like land. And **if** it is the opinion of **the Rabbis,** then **even if he** first **fixed** the duct to the ground **and** only **afterward he hollowed it out,** the duct should **also** be treated like a vessel, and the water flowing through it should be considered drawn water, as the Rabbis do not differentiate with regard to the stage at which the baker's board was affixed to the wall.

לְעוֹלָם רַבִּי אֱלִיעֶזֶר הִיא, וְשָׁאנֵי פְּשׁוּטֵי כְּלֵי עֵץ, דְּטוּמְאָה דְּרַבָּנַן.

The Gemara responds: **Actually,** one can explain that the *baraita* **is** in accordance with the opinion of **Rabbi Eliezer, but** the *halakha* governing **flat wooden vessels**[H] without a receptacle, such as a baker's board, **is different, as** they are vessels susceptible to **ritual impurity** only **by rabbinic law,**[N] but by Torah law they are not vessels susceptible to ritual impurity. Therefore, Rabbi Eliezer agrees that when the baker's board is affixed to the wall, it is no longer subject to the rabbinic decree. A hollowed-out duct, however, is a vessel susceptible to ritual impurity by Torah law, and it remains so even if afterward it was affixed to the ground. Therefore, the water flowing through it invalidates a ritual bath.

מִכְּלָל דִּשְׁאִיבָה דְּאוֹרָיְיתָא?

The Gemara asks: **By inference,** from the fact that Rabbi Eliezer is more stringent in the case of the duct and distinguishes between a duct that was first hollowed out and only afterward affixed to the ground, and one that was first affixed to the ground and only afterward hollowed out, does it not follow **that** the *halakha* governing **drawn** water, i.e., that drawn water added to a ritual bath that does not already contain the necessary quantity of water invalidates it, applies **by Torah law?**

HALAKHA

Flat wooden vessels – פְּשׁוּטֵי כְּלֵי עֵץ: Wooden vessels lacking a receptacle, which are known as flat wooden vessels, are susceptible to ritual impurity only by rabbinic law, and some are not susceptible to any impurity at all. This does not apply to flat wooden vessels that are fit for sitting or lying upon and, consequently, are susceptible to ritual impurity imparted by treading. That is to say, if a man who experiences a gonorrhea-like discharge [*zav*], or the like, treads, lies, or sits on such vessels, they become ritually impure by Torah law. Since they are susceptible to impurity imparted by treading by Torah law, they are susceptible to all types of impurity by rabbinic law (Rambam *Sefer Tahara*, *Hilkhot Kelim* 1:10, 23:1).

NOTES

Flat wooden vessels…as they are susceptible to ritual impurity by rabbinic law – פְּשׁוּטֵי כְּלֵי עֵץ דְּטוּמְאָה דְּרַבָּנַן: According to the Rashbam, flat wooden vessels are not susceptible to ritual impurity at all, neither by Torah law nor rabbinic law. The only exceptions are flat wooden vessels that are fit for sitting or lying upon, which are susceptible to ritual impurity by Torah law. Therefore, according to the Rashbam, this statement is the Gemara's initial assumption that is abandoned at the conclusion of the discussion.

The majority of the early commentaries disagree. All agree that flat wooden vessels that are fit for sitting or lying upon are susceptible to ritual impurity by Torah law. Also, all agree that flat wooden vessels that do not serve humans or their utensils directly, such as arrows, are not susceptible to ritual impurity at all. The early commentaries disagree about flat wooden vessels that serve humans or their utensils, e.g., tables, at which a person eats or upon which he rests his utensils. Some hold that they are susceptible to ritual impurity by Torah law (Ramban; Rashba), while others hold that their susceptibility to ritual impurity is by rabbinic law (Rambam; *Tosafot*). All agree, apart from the Rashbam, that a baker's board is susceptible to ritual impurity only by rabbinic law since it does not serve any direct human use.

וְהָא קַיְימָא לַן: דְּרַבָּנַן! וְעוֹד, הָאָמַר רַבִּי יוֹסֵי בֶּן רַבִּי חֲנִינָא: בְּדַף שֶׁל מַתֶּכֶת מַחְלוֹקֶת!

But this is difficult, as **we maintain** that the *halakha* that drawn water invalidates a ritual bath applies only by **rabbinic** decree. **And furthermore, doesn't Rabbi Yosei ben Rabbi Ḥanina say** that the **dispute** between Rabbi Eliezer and the Rabbis is **with regard to a board of metal,**[N] and a metal vessel, even if it is flat and lacks a receptacle, is susceptible to ritual impurity by Torah law? This means that, according to Rabbi Eliezer, even a vessel that is susceptible to ritual impurity by Torah law loses its status as a vessel when it is affixed to the ground. Consequently, the question returns: Whose opinion is cited in the *baraita* that states that if one first hollowed out a duct and afterward fixed it to the ground, it is still considered a vessel and water flowing through it invalidates a ritual bath, but if he first fixed it to the ground and afterward hollowed it out, the water flowing through it does not invalidate a ritual bath?

NOTES

With regard to a board of metal – בְּדַף שֶׁל מַתֶּכֶת: According to all opinions, a metal vessel, even if it is flat, is susceptible to ritual impurity by Torah law. The dispute here relates to the effect of fixing the baker's metal board to the wall: Is the board, which is susceptible to impurity by Torah law, considered part of the wall, and therefore treated like the ground, which is not susceptible to impurity, or is its status as a vessel not capable of being nullified in this manner?

לְעוֹלָם רַבָּנַן הִיא, וְשָׁאנֵי שְׁאִיבָה דְּרַבָּנַן.

The Gemara answers: **Actually,** one can explain that the *baraita* **is in** accordance with the opinion of **the Rabbis,**[N] who deem the baker's metal board susceptible to ritual impurity even when it is fixed to a wall, **but** the *halakha* governing **drawn** water added to a deficient ritual bath **is different,** because drawn water invalidates a deficient ritual bath only **by rabbinic law,**[H] and therefore the Rabbis were lenient.

אִי הָכִי, אֲפִילּוּ חֲקָקוֹ וּלְבַסּוֹף קְבָעוֹ נַמִּי! שָׁאנֵי הָתָם, דְּאִיכָּא תּוֹרַת כְּלִי עָלָיו בְּתָלוּשׁ.

The Gemara asks: **If so,** then **even** if one first **hollowed out** the duct **and** only **afterward fixed it** to the ground, water flowing through it should not invalidate the ritual bath **as well.** The Gemara answers: **It is different there,** where the duct was hollowed out before being affixed to the ground, as the duct **had the status of a vessel**[N] **when** it was still **detached** from the ground, and therefore the Rabbis were not willing to be lenient to such an extent and rule that water flowing through the duct does not invalidate a ritual bath.

בָּעֵי רַב יוֹסֵף: מֵי גְשָׁמִים שֶׁחָשַׁב עֲלֵיהֶם לְהָדִיחַ אֶת הָאִיצְטְרוּבְּלִין, מַהוּ לִזְרָעִים?

§ **Rav Yosef raises a dilemma:** With regard to **rainwater** that was falling and the owner consciously **desired** that it should fall **so that it would wash** his immovable **lower millstones,**[N] **what is the** *halakha* **with regard to the seeds** in the millstones? The verse "But if any water be put upon the seed…it shall be unclean to you" (Leviticus 11:38) teaches that seeds and other food become susceptible to ritual purity only after they have been detached from the ground, and water, or another of the seven liquids specified in the mishna (*Makhshirin* 6:4), has been put on them. The food must be exposed to the liquid willfully by the owner; that is, he must desire or at least be pleased that the food should become wet. Rav Yosef asks about a case where the owner wants the rain to fall on the millstones: Does that water make the seeds upon which it falls susceptible to ritual impurity?

אַלִּיבָּא דְּרַבִּי אֱלִיעֶזֶר דְּאָמַר: כָּל הַמְחוּבָּר לְקַרְקַע הֲרֵי הוּא כְּקַרְקַע – לָא תִּיבָּעֵי לָךְ, כִּי תִּיבָּעֵי לָךְ – אַלִּיבָּא דְּרַבָּנַן דְּאָמְרִי: אֵינוֹ כְּקַרְקַע, מַאי? תֵּיקוּ.

The Gemara clarifies Rav Yosef's question: **Do not raise this dilemma according to** the opinion **of Rabbi Eliezer, who says: Anything attached to the ground** has the same legal status **as the ground.** Since the lower millstones are attached to the ground, they therefore have the same legal status as the ground, and water that falls on the ground, even if it is pleasing to the owner, does not make food susceptible to ritual impurity. **When should you raise this dilemma?** Raise it **according to** the opinion **of the Rabbis, who say:** It does **not** have the same legal status **as the ground. What** is the *halakha* with respect to imparting susceptibility to ritual impurity? The Gemara concludes: An answer to this question was not found; therefore, the dilemma **shall stand** unresolved.

שְׁלַח לֵיהּ רַב נְחֶמְיָה בְּרֵיהּ דְּרַב יוֹסֵף לְרַבָּה בְּרֵיהּ דְּרַב הוּנָא זוּטֵי לִנְהַרְדְּעָא: כִּי אָתְיָא הַךְ אִיתְּתָא לְקַמָּךְ,

§ **Rav Neḥemya, son of Rav Yosef, sent** a message **to Rabba son of Rav Huna the Short at Neharde'a: When this woman** bearing this letter **comes before you,**

HALAKHA

Drawn water…invalidates a deficient ritual bath by rabbinic law – **שְׁאִיבָה דְּרַבָּנַן**: Some maintain that even if a ritual bath is filled entirely with drawn water, it is invalid only by rabbinic law (Rambam; Rabbeinu Yitzḥak of Dampierre; *Ge'onim*). The *Levush* maintains that this is also the opinion of the *Shulḥan Arukh*. The Rema, citing Rabbi Shimshon of Saens and the Rosh, writes that only if less than half of the ritual bath's minimum volume is completed by drawn water is it invalid by rabbinic law, but if half or more is completed by drawn water it is invalid by Torah law (Rambam *Sefer Tahara*, *Hilkhot Mikvaot* 4:1–2; *Shulḥan Arukh*, *Yoreh De'a* 201:3, and in the comment of Rema, and see *Taz* on 201:70).

NOTES

Actually it is the opinion of the Rabbis – **לְעוֹלָם רַבָּנַן הִיא**: The Gemara's conclusion here is that the *baraita* about the hollowed-out duct can be explained in accordance with the opinion of the Rabbis about a baker's metal board, and the apparent contradiction is resolved as follows: A baker's metal board is susceptible to ritual impurity by Torah law, and therefore fixing it to a wall does not nullify that susceptibility; but drawn water invalidates a ritual bath only by rabbinic decree, and therefore the Rabbis are lenient with regard to water flowing into a ritual bath through a duct that was hollowed out only after it was attached to the ground (Rashbam).

It had the status of a vessel – **תּוֹרַת כְּלִי עָלָיו**: Since this duct was already hollowed out, it is considered a vessel, even if later it was attached to the ground. If water flowing through such a duct would not invalidate a ritual bath, this would negate the rabbinic decree relating to drawn water (Rashbam).

So that it would wash his lower millstones – **לְהָדִיחַ אֶת הָאִיצְטְרוּבְּלִין**: The Rashbam interprets this as a general question as to whether an item that was movable and was later attached to the ground is considered as attached or detached with regard to susceptibility to ritual impurity. Many early commentaries maintain that the question is specifically about stationary millstone bases, as if it were a general question it should have been asked in a general manner, without mentioning millstone bases. They explain that the Gemara assumes that certain items that had been movable but were later attached to the ground, such as a wall, are treated like the ground with regard to susceptibility to ritual impurity, while others, like a baker's metal board, are considered detached even if they were physically fixed to a wall or the like. Therefore, the question here is whether the Rabbis, who exclude even the stationary mortar from the sale of a house but include the stationary millstone base, consider the millstone base attached to the ground for the purpose of susceptibility to ritual impurity or whether they include the stationary millstone base in the sale of a house solely because the seller sells generously, but with regard to susceptibility to ritual impurity they consider it portable (*Tosafot*; Ri Migash; Rid).

אגבה עישור נכסי אפילו מאצטרובלי דריחיים. אמר רב אשי: כי הוינן בי רב כהנא, מגבינן אפילו מעמלא דבתי.

collect for her one-tenth of her father's **estate,**[N] in keeping with the rabbinic ordinance that states that if a man dies, his sons are obligated to give his daughter a tenth of his landed properties as a dowry, and collect it **even from** his immovable **lower millstones,**[NH] as they too are considered landed property. **Rav Ashi said: When we were** students **in Rav Kahana's house we would collect** for this purpose **even from the rent of houses;**[NH] since this money is earned from real estate, it too has the status of landed property and is included in the dowry calculations.

מתני׳ המוכר את החצר – מכר בתים, בורות שיחין ומערות, אבל לא את המטלטלין; בזמן שאמר לו: ״הוא וכל מה שבתוכו״ – הרי כולן מכורין. בין כך ובין כך, לא מכר לא את המרחץ ולא את בית הבד שבתוכה. רבי אליעזר אומר: המוכר את החצר – לא מכר אלא אוירה של חצר.

MISHNA One **who sells a courtyard**[H] without specifying what is included in the sale **has sold** with it **the houses, pits, ditches, and caves** found in the courtyard, **but** he has **not** sold **the movable property.**[N] **When** the seller **says to** the buyer: I am selling you **it and everything that is in it, all these** components **are sold** along with the courtyard, even the movable property. **Both** in **this** case, where he executes the sale without specification, **and** in **that** case, where he adds the phrase that includes the movable property, **he has not sold the bathhouse, nor** has he sold **the olive press that is in** the courtyard, as each is an entity with a discrete purpose and not an integral part of the courtyard. **Rabbi Eliezer says:** One **who sells a courtyard** without specifying what is included in the sale **has sold only the airspace,** i.e., the open space, **of the courtyard,** but nothing found in the courtyard, not even the houses.

גמ׳ תנו רבנן: המוכר את החצר – מכר בתים החיצונים ובתים הפנימים ובית החולסאות; חנויות פתוחות לתוכה – נמכרות עמה, ושאין פתוחות לתוכה – אין נמכרות עמה; פתוחות לכאן ולכאן – [אלו] ואלו נמכרות עמה. רבי אליעזר אומר: המוכר את החצר – לא מכר אלא מילוסא של חצר.

GEMARA **The Sages taught** in a *baraita* (*Tosefta*, 3:1): One **who sells a courtyard has sold** with it **the outer houses** that can be accessed directly from the courtyard, **and the inner houses** that can be entered only via the outer houses, **and the area of the sand fields** [*uveit haḥolsaot*].[NL] As for the **stores,** those **that open into** the courtyard **are sold** along **with it;** those that **do not open into it,** but rather open into the public domain, even if they are located in the courtyard, **are not sold** along **with it;** and those that **open** both **into this** courtyard **and into that** other public domain are grouped together with those that open into this courtyard alone, and both **these and those are sold with it. Rabbi Eliezer says:** One **who sells a courtyard** without specifying what is included in the sale **has sold only the open space of the courtyard.**

NOTES

One-tenth of the estate – עישור נכסי: One of the stipulations in a marriage contract is that a father must provide a dowry for each of his daughters. If the daughter marries during the father's lifetime, he gives a sum that accords with the prevalent custom, as well as with his capabilities and personality. If she marries after the death of her father, the court assesses how much the father would likely have provided. When the court has some basis for such an assessment, e.g., when the father had married off one of his daughters during his lifetime, the court uses that to set the sum of the dowry. When there is no clear basis upon which to make such an estimate, the Sages enacted that the dowry should be one-tenth of the landed property of the father's estate.

From his lower millstones – מאצטרובלי דריחיים: Even though the lower millstones are not part of the ground, since they are considered part of a house for the purpose of a sale, they are also considered land with regard to the one-tenth of the deceased's estate that must be given to his daughter as her dowry.

From the rent of houses – מעמלא דבתי: Most of the commentaries interpret this term as referring to the money a landlord receives from rentals. Rabbeinu Gershom understands that it means the manure that is produced in the courtyards and the houses. With regard to the rent money, *Tosafot* state that the reference is to uncollected rent money, as once the heirs have collected the money it is considered movable property from which the dowry cannot be collected. The Ri Migash writes that the dowry can be collected from the rent only for the period during which the father was still alive, but not from the rent for later periods.

Movable property – מטלטלין: The reference here is to movable property that is associated with the house, e.g., furniture and other items usually used in a house. This does not include movable property stored there, but not associated specifically with the house, e.g., merchandise or work tools (Rashbam).

Area of sand fields – בית החולסאות: Some early commentaries had a version of the text according to which the sand fields are not included in the sale (Rabbeinu Barukh; Rabbeinu Gershom; Rashbam). Many commentaries explain the term as referring to a place containing high-quality sand from which glass is produced (Rabbeinu Ḥananel; Ri Migash; Rashbam). Others explain that it means a building built of stones from which glass is produced, making it an exceptional building in its own right, yet nevertheless it is considered part of the courtyard (*Nimmukei Yosef*). Yet others argue that courtyards do not normally contain such a building, and therefore they interpret the term as referring to a building without floorboards where the floor is comprised of sand. Such a building is generally not used for dwelling, but for storage (Ramah). Still others propose that this is referring to a rocky area within the courtyard (Rabbeinu Gershom; Rabbeinu Barukh).

HALAKHA

From immovable lower millstones – מאצטרובלי דריחיים: If a man dies leaving an unmarried daughter, and the court has no way to determine how much he would have given his daughter for her dowry, she is granted one-tenth of her father's landed property. The *Tur* writes that the daughter's dowry is also collected from his immovable lower millstones (Rambam *Sefer Nashim*, *Hilkhot Ishut* 20:3, 5; *Tur*, *Even HaEzer* 113; *Shulḥan Arukh*, *Even HaEzer* 113:2).

From the rent of houses – מעמלא דבתי: A daughter's dowry can also be collected from the rent generated by property left by her father, in accordance with the opinion of Rav Ashi. This is the *halakha* only if the payment date has not arrived and the heirs have not collected the rent for the time that has passed. If the rental period has concluded and the money for rent has been collected, the dowry cannot be collected from that money (Rema, citing *Tur*). Nowadays, when the marriage contract payment and its stipulations are collected from movable property, a daughter's dowry may also be collected from movable property (Rambam *Sefer Nashim*, *Hilkhot Ishut* 20:5; *Shulḥan Arukh*, *Even HaEzer* 113:2–3, and in the comment of Rema).

One who sells a courtyard – המוכר את החצר: When one sells a courtyard to another, the sale includes its pits, ditches, and caves, and all its houses, even houses that do not open into the courtyard, including those used to store sand. The courtyard's stores that open into the courtyard are also included in the sale. These are stores designated for supplying the needs of the courtyard's residents (*Sma*). Stores that open both into the courtyard and into other places, such as the public domain, but the majority of whose business is with residents of the courtyard, are also included in the sale. Stores that do not meet the above criteria are not included in the sale.

Movable property is also not included in the sale. This refers to items that are not normally considered part of the sale of a house (Rema). But if it is stipulated that the sale includes the courtyard and everything that is in it, then even the movable property is included in the sale, but food is not (Rema, citing *Tur*). In any case, even if it was stipulated that the sale includes everything that is in the courtyard, it includes neither the olive press nor the bathhouse. Some maintain that if the borders of the courtyard are specified, the buyer acquires these as well (*Nimmukei Yosef*, citing Rashba). The *Sma* adds that this is the *halakha* only if the seller writes that he is selling everything contained within those boundaries (Rambam *Sefer Kinyan*, *Hilkhot Mekhira* 25:6; *Shulḥan Arukh*, *Ḥoshen Mishpat* 215:1, and in the comment of Rema).

LANGUAGE

Sand fields [*ḥolsaot*] – חולסאות: Some maintain that the source of this word is the Greek χάλιξ, *khalix*, meaning gravel stones. The word could have been altered after entering Aramaic, under the influence of the word for clay, *ḥarsit*.

אָמַר מָר: פְּתוּחוֹת לְכָאן וּלְכָאן – נִמְכָּרוֹת עִמָּהּ. וְהָא תָּנֵי רַבִּי חִיָּיא: אֵין נִמְכָּרוֹת עִמָּהּ! לָא קַשְׁיָא: הָא דְּרוֹב תַּשְׁמִישְׁתַּיְיהוּ לְגוֹ, הָא דְּרוֹב תַּשְׁמִישְׁתַּיְיהוּ לְבַר.

The Master said in the *baraita*: Stores that **open** both **into this** courtyard **and into that** public domain **are sold** along **with** the courtyard. The Gemara raises an objection: **But didn't Rabbi Ḥiyya teach** a *baraita* that states that such stores **are not sold with** the courtyard? The Gemara answers that this is **not difficult: This** *baraita*, that teaches that the stores are sold along with the courtyard, is referring to a case **where the majority of their use is from within,** i.e., the stores are mainly accessed from within the courtyard, while **that** *baraita* of Rabbi Ḥiyya, that teaches that the stores are not sold along with the courtyard, is referring to a case **where the majority of their use is from without,** i.e., the stores are accessed mainly from the public domain.

רַבִּי אֱלִיעֶזֶר אוֹמֵר: הַמּוֹכֵר אֶת הֶחָצֵר – לֹא מָכַר אֶלָּא אֲוִירָהּ שֶׁל חָצֵר. אֲמַר רַבָּה: אִי דַּאֲמַר לֵיהּ "דִּירָתָא" – דְּכוּלֵּי עָלְמָא לָא פְּלִיגִי דְּבָתֵּי מַשְׁמַע, כִּי פְּלִיגִי – דַּאֲמַר לֵיהּ "דַּרְתָּא", מָר סָבַר: תַּרְבִּיצָא מַשְׁמַע, וּמָר סָבַר: בָּתֵּי מַשְׁמַע.

The mishna teaches, and it was similarly taught in the *baraita*, that **Rabbi Eliezer says:** One **who sells a courtyard has sold only the airspace of the courtyard,** and he has sold nothing found in the courtyard, not even the houses. To clarify the disagreement between the unattributed opinion in the mishna and Rabbi Eliezer, **Rabba said: If** the seller **said to** the buyer that he is selling him ***dirata***, i.e., the place of residence, **everyone agrees that he means** to sell **the houses** and that they are also included in the sale. **When they disagree,** it is **where he said to him** that he is selling him ***darta***, i.e., the courtyard. One **Sage,** Rabbi Eliezer, **holds** that **he means** to sell only **the garden,** i.e., the space between the houses, **and one Sage,** the unattributed first opinion in the mishna, **holds** that **he means** to sell also **the houses.**

אִיכָּא דְּאָמְרִי, אֲמַר רַבָּה: אִי דַּאֲמַר לֵיהּ "דַּרְתָּא" – דְּכוּלֵּי עָלְמָא לָא פְּלִיגִי דְּבָתֵּי מַשְׁמַע, כִּי פְּלִיגִי – דַּאֲמַר לֵיהּ "חָצֵר", מָר סָבַר: חָצֵר – אֲוִירָא מַשְׁמַע, וּמָר סָבַר: כַּחֲצַר הַמִּשְׁכָּן.

Some state a different version of this discussion, according to which **Rabba says: If** the seller **says to** the buyer that he is selling him ***darta***, **everyone agrees that he means** to sell also **the houses** and that they are included in the sale. **When they disagree,** it is **where he said to him** that he is selling him the ***ḥatzer***, the Hebrew term for courtyard. One **Sage,** Rabbi Eliezer, **holds** that when he says ***ḥatzer***, **he means** to sell him only **the airspace,** i.e., the open space of the courtyard itself, **and** one **Sage,** the unattributed first opinion in the mishna, **holds** that houses are also included in the sale, just **as the courtyard of the Tabernacle** included the Tabernacle itself.

וְאָמַר רַבָּה אָמַר רַב נַחְמָן: מָכַר לוֹ חוֹלְסִית וּמְצוּלָה, הֶחֱזִיק בַּחוֹלְסִית – לֹא קָנָה מְצוּלָה, הֶחֱזִיק בַּמְּצוּלָה – לֹא קָנָה חוֹלְסִית. אִינִי? וְהָא אָמַר שְׁמוּאֵל: מָכַר לוֹ עֶשֶׂר שָׂדוֹת בְּעֶשֶׂר מְדִינוֹת, כֵּיוָן שֶׁהֶחֱזִיק בְּאַחַת מֵהֶן – קָנָה כּוּלָּן!

§ **And Rabba says** that **Rav Naḥman says:** If one **sold** another **a sand field** for glass making, **and a pond**[N] for fishing or some other purpose, if the buyer **took possession of the sand field**[N] in order to finalize the transaction, **he has not acquired the pond** and must therefore perform a separate act of acquisition for it. Conversely, if **he took possession of the pond, he has not acquired the sand field.** The Gemara asks: **Is that so? But doesn't Shmuel say:** If one **sold** another **ten fields in ten** different **regions,** all in a single bill of sale, **once he takes possession of one of them, he has acquired them all;** and the two cases seem to be analogous.

הָתָם הוּא דְּסַדְנָא דְּאַרְעָא חַד הוּא, וְכוּלָּהּ חֲדָא תַּשְׁמִישְׁתָּא הוּא, אֲבָל הָכָא – הָא תַּשְׁמִישְׁתָּא לְחוּד, וְהָא תַּשְׁמִישְׁתָּא לְחוּד.

The Gemara rejects the parallel: **There,** in the case of the ten fields, **the land is** all located in **one** geographic **block, and it all has one use,** i.e., to be farmed. The buyer, therefore, acquires all of the fields when he takes possession of one of them, even if they are not adjacent. **But here,** in the case of the sand field and the pond, **this,** the sand field, has **a distinct use,** i.e., to supply sand for glass making, **and that,** the pond, has **a distinct use,** i.e., for fishing. Therefore, taking possession of one of them does not effect a transfer of the other.

וְאִיכָּא דְּאָמְרִי,

And some state a different version of the previous discussion.

NOTES

Pond – מְצוּלָה: Some interpret this as a river or stream from which gold may be extracted (Rabbeinu Ḥananel; Rashbam). The Rashbam suggests an alternative explanation that it is a place for fishing. The Ri Migash explains that this is a water hole in the courtyard. The Rambam explains this section of the Gemara as teaching about the sale of two fields, located in different types of terrain, to one person. In his opinion one field is in a valley, while the other field is in a mountainous area. If the buyer took possession of one field, he has not acquired the other.

Took possession of the sand field – הֶחֱזִיק בַּחוֹלְסִית: One of the ways to effect acquisition of real estate is by taking physical possession of the property, as explained in the third chapter of this tractate. When a buyer performs an act that enhances the property, this is an act of acquisition, which finalizes the transfer of ownership. The issue here is whether an act of acquisition that is performed with one property can effect the acquisition of another property located in a different place, when the two properties are being sold together.

אָמַר רַבָּה אָמַר רַב נַחְמָן: הֶחֱזִיק בַּחוּלְסִית קָנָה מְצוּלָה. פְּשִׁיטָא, דְּהָא אָמַר שְׁמוּאֵל: מָכַר לוֹ עֶשֶׂר שָׂדוֹת וכו׳! מַהוּ דְּתֵימָא: הָתָם הוּא דְּסַדְנָא דְּאַרְעָא חַד הוּא, אֲבָל הָכָא הָא תַּשְׁמִישְׁתָּא לְחוּד וְהָא תַּשְׁמִישְׁתָּא לְחוּד, קָא מַשְׁמַע לַן.

Rabba actually **said** that **Rav Naḥman said:** If one sold another a sand field and a pond, and the buyer **took possession of the sand field, he has** also **acquired the pond.**[H] The Gemara asks: This is **obvious, as Shmuel says:** If one **sold ten fields to** another in ten different regions, once he takes possession of one of them, he has acquired them all. The Gemara explains why Rav Naḥman's statement was nevertheless necessary: It is necessary **lest you say** that **there,** in the case of the ten fields, **the land is** all located in **one** geographic **block** with a single use, and therefore all the fields are acquired together. **But here,** in the case of the sand field and the pond, **this,** the sand field, has **a distinct use, and that,** the pond, has a **distinct use,** and therefore taking possession of one of them should not effect acquisition of the other. Therefore, Rav Naḥman **teaches us** that if the buyer took possession of the sand field, he has acquired the pond as well.

מתני׳ הַמּוֹכֵר בֵּית הַבַּד – מָכַר אֶת הַיָּם וְאֶת הַמָּמֶל וְאֶת הַבְּתוּלוֹת, אֲבָל לֹא מָכַר אֶת הָעֲבִירִים וְאֶת הַגַּלְגַּל וְאֶת הַקּוֹרָה, וּבִזְמַן שֶׁאָמַר לוֹ: ״הוּא וְכָל מַה שֶּׁבְּתוֹכוֹ״ – הֲרֵי כּוּלָּן מְכוּרִין; רַבִּי אֱלִיעֶזֶר אוֹמֵר: הַמּוֹכֵר בֵּית הַבַּד – מָכַר אֶת הַקּוֹרָה.

MISHNA One **who sells an olive press**[H] without specifying what is included in the sale **has sold** with it **the *yam***[N] **and the *memel* and the *betulot*,**[N] the immovable elements of the olive press. **But he has not sold** with it **the *avirim* and the *galgal* and the *kora*,** the movable utensils of the olive press. **When** the seller **says to** the buyer: I am selling you **it and everything that is in it, all these** components **are sold** along with the olive press, even the movable utensils. **Rabbi Eliezer says: One who sells an olive press has sold the *kora*** as well, as it is the most fundamental element of the olive press.

HALAKHA

If he took possession of the sand field he has acquired the pond – הֶחֱזִיק בַּחוּלְסִית קָנָה מְצוּלָה: If one purchased ten fields from another and paid him in full, once he takes possession of one of the fields he has acquired them all, even if they are in ten different regions. The same applies to houses or a combination of fields and houses (Rema, citing *Nimmukei Yosef*). This is the *halakha* even if they are not all used in the same manner, e.g., if one is on a mountaintop while another is in a valley, according to the Rambam's interpretation of the terms used in the Gemara. The above is in accordance with the second version of Rav Naḥman's opinion. If the buyer did not pay in full, he has acquired property only in accordance with the amount he paid. If he received the fields as a gift, he acquires all of them by taking possession of one. Some (Rema, citing Rosh; see *Sma*) hold that even in the case of a gift, he acquires only those properties with regard to which he performs some act of possession (Rambam *Sefer Kinyan, Hilkhot Mekhira* 1:19; *Shulḥan Arukh, Ḥoshen Mishpat* 192:12).

One who sells an olive press – הַמּוֹכֵר בֵּית הַבַּד: One who sells an olive press without specifying what is included in the sale has sold the large millstone that is attached to the ground upon which the olives are ground, the cedar posts that support the beam during the grinding, the vats, the containers for the ground olives, and the planks placed around the olives to prevent their dispersal (Rema, citing *Tur*), but he has not sold the upper millstone. If the seller says that he is selling the olive press and everything that is in it, the sale includes the upper millstone as well. But even if the seller uses the phrase: The olive press and everything that is in it, nevertheless, the pressing utensils, the wheel used to rotate the stone, and the beam are not included in the sale (Rambam, citing a different version of the text of the mishna and the *baraita*; *Maggid Mishne*). Some say that if the seller says that he is selling the olive press and everything that is in it, all of these components are included in the sale (Rema, citing *Tur*), in accordance with the standard version of the mishna, as opposed to the opinion provided in the *baraita*, but the sacks, whether they are made of leather or of wool, are not included in the sale (Rambam *Sefer Kinyan, Hilkhot Mekhira* 25:7; *Shulḥan Arukh, Ḥoshen Mishpat* 215:2).

NOTES

Has sold the *yam* – מָכַר אֶת הַיָּם: According to one explanation of this and the following mishna, anything attached to the ground is included in the sale, while movable items are not included in the sale (Rashbam). According to another explanation, some of the items sold together with the olive press are movable, but they are included in the sale, either because they have no independent significance and are therefore subsumed under the general sale, or because they are used only in an olive press and are therefore assumed to be sold along with it (Rabbeinu Tam in *Tosafot*; Ramah). The Ramah adds that items that are essential for an olive press and cannot be borrowed from others even in exigent circumstances are included in the sale, while items that can be borrowed are not included in the sale, since the buyer can operate the olive press even without owning them.

The *yam* and the *memel* and the *betulot* – אֶת הַיָּם וְאֶת הַמָּמֶל וְאֶת הַבְּתוּלוֹת: The various terms used here are explained in the Gemara, but the meanings of these explanations are not always clear. Even the early commentaries differed in their interpretations of these terms, both because they relied upon different sources and traditions, and because of differences in what was customary in their respective localities. It is also likely that in different places there were different ways of producing olive oil, and it is possible that the mishna and the *baraitot* refer to different methods of oil production.

גמ׳ יָם – טְלָפְחָא. מֶמֶל – אֲמַר רַבִּי אַבָּא בַּר מֶמֶל: מַפְרַכְתָּא. בְּתוּלוֹת – אֲמַר רַבִּי יוֹחָנָן: כְּלוֹנְסוֹת שֶׁל אֶרֶז שֶׁמַּעֲמִידִין בָּהֶן אֶת הַקּוֹרָה. עֲבִירִים – כִּבְשֵׁי. גַּלְגַּל – חוּמְרְתָא. קוֹרָה – קוֹרָה.

GEMARA The Gemara explains the terms used in the mishna. The ***yam*** is the **lentil,**[N] the round stationary container into which the olives are placed before being crushed. As for the ***memel*****, Rabbi Abba bar Memel said:** This is the **crusher,**[N] the utensil used to pound and crush the olives. As for the ***betulot*****, Rabbi Yoḥanan said:** These are the **cedar posts**[N] **[*klonsot*]**[L] **that support the beam** of the olive press. The ***avirim*** are the **pressers,**[N] wooden boards that are placed on top of the crushed olives, and upon which the beam is lowered in order to press the olives. The ***galgal*** is the ***ḥumrata*****,**[LN] a round stone that is placed on the beam to weigh it down. The ***kora*** is the heavy wooden **beam** used to press down upon the olives and thereby extract the oil.

תָּנוּ רַבָּנַן: הַמּוֹכֵר בֵּית הַבַּד – מָכַר אֶת נְסָרִים וְאֶת הַיְּקָבִים וְאֶת הַמַּפְרֵכוֹת, וְאֶת הָרֵיחַיִם הַתַּחְתּוֹנוֹת אֲבָל לֹא הָעֶלְיוֹנָה, וּבִזְמַן שֶׁאָמַר לוֹ: ״הוּא וְכָל מַה שֶּׁבְּתוֹכוֹ״ – הֲרֵי כּוּלָּן מְכוּרִין; בֵּין כָּךְ וּבֵין כָּךְ, לֹא מָכַר לֹא אֶת הָעֲבִירִים וְלֹא אֶת הַשַּׂקִּין וְלֹא אֶת הַמַּרְצוּפִין;

The Sages taught in a *baraita* (*Tosefta*, 3:2): One **who sells an olive press** without specifying what is included in the sale **has sold** with it **the boards**[N] that are fixed in place to hold the olives; **and the vats**[N] for collecting the oil, **and the crushers,**[N] used to pound and crush the olives before pressing them, **and the lower millstone,**[N] i.e., the stationary millstone base; **but not the upper** millstone. **But when** the seller **says to** the buyer: I am selling you **it and everything that is in it, all these** components **are sold. Both** in **this** case, where he executes the sale without specification, **and** in **that** case, where he adds the phrase that he is selling everything that is in the olive press, **he has not sold the** wooden **boards** that are placed on top of the crushed olives when they are being pressed, **nor** has he sold **the sacks, nor** has he sold **the leather bags** for carrying the olives, as these are all movable goods that are not specifically part of the olive press.

רַבִּי אֱלִיעֶזֶר אוֹמֵר: הַמּוֹכֵר בֵּית הַבַּד – מָכַר אֶת הַקּוֹרָה, שֶׁלֹּא נִקְרָא בֵּית הַבַּד אֶלָּא עַל שׁוּם קוֹרָה.

Rabbi Eliezer says: One **who sells an olive press has sold the** heavy wooden **beam** used to press down upon the olives, **as it is called an olive press [*beit habad*]**[L] **only due to this beam,** the most essential part of the press, and this beam is otherwise known as a *bad*.

LANGUAGE

Posts [*klonsot*] – כְּלוֹנְסוֹת: Apparently derived from the Latin columnas, which means columns, in rabbinic literature the term refers to wooden beams or branches. Some suggest that it derives from a similar Greek form, the word κλωνός, *klonos*.

Ḥumrata **– חוּמְרְתָא:** Apparently related to the Middle Persian word for a seal, muhr. According to various commentaries it is used here for a ring-like round stone with a hole in the middle or a screw-shaped round wooden object.

Olive press [*beit habad*] – בֵּית הַבַּד: The literal meaning of the Hebrew *beit habad* is: The beam house, which underlies Rabbi Eliezer's statement that an olive press is called by that name because of its most essential element, the beam.

Ancient olive press in Tel Hatzor

NOTES

Yam **is the lentil – יָם טְלָפְחָא:** According to all opinions this is a round object, which is why it is called a lentil in Aramaic, but its exact definition is disputed among the commentaries. The Rashbam defines it as a large vessel similar to a kneading trough, into which the olives are placed for pressing, and it is either attached to the ground or hollowed out of clay or stone. Rabbeinu Gershom interprets the word in a similar manner. This is like Rashi's explanation (*Avoda Zara* 75a) that the lentil is the olive press itself. Some explain that this is a round stone, similar to a millstone, which has a receptacle where the olives are ground (Ri Migash; Rambam's Commentary on the Mishna). Similarly, the Meiri (*Avoda Zara* 75a) explains that it is a round receptacle where the olives are initially pounded before they are placed under the beam of the olive press. Others explain that these lentils are large clay balls placed upon the mounds of olives in order to weigh them down and extract their oil (*Tosafot*, citing *Arukh*; *Ge'onim*).

The crusher – מַפְרַכְתָּא: According to all of the commentaries this refers to a utensil used to crush and mash the olives. The first interpretation presented by the Rashbam, citing Rabbeinu Ḥananel (see *Arukh*), is that this refers to a hollowed-out stone, similar to a mortar, into which the olives are placed to be crushed with a special wooden pestle. This is similar to one of the interpretations of the lentil in the previous note. A second interpretation mentioned by the Rashbam is that this refers to the wooden pestle itself. Similarly, the Meiri explains that this is a pestle for pounding the olives in the lentil before they are pressed by the beam. Others explain that this is the upper stone that grinds the olives in the lentil (Rambam's Commentary on the Mishna; Ri Migash; and see *Arukh*).

Cedar posts – כְּלוֹנְסוֹת: Some of the early commentaries explain that this term refers to the posts upon which the beam was placed when not in use. The Rashbam suggests that bars were passed through these posts, and the beam rested upon them. The Meiri proposes that these posts were a sort of track, upon which the beam was raised and lowered via a wheel or pulley.

Pressers – כִּבְשֵׁי: These are wooden panels placed on top of the olives in order to distribute the weight of the crossbeam across all of them. They are not included in the sale of the olive press because they are portable and not utilized exclusively for the olive press. According to Rabbeinu Gershom, these are wooden blocks that were placed on top of the wooden panels.

Ḥumrata **– חוּמְרְתָא:** This word refers to a round and ring-shaped item. According to Rabbeinu Ḥananel and the *Arukh*, it refers to a ring-shaped round stone with a hole in the middle that was placed on the head of the beam in order to add to the weight and pressure applied to the olives. Many commentaries explain that this refers to a large wooden gear that was used to raise and lower the beam (Ri Migash; Rambam's Commentary on the Mishna; Rabbeinu Gershom; Rashbam). The Ramah integrates the two interpretations and describes it as a round stone, inside of which the wooden gear would rotate.

Boards [*nesarim*] – נְסָרִים: There are several versions and interpretations of this term. The Rashbam explains that these are boards that are fixed in the ground to keep the olives from being dispersed, as opposed to the pressers, which are boards used to press down upon the olives. Rabbeinu Gershom suggests that these are actually identical to the pressers. These wooden objects can also be interpreted as ducts through which the oil flows into the vat (Meiri). Instead of *nesarim*, some versions read *beit ha'asurim*, which in this context refers to the pit in which the oil is collected after it flows out of the olive press (Ri Migash). The *Tosefta* reads *yetzarim*, which the Rashbam understands as referring to the baskets that held the olives while they were being pressed.

Vats – יְקָבִים: Some explain that this refers to the vat hollowed out of stone into which the oil would flow (Rabbeinu Barukh). Others say this refers to the baskets in which the olives were brought to the press (*Tosafot*, citing *Arukh*; Rabbeinu Gershom). The Ri Migash explains that this term refers to the pit into which pressed wine would flow, and a similar pit formed part of an olive press. According to the Rashbam the term refers to the lentil, where the olives were placed for crushing.

Crushers – מַפְרֵכוֹת: The majority of the early commentaries maintain that this term refers to the *memel* mentioned in the mishna, a utensil used to crush olives (Rashbam; Ri Migash). Rabbeinu Barukh and the Rambam in *Mishne Torah* explain that it refers to trenches in which the pressed olives would be rinsed with water.

The lower millstone – הָרֵיחַיִם הַתַּחְתּוֹנוֹת: This term refers to the lower stationary part of the millstone. The Ri Migash understands it to be identical to the lentil, where the olives were crushed. The Rashbam distinguishes between crushing and grinding olives and explains that the olives were pressed only after they were crushed in the lentil and then ground on the millstone. According to another interpretation, the *baraita* describes a different process for extracting olive oil in which a millstone was used to press the olives (Meiri).

מתני׳ הַמּוֹכֵר אֶת הַמֶּרְחָץ – לֹא מָכַר אֶת הַנְּסָרִין וְאֶת הַסְּפָלִין וְאֶת הַבִּלָּנִיּוֹת; בִּזְמַן שֶׁאָמַר לוֹ: ״הִיא וְכָל מַה שֶּׁבְּתוֹכָהּ״ – הֲרֵי כּוּלָּן מְכוּרִין; בֵּין כָּךְ וּבֵין כָּךְ, לֹא מָכַר לֹא אֶת הַמְּגוּרוֹת שֶׁל מַיִם וְלֹא אֶת אוֹצָרוֹת שֶׁל עֵצִים.

MISHNA One who sells a bathhouse[H] without specifying what is included in the sale **has not sold** with it **the boards**[N] that are placed on the floor, **nor** has he sold **the basins**[N] **or the curtains** [*habilaniyot*].[LN] **When** the seller **says to** the buyer: I am selling you **it and everything that is in it, all these** components **are sold** along with the bathhouse. **Both** in **this** case, where he executes the sale without specification, **and** in **that** case, where he adds the phrase that he is selling everything that is in the bathhouse, **he has not sold the tanks of water, nor** has he sold **the storerooms for wood,** as an explicit sales agreement is required for these matters.

גמ׳ תָּנוּ רַבָּנַן: הַמּוֹכֵר אֶת הַמֶּרְחָץ – מָכַר אֶת בֵּית הַנְּסָרִין וְאֶת בֵּית הַיְּקָמִין, וְאֶת בֵּית הַסְּפָלִים וְאֶת בֵּית הַוִּילָאוֹת, אֲבָל לֹא אֶת נְסָרִין עַצְמָן וְלֹא יְקָמִין עַצְמָן, וְלֹא סְפָלִים עַצְמָן וְלֹא וִילָאוֹת עַצְמָן, וּבִזְמַן שֶׁאָמַר לוֹ: ״הִיא וְכָל מַה שֶּׁבְּתוֹכָהּ״ – הֲרֵי כּוּלָּן מְכוּרִין; בֵּין כָּךְ וּבֵין כָּךְ, לֹא מָכַר לוֹ אֶת הַבְּרֵיכוֹת הַמְּסַפְּקוֹת לוֹ מַיִם, בֵּין

GEMARA **The Sages taught** in a *baraita* (*Tosefta*, 3:3): **One who sells a bathhouse** without specifying what is included in the sale **has sold** with it **the storeroom** for **the boards,**[N] **and the storeroom** for **the** implements called *yekamin*,[LN] **and the storeroom for the basins,**[N] **and the storeroom for the curtains** [*vilaot*],[LN] **but he has not sold the boards themselves, nor the** *yekamin*[N] **themselves, nor the basins themselves, nor the curtains themselves. When** the seller **says to** the buyer: I am selling you **it and everything that is in it, all these** components **are sold** along with the bathhouse. **Both** in **this** case, where he executes the sale without specification, **and** in **that** case, where he adds the phrase that he is selling everything that is in the bathhouse, **he has not sold him the pools that supply him with water, whether**

LANGUAGE

Curtains [*bilaniyot*] – בִּלָּנִיּוֹת: This apparently refers to curtains, deriving from the Greek word βηλός, *bēlos*, meaning threshold. Some have suggested that it derives from the Latin balnearia, meaning, among other things, bathhouse accessories.

Yekamin – יְקָמִין: The correct reading and interpretation of this word is not clear. None of the suggested meanings give a clear indication of the source of the word. Some rely upon the textual version of the *Tosefta*, *kamin*, and assume that it derives from the Greek κάμινος, *kaminos*, which means an oven or furnace. According to this, the reference here might be to a portable oven, and the room mentioned in the *baraita* would be the room where this oven is placed to heat the water, hot water being extensively used in the bathhouse.

Curtains [*vilaot*] – וִילָאוֹת: From the Latin velum, although its Aramaic form may be derived from the Greek βηλός, *bēlos*, meaning threshold, indicating a screen or a curtain.

HALAKHA

One who sells a bathhouse – הַמּוֹכֵר אֶת הַמֶּרְחָץ: One who sells a bathhouse without specifying what is included in the sale has sold the board room where people sit after removing their clothing, the storeroom for the basins in which the bathers receive water, the room where people sit on benches while they are still clothed, and the towel room in which they dry themselves. The boards, the basins, the benches, and the towels themselves are not included in the sale. If the seller says to the buyer: I am selling you the bathhouse, and everything that is in it, then all these components are included. In any case, the sale does not include the pools that supply water to the bathhouse or the storerooms for the firewood (Rambam *Sefer Kinyan*, *Hilkhot Mekhira* 25:9; *Shulḥan Arukh*, *Ḥoshen Mishpat* 215:3).

NOTES

Boards – נְסָרִין: This term refers to boards that were placed on the floor of the bathhouse to protect the bather's feet either from dirt or from the scorching heat, as the bathhouse was heated from beneath the floor (Rashbam; Rabbeinu Gershom). According to another explanation, these boards were used to cover the water in the pools to preserve its heat (*Tosafot*). The Ri Migash proposes that these boards served as benches, either to place utensils upon them or for the bathers to sit upon (Ri Migash).

Basins – סְפָלִין: These are large utensils that were used to carry the water for bathing (Rashbam). Some commentaries have a version of the text that replaces this word, meaning basins, with the similarly spelled word for benches, and they assume that they were seats for the bathers (Rambam's Commentary on the Mishna; Rabbeinu Barukh).

Curtains [*bilaniyot*] – בִּלָּנִיּוֹת: Most commentaries have a version of the text that replaces this word with *vilonot*, the standard term for curtains. In any case, the term refers to curtains hung for purposes of modesty. Others understand that it refers to towels that the bathers used to dry themselves (Rambam's Commentary on the Mishna).

The storeroom for the boards – בֵּית הַנְּסָרִין: The most straightforward explanation is that this term refers to the room in which the bathhouse's boards were stored (Rashbam). One commentary understands it as referring to an inner room that was so hot that its floor had to be covered with boards to enable people to walk there (Rabbeinu Barukh).

The storeroom for the implements called *yekamin* – בֵּית הַיְּקָמִין: This is the room for storing the *yekamin* (Rashbam), which are explained in a later note. Some commentaries have a version of the text replacing *yekamin* with *kamim*, meaning those who stand or stay, and they interpret this room not as a storeroom, but as an external room, cooler than the internal ones, in which bathers spent most of their time in the bathhouse (Rabbeinu Barukh).

The storeroom for the basins – בֵּית הַסְּפָלִים: According to the alternative version of the text, this was called the bench storeroom. Alternatively, it is the room where people sat on benches and removed their clothes before bathing (Rabbeinu Barukh).

The storeroom for the curtains – בֵּית הַוִּילָאוֹת: This is the room for storing curtains (Rashbam). Others explain that it is a room with curtains partitioning off sections for people to bathe or clean themselves privately (Rabbeinu Barukh; Ri Migash).

Yekamin – יְקָמִין: Some interpret this term to mean tubs (Rashbam). Similarly, others interpret this term to mean wooden basins holding water for bathing (Ri Migash; Meiri). Others interpret it as a term for scarves with which the bathers cover their heads (Rabbeinu Gershom; *Arukh*). Additionally, some commentaries have an alternative version with the word *yekavim*, vats (Rav Hai Gaon).

בִּימוֹת הַחַמָּה וּבִימוֹת הַגְּשָׁמִים, וְלֹא בֵּית כִּינּוּס הָעֵצִים; וְאִם אָמַר לוֹ: ״בֵּית הַמֶּרְחָץ וְכׇל תַּשְׁמִישָׁיו אֲנִי מוֹכֵר לָךְ״ – כּוּלָּן מְכוּרִין.

in the summer season[N] **or in the rainy season, nor** has he sold him **the storeroom for the wood.**[N] **But if** the seller **says to** the buyer: **I am selling you the bathhouse and all of its accompaniments,**[H] **all these** components **are sold.**

הַהוּא דַּאֲמַר לֵיהּ לְחַבְרֵיהּ: ״בֵּית הַבַּד וְכׇל תַּשְׁמִישָׁיו אֲנִי מוֹכֵר לָךְ״, הֲוָיא הָנְהוּ חָנְוָאתָא אַבָּרַאי דַּהֲווֹ שָׁטְחוּ בְּהוּ שׁוּמְשְׁמֵי, אֲתָא לְקַמֵּיהּ דְּרַב יוֹסֵף.

The Gemara relates: There was a certain person **who said to another: I am selling you** this **olive press and all of its accompaniments. There were certain stores**[N] **outside** of the olive press, **where,** in addition to the ordinary services that these stores provided, **sesame seeds would** also **be spread out** to dry before they would be pressed for their oil. The seller and the buyer disagreed about whether these stores were included in the sale, and the buyer **came before Rav Yosef,** presenting him with his claim to ownership of the stores.

אֲמַר לֵיהּ: תָּנֵינָא, אִם אָמַר: ״בֵּית הַמֶּרְחָץ וְכׇל תַּשְׁמִישָׁיו אֲנִי מוֹכֵר לָךְ״ – הֲרֵי כּוּלָּן מְכוּרִין. אֲמַר לֵיהּ אַבָּיֵי, וְהָא תָּנֵי רַבִּי חִיָּיא: אֵין כּוּלָּן מְכוּרִין! אֶלָּא אָמַר רַב אָשֵׁי: חָזֵינַן, אִי אֲמַר לֵיהּ: ״בֵּית הַבַּד וְכׇל תַּשְׁמִישָׁיו וְאִלֵּין מִצְרָנָהָא״ – קָנֵי, וְאִי לָא – לָא קָנֵי.

Rav Yosef **said to him: We learned** in the previously cited *baraita* that **if** the seller **says** to the buyer: **I am selling you the bathhouse**[N] **and all of its accompaniments, all these** components **are sold.** Rav Yosef held that in this case too, the disputed stores were sold. **Abaye said to** Rav Yosef: **But didn't Rabbi Ḥiyya teach** in a *baraita*: **They are not all sold? Rather,** the issue should be resolved as **Rav Ashi said: We consider** the seller's statement, and **if he said to** the buyer: I am selling you **the olive press and all of its accompaniments, and these are its boundaries,**[H] and he included the area of the stores within those boundaries, the buyer **has acquired** those stores, **but if** the seller does **not** say this, **he has not acquired** them, as they are not actually part of the olive press.

מתני׳ הַמּוֹכֵר אֶת הָעִיר – מָכַר בָּתִּים, בּוֹרוֹת שִׁיחִין וּמְעָרוֹת, מֶרְחֲצָאוֹת וְשׁוֹבָכוֹת, בֵּית הַבַּדִּין וּבֵית הַשְּׁלָחִין, אֲבָל לֹא אֶת הַמִּטַּלְטְלִין; וּבִזְמַן שֶׁאָמַר לוֹ: ״הִיא וְכׇל מַה שֶּׁבְּתוֹכָהּ״, אֲפִילּוּ הָיוּ בָּהּ בְּהֵמָה וַעֲבָדִים – הֲרֵי כּוּלָּן מְכוּרִין. רַבָּן שִׁמְעוֹן בֶּן גַּמְלִיאֵל אוֹמֵר: הַמּוֹכֵר אֶת הָעִיר – מָכַר אֶת הַסַּנְטֵר.

MISHNA **One who sells a city**[HB] without specifying what is included in the sale **has sold** with it **the houses, the pits,** the **ditches and caves, the bathhouses and the dovecotes,** and **the olive presses and** ***beit hashelaḥin***, as will be explained in the Gemara, **but** he has **not** sold **the movable property**[N] in the city. **But when** the seller **says to** the buyer: I am selling you **it and everything that is in it, even if there were cattle and** Canaanite **slaves in** the city, **all these** entities **are sold. Rabban Shimon ben Gamliel says: One who sells a city has sold** with it **the** ***santar***,[N] the meaning of which will be explained in the Gemara.

HALAKHA

The bathhouse and all of its accompaniments – בֵּית הַמֶּרְחָץ וְכׇל תַּשְׁמִישָׁיו: When one sells a bathhouse, he has not sold the pools that supply its water, whether in the summer or in the rainy season, even if he writes in the bill of sale that he is selling the bathhouse and everything that is in it. If he states: I am selling you the bathhouse and all of its accompaniments, the pools are included in the sale even if they are external to the bathhouse. The *Tur* writes that this applies only if they are within the boundaries of the area sold, as defined by the seller, and only if he wrote: And these are its boundaries (Rambam *Sefer Kinyan, Hilkhot Mekhira* 25:9; *Shulḥan Arukh, Ḥoshen Mishpat* 215:3).

The olive press and all of its accompaniments, and these are its boundaries – בֵּית הַבַּד וְכׇל תַּשְׁמִישָׁיו וְאִלֵּין מִצְרָנָהָא: If one sells an olive press to another and there are stores outside of the press where olives or sesame seeds are spread out to dry, and the seller delineates the external boundaries of the area included in the sale, and says to the buyer: I am selling you the olive press and all of its accompaniments, the buyer has acquired those stores, provided that they are found within the specified boundaries. Otherwise, he acquires only that which is within the olive press itself, in accordance with the conclusion of Rav Ashi (Rambam *Sefer Kinyan, Hilkhot Mekhira* 25:8; *Shulḥan Arukh, Ḥoshen Mishpat* 215:2).

One who sells a city – הַמּוֹכֵר אֶת הָעִיר: When one sells a city, then the houses, pits, ditches, caves, bathhouses, dovecotes, olive presses, and fields requiring irrigation that are within or adjacent to the city are included in the sale. But the sale does not include the movable property found in the city. If the seller writes for the buyer that he is selling the city and everything that is in it, the buyer acquires the movable property as well, including even the livestock and the Canaanite slaves (Rambam *Sefer Kinyan, Hilkhot Mekhira* 26:1; *Shulḥan Arukh, Ḥoshen Mishpat* 215:4 and *Sma* there).

BACKGROUND

One who sells a city – הַמּוֹכֵר אֶת הָעִיר: From here and other places it appears that in addition to the larger cities, which were public property, there were also smaller settlements that were similar to cities and were privately owned. From the context it seems that the mishna is discussing an estate, like a large farm, on which stood several buildings, all owned by the same person. The residents of the estate were the city owner's tenants, and the land and its equipment were his property.

NOTES

In the summer season – בִּימוֹת הַחַמָּה: The Rashbam explains that the novelty here is that the pools are not included in the sale of the bathhouse even during the summer, when they contain little water and might be assumed to be insignificant and subsumed under the classification of the bathhouse itself. According to another explanation, the pools excluded from the sale are those that collect sufficient water to provide not only for the winter, but even for the summer when water is scarce. But it is possible that pools that provide only for the winter are deemed insignificant and are therefore included in the sale of the bathhouse (*Tosefot HaRosh*).

Storeroom for the wood – בֵּית כִּינּוּס הָעֵצִים: The early commentaries note that while wood is needed to heat the bathhouse, nevertheless, since people store wood for many other purposes as well, the wood storage chamber is not considered an integral part of the bathhouse.

Certain stores – הָנְהוּ חָנְוָאתָא: The Rashbam and others write that these were ordinary stores that sold food and the like, but during the sesame harvest season they also served as a place to spread out the sesame seeds to dry before extracting their oil in the olive press. Consequently, in addition to their commercial use that was totally unconnected to the olive press, these stores sometimes provided a secondary function related to the olive press. The dispute here is whether this suffices for the stores to be subsumed in the category of all of the olive press's accompaniments and included in the sale. There is also an unattributed opinion that the principle service provided by these stores was the drying of the sesame seeds.

He said to him: We learned that if he says to the buyer, I am selling you a bathhouse – אֲמַר לֵיהּ תָּנֵינָא אִם אָמַר בֵּית הַמֶּרְחָץ: The ruling with regard to a bathhouse is then extended to the case of an olive press (Rashbam). The Ramah writes that this is the textual version of Rav Hai Gaon. The Rif and many other early commentaries have a version of the Gemara that reads: Olive press, in place of: Bathhouse.

But not the movable property – אֲבָל לֹא אֶת הַמִּטַּלְטְלִין: Even the movable property that serves the needs of the city, e.g., household equipment such as a stove or an oven, is excluded from the sale, and all the more so commodities, such as wheat or barley, are excluded as well (Rashbam).

Has sold the *santar* – מָכַר אֶת הַסַּנְטֵר: Even if the seller did not specify that he was selling the city and everything that is in it, the *santar* is still included in the sale, as the *santar* is an integral part of the city and the sale would be incomplete without him (Ri Migash; Ramah).

גמ׳ אֲמַר לֵיהּ רַב אַחָא בְּרֵיהּ דְּרַב אָוְיָא לְרַב אַשִׁי, שָׁמְעַתְּ מִינַּהּ: עַבְדָּא כְּמִטַּלְטְלָא דָּמֵי, דְּאִי כְּמְקַרְקַע דָּמֵי, נִיזְדַּבַּן אַגַּב מָתָא. וְאֶלָּא מַאי? עַבְדָּא כְּמִטַּלְטְלָא דָּמֵי, מַאי ״אֲפִילּוּ״?

GEMARA Rav Aḥa, son of Rav Avya, said to **Rav Ashi: Learn from** the mishna that the legal status of a Canaanite **slave is like** that **of movable property, as if** it is **like** that of **land,** the slave **should be sold along with the city.** Rav Ashi responded: **Rather, what** do you claim, that the legal status of a Canaanite **slave is like** that of **movable property?** If that is the case, **what** is the meaning of the mishna's statement that **even** if there were cattle and Canaanite slaves in the city, they are all sold? This is obvious, as the slaves should be treated no differently than the rest of the city's movable property.

אֶלָּא מַאי אִית לָךְ לְמֵימַר, שָׁאנֵי בֵּין מִטַּלְטְלָא דְּנָיֵיד מִמִּטַּלְטְלָא דְּלָא נָיֵיד? אֲפִילּוּ תֵּימָא: עַבְדָּא כְּמְקַרְקַע דָּמֵי, שָׁאנֵי בֵּין מְקַרְקַע דְּנָיֵיד לִמְקַרְקַע דְּלָא נָיֵיד.

Rather, what have you to say? You must explain that there is **a difference between movable property that moves about** by itself, such as slaves, **and movable property that does not move about** by itself, i.e., inanimate objects. In exactly the same manner, one can claim that **even if you say** that the legal status of a Canaanite **slave is like** that of **land,** there **is a difference between land that moves about** by itself, i.e., slaves, **and land that does not move about** by itself.

״רַבָּן שִׁמְעוֹן בֶּן גַּמְלִיאֵל אוֹמֵר: הַמּוֹכֵר אֶת הָעִיר – מָכַר אֶת הַסַּנְטָר״. מַאי סַנְטָר? הָכָא תַּרְגִּימוּ: בַּר מַחֲוָונִיתָא; שִׁמְעוֹן בֶּן אַבְטוֹלְמוֹס אוֹמֵר: בָּאגֵי. מַאן דְּאָמַר בַּר מַחֲוָונִיתָא, כׇּל שֶׁכֵּן בָּאגֵי; מַאן דְּאָמַר בָּאגֵי, אֲבָל בַּר מַחֲוָונִיתָא לָא מִיזְדַּבַּן.

§ The mishna teaches: **Rabban Shimon ben Gamliel says:** One **who sells a city has sold** with it **the** *santar*.[L] The Gemara asks: **What** is the meaning of the term *santar*?[N] **Here** in Babylonia **they interpreted** it to mean the land **registrar** [*bar mahavanita*][LN] in charge of keeping track of property boundaries. **Shimon ben Avtolemos** disagrees and **says** that it is referring to **the fields**[N] that surround the city. The Gemara comments: **The one who says** that *santar* means the land **registrar** understands that according to Rabban Shimon ben Gamliel, when one sells a city, **all the more** so are **the fields** that surround the city included in the sale. **But the one who says** that it means **the fields** that surround the city holds that the land **registrar** is **not sold** with the city.

תְּנַן: בֵּית הַבַּדִּים וּבֵית הַשְּׁלָחִין; סַבְרוּהָ: מַאי ״שְׁלָחִין״ – בָּאגֵי, דִּכְתִיב: ״וְשֹׁלֵחַ מַיִם עַל פְּנֵי חוּצוֹת״; בִּשְׁלָמָא לְמַאן דְּאָמַר בַּר מַחֲוָונִיתָא, אֲמַר תַּנָּא קַמָּא: בָּאגֵי מִיזְדַּבְּנִי, בַּר מַחֲוָונִיתָא לָא מִיזְדַּבַּן, וְאָתָא רַבָּן שִׁמְעוֹן בֶּן גַּמְלִיאֵל לְמֵימַר: אֲפִילּוּ בַּר מַחֲוָונִיתָא נַמִי מִיזְדַּבַּן; אֶלָּא לְמַאן דְּאָמַר בָּאגֵי, תַּנָּא קַמָּא נַמִי הָכִי קָאָמַר!

The Gemara attempts to adduce proof in support of one of the opinions: **We learned** in the mishna here that **the olive presses and** *beit hashelaḥin* are sold along with the city. The Sages initially **maintained: What** is meant by *shelaḥin*? This is referring to irrigated **fields,** fields that require additional irrigation to supplement the rain that they receive. **As it is written:** "Who gives rain upon the earth **and sends** [*shole'aḥ*] **water upon the fields**" (Job 5:10). **Granted, according to the one who says** that *santar* means the land **registrar, the first** *tanna* of the mishna **said** that **the fields** that surround the city **are sold** with the city, but the land **registrar is not sold, and Rabban Shimon ben Gamliel comes to say** that **even** the land **registrar is sold. But according to the one who says** that *santar* means **fields, this** is what **the first** *tanna* **is saying as well.** In what way, then, does Rabban Shimon ben Gamliel disagree with the first *tanna*?

מִי סָבְרַתְּ מַאי ״שְׁלָחִין״ – בָּאגֵי? לָא, מַאי ״שְׁלָחִין״ – גִּינּוּנִיָּיתָא, שֶׁנֶּאֱמַר: ״שְׁלָחַיִךְ פַּרְדֵּס רִמּוֹנִים״, אֲבָל בָּאגֵי לָא מִיזְדַּבְּנִי; וְאָתָא רַבָּן שִׁמְעוֹן בֶּן גַּמְלִיאֵל לְמֵימַר: אֲפִילּוּ בָּאגֵי נַמִי מִזְדַּבְּנִי.

The Gemara rejects this proof: **Do you maintain** that **what** is meant by *shelaḥin* is irrigated **fields?** This is not the case. Rather, **what** is meant by *shelaḥin*? This is referring to **gardens** found within the city, **as it is stated: "Your shoots** [*shelaḥayikh*] **are an orchard of pomegranates"** (Song of Songs 4:13). **But the fields** that surround the city **are not sold. And Rabban Shimon ben Gamliel comes to say** that **even the fields are sold as well.** This is one version of the discussion.

אִיכָּא דְּאָמְרִי: סַבְרוּהָ מַאי ״שְׁלָחִין״ – גִּינּוּנִיָּאתָא; בִּשְׁלָמָא לְמַאן דַּאֲמַר בָּאגֵי, אֲמַר תַּנָּא קַמָּא: גִּנּוּנִיָּיתָא מִיזְדַּבַּן, בָּאגֵי לָא מִיזְדַּבְּנִי, וְאָתָא רַבָּן שִׁמְעוֹן בֶּן גַּמְלִיאֵל לְמֵימַר: אֲפִילּוּ בָּאגֵי מִיזְדַּבְּנִי;

Some say that the discussion took place as follows: The Sages initially **assumed** that **what** is meant by *shelaḥin*? This is referring to **gardens** found within the city. **Granted, according to the one who said** that *santar* means **the fields** that surround the city, **the first** *tanna* of the mishna **said** that **the gardens** found within the city **are sold** along with the city, but **the fields** that surround the city **are not sold, and Rabban Shimon ben Gamliel comes to say** that **even the fields** that surround the city **are sold.**

LANGUAGE

Santar – סַנְטָר: The commentaries disagree over the exact meaning and derivation of this word. Some assert that it derives from the Greek συντηρέω, *suntēreo*, meaning to guard or to hold rights or commitments. Others propose that it comes from the Latin saltarius, meaning the guardsman of the fields, with the letter n substituted for the letter l. Many others maintain that it stems from the Hebrew root *natar* with the letter *samekh* added at the beginning, and it means guard.

Registrar [*bar mahavanita*] – בַּר מַחֲוָונִיתָא: The Aramaic word *mahavei* means show, and so this term literally means: The man who shows. The word does not give any indication of what he is showing, nor does it indicate whether he is a guard or if he is the one responsible for showing the boundaries of the fields.

Here, *bar* is referring to someone who possesses a certain quality or profession, as in the term *bar mitzva*, which means: One who is able to perform the mitzvot. This usage is found in other Hebrew expressions, for example a *ben ḥayil*, a hero, one who possesses the quality of bravery and valor.

NOTES

What is the *santar* – מַאי סַנְטָר: It is clear from other sources that the term *santar* is referring to a person; but it is also known that the word had originally referred to fields, and that the name was then adopted to refer to the person in charge of keeping track of the fields. The disagreement here is about which of the two possible meanings of the word is correct in this context (Ramban; Rashba).

The land registrar [*bar mahavanita*] – בַּר מַחֲוָונִיתָא: Rav Hai Gaon in his *Sefer HaMikkaḥ VehaMimkar* and most of the early commentaries explain that *bar mahavanita* is referring to a slave who was in charge of keeping track of the city limits, property boundaries, and the land taxes that applied in each part of the city. For this reason, it would be impossible to maintain normal function of the city without this slave. Other commentaries propose that *bar mahavanita* is referring to the city watchman (Rabbeinu Ḥananel; Rambam's Commentary on the Mishna; Rabbi Ovadya Bartenura).

The fields – בָּאגֵי: This is referring to fields that are adjacent to the city but not inside it, as all the land inside the city is obviously sold with the city (Rashbam). According to many opinions, these fields, as well those referred to by the term *shelaḥin*, are fields that are not irrigated; rather, they require rain, as the verse (Job 5:10) states: "And sends [*shole'aḥ*] waters upon the fields" (Rashbam; Rabbeinu Gershom; Ramah). By contrast, others explain, based on the same verse, that the reference here is to fields that require irrigation in addition to the rainwater that they receive (*Tosafot*; Ramban; Rambam).

אֶלָּא לְמַאן דְּאָמַר בַּר מַחֲוָונִיתָא, אֲמַר תַּנָּא קַמָּא גִּינּוּנִיָּיתָא, וּמְהַדַּר לֵיהּ רַבָּן שִׁמְעוֹן בֶּן גַּמְלִיאֵל בַּר מַחֲוָונִיתָא?! מִי סָבְרַתְּ מַאי "שְׁלָחִין" – גִּינּוּנִיָּיתָא? לָא, מַאי "שְׁלָחִין" – בָּגֵי, דִּכְתִיב: "וְשֹׁלֵחַ מַיִם עַל פְּנֵי חוּצוֹת", אֲבָל בַּר מַחֲוָונִיתָא לָא מִזְדַּבַּן, וְאָתָא רַבָּן שִׁמְעוֹן בֶּן גַּמְלִיאֵל לְמֵימַר דַּאֲפִילּוּ בַּר מַחֲוָונִיתָא נַמִי מִזְדַּבַּן.

But according to the one who says that *santar* means the land **registrar,** is it reasonable that **the first *tanna*** of the mishna **said** that the **gardens** within the city are included in the sale of the city, **and Rabban Shimon ben Gamliel responded to him** that the land **registrar** is included? How are the two connected? The Gemara answers: **Do you maintain** that **what** is meant by ***shelaḥin*** is **gardens?** This is **not** the case. Rather, **what** is meant by ***shelaḥin?*** This is referring to **the fields** that surround the city, **as it is written:** "Who gives rain upon the earth **and sends [*sholeaḥ*] waters upon the fields**" (Job 5:10). According to the first *tanna*, it is specifically the fields that are sold with the city, **but** the land **registrar is not sold. And Rabban Shimon ben Gamliel comes to say** that **even** the land **registrar is also sold.**

תָּא שְׁמַע, רַבִּי יְהוּדָה אוֹמֵר: סַנְטָר אֵינוֹ מָכוּר, אַנְקוֹלְמוּס מָכוּר; מַאי לָאו מִדְּאַנְקוֹלְמוּס גַּבְרָא, סַנְטָר נַמִי גַּבְרָא! מִידֵּי אִירְיָא? הָא כִּדְאִיתָא וְהָא כִּדְאִיתָא.

The Gemara suggests: **Come** and **hear** a proof from the following *baraita*: **Rabbi Yehuda says:**[N] **The *santar* is not sold** with the city, but **the city scribe [*ankolemus*]**[L] **is sold** with it. **What, is it not** clear **from** the fact **that the city scribe is a man** that **the *santar* is also a man?** The Gemara rejects this proof: **Are the cases comparable? This** case is **as it is, and that** case is **as it is,** and *santar* means fields, and not the land registrar.

וּמִי מָצֵית אָמְרַתְּ הָכִי? וְהָא קָתָנֵי סֵיפָא: אֲבָל לֹא שְׁיָירֶיהָ וְלֹא בְּנוֹתֶיהָ, וְלֹא חוֹרָשִׁין הַמּוּקְצִין לָהּ, וְלֹא בֵּיבָרִין שֶׁל חַיָּה וְשֶׁל עוֹפוֹת וְשֶׁל דָּגִים; וְאָמְרִינַן, מַאי שְׁיָירֶיהָ? בִּיזְלֵי, מַאי בִּיזְלֵי? אֲמַר רַבִּי אַבָּא: פִּיסְקֵי בָּגֵי. פִּיסְקֵי בָּגֵי הוּא דְּלָא מִזְדַּבְּנִי, הָא בָּגֵי עַצְמָן מִזְדַּבְּנִי!

The Gemara asks: **How can you say** that according to Rabbi Yehuda the fields surrounding the city are not sold along with it? **But isn't it taught in the latter clause** of this *baraita*: **But** when one sells a city he has **not** sold **its remnants,**[H] **and not its daughters,** i.e., the nearby rural villages, **and not the woods that are set aside** and designated **for the city, and not the enclosures [*beivarin*]**[LH] **for animals, for birds, and for fish. And we said** in explanation: **What** is meant by **its remnants? *Bizlei.***[L] The Gemara asks: **What** is the meaning of ***bizlei?*** **Rabbi Abba said: The strips of the fields**[N] that are separated from the main fields by a stretch that cannot be cultivated. From here, it may be inferred that **it is the strips of the fields that are not sold** with the city, **but the fields themselves are sold** with it.

אֵיפוּךְ, רַבִּי יְהוּדָה אוֹמֵר: סַנְטָר מָכוּר, אַנְקוֹלְמוּס אֵינוֹ מָכוּר.

The Gemara suggests: **Reverse** the statement found in the *baraita* so that **Rabbi Yehuda**[N] **says** that **the *santar*,** now understood to mean fields, **is sold** with the city, but the **city scribe is not sold** with it.

וּמִי מָצֵית אָמְרַתְּ: רַבִּי יְהוּדָה כְּרַבָּן שִׁמְעוֹן בֶּן גַּמְלִיאֵל סְבִירָא לֵיהּ? וְהָא רַבִּי יְהוּדָה כְּרַבָּנַן סְבִירָא לֵיהּ! דְּקָתָנֵי סֵיפָא: אֲבָל לֹא שְׁיָירֶיהָ וְלֹא בְּנוֹתֶיהָ, וְאִילּוּ רַבָּן שִׁמְעוֹן בֶּן גַּמְלִיאֵל הָאָמַר: מָכַר אֶת הָעִיר – מָכַר בְּנוֹתֶיהָ, דְּתַנְיָא: הַמּוֹכֵר אֶת הָעִיר – לֹא מָכַר אֶת בְּנוֹתֶיהָ, רַבָּן שִׁמְעוֹן בֶּן גַּמְלִיאֵל אוֹמֵר: הַמּוֹכֵר אֶת הָעִיר – מָכַר בְּנוֹתֶיהָ!

The Gemara asks: **How can you say** that **Rabbi Yehuda holds in accordance with** the opinion of **Rabban Shimon ben Gamliel,** to the point that you adduce proof from the words of Rabbi Yehuda with regard to the opinion of Rabban Shimon ben Gamliel? **But** doesn't **Rabbi Yehuda hold in accordance with** the opinion of **the Rabbis? As it is taught in the latter clause** of that same *baraita*: **But** when one sells a city he does **not** sell **its remnants, and** he does **not** sell **its daughters,** i.e., the nearby rural villages. **Whereas** with regard to **Rabban Shimon ben Gamliel, doesn't he say** that one **who sold a city sold its daughters** along with it, i.e., the nearby rural villages, **as it is taught** in a *baraita*: One **who sells a city has not sold its daughters; Rabban Shimon ben Gamliel** disagrees and **says:** One **who sells a city has sold its daughters.**

רַבִּי יְהוּדָה סָבַר לֵיהּ כְּוָותֵיהּ בַּחֲדָא, וּפָלֵיג עֲלֵיהּ בַּחֲדָא.

The Gemara answers: This does not prove that Rabbi Yehuda disagrees with Rabban Shimon ben Gamliel, as it may be suggested that **Rabbi Yehuda holds in accordance with** the opinion of Rabban Shimon ben Gamliel **with regard to one** issue, that the fields that surround the city are included in the sale, **and disagrees with him with regard to** another issue, as according to Rabbi Yehuda the nearby villages are not sold along with the city.

NOTES

Rabbi Yehuda says – רַבִּי יְהוּדָה אוֹמֵר: The text here is the Rashbam's version of the text. There is another version from the *ge'onim*, cited by the early commentaries. According to this other version, which is the version found in the *Tosefta* (see *Tosafot*), the *baraita* states the opposite, that the *santar* is included in the sale but the city scribe is not. A similar version is also found in the Ramban, Rashba, and other commentaries. In terms of the Gemara's conclusion, the different versions are not at odds, but they differ in the way that they adduce proof from the statement of Rabbi Yehuda and in the way that they discuss his opinion.

The strips of the fields – פִּיסְקֵי בָּגֵי: This is referring to portions of land that are separated from the rest of the fields by stones and rocky ground (Rashbam) or by streams and riverbeds (Ra'avad). According to Rabbeinu Gershom these are small fields that serve as grazing ground.

Reverse the statement of Rabbi Yehuda – אֵיפוּךְ רַבִּי יְהוּדָה: According to this, when Rabbi Yehuda spoke of the *santar*, he was referring to the fields that surround the city and not the person responsible for them, in which case Rabbi Yehuda's opinion is identical to the opinion of Rabban Shimon ben Gamliel.

LANGUAGE

City scribe [*ankolemus*] – אַנְקוֹלְמוּס: According to the *Arukh*, the word *ankolemus* is derived from the Greek κάλαμος, *kalamos*, meaning a reed that may be used as a pen, and it is referring to the city scribe who is responsible for the official records of the city. It seems, however, that the more correct version of the word is *ikonomos*, as it appears in the Jerusalem Talmud, a term that is derived from the Greek οἰκονόμος, *oikonomos*, meaning household manager.

Enclosures [*beivarin*] – בֵּיבָרִין: From the Latin vivarium, an animal pen or a fishpond.

Bizlei – בִּיזְלֵי: Apparently similar in meaning to the Hebrew *badal*, meaning a small piece. As explained in the Gemara, the word refers here to small strips of land or portions of fields.

HALAKHA

But he has not sold its remnants – אֲבָל לֹא שְׁיָירֶיהָ: One who sells a city has also sold the fields that are known to be part of the city, as the *halakha* is in accordance with the latter formulation of Rabbi Yehuda's statement (*Beit Yosef*). He has also sold the woods that are adjacent to it. He has not sold the strips of land that are separated from the city by rocks and other barriers (Rema), nor has he sold the nearby villages or the forests that are distant from the city (Rambam *Sefer Kinyan*, *Hilkhot Mekhira* 26:1; *Shulḥan Arukh*, *Ḥoshen Mishpat* 215:4).

And not the enclosures – וְלֹא בֵּיבָרִין: When one sells a city, the enclosures for animals, birds, and fish are included in the sale even if they are located at a distance from the city, provided that their openings face the city. Enclosures that do not face the city, the city's portion of a sea, and its portion of dry land are not included in the sale. This is in accordance with the Gemara's conclusion, according to the version of the *ge'onim* (Rambam *Sefer Kinyan*, *Hilkhot Mekhira* 26:1; *Shulḥan Arukh*, *Ḥoshen Mishpat* 215:4).

״וְלֹא בֵּיבָרִין שֶׁל חַיָּה וְשֶׁל עוֹפוֹת וְשֶׁל דָּגִים״. וּרְמִינְהִי: הָיוּ לָהּ בָּנוֹת – אֵין נִמְכָּרוֹת עִמָּהּ; הָיָה לָהּ חֵלֶק אֶחָד בַּיָּם וְחֵלֶק אֶחָד בַּיַּבָּשָׁה, בֵּיבָרִים שֶׁל חַיָּה וְשֶׁל עוֹפוֹת וְשֶׁל דָּגִים – הֲרֵי אֵלּוּ נִמְכָּרִים עִמָּהּ!

§ The *baraita* teaches: When one sells a city he has not sold, among other things, **the enclosures for animals, for birds, and for fish. And** the Gemara **raises a contradiction** from another *baraita*: **If** the city **has daughters,** i.e., nearby villages, they **are not sold** along **with it. If it has one part on the sea**[N] **and one part on dry land,** or if it has **enclosures for animals, for birds, or for fish, these are** all **sold** along **with** the city.

לָא קַשְׁיָא: הָא דִּנְגִיחַ קָאֵיהִי לְגוֹ, וְהָא דִּנְגִיחַ קָאֵיהִי לְבַר. וְהָא קָא תָּנֵי: וְלֹא אֶת חוֹרָשִׁין הַמּוּקְצִין לָהּ! אֵימָא: הַמּוּקְצִין הֵימֶנָּה.

The Gemara answers that this is **not difficult,** as a distinction can be made between different cases: **Here,** the one *baraita* addresses animal enclosures **whose openings face**[N] **inward,** i.e., toward the city, and they are therefore considered a part of the city, whereas **there,** the other *baraita* addresses animal enclosures **whose openings face outward,** i.e., away from the city, and therefore they are not included in its sale. The Gemara raises a difficulty: **But doesn't** the *baraita* **teach: And** he has **not** sold **the woods that are set aside for** the city,[N] indicating that they face the city, and nevertheless they are not sold along with the city? The Gemara answers: **Say** that the *baraita* should be emended so that it reads instead: And he has not sold the woods **that are set apart** from the city, i.e., that are at a distance and do not face the city.

מתני׳ הַמּוֹכֵר אֶת הַשָּׂדֶה – מָכַר אֶת הָאֲבָנִים שֶׁהֵם לְצָרְכָּהּ, וְאֶת הַקָּנִים שֶׁבַּכֶּרֶם שֶׁהֵם לְצָרְכּוֹ, וְאֶת הַתְּבוּאָה שֶׁהִיא מְחוּבֶּרֶת לַקַּרְקַע, וְאֶת חִיצַת הַקָּנִים שֶׁהִיא פְּחוּתָה מִבֵּית רוֹבַע, וְאֶת הַשּׁוֹמֵירָה שֶׁאֵינָהּ עֲשׂוּיָה בְּטִיט, וְאֶת הֶחָרוּב שֶׁאֵינוֹ מוּרְכָּב, וְאֶת בְּתוּלַת הַשִּׁקְמָה;

MISHNA One **who sells a field**[H] without specifying what is included in the sale **has sold the stones** in the field **that are for its use,**[N] **and the reeds in the vineyard**[N] **that are for its use, and the produce that is still attached to the ground, and the cluster of reeds that occupy less than the area required for sowing a quarter-kav of seed** [*beit rova*],[B] **and the watch station that is not plastered with clay,**[N] **and the young carob tree that has not** yet **been grafted,**[B] **and the untrimmed sycamore**[B] that is still young.

NOTES

If it has one part on the sea – חֵלֶק אֶחָד בַּיָּם: According to one explanation, this is referring to a city where the majority of it is located on the mainland while a minority is situated on the sea, or conversely, the majority of the city is situated on the sea, with a minority on the mainland (Ramah). Alternatively, this is referring to areas that are located outside the city, either at a distance or on the sea, but which are called by the same name as the city (Rashbam). According to Rav Hai Gaon, this is referring to an island, or part of an island, that is considered part of the city, while the Ra'avad explains that these areas are forests that serve the city. The different explanations of this passage depend in part on the text of the *baraita*, which, according to some early commentaries, states the opposite, that this land is not sold along with the city (see Ri Migash; Ra'avad; Ramah). The Jerusalem Talmud cites two conflicting *baraitot*, which Rav Ḥisda reconciles by distinguishing between whether this land is situated within or outside the border of the city.

Whose openings face [*negiaḥ ka'ihi*] – נְגִיחַ קָאֵיהִי: There are several different versions of the phrase *negiaḥ ka'ihi*. According to the version found in the *Arukh* and the Ritva, the phrase is one word, *negahakayhu*. The commentaries agree that the phrase means that their openings face the city, but they disagree about the literal meaning of the words. According to the Ritva, *naga* means an opening, and *ka'ihu* means their position or place; therefore, the entire phrase means that the place of their opening faces the city. According to the Ra'avad, *negiaḥ* means pulling; therefore, the expression means that the opening extends toward the city.

And not the woods that are set aside for the city [*hamuktzin lah*] – וְלֹא אֶת חוֹרָשִׁין הַמּוּקְצִין לָהּ: According to some commentaries, these woods, like the animal enclosures, are defined areas used for hunting, and therefore the words *muktzin lah* indicate that they face the city. The Gemara answers that in fact the words are *muktzin heimena*, which indicate that they do not face the city (Rashbam; see Ra'avad). Others explain that *muktzin lah* means that these woods are in close proximity to the city, and the Gemara answers that they are actually found at a distance from it (Ri Migash), or that the woods are more easily reached from a different city (Ramah). Alternatively, the words *muktzin lah* mean that the residents of the city are permitted to enter the woods, and the Gemara answers that the woods are *muktzin heimena*, meaning that the residents of the city are not permitted to enter them (Meiri).

The stones that are for its use – הָאֲבָנִים שֶׁהֵם לְצָרְכָּהּ: The general assumption is that when one sells land, anything that is attached to and relevant to the function of the ground is included in the sale, while movable items are not. But with regard to the sale of a field or a vineyard, certain items are included in the sale not because they are attached to the ground, but because they are required for working the land and are designated for this purpose.

And the reeds in the vineyard – וְאֶת הַקָּנִים שֶׁבַּכֶּרֶם: This mishna proves that a vineyard that is located within a field is included in the sale of the field (Rashbam; *Nimmukei Yosef*). By contrast, the *Levush* understands that the mishna is referring to a case where the vineyard was explicitly included in the sale (see *Tosefot Yom Tov*). This is also the opinion of the Meiri.

That is not plastered with clay – שֶׁאֵינָהּ עֲשׂוּיָה בְּטִיט: *Tosafot* point out that there are two opposite versions of this statement. The version here is the version of the Rashbam. According to the version of the *ge'onim*, if the watch station is plastered with clay, it is included in the sale of the field, whereas if it is not plastered with clay, it is not included. According to the Rashbam's version, a watch station that is not plastered is an unimportant structure, and therefore it is included in the sale of the field, while one that is plastered is significant enough in its own right to be excluded from the sale. According to the version of the *ge'onim*, a plastered watch station is a permanent structure found in the field, and therefore it is included in the sale, while one that is not plastered is considered to be mobile and therefore it is not included in the sale.

HALAKHA

One who sells a field – הַמּוֹכֵר אֶת הַשָּׂדֶה: One who sells a field has sold all the items that are designated for its use and all the items that are always found in the field (*Sma*), as is explained in detail in the Gemara. The stones in the field that are designated for its use are included in this category. Also included in the sale are the reeds in a vineyard that support the vines; the produce that is still attached to the ground; the clusters of reeds, or according to the version of the Rif, the partitions of reeds that occupy less than the area required for sowing a quarter-*kav* of seed; and young carob or sycamore trees. The sale also includes any watch station that is plastered with clay, in accordance with the Rif and Rambam's version of the text. The sale does not include the stones that are not designated for use in the field or the reeds that are not designated for use in the vineyard. But if the seller specified that he is selling the field or the vineyard and everything that is in it, these are included in the sale. In any event, the sale does not include the clusters of reeds that occupy at least an area necessary for sowing a quarter-*kav* of seed; a watch station that is not plastered with clay, even if it is attached to the ground; and mature carob and sycamore trees (Rambam *Sefer Kinyan*, *Hilkhot Mekhira* 26:2–3; *Shulḥan Arukh*, *Ḥoshen Mishpat* 215:5).

BACKGROUND

The area required for sowing a quarter-*kav* of seed [*beit rova*] – בֵּית רוֹבַע: The minimum amount of space required in order to sow one quarter-*kav* of seed is 104⅙ square cubits, equal to 24 sq m according to Rabbi Ḥayyim Na'e, and 35 sq m according to the Ḥazon Ish.

Young carob tree that has not been grafted – חָרוּב שֶׁאֵינוֹ מוּרְכָּב: Carob trees grow wild in nature, yet by and large they are small with poor fruit. In contrast, cultivated carob trees are tall and grow fine carobs. The wild carobs, however, are stronger than the cultivated ones, and for this reason to this day carobs are grown from the seeds of wild carob trees, with the branches of cultivated carobs grafted onto them. A carob grown from such a graft retains the strength of the initial planting yet grows branches and fruits like the cultivated carobs. These carob trees are considered superior to carob trees that have not been grafted, i.e., the wild variety of carob trees.

Untrimmed sycamore – בְּתוּלַת הַשִּׁקְמָה: The sycamore, *Ficus sycomorus*, is a tall, broad tree of the fig species. Even though the fruits of the sycamore are edible, it is usually grown for its wood, as sycamore beams are large, wide, and relatively lightweight. The sycamore is usually left to grow for several years until it reaches sizable dimensions, whereupon it is cut down for its wood. The stump is then left for several years to grow back again, after which time more wood is harvested.

Old sycamore with a hollow trunk in Ramat Gan, Israel

אֲבָל לֹא מָכַר לֹא אֶת הָאֲבָנִים שֶׁאֵינָן לְצׇרְכָּהּ, וְלֹא אֶת הַקָּנִים שֶׁבַּכֶּרֶם שֶׁאֵינָן לְצׇרְכּוֹ, וְלֹא אֶת הַתְּבוּאָה שֶׁהִיא תְּלוּשָׁה מִן הַקַּרְקַע; בִּזְמַן שֶׁאָמַר לוֹ: ״הִיא וְכׇל מַה שֶּׁבְּתוֹכָהּ״ – הֲרֵי כּוּלָּן מְכוּרִין; בֵּין כָּךְ וּבֵין כָּךְ, לֹא מָכַר לֹא אֶת חִיצַת הַקָּנִים שֶׁהִיא בֵּית רוֹבַע, וְלֹא אֶת הַשּׁוֹמֵירָה שֶׁהִיא עֲשׂוּיָה בְּטִיט, וְלֹא אֶת הֶחָרוּב הַמּוּרְכָּב, וְלֹא אֶת סַדַּן הַשִּׁקְמָה.

But he has not sold along with the field **the stones that are not** designated **for use** in the field, **and not the reeds in the vineyard that are not** designated **for its use, and not the produce that is** already **detached from the ground. When** the seller **says to** the buyer: I am selling you **it and everything that is in it, all these** components **are sold** along with the field. **Both** in **this** case, where he executes the sale without specification, **and in that** case, where he adds the phrase that he is selling everything that is in the field, **he has not sold the cluster of reeds that** occupy **a *beit rova*** or more, as they are considered a separate field, **and** he has **not** sold **the watch station that is plastered with clay, and not the carob tree that has been grafted, and not the sycamore trunk.** All of these entities are significant in their own right and have a status independent from that of the fields, and they are therefore not included in the sale of the field.

Perek **IV**
Daf **69** Amud **a**

גמ׳ מַאי אֲבָנִים שֶׁהֵן לְצׇרְכָּהּ? הָכָא תַּרְגִּימוּ: אַבְנֵי דְּאַכְפָּא. עוּלָּא אָמַר: אֲבָנִים הַסְּדוּרוֹת לַגָּדֵר. וְהָא תָּנֵי רַבִּי חִיָּיא: אֲבָנִים צְבוּרוֹת לַגָּדֵר! תְּנֵי: סְדוּרוֹת.

GEMARA The mishna teaches that one who sells a field has sold the stones in the field that are for its use. The Gemara clarifies: **What** is meant by **stones that are for its use?**[H] **Here** in Babylonia **they interpreted** it as follows: **Stones** placed **on the sheaves**[N] in the field to protect them from being scattered by the wind. **Ulla says:** The mishna is referring to **stones that are arranged for** the future building of **a fence**[N] for the field. The Gemara asks: **But didn't Rabbi Ḥiyya teach** in a *baraita* that they are **stones that are piled up for** the future building of **a fence,** and not necessarily arranged? The Gemara answers: **Teach** that Rabbi Ḥiyya said: They are stones that are **arranged** for the future building of a fence.

הָכָא תַּרְגִּימוּ: אַבְנֵי דְּאַכְפָּא; לְרַבִּי מֵאִיר – דְּמִתַּקְּנָן אַף עַל גַּב דְּלָא מַחְתָּן, לְרַבָּנַן – הוּא דְּמַחְתָּן.

The Gemara elaborates on the two explanations: It was stated that **here** in Babylonia **they interpreted** the mishna as referring to **stones** that are placed **on the sheaves. According to Rabbi Meir** this should be understood as referring to stones **that are ready**[N] to be used to protect the sheaves, **even though they are not** yet **placed** on them. This is in keeping with Rabbi Meir's opinion that whenever a place is sold, all the accompaniments that are necessary for its proper utilization are included in the sale (see 78b). **According to the Rabbis,** the mishna is referring specifically to stones **that are** already **placed**[N] on the sheaves.

וּלְעוּלָּא דְּאָמַר: אֲבָנִים הַסְּדוּרוֹת לַגָּדֵר; לְרַבִּי מֵאִיר – דְּמִתַּקְּנָן אַף עַל גַּב דְּלָא סַדְרָן, לְרַבָּנַן – הוּא דְּסַדְרָן.

And according to Ulla, who says that the mishna is referring to **stones that are arranged for** the future building of **a fence** for the field, **according to Rabbi Meir,** stones **that are ready** to be used for building a fence are also included in the sale, **even though they are not** yet **arranged** for that purpose. **According to the Rabbis,** the mishna is referring specifically to stones **that are** already **arranged** for building a fence.[N]

NOTES

Stones placed on the sheaves [*de'akhpa*] – אַבְנֵי דְּאַכְפָּא: Most of the commentaries agree with the Rashbam that *akhpa* means sheaves and that the phrase is referring to stones that are placed on the sheaves in the field to prevent them from being scattered by the wind. According to the Meiri, the stones are prepared in a special manner, as they are flat on one side. Others explain that the expression means stones that are carried on one's shoulder [*katef*] (Rabbeinu Yehonatan of Lunel). According to the Ramah, the expression is referring to stones that are loaded on the branches of trees that shed their fruit prematurely.

Arranged for a fence – סְדוּרוֹת לַגָּדֵר: According to some opinions, this is referring to stones that are arranged one on top of the other like a wall, but without clay or mortar (first explanation of Ra'avad; Ramah). Others explain that it means stones that were selected to be used to build a fence (Meiri), or stones that are used as a fence during specific seasons but at the moment do not serve as a fence (second explanation of Ra'avad; see *Tosefta* 3:6).

That are ready – דְּמִתַּקְּנָן: According to the Rashbam and Rav Hai Gaon in *Sefer HaMikkaḥ VehaMimkar*, this means that the stones were designated for this use. Rabbeinu Gershom and others explain that they were chiseled and planed so as to be fit for this purpose.

That are placed – הוּא דְּמַחְתָּן: Some of the commentaries explain that the stones were already placed on the sheaves. *Tosafot* and others explain that since the sheaves themselves are not sold along with the field, it does not matter whether or not the stones were resting on them at the time of the sale. Rather, the question is whether the stones were ever used for this purpose, or whether they were merely intended for this use without ever actually having been used. According to the Rashbam, it means that they were placed inside the field.

That are arranged – הוּא דְּסַדְרָן: The stones are already arranged, one on top of the other (Rashbam). Alternatively, they are arranged in a row alongside the area where a fence will be built (Meiri).

HALAKHA

The stones that are for its use – אֲבָנִים שֶׁהֵן לְצׇרְכָּהּ: Stones that are arranged for building a fence and stones that are placed on the sheaves are included in the sale of the field, in accordance with both the interpretation given in Babylonia and the explanation of Ulla, as the two do not contradict each other. If the stones have not yet been arranged for a fence or placed on sheaves but are merely intended to be used for these purposes, they are not included in the sale. The Rema writes that there are those who say that if the stones had, at some point in the past, been placed on the sheaves, they are included in the sale (*Tur*, citing *Tosafot*). The *halakha* is in accordance with the opinion of the Rabbis (Rambam *Sefer Kinyan*, *Hilkhot Mekhira* 26:2; *Shulḥan Arukh*, *Ḥoshen Mishpat* 215:5).

"וְאֶת הַקָּנִים שֶׁבַּכֶּרֶם שֶׁהֵן לְצָרְכּוֹ". קָנִים מַאי עֲבִידְתַּיְיהוּ? אָמְרִי דְּבֵי רַבִּי יַנַּאי: קָנִים הַמְחוּלָּקִין שֶׁמַּעֲמִידִים תַּחַת הַגְּפָנִים; לְרַבִּי מֵאִיר – דִּמְשַׁפְיָין אַף עַל גַּב דְּלָא מוּקְמָן, לְרַבָּנַן – הוּא דְּמוּקְמָן.

The Gemara continues with its clarification of the mishna, which teaches that one who sells a field has **also sold the reeds in the vineyard**[H] **that are for its use.** The Gemara asks: With regard to the **reeds, what is their purpose** in the vineyard? The Sages **of the school of Rabbi Yannai said:** These are **reeds that are split**[BN] on top and **placed under the vines** so that the boughs of the vines can rest on them. **According to Rabbi Meir,** this is referring to reeds **that have been smoothed** and made ready for this purpose, **even though they are not** yet **set in their place. According to the Rabbis,** the mishna refers specifically to reeds **that are** already **set in their place.**

"וְאֶת הַתְּבוּאָה הַמְחוּבֶּרֶת לַקַּרְקַע" וכו'. וְאַף עַל גַּב דִּמְטַאי לְמֵיחְצַד. "וְאֶת חִיצַת הַקָּנִים שֶׁפְּחוּתָה מִבֵּית רוֹבַע". וְאַף עַל גַּב דְּאַלִּימֵי.

The Gemara continues expounding the mishna, which includes among the components that are sold with a field **the produce**[H] **that is still attached to the ground.** The Gemara comments: **Even though** the time **has** already **come** for the produce **to be cut down,**[N] it is included in the sale since it is still attached to the ground. The mishna also includes among the things that are sold with a field **the cluster of reeds**[H] **that** occupy **less than a** ***beit rova.*** The Gemara notes: **Even though** these reeds **are thick,** they are still classified as part of the field.

"וְאֶת הַשּׁוֹמֵירָה שֶׁאֵינָהּ עֲשׂוּיָה בְּטִיט". אַף עַל גַּב דְּלָא קְבִיעָא בְּאַרְעָא. "וְאֶת הֶחָרוּב שֶׁאֵינוֹ מוּרְכָּב, וְאֶת בְּתוּלַת הַשִּׁקְמָה". אַף עַל גַּב דְּאַלִּימֵי.

The mishna teaches that one who sells a field sells with it **the watch station**[H] **that is not plastered with clay.** The Gemara comments: **Even though it is not fixed in the ground** and can still be moved, since it is not plastered, it is not significant enough to be considered an independent entity, and it is considered part of the field. The mishna also includes the following among the components that are sold with a field: **And the carob tree that has not been grafted, and the untrimmed sycamore.** The Gemara notes: **Even though they are** big and **thick,** since they have not yet reached the stage of grafting, in the case of the carob, or trimming, in the case of the sycamore, they are considered part of the field.

"אֲבָל לֹא מָכַר אֶת הָאֲבָנִים שֶׁאֵינָן לְצָרְכָּהּ". לְרַבִּי מֵאִיר – דְּלָא מִתַּקְנָן, לְרַבָּנַן – דְּלָא מַחְתָן.

The Gemara proceeds to explain the second half of the mishna, which teaches: **But he has not sold** along with the field **the stones that are not** designated **for use** in the field. On the assumption that the mishna speaks of stones that are placed on the sheaves to prevent them from being scattered, **according to Rabbi Meir,** the mishna is referring to stones **that are not ready** to be used for this purpose, whereas **according to the Rabbis,** even if the stones are ready to be used to protect the sheaves, they are not included in the sale if **they are not** yet **placed** on them.

וּלְעוּלָּא דְּאָמַר: אֲבָנִים הַסְּדוּרוֹת לַגָּדֵר; לְרַבִּי מֵאִיר – דְּלָא מִתַּקְנָן, לְרַבָּנַן – דְּלָא סִדְרָן.

And according to Ulla, who says that the mishna is referring to **stones that are arranged for** the future building of **a fence** for the field, **according to Rabbi Meir,** this clause addresses a case **where** the stones **were not ready** to be used for this purpose, whereas **according to the Rabbis,** it addresses a case **where** the stones **were not** yet **arranged** for building a fence, even though they were ready to be used for that purpose.

HALAKHA

The reeds in the vineyard – קָנִים שֶׁבַּכֶּרֶם: Reeds that have been smoothed and placed under the vines to support them are included in the sale of a vineyard. If they were not yet placed under the vines, even if they were smoothed so that they could be used in this manner, they are not included in the sale as the *halakha* is in accordance with the Rabbis (Rambam *Sefer Kinyan, Hilkhot Mekhira* 26:2; *Shulḥan Arukh, Ḥoshen Mishpat* 215:5).

The produce – הַתְּבוּאָה: When one sells a field, the sale includes the produce that is still attached to the ground, even if it is ready to be harvested. Produce that has already been harvested is not included in the sale, even if it still needs to be left in the field (Rambam *Sefer Kinyan, Hilkhot Mekhira* 26:2; *Shulḥan Arukh, Ḥoshen Mishpat* 215:5).

The cluster of reeds – חִיצַת הַקָּנִים: If a cluster of reeds occupies less than a *beit rova*, it is included in the sale of a field, even if the reeds are thick. If it occupies more than a *beit rova*, it is not included in the sale, even if the reeds are thin (Rambam *Sefer Kinyan, Hilkhot Mekhira* 26:2; *Shulḥar Arukh, Ḥoshen Mishpat* 215:5).

The watch station – הַשּׁוֹמֵירָה: A watch station that is plastered with clay is included in the sale of a field or vineyard, even if it is not attached to the ground, and a watch station that is not plastered with clay is not included in the sale, even if it is attached to the ground. This is in accordance with the Rif and Rambam's version of the mishna and Gemara (Rambam *Sefer Kinyan, Hilkhot Mekhira* 26:2; *Shulḥan Arukh, Ḥoshen Mishpat* 215:5).

BACKGROUND

Reeds that are split – קָנִים הַמְחוּלָּקִין: It was customary in some places to build permanent structures on which to trellis the vines. Sometimes, they would simply position canes, usually reeds, under the vines to support the boughs that had grown that year and keep the clusters of grapes off the ground and protect them from damage. These reeds were used for a year and then removed. The vine was then pruned, and new reeds were put in place for the next year.

The thin outer husks of the reeds were removed in order to prevent water from entering between the reed and the husk, causing the reed to rot over time. According to one version of the discussion here, this is what is meant by the expression: Reeds that are split. Other commentaries explain that split reeds are reeds whose tops have been split so that the vines can rest upon them.

NOTES

Reeds that are split [*hameḥullakin*] – קָנִים הַמְחוּלָּקִין: Some explain that these are reeds that are split [*meḥulak*] on top so that the boughs of the vines can rest on them (Rashbam; Meiri). Others explain that these are reeds that were made smooth [*ḥalak*] through the removal of their outer husks to prevent them from rotting (*Arukh*; Rabbeinu Gershom; *Tosafot*).

Even though the time has come for it to be cut down – וְאַף עַל גַּב דִּמְטַאי לְמֵיחְצַד: The Gemara is not referring to produce that is fully ripe and ready to be harvested, as in such a case the produce would certainly be considered as though it were already cut down. Rather, the Gemara speaks of produce that is sufficiently ripe to be cut down, but would still benefit from remaining attached to the ground (Ritva).

״וְלֹא אֶת הַקָּנִים שֶׁבַּכֶּרֶם שֶׁאֵינָן לְצָרְכּוֹ״. לְרַבִּי מֵאִיר – דְּלָא מְשַׁפְּיָין, לְרַבָּנַן – דְּלָא מוֹקְמָן. ״וְלֹא אֶת הַתְּבוּאָה הַתְּלוּשָׁה מִן הַקַּרְקַע״. וְאַף עַל גַּב דִּצְרִיכָא לְאַרְעָא.

The mishna teaches that one who sells a field has **not** sold **the reeds in the vineyard that are not** designated **for its use.** The Gemara explains: **According to Rabbi Meir,** this is referring to a case **where** the reeds **are not smoothed,** whereas **according to the Rabbis,** the reference is to reeds **that are not** yet **set in their place,** even if they are smoothed. The mishna further teaches: One who sells a field has also **not** sold **the produce that is detached from the ground.** The Gemara comments: The produce is not included in the sale **even though it** still **requires the ground,**[N] that is, it needs to be left in the field in order to dry out completely.

״וְלֹא אֶת חִיצַּת הַקָּנִים שֶׁהִיא בֵּית רוֹבַע״. וְאַף עַל גַּב דִּקְטִינֵי. אָמַר רַבִּי חִיָּיא בַּר אַבָּא אָמַר רַבִּי יוֹחָנָן: לֹא חִיצַּת הַקָּנִים בִּלְבַד, אֶלָּא אֲפִילּוּ עֲרוּגָה קְטַנָּה שֶׁל בְּשָׂמִים וְיֵשׁ לָהּ שֵׁם בִּפְנֵי עַצְמָהּ – אֵינָהּ נִמְכֶּרֶת עִמָּהּ. אֲמַר רַב פַּפָּא: וְהוּא דְּקָרוּ לָהּ וַורְדָּא דִּפְלָנְיָא.

The mishna teaches that one who sells a field has **not** sold **the cluster of reeds that occupy a** ***beit rova.*** The Gemara comments: **And** this is so **even though they are thin,** as since they occupy the area of a *beit rova* they are considered a separate entity and are not part of the field. Concerning this ruling, **Rabbi Ḥiyya bar Abba says** that **Rabbi Yoḥanan says:** It is **not only a cluster of reeds** that is considered a separate entity, and therefore not included in the sale; **rather, even a small garden bed of spices**[H] that does not occupy the area of a *beit rova* **but has a distinct name is not sold** along **with** the field. **Rav Pappa said:** What **this** means is **that** people **call it the roses** [***vardda***][L] **of so-and-so,** thereby establishing for it a name of its own.

״וְלֹא הַשּׁוֹמֵירָה הָעֲשׂוּיָה בְּטִיט״. וְאַף עַל גַּב דִּמְחַבְּרָא בְּאַרְעָא. ״וְלֹא אֶת חָרוּב הַמּוּרְכָּב וְלֹא סַדַּן הַשִּׁקְמָה״. וְאַף עַל גַּב דִּקְטִינֵי.

The mishna teaches that the sale does **not** include **the watch station that is plastered with clay.** The Gemara comments: **And** this is the *halakha* **even though it is attached to the ground,** as it is still considered a separate entity and not part of the field. The mishna teaches: He has also **not** sold **the carob tree that has been grafted, and** he has **not** sold **the sycamore trunk.** The Gemara notes: **Even though they are small,** they are considered their own entity.

בָּעֵי רַבִּי אֶלְעָזָר: מַלְבֵּנוֹת שֶׁל פְּתָחִים, מַהוּ? הֵיכָא דִּמְחַבְּרִי בְּטִינָא לָא תִּיבָּעֵי לָךְ – דְּהָא מְחַבַּר, כִּי תִּיבָּעֵי לָךְ – דִּנְקִיטֵי בְּסִיכֵּי, מַאי? תֵּיקוּ.

Apropos the discussion of a watch station that is attached to the ground, the Gemara cites a discussion about the sale of a house: **Rabbi Elazar raised the dilemma:** With regard to wooden **door frames,**[NB] **what is** the *halakha*? Are they sold together with the house, or not? The Gemara explains the question: **Do not raise the dilemma** in a case **where** the frames **are attached** to the house **with clay, as they are** certainly **attached** to the house and sold along with it. **When you can raise this dilemma is where they are connected** only **with small wooden pegs. What** is the ruling in that case? No resolution was found for this question, and so the dilemma **shall stand** [***teiku***][L] unresolved.

NOTES

It still requires the ground – דִּצְרִיכָא לְאַרְעָא: The produce would benefit from remaining in the field until it dries out completely. Nevertheless, since it was already cut down and can be moved, it is not included in the sale (Rashbam; Rabbeinu Gershom).

Door frames – מַלְבֵּנוֹת שֶׁל פְּתָחִים: According to the Rashbam, both this and the following dilemma are mentioned here because the distinctions that are drawn are similar to the distinction made here as to whether the item is or is not plastered with clay. Based on this explanation, Rabbi Zeira is asking whether door frames are included in the sale of a house. This also seems to be the understanding of the Rambam and the *Shulḥan Arukh*. Others understand Rabbi Zeira's dilemma as a continuation of the previous discussion. According to this, he is not asking about the door frames of houses, but about the door frame of a watch station, and the question is whether it is sold along with the watch station, when the watch station itself is included in the sale (*Tosafot*; *Tosefot HaRosh*; Ramban).

HALAKHA

A small garden bed of spices – עֲרוּגָה קְטַנָּה שֶׁל בְּשָׂמִים: With regard to one who sells a field, even if he says that he is selling the field and everything that is in it, he has not included in the sale a small garden bed of spices that has its own name, for example, if it is called the rose garden of so-and-so (Rambam *Sefer Kinyan*, *Hilkhot Mekhira* 26:3; *Shulḥan Arukh*, *Ḥoshen Mishpat* 215:5).

LANGUAGE

Roses [*vardda*] – וַורְדָּא: Apparently from the Middle Iranian word ward, meaning a rose.

It shall stand [*teiku*] – תֵּיקוּ: Various explanations have been offered with regard to the etymology of this term. One explanation is that the word is an abbreviated version of *tikom*, let it stand. Another is that its source is the word *tik*, a case or pouch, whose contents are unknown. Similarly, the resolution of the matter at hand is unknown to us as if it were hidden inside a case (*Arukh*). Although not the literal meaning, some suggest that the term is an acrostic, meaning: The Tishbite, i.e., Elijah the Prophet, will resolve questions and dilemmas (*Tosafot Yom Tov*). This alludes to the belief that upon Elijah's return to announce the advent of the Messiah, he will also reveal the solutions to outstanding halakhic difficulties.

BACKGROUND

Door frames – מַלְבֵּנוֹת שֶׁל פְּתָחִים: The wooden frames of doorways, i.e., the lintels and crossbeam, as well as the window frames, were not part of the stone or brick structure of the buildings. Rather, they were inserted afterward into the openings left for them. In order to strengthen the frame, any space between the frame and the stone was filled in either with clay, which also served as a sealant, or with small wooden pegs.

Wooden pegs inserted in between the stones to strengthen the door frame

בָּעֵי רַבִּי זֵירָא: מַלְבְּנוֹת שֶׁל חַלּוֹנוֹת, מַהוּ? מִי אָמְרִינַן: לְנוֹי בְּעָלְמָא הוּא דַּעֲבִידִי, אוֹ דִּלְמָא כֵּיוָן דִּמְחַבְּרִי – מְחַבְּרִי? תֵּיקוּ.

Rabbi Zeira raises a similar **dilemma** about what is included in the sale of a house: With regard to **window frames**[B] **what is** the *halakha*? Are they sold together with the house, or not? **Do we say** that **they serve merely** as **an ornament,** and are not included in the sale, and the seller can remove them from the house and keep them for himself? **Or perhaps, since they are attached** to the window, **they are attached.** The dilemma **shall stand** unresolved.

בָּעֵי רַבִּי יִרְמְיָה: מַלְבְּנוֹת שֶׁל כַּרְעֵי הַמִּטָּה, מַהוּ? כָּל הֵיכָא דְּמִטַּלְטְלִי בַּהֲדָהּ לָא תִּיבְּעֵי לָךְ – דְּהָא מִטַּלְטְלִי, כִּי תִּיבְּעֵי לָךְ – הֵיכָא דְּלָא מִטַּלְטְלִי, מַאי? תֵּיקוּ.

And similarly, **Rabbi Yirmeya raised a dilemma:** With regard to **stands for the legs of a bed**[BNH] that are placed under the legs to prevent them from being damaged by moisture, **what is** the *halakha*? The Gemara explains the question: **Do not raise the dilemma wherever** the stands **move** along **with** the bed, **as they move** along with it and are therefore not considered part of the house. **Where you can raise this dilemma is where they do not move** along with the bed. **What** is the ruling in that case? No resolution was found for this question either, and therefore the dilemma **shall stand** unresolved.

״וְלֹא אֶת חָרוּב הַמּוּרְכָּב וְלֹא סַדַּן הַשִּׁקְמָה״ וכו׳.

The mishna teaches: One who sells a field has **not** sold **the carob tree that has been grafted, and** he has **not** sold **the sycamore trunk.**

BACKGROUND

Window frames – מַלְבְּנוֹת שֶׁל חַלּוֹנוֹת: This is referring to wooden window frames. In those days there were no glass window panes, so these frames had no actual use; rather, they served an aesthetic purpose.

Stands for the legs of a bed – מַלְבְּנוֹת שֶׁל כַּרְעֵי הַמִּטָּה: In order to protect the legs of a bed, wooden boxes were placed under the legs, like shoes for the bed legs. This would protect the bed's legs from moisture and also from getting worn down if dragged.

Stands for the legs of the bed

NOTES

Stands for the legs of a bed – מַלְבְּנוֹת שֶׁל כַּרְעֵי הַמִּטָּה: In order to protect the legs of a bed from moisture and from getting worn down when dragged, pieces of wood would be placed under the legs of the bed and attached to them (Rashbam). According to the Ra'avad, the reference here is to wooden partitions that were placed around the bed, for ornamentation or to prevent the user from falling off the bed. They were not attached to the bed itself and were sometimes used alone. According to these opinions, the Gemara's question is whether they are included in the sale of the bed. Alternatively, the question is whether stands for the legs of a bed that are attached to the ground are included in the sale of the house (Rambam; Ri Migash).

HALAKHA

Door frames, window frames, stands for the legs of a bed – מַלְבְּנוֹת שֶׁל פְּתָחִים, חַלּוֹנוֹת, כַּרְעֵי הַמִּטָּה: When one sells a house, the door frames that are attached to the house with clay are included in the sale. The Rema writes that some say that if the frames are attached with wooden pegs, they are not included in the sale, as the Gemara never reached a conclusion about this matter, and the burden of proof, to demonstrate that he is entitled to them, falls upon the buyer. The *Sma* questions the necessity of stating this, as no one disagrees (see *Pitḥei Teshuva*). One who sells a house has not sold the window frames, even if they are attached to the house with clay, as they are intended to serve only as an ornament. This is in accordance with the Rambam's explanation of the Gemara. Similarly, he has not sold the stands for the legs of a bed. If he wrote that he is selling the house and everything that is in it, all of these are included in the sale (Rambam *Sefer Kinyan*, *Hilkhot Mekhira* 25:5; *Shulḥan Arukh*, *Ḥoshen Mishpat* 214:11).

מְנָא הָנֵי מִילֵּי? אָמַר רַב יְהוּדָה אָמַר רַב, דְּאָמַר קְרָא: ״וַיָּקָם שְׂדֵה עֶפְרוֹן אֲשֶׁר בַּמַּכְפֵּלָה״ וגו׳, מִי שֶׁצָּרִיךְ לִגְבוּל סָבִיב, יָצְאוּ אֵלּוּ שֶׁאֵין צְרִיכִין לִגְבוּל סָבִיב. אָמַר רַב מְשָׁרְשִׁיָּא: מִכָּאן לִמְצָרִים מִן הַתּוֹרָה.

The Gemara asks: **From where are these matters,** i.e., that a grafted carob and a sycamore trunk are not included in the sale of a field, derived? **Rav Yehuda said that Rav said: As the verse states: "So the field of Ephron, which was in Machpelah,** which was before Mamre, the field, and the cave that was within it, and all the trees that were in the field, that were in all the boundaries around, were established for Abraham as a possession" (Genesis 23:17–18). This teaches that **anything that requires a boundary**[N] around it, as it does not have natural demarcations, is included in the sale of a field. This **excludes these** trees, i.e., the grafted carob and the sycamore trunk, **which do not require a boundary around** them, as they stand out individually on their own. **Rav Mesharshiyya says: From here** there is a source **that** the acquisition of the actual **boundaries** in a sale **is from the Torah.**[N]

אָמַר רַב יְהוּדָה: הַאי מַאן דְּמְזַבֵּן אַרְעָא לְחַבְרֵיהּ, צָרִיךְ לְמִכְתַּב לֵיהּ: ״קְנֵי לָךְ דִּיקְלִין וְתָאלִין וְהוּצִין וְצִיצִין״. וְאַף עַל גַּב דְּכִי לָא כְּתַב לֵיהּ הָכִי קָנֵי, אֲפִילּוּ הָכִי – שׁוּפְרָא דִּשְׁטָרָא הוּא.

§ **Rabbi Yehuda said: One who sells land to another**[H] **must write for him** the following in the bill of sale: **Acquire for yourself the palm trees and the dates**[N] **and the branches and the seedlings.**[N] **And even if he did not write this for him** the buyer would still **acquire** all of these entities, as demonstrated by the mishna that it is only a grafted carob and a sycamore trunk that are excluded from the sale of a field. **Even so, it is an enhancement of the bill** of sale that he write all of the details of the transaction so that there be no possible room for disagreement.

אֲמַר לֵיהּ: ״אַרְעָא וְדִיקְלֵי״; חָזֵינַן, אִי אִית לֵיהּ דִּיקְלֵי – יָהֵיב לֵיהּ תְּרֵי דִּיקְלֵי, וְאִי לֵית לֵיהּ – זָבֵין לֵיהּ תְּרֵי דִּיקְלֵי, וְאִי מְשַׁעְבְּדִי – פָּרֵיק לֵיהּ תְּרֵי דִּיקְלֵי.

If the seller **said to** the buyer: I am selling you **the land and palm trees,**[HN] **we consider** the situation. **If he has palm trees, he must give him two palm trees**[N] as two is the minimum number of trees that would justify being called: Trees, in the plural. **And if he has no** palm trees,[N] **he must buy two palm trees for him** somewhere else. **And if** he has palm trees, but **they are mortgaged** to another person, **he must redeem two palm trees** and give them to the buyer.

HALAKHA

One who sells land to another – מַאן דִּמְזַבֵּן אַרְעָא לְחַבְרֵיהּ: One who sells an orchard to another must write in the bill of sale: Acquire for yourself the palm trees and the branches and the dates. According to the *Tur*, it is only advisable to do so but the sale is valid even if he does not do so. Similarly, one who sells a field should specify the names of all of the types of trees that are found in the field (*Tur*). This is an enhancement of the bill of sale that prevents future claims. Nevertheless, all of these entities are acquired even if they were not explicitly mentioned in the bill of sale (Rambam *Sefer Kinyan*, *Hilkhot Mekhira* 24:14; *Shulḥan Arukh*, *Ḥoshen Mishpat* 216:1).

The land and palm trees – אַרְעָא וְדִיקְלֵי: If the seller says to the buyer that he is selling him the land and palm trees, the sale is valid even if the land contains no palm trees, provided that the seller gives him two palm trees somewhere else, and the buyer cannot claim that he had intended to buy only a field that contained palm trees. Some explain that in any event, the seller is obligated to purchase palm trees for the buyer (Ra'avad, citing Rif). The Rema writes that some say that this is considered two sales, so that even if the field contains palm trees, the seller must still give the buyer two palm trees from another field of his; but if the seller has no other palm trees, he is not obligated to purchase them for the buyer (Rambam *Sefer Kinyan*, *Hilkhot Mekhira* 24:13; *Shulḥan Arukh*, *Ḥoshen Mishpat* 216:5, and in the comment of Rema).

NOTES

Anything that requires a boundary – מִי שֶׁצָּרִיךְ לִגְבוּל: The proof is not found in the words cited by the Gemara, but in the continuation of the verse, which ostensibly states the same idea twice: "And all the trees that were in the field, that were in all the boundaries around." Two *halakhot* can be derived from here. The first is that when one sells a field without specification, in the way that Ephron sold his field to Abraham, the trees are included in the sale. The second is that only trees that require a boundary are included in the sale (Rashbam).

The commentaries explain the phrase: Anything that requires a boundary, to mean as follows: Any small or unimportant tree that is not referred to as an independent item, and must be marked by its boundary to define it, is included in the sale of the land. By contrast, significant trees that are known by a name are not included in the sale even when they are not marked by a boundary (Ri Migash). Alternatively, only small trees that require a protective border, i.e., a fence, are sold with the field, while large trees that have no need for such a border are not included in the sale (Rabbeinu Gershom).

From here there is a source that the acquisition of the actual boundaries is from the Torah – מִכָּאן לִמְצָרִים מִן הַתּוֹרָה: The Rashbam explains that when one sells a field, he sells along with it the boundaries of the field, including whatever is planted on them. This opinion is cited by Rabbeinu Gershom and the Ritva, who agrees that this is, in fact, the *halakha*, but he does not think that it fits in easily with the wording of the Gemara. Rabbeinu Gershom explains that the verse teaches that at the time of the sale the boundaries must be defined. Rav Hai Gaon and the Rashba point out that even if this was not done, the sale is still valid. Similarly, other early commentaries explain that the verse teaches that defining or failing to define boundaries has halakhic repercussions. This is the opinion of the Ra'avad, who holds that if the boundaries were not mentioned, the seller can claim that he sold only the area required for sowing nine *kav* of seed. Similarly, if he sold a field in a valley that does not have clearly delineated boundaries, unless the boundaries are specified, the seller can claim that he sold a field in a different location.

Palm trees [*dikelin*] and dates [*talin*] – דִּיקְלִין וְתָאלִין: *Talin* is generally understood as referring to palm trees. Accordingly, the Rashbam explains that *dikelin* and *talin* are respectively large and small palm trees. Others explain that these terms refer to other types of tall trees (*Arukh*). The Rambam, who perhaps had a different version of the text, seems to have understood *talin* to mean dates, the fruit of the palm tree.

Branches [*hutzin*] and seedlings [*tzitzin*] – הוּצִין וְצִיצִין: According to the Rashbam, these are types of palm trees that do not produce fruit. Others explain that *hutzin* is referring to all types of shrub-like trees, and *tzitzin*, or according to the version of the *Arukh*, *tzinin*, are young palm trees (Rabbeinu Gershom; *Arukh*). According to the Rambam, the text does not mention *tzitzin*, and *hutzin* is referring to palm leaves.

The land and palm trees – אַרְעָא וְדִיקְלֵי: According to the Rashbam and other early commentaries, the seller is understood to be selling the field and the palm trees separately. He is therefore obligated to provide the buyer with another two palm trees, in addition to the palm trees that are found in the field that is being sold, either from another field that he owns, or by buying or redeeming them. Other early commentaries disagree and explain that in the case at hand there is only one sale taking place.

He must give him two palm trees – יָהֵיב לֵיהּ תְּרֵי דִּיקְלֵי: Most of the commentaries explain that he must give him at least two palm trees, but this does not negate the buyer's right to the palm trees in the purchased field. The Rashbam cites an opinion, which is also the opinion of *Tosafot*, that the seller is obligated to give the buyer only two trees in the purchased field. According to this, if the seller had not specified that any trees were included in the sale, all of the trees in the field would be included. Once he says explicitly that he is selling him palm trees, he sells only two palm trees, as this is the minimum number of trees that would justify being called trees.

And if he has no palm trees – וְאִי לֵית לֵיהּ: If he does not own any palm trees he must buy some, or else he must reduce the price of the field by the price of two palm trees (Rashbam).

"אַרְעָא בְּדִיקְלֵי" – חָזֵינַן, אִי אִית בָּהּ דִּיקְלֵי – יָהֵיב לֵיהּ, וְאִי לָאו – מִקַּח טָעוּת הוּא. "אַרְעָא בֵּי דִיקְלֵי" – לֵית לֵיהּ דִּיקְלֵי, דְּחַזְיָא לְדִיקְלֵי קָאָמַר לֵיהּ. אֲמַר לֵיהּ: "לְבַר מִדִּיקְלָא פְּלָנְיָא" – חָזֵינַן, אִי דִּיקְלָא טָבָא הוּא – שִׁיּוּרֵי שַׁיְּירֵיהּ, אִי דִּיקְלָא בִּישָׁא הוּא – כׇּל שֶׁכֵּן הָנָךְ.

If the seller said to the buyer: I am selling you **land with palm trees, we consider** the situation. **If there are palm trees on** the land, **he must give him** the land, **and if not, this is a mistaken transaction**[N] and the sale is void. If the seller said to the buyer: I am selling you **land of palm trees,**[H] the buyer **has no** claim to receive **palm trees.** Therefore, if the land has no palm trees, this is not a mistaken transaction, as the seller meant to **say to him** that the land **was fit for palm trees,** and not that it already contained them. Furthermore, if the seller **said to** the buyer that he is selling the land **except for such and such a palm tree,**[H] **we consider** the situation. **If it is a good palm tree,**[N] we assume that **he retained** only **that** one for himself and did not include it in the sale, but **if it is a bad palm tree,** we assume that **all the more so** did he retain for himself **the other** ones that are of higher quality.

אֲמַר לֵיהּ: "לְבַר מֵאִילָנֵי", אִי אִית לֵיהּ אִילָנֵי – לְבַר מֵאִילָנֵי, אִי אִית לֵיהּ דִּיקְלֵי – לְבַר מִדִּיקְלֵי, אִי אִית לֵיהּ גּוּפְנֵי – לְבַר מִגּוּפְנֵי,

If the seller **said to** the buyer that he is selling him the entire field **except for the trees,** we consider the situation. **If he has** different types of **trees** in the field, for example, olive and fig trees, he has sold the entire field **except for the trees. If he has** only **palm trees** in the field, we assume that he meant to sell the entire field **except for the palm trees,** even though one does not ordinarily refer to palm trees by the more general term: Trees. Similarly, **if he has** only **grapevines** in the field, the buyer acquires everything **except for the grapevines.**

אִילָנֵי וְגוּפְנֵי – לְבַר מֵאִילָנֵי, אִילָנֵי וְדִיקְלֵי – לְבַר מֵאִילָנֵי, גּוּפְנֵי וְדִיקְלֵי – לְבַר מִגּוּפְנֵי.

If the field has both **trees and grapevines,** he has sold everything **except for the trees;**[H] therefore, the buyer does not acquire the trees, which the seller excluded from the sale, but he does acquire the grapevines. Similarly, if in the field there are both **trees and palm trees,** he has sold everything **except for the trees.**[N] If there are no other trees in the field, but only **grapevines and palm trees,**[N] everything, including the palm trees, is sold **except for the grapevines,** which we assume the seller reserved for himself.

אָמַר רַב: כׇּל שֶׁעוֹלִין לוֹ בְּחֶבֶל – הָוֵי שִׁיּוּר, כׇּל שֶׁאֵין עוֹלִין לוֹ בְּחֶבֶל – לָא הָוֵי שִׁיּוּר;

Rav says: If the seller specified that he is selling a field but not the trees, **any** tree that is so tall **that one must climb it by rope** in order to harvest its fruit **is retained** and is not included in the sale, and **any** tree **that one need not climb by rope is not retained** and is sold along with the field.

NOTES

Land with palm trees…mistaken transaction – אַרְעָא בְּדִיקְלֵי...מִקַּח טָעוּת: The principle that there is no claim of exploitation with regard to the sale of land applies only to the matter of the purchase price. But if the seller claims that a field has certain characteristics, e.g., that it is of a certain size, and it turns out that the claims are untrue, this is considered a mistaken transaction and the sale is nullified.

A good palm tree – דִּיקְלָא טָבָא: The seller is not pointing out the best or the worst palm tree. Rather, if he chose a good tree, even if there are better ones, he demonstrates that he wishes to retain something for himself from the field, but if he spoke of a bad one, it means that he is excluding all of the palm trees from the sale (Rashbam; Ri Migash). According to the Rashbam, a bad palm tree is one that does not produce a *kav* of dates.

Except for the trees – לְבַר מֵאִילָנֵי: The principle here is that one speaks precisely and if he mentions trees, he does not mean to include palm trees or grapevines. But if the field consists exclusively of grapevines or palm trees, since they are a kind of tree, it is understood that he is referring to them (Rashbam).

Grapevines and palm trees – גּוּפְנֵי וְדִיקְלֵי: If the seller says that he is selling everything except for the trees, and there are only grapevines and palm trees in the field, it is understood that he means to reserve the grapevines for himself. Some commentaries explain that this is because grape vines are more commonly referred to as trees than are palm trees (Rashbam; Rabbeinu Gershom). The Rashbam cites and rejects another explanation, which is the explanation of the Ramah, that since grapevines are preferred to palm trees, it is assumed that he would have chosen to withhold them for himself. The Ramah adds that the buyer is at a disadvantage and cannot claim that the seller is referring to the one and not the other.

HALAKHA

Land with palm trees…land of palm trees – אַרְעָא בְּדִיקְלֵי...אַרְעָא בֵּי דִיקְלֵי: If the seller says to the buyer that he is selling him land with palm trees, and the field contains two palm trees, the sale is valid. If the land has no palm trees, it is a mistaken transaction and the buyer can renege on the sale. If the seller said that he is selling him land of palm trees, the sale is valid even if the land contains no palm trees, and the seller is not obligated to give the buyer palm trees somewhere else. This is because his statement is interpreted to mean that he is selling him land that is fit for palm trees. In any event, whether he said that he is selling land of palm trees or with palm trees, if the land contains palm trees, they are acquired by the buyer (Rambam *Sefer Kinyan, Hilkhot Mekhira* 24:13; *Shulḥan Arukh, Ḥoshen Mishpat* 216:5).

Except for such and such a palm tree – לְבַר מִדִּיקְלָא פְּלָנְיָא: If the seller says to the buyer that he is selling him land, except for such and such palm tree, and that tree was of high quality, as it produces a *kav* of fruit (Rema, citing *Tur* and Rosh), the seller is presumed to have retained for himself only that tree, and the buyer acquires the rest of the palm trees. If the reserved tree was of poor quality, the buyer does not acquire that tree or any other palm trees in the field. The Rema writes that some say that the buyer does not acquire those palm trees that are superior to it, but he does acquire those that are equivalent or inferior to it (*Tur* and Rosh). *Nimmukei Yosef*, citing Rashba, says that if aside from the palm tree the field contains other varieties of trees, the buyer acquires all of the trees of those other varieties (Rambam *Sefer Kinyan, Hilkhot Mekhira* 24:11; *Shulḥan Arukh, Ḥoshen Mishpat* 216:3).

Except for the trees – לְבַר מֵאִילָנֵי: If one sells a field and writes in the bill of sale that the sale does not include the trees in the field, and there is only one variety of tree in the field, whether the field contains palm trees, grapevines, or any other type of tree or vine, these trees are not included in the sale. If there are both palm trees and grapevines in the field, the seller is presumed to have retained for himself the grapevines. If there are either grapevines or palm trees, as well as another type of tree, he retains the trees of the other type (Rema), in accordance with the principle that one who sells, sells generously (see Ra'avad, *Mishne LaMelekh*, and *Maggid Mishne*). If the field contains only palm trees (*Sma*, citing *Tur*) and he specified that he is retaining the palm trees, the seller retains only the palm trees that are so large that they must be climbed by rope to harvest their fruit. But if all of the palm trees are shorter than this, the seller retains them all (*Tur*). If the seller specified that he is retaining other types of trees that are found in the field, the only trees that are retained by the seller are those that are so large that, when plowing, the ox's yoke does not bend them back. This is in accordance with the Gemara's conclusion (70a). If all of the trees are so young that they are bent back by the yoke, they are all excluded from the sale (Rambam *Sefer Kinyan, Hilkhot Mekhira* 24:12; *Shulḥan Arukh, Ḥoshen Mishpat* 216:4).

וְדַיָּינֵי גוֹלָה אָמְרִי: כָּל שֶׁהָעוֹל כּוֹבְשׁוֹ – לָא הָוֵי שִׁיּוּר, כָּל שֶׁאֵין הָעוֹל כּוֹבְשׁוֹ – הָוֵי שִׁיּוּר. וְלָא פְּלִיגִי: הָא בְּדִיקְלֵי, הָא בְּאִילָנֵי.

But the judges of the exile, Shmuel and Karna, **say: Any** tree **that is bent back**[N] **by the yoke** of oxen as the animals plow the ground under the tree, and in this way the tree does not impede the plowing, **is not retained** by the seller, as it is not a significant tree. **Any** tree **that is not bent** back **by the yoke** of the oxen **is retained** by the seller and not included in the sale. The Gemara comments: **And** these *amora'im* **do not disagree** with regard to the *halakha*: **That** which Rav said, that the only trees that the seller retains for himself and excludes from the sale are those that must be climbed by means of a rope, was said **with regard to palm trees,** while **that** which the judges of the exile said, that the only trees that are retained are those that are not bent back by the yoke of the oxen, was said **with regard** to other types of **trees.**

בְּעָא מִינֵּיהּ רַב אַחָא בַּר הוּנָא מֵרַב שֵׁשֶׁת: "חוּץ מֵחָרוּב פְּלוֹנִי", "חוּץ מִסַּדָּן פְּלוֹנִי", מַהוּ? אוֹתוֹ חָרוּב הוּא דְּלָא קָנֵי, הָא שְׁאָר חֲרוּבִים קָנֵי, אוֹ דִּלְמָא שְׁאָר חֲרוּבִין נַמִי לָא קָנֵי? אֲמַר לֵיהּ: לֹא קָנָה.

§ The Gemara cites a discussion related to the mishna's ruling that a grafted carob tree and a sycamore trunk are not included in the sale of the field: **Rav Aḥa bar Huna raised a dilemma before Rav Sheshet:** If one selling a field said to the buyer: I am selling you the entire field **except for such and such** grafted **carob tree,**[N] or **except for such and such** sycamore **trunk,** and there were other grafted carob trees or sycamore trunks in the field, **what is** the *halakha*? The Gemara explains the two sides of the question: Does the seller mean to say that **it is this carob tree that** the buyer **does not acquire, but he does acquire the other carob trees, or perhaps** he means that **he also does not acquire the rest of the carob trees?** Rav Sheshet **said to him** in response: The buyer does **not acquire** any of them.

אֵיתִיבֵיהּ: "חוּץ מֵחָרוּב פְּלוֹנִי", "חוּץ מִסַּדָּן פְּלוֹנִי" – לֹא קָנָה; מַאי לָאו, אוֹתוֹ חָרוּב הוּא דְּלָא קָנָה, הָא שְׁאָר חֲרוּבִין קָנָה?

Rav Aḥa **raised an objection to** Rav Sheshet from a *baraita* that states: If the seller said to the buyer: I am selling you this field **except for such and such carob tree,**[H] or **except for such and such** sycamore **trunk,** the buyer does **not acquire** it. **What, is it not** that **it is this carob tree that he does not acquire, but he does acquire the other carob trees?**

אֲמַר לֵיהּ: לָא, אֲפִילּוּ שְׁאָר חֲרוּבִין נַמִי לֹא קָנָה. תֵּדַע, דְּאִילּוּ אָמַר לֵיהּ: "שָׂדִי מְכוּרָה לְךָ חוּץ מִשָּׂדֶה פְּלוֹנִית" – הַהִיא הוּא דְּלָא קָנֵי, הָא אַחֲרָנְיָיתָא קָנֵי? אֶלָּא לֹא קָנָה, הָכָא נַמִי לֹא קָנָה.

Rav Sheshet **said to him: No,** what this means is that **he does not acquire even the other carob trees. Know** that this is correct, **as if** a person selling a field **said to** the buyer: **My field is sold to you except for such and such field**[N] that is adjacent to it, would you say that **it is** only **that** adjacent field **that he does not acquire, but he acquires** all **the other** fields owned by the seller? This is clearly not the case, as the seller explicitly stated that he is selling a certain field, not all of his fields. **Rather,** everyone would agree that the buyer does **not acquire** the other fields. Therefore, **here too,**[N] the buyer does **not acquire** the other carob trees.

וְאִיכָּא דְּאָמְרִי, בְּעָא מִינֵּיהּ רַב אַחָא בַּר הוּנָא מֵרַב שֵׁשֶׁת: "חוּץ מֵחֲצִי חָרוּב פְּלוֹנִי", "חוּץ מֵחֲצִי סַדָּן פְּלוֹנִי", מַהוּ? שְׁאָר חֲרוּבִין וַדַּאי לָא קָנֵי, הָא מַה שֶּׁשִּׁיֵּיר בְּאוֹתוֹ חָרוּב קָנֵי, אוֹ דִּלְמָא אֲפִילּוּ מַה שֶּׁשִּׁיֵּיר בְּאוֹתוֹ חָרוּב נַמִי לָא קָנֵי? אֲמַר לֵיהּ: לָא קָנֵי.

And there are those **who say** that the discussion took place as follows: **Rav Aḥa bar Huna raised a dilemma before Rav Sheshet:** If one selling a field said to the buyer: I am selling you the entire field **except for half of such and such carob tree,**[N] or **except for half of such and such** sycamore **trunk, what is** the *halakha*? The Gemara explains the two sides of the question: Do we say that the buyer **certainly does not acquire the other carob trees, but he does acquire what remains from that carob tree** that was mentioned, that is, the half of the carob tree that the seller did not specifically retain for himself? **Or perhaps he does not acquire even what remains from that carob tree?** Rav Sheshet **said to him:** Even what remains from that carob tree the buyer does **not acquire.**

NOTES

Bent back [*kovsho*] – כּוֹבְשׁוֹ: Most of the commentaries explain that *kovsho* means that the tree is bent back by the yoke, as it is young and short. Another explanation of *kovsho* is that the tree is covered by the yoke as the oxen pass by with the yoke on their backs, as it is not tall enough to reach the yoke (Ri Migash).

Except for such and such carob tree – חוּץ מֵחָרוּב פְּלוֹנִי: Since the carob trees would normally be excluded from the sale in any case, there is room to clarify what the seller meant when he excluded a specific carob tree, or a part of it, from the sale. He might have meant to waive his right to the other carob trees in the field, and retain only this one. Or perhaps he did not mean to sell any of the trees, but he specified one particular tree for another reason: Either to state that he wishes to reserve for himself a right of way to access the tree, in accordance with the opinion of Rabbi Akiva in an earlier mishna (64a), or, according to the Rabbis, to enhance the bill of sale and thereby prevent any possible future claim of the buyer to this specific tree (Rashbam).

Most of the early commentaries disagree with the Rashbam, who assumes that according to Rabbi Akiva, one who sells a field without specification does not have a right of way to access his carob trees. This would then be the *halakha*, as the *halakha* is in accordance with Rabbi Akiva. Nevertheless, it is apparent from later passages that even when one sells a field without specification, the seller has such a right of way. They explain that the seller specified a particular carob tree for another reason, in accordance with a different version of the text. The Ramban and the Rashba point out that this issue does not appear in the Rambam or the Rif, which proves that this entire issue is only a problem for the Rabbis, who disagree with Rabbi Akiva. In practice, superfluous clauses such as this one have no effect on the sale.

Except for such and such field – חוּץ מִשָּׂדֶה פְּלוֹנִית: Here, the seller specifies that the adjacent field is not included in the sale. In this case as well, this added clause is unnecessary, as he sold only a specific field.

Rather, the buyer does not acquire the other fields, therefore here too – אֶלָּא לֹא קָנָה הָכָא נַמִי: The version of the text here is the version of the Rashbam. The Rashbam himself cites and rejects another version of the text. The majority of the early commentaries reject the Rashbam's version and explanation of the text, in favor of the alternative version, which is the version of Rabbeinu Ḥananel. This variant version, which was found in ancient manuscripts and was transmitted as a tradition from the time of the *ge'onim*, states: Rather, for the value, here too for the value. Rabbeinu Ḥananel explains that he received a direct tradition from his teachers that the Gemara should be understood as follows: When the seller says that he is selling his field, except for such and such field, he means that he is selling the first field, minus an area worth the value of the adjacent field. The same is true with regard to one who says that he is selling a field except for such and such carob, as he means to remove from the sale an area worth the value of the carob tree (see *Sefer HaMikkaḥ VehaMimkar Sha'ar* 19 and Ramban).

And there are those who say…except for half of such and such carob tree – וְאִיכָּא דְּאָמְרִי...חוּץ מֵחֲצִי חָרוּב: The premise of this discussion is that if the owner of the field had said: Except for such and such carob tree, the buyer also does not acquire ownership of the other carob trees in the field (Rashbam).

HALAKHA

Except for such and such carob tree – חוּץ מֵחָרוּב פְּלוֹנִי: If the owner of a field that contains grafted carob trees says to the buyer that he is selling him the field, except for a specific grafted carob tree (*Sma*), the buyer does not acquire that or any of the other carob trees in the field. This is because it is presumed that when the seller specified that one particular carob tree is excluded from the sale, he did so only in order to retain a right of way to access that tree, in accordance with the Rashbam's version of the text and his explanation (Rema, citing *Tur*). The Rambam and the *Shulḥan Arukh* do not cite this *halakha*, in accordance with Rabbeinu Ḥananel's version of the text (*Shulḥan Arukh, Ḥoshen Mishpat* 216:4 in the comment of Rema).

אֵיתִיבֵיהּ: ״חוּץ מֵחֲצִי חָרוּב פְּלוֹנִי״, ״חוּץ מֵחֲצִי סַדָּן פְּלוֹנִי״ – שְׁאָר חֲרוּבִין לֹא קָנָה; מַאי לָאו, שְׁאָר חֲרוּבִין הוּא דְּלָא קָנָה, הָא מַה שֶּׁשִּׁיֵּיר בְּאוֹתוֹ חָרוּב קָנָה?

Rav Aḥa **raised an objection to** Rav Sheshet from a *baraita* that states: If the seller said to the buyer: I am selling you the entire field **except for half of such and such carob tree,**[H] or **except for half of such and such** sycamore **trunk,** the buyer does **not acquire the other carob trees. What, is it not that it is the other carob trees that he does not acquire, but what remains of that carob tree he does acquire?**

אֲמַר לֵיהּ: לָא, אֲפִילּוּ מַה שֶּׁשִּׁיֵּיר בְּאוֹתוֹ חָרוּב נַמִי לֹא קָנָה. תֵּדַע, דְּאִילּוּ אָמַר לֵיהּ: ״שָׂדִי מְכוּרָה לָךְ חוּץ מֵחֲצִי שָׂדֶה פְּלוֹנִי״ – הַהוּא הוּא דְּלָא קָנָה, הָא אִידָּךְ קָנָה? אֶלָּא לָא קָנֵי, הָכָא נַמִי לָא קָנֵי.

Rav Sheshet **said to him: No,** what this means is that **he does not acquire even what remains of that carob tree. Know** that this is correct, **as if** a person selling a field **said to** the buyer: **My field is sold to you except for half of such and such field** that is adjacent to it, would you say that **it is** only **that** half of the field **that he does not acquire, but he acquires the other** half of the field? This is clearly not the case, as the seller explicitly stated that he is selling a certain field and nothing else. **Rather,** everyone would agree that the buyer does **not acquire** the other half of the field. Therefore, **here too,** the buyer does **not acquire** what remains of the carob tree.

בְּעָא מִינֵּיהּ רַב עַמְרָם מֵרַב חִסְדָּא: הַמַּפְקִיד אֵצֶל חֲבֵירוֹ בִּשְׁטָר, וְאָמַר לוֹ ״הֶחֱזַרְתִּים לָךְ״, מַהוּ? מִי אָמְרִינַן: מִיגּוֹ דְּאִי בָּעֵי אָמַר ״נֶאֶנְסוּ״ מְהֵימַן – הַשְׁתָּא נַמִי מְהֵימַן, אוֹ דִּלְמָא אָמַר לֵיהּ ״שְׁטָרָךְ בְּיָדִי מַאי בָּעֵי״? אֲמַר לֵיהּ: מְהֵימַן.

§ **Rav Amram raised a dilemma**[N] **before Rav Ḥisda:** If one **deposits** certain items **with another** and receives **a document**[H] signed by witnesses testifying that he deposited these items with this individual, **and** the bailee later **says to him: I returned** the items **to you,** but the document is still in the hands of the depositor, **what is the** *halakha*? **Do we say that since if** the bailee **wanted to** lie **he** could have **said** that the items **were taken** from him **under circumstances beyond his control,**[N] and **he would have been deemed credible;** therefore **now too,** when he claims that he returned the items, **he is deemed credible** as well? **Or perhaps,** the one who deposited the items can **say to him:** If you returned the items, **what is your document doing in my possession?**[N] Upon return of the deposit, you should have retrieved the document. Rav Ḥisda **said to him:** The bailee **is deemed credible.**

וְלֵימָא לֵיהּ ״שְׁטָרָךְ בְּיָדִי מַאי בָּעֵי״! אֲמַר לֵיהּ: וְלִיטַעְמִיךְ, וְכִי אָמַר לֵיהּ ״נֶאֶנְסוּ״, מִי מָצֵי אָמַר לֵיהּ ״שְׁטָרָךְ בְּיָדִי מַאי בָּעֵי״? אֲמַר לֵיהּ:

Rav Amram asked: **But let** the depositor **say to** the bailee: If you returned the items, **what is your document doing in my possession?** Rav Ḥisda **said to him: And according to your reasoning, if** the bailee had **said to him** that the items **were taken** from him **under circumstances beyond his control, would he be able to say to him: What is your document doing in my possession?** Since this claim could not have been stated had the bailee stated the alternative claim, it can also not be stated when the bailee claims that the items were returned. Rav Amram **said to him:**

Perek **IV**
Daf **70** Amud **b**

סוֹף סוֹף כִּי אָמַר לֵיהּ ״נֶאֶנְסוּ״ לָאו שְׁבוּעָה בָּעֵי? הָכָא נַמִי, מַאי נֶאֱמָן? נֶאֱמָן בִּשְׁבוּעָה.

Ultimately, even **when** the bailee **says to** the depositor that the items were **taken** from him **under circumstances beyond his control, is he not required to take an oath?**[N] How, then, can you assert that he is deemed credible to claim that he returned the items without taking an oath? Rav Ḥisda said to him: **Here too, what** did I mean when I said that he is **deemed credible?** It means that **he is deemed credible when** he takes **an oath.**

HALAKHA

Except for half of such and such carob tree – חוּץ מֵחֲצִי חָרוּב פְּלוֹנִי: If the owner of a field said that he is selling the field but not half of such and such carob tree, the buyer also does not acquire the other half of the carob tree (*Tur*, *Ḥoshen Mishpat* 216).

If one deposits items with another and receives a document – הַמַּפְקִיד אֵצֶל חֲבֵירוֹ בִּשְׁטָר: If one deposits an item with another and receives a document acknowledging that the deposit had been made, and the bailee later claims that he returned the item, the bailee must take an oath while holding a sacred object, just as he would be obligated to do had he claimed that the item was lost under circumstances beyond his control, and he is then exempt from payment. This is in accordance with the statement of Rav Ḥisda and the Gemara's conclusion that the bailee is deemed credible upon taking an oath. Many authorities hold that this oath is mandated by Torah law (*Sma*; *Baḥ*; Maharshal; *Ketzot HaḤoshen*), while others (*Shakh*) maintain that it was instituted by rabbinic decree, in a manner similar to oaths mandated by Torah law (Rambam *Sefer Mishpatim*, *Hilkhot Sekhirut* 2:12; *Shulḥan Arukh*, *Ḥoshen Mishpat* 121:5, 296:2).

NOTES

Rav Amram raised a dilemma – בְּעָא מִינֵּיהּ רַב עַמְרָם: This question is out of place here, and in terms of its content it should be found in tractate *Bava Metzia*. The Rashbam explains that this discussion was recorded here because both it and the previous discussion mention the opinion of the judges of the exile.

Since if the bailee wanted to lie he could have said that the items were taken under circumstances beyond his control – דְּאִי בָּעֵי אָמַר נֶאֶנְסוּ: Similarly, if this were a case of an unpaid bailee, he could claim that the items were lost or stolen. The Gemara speaks specifically of the claim that the items were taken from the bailee under circumstances beyond his control because this claim exempts the bailee whether he was a paid bailee or an unpaid one (Rabbeinu Gershom).

Or perhaps…what is your document doing in my possession – אוֹ דִּלְמָא...שְׁטָרָךְ בְּיָדִי מַאי בָּעֵי: Here, the depositor can claim that if, in fact, his items had been returned to him, the bailee would have demanded that the document be returned and destroyed so that it could not be presented against him a second time. The Rashbam explains that this argument impairs the bailee's claim that had he wanted to lie he could have put forward a more advantageous claim [*miggo*], and consequently this *miggo* claim no longer grants him credibility, as it is counteracted by the document. According to this opinion, like a *miggo* claim that is opposed by the testimony of witnesses, the document serves as evidence that casts doubt on the bailee's credibility.

NOTES

Is he not required to take an oath – לָאו שְׁבוּעָה בָּעֵי: The Rashbam explains that Rav Amram is challenging Rav Ḥisda's ruling, which seemed to have been that the bailee is deemed credible without having to take an oath. Rav Amram challenges Rav Ḥisda's ruling by claiming that the bailee is deemed credible when claiming that he returned the deposit only due to the fact that he could have made the more advantageous claim that the deposit was taken from him under circumstances beyond his control. Since, were he to claim that, he would have been liable to take an oath in order to be exempted from responsibility, the same should apply when he claims that the deposit was returned.

לֵימָא, בִּפְלוּגְתָּא דְּהָנֵי תַּנָּאֵי; דְּתַנְיָא: שְׁטַר כִּיס הַיּוֹצֵא עַל הַיְּתוֹמִים – דַּיָּינֵי גוֹלָה אָמְרִי: נִשְׁבָּע וְגוֹבֶה כּוּלּוֹ, וְדַיָּינֵי אֶרֶץ יִשְׂרָאֵל אָמְרִי: נִשְׁבָּע וְגוֹבֶה מֶחֱצָה.

The Gemara suggests: **Let us say** that Rav Amram and Rav Ḥisda disagree **with regard to** the issue that is the subject of **the dispute between these *tanna'im*, as a *halakha* is taught** in a *baraita* with regard to **a purse document,**[N] i.e., a document that records an arrangement whereby one gives another money as an investment in a joint venture on condition that the profits will be divided equally between the two parties. If the person who received the money died, and this document **was presented** by the lender **against the orphans,**[H] **the judges of the exile say** that the lender **takes an oath** that the money had never been returned to him, **and** he **collects the entire** sum.[N] **And the judges of Eretz Yisrael**[P] **say** that he **takes an oath and collects** only **half**[N] of the sum.

וּדְכוּלֵּי עָלְמָא אִית לְהוּ דִּנְהַרְדְּעֵי, דְּאָמְרִי נְהַרְדְּעֵי: הַאי עִיסְקָא – פַּלְגָּא מִלְוֶה וּפַלְגָּא פִּקָּדוֹן;

And it is understood **that everyone agrees with** the opinion of the Sages **of Neharde'a, as** the Sages **of Neharde'a say:** With regard to **this joint venture,**[NH] whereby one person gives money to another on condition that it will be used for business purposes and that the profits will be divided equally between the two parties, **half** of the invested money is considered **a loan,** for which the borrower is exclusively liable, **and half** is considered **a deposit,** so that if it is lost under circumstances beyond his control, the borrower is exempt from the liability to return it.

מַאי לָאו בְּהָא קָא מִיפַּלְגִי, דְּמָר סָבַר: מָצֵי אָמַר לֵיהּ "שְׁטָרָךְ בְּיָדִי מַאי בָּעֵי", וּמָר סָבַר: לָא אָמְרִי?

According to this assumption, everyone agrees that the claimant can recover from the orphans by means of an oath the half of the money that is considered a loan, just as he would have been able to demand that money from their father. Concerning the half that is considered a deposit, **what, is it not with regard to this** point that **they disagree, as one Sage,** the judges of the exile, **holds** like Rav Amram **that** the depositor **can say to** the bailee: **What is your document doing in my possession?** Therefore, neither the father nor his children are deemed credible to claim that they had returned the half that is considered a deposit, and the investor can collect that half as well. **And one Sage,** the judges of Eretz Yisrael, **holds** like Rav Ḥisda, that one **cannot assert** this claim, and therefore the investor can collect only the half that is considered a loan. But as for the half that is considered a deposit, the father would have been deemed credible in his claim that he had already returned it.

לֹא, דְּכוּלֵּי עָלְמָא אִית לְהוּ דְּרַב חִסְדָּא, וְהָכָא בְּהָא קָמִיפַּלְגִי, דְּמָר סָבַר: אִם אִיתָא דִּפְרָעֵיהּ מֵימַר הֲוָה אָמַר, וּמָר סָבַר: אֵימוּר מַלְאַךְ הַמָּוֶת הוּא דְּאַנְסֵיהּ.

The Gemara rejects this opinion: **No, everyone,** i.e., both the judges of the exile and the judges of Eretz Yisrael, **agrees with the** opinion **of Rav Ḥisda,** that the father can claim that he returned the money. **And here, they disagree about** the following issue, **as** one **Sage,** the judges of the exile, **holds** that **if it is so** that he had in fact **repaid** the money, **he would have told**[N] his children that he repaid it. Since he did not tell them, it may be assumed that he never repaid the money. **And one Sage,** the judges of Eretz Yisrael, **holds** that you can **say** that **it was the Angel of Death**[N] **that prevented him** from doing so, meaning he died before he had the opportunity to give his children a detailed report concerning his financial affairs.

NOTES

Purse document – **שְׁטַר כִּיס**: This is referring to a document that attests that one gave another a purse of money to be part of a joint venture. In the case at hand, the recipient died, and the investor demands reimbursement from the orphaned heirs. Money given in this manner, as part of a joint venture, has a special halakhic status, as one who is in possession of a standard promissory note that records a loan extended to the father can certainly collect the money from the orphans.

Rav Hai Gaon and other *ge'onim* point out that this is a case where nothing tangible remains from the joint venture, such as merchandise or some other item acquired by way of this business arrangement. If anything tangible remains from the venture, the investor would be able to collect it even from the orphans, and the orphans would not be able to claim that their father had later purchased the business from the investor (cited in Ritva and *Nimmukei Yosef*).

And collects the entire sum – **וְגוֹבֶה כּוּלּוֹ**: Everyone agrees that he can collect the first half, which is considered a loan, by means of an oath, in accordance with the *halakha* concerning one who collects payment from orphans. He is also deemed credible to collect the second half, which is considered a deposit, because of the document that is in his possession.

Takes an oath and collects half – **נִשְׁבָּע וְגוֹבֶה מֶחֱצָה**: Since he is able to collect only half of the sum, he takes an oath only with regard to that half. In order to prevent an appearance of falsehood, he must take an oath stating that he has a monetary claim which amounts to no less than half of the sum of money (*Tosafot*).

This joint venture – **הַאי עִיסְקָא**: In the joint venture referred to here, the investor gives a sum of money to another, with the understanding that the recipient will use it for some sort of business enterprise, and that they will share the profits. The profits received by the investor could be seen as a type of interest, but instead the arrangement is considered a joint enterprise, where one party invests his money while the other invests his energy. In fact, this model is the basis of the *heter iska*, a halakhic convention developed in order to structure business transactions in such a manner as to avoid violating the prohibition of interest.

Various enactments were introduced to differentiate a joint enterprise from a loan with interest. For example, the manager does not bear total financial liability. Unlike a borrower, he is not liable for all of the money if it is lost under circumstances beyond his control. Rather, he is liable only for half of the sum. The other half is treated as a deposit. With regard to the division of profits as well, the Sages decreed that the investor's profit may not be in proportion to his investment. He must either assume greater liability in the case of a loss or receive a smaller proportion of the profits.

He would have told – **מֵימַר הֲוָה אָמַר**: *Tosafot* point out that this assumption, that had the father repaid the money he would have told his children, is valid only with regard to a loan that was recorded in a document, as it is assumed that he would have told them that even though the document is not in his possession, the debt was repaid. But in the case of a loan made by oral agreement, he would not have been concerned with telling his children that it was repaid.

The Angel of Death – **מַלְאַךְ הַמָּוֶת**: That is to say, he died suddenly and did not have a chance to tell his children (Rashbam). The Ritva adds that even if his death was not sudden, perhaps he thought that he would still have an opportunity to inform them at some later point, but he died before he had a chance to speak to them.

PERSONALITIES

Judges of Eretz Yisrael – **דַּיָּינֵי אֶרֶץ יִשְׂרָאֵל**: According to the Talmud (*Sanhedrin* 17b), this appellation was bestowed upon the *amora'im* Rav Ami and Rav Asi, a pair of Babylonian Sages who emigrated to Eretz Yisrael, where they were ordained by Rabbi Yoḥanan and included among his most important disciples. These Sages were considered the leading authorities of the generation following Rabbi Yoḥanan. They instituted ordinances, and even the other disciples of Rabbi Yoḥanan, such as Rabbi Abbahu, addressed questions to them.

HALAKHA

A purse document that was presented against the orphans – **שְׁטַר כִּיס הַיּוֹצֵא עַל הַיְּתוֹמִים**: If one gave another person money as an investment in a joint venture, and the person who received the money died, and the investor now demands that the orphans return to him the money that he had given to their deceased father, and he has a document given to him by the father attesting to the arrangement, he takes an oath with regard to half of the sum, which was considered a loan. This oath is taken in the manner of an oath mandated by Torah law, while holding a sacred object. After taking the oath, the investor receives half of the money. He cannot collect the other half, which was considered a deposit, even by means of taking an oath, in accordance with the opinion of the judges of Eretz Yisrael (Rambam *Sefer Kinyan*, *Hilkhot Sheluḥin VeShutafin* 7:1; *Shulḥan Arukh*, *Ḥoshen Mishpat* 108:4).

Joint venture – **עִיסְקָא**: According to rabbinic decree, if one gives another money as an investment in a joint venture, half of the money is considered a loan, and the recipient is liable to return it even if it was lost because of circumstances beyond his control. The other half is considered a deposit, and if it was lost or stolen he is not liable to return it (see Ra'avad and *Kesef Mishne*). Half of the profits of the enterprise are given to the investor, provided that the venture was conducted in the permitted manner, for example, where the investor paid the manager every day as an unemployed laborer. Different opinions of the early commentaries are cited in the *Shakh* and *Taz* with regard to how much he is paid. If the manager has another business, it suffices if the investor pays him even only one dinar for the entire period of their joint venture (Rambam *Sefer Kinyan*, *Hilkhot Sheluḥin VeShutafin* 6:2; *Shulḥan Arukh*, *Yoreh De'a* 177:2).

שָׁלַח רַב הוּנָא בַּר אָבִין: הַמַּפְקִיד אֵצֶל חֲבֵירוֹ בִּשְׁטָר, וְאָמַר לוֹ ״הֶחֱזַרְתִּיו לָךְ״ – נֶאֱמָן, וּשְׁטַר כִּיס הַיּוֹצֵא עַל הַיְּתוֹמִין – נִשְׁבָּע וְגוֹבֶה כּוּלּוֹ.

Apropos this discussion, it is related that **Rav Huna bar Avin sent** the following ruling: If one **deposits** an item **with another** and receives a **document** attesting to the deposit, **and** the bailee later **says to him: I returned** the item **to you,** the bailee is **deemed credible** even if the document is still in the hands of the depositor. **And** with regard to a **purse document** attesting to a joint venture **that was presented** by the lender to support his claim **against the** borrower's **orphans,** the lender **takes an oath** that the money had never been returned to him **and collects the entire** sum from the orphans.

תַּרְתֵּי? שָׁאנֵי הָתָם, דְּאִם אִיתָא דִּפְרָעֵיהּ מֵימַר הֲוָה אָמַר.

The Gemara asks: Don't these **two** *halakhot* contradict each other? If the father is deemed credible when he claims that he repaid a loan, the court should present this claim on behalf of his orphans. The Gemara answers: **It is different there, as if it is so** that the father had, in fact, **repaid** the money, **he would have told** his children that he repaid it. Since he did not tell them anything about it, it may be assumed that he never repaid the money.

רָבָא אָמַר, הִלְכְתָא: נִשְׁבָּע וְגוֹבֶה מֶחֱצָה. אֲמַר מָר זוּטְרָא: הִלְכְתָא כְּדַיָּינֵי גוֹלָה. אֲמַר לֵיהּ רָבִינָא לְמָר זוּטְרָא, הָא אָמַר רָבָא: נִשְׁבָּע וְגוֹבֶה מֶחֱצָה! אֲמַר לֵיהּ: אֲנַן דְּדַיָּינֵי גוֹלָה

Rava said: With regard to the case of a purse document that was presented to support a claim against orphans, **the** *halakha* is that the claimant **takes an oath** that the money had never been returned to him **and** then **collects half**[N] of the sum recorded in the document, in accordance with the judges of Eretz Yisrael. The Gemara relates that two generations later, **Mar Zutra said: The** *halakha* **is in accordance with** the opinion of **the judges of the exile. Ravina said to Mar Zutra: Didn't Rava say** that the claimant **takes an oath and collects half** of the sum? Mar Zutra **said to him:** With regard to the opinion **of the judges of the exile, we**

NOTES

The ***halakha*** **is that the claimant takes an oath and collects half** – הִלְכְתָא נִשְׁבָּע וְגוֹבֶה מֶחֱצָה: According to some early commentaries, the orphans are required to take the oath that is imposed upon heirs who were not informed by their father that he owes this money (Rashbam; Ra'ah). Others hold that they are not required to take this oath, as it was instituted only in situations where orphans collect money from other orphans (Ramban; Rashba).

אִיפְּכָא מַתְנִינַן לַהּ.

learned the reverse, that is to say, according to our version of the *baraita*, it is the judges of the exile who maintain that the claimant collects only half the sum, which corresponds to the *halakha* taught by Rava.

מתני׳ לֹא אֶת הַבּוֹר וְלֹא אֶת הַגַּת וְלֹא אֶת הַשּׁוֹבָךְ, בֵּין חֲרֵבִין בֵּין יְשׁוּבִין. וְצָרִיךְ לִיקַּח לוֹ דֶּרֶךְ, דִּבְרֵי רַבִּי עֲקִיבָא; וַחֲכָמִים אוֹמְרִים: אֵינוֹ צָרִיךְ.

MISHNA In continuation of the previous mishna (68b) discussing one who sells a field, the mishna teaches that even if he says that he is selling it and everything that is in it, has sold **neither the cistern,**[H] **nor the winepress, nor the dovecote, whether** it is **abandoned or utilized,** as these items are not part of the field itself. **And** the seller **must purchase** for himself **a path** through the buyer's domain to reach whatever remains his. This is **the statement of Rabbi Akiva,** who holds that one who sells, sells generously; therefore, whatever is not explicitly excluded from the sale is assumed to be sold, and it is presumed that the seller did not retain for himself the right to the path that he requires to access his property. **And the Rabbis say:** The seller **need not** purchase a path through the buyer's domain, as it is assumed that since the seller withholds these items for himself, he also reserves a path to reach them.

וּמוֹדֶה רַבִּי עֲקִיבָא, בִּזְמַן שֶׁאָמַר לוֹ ״חוּץ מֵאֵלּוּ״ – שֶׁאֵינוֹ צָרִיךְ לִיקַּח לוֹ דֶּרֶךְ. מְכָרָן לְאַחֵר – רַבִּי עֲקִיבָא אוֹמֵר: אֵינוֹ צָרִיךְ לִיקַּח לוֹ דֶּרֶךְ, וַחֲכָמִים אוֹמְרִים: צָרִיךְ לִיקַּח לוֹ דֶּרֶךְ.

And Rabbi Akiva concedes that when the seller **says to** the buyer in the bill of sale that he is selling the field **apart from these** things, i.e., the cistern and the winepress, **he need not purchase for himself a path** through the buyer's domain. Since these items would have been excluded from the sale even if he had said nothing, it is assumed that he also meant to reserve for himself the right to access them. But if the seller kept the field but **sold** the cistern and winepress **to another** person, **Rabbi Akiva says:** The buyer **need not purchase for himself a path** through the seller's domain to reach what he has bought, since a seller sells generously. **But the Rabbis say: He must purchase for himself a path** through the seller's domain.

HALAKHA

Neither the cistern – לֹא אֶת הַבּוֹר: If one buys a field from another, even if the seller says to him that he is selling the field and everything contained in it, he does not acquire items that have their own separate name and identity, even if they are fixed in the ground, such as a pit, cistern, or dovecote. This is the *halakha* whether or not they are currently in use. The seller is required to purchase a path if he wishes to access these items, in accordance with the opinion of Rabbi Akiva. If the seller explicitly stated that he is excluding the pit, cistern, and dovecote from the sale, he has retained a path to them and does not need to purchase one, as Rabbi Akiva concedes to the Rabbis in this case (Rambam *Sefer Kinyan, Hilkhot Mekhira* 26:3–4; *Shulḥan Arukh, Ḥoshen Mishpat* 215:5).

במה דברים אמורים – במוכר, אבל בנותן מתנה – נותן את כולה. האחין שחלקו, זכו בשדה – זכו בכולה. המחזיק בנכסי הגר, החזיק בשדה – החזיק בכולה.

In what case **is this statement,** that these items are excluded, **said?** It is said **with regard to one who sells** a field, **but with regard to one who gives** it away **as a gift,**[H] it is assumed that **he gives all of it,**[N] including everything found in the field. Similarly, with regard to **brothers who divide**[H] their father's estate among themselves, when they each **acquire** a **field** as part of their inheritance, **they acquire all of it,** including the items that would be excluded from a sale. So too, with regard to **one who takes possession of the property of a convert,**[N] when **he takes possession of a field, he takes possession of all of it.**

המקדיש את השדה – הקדיש את כולה; רבי שמעון אומר: המקדיש את השדה – לא הקדיש אלא את החרוב המורכב ואת סדן השקמה.

One who consecrates a field has consecrated all of it. Rabbi Shimon says: One who consecrates a field has not consecrated any of the items that are ordinarily excluded from a sale **except for the grafted carob tree**[N] **and the sycamore trunk.**

גמ׳ מאי שנא מכר ומאי שנא מתנה? פירש יהודה בן נקוסא לפני רבי: זה פירש וזה לא פירש.

GEMARA The Gemara asks: In **what** way **is a sale different from** a gift, **and in what** way **is a gift different from** a sale? Why does the mishna distinguish between the two with regard to what is retained by the prior owner? **Yehuda ben Nekosa explained before Rabbi** Yehuda HaNasi: The difference between the cases is that **this** one, the seller, **specified** that certain items were not included in the sale, **and that** one, the donor, **did not specify.**

האי זה פירש וזה לא פירש, זה לא פירש וזה לא פירש הוא! אלא, זה היה לו לפרש, וזה לא היה לו לפרש.

The Gemara asks: How can it be suggested that **this** one **specified and that** one **did not specify,** when in fact **this** one **did not specify, and that** one **did not specify,** as in neither case did the prior owner specify what items he was reserving for himself? **Rather,** the difference is that **this** one, the buyer, **should have specified**[N] that those items that are not integral parts of the field are nevertheless included in the sale, and since he neglected to do so, he suffers the loss. **But** in the case of a gift, **that** one, the recipient, **should not have specified** what was included in the gift, as it would have been inappropriate for him to act in this manner.

HALAKHA

With regard to one who gives a gift – בנותן מתנה: With regard to one who sells a house, courtyard, olive press, or field, he reserves for himself some of the items found there, as it was the responsibility of the buyer to specify that he wanted any of those items to be included in the sale. But if he gives one of these items to another as a gift, the recipient acquires everything that is appended to it, so long as the giver did not specify that he is reserving the item for himself. The Rema writes that this applies only to items that are situated within the property given as a gift. But if they are outside of it, the *halakha* governing a gift is the same as that concerning a sale, and the recipient does not acquire them (Rambam *Sefer Kinyan, Hilkhot Mekhira* 26:5; *Shulḥan Arukh, Ḥoshen Mishpat* 215:6).

Brothers who divide – האחין שחלקו: In the case of brothers who divide their father's property among themselves, where they each acquire a field as part of their inheritance, they acquire the items that are fixed in the field, such as a pit, cistern, and dovecote. This is also the *halakha* with regard to one who takes possession of the property of a convert (*Sma*). Similarly, one who consecrates his field has consecrated these items as well (Rambam *Sefer Kinyan, Hilkhot Mekhira* 26:6; *Shulḥan Arukh, Ḥoshen Mishpat* 215:7).

NOTES

He gives all of it – נותן את כולה: That is to say, he gives all of the items that would not be included had this been a sale and not a gift. But he does not give produce that is detached from the ground and left in the field or other items that are found there, as they are clearly not part of the field and not included in the gift (Rashbam). The Ri Migash adds that anything that is not included within the gifted item's boundaries is not included in the gift. For example, if one gives a house as a gift, the gallery is not included, as it is only adjacent to the house but not a part of it. The Ramah disagrees.

One who takes possession of the property of a convert – המחזיק בנכסי הגר: The Rashbam explains that even though one who takes possession of a field that had belonged to a convert does not acquire the adjoining property if it is separated from it by a fence, he does acquire the sycamore trunk, even though it is considered a separate entity, because it is not separated from the field by a fence. The Ramah adds that after one takes possession of a field that had belonged to a convert, if he is then standing next to it, the field has the status of a courtyard that is consciously secured by its owners, and effects acquisition on his behalf of all movable items found in the field.

Except for the grafted carob tree – אלא את החרוב: As the Gemara later explains, Rabbi Shimon holds that in principle, the *halakha* in the case of one who consecrates a field is comparable to the *halakha* in the case of a sale, and it is not comparable to the case of one who gives a gift. There is a specific reason why the carob and sycamore are consecrated, as they draw nutrients from the field, and it is assumed that the owner does not wish to derive benefit from consecrated property.

This one should have specified – זה היה לו לפרש: The Rashbam offers two explanations as to who should have made the specification. According to his first explanation, since one who gives a gift usually gives generously, he should have specified any item that he meant to reserve for himself. By contrast, since one who sells does so only because he needs the money, he sells the minimum amount necessary to complete the sale. The Ritva adds that the seller relies on the fact that everyone knows that he is selling as little as possible, and because it is in his interest that the sale should take place, he avoids mentioning the items that are not included in the sale.

According to the Rashbam's second explanation, it is the buyer who should have specified what is included in the sale, as he generally tries to get the most for his money. Therefore, unless he specified differently, it is assumed that he agreed to the standard conditions of the sale. The recipient of a gift, by contrast, is embarrassed to demand that he receive additional items, as everything that he receives is a gift. Therefore, the responsibility falls upon the giver (Rashbam, citing Rabbeinu Ḥananel; Rabbeinu Gershom; Rambam's Commentary on the Mishna). A similar dispute appears in the Jerusalem Talmud, where it is discussed whether the reason for the distinction between a sale and a gift is that one who gives a gift gives generously, or that a buyer, as opposed to the recipient of a gift, takes care to specify what is included in the transaction.

הַהוּא דַּאֲמַר לְהוּ: הֲבוּ לֵיהּ לִפְלָנְיָא בֵּיתָא דְּמַחֲזִיק מְאָה גּוּלְפֵי, אִשְׁתַּכַּח דַּהֲוָה מַחֲזִיק מְאָה וְעֶשְׂרִין. אֲמַר מָר זוּטְרָא: מְאָה אֲמַר לֵיהּ, מְאָה וְעֶשְׂרִין לָא אֲמַר לֵיהּ.

It is related that there was **a certain** person **who said to** others:[N] **Give to so-and-so my house containing 100 barrels** [*gulfei*][HL] as a gift. **It was found that there was** a house in his possession that **contained 120** barrels. **Mar Zutra said:** The owner **said to him** that he was giving him a house containing 100 barrels,[N] **and** he **did not say to him** that he was giving him a house containing 120 barrels. Therefore, the recipient receives only the portion of the house that holds 100 barrels, and not the rest of the house.

רַב אַשִׁי אֲמַר, מִי לָא תְּנַן: בַּמֶּה דְּבָרִים אֲמוּרִים – בְּמוֹכֵר, אֲבָל בְּנוֹתֵן מַתָּנָה – נוֹתֵן אֶת כּוּלָּן? אַלְמָא מַאן דְּיָהֵיב מַתָּנָה – בְּעַיִן יָפָה יָהֵיב, הָכָא נַמִּי מַאן דְּיָהֵיב מַתָּנָה – בְּעַיִן יָפָה יָהֵיב.

Rav Ashi said: Didn't we learn in the mishna here: **In what case is this statement said?** It is said **with regard to one who sells** a field, **but with regard to one who gives** it away **as a gift,** it is assumed that **he gives all of it. Apparently, one who gives a gift**[N] **gives generously. Here too,** then, say that **one who gives a gift gives generously,** even if he is not always precise in his wording. Therefore, it should be assumed that the donor intended to give the recipient the entire house, which contains more than 100 barrels.

״הַמַּקְדִּישׁ אֶת הַשָּׂדֶה – הִקְדִּישׁ״ וכו׳. אֲמַר רַב הוּנָא, אַף עַל גַּב דַּאֲמוּר רַבָּנַן: הַקּוֹנֶה שְׁנֵי אִילָנוֹת בְּתוֹךְ שֶׁל חֲבֵירוֹ – הֲרֵי זֶה לֹא קָנָה קַרְקַע, מָכַר קַרְקַע וְשִׁיֵּיר שְׁנֵי אִילָנוֹת לְפָנָיו – יֵשׁ לוֹ קַרְקַע; וַאֲפִילּוּ לְרַבִּי עֲקִיבָא דְּאָמַר: מוֹכֵר בְּעַיִן יָפָה מוֹכֵר, הָנֵי מִילֵּי גַּבֵּי בּוֹר וְדוּת דְּלָא קָא מַכְחֲשִׁי בְּאַרְעָא, אֲבָל אִילָנוֹת דְּקָא מַכְחֲשִׁי בְּאַרְעָא,

§ The mishna teaches: **One who consecrates a field,** has consecrated all of it. **Rav Huna said: Even though the Rabbis said:**[N] **If one buys two trees in the field of another,**[H] **he does not acquire** any of **the land** but acquires only the trees, and if **he sells land** to another, **and he retains two trees for himself,**[H] **he** also **retains the land**[N] around those trees, that does not always apply. Rav Huna elaborates: **And even according to Rabbi Akiva, who says** that **one who sells, sells generously** and does not retain anything for himself, **this does not always apply,** as **this statement** applies only **with regard to a pit and a cistern, which do not weaken the land,** and therefore the seller feels no need to protect himself from the potential claims of the buyer. **But** with regard to **trees, which do weaken the land,** as they draw water and nutrients from the soil,

HALAKHA

Give to so-and-so my house containing 100 barrels – הֲבוּ לֵיהּ לִפְלָנְיָא בֵּיתָא דְּמַחֲזִיק מְאָה: If a man on his deathbed said: Give to so-and-so a house that contains 100 barrels, and his property includes only a house that holds 120 barrels, the recipient receives this house, even though it is larger than the one he was promised. If it contains even more than 120 barrels, he does not acquire the house, as one would not be mistaken with regard to such a large amount (*Baḥ* and *Nimmukei Yosef*, citing Ritva). According to the *Nimmukei Yosef* himself, even if the house holds more than 120 barrels, the recipient acquires the entire house (*Shulḥan Arukh, Ḥoshen Mishpat* 253:14 and *Shakh* there).

If one buys two trees in the field of another – הַקּוֹנֶה שְׁנֵי אִילָנוֹת בְּתוֹךְ שֶׁל חֲבֵירוֹ: If one buys two trees in a field belonging to another, he does not acquire the land under the trees. Therefore, if the trees died or were cut down, the buyer has no right to any part of the field, and he cannot plant new trees in place of the dead trees. The buyer does, however, have the right to use the land under and around the trees to tend to his trees and harvest their fruit. In addition, he has a right to use a path to access his trees (Rambam *Sefer Kinyan, Hilkhot Mekhira* 24:6; *Shulḥan Arukh, Ḥoshen Mishpat* 216:9, and in the comment of Rema).

If he sells land and retains two trees for himself – מָכַר קַרְקַע וְשִׁיֵּיר שְׁנֵי אִילָנוֹת לְפָנָיו: One who sells a field and reserves for himself two trees in the field has also reserved for himself the land under and around those trees (Rambam *Sefer Kinyan, Hilkhot Mekhira* 24:8; *Shulḥan Arukh, Ḥoshen Mishpat* 216:12).

LANGUAGE

Barrels [*gulfei*] – גּוּלְפֵי: Some explain that this word is derived from the Greek κάλπη, *kalpē*, meaning a bottle or a container for water.

NOTES

A certain person who said to others – הַהוּא דַּאֲמַר לְהוּ: The Ritva notes that this person was on his deathbed, and therefore it is a mitzva to fulfill his instructions, but in general this wording is not effective in conferring ownership.

The owner said to him 100 barrels – מְאָה אֲמַר לֵיהּ: Because the donor said to give a house that contains 100 barrels, the recipient receives only an area of the house that holds 100 barrels (Rashbam). The Ritva cites some commentaries who explain that according to Mar Zutra, since this house does not meet the donor's criteria, the intended recipient receives nothing. The Ritva rejects this opinion, as the donor was on his deathbed, and it is a mitzva to fulfill his instructions. Therefore, in any event the heirs would have to buy for the other person a house that holds 100 barrels.

Apparently, one who gives a gift – אַלְמָא מַאן דְּיָהֵיב מַתָּנָה: Since it is assumed that a donor acts generously, he must have intended to give this house and was simply mistaken about its size. The Ritva asks how this is related to the presumption with regard to a donor's generosity, as the real question seems to be whether the donor was referring to this house or to a different house. He explains that since a donor gives generously, although he speaks modestly and promises only a field or a small house, he actually intends to give more. The Ritva also qualifies this presumption with regard to the donor's generosity, explaining that the entire house is not given to the recipient if the difference between the promised area and the actual area exceeds the amount in the case reported here. The Meiri also explains that this presumption applies only when the discrepancy between the two amounts is about one-sixth, as it is assumed that the donor did not speak precisely, nor was he mistaken. If the house was much larger, it cannot be assumed that the donor intended to give all of it.

Even though the Rabbis said – אַף עַל גַּב דַּאֲמוּר רַבָּנַן: The Rashbam explains that this is in contrast to Rabbi Akiva, who holds that one who sells, sells generously, and a seller therefore includes the land in the sale. Other commentaries understand the opinion of the Rabbis, that the land is sold along with the trees only when three trees are sold, as not related to the matter of whether or not a seller sells generously. Rather, it depends on whether the land around the trees is considered to be a separate entity or included with the trees that are sold (*Tosafot*; Rashba).

He retains the land – יֵשׁ לוֹ קַרְקַע: This means that he enjoys a permanent right to use the land. Therefore, if the tree dies, he can plant another in its place. In addition, he can plant other produce in the ground underneath and around the tree.

אִם אִיתָא דְּלָא שַׁיֵּיר, לֵימָא לֵיהּ: ״עֲקוֹר אִילָנָךְ שְׁקוֹל וְזִיל״.

if it is so that the prior owner **did not retain** some of the land for himself, **let** the buyer **say to him: Uproot**[N] **your trees, take** them, **and go,** as the trees draw water and nutrients from the soil, causing damage to the buyer's land. Therefore, the seller must have retained for himself the land needed for these trees.

תְּנַן, רַבִּי שִׁמְעוֹן אוֹמֵר: הַמַּקְדִּישׁ אֶת הַשָּׂדֶה – לֹא הִקְדִּישׁ אֶלָּא חָרוּב הַמּוּרְכָּב וְסַדַּן הַשִּׁקְמָה; וְתָנֵי עֲלַהּ, אָמַר רַבִּי שִׁמְעוֹן: מָה טַעַם? הוֹאִיל וְיוֹנְקִין מִשְּׂדֵה הֶקְדֵּשׁ;

The Gemara raises an objection: **We learned** in the mishna here that **Rabbi Shimon says: One who consecrates a field has not consecrated** any of the items that are ordinarily excluded from a sale **except for the grafted carob tree and the sycamore trunk. And it is taught with regard to** this in a *baraita*: **Rabbi Shimon said: What is the reason** that it is specifically the carob tree and the sycamore trunk that are consecrated? **Since** they **draw** their **nutrients from a consecrated field,**[N] the owner must have had in mind to consecrate them as well, as otherwise his trees would be nurtured from consecrated property.

וְאִי סָלְקָא דַּעְתָּךְ שִׁיּוּרֵי שַׁיֵּיר, כִּי קָא יָנְקִי – מִדְּנַפְשֵׁיהּ קָא יָנְקִי!

And if it enters your mind, as Rav Huna claims, that when the seller retains certain trees for himself, he also **retains** the land around them so that they will be nurtured from soil that belongs to him, what is the reason for Rabbi Shimon's ruling? **When** these trees **draw** their **nutrients, they draw** their **nutrients from** the ground that the consecrator had retained for himself that still **belongs to him,** not from consecrated property.

רַבִּי שִׁמְעוֹן דְּאָמַר – כְּרַבִּי עֲקִיבָא, וְרַב הוּנָא דְּאָמַר – כְּרַבָּנַן.

The Gemara answers: The assumption that Rav Huna's statement is true according to everyone must be reconsidered. Rather, **Rabbi Shimon, who says** that one who consecrates his field does not retain for himself the land around the trees, holds **in accordance with** the opinion of his teacher, **Rabbi Akiva.**[N] According to Rabbi Akiva, one who sells, sells generously, and there is no presumption that he retained some item or right for himself unless this was stated explicitly. Therefore, Rabbi Shimon rules that one who consecrates his field has also consecrated the carob trees, as otherwise they would draw nutrients from consecrated land. **And Rav Huna, who says** that when a seller retains trees for himself he also retains the land around them, holds **in accordance with** the opinion of **the Rabbis,** who say that one who sells, sells sparingly.

כְּרַבָּנַן, פְּשִׁיטָא! נָפְקָא מִינַּהּ, דְּאִי נָפְלִי הָדַר שָׁתֵיל לְהוּ.

The Gemara asks: If Rav Huna's statement is only **in accordance with** the opinion of **the Rabbis,** then isn't his statement **obvious?**[N] What novel idea is he adding? The Gemara answers: The practical **difference** is **that** while one might have thought that the prior owner retains a right to the land only for the sake of trees that were there, this is not the case. Rather, he retains absolute ownership of the land, and therefore, **if the** trees **fall** or die **he can plant them again.**[N]

NOTES

Let the buyer say to him, uproot – לֵימָא לֵיהּ עֲקוֹר: The early commentaries disagree as to whether the Gemara means that the buyer could demand that he uproot the tree immediately, since it draws nutrients from soil that belongs to him (*Tosafot*; Rid; Ramban), or if it is referring only to a case where the tree dried up and died (Rashbam). Others explain that in principle, the owner of the field cannot be forced to uproot the trees immediately, as the *halakha* is that if someone buys two trees in a field belonging to another, even though he does not own the ground underneath them, the trees remain in the field. The buyer is limited only insofar as that if the trees die, he cannot plant new trees in their place. The same would then be the *halakha* in the case of one who sells a field but retains ownership of the trees. Even though this is, in fact, the *halakha*, in order to avoid an unpleasant situation where the buyer is unaware of this and demands that the trees be uprooted, it is assumed that the owner of the field reserves for himself the right to the ground under the trees (Rashba; Ran).

Since they draw their nutrients from a consecrated field – הוֹאִיל וְיוֹנְקִין מִשְּׂדֵה הֶקְדֵּשׁ: In any case where the owner of a field retains or sells the trees, it is the right of the owner of the trees that they continue to draw nutrients from the field. In truth, this should also be the case with regard to a consecrated field, so that if someone consecrates his field but reserves the trees for himself, he also reserves the right that his trees draw nutrients from the field (Ritva). The dispute between the Rabbis and Rabbi Shimon is only with regard to whether there is a concern that people will not know that this is the *halakha*, and therefore they will assume that the owner of the trees is deriving benefit from consecrated property (Ritva).

Rabbi Shimon who says in accordance with Rabbi Akiva – רַבִּי שִׁמְעוֹן דְּאָמַר כְּרַבִּי עֲקִיבָא: According to this explanation, Rabbi Shimon agrees with Rabbi Akiva, that one who sells, sells generously, and he does not reserve anything for himself. Likewise, one who consecrates does so generously. The reason, then, that Rabbi Shimon holds that the cistern and winepress are not consecrated is that they are not included in the term field (Rashbam).

In accordance with the opinion of the Rabbis, isn't his statement obvious – כְּרַבָּנַן פְּשִׁיטָא: According to the Rabbis, the seller always sells sparingly. And while it is true that they never explicitly stated that the seller reserves the land for his trees, this can be deduced from their ruling that a seller reserves the right to use a path to access the pit and winepress that he kept for himself. If in that case, he reserves a path even though the pit and winepress do not damage the land, all the more so would he reserve the land around the trees, as the trees draw their nutrients from it.

If the trees fall he can plant them again – דְּאִי נָפְלִי הָדַר שָׁתֵיל לְהוּ: The novelty of Rav Huna's statement is to emphasize that the right of the owner of the trees to the land is not a temporary one that can be utilized only for the trees that he reserved. Rather, it is a permanent right that gives him ownership of the land. For this reason, he is allowed to plant new trees in place of the old ones (Rashbam).

וּמִי מָצֵית מוֹקְמַתְּ לַהּ לְרַבִּי שִׁמְעוֹן כְּרַבִּי עֲקִיבָא? וְהָא תַּנְיָא: הִקְדִּישׁ שְׁלֹשָׁה אִילָנוֹת מִמֶּטַע עֲשָׂרָה לְבֵית סְאָה – הֲרֵי הִקְדִּישׁ אֶת הַקַּרְקַע וְאֶת הָאִילָנוֹת שֶׁבֵּינֵיהֶם, לְפִיכָךְ כְּשֶׁהוּא פּוֹדֶה – פּוֹדֶה בֵּית זֶרַע חוֹמֶר שְׂעוֹרִים בַּחֲמִשִּׁים שֶׁקֶל כֶּסֶף;

The Gemara asks: **But can you establish that** the opinion of **Rabbi Shimon is in accordance with** the opinion of **Rabbi Akiva,** that one who sells or consecrates property does so generously? **But isn't it taught** in a *baraita*: **If one consecrates three trees**[H] in a field **where ten** trees are **planted in an area required for sowing one** *se'a* **of seed** [*beit se'a*],[N] **he has consecrated** not only those trees, but also **the land and the young trees**[N] **between them? Therefore,** if this is an ancestral field[B] of his, **when he redeems** them, **he redeems** the land and everything contained within it according to the standard rate established by the Torah, whereby **an area fit for the sowing of a** *homer*,[B] i.e., a *kor*, of **barley seed**[N] is redeemed **for fifty silver shekels.**

פָּחוֹת מִכָּאן אוֹ יוֹתֵר עַל כֵּן, אוֹ שֶׁהִקְדִּישָׁן בְּזֶה אַחַר זֶה – הֲרֵי זֶה לֹא הִקְדִּישׁ לֹא הַקַּרְקַע וְלֹא אֶת הָאִילָנוֹת שֶׁבֵּינֵיהֶם, לְפִיכָךְ כְּשֶׁהוּא פּוֹדֶה – פּוֹדֶה אֶת הָאִילָנוֹת בְּשָׁוְויֵהֶן; וְלֹא עוֹד, אֶלָּא אֲפִילּוּ הִקְדִּישׁ אֶת הָאִילָנוֹת וְחָזַר וְהִקְדִּישׁ אֶת הַקַּרְקַע, כְּשֶׁהוּא פּוֹדֶה – פּוֹדֶה אֶת הָאִילָנוֹת בְּשָׁוְויֵהֶן, וְחוֹזֵר וּפוֹדֶה בֵּית זֶרַע חוֹמֶר שְׂעוֹרִים בַּחֲמִשִּׁים שֶׁקֶל כֶּסֶף;

The *baraita* continues: If the ratio of land to trees was **less than this,**[N] and the trees were planted more densely, **or** if the ratio of land to trees was **more than this,**[N] and the trees were planted less densely, **or if he consecrated** each of the trees separately, **one after the other,**[N] **this** person **has consecrated neither the land nor the** young **trees between them. Therefore, when he redeems** them, **he redeems the trees in accordance with their worth. And moreover, even if one consecrates the trees** where they are planted more densely, less densely, or one after the other, **and then** afterward **he consecrates the land,** so that everything belongs to the Temple treasury, **when he redeems** them, **he redeems the trees** separately **in accordance with their worth, and then he redeems** the land according to the standard rate, where **an area fit for the sowing of a** *homer* of **barley seed** is redeemed **for fifty silver shekels.**

HALAKHA

If one consecrates three trees – הִקְדִּישׁ שְׁלֹשָׁה אִילָנוֹת: If one consecrates trees, they are redeemed according to their value. If he consecrates three trees that are planted within a *beit se'a* and he does not specify that he is consecrating only the trees, he has also consecrated the land and the trees between them. If the trees were planted more or less densely or if he consecrated them separately, one after the other, neither the land nor the trees between them are consecrated. If one first consecrated the trees and only afterward consecrated the land, he redeems the trees according to their value, and he redeems the land according to the calculation of one *sela* and one *pundeyon* per year for every parcel of land in which a *homer* of barley seed can be sown (Rambam *Sefer Hafla'a*, *Hilkhot Arakhin VaHaramim* 4:16–18, and *Kesef Mishne* and *Lehem Mishne* there).

NOTES

Where ten trees are planted in a *beit se'a* – מִמֶּטַע עֲשָׂרָה לְבֵית סְאָה: The trees were planted in such a manner that ten trees could be planted in a *beit se'a*, i.e., each tree was cultivated in an area of 250 square cubits. The Rashbam explains that the *baraita* is referring to three young trees, as three fully grown trees would require a full *beit se'a*.

And the trees – וְאֶת הָאִילָנוֹת: Rashbam and Rabbeinu Gershom explain that the *baraita* is referring to young trees planted between the grown trees. *Tosafot* explain that it is referring to trees that do not bear fruit that are situated between fruit-bearing trees.

He redeems an area fit for the sowing of a *homer* of barley seed – פּוֹדֶה בֵּית זֶרַע חוֹמֶר שְׂעוֹרִים: Since by consecrating the trees he is regarded as having consecrated the land, when he redeems them, he redeems them as one redeems land. The Torah establishes that an ancestral field is redeemed at the rate of fifty silver shekels for a parcel of land in which a *homer* of barley seed can be sown for the entire fifty-year Jubilee period. This is equivalent to one *sela* and one *pundeyon* for each year.

Less than this – פָּחוֹת מִכָּאן: If the trees were planted more densely than this, there is insufficient area to support the amount of trees planted, and they are not considered to be permanently planted, as they will ultimately be uprooted (Rashbam; Rabbeinu Gershom).

More than this – יוֹתֵר עַל כֵּן: If the trees were planted less densely, so that there is more space between each tree, the trees are regarded as if they were consecrated individually and the land between them is not consecrated (Rashbam).

One after the other – בְּזֶה אַחַר זֶה: By consecrating each tree individually, or by consecrating the trees individually and then consecrating the land, he demonstrates that his intent was not to consecrate the land, but only to consecrate the trees. Therefore, he redeems the trees in accordance with their worth, and then afterward he redeems the land according to the standard rate, as the trees and the land were consecrated separately.

BACKGROUND

Ancestral field – שְׂדֵה אֲחוּזָּה: An ancestral field is a field that one inherits from his ancestors within his family holdings in Eretz Yisrael. When the Jewish people entered and conquered Eretz Yisrael, it was divided among the tribes and among households within the tribes. Ancestral land can be sold only until the Jubilee Year, at a price that takes into consideration the number of years remaining from the date of sale until the Jubilee Year. If the seller of the field obtains some money in the interim, he may buy back his field after two years have passed. If one consecrates an ancestral field, he may redeem it at a set price that takes into account the number of years remaining until the Jubilee Year. If one did not redeem his field, and the Temple treasurers sold it to someone else, it does not revert to its owner in the Jubilee Year but to the priests who are on the priestly watch when the Jubilee Year begins (see Leviticus 27:16–21).

An area fit for the sowing of a *homer* – בֵּית זֶרַע חוֹמֶר: This is an area fit for the sowing of the biblical measurement of a *homer*, the equivalent of a *kor* in the terminology of the Sages, of barley seeds. A *kor* is the largest measurement of volume mentioned by name in the sources. According to the standard method of converting talmudic measurements of Rabbi Hayyim Na'e, a *kor* is approximately 248 ℓ and according to the Hazon Ish it is 430 ℓ.

מני? אי רבי עקיבא – הא אמר: מוכר בעין יפה מוכר, וכל שכן מקדיש! אי רבנן – הא אמרי: מוכר הוא דבעין רעה מוכר, אבל מקדיש בעין יפה מקדיש! אלא פשיטא רבי שמעון היא;

The Gemara clarifies: **Whose** opinion is expressed in the *baraita*? **If** it is the opinion of **Rabbi Akiva, doesn't he say** that **one who sells, sells generously,**[N] **and all the more so one who consecrates** does so generously? This being the case, even if the trees were consecrated one after the other, some of the land should be consecrated along with them. And **if** the *baraita* reflects the opinion of **the Rabbis, don't they say** in the mishna that **it is** specifically **the seller who sells sparingly, but one who consecrates, consecrates generously,**[H] and therefore the pit and the winepress are consecrated along with the field? Therefore, the *halakha* stated here is not in accordance with their opinion either. **Rather,** it is **obvious** that the *baraita* **is** in accordance with the opinion of **Rabbi Shimon**[N] in the mishna here, that even one who consecrates a field does not consecrate the cistern and the winepress along with it.

ורבי שמעון אליבא דמאן? אי אליבא דרבי עקיבא, הא אמר: מוכר בעין יפה מוכר, וכל שכן מקדיש! אלא פשיטא אליבא דרבנן, וקא סבר רבי שמעון: כי היכי דמוכר בעין רעה מוכר, מקדיש נמי בעין רעה מקדיש, ומשייר ארעא;

And the opinion of **Rabbi Shimon** is **in accordance with** the opinion **of whom? If** it is **in accordance with** the opinion **of Rabbi Akiva, doesn't he say** that **one who sells, sells generously, and all the more so one who consecrates** does so generously? **Rather,** it is **obvious** that his opinion is **in accordance with** the opinion **of the Rabbis,** who disagree with Rabbi Akiva and say that one who sells, sells sparingly. **And Rabbi Shimon** disagrees with the Rabbis insofar as **he** himself **holds** that **just as one who sells, sells sparingly, one who consecrates also consecrates sparingly and retains the land** around the trees for himself.

NOTES

One who sells, sells generously – מוכר בעין יפה מוכר: The Rashbam and the majority of commentaries explain that the proof that the *baraita* is not in accordance with the opinion of Rabbi Akiva is that the *baraita* distinguishes between one who consecrates three trees, who has consecrated the land between them, and one who consecrates two trees, who has not consecrated the land between them. This is in accordance with the opinion that one who sells, sells sparingly, and therefore the land is not included.

Many commentaries disagree and explain that the proof is not related to the distinction made here between two and three trees, as even Rabbi Akiva agrees that if one sells two trees, the land between them is not included in the sale. Rather, the proof is based on the statement in the *baraita* that one who consecrates a field of trees redeems the land and everything contained within it according to the standard rate established by the Torah. Since the *baraita* does not state that the land and the trees are redeemed separately, in which case the Temple treasury would receive a more generous sum of money, apparently one who consecrates does so sparingly (Rashba; *Tosafot* on 37b, citing Rabbeinu Yitzḥak of Dampierre; Ritva; Ran). This is also the interpretation of the *baraita* according to one opinion in tractate *Arakhin*.

It is obvious that the *baraita* is in accordance with Rabbi Shimon – פשיטא רבי שמעון היא: Rabbi Shimon's opinion in the mishna is that whether one sells or consecrates, he does so sparingly. For this reason, one who consecrates a field does not consecrate the pit and winepress found in the field. Only carob and sycamore trees are consecrated along with the field, as they will draw nutrients from consecrated ground.

HALAKHA

One who consecrates, consecrates generously – מקדיש בעין יפה מקדיש: If one consecrated a field that was full of trees, the trees are sanctified along with field, even though he never specified that this was his intention, as one who consecrates property does so generously. For the same reason, if he wishes to redeem what he consecrated, the trees are redeemed according to their value, and the land is redeemed according to the calculation of one *sela* and one *pundeyon* per year for every parcel of land in which a *ḥomer* of barley seed can be sown (Radbaz; *Kesef Mishne*; *Leḥem Mishne*). This is in accordance with the opinion of Rav Huna in tractate *Arakhin*. According to the Ra'avad, the trees are not redeemed separately; rather, they are redeemed along with the land, in accordance with the opinion of Rav Pappa in tractate *Arakhin* (Rambam *Sefer Hafla'a*, *Hilkhot Arakhin VaḤaramim* 4:15).

Perek **IV**
Daf **72** Amud **b**

ואלא קשיא: הואיל ויונקין משדה הקדש!

The Gemara concludes stating the difficulty: **But** this is **difficult,** as Rabbi Shimon himself said that the grafted carob tree and the sycamore trunk are consecrated along with the field **since they draw** their **nutrients from a consecrated field,** indicating that one who consecrates acts generously and does not retain the land around the trees for himself.

אלא, רבי שמעון לדבריהם דרבנן קאמר להו: לדידי, כי היכי דמוכר בעין רעה מוכר, מקדיש נמי בעין רעה מקדיש, ושיורי משייר. לדידכו, אודו לי מיהא דלא הקדיש אלא חרוב המורכב וסדן השקמה. ואמרי ליה רבנן: לא שנא.

The Gemara explains: **Rather,** it must be understood that when **Rabbi Shimon** stated his ruling in the mishna, he was not expressing his own opinion. Rather, **he was speaking to the Rabbis in accordance with their statement,**[N] and he meant to say: **According to my** opinion, **just as one who sells, sells sparingly, so too, one who consecrates, consecrates sparingly and retains** for himself land to nurture the trees. Therefore, when one consecrates a field, even the sycamore and carob tree are not consecrated along with it. But **according to your** opinion, that one who consecrates does so generously, **agree with me**[N] **at least that** one who consecrates a field **has consecrated only the grafted carob and the sycamore trunk,** because they draw nutrients from consecrated ground, but he has not consecrated the other items that are not integral parts of the field. **And the Rabbis said to him: There is no difference**[N] between the two in this regard. Since one who consecrates an item does so generously, everything found in the field is consecrated.

NOTES

He was speaking to the Rabbis in accordance with their statement – לדבריהם דרבנן קאמר להו: This means that the opinion expressed by the Sage is not his own opinion. Rather, he is engaging in a dispute with other Sages and stating that even according to their own reasoning, their opinion must be adjusted. Wherever this argument is used, the Sage's statement proves nothing about his own opinion.

According to your opinion agree with me – לדידכו אודו לי: Rabbi Shimon is saying that according to the opinion of the Rabbis, that one who sells does so sparingly, the same should be true with regard to one who consecrates his property. Although it could be argued that one who consecrates offers more than one who sells, that is true only where there is a reason to reach this conclusion, e.g., in the case of the carob and sycamore, which draw nutrients from consecrated property. With regard to a cistern, a winepress, and other similar items, there is no reason to say that they should be consecrated (Rashbam).

There is no difference – לא שנא: The Rabbis hold that one who consecrates his property is considered as one who gives a gift, as he too acts of his own volition, and therefore, he gives generously of his possessions (Rashbam).

בְּמַאי אוֹקִימְתָּא לְהָ? כְּרַבִּי שִׁמְעוֹן; אֵימָא סֵיפָא: וְלֹא עוֹד, אֶלָּא אֲפִילּוּ הִקְדִּישׁ אֶת הָאִילָנוֹת וְחָזַר וְהִקְדִּישׁ אֶת הַקַּרְקַע, כְּשֶׁהוּא פּוֹדֶה – פּוֹדֶה אֶת הָאִילָנוֹת בְּשָׁוְויֵיהֶן, וְחוֹזֵר וּפוֹדֶה בֵּית זֶרַע חוֹמֶר שְׂעוֹרִים בַּחֲמִשִּׁים שֶׁקֶל כֶּסֶף;

The Gemara returns to the *baraita* that it had concluded was taught according to the opinion of Rabbi Shimon, and asks: **In accordance with which opinion did you interpret** the *baraita* discussing consecrated property? It was interpreted **in accordance with** the opinion of **Rabbi Shimon.** But **say the last clause: And moreover, even if one consecrates the trees and then** afterward **he consecrates the land, when he redeems** them, **he redeems the trees** separately **in accordance with their worth, and then he redeems** the land according to the standard rate, where **an area fit for the sowing of a** ***ḥomer*** **of barley seed** is redeemed **for fifty silver shekels.**

וְאִי רַבִּי שִׁמְעוֹן, לֵיזִיל בָּתַר פִּדְיוֹן וְנִיפָּרְקוּ אַגַּב אַרְעַיְיהוּ, דְּהָא שָׁמְעִינַן לֵיהּ לְרַבִּי שִׁמְעוֹן דְּאָזֵיל בָּתַר פִּדְיוֹן!

And if the *baraita* is in accordance with the opinion of **Rabbi Shimon, let him follow** the character of the field at the time of its **redemption, and** so the trees should **be redeemed along with their land,** as at the time of the redemption both the trees and the land are consecrated. **As we have** already **heard that Rabbi Shimon follows** the time of the redemption, i.e., he determines the price at which a field is redeemed based on the time it is being redeemed.

דְּתַנְיָא: מִנַּיִן לַלּוֹקֵחַ שָׂדֶה מֵאָבִיו וְהִקְדִּישָׁהּ וְאַחַר כָּךְ מֵת אָבִיו, מִנַּיִן שֶׁתְּהֵא לְפָנָיו כִּשְׂדֵה אֲחוּזָּה? תַּלְמוּד לוֹמַר: ״וְאִם אֶת שְׂדֵה מִקְנָתוֹ אֲשֶׁר לֹא מִשְּׂדֵה אֲחֻזָּתוֹ״, שָׂדֶה שֶׁאֵין רְאוּיָה לִהְיוֹת שְׂדֵה אֲחוּזָּה, יָצְתָה זוֹ שֶׁרְאוּיָה לִהְיוֹת שְׂדֵה אֲחוּזָּה, דִּבְרֵי רַבִּי יְהוּדָה וְרַבִּי שִׁמְעוֹן.

As it is taught in a *baraita*: **From where** is it derived that **with regard to one who purchases a field from his father and consecrates it,**[H] **and afterward his father dies,** so the field would now be considered his as an inheritance, **from where** is it derived **that** with regard to its redemption **it should be** considered **before him as an ancestral field**[N] and not a field that he purchased? **The verse states** about a field that was purchased: **"And if** he sanctifies to the Lord **a field that he has bought, which is not of his ancestral fields"** (Leviticus 27:22). The verse speaks specifically of **a field that is not fit** at the time of its consecration **to be an ancestral field,** meaning that he never could have inherited it in the future. This specification **excludes this** field **that was fit to be an ancestral field** from this *halakha*, since eventually it would have become his through inheritance, even had he not purchased it. This is **the statement of Rabbi Yehuda and Rabbi Shimon.**

רַבִּי מֵאִיר אוֹמֵר: מִנַּיִן לַלּוֹקֵחַ שָׂדֶה מֵאָבִיו וּמֵת אָבִיו וְאַחַר כָּךְ הִקְדִּישׁ, מִנַּיִן שֶׁתְּהֵא לְפָנָיו כִּשְׂדֵה אֲחוּזָּה? תַּלְמוּד לוֹמַר: ״וְאִם אֶת שְׂדֵה מִקְנָתוֹ אֲשֶׁר לֹא מִשְּׂדֵה אֲחֻזָּתוֹ״, שָׂדֶה שֶׁאֵינָהּ שְׂדֵה אֲחוּזָּה, יָצְתָה זוֹ שֶׁהִיא שְׂדֵה אֲחוּזָּה;

The *baraita* continues: **Rabbi Meir** learns a different *halakha* from this verse, and he **says: From where** is it derived **that** in the case of **one who purchases a field from his father, and his father dies, and afterward he consecrates** the field, **from where** is it derived **that it should be** considered **before him like an ancestral field? The verse states: "And if** he sanctifies to the Lord **a field that he has bought, which is not of his ancestral fields."** The verse refers specifically to **a field that is not** now **an ancestral field** at the time of its consecration. This specification **excludes this** field, **as** after the death of the father, **it is an ancestral field.**

וְאִילּוּ רַבִּי יְהוּדָה וְרַבִּי שִׁמְעוֹן, הֵיכָא דְּמֵת אָבִיו וְאַחַר כָּךְ הִקְדִּישָׁהּ לָא צְרִיכִי קְרָא, כִּי אִצְטְרִיךְ קְרָא – הֵיכָא דְּהִקְדִּישָׁהּ וְאַחַר כָּךְ מֵת אָבִיו;

But according to **Rabbi Yehuda and Rabbi Shimon, a verse is not required** to teach that, in a case **where his father dies and afterward he consecrates** the field, it is considered to be an ancestral field, as this is obvious. **A verse is required** only to teach the *halakha* in a case **where he consecrates** the field after having bought it, **and afterward his father dies.**

מְנָא לְהוּ? אִי מֵהַאי קְרָא, אֵימָא: לְכִדְרַבִּי מֵאִיר הוּא דְּאָתָא! אֶלָּא, לָאו מִשּׁוּם דְּאָזְלִי בָּתַר פִּדְיוֹן?

The Gemara asks: **From where do** Rabbi Yehuda and Rabbi Shimon arrive at this conclusion? **If** they derive it only **from this verse,** you can **say that** the verse **came** to be interpreted **in accordance with** the opinion of **Rabbi Meir,**[N] as opposed to the opinions of Rabbi Yehuda and Rabbi Shimon, as there is no clear proof from the verse to support either opinion. **Rather, is it not due to** the fact **that they follow** the time of the **redemption,** and at the time of the redemption the father is dead, and the field is the son's ancestral field that is currently in the possession of the Temple treasury?

NOTES

That it should be before him as an ancestral field – **שֶׁתְּהֵא לְפָנָיו כִּשְׂדֵה אֲחוּזָּה**: The Rashbam and others explain that the distinction between a purchased field and an ancestral field has practical ramifications with regard to the sum that one must pay in order to redeem the field. With regard to an ancestral field, there is a set price that is not affected by the actual value of the field. By contrast, a purchased field is redeemed according to its market value. The Maharsha points out that the distinction between the two types of fields is not obvious and is subject to dispute in tractate *Arakhin*. Rashi, in his commentary on the Torah, offers a different explanation, that the practical difference between a purchased field and an ancestral field relates to a subject explicitly discussed in the Bible (see Leviticus, chapter 27): If a purchased field was consecrated but not redeemed, it returns to its prior owner in the Jubilee Year, while an ancestral field that was not redeemed is divided among the priests.

Say that it came to be interpreted in accordance with Rabbi Meir – **אֵימָא לְכִדְרַבִּי מֵאִיר הוּא דְּאָתָא**: When deriving a *halakha* from a superfluous element in a verse, one derives a *halakha* that is closest conceptually to that which is explicitly stated in the verse. In this case, this would be the *halakha* taught by Rabbi Meir, that a field is considered an ancestral field even if it had been purchased by the son from the father, provided that it was consecrated after the father's death. This principle does not apply when the verse itself indicates that a more novel *halakha* should be derived from it, but in this case the verse gives no such indication. It also does not apply when the basic assumption underlying any derivation from the verse suggests a more novel *halakha*. In this case, the underlying assumption of Rabbi Shimon is that one follows the time of the redemption (Rashbam).

HALAKHA

With regard to one who purchases a field from his father and consecrates it – **לַלּוֹקֵחַ שָׂדֶה מֵאָבִיו וְהִקְדִּישָׁהּ**: If one purchases a field from his father, or from someone else from whom he would inherit, and he consecrates the field, whether he does so before or after his father's death, the field is considered an ancestral field, and it is redeemed according to the calculation of one *sela* and one *pundeyon* per year for every parcel in which a *ḥomer* of barley seed can be sown. This is in accordance with the statement of Rabbi Yehuda and Rabbi Shimon (Rambam *Sefer Hafla'a*, *Hilkhot Arakhin VaḤaramim* 4:28).

אָמַר רַב נַחְמָן בַּר יִצְחָק: לְעוֹלָם בְּעָלְמָא רַבִּי יְהוּדָה וְרַבִּי שִׁמְעוֹן לָא אָזְלִי בָּתַר פִּדְיוֹן, וְהָכָא קְרָא אַשְׁכְּחוּ וּדְרוּשׁ: אִם כֵּן, לִכְתּוֹב קְרָא: "וְאִם אֶת שְׂדֵה מִקְנָתוֹ אֲשֶׁר לֹא אֲחוּזָּתוֹ", אִי נַמִּי: "שְׂדֵה אֲחוּזָּתוֹ", מַאי "אֲשֶׁר לֹא מִשְּׂדֵה אֲחֻזָּתוֹ"? אֶת שֶׁאֵינָהּ רְאוּיָה לִהְיוֹת שְׂדֵה אֲחוּזָּה, יָצְתָה זוֹ שֶׁרְאוּיָה לִהְיוֹת שְׂדֵה אֲחוּזָּה.

Rav Naḥman bar Yitzḥak says: Actually, I can say to you that **generally** speaking, **Rabbi Yehuda and Rabbi Shimon do not follow** the time of the **redemption,** and therefore their ruling here is not based on this premise. **But here they found a verse and interpreted it,** as, if the verse is to be understood as it was explained by Rabbi Meir, then **let the verse write: And if** he sanctifies to the Lord **a field that he has bought, which is not his ancestral estate, or** let it write: Which is not **his ancestral field. What** is meant by the expression: **"Which is not of his ancestral fields"** (Leviticus 27:22)?[N] It means that **a field that is not fit to** ever **be an ancestral field** is considered a purchased field. That **excludes this field, as it is fit to be an ancestral field.** Based on this explanation, the *baraita* that addresses one who consecrates trees can, in fact, be understood to be in accordance with the opinion of Rabbi Shimon.

אָמַר רַב הוּנָא: חָרוּב הַמּוּרְכָּב וְסַדַּן הַשִּׁקְמָה – תּוֹרַת אִילָן עָלָיו וְתוֹרַת קַרְקַע עָלָיו; תּוֹרַת אִילָן עָלָיו, דְּהֵיכָא דְּאַקְדֵּישׁ אוֹ זְבֵין שְׁנֵי אִילָנוֹת וְהַאי – יֵשׁ לוֹ קַרְקַע; תּוֹרַת קַרְקַע עָלָיו, דְּלָא מִזְדַּבַּן אַגַּב אַרְעָא.

§ **Rav Huna says: A grafted carob and a sycamore trunk have** both **the status of a tree and the status of land.** Each of these **has the status of a tree,**[N] **so if one consecrates or buys two trees and this** carob or sycamore, **he has** also consecrated or bought **the land** between them, as the sycamore or carob joins with the other two trees to form a unit of three trees that take their land with them. And each **has the status of land, as it is not sold along with land,** as explained in the mishna, that one who sells a field has not sold a grafted carob or a sycamore trunk that is in the field.

וְאָמַר רַב הוּנָא: עוֹמֶר שֶׁיֵּשׁ בּוֹ סָאתַיִם – תּוֹרַת עוֹמֶר עָלָיו וְתוֹרַת גָּדִישׁ עָלָיו; תּוֹרַת עוֹמֶר עָלָיו, דִּשְׁנֵי עוֹמָרִים שִׁכְחָה, שְׁנַיִם וְהוּא – אֵינָן שִׁכְחָה;

And Rav Huna says in a similar fashion: A large **sheaf** of grain **that contains two** ***se'a*** has both **the status of a sheaf and the status of a heap** with regard to the *halakhot* of forgotten sheaves that must be left for the poor. **It has the status of a sheaf,** as the principle is that **two sheaves** that were inadvertently **left in the field are** considered **forgotten** sheaves[NH] that must be left for the poor, whereas three sheaves need not be left for the poor, but rather the owner of the field may go back and take them for himself. In this regard a two-se'a sheaf is considered one sheaf, so if one forgot **two** sheaves **and** also **this** sheave that contains two *se'a*, the three together are three sheaves and **are not** considered **forgotten** sheaves that must be left for the poor.

תּוֹרַת גָּדִישׁ עָלָיו, דִּתְנַן: עוֹמֶר שֶׁיֵּשׁ בּוֹ סָאתַיִם, שְׁכָחוֹ – אֵין שִׁכְחָה.

And **it has the status of a heap, as we learned** in a mishna (*Pe'a* 6:6): In the case of **a sheaf that contains two** ***se'a***,[H] **if one forgets it** in a field, it is **not** considered **a forgotten** sheaf that must be left for the poor, as its size and importance grant it the status of a heap, rather than a sheaf.

NOTES

What is meant by, which is not of his ancestral field – מַאי אֲשֶׁר לֹא מִשְּׂדֵה אֲחֻזָּתוֹ: Rabbi Yehuda and Rabbi Shimon derive from the superfluous letter *mem*, meaning "of" in the verse, that the verse refers to fields that will never be fit to be ancestral fields. Therefore, any field that can be regarded as an ancestral field is not considered a purchased field.

Each has the status of a tree – תּוֹרַת אִילָן עָלָיו: Despite their great importance, which confers upon a grafted carob or a sycamore trunk the status of land, they are both still considered trees, and therefore they retain the *halakhot* associated with all trees. Therefore, when a grafted carob or a sycamore trunk is sold along with two other trees, it is considered the third tree, and the buyer acquires the land between them. The same principle applies with regard to large sheaves, which are discussed in the continuation of the Gemara. Despite its size, a large sheaf still combines with two other sheaves, and as a result they are not considered forgotten sheaves that must be left for the poor.

Forgotten sheaves – שִׁכְחָה: The mitzvah to leave forgotten sheaves for the poor appears in the Torah (Deuteronomy 24:19) and is explained in detail in tractate *Pe'a*. The essence of the mitzva is that if one forgets a sheaf while gathering sheaves in the field, it is not permitted for him to go back and take it, as it belongs to the poor. This *halakha* does not apply to sheaves that have special importance because of their number, size, or placement, because one would remember within a short amount of time that he did not collect them. Therefore, a large sheave that contains two *se'a* or more is not treated as a forgotten sheaf that must be left for the poor.

HALAKHA

As two sheaves left in the field are considered forgotten sheaves – דִּשְׁנֵי עוֹמָרִים שִׁכְחָה: If one forgot two separate sheaves of grain in his field, they are considered forgotten sheaves and must be left for the poor. If he forgot three separate sheaves, they are not considered forgotten sheaves, and it is permitted for the owner to go back and take them for himself (Rambam *Sefer Zera'im, Hilkhot Mattenot Aniyyim* 5:14).

A sheaf that contains two ***se'a*** **– עוֹמֶר שֶׁיֵּשׁ בּוֹ סָאתַיִם:** A large sheaf of grain containing two *se'a* that was forgotten by its owner in the field is not considered a forgotten sheaf. This is because the Sages derived from the phrase in the verse: "And have forgotten a sheaf in the field" (Deuteronomy 24:19), that this mitzva applies only to sheaves, and not to heaps, and a sheaf of this size is considered a heap (Rambam *Sefer Zera'im, Hilkhot Mattenot Aniyyim* 5:18).

אָמַר רַבָּה בַּר בַּר חָנָה אָמַר רֵישׁ לָקִישׁ: חָרוּב הַמּוּרְכָּב וְסַדַּן הַשִּׁקְמָה – בָּאנוּ לְמַחֲלוֹקֶת רַבִּי מְנַחֵם בַּר יוֹסֵי וְרַבָּנַן.

§ **Rabba bar bar Ḥana says** that **Reish Lakish says:** With regard to whether **a grafted carob and a sycamore trunk** are consecrated along with a field that one has consecrated, **we have arrived at the dispute between Rabbi Menaḥem bar Yosei and the Rabbis,** as Rabbi Menaḥem bar Yosei rules that they are not consecrated, whereas the Rabbis rule that they are.

Perek **IV**
Daf **73** Amud **a**

וְלֵימָא: מַחֲלוֹקֶת רַבִּי שִׁמְעוֹן וְרַבָּנַן! הָא קָא מַשְׁמַע לַן, דְּרַבִּי מְנַחֵם בְּרַבִּי יוֹסֵי כְּרַבִּי שִׁמְעוֹן סְבִירָא לֵיהּ.

הדרן עלך המוכר את הבית

The Gemara asks: **But let us say** that this is **the dispute**[N] **between Rabbi Shimon and the Rabbis,** as it was concluded previously that according to Rabbi Shimon himself, even the carob and sycamore trees are not consecrated. The Gemara answers: Reish Lakish **teaches us this,**[N] **that Rabbi Menaḥem, son of Rabbi Yosei, holds in accordance with** the opinion of **Rabbi Shimon,** and therefore Rabbi Shimon is not the only Sage who holds this opinion.

NOTES

But let us say that this is the dispute – וְלֵימָא מַחֲלוֹקֶת: The Rashbam explains the Gemara's question as follows: If Reish Lakish had taught that this is the dispute between the Rabbis and Rabbi Shimon, he would have taught a novel idea, that Rabbi Shimon himself disagrees with the Rabbis with regard to the consecration of carob and sycamore trees, and although he states in the mishna that they are consecrated, he speaks there according to the opinion of the Rabbis, while he himself holds that they are not consecrated.

Teaches us this – הָא קָא מַשְׁמַע לַן: According to the Rashbam, this means that the fact that Rabbi Menaḥem, son of Rabbi Yosei, holds in accordance with the opinion of Rabbi Shimon is a more novel concept, as his opinion is not found in the mishna, whereas Rabbi Shimon's own opinion can be deduced by comparing his statements in the mishna and the *baraita*. The Ramah explains that from here it is evident that the *halakha* is not in accordance with Rabbi Menaḥem, son of Rabbi Yosei, as his opinion is identical to the opinion of Rabbi Shimon, which is not accepted as the *halakha*.

Summary of **Perek IV**

This chapter analyzed the sale of various types of landed property, what is included in the sale of land, and how the boundaries of sold property are established. The Gemara's discussion revolved around properties such as a house, courtyard, olive press, bathhouse, field, vineyard, and even an entire city.

The principle that emerges is that when one sells one of these properties without specifying what is included in the sale, any item situated on the property is included in the sale, provided that it is affixed to the ground and serves a function with regard to that property. Similarly, when one sells a field, the trees in the field are included in the sale. By contrast, items that are attached to the ground are not included in the sale of the property if they are considered important in their own right, for example, a cistern when a house is sold; or a dovecote, sycamore trees, or carob trees in a field.

In general, movable property is not included in the sale of land, even if it serves a purpose on the land. Nevertheless, in the case of a field, movable property found in the field is included in the sale, provided that it serves a function in either working or protecting the field.

All of the above applies when the seller sells the land without specifying what is included in the sale. If he explicitly states that he is selling the land and everything that is in it, all the movable property that serves any function with regard to the land is included in the sale, but other movable property, such as money or merchandise, is still excluded. In the case of the sale of a field, this specification is even more inclusive, as it includes all of the movable property found in the field, even items such as harvested produce that was left in the field.

Since the presumption is that a seller sells generously, if certain fixed items that were not included in the sale are situated on the land transferred to the buyer, the seller is obligated to purchase a path in order to access those items. If he states that he is reserving such a path for himself, or if he specifies that he is excluding these items from the sale, he is not required to purchase a path. One who sells a field and retains the trees for himself is not required to purchase a path, as he reserves for himself the land needed to tend the trees even without specifying his intent.

All of these limitations with regard to what is included in the transaction apply only in the case of a sale, as the seller relies on the fact that the buyer could have stipulated that he wanted specific items to be included in the sale. But in cases where one gives the property as a gift or consecrates it, all movable property found in the land is included, with the exception of those items that are clearly not connected to the land. The *halakha* is the same with regard to one who takes possession of land that had belonged to a convert or brothers who divide between themselves the property of their father's estate.

With regard to the boundaries of the land being sold, the Gemara established that when one sells a house, the sale does not include the gallery or a room behind the house. It also does not include the pit, cistern, tunnels, or roof, as these are all considered separate entities. Additionally, the seller has not sold that which is found above the roof or below the ground unless he specifies that he is also selling the depths and the heights of the house. With regard to the sale of a city, everything within the city's borders is sold, but the nearby villages and lands are not, unless they serve some function only for that city.

When one sells a field that is situated between two other fields, he must delineate the boundaries on all sides. If only some of the boundaries were specified, the buyer receives the smallest area that those boundaries can define. Similarly, when one sells a house or field that is part of a larger unit and specifies only the boundaries of the larger area as opposed to the land that is being sold, it is assumed that the seller expanded the boundaries for the buyer but he in fact meant to sell him only the particular house or field.

My Notes

My Notes

My Notes

הַמּוֹכֵר אֶת הַבַּיִת – [א] לֹא מָכַר יָצִיעַ, וְאע"פ שֶׁהִיא פְּתוּחָה לְתוֹכוֹ; [ב] וְלֹא אֶת הַחֶדֶר שֶׁלִּפְנִים הֵימֶנּוּ; [ג] וְלֹא אֶת הַגַּג בִּזְמַן שֶׁיֵּשׁ לוֹ מַעֲקֶה גָּבוֹהַּ עֲשָׂרָה טְפָחִים; ר' יְהוּדָה אוֹמֵר: אִם יֵשׁ לוֹ צוּרַת פֶּתַח, אע"פ שֶׁאֵינוֹ גָּבוֹהַּ י' טְפָחִים – אֵינוֹ מָכוּר.§ **גמ'** מַאי יָצִיעַ? הָכָא תַּרְגִּימוּ: אַפְּתָא. רַב יוֹסֵף אֲמַר: [ד] בִּדְקָא חֲלִילָה. לְמַאן דְּאָמַר אַפְּתָא לָא מִזְדַּבְּנָא, כ"ש בִּדְקָא חֲלִילָה לָא מִזְדַּבְּנָא; לְמ"ד בִּדְקָא חֲלִילָה, אֲבָל אַפְּתָא מִזְדַּבְּנָא. תָּאנֵי רַב יוֹסֵף, שָׁלֹשׁ שֵׁמוֹת יֵשׁ לוֹ: יָצִיעַ, צֶלַע, תָּא; יָצִיעַ – דִּכְתִיב: °"הַיָּצִיעַ הַתַּחְתּוֹנָה חָמֵשׁ בָּאַמָּה רָחְבָּהּ". צֶלַע – דִּכְתִיב: °"וְהַצְּלָעוֹת צֵלָע אֶל צֵלָע שָׁלֹשׁ וּשְׁלֹשִׁים פְּעָמִים". תָּא – דִּכְתִיב: °"וְהַתָּא קָנֶה אֶחָד אוֹרֶךְ וְקָנֶה אֶחָד רֹחַב וּבֵין הַתָּאִים חָמֵשׁ אַמּוֹת". וְאִי בָּעֵית אֵימָא, מֵהָכָא: *כּוֹתֶל הַהֵיכָל שֵׁשׁ, וְהַתָּא שֵׁשׁ, כּוֹתֶל הַתָּא חָמֵשׁ. אֲמַר מָר זוּטְרָא: [ה] וְהוּא דְּהָוֵי אַרְבַּע אַמּוֹת. אֲמַר לֵיהּ רָבִינָא לְמָר זוּטְרָא: לְדִידָךְ דְּאָמְרַתְּ עַד דְּהָוֵי אַרְבַּע אַמּוֹת, אֶלָּא מֵעַתָּה, גַּבֵּי בּוֹר *דִּתְנַן: לֹא אֶת הַבּוֹר וְלֹא אֶת הַדּוּת, אַף עַל פִּי שֶׁכָּתַב לוֹ "עוּמְקָא וְרוּמָא", ה"נ אִי הָווּ אַרְבַּע אַמּוֹת – אִין, אִי לָא – לָא? הָכִי הַשְׁתָּא?! הָתָם הָא תַּשְׁמִישְׁתָּא לְחוּד וְהָא תַּשְׁמִישְׁתָּא לְחוּד, הָכָא אִידִי וְאִידִי חֲדָא תַּשְׁמִישְׁתָּא הִיא, אִי הָוֵי ד' אַמּוֹת – חֲשִׁיב, וְאִי לָא – לָא חֲשִׁיב.§ "וְלֹא אֶת הַחֶדֶר שֶׁלִּפְנִים הֵימֶנּוּ".§ הַשְׁתָּא יָצִיעַ לָא מִיזְדַּבַּן, חֶדֶר מִיבַּעְיָא?!

לָא

הַמּוֹכֵר אֶת הַבַּיִת. סְתָם. הַיָּצִיעַ. בַּגְּמָרָא מְפָרֵשׁ. וְאֵינוֹ בִּכְלַל בַּיִת. אע"פ שֶׁפָּתוּחַ הַיָּצִיעַ לְתוֹכוֹ שֶׁל בַּיִת, דְּאִיכָּא לְמֵימַר דְּכֵיוָן דְּתַשְׁמִישׁוֹ לַבַּיִת מְכָרוֹ עִם הַבַּיִת, אפ"ה אֵינוֹ מָכוּר. וְלֹא אֶת הַחֶדֶר. אע"פ שֶׁהוּא לִפְנִים מִן הַבַּיִת וּפָתוּחַ לְתוֹכוֹ, וּדְרִיסָתָהּ לַבַּיִת. דְּכֵיוָן דְּאֵין תַּשְׁמִישׁוֹ כְּשֶׁל בַּיִת, שֶׁאֵינוֹ עָשׂוּי אֶלָּא לְהַצְנִיעַ שָׁם חֲפָצָיו לִשְׁמוֹר כְּמִין תֵּיבָה, הִלְכָּךְ אֵינוֹ בִּכְלַל בַּיִת. בִּזְמַן שֶׁיֵּשׁ לוֹ מַעֲקֶה כו'. הָוֵי חָשׁוּב בִּפְנֵי עַצְמוֹ, וְלָא בָּטֵיל אַגַּב בַּיִת. **גמ'** אַפְּתָא. אפנטמ"ן, כְּגוֹן נָמוּךְ אֵצֶל הַבַּיִת, מִצִּדּוֹ אוֹ מֵאֲחוֹרָיו. בִּדְקָא חֲלִילָה. אִיהוּ נַמִי כְּמִין אַפְּתָא סָמוּךְ לַבַּיִת, אֶלָּא שֶׁעָשׂוּי חַלּוֹנוֹת חַלּוֹנוֹת לְנוֹי, לודר"ש בְּלַעַ"ז וְהַיְינוּ לְשׁוֹן חֲלִילָה – עַל שֵׁם שֶׁכְּתָלָיו חָלוּל כָּל סְבִיבֶיהָ וְעָשׂוּי חַלּוֹנוֹת, כֵּן נִרְאֶה בְּעֵינַי. כ"ש בִּדְקָא חֲלִילָה. דְּאֵינוֹ מָכוּר, דְּאֵין תַּשְׁמִישׁוֹ דּוֹמֶה לְתַשְׁמִישׁוֹ שֶׁל בַּיִת כְּלָל, שֶׁהֲרֵי לְנוֹי עָשׂוּי, וּלְהָקֵר שָׁם. אֲבָל אַפְּתָא. שֶׁהוּא סָתוּם כְּבַיִת – דָּמֵי תַּשְׁמִישׁוֹ לְתַשְׁמִישׁ דְּבַיִת טְפֵי, וּמִזְדַּבְּנָא בִּכְלַל בַּיִת. הַיָּצִיעַ הַתַּחְתּוֹנָה וגו'. ג' הָיוּ זוֹ עַל גַּב זוֹ כו', וְכָל אַחַת וְאַחַת מַרְחֶבֶת אַמָּה מֵחֲבֶרְתָּהּ, בִּשְׁבִיל שֶׁהָיוּ כּוֹנְסִין אֶת הַחוֹמָה אַמָּה לְהוֹשִׁיב רָאשֵׁי קוֹרוֹת שֶׁל תִּקְרָה הַמַּפְסֶקֶת בֵּין יָצִיעַ לְיָצִיעַ, כִּדְכְתִיב: "כִּי מִגְרָעוֹת" דְּהַיְינוּ כְּנִיסַת הַחוֹמָה "נָתַן לַבַּיִת סָבִיב לְבִלְתִּי אֲחוֹז בְּקִירוֹת הַבַּיִת", כְּלוֹמַר, שֶׁלֹּא יִצְטָרֵךְ לִנְקוֹב אֶת קִירוֹת הַבַּיִת לִתְחוֹב שָׁם רָאשֵׁי קוֹרוֹת. דִּכְתִיב. בִּיחֶזְקֵאל. הַצְּלָעוֹת צֵלָע אֶל צֵלָע וגו'. וּפְשָׁטֵיהּ דִּקְרָא בְּתָאִים מַיְירֵי. קָנֶה אֶחָד אוֹרֶךְ וגו'. הַיְינוּ שֵׁשׁ אַמּוֹת, שֶׁכֵּן מִדַּת הַקָּנֶה כִּדְמְפָרֵשׁ בִּיחֶזְקֵאל. וְאַיָּצִיעַ הַתִּיכוֹנָה קָאֵי, דַּהֲוָיָא שֵׁשׁ אַמּוֹת. וְאִיבָּעֵית אֵימָא מֵהָכָא. נָפְקָא לָן דְּתָא הַיְינוּ בִּנְיָן שֶׁאֲחוֹרֵי בַּיִת, דְּהַיְינוּ יָצִיעַ – דְּקָחָשֵׁיב תָּא אֲחוֹרֵי הַהֵיכָל. כּוֹתֶל הַהֵיכָל שֵׁשׁ כו'. מִשְׁנָה בְּמַסֶּכֶת מִדּוֹת, דְּקָחָשֵׁיב אוֹרֶךְ הַהֵיכָל מִן הַמִּזְרָח לַמַּעֲרָב מֵאָה אַמָּה: כּוֹתֶל הָאוּלָם חָמֵשׁ כו'. וּמִדְּקָא חָשֵׁיב תָּא לְבַסּוֹף – ש"מ הַיְינוּ יָצִיעַ. כּוֹתֶל הַהֵיכָל שֵׁשׁ. עוֹבִי הַכּוֹתֶל שֶׁאֲחוֹרֵי בֵּית קָדְשֵׁי הַקֳּדָשִׁים. וְהַתָּא שֵׁשׁ. חֲלָלוֹ שֶׁל תָּא, מִן הַמִּזְרָח לַמַּעֲרָב. וְכוֹתֶל הַתָּא. כּוֹתֶל מַעֲרָבִי שֶׁלּוֹ עָבְיוֹ חָמֵשׁ. אֲמַר מָר זוּטְרָא. הָא דִּתְנַן: לֹא מָכַר אֶת הַיָּצִיעַ – וְהוּא דְּאִיכָּא ד' אַמּוֹת עַל ד' אַמּוֹת, חָשׁוּב בִּפְנֵי עַצְמוֹ, וְאִי לָא – לָא. לא אֶת הַבּוֹר. סֵיפָא דְּמַתְנִי' דְּהַמּוֹכֵר אֶת הַבַּיִת לֹא מָכַר אֶת הַיָּצִיעַ הִיא, וְקָאָמַר דְּגַם אֶת הַבּוֹר וְאֶת הַדּוּת אֵינוֹ בִּכְלַל בַּיִת. בּוֹר. בַּחֲפִירָה, דּוּת – בְּבִנְיָן. אע"פ שֶׁכָּתַב לוֹ. "בַּיִת זֶה אֲנִי מוֹכֵר לְךָ וְעוּמְקֵהּ וְרוּמֵהּ". דְּלָא אֲתָא לְרַבּוּיֵי אֶלָּא עֲלִיּוֹת וּמַעֲקֶה וְקַרְקָעִית הַבַּיִת, שֶׁאִם רָצָה מוֹכֵר לַחְפּוֹר תַּחַת הַבַּיִת – לוֹקֵחַ מְעַכֵּב עָלָיו. ה"נ. גַּבֵּי בּוֹר וְדוּת, אִי הָוֵי ד' אַמּוֹת – אֵינוֹ מָכוּר. וְאִי לָא – לָא חֲשִׁיב בִּפְנֵי עַצְמוֹ, וּמִזְדַּבַּן בַּהֲדֵי בַּיִת? בִּתְמִיָּה, וַהֲלֹא סְתָם בּוֹר לָא הָוֵי אַרְבַּע אַמּוֹת רוֹחַב, דְּבוֹר קָצָר הוּא! בּוֹר וְדוּת תַּשְׁמִישְׁתֵּיהּ לְחוּד. שֶׁעֲמוּקִּים הֵם, וְתַשְׁמִישָׁן לַמַּיִם. וּבַיִת תַּשְׁמִישְׁתָּא לְחוּד. לְפִיכָךְ אֵינוֹ בִּכְלַל בַּיִת, אע"ג דְּלָא הָוֵי ד' אַמּוֹת. אֲבָל יָצִיעַ וּבַיִת – חֲדָא תַּשְׁמִישְׁתָּא הָוֵי הוּא, מְקוֹם דִּירָה. לא חֲשִׁיב. וּבָטֵיל לְגַבֵּי בַּיִת. הַשְׁתָּא יָצִיעַ. שֶׁתַּשְׁמִישְׁתֵּיהּ שָׁוֶה לְגַמְרֵי לְשֶׁל בַּיִת – אָמְרַתְּ: לָא מִיזְדַּבַּן לַהֲדֵי בַּיִת. חֶדֶר. הֶעָשׂוּי לִשְׁמִירַת מָמוֹנוֹ, וְאֵין (א) דּוֹמֶה הַתַּשְׁמִישׁ לְשֶׁל בַּיִת – לֹא כָּל שֶׁכֵּן? וְאַמַּאי אִיצְטְרִיךְ לְמֶיהְדַּר וּלְמִיתְנֵיהּ?

לָא

המוכר את הבית. תני רב יוסף ג' שמות יש לה יציע צלע ותא. אליבא דקרא קאי. דיציע דמתני' כבר פירש רב יוסף גופיה דהוי בדקא חלילה. ויציע דבהמ"ק לא מצינו בשום מקום שהיה עשוי כמין חלונות. **והצלעות** צלע אל צלע. וכתיב בההוא קרא "ולא (ב) היו אוחזים בקירות הבית", ובקרא דיציע כתיב "לבלתי אחוז בקירות הבית" — ש"מ דצלע ויציע חד הוא. **ואיבעית** אימא מהכא כותל ההיכל שש. תימה לר"ת ולר"י דבתר קרא מייתי משנה, דהוי כמו "יהודה ועוד לקרא"(ג) בפ"ק דקדושין (דף ו.)! ואומר ר"י: דהתם לא קפיד אלא אלשון "ועוד", אבל הכא דלא קאמר "ועוד" — אתי שפיר. וכענין זה מצינו בכמה מקומות (ב"ק דף נב:): דבר זה כתוב בתורה ושנוי בנביאים ומשולש בכתובים ושנוי במשנה. **והתא** שש. בתיכונה איירי, דאותה היתה שש. אבל תחתונה לא היתה אלא חמש, כדכתיב "והיציע התחתונה חמש באמה רחבה" וגו'. ונראה דלכך לא נקט התחתונה — משום דכנגד התחתונה היה כותל ההיכל עביו שבע. אע"פ שכותל מזרחי של היכל שלא היה בו תאים היה שש עביו למעלה ולמטה, שאר כתלי ההיכל שהיו בהן מגרעות היו למטה עבין ז', וכנגד התיכונה עביו שש. כי המגרעת היא אמה, ולכך התיכונה רחבה מן התחתונה אמה. ולכך נקט תיכונה, משום דניחא ליה למינקט בכותל היכל מערב שש, כמו שמונה התם בכותל מזרח. ואם הוה נקט בתחתונה — הוה צריך למימר "כותל היכל שבע, והתא חמש", וניחא ליה למינקט שש במערב כמו במזרח. ועוד נראה לר"י: דהמגרעות היו בין בכותל ההיכל בין בשלשה כותלי התא, והמגרעת היתה חצי אמה מכל צד, והיתה כותל ההיכל מלמטה שש ומחצה, וכנגד התיכונה שש. והשתא ניחא, דכל התאים היו מרובעים: התחתונה חמש על חמש, והתיכונה שש על שש, והעליונה שבע על שבע. והא דתנן במס' מדות (פ"ד מ"ד): התחתונה רחבה ה' ורובד שש, אמצעית שש ורובד שבע — המגרעת קרי רובד, לפי שהוא כעין שורה בולטת. דרובד היינו שורה, כדתנן במסכת תמיד (פ"א מ"א): בית גדול היה ומוקף רובד של אבן. ומפרש בגמ' דהיינו איצטוונית. ועוד יש לפרש: דבבית שני היתה יציע התחתונה שש, והיה חלוק מבית ראשון, כמו שמצינו שחלוקין תאים שלעתיד במשכן דיחזקאל, דכתיב התם "ורוחב הצלע ד' אמות" — ה"נ שמא כך היו חלוקין מבית ראשון, ומצינא למימר דחשיב שפיר מלמטה.

לא

עין משפט נר מצוה

א א מיי' פכ"ה מהל' מכירה הל' א סמג עשין פב טוש"ע ח"מ סי' ריד סעיף א:

ב ב ג מיי' שם הל' ב טוש"ע שם סעיף ב:

ג ד ה מיי' שם הל' א טוש"ע שם סעיף א:

רבינו גרשום

המוכר את הבית. סתם: יציע. מפרש בגמ': שהיא פתוחה לתוכו. דמהו דתימא כיון דתשמישו בבית מכרו אפ"ה אינו מכור: בזמן שיש לו מעקה גבוה י' טפחים. דבר חשוב בפני עצמו לא מכרו. וכן היו רגילין שהיו משתמשין בגגותיהן: אפתא דהכא הוי עליה ולא כההוא אפתא דסוף חזקת הבתים: בדקא חלילה. הוא פרוזדור שעושין בפני הבית ולועזין פוריי"א: מ"ד אפתא. אינו מוכר אע"פ שפתוח לבית כל שכן בדקא חלילה שלפני הבית שפתוח לחצר ולבית ודבר חשוב לעצמו: אבל מאן דאמר דבדקא חלילה. לא מיזדבנא דחשיבא: ג' שמות יש לו. במקרא: והיציע התחתונה. אלו לשכות שהיו בנויות חוץ לכותל בהמ"ק תחתים שנים ושלישים זו על גב זו. וכי האי גוונא היו בנויות דקי"ל דכותל ההיכל עביו שש אמות מלמטה כנגד היציע התחתונה והיא היתה חמש באמה רחבה וכנס אמה מכותל ההיכל כנגד תקרה של יציע התחתונה ועל אותה כניסה שוכבות קצות קורותיו של יציע וממנו ולמעלה כנגד יציע התיכונה היה עביו של כותל היכל חמש אמה ולהכי הוה תיכונה שש באמה רחבה וכנגד תקרה של תיכון כנס אמה בכותל היכל שעל אותה כניסה קצות קורות תיכון שוכבות וכנגד היציע שלישי היה עובי הכותל היכל ד' אמות. ולהכי והשלישית שבע באמה רחבה וכנס עוד אמה מקום שקורותיו שוכבות. נמצא מן תקרה השלישית ולמעלה עביו של כותל ג' אמה והיינו כי מגרעות היינו כניסות לבלתי אחוז בקירות הבית כדי שלא יהיו צריכין לנקוב הכותל בשביל הנחת הקורות שלא יהא הכותל רעוע: והצלעות צלע אל צלע. לא יהיו אחוזות בקירות הבית אלא כדאמרן במגרעות: והתא. היינו יציע: ובין התאים. כלומר בין תא לתא ה' אמות: ואיבעית אימא מהכא. מצי יליף דתא היינו יציע של אחר הבית דקא חשיב במדות דכותל ההיכל עביו שש והתא שש היינו יציע: אמר מר זוטרא. היכי אמרי' מכר את הבית סתם דלא מכר את היציע והוא דהויא יציע ד' אמות ברוחב דמקום חשוב בפני עצמו הוא: ה"נ. בור ודות אי הוי ד' רוחב אין מכורין אי לא לא והא בור לא הוי ד' אמות רוחב: האי תשמישתא. דבית לחוד הוא שהולכין בו ושוכבין בו ובור ודות עומדין לתשמיש אחר מש"ה אפי' פחות מד' אמות לא מכר אבל הכא גבי בית ויציע אידי ואידי חדא תשמיש מקום דירה. הלכך אי הוי ד' אמות חשוב הוא לעצמו ולא מכר ואי לא לא: השתא יציע. דתשמיש הבית הוא אמרת לא מזדבנא. חדר בפני עצמו דלאו תשמיש בית הוא אלא לישן בו או להצניע בו חפצים מיבעיא דלא מזדבן:

דמצר

הגהות הב"ח

(א) רשב"ם ד"ה חדר וכו' [ו]אין תשמישו דומה לשל [ב]ית: (ב) תום' ד"ה [ו]הצלעות וכו' ולא יהיו [א]חוזים בקירות הבית: (ג) ד"ה ואיבעית וכו' [ו]עוד לקרא להכי מקשה בפ"ק דקדושין:

תורה אור: מ"א ו; יחזקאל מח; שם מ

מדות פ"ד מ"ו

לקמן סד.

ד א מיי' פכ"ה מהל' מכירה הל' ב סמג עשין פב טוש"ע ח"מ סי' ריד סעיף ג:
ה ב ג ד מיי' שם פכ"א הלכה יז סמג שם טוש"ע ח"מ סי' ריח סעיף ז:
ו ה ו מיי' שם וסמג שם טוש"ע ח"מ סי' ריח סעיף כב:
ז ז מיי' שם פכ"ד הל' יד סמג שם טוש"ע ח"מ סי' רעז סעיף ב:
ח ח ט מיי' שם פכ"א הל' כ טוש"ע שם סי' ריח סעיף כג:
ט י כ ל מיי' שם הל' יח טוש"ע שם סעיף כד:

לא צריכא דאע"ג דמצר ליה מצרי אבראי; כדרב נחמן, דאמר רב נחמן אמר רבה בר אבוה: ב המוכר בית לחבירו בבירה גדולה, אע"פ שמצר לו מצרים החיצונים — מצרים הרחיב לו. היכי דמי? אילימא דקרו ליה לבית בית, ולבירה בירה — פשיטא, בית זבין ליה, בירה לא זבין ליה! אלא דלבירה נמי קרו לה בית — כוליה זבין ליה! ג לא צריכא, *דרובא קרו ליה לבית בית, לבירה בירה, ואיכא נמי דלבירה קרו ליה בית. מהו דתימא כוליה זבין ליה, קמ"ל, ד מדהוה ליה למכתב "ולא שיירית בזביני אלין (א) כלום" ולא כתב, שמע מינה: שיורי שייר. ואמר רב נחמן אמר רבה בר אבוה: ה המוכר שדה לחבירו בבקעה גדולה, אע"פ שמצר לו מצרים החיצונים — מצרים הרחיב לו. היכי דמי? אילימא דקרו ליה לשדה שדה, ולבקעה בקעה — פשיטא, שדה זבין ליה, בקעה לא זבין ליה! ואלא דלבקעה נמי קרו לה שדה — כולה זבין ליה! ו לא צריכא, דאיכא דלשדה קרו ליה שדה, ולבקעה — בקעה, ואיכא נמי דלבקעה קרו לה שדה, מהו דתימא כוליה זבין ליה, קמ"ל, מדהוה ליה למכתב ליה "לא שיירית בזביני אלין קדמי כלום" ולא כתב ליה, שמע מינה: שיורי שייר. וצריכא, דאי אשמעינן בית — משום דהא תשמישתא לחוד והא תשמישתא לחוד, אבל בקעה דכולה חדא תשמישתא היא — אימא כוליה זבין ליה; ואי אשמעינן בקעה — משום דלא הוה ליה למימצר ליה, אבל בית דהוה ליה למימצר ליה ולא מצר ליה — כוליה זבין ליה, צריכא. כמאן אזלא הא דאמר רב מרי *(בריה) דבת שמואל *(בר שילת) משמיה דאביי: ז האי מאן דמזבני ליה מידי לחבריה, צריך למכתב ליה "לא שיירית בזביני אלין קדמי כלום", כמאן? כרב נחמן אמר רבה בר אבוה. ח ההוא דא"ל לחבריה: "ארעא דבי חייא מזבננא לך", הואי ליה תרתי ארעתא דהוה מתקרין "דבי חייא". אמר רב אשי: ט חדא אמר ליה, תרתי לא א"ל. ואי א"ל "ארעתא" (ב) י סתמא — מיעוט ארעתא כ שתים. ואי א"ל "כל ארעתא" — כל ארעתא דאית ליה, לבר מבוסתני ופרדיסי. ל ואי א"ל "זיהרא" — אפי' (ג) בי בוסתני ופרדיסי, לבר מבתי ועבדי.
ואי

לא צריכא אע"ג דמצר ליה מצרים אבראי. מספקא לר"י ביליע, אי אמרינן נמי מצרים הרחיב לו, ממשנה יתירה, או שמא דוקא בחדר, דתשמיש אחרינא הוא כדאמר הכא, אבל יציע קנה.
אלא דקרו לה לבירה נמי בית. פי' ריב"ס: אלא דכולי עלמא, כשמזכירין בית סתם — כל הבירה משמע. וכשרוצין (ה) להזכיר בית אחד בלא בירה — צריכין לפרש ולומר: בית אחד בלא בירה אני אומר. א"כ, אפי' לא מצר מצרים החיצונים כולה זבין ליה. ומתוך לשון הקונטרס משמע נמי שרוצה לפרש כן. ולפי' זה, הא דכתיב בכל הספרים "לבירה נמי בית", היינו: כמו שקורין לבירה בירה — קורין נמי לבירה בית. וקשה לר"י: דא"כ ה"ל לשנויי: "לא צריכא דקרו נמי לבית בית, וקרו כולי עלמא לבית בית, ולבירה בית", ואמאי איצטריך למימר: דאיכא דקרו לבירה בירה. פי': ולא בית, ואיכא נמי דקרו לבירה בית! ונראה לר"י דה"פ: ואלא דקרו לבירה נמי בית, כמו שקורין לבית בית — כוליה זבין ליה, כיון דמצר לו מצרים החיצונים. ובתר הכי משני דלאו כולי עלמא קרו לבירה בית, אלא איכא דקרו לבירה בירה ולא בית. שמע מינה שיורי שייר. וא"ת: ונימא הדמים מודיעים, כדקאמר ר' יהודה גבי מכר לו את הצמד, ב"המוכר את הספינה" (לקמן דף עז:): הדבר ידוע שאין הצמד שוה מאתים כו' — ה"נ נימא: הדבר ידוע שאין הבית שוה כל כך, אלא כל הבירה קאמר! וי"ל: דהכא כרבנן דר' יהודה, דאמרי: אין הדמים ראיה. והיא דריש "המוכר פירות" (לקמן דף צב.) דפריך: וניחזי, אי דמי רדיא לרדיא — נפרש כשנגיע שם בע"ה. ועוד אומר ר"י: דשמעתין אתיא אפי' כר' יהודה, דגבי קרקע לא שייכא הודעת דמים, דפעמים קונה אדם קרקע הרבה יותר ממה שהיא שוה כדאמר בפ' "מי שהיה נשוי" (כתובות דף צא:): ההוא גברא דהוו מסקי ביה אלפא זוזי כו', הוו ליה תרי אפדני, זבן חדא בחמש מאה וחדא בחמש מאה, אתא בע"ח וטרפה לחדא מינייהו, הדר קא טריף לאידך. שקל אלפא זוזי, ואמר ליה: אי שויא לך באלפא זוזא — לחיי, ואי לא — שקול אלפא זוזי ואיסתלק. ומה שפירש רבינו שמואל דלא שייך בקרקע הודעת דמים, משום דאין אונאה בקרקעות — אין נראה לר"י, דזה אינו בשביל ששוה יותר, דהא הקדשות ועבדים נמי אין להם אונאה! אלא גזירת הכתוב הוא, ושייך שפיר הודעת דמים. ועוד: דהא ביטול מקח יש להן. ארעתא תרתי משמע. והא דאמר ב"השואל" (ב"מ דף קג. ושם ד"ה פרדסי): האי מאן דמשאיל מרא לחבריה למירפק ביה פרדסי — רפיק ביה כל "פרדסי" דאית ליה. ולא אמר: "פרדסי" תרתי משמע! התם דרך הוא שמשאיל לו לכל מה שצריך. אבל הכא, בשביל שימכור אדם שתי שדות — לא ימכור כל שדותיו. וי"מ: דהתם יד המשאיל על התחתונה, דשואל מוחזק, אבל הכא — יד לוקח על התחתונה, שהמוכר מוחזק. ואין נראה לר"י, דהתם נמי, הואיל וסופה לחזור לבעליה — הוי משאיל מוחזק, כדאמר רב נחמן (שם דף קב:): דקרקע בחזקת בעליה עומדת, הואיל וסופה לחזור לבעליה. ואין לומר דיש לחלק בין קרקע למטלטלין, דאין חזקת השוכר חשובה בקרקע כמו במטלטלין, כדאשכחן (לקמן דף לב.) גבי מוכר שור לחבירו ונמצא נגחן, דאזלי בתר מוחזק במעות עתה, אף על פי שתחלה היו של לוקח, ולא אמרינן בחזקת בעלים הראשונים קיימא. דאין נראה לחלק, דהא מיירי התם רב נחמן אפילו בא בסוף החדש שנגמרה חזקתו שדר בה, אפילו הכי מוקמן בחזקת בעלים. וכן ב"המקבל" (ב"מ קי.): מלוה אומר חמש ולוה אומר שלש — פירות בחזקת אוכליהן. ופריך: אמאי לא מוקמן בחזקת בעלים? אף על פי שהפירות כבר אכלן מלוה — אם כן לא הוי טעמא משום דחזקת קרקע גרועה, אלא משום דסופה לחזור. וריב"ס מחלק בין "פרדיסי" ל"ארעתא". וה"נ אי אמר "מקרקעי" — הוי אמר כל הקרקעות שיש לו, כדמוכח לקמן ב"מי שמת" (דף קמח:).
ואי

לא צריכא. למיתני לא מכר את החדר, אלא (ד) דמצר לו מוכר ללוקח בשטר מכירה מצרים חיצונים שחוץ לחדר. דסד"א מכר את החדר, שהרי בתוך המצרים הוא — קמ"ל מתני' דלא מכר אלא בית, והאי דמצר חוץ לחדר, וכתב "ביתו של פלוני מן המערב" — מצרים הרחיב לו. כדרב נחמן. שלא ידע לפרש ולומר "חדר שלי היא מתערבו של בית", דאין זה מצר הניכר לאנשי העיר, והלכך כתב מצרים הניכרים. בבירה גדולה. בית גדול הוא, ופתוחין לו בתים סביבותיו. ואין הבירה עשויה לתשמיש אלא לישיבה והילוך בני הבתים. והכל בית אחד הוא, כדכתיב: "הבירה אשר הכינותי" (דה"א כט). המוכר בית לחבירו. וכגון שהיה עומד באחד מבתי הבירה, ואמר לו "בית זה אני מוכר לך". כוליה זבין ליה. דכיון דליכא דקרו לבית בית ולבירה בירה, אלא כולה ביחד מיקריא בית — איהו בית זבין ליה, וקנה הכל. דאיכא דקרו לבית. שבבירה בית, ולבירה עצמה קרו בירה. מהו דתימא. כיון דמצר ליה מיצרי בראי, וכולה מיקריא בית — כולה זבין ליה. קמ"ל. רב נחמן, דלא אמרינן הכי. משום דהוה ליה למכתב. למוכר: "ולא שיירית בזביני אלין שבתוך ארבעה המצרים קדמי כלום". שהרי כך תיקנו חכמים לכתוב, בשביל שיש בני אדם שמרחיבין המצרים בשטר המכירה, ואינם מוכרים כל מה שבתוך המצרים, ואיהו לא כתב ליה, ש"מ כו'. בבקעה גדולה. שיש בה שדות הרבה והן שלו. וכגון שהיה עומד באחד מן השדות, ואמר לו "שדי זו אני מוכר לך". והדמים מודיעין ליכא למימר, לא גבי בירה ולא גבי בקעה, דהא אין אונאה לקרקעות. וצריכא. לאשמועינן גבי בירה ובקעה, דמצרים הרחיב לו. משום דהא תשמישתא לחוד כו'. בית ובירה אין תשמישן שוה, לפיכך אין בירה בכלל בית, ואמרי' מצרים הרחיב לו. אבל שדות שבבקעה, שהכל עומד לחרישה — אימא דכולה זבין, דבקעה בכלל שדה. דלא הוה ליה למימצר. לחוד, דלא ידע מוכר היאך ימצא שדה אחת בתוך שדותיו, והלכך הוצרך להרחיב מצרים, ולכתוב "שדה ראובן מן המזרח ושדה שמעון מן המערב", וכן לכל ד' רוחות. אבל גבי בירה, שעשויה בניינין משופין זה מזה בין ברוחב בין באורך בין בגובה ועובי הכתלים, והיה יכול למצור ולכתוב אותו בית שעשוי כן וכן מהמזרח, וכן לכל רוח ורוח, ומדלא עשה כן — איכא למימר דכולה זבין, צריכא. כמאן כרב נחמן אמר רבה בר אבוה. דמשום דס"ל דאמרינן בעלמא מצרים הרחיב לו, הלכך תקינו לכתוב כן, דלא ליטעון מוכר "מצרים הרחבתי", ויפסיד לוקח. ארעא דבי רבי חייא. שקנה מרבי חייא. ארעא לשון יחיד אמר ליה, ויטול הלוקח הפחותה שבשתיהן, דיד בעל השטר על התחתונה. ומפרש גמרא ואזיל. ואי א"ל. איניש לחבריה. ארעתא. מזבינא לך. בוסתני. גנות. ופרדסי. כרמים. זיהרא. כל הקרקעות קרויין כן.
ואי

גי' רש"ל דאיכא

[נ"ל ברה]

[כרב אלפס וכרא"ש ליתא]

הגהות הב"ח
(א) גמ' ולא שיירית בזביני אלין קדמי כלום: (ב) שם ואי א"ל ארעתא מיעוט כצ"ל ותיבת סתמא נמחק: (ג) שם אפי' בוסתני כצ"ל ותיבת בי נמחק: (ד) רשב"ם ד"ה לא צריכא וכו' אלא כגון דמצר: (ה) תוס' ד"ה אלא וכו' וכשרוצין להזכיר בית.

רבינו גרשום
דמצר לו מצרי אבראי: שאמר לו מצר פלוני רוח דרומי וכן לכל מצר ומצר והיציע חדר זה לפנים מן המצרים וחוצה לחדר מצר ליה מצריו וסד"א הואיל דחוץ לחדר מצר לו וקלט החדר עם הבית דמכר לו החדר נמי קמ"ל דלא מכר: כרב נחמן וכו' בבירה גדולה. פלטורין: אע"פ שמצר לו מצרים החיצונים. שחוץ מן הבירה לא מצי למיטען ליה עם אותן המצרים דמצרת לי מכרת לי הכל. אפ"ה לא מכר לו אלא בית א' בלבד בבירה וזה שמצר לו כן מבחוץ מצרים הרחיב לו שלא היה יודע היאך לומר מפני שיש למוכר בתחום סביב לזה שמכר. ואיכא נמי אינשי דקרו לבירה כולה נמי בית. מהו דתימא כוליה [זבין ליה] קמ"ל דלא. מדהוה ליה למכתב. אי איתא דכולה מכר ליה הו"ל למכתב לא שיירית בזביני אלין קדמי בין המצרים כלום ולא כתב ליה ש"מ שיורי שייר לפניו ולא מכר לו אלא בית בלבד ומצרים הרחיב לו: מצרים החיצונים. שסביב לכל הבקעה לא מכר אלא שדה אחת בלבד: וצריכא לאשמועינן. בין גבי שדה בבקעה בין גבי בית בבירה גדולה: דאי אשמועינן בית. ה"א מש"ה שיורי שייר ולא מכר לו כי אם הבית לחוד משום דבית תשמיש לחוד ופלטין תשמיש לחוד ולא דמי האי תשמיש להאי תשמיש אבל גבי שדה ובקעה אימא דלא שייר כלום משום דכולה חדא תשמישתא הוא לזריעה: אימא. הואיל ומצר לו מצרים החיצונים דכולה בין הואיל דאיכא דקרו לבקעה נמי שדה קמ"ל דלא מדהוה ליה למכתב לא שיירית בתוך מצרים הללו לעצמי כלום ולא כתב ש"מ שיורי שייר: ואי אשמועינן שדה. ה"א מש"ה שייר דלא הוה ליה למוכר למימצר ליה דלא ידע היכי מצי מצר ליה שדה אחת בתוך שדותיו דיש לו שדות למוכר כל סביבותיו ומש"ה מצר לו מצרים החיצונים דלא אפשר ליה בלאו הכי דלא מינכר מלתא. אבל בית אימא דלא שייר לעצמו כלום היכא דמצר ליה מצרים החיצונים משום דאם איתא דשייר מצי למימצר ליה הכי בית זה שאני מוכר לך מצר מזרחי בית שסמוך לחצר ומצר דרומי גינתי ומצר מערבי פרדסי או בית העצים או בית הבקר הואיל דלא דמיין תשמישייהו אהדדי מצי מצר ליה והואיל ולא מצר ליה כוליה זבין ליה קמ"ל מדהוה ליה למכתב לא שיירית בין המצרים הללו לפני כלום ולא כתב ליה (קמ"ל) [ש"מ] דשיורי שייר: ארעתא דבי חייא. קרקע שקנה מן חייא. אמר רב אשי. ארעא חדא משמע דקאמר ליה ולא ארעתא דמשמע תרתי: ואי א"ל מזבינא לך כל ארעתא דאית לי. זבין ליה הכל שהן בני זריעה: לא מבוסתני. גינה של אילנות: ופרדיסי. גינת ירק: ואי א"ל זיהרא. מזבינא לך דמשמע כל נחלות שיש לי מכרנא לך אפי' בוסתני ופרדיסי דנחלות נינהו: בר מבתי ועבדי. דנכסים נינהו ועבדא כמקרקעי דמי: מכר

י א מיי' פכ"א מהל' מכירה הל' יח סמג עשין פב טוש"ע ח"מ סי' ריח סעיף כג:
יא ב ג מיי' שם הל' יג סמג שם טוש"ע ח"מ סי' ריט סעיף ג:
יב ד ה מיי' שם הל' יד טוש"ע שם סעיף ב:
יג ו מיי' שם הל' טז טוש"ע שם סעיף ז:

א וְאִי אֲמַר לֵיהּ "נִכְסֵי" – אֲפִילּוּ בָּתֵּי וְעַבְדֵי. מָצַר לוֹ מֶצֶר אֶחָד אָרוֹךְ וּמֶצֶר אֶחָד קָצָר – אֲמַר רַב: ב לֹא קָנָה אֶלָּא כְּנֶגֶד הַקָּצָר. אֲמַרוּ לֵיהּ רַב כָּהֲנָא וְרַב אַסִּי לְרַב: וְיִקְנֶה כְּנֶגֶד רֹאשׁ תּוֹר! שָׁתֵיק רַב. ג וּמוֹדֶה רַב, הֵיכָא דְּאִיכָּא מֶצֶר רְאוּבֵן וְשִׁמְעוֹן מֵחַד גִּיסָא וּמֶצֶר לֵוִי וִיהוּדָה מֵחַד גִּיסָא, מִדַּהֲוָה לֵיהּ לְמִכְתַּב (א) לֵיהּ דִּרְאוּבֵן כְּנֶגֶד לֵוִי וּדְשִׁמְעוֹן כְּנֶגֶד יְהוּדָה, וְלָא כְּתַב לֵיהּ, שְׁמַע מִינַּהּ: כְּנֶגֶד רֹאשׁ תּוֹר הוּא דְּאָמַר לֵיהּ. ד מֶצֶר רְאוּבֵן מִזְרָח וּמַעֲרָב, וּמֶצֶר שִׁמְעוֹן צָפוֹן וְדָרוֹם – ה צָרִיךְ לְמִכְתַּב לֵיהּ: מֶצֶר רְאוּבֵן רוּחִין תְּרֵין, וּמֶצֶר שִׁמְעוֹן רוּחִין תְּרֵין. ו אִיבַּעְיָא לְהוּ: סִיֵּים לוֹ אֶת הַקְּרָנוֹת, מַהוּ? כְּמִין *גַּאם, מַהוּ? בְּסֵירוּגִין

רש"י

וְאִי אָמַר לֵיהּ נִכְסֵי אֲפִילּוּ בָּתֵּי וְעַבְדֵי. אֲבָל מִטַּלְטְלֵי לָא, עַד דְּאָ"ל "כָּל נִכְסַיי". מֵצַר לוֹ. הַמּוֹכֵר שָׂדֶה לַחֲבֵירוֹ בִּשְׁטַר הַמְּכִירָה, מֶצֶר מַעֲרָבִי אָרוֹךְ מֵאָה אַמָּה, וּמֶצֶר מִזְרָחִי כְּנֶגְדּוֹ קָצָר נ' אַמָּה, שֶׁלֹּא הִגִּיעַ אֶלָּא עַד חֲצִי הַשָּׂדֶה, וּמֶצֶר שֶׁל צָפוֹן וְדָרוֹם מִיָּמִין וּשְׂמֹאל מִן הַמִּזְרָח עַד הַמַּעֲרָב, כָּזֶה: אֶלָּא כְּנֶגֶד הַקָּצָר. כְּנֶגֶד מֶצֶר מִזְרָחִי יִקְנֶה, דְּהַיְינוּ חֲצִי הַשָּׂדֶה, וּמֶצֶר מַעֲרָבִי שֶׁהוּא אָרוֹךְ – מַצְרִיס הִרְחִיב לוֹ, דְּמֶצֶר שָׁלֵם הוּצְרַךְ לִכְתּוֹב בַּשְּׁטָר.

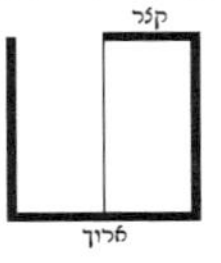

וְיִקְנֶה כְּנֶגֶד רֹאשׁ תּוֹר. כְּלוֹמַר, הָא אִיכָּא לְמֵימַר דְּדַוְקָא כָּתַב לוֹ מֶצֶר מַעֲרָב אָרוֹךְ וּמֶצֶר מִזְרָח קָצָר, (ב) הַיְינוּ כְּדֵי לִקְנוֹת מֶצֶר מַעֲרָב מֵאָה אַמָּה בְּאוֹרֶךְ הַמֶּצֶר, וּמֶצֶר מִזְרָח חֲמִשִּׁים אַמָּה. וְה"ד – כְּגוֹן שֶׁיִּקְנֶה כָּל הַשָּׂדֶה בַּאֲלַכְסוֹן, כְּנֶגֶד רָאשֵׁי הַשּׁוּרוֹת שֶׁל מִזְרָח וּמַעֲרָב, כָּזֶה: וּמוֹדֶה רַב. מִקַּמֵּי דְּאִישְׁתִּיק. אֲבָל בָּתַר דְּאִישְׁתִּיק – אוֹדֵי בְּתַרְוַיְיהוּ. הֵיכָא

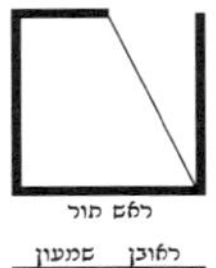

דְּאִיכָּא מֶצֶר רְאוּבֵן וְשִׁמְעוֹן מִזְרָח וּמֶצֶר לֵוִי וִיהוּדָה כְּנֶגְדָּן בַּמַּעֲרָב. וְרוֹחַב הַשָּׂדֶה ק' אַמָּה, וְהָוֵי מֶצֶר לֵוִי כְּנֶגֶד רְאוּבֵן נ' אַמָּה, וְכֵן מֶצֶר יְהוּדָה כְּנֶגֶד שִׁמְעוֹן נ' אַמָּה, וְכָתַב לוֹ בַּשְּׁטָר: מֶצֶר רְאוּבֵן וְשִׁמְעוֹן מִן הַמִּזְרָח, וּמֶצֶר יְהוּדָה מִן הַמַּעֲרָב, דְּהַיְינוּ מֶצֶר מַעֲרָבִי *קָצָר, וְלֵוִי לֹא הִזְכִּיר – הָכָא מוֹדֶה רַב דְּיִקְנֶה כְּנֶגֶד רֹאשׁ תּוֹר. דְּאִי הֲוָה בָּעֵי מוֹכֵר לְהַקְנוֹת כְּנֶגֶד הַקָּצָר – הָכִי הֲוָה לֵיהּ לְמִיכְתַּב: וְשִׁמְעוֹן כְּנֶגֶד (חֲצִי) יְהוּדָה,

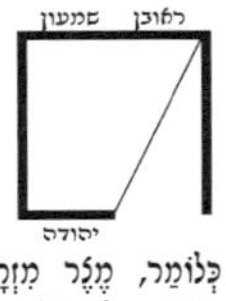

כְּלוֹמַר, מֶצֶר מִזְרָחִי שֶׁהוּא אָרוֹךְ לֹא יִקְנֶה אֶלָּא יְהוּדָה כְּנֶגֶד שִׁמְעוֹן, דְּהַיְינוּ חֲצִי הַשָּׂדֶה, וּמִדְּלָא כָּתַב הָכִי – ש"מ כְּנֶגֶד רֹאשׁ תּוֹר קָאָמַר לֵיהּ. אֲבָל לְעֵיל בְּמִילְּתֵיהּ דְּרַב מַיְירֵי כְּגוֹן רְאוּבֵן וְשִׁמְעוֹן מֶצֶר מִזְרָחִי, וִיהוּדָה מֶצֶר מַעֲרָב כְּנֶגֶד שְׁנֵיהֶן, וְכָתַב לוֹ: יְהוּדָה מֶצֶר מַעֲרָב וְשִׁמְעוֹן מֶצֶר מִזְרָח, דְּהַיְינוּ אֶחָד אָרוֹךְ וְאֶחָד קָצָר – הָתָם לֹא קָנָה אֶלָּא כְּנֶגֶד הַקָּצָר, וּמֶצֶר מַעֲרָב הִרְחִיב לוֹ, שֶׁלֹּא יָכוֹל לְפָרֵשׁ "וְשִׁמְעוֹן כְּנֶגֶד חֲצִי יְהוּדָה" כִּי הָכָא, שֶׁאֵין כּוֹתְבִין חֲצִי מֶצֶר, וְהוּצְרַךְ לִכְתּוֹב מֶצֶר שָׁלֵם. נִרְאֶה דְּה"ג: מִדַּה"ל לְמִיכְתַּב רְאוּבֵן כְּנֶגֶד לֵוִי, (ג) דְּמַשְׁמַע שֶׁמָּצַר לוֹ מֶצֶר רְאוּבֵן וְשִׁמְעוֹן אָרוֹךְ, וּמֶצֶר לֵוִי הוּא הַקָּצָר. אֲבָל יְהוּדָה לֹא הִזְכִּיר. וְנִרְאִין כֵּן הַדְּבָרִים לְהַעֲמִיד הַחִסָּרוֹן שֶׁל מֶצֶר בִּיהוּדָה הָאַחֲרוֹן. וּבְפֵירוּשֵׁי ר' חֲנַנְאֵל מֵרוֹמָא גָּרְסִינַן: מִדַּה"ל לְמִיכְתַּב מֶצֶר לֵוִי כְּנֶגֶד מֶצֶר רְאוּבֵן, וְכַיּוֹצֵא בּוֹ מֶצֶר יְהוּדָה כְּנֶגֶד מֶצֶר שִׁמְעוֹן. וּמִשָּׁם יֵשׁ לִלְמוֹד שֶׁכָּתוּב בַּסְּפָרִים שֶׁלָּהֶן: מִדַּהֲוָה לֵיהּ לְמִיכְתַּב לֵוִי כְּנֶגֶד רְאוּבֵן וְלֹא כָּתַב כו', וְכֵן עִיקָּר. מֶצֶר רְאוּבֵן מִזְרָח וּמַעֲרָב כו'. הַמּוֹכֵר שָׂדֶה לַחֲבֵירוֹ וְרוֹצֶה לִכְתּוֹב מְצָרֶיהָ, וְיֵשׁ לִשְׁכֵנוֹ רְאוּבֵן ב' שָׂדוֹת אַחַת בַּמִּזְרָח וְאַחַת בַּמַּעֲרָב (וּלְשִׁמְעוֹן שְׁכֵנוֹ שְׁתֵּי שָׂדוֹת אַחַת בַּצָּפוֹן וְאַחַת בַּדָּרוֹם) – לֹא יִכְתּוֹב לוֹ סְתָם "שָׂדֶה זוֹ שֶׁאֲנִי מוֹכֵר לְךָ הֲרֵי הִיא בְּתוֹךְ שְׂדוֹת רְאוּבֵן וְשִׁמְעוֹן", דְּאָתֵי לְמִיפְלַג לֵיהּ בַּאֲלַכְסוֹן כָּזֶה: וְנִמְצָא שֶׁנּוֹטֵל אֵצֶל מֶצֶר רְאוּבֵן וְשִׁמְעוֹן. אֲבָל כְּשֶׁכּוֹתֵב "מֶצֶר רְאוּבֵן רוּחִין תַּרְתֵּין, וּמֶצֶר שִׁמְעוֹן רוּחִין תַּרְתֵּין" – הֲרֵי אַרְבַּע רוּחוֹת. וְכ"ש אִם יִכְתּוֹב לוֹ בְּפֵירוּשׁ "מֶצֶר רְאוּבֵן מִזְרָח וּמַעֲרָב, מֶצֶר שִׁמְעוֹן צָפוֹן וְדָרוֹם"

– דְּשַׁפִּיר דָּמֵי. סִיֵּים לוֹ אֶת הַקְּרָנוֹת. לְשׁוֹן סִימָן. שֶׁהָיוּ שְׂדוֹת הַרְבֵּה שֶׁל בְּנֵי אָדָם מַקִּיפִין אוֹתוֹ, וְלֹא כָּתַב אֶלָּא אַרְבַּע שָׂדוֹת שֶׁל ד' קַרְנוֹת הַשָּׂדֶה, אֲבָל אָרְכָּהּ וְרָחְבָּהּ לֹא מָצַר כְּלָל. מִי אָמְרִינַן: אֵין דֶּרֶךְ לִמְכּוֹר קַרְנוֹת הַשָּׂדֶה, אֶלָּא כָּל הַשָּׂדֶה שֶׁבְּתוֹךְ הַקְּרָנוֹת מָכַר לוֹ, דְּמִשּׁוּם הָכִי סִיֵּים לוֹ קַרְנוֹתָיו. אוֹ דִּלְמָא לֹא מָכַר לוֹ אֶלָּא תֶּלֶם בַּאֲלַכְסוֹן, מִקֶּרֶן לְקֶרֶן, שְׁתֵּי וָעֵרֶב כָּזֶה: כְּמִין גַּאם. אוֹת יְוָנִית, וְדוֹמֶה לְכָ"ף. כְּגוֹן שֶׁמָּצַר לוֹ קֶרֶן דְּרוֹמִית מִזְרָחִית וְקֶרֶן צְפוֹנִית מַעֲרָבִית, וְנִמְצָא שֶׁמָּצַר תְּחִלַּת כָּל רוּחַ כָּזֶה: אִם תִּמְצָא לוֹמַר גַּבֵּי סִיֵּים לוֹ אֶת הַקְּרָנוֹת דְּלֹא קָנָה אֶלָּא כְּנֶגֶד הַקְּרָנוֹת – הַיְינוּ מִשּׁוּם דְּהָתָם לֹא סִיֵּים אֶת הָרוּחוֹת, אֲבָל הָכָא שֶׁמָּצַר תְּחִלַּת כָּל הָרוּחוֹת – כְּמִי שֶׁמָּצַר אֶת כּוּלָּן דָּמֵי, וְקָנָה הַכֹּל. אוֹ דִּלְמָא לֹא קָנָה אֶלָּא בַּאֲלַכְסוֹן, כָּזֶה:

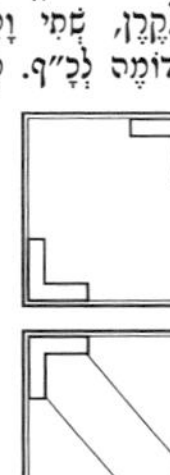

תוספות

ואי א"ל נכסי אפילו בתים ועבדים. אבל מטלטלין לא. ואע"ג דאמר ב"מי שמת" (לקמן דף קנ:): "כל נכסיי לפלוני", גלימא איקרי נכסי – לשון "נכסיי" שאני, דמשמע ריבוי יותר מ"נכסי" דהכא. אבל אין לחלק משום דהתם אמר "כל נכסי", דא"כ הו"ל לחלק התם כדמחלק התם בין "מטלטלי" ל"כל מטלטלי". ועוד י"ל: דהתם מיירי במתנה, דבעין יפה נותן, והכא במכר. **מצר** אחד ארוך ומצר אחד קצר. ומיירי שמצר לכל ד' רוחות, כדפי' הקונט'. דאי לא מצר אלא מזרח ומערב ולא מצר לפון ודרום – א"כ היכי קאמר ליה רב אסי: וניקני כנגד ראש תור? אדרבה, ה"ל למפרך דלא ליקני אלא תלם אחד במזרח ותלם אחד במערב, דהא אית ליה לרב אסי לקמן במצר לו מצר ראשון ושני ושלישי, ומצר רביעי לא מצר לו – דלא קנה אלא תלם אחד על פני כולו. ומה שהקשה רבינו יצחק לפירוש הקונטרס: אי מארבע רוחות מצר לו אמאי לא קנה אלא כנגד הקצר, דאם כן אמאי מצר לו מצר רביעי? לאו פירכא היא, דמצינן למימר:

מצריס הרחיב לו. **ומודה** רב. פי' בקונטרס: קודם ששתק. משמע דבשתק מודה להו. אע"ג דלקמן (עמוד ב) שתק (*רבא) לאביי אע"ג דלא הודה לו, אלא שלא חש להשיבו – הכא ליכא למימר הכי, דרב כהנא ורב אסי הוו כמו תלמיד חבר לרב, כדאמרי' (סנהדרין דף לו:) דלסבריה לא הוו צריכי. וברוב מקומות רב מודה כששתק להם, בפ"ק דב"ק (דף יא. ושם) גבי אין שמין לא לגנב ולא לגזלן, דקאמרי': אדרבה, מדאמרו ליה רב כהנא ורב אסי לרב דינא הכי, ושתיק – ש"מ שמין, ולא אמר הא דשתיק משום דלא חש להשיב. ובפ"ק דבילה (דף ו. ושם) גבי אפרוח שנולד ביו"ט, דא"ל רב כהנא ורב אסי לרב: וכי מה בין זה לעגל שנולד מן הטרפה? ושתיק רב. אמר רב יוסף: מאי טעמא שתיק רב? לימא להו: הואיל ומוכן אגב אמו לכלבים. וכן ב"איזהו נשך" (ב"מ דף סט:) גבי ספינה, אמר רב: אגרא ופגרא. א"ל רב כהנא ורב אסי לרב: אי אגרא לא פגרא, אי פגרא לא אגרא. שתיק רב. אמר רב ששת: מאי טעמא שתיק רב? לא שמיע ליה הא דתניא כו'. משמע בכל הנהו, דלא מפני שלא חש להשיב שתק, אלא מפני שהודה. **מדהוה** ליה למיכתב מצר שמעון כנגד יהודה. פירוש: כנגד יהודה לבד, ולא הו"ל למיכתב ראובן, ומדכתב ראובן – שמע מינה כנגד ראש תור קאמר ליה. וגירסא זו אינה נראה, דלמה ליה למינקט כה"ג, דהשתא דלג לוי? יהודה היה לו לדלג, שהוא אחרון! לכך גרים רשב"ס: מדה"ל למיכתב ראובן כנגד לוי, והשתא דלג יהודה. ומ"מ קשיא לר"ת, דהכי הוה ליה למימר: מדלא הו"ל למיכתב שמעון וכתב – שמע מינה כנגד ראש תור קאמר ליה. ונראה לר"ת כגירסא ראשונה. ולא קאי אעיקר מילתיה דרב, דקאמר לא קנה אלא כנגד הקצר – דא"כ הו"ל למימר: מדלא הו"ל למיכתב ראובן. אלא קאי אדיוק, דכי היכי דקאמר רב דלא קנה אלא כנגד הקצר – ה"נ אם מצר מצר ראובן ושמעון מצד מזרח, ומצר לוי חצי שדה מצד מערב, ואצל לוי קרקע עולם – דמודה רב דקנה כנגד הארוך, כיון שלא מצא מה למצור. והא קאמר, דהיכא דמוצא למצור, כגון לוי ויהודה מן המערב – מודה רב דלא קנה כנגד הארוך אם דלג יהודה. וגרסינן: מדהו"ל למיכתב יהודה כנגד שמעון. דאי גרסינן שמעון כנגד יהודה הלשון דחוק. ופי' מגומגם, דלא קאי אדברי רב אלא אדיוק. ואין להקשות: אמאי לא קאמר גמרא מודה רב אעיקר דבריו, כדפירש הקונטרס? ולימא: מדלא הו"ל למיכתב! כי שמא לא חשש הגמרא לפרש זה, דפשיטא דלא אמר הכא דלא קנה אלא כנגד הקצר, דודאי לא מצר לו מצר שמעון בחנם, ולא הוצרך לפרש אלא אמאי לא קנה כנגד הארוך, כיון שמצר לו מצר שמעון. **מצר** ראובן לרוחין תרין. אע"פ שאם היה כותב לו קרקע שבין שדות ראובן ובין שדות שמעון לא הייני יכולין לומר שיקנה חצי (ד) שדה כזה: דאם כן לא הוי בין שדות ראובן ושמעון (בזוית). ומיהו *)קאמר דקנה באלכסון מקרן לקרן, דהויא בין שדות שמעון וראובן בזוית. **כמין** גאם. פירש ר"י: מזרח ודרום, דהיינו משתי רוחות. וקשה לפירושו: דאם כן, אמאי צריך למיכתב לעיל "מצר ראובן לרוחין תרין ומצר שמעון לרוחין תרין" אי קני כמין גאם! ופירוש הקונטרס נראה עיקר.

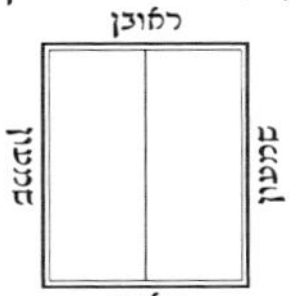

*) נ"א הוה אמינא

איתמר

רבינו גרשום

מכר לו שדה ומצר לו מצר אחד ארוך. כגון מצר מזרחי ראובן על פני כל השדה שמכר לו ומצר אחר קצר כגון למערב השדה מצר שמעון ולא היה מגיע מיצרו אלא עד חצי השדה שמכר לו: אמר רב. הואיל וכן לא אזלינן בתר מצר הארוך אלא בתר מצר הקצר ולא קנה בשדה אלא כשיעור משך מצרו של שמעון כנגדו עד מצר ראובן: אמרו ליה רב הונא ורב אסי. אמאי אמרת דלא קנה אלא שוה בשוה כנגד הקצר של שמעון ליקני כנגד ראש תור. כלומר היכא דאין מגיע מצר שמעון אלא כנגד חצי של ראובן ימשך מסוף מצר שמעון אצל השדה באלכסון עד סוף מצר ראובן וכך יקנה והיינו כעין ראש תור שמלמעלה מרוחב ומלמטה מקצר: ומודה רב היכא דאיכא מצר ראובן ושמעון לצד מזרח השדה ומצר לוי ויהודה לצד מערב ואמר לו שדה זו שאני מוכר לך מצד מזרחי עומד ראובן ושמעון ומצד מערב שסמוך לדרום עומד מצר לוי ומצר יהודה לא מצר לו שסמוך ללוי היינו מצר לוי מצר אחד ארוך ומצר אחד קצר מדהו"ל למכתב נמי ומצר שמעון כנגד יהודה ולא כתב ליה אלא מצר ראובן ושמעון למזרח ומצר לוי למערב ולא כתב יהודה ש"מ דלא ניחא ליה דניקני ליה מסוף מצר לוי ועד יהודה אלא כעין ראש תור ולא יותר כמו שמצויירין. ואם אותה שדה שמכר לו היו לו לראובן משני צידיה בשדות כשיעור ארכה אחת במזרח ואחת במערב וכן לשמעון אחת לצפונה ואחת לדרומה צריך למכתב ליה המוכר מצר ראובן לרוחין תרין וכו' ואי כתב ליה הכי מקנה ליה כל השדה כולה מקצה לקצה לד' רוחותיה. אבל אי לא כתב ליה אלא מצר ראובן מזרח ומערב יש לומר שמא לצד מזרח קנה כולו ולצד מערב מעט וכן נמי מצד צפון קנה כולה ומצד דרום קצת מן דרום *). ואיכא למימר דשייר בשדה מקצת: איבעיא להו סיים לו הקרנות שעל זוית אחד של שדה קרן של מצר ראובן ועל זוית אחר קרן של מצר שמעון ועל זוית שלישי קרן מצר לוי ועל זוית רביעי קרן מצר יהודה (כי האי גוונא) ולא מצר לו כל אורך השדה על פני כולה ולא כל הרוחב אלא הזווית מהו מי אמרי' הואיל דמצר ד' קרנותיה כולה מכרה לו השדה על פני כולה או דלמא כיון דלא מצר לו כל ארכה וכל רחבה אלא הקרנות לא מכר לו אלא רצועות באלכסון ההולכות מקרן לקרן ב' רצועות ולא יותר (כי האי גוונא): כמין גמא מהו. שמצר לו מצרים שתים ראובן ארכה מצד אחד ושמעון רחבה מצד אחד ולא יותר מהו מי אמרי' נותנה לו בריבוע על פני כולה או דלמא כיון שלא מצר לו אלא ב' רוחות לא קנה אלא שתי רצועות כנגד המצר (הכי). מצר לו בסירוגין

מצר לו מזרחית לפונית שהוא כמין גמא ועלתה איבעיא זו בתיקו וקי"ל כל תיקו דממונא לקולא ויד הקונה על התחתונה ואינו לוקח אלא בפחות שכך הדין שלא להוציא ממון מיד מחזיקו בספק וי"א חולקין מפני שהוא ספק וכל ספיקא דממונא חולקין ולא נתברר לנו להכריע הלכה למעשה זה פי' רבינו חננאל. ערוך ערך גם ול"ע שלא הביאו שום אחד מהפוסקים וגם תדע שפי' ר"ח כמו שפירש ר"י בתוספות ד"ה כמין גאם.

הגהות הב"ח

(א) גמ' מדהוה ליה למכתב מצר דראובן כנגד לוי (ודשמעון כנגד יהודה) תא"מ. ונ"ב גירסת התוס' היתה דשמעון כנגד יהודה ורשב"ם היה גורס במקומו דראובן כנגד לוי והמדפיס הכניס שתי הגירסות בפנים: (ב) רשב"ם ד"ה ויקנה כנגד וכו' מזרח קצר כדי כצ"ל ותיבת היינו נמחק: (ג) ד"ה היכא דאיכא כו' מדהוה ליה למכתב ראובן כנגד לוי כזה:

(ד) תוס' ד"ה מצר וכו' חצי שדה כזה:

*) הגיוריס עי' בסוף המסכתא

בְּסֵירוּגִין מַהוּ? אתֵיקוּ. מָצַר לוֹ מֶצֶר רִאשׁוֹן וּמֶצֶר שֵׁנִי וּמֶצֶר שְׁלִישִׁי, וּמֶצֶר רְבִיעִי לֹא מָצַר לוֹ — אָמַר רַב: בקָנָה הַכֹּל חוּץ מִמֶּצֶר רְבִיעִי. וּשְׁמוּאֵל אָמַר: אֲפִי' מֶצֶר רְבִיעִי. (א) וְרַב אַסִי אָמַר: לֹא קָנָה אֶלָּא תֶּלֶם אֶחָד עַל פְּנֵי כּוּלָּהּ; סָבַר לָהּ כְּרַב, דַּאֲמַר: שִׁיּוּרֵי שַׁיֵּיר, וּמִדְּשַׁיֵּיר בְּמֶצֶר — שַׁיֵּיר נַמִי (ב) בְּכוּלְּהִי. אֲמַר רָבָא, הִלְכְתָא: קָנָה הַכֹּל חוּץ מִמֶּצֶר רְבִיעִי. וְלָא אֲמַרַן אֶלָּא דְּלָא מִבְלַע, אֲבָל מִבְלַע — קָנָה. וְכִי לָא מִבְלַע נַמִי — לָא אֲמַרַן אֶלָּא דְּאִיכָּא עֲלֵיהּ רִיכְבָּא דְּדִיקְלָא וְהָוֵי תִּשְׁעַת קַבִּין, אֲבָל לֵיכָּא עֲלֵיהּ רִיכְבָּא דְּדִיקְלָא, וְלָא הָוֵי תִּשְׁעַת קַבִּין — (ג) קָנָה. מִכְּלָל דְּכִי מוּבְלָע, אע"ג דְּאִיכָּא עֲלֵיהּ רִיכְבָּא דְּדִיקְלָא וְהָוֵי תִּשְׁעַת קַבִּין — (ד) קָנָה. אִיכָּא דְּאָמְרִי: אֲמַר רָבָא, הִלְכְתָא: קָנָה הַכֹּל, וַאֲפִילּוּ מֶצֶר רְבִיעִי. וְלָא אֲמַרַן אֶלָּא דְּמִבְלַע, אֲבָל לָא מִבְלַע — לָא קָנֵי. וְכִי מִבְלַע נַמִי — לָא אֲמַרַן אֶלָּא דְּלֵיכָּא עֲלֵיהּ רִיכְבָּא דְּדִיקְלָא, וְלָא הָוֵי תִּשְׁעַת קַבִּין, אֲבָל אִיכָּא עֲלֵיהּ רִיכְבָּא דְּדִיקְלָא וְהָוֵי תִּשְׁעַת קַבִּין — לָא קָנֵה. מִכְּלָל דְּכִי לָא מוּבְלָע, אַף עַל גַּב דְּלֵיכָּא עֲלֵיהּ רִיכְבָּא דְּדִיקְלָא, וְלָא הָוֵי תִּשְׁעַת קַבִּין — לָא קָנֵי גשְׁמְעִינַן מִתַּרְוַיְיהוּ לִישָּׁנֵי דְּרָבָא, דִּבְשָׂדֶה לָא שַׁיֵּיר וְלָא מִידֵי. דוְשָׁמְעִינַן נַמִי, דְּהֵיכָא דְּמִבְלַע, וְלֵיכָּא עֲלֵיהּ רִיכְבָּא דְּדִיקְלָא, וְלָא הָוֵי תִּשְׁעַת קַבִּין — קָנֵה; הלָא מִבְלַע, וְאִיכָּא עֲלֵיהּ רִיכְבָּא דְּדִיקְלָא, וְהָוֵי ט' קַבִּין — לָא קָנֵה; מִבְלַע וְאִיכָּא עֲלֵיהּ, לָא מִבְלַע וְלֵיכָּא עֲלֵיהּ — אִתְּמַר לָהּ לְהַאי גִּיסָא וְאִתְּמַר לָהּ לְהַאי גִּיסָא, א)ושׁוּדָא דְּדַיָּינֵי.§ אֲמַר רַבָּה: ז"פַּלְגָא דְּאִית לִי בְּאַרְעָא" — פַּלְגָא, "פַּלְגָא בְּאַרְעָא דְּאִית לִי" — רִיבְעָא. א"ל אַבַּיֵי: מַאי שְׁנָא הָכִי וּמ"ש הָכִי? אִישְׁתִּיק. אֲמַר אַבַּיֵי: אֲנָא סְבַרִי, מִדְּאִישְׁתִּיק קַבּוּלֵי קַבְּלָהּ; וְלָא הִיא, חֲזֵינָא הָנְהוּ שְׁטָרֵי דְּנָפְקִי מִבֵּי מָר, וּכְתִיב בְּהוּ הָכִי: "פַּלְגָא דְּאִית לִי בְּאַרְעָא" — פַּלְגָא, "פַּלְגָא בְּאַרְעָא דְּאִית לִי" — רִיבְעָא. וַאֲמַר רַבָּה: "מְצַר אַרְעָא דְּמִינָּהּ (ה) פַּלְגָא" — פַּלְגָא, "מְצַר אַרְעָא דְּמִינָּהּ פְּסִיקָא" — ט' קַבִּין. א"ל אַבַּיֵי: מַאי שְׁנָא הָכִי וּמ"ש הָכִי? אִישְׁתִּיק. סְבוּר מִינָּהּ: אִידִי וְאִידִי פַּלְגָא,

ולא

רשב"ם

בְּסֵירוּגִין מַהוּ. כְּגוֹן שֶׁהָיוּ מַקִּיפִין אוֹתוֹ שְׁמוֹנָה בְּנֵי אָדָם, שְׁנַיִם לְכָל רוּחַ: רְאוּבֵן וְשִׁמְעוֹן מִן הַמִּזְרָח, לֵוִי וִיהוּדָה מִן הַצָּפוֹן, יִשָּׂשכָר וּזְבוּלוּן מִן הַמַּעֲרָב, יוֹסֵף וּבִנְיָמִין מִן הַדָּרוֹם. וְכָתַב: רְאוּבֵן מֶצֶר מִזְרָח, לֵוִי מֶצֶר צָפוֹן, יִשָּׂשכָר מֶצֶר מַעֲרָב, יוֹסֵף מֶצֶר דָּרוֹם. אִם תִּמְצָא לוֹמַר כְּמִין גַּאם לֹא קָנָה אֶלָּא בָּאֲלַכְסוֹן — הַיְינוּ מִשּׁוּם דְּדֶרֶךְ לִמְכּוֹר תֶּלֶם אֶחָד בֵּין ב' שָׂדוֹת, אֲבָל אֵין דֶּרֶךְ לִמְכּוֹר בְּסֵירוּגִין. וְרַגְלַיִם לַדָּבָר, דְּטוֹרַח הָיָה לוֹ לִכְתּוֹב כּוּלָּם, וְדִלְגַם בְּסֵירוּגִין לִיתֵּן מֶצֶר בְּכָל ד' רוּחוֹת. אוֹ דִּלְמָא ה"נ לֹא מָכַר אֶלָּא כְּנֶגֶד אוֹתָן שֶׁל מֶצֶר, וּבַאֲלַכְסוֹן, כָּזֶה:

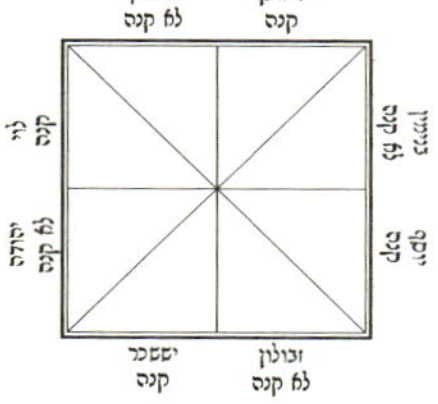

קָנָה הַכֹּל. כָּל מַה שֶּׁמּוּבְלָע בְּתוֹךְ ג' הַמְּצָרִים. חוּץ מִמֶּצֶר ד'. הַתֶּלֶם עַצְמוֹ שֶׁל מֶצֶר רְבִיעִי לֹא קָנָה, דִּלְהָכִי אַהֲנֵי מַאי דְּלֹא כָּתַב מֶצֶר רְבִיעִי. **אֲפִילּוּ** מֶצֶר רְבִיעִי. דְּהַאי דְּלָא כְּתָבֵיהּ — מִשּׁוּם דְּלֹא צָרִיךְ. **תֶּלֶם אֶחָד עַל פְּנֵי כּוּלָּהּ.** אֵצֶל ג' הַמְּצָרִים, כְּמִין חי"ת. **סָבַר לָהּ.** רַב אַסִי כְּרַב, דְּאָמַר דְּהַאי דְּלָא כְּתָבֵיהּ — מִשּׁוּם דְּשִׁיּוּרֵי שַׁיֵּיר לְעַצְמוֹ מִן הַשָּׂדֶה. וַעֲדִיפָא דְּרַב אַסִי מִדְּרַב, דְּקָסָבַר רַב אַסִי: מִדְּשַׁיְּירֵיהּ לַמֶּצֶר — שַׁיְּירֵיהּ נַמִי לְכוּלָּהּ שָׂדֶה שֶׁכְּנֶגֶד הַמֶּצֶר. וּמִיהוּ, אַהֲנֵי ג' מְצָרִים שֶׁכָּתַב לִקְנוֹת פּוּרְתָּא, דְּהַיְינוּ תֶּלֶם אֶחָד אֵצֶל הַמְּצָרִים. **וְלָא אֲמָרַן.** דְּלֹא קָנָה מֶצֶר רְבִיעִי אֶלָּא דְּלָא מִבְלַע בְּתוֹךְ שְׁנֵי הַמְּצָרִים שֶׁמִּכָּאן וּמִכָּאן, אֶלָּא הוֹלֵךְ עַל פְּנֵי שְׁנֵיהֶם, כָּזֶה:

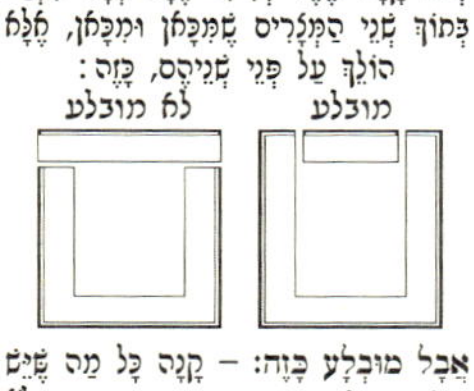

אֲבָל מוּבְלָע כָּזֶה: — קָנָה כָּל מַה שֶּׁיֵּשׁ בְּתוֹךְ הַמְּצָרִים. הָכִי גָּרְסִינַן: וְכִי לֹא מוּבְלָע נַמִי לֹא אֲמָרַן אֶלָּא בִּדְאִיכָּא עֲלֵיהּ רִיכְבָּא דְּדִיקְלָא וְהָוֵי תִּשְׁעַת קַבִּין אֲבָל לֵיכָּא עֲלֵיהּ רִיכְבָּא דְּדִיקְלָא וְלָא הָוֵי תִּשְׁעַת קַבִּין אַף עַל גַּב דְּלָא מוּבְלָע נַמִי קָנָה מִכְּלָל דְּכִי מוּבְלָע אע"ג דְּאִיכָּא עֲלֵיהּ רִיכְבָּא דְּדִיקְלָא וְהָוֵי ט' קַבִּין קָנֵה. וְאַמַּאי דְּקָאָמַר רָבָא בְּהֶדְיָא "חוּץ מִמֶּצֶר רְבִיעִי" קָאֵי, וְאוֹקְמָהּ בִּדְלֹא מוּבְלָע, וְקָמְפָרֵשׁ: וְכִי לֹא מוּבְלָע נַמִי דַּאֲמָרַן לֹא קָנָה — לֹא אֲמָרַן אֶלָּא דְּאִיכָּא עֲלֵיהּ הַרְכָּבַת דְּקָלִים הַנְּטוּעִים שָׁם, אִי נַמִי, דְּהָוֵי הַהוּא מֶצֶר תִּשְׁעַת קַבִּין כְּשִׁיעוּר שָׂדֶה בְּפֶרֶק רִאשׁוֹן (לעיל דף יא.), דְּכֵיוָן דַּחֲשִׁיב — שַׁיְּירֵיהּ לְעַצְמוֹ. וְקָדַיֵּיק גְּמָרָא: מִכְּלַל דִּבְרֵי דְּרָבָא אָנוּ לְמֵדִים, מִדְּאוֹקְמֵיהּ לְהַאי "חוּץ מִמֶּצֶר רְבִיעִי" בְּתַרְתֵּי לְרֵיעוּתָא, בִּדְלֹא מוּבְלָע וּכְגוֹן דְּאִיכָּא עֲלֵיהּ רִיכְבָּא דְּדִיקְלֵי — מִכְּלָל דְּאִי מוּבְלָע, אע"ג דְּאִיכָּא עֲלֵיהּ רִיכְבָּא דְּדִיקְלֵי — קָנֶה, דְּלֵיכָּא אֶלָּא חֲדָא לְרֵיעוּתָא. **אִיכָּא דְּאָמְרִי** כו' וַאֲפִי' מֶצֶר רְבִיעִי וְלֹא אֲמָרַן אֶלָּא דְּמִיבְלַע אֲבָל לֹא מִיבְלַע לֹא קָנֵי וְכִי מִיבְלַע נַמִי לֹא אֲמָרַן אֶלָּא דְּלֵיכָּא עֲלֵיהּ רִיכְבָּא דְּדִיקְלָא וְלֹא הָוֵי תִּשְׁעַת קַבִּין אֲבָל אִיכָּא כו' אע"ג דְּמִיבְלַע נַמִי לֹא קָנֶה מִכְּלָל דְּכִי לֹא מִיבְלַע אע"ג דְּלֵיכָּא עֲלֵיהּ כו' לֹא קָנֵי. ה"ג לָהּ. וְהָכִי פֵּירוּשָׁא: מִדְּאוֹקְמֵיהּ רָבָא לְהַאי "וַאֲפִי' מֶצֶר רְבִיעִי" בְּתַרְתֵּי לְטִיבוּתָא, בִּדְמִיבְלַע וְלֵיכָּא עֲלֵיהּ — מִכְּלָל דְּאִי לֹא מִיבְלַע, אע"ג דְּלֵיכָּא עֲלֵיהּ כו' — לֹא קָנָה, מִשּׁוּם דְּאִיכָּא חֲדָא לְרֵיעוּתָא. וְקָפָסֵיק גְּמָרָא: וְשָׁמְעִינַן מֵהָנֵי תְּרֵי לִישָּׁנֵי דְּרָבָא כו'. דְּאע"ג דִּפְלִיגֵי כִּדְלְקַמָּן, בְּהָכִי מִיהָא לֹא פְּלִיגֵי. וְכֵן הֲלָכָה, דְּהַקַּרְקַע לֹא שַׁיֵּיר אֶלָּא בְּמֶצֶר רְבִיעִי, דְּהַיְינוּ כְּרַב. וְהֵיכָא דְּמִיבְלַע וְלֵיכָּא עֲלֵיהּ — קָנֶה, דְּאִיכָּא תַּרְתֵּי לְטִיבוּתָא. וְהֵיכָא דְּלֹא מִיבְלַע וְאִיכָּא עֲלֵיהּ כו' — לֹא קָנָה, דְּאִיכָּא תַּרְתֵּי לְרֵיעוּתָא. מִיבְלַע וְאִיכָּא עֲלֵיהּ, א"נ לֹא מִיבְלַע וְלֵיכָּא עֲלֵיהּ, דְּהַיְינוּ חֲדָא לְטִיבוּתָא וַחֲדָא לְרֵיעוּתָא — אָמְרֵי לָהּ בִּתְרֵי לִישָּׁנֵי וְאִיפְּכָא דְּרָבָא, לְלִישָּׁנָא קַמָּא — קָנֶה, לְלִישָּׁנָא בַּתְרָא — לֹא קָנָה. וְקָפָסֵיק גְּמָרָא: שׁוּדָא דְּדַיָּינֵי הִלְכְתָא הַדַּיָּינִין. מֵאַחַר דְּמִסְפְּקָא לַן — נַעֲבִיד שׁוּדָא, הַכֹּל לְפִי הָעִנְיָן שֶׁיִּרְאוּ הַדַּיָּינִין וְיַכִּירוּ הַמּוֹכֵר, עֵינוֹ יָפָה אוֹ רָעָה, הַכֹּל לְפִי אוֹמֶד דַּעְתָּם. וּמִיהוּ, בִּשְׁאָר מְקוֹמוֹת דְּמִסְפְּקָא לָן בִּתְרֵי לִישָּׁנֵי הִלְכְתָא כְּמַאן — לֹא אָמְרִינַן שׁוּדָא דְּדַיָּינֵי עַד שֶׁיִּפָּרֵשׁ כִּי הָכָא, אֶלָּא הַמּע"ה. **אָמַר רַבָּה.** רְאוּבֵן וְשִׁמְעוֹן שֶׁהָיָה לָהֶם שָׂדֶה בְּשׁוּתָּפוּת, וּמָכַר רְאוּבֵן אֶת חֶלְקוֹ לְאִינִישׁ מֵעָלְמָא וְכָתַב לוֹ כֵּן "פַּלְגָא דְּאִית לִי בְּאַרְעָא", כְּלוֹמַר: הַחֲצִי שֶׁיֵּשׁ לִי בְּשָׂדֶה זוֹ אֲנִי מוֹכֵר לְךָ. **פַּלְגָא.** כְּלוֹמַר, כָּל חֲצִי הַשָּׂדֶה מָכַר, וְלֹא שַׁיֵּיר לְעַצְמוֹ כְּלוּם. אֲבָל אִם כָּתַב לוֹ "פַּלְגָא בְּאַרְעָא דְּאִית לִי אֲנִי מוֹכֵר לְךָ". **רִיבְעָא.** זָבִין לֵיהּ רְבִיעַ הַשָּׂדֶה, דְּהַיְינוּ חֲצִי חֶלְקוֹ. דְּהָכִי קָאָמַר לֵיהּ: הַחֲצִי אֲנִי מוֹכֵר לְךָ מִקַּרְקַע שֶׁלִּי. נִמְצָא מֵחֲצִי הַשָּׂדֶה שֶׁיֵּשׁ לוֹ מָכַר הַחֲצִי, דְּהַיְינוּ רְבִיעַ כָּל הַשָּׂדֶה. **א"ל אַבַּיֵי מַאי שְׁנָא הָכִי כו'.** כִּי הֵיכִי דְּ"פַלְגָא דְּאִית לִי בְּאַרְעָא" פַּלְגָא — הָכִי נַמִי "פַּלְגָא בְּאַרְעָא דְּאִית לִי" פַּלְגָא! דְּהָכִי מַשְׁמַע: פַּלְגָא אֲנִי מוֹכֵר לְךָ בְּאוֹתָהּ אַרְעָא. וְהַאי דִּמְסַיֵּים "דְּאִית לִי" — אַמַּאי דְּקָאָמַר "פַּלְגָא" קָאֵי, כְּלוֹמַר: אוֹתוֹ חֲצִי שֶׁיֵּשׁ לִי אֲמַרְתִּי לְךָ לִמְכּוֹר. **מִבֵּי מָר.** רַבָּה, (ו) וּכְתִיב הָכִי בְּהָנְהוּ שְׁטָרֵי מְכִירָה: פַּלְגָא דְּאִית לִי בְּאַרְעָא — פַּלְגָא כו'. כְּלוֹמַר, אוֹתוֹ שְׁטָר שֶׁהָיָה כָּתוּב בְּרֹאשׁוֹ: אֵיךְ פְּלוֹנִי אָמַר לָנוּ "הֱווּ (ז) עֵדִים שֶׁאֲנִי מוֹכֵר לִפְלוֹנִי פַּלְגָא דְּאִית לִי בְּאַרְעָא" — הָיָה מוֹכִיחַ בְּסוֹפוֹ שֶׁפַּלְגָא הָיָה מוֹכֵר לוֹ, שֶׁכָּךְ הָיָה כָּתוּב: וְקָנָה פְּלוֹנִי מִן פְּלוֹנִי חֲצִי הַשָּׂדֶה בְּכָךְ וְכָךְ מָמוֹן. וְאוֹתוֹ שֶׁכָּתוּב בּוֹ "פַּלְגָא בְּאַרְעָא דְּאִית לִי" — הָיָה מְפָרֵשׁ בְּסוֹף הַשְּׁטָר שֶׁהִקְנָה לָזֶה הַלּוֹקֵחַ רְבִיעַ הַשָּׂדֶה. **מֶצֶר אַרְעָא** דְּמִינָּהּ פַּלְגָא **פַּלְגָא.** רְאוּבֵן שֶׁהָיָה לוֹ שָׂדֶה, וּמָכַר מִקְצָתוֹ לְשִׁמְעוֹן לְצַד מַעֲרָב, וּמִצַּד מִזְרָח עִכֵּב לְעַצְמוֹ, וְלֹא פֵּירֵשׁ כַּמָּה מָכַר וְכַמָּה שַׁיֵּיר לְעַצְמוֹ, אֶלָּא כָּךְ כָּתַב הַמְּצָרִים: שָׂדֶה פְּלוֹנִי שֶׁאֲנִי מוֹכֵר לִפְלוֹנִי, מִצַּד מַעֲרָב לֵוִי, וּמִצַּד מִזְרָח אַרְעָא דְּמִינָּהּ פַּלְגָא — הַקַּרְקַע עַצְמָהּ שֶׁהָיְתָה שֶׁלִּי, שֶׁחֲלַקְתִּיהָ מִמֶּנָּה זוֹ שֶׁמָּכַרְתִּי, הוּא מֶצֶר מִזְרָחִי שֶׁלָּהּ — פַּלְגָא מָכַר לוֹ. דְּהָא קָאָמַר "דְּמִינָּהּ פַּלְגָא", דְּמַשְׁמַע חֲלוּקָה לַחֲצָאִין. דְּמִינָּהּ **פְּסִיקָא.** מַשְׁמַע: שָׂדֶה הָרְאוּיָה לִפְסוֹק מִקַּרְקַע אַחֶרֶת, דְּהַיְינוּ לְכָל הַפָּחוֹת תִּשְׁעָה קַבִּין, כִּדְתְנַן בְּפֶ' רִאשׁוֹן (לעיל יא.): אֵין חוֹלְקִין אֶת הֶחָצֵר כו'

ולא

תוספות

איתמר להאי גיסא ואיתמר להאי גיסא שודא. אע"ג דבעלמא בכל דוכתי, אמרינן: המוציא מחבירו עליו הראיה ואוקי ממונא בחזקת מריה, בין היכא דמספקא בעובדא היכי הוה, כגון לעיל (דף לג:) דאמר: דאיכא סהדי למר ואיכא סהדי למר — היכא דקיימא ארעא תיקום, בין מספקא לן בדינא, כההיא דסוף "השואל" (ב"מ דף קג:) דמוקי שמואל למתני' באחד ששכר מרחץ בבא באמצע החדש, לכך יחלוקו, דמספקא לן אי תפוס לשון ראשון או אחרון. אבל בא בתחלת החדש — כולו למשכיר, בסוף החדש — כולו לשוכר, דהמע"ה. אלא שכאן נראה לחכמים לעשות שודא. וגבי קדשה בעשרים ונתן לה ל' אלאין, בפ' "מי שמת" (לקמן דף קמה.), דמספקא לן לרבי יוסי אי קדושין לטיבועין ניתנו אי לאו, ואין מונה לה בכסף כתובה מכסף קדושין אלא מחצה, והיינו חולקין, ולא בעי למימר המע"ה, אע"ג דמכתמא לא סבר כסומכוס, דלית הלכתא הכי. ועוד, דאוקי שמואל מתני' דסוף "השואל" דאיירי בה ר' יוסי בבא באמצע החדש, היינו כרבנן דסומכוס. וכן לרב אסי בפ"ק דבבא קמא (דף ט שם) גבי אחין שחלקו ובא בעל חוב וטרף חלקו של אחד מהן, דאמרינן נוטל רביע בקרקע כו' — דמספקא ליה אי כיורשים אי כלקוחות דמו, וחולקין, ולא אמר המע"ה. וב"יש נוחלין" (לקמן דף קכד:) נמי, גבי בכור שאינו נוטל פי שנים במלוה, דהו"ל ראוי, ובמלוה שפמו אמר התם (דף קכו.) דפליג משום (ח) דהמע"ה, דמספקא לן אי גמר ומשעבד נכסיו כל כך שיהא אביו מוחזק כדי שיטול בהן פי שנים, או לא, וחולקים מספיקא. וכן (ב"מ דף פג.) דדרו באגרא ואיתבר — משלם פלגא, מאי טעמא, כפיש לחד וזוטר לתרי — קרוב לפשיעה וקרוב לאונס. בכל אלו היה נראה לחכמים שיחלוקו. והיכא דלא מפרש גמרא מידי — אית לן למימר המע"ה. והיכא דלא איתמר הלכתא לא כמר ולא כמר, וס"ל לדיין כחד מינייהו, ועבד — מאי דעבד עבד. דהכי אמר בפרק "כל הנשבעין" (שבועות דף מח:): השתא דלא איתמר לא כמר ולא כמר, דעבד כמר — עבד, ודעבד כמר — עבד. ואי מספקא לדיין כמאן הלכת' — המע"ה. **חזינא** להנהו שטרי דכתב בהו פלגא דאית לי בארעא פלגא. כלומר, היו מגבין פלגא. פלגא בארעא דאית לי ריבעא — היו מגבין אותו ריבעא.

אין

יד א מיי' פכ"א מהל' מכירה הל' עז סמג עשין פב טוש"ע ח"מ סי' ריט סעיף ז [ושודא דדיינא]:

טו ב ג ד ה ו מיי' שם הל' טו וסמג שם טוש"ע שם סעיף ב:

טז ז מיי' שם הל' כג וסמג שם טוש"ע ח"מ סי' ריח סעיף כח:

רבינו גרשום

בסירוגין מהו. כגון שהיו עומדין על המצרים ראובן ושמעון ולוי על רוח מזרחית יהודה יששכר זבולון על רוח דרומית ובנימין דן ונפתלי על רוח מערבית גד ואשר ויוסף על רוח צפונית ובין הני מצרים מכר לו שדה וכתב ליה מצר ראובן ולא כתב ליה מצר שמעון וכתב לו מצר לוי וכן לכל רוח דלג מצר האמצעי שלא כתב לו. מהו מי אמרי' הואיל דמצר לו מצר לכל רוח הכל מצר לו וקנה בריבוע כל השדה על פני כולה או לא קנה אלא כנגד המצר ד' שדות (כעין צורתו) דמאי דמצר ליה קנה ומאי דלא מצר ליה לא קנה תיקו: מצר לו מצר ראובן עד דרך שביל אחד שבמזרח ומצר שני שביל שני ומצר שלישי שביל שלישי ומצר רביעי לא כתב לו: אמר רב קנה הכל. השדה והמצר חוץ ממצר רביעי משום דשיירה ולא כתבו: אלא תלם אחד על פני כל המצרים. משלש רוחות דמצר לו סמוך למצר: כרב דאמר. שייר המצר רביעי שלא קנה וקא מוסיף רב אסי מדשייר למצר שייר לכולה שדה חוץ מתלם אחד שקנה. והני מילי דלא קנה מצר רביעי היכא דלא מובלע המצר בתוך השדה שהמצר עמוק ונמוך מן השדה או גבוה יותר מן השדה שנראה כמו שאינו מן השדה: אבל מיבלע בשדה. דהמצר שוה עם השדה דמי כשדה עצמה ומכרו: וכי מבלע נמי לא אמרן דקני. דליכא עליה דההוא מצר ריכבא. שורה של דקלים. דלא כשדה אחרת דמי ולא הוי ארוך כל כך כמקום זריעת ט' קבין דהיינו שיעור שדה קטנה: אבל אי איכא כו' לא קנה. משום דכשדה אחרת דמיא: ואיכא דאמרי כו'. ה"ג וכי לא מבלע נמי לא אמרן אלא דאיכא עליה ריכבא דדיקלא ואי נמי הוי כו' אבל ליכא עליה ריכבא ולא הוי ט' קבין קנה. דייקי' מהאי לישנא בתרא מכלל דכי מיבלע אע"ג דאיכא עליה ריכבא והוי ט' קבין קני. ושמעינן מתרוייהו לישנא דבשדה לא שייר דבמצר פליגי ולא בשדה ושמעינן נמי מתרוייהו לישני דהיכא דמיבלע וכו' קני. ושמעינן נמי מתרוייהו דהיכא דלא מיבלע ואי איכא ריכבא אי הוי ט' קבין לא קני דכשדה בפני עצמה דמיא. אבל מיבלע ואיכא עליה ריכבא איתמר להך גיסא ללישנא קמא דלא קני דכשדה בפני עצמה דמיא ואיתמר להך גיסא ללישנא בתרא דייקא מיניה דקנה. ולהיכא נמי דלא מבלע ולא איכא עליה ריכבא איתמר להך גיסא בלישנא

א) [קדושין עב. וש"נ]

רבינו גרשום

בלישנא קמא משמע דלא קנה ואיתמר להך גיסא ללישנא בתרא משמע דקנה דלאו כשדה אחרת דמיא דהואיל דליכא עליה ריכבא דדיקלי: שודא דדייני. שאם יראו ב"ד שדעתו של מוכר קרובה ללוקח שהוא אוהבו או שקרובו ומוכר לו בעין יפה יתננה לחלקו של לוקח ואם לאו למוכר: אמר רבה. אם היה בין שני שותפין קרקע ואמר אחד לאיניש דעלמא מזבינא לך פלגא דאית לי בארעא משמע דכל חלקו מקני ליה וקנה הלוקח ההוא פלגא דאית ליה כולה. אבל אמר ליה כי האי לישנא פלגא בארעא דאית לי מזבינא לך משמע דמההיא פלגא דמגיע לחלקו מזבין ליה החצי והיינו ריבעא דכולה שדה קנה: א"ל אביי. מ"ש בהאי לישנא דקנה פלגא מ"ש באידך דלא קנה אלא ריבעא: דקבולי קבלה. דאידי ואידי פלגא: מבי מר. מבי רבה: אמר רבה. אם יש לב' שותפין קרקע וחלקוה ביניהן ואמר חד מן השותפין לאחר קרקע שלי אני מוכר לך ומצר לו ללוקח מצד אחד מצר ארעא דמינה פליגא כלומר חלק שותפי שחלק עמי הוא מצר אחד ודאי אמרי' דאית ליה פלגא ללוקח שכל חלקו מכר לו עד חלק שותפו: אבל אי אמר ליה בהאי לישנא קרקע שלי אני מוכר לך ומצר לו מצר אחד בהאי לישנא לרוח פלוני ארעא דמינה פסיקא לא קנה בה הלוקח אלא שדה של ט' קבין דאמרי דהכי אמר ליה המוכר ללוקח לרוח פלוני מצר ארעא דילי דמינה פסיקא ההוא שדה דזביני לך כלומר שפסקתי מקרקע שלי שיעור שנחשב שדה ומכרתי לך והשאר שיירתי לי ולא קנה כל חלקו: א"ל אביי. מ"ש בהאי לישנא דקנה פלגא ומ"ש בהאי לישנא דלא קנה אלא ט' קבין בלבד: בין מצר ארעא. דמינה פסיקא. הכל אחד: אי א"ל ואלין מצרנהא האחרים ופירשן למזרח מצר פלוני למערב מצר פלוני וכן כולם:

הגהות הב"ח

(א) גמ' אפי' מצר רביעי קנה ורב אסי: (ב) שם שייר נמי בכולה שדה אמר רבה: (ג) שם ולא הוי ט' קבין קנה אע"ג דלא מבלע קנה מכלל דכי מובלע וכו': (ד) שם והוי ט' קבין לא קנה: (ה) שם דמינה פליגא פלגא: (ו) רשב"ם ד"ה מבי מר רבה כו' כהנהו שטרי מכירה הכי הס"ד ואח"כ מה"ד וכתיב בהו: (ז) בא"ד הוו עלי עדים: (ח) תוס' ד"ה איתמר וכו' דפליג משום דהמספקא כל"ל ותיבת דהמע"ה נמחק.

וְלָא הִיא, דַּאֲמַר רַב יֵימָר בַּר שֶׁלֶמְיָה: אלְדִידִי מְפָרְשָׁא לִי מִינֵּיהּ דְּאַבַּיֵי: בֵּין "מְצַר אַרְעָא דְּמִינָּהּ פַּלְגָא" וּבֵין "מְצַר אַרְעָא דְּמִינָּהּ פְּסִיקָא", אִי א"ל "אִלֵּין מַצְרָנָהָא" — פַּלְגָא, לָא א"ל "אִלֵּין מַצְרָנָהָא" — תִּשְׁעָה קַבִּין.§ בפְּשִׁיטָא, אֲמַר "יַחֲלוֹק פְּלוֹנִי בִּנְכָסַי" — פַּלְגָא, "תְּנוּ חֵלֶק לִפְלוֹנִי בִּנְכָסַי", מַאי? אֲמַר רָבִינָא בַּר קִיסִי: גתָּא שְׁמַע, דְּתַנְיָא: *דהָאוֹמֵר "תְּנוּ חֵלֶק לִפְלוֹנִי בְּבוֹר" — סוּמָכוֹס אוֹמֵר: אֵין פָּחוֹת מֵרְבִיעַ, "לְחָבִית" — אֵין פָּחוֹת מִשְּׁמִינִית, "לְקְדֵרָה" — אֵין פָּחוֹת מִי"ב, "לְטָפִיחַ" — אֵין פָּחוֹת מִשִּׁשָּׁה עָשָׂר. תָּנוּ רַבָּנַן: הבֶּן לֵוִי שֶׁמָּכַר שָׂדֶה לְיִשְׂרָאֵל, וְאָמַר לוֹ "עַל מְנָת שֶׁמַּעֲשֵׂר רִאשׁוֹן שֶׁלִּי" — מַעֲשֵׂר רִאשׁוֹן שֶׁלּוֹ; וְאִם אָמַר "לִי וּלְבָנַי", מֵת — יִתֵּן לְבָנָיו; וְאִם אָמַר לוֹ "כָּל זְמַן שֶׁהַשָּׂדֶה זוֹ בְּיָדְךָ", מְכָרָהּ וְחָזַר וּלְקָחָהּ — אֵין לוֹ עָלָיו כְּלוּם. אַמַּאי? ואֵין אָדָם מַקְנֶה דָּבָר שֶׁלֹּא בָּא לָעוֹלָם! זכֵּיוָן דַּאֲמַר לֵיהּ "עַל מְנָת שֶׁמַּעֲשֵׂר רִאשׁוֹן שֶׁלִּי", שִׁיּוּרֵי שַׁיְּרֵיהּ לִמְקוֹם מַעֲשֵׂר. *אָמַר רֵישׁ לָקִישׁ, חזֹאת אוֹמֶרֶת: הַמּוֹכֵר בַּיִת לַחֲבֵירוֹ, וְאָמַר לוֹ "עַל מְנָת שֶׁדְּיוֹטָא הָעֶלְיוֹנָה שֶׁלִּי" — דְּיוֹטָא הָעֶלְיוֹנָה שֶׁלּוֹ.

לְמַאי

וְלֹא אֶת הַשָּׂדֶה עַד שֶׁיְּהֵא בּוֹ ט' קַבִּין לָזֶה וְט' קַבִּין לָזֶה. "פְּסִיקָא" מַשְׁמַע: מְחוּתָּךְ מִמֶּנָּה, הַמּוּעָט מִן הַמְּרוּבֶּה. אִי אֲמַר לֵיהּ וְאִלֵּין מַצְרָנָהָא. "מֶצֶר מִזְרָח אַרְעָא דְּמִינָּהּ פַּלְגָא, מֶצֶר מַעֲרָב פְּלוֹנִי", וְכֵן הוֹלֵךְ וְחוֹשֵׁב כָּל הַמְּצָרִים. וְהִלְכָּךְ הַאי "וְאִלֵּין מַצְרָנָהָא" — יִתּוּר לָשׁוֹן הוּא, לְיַיפּוֹת כֹּחוֹ. וּלְקַמָּן בִּשְׁמַעְתִּין נַמִי חֲזִינָא יִתּוּר לָשׁוֹן טוּבָא לְיַיפּוֹת כֹּחַ. וְה"ק אַבַּיֵי לְעֵיל: מַאי שְׁנָא הָכִי וּמַאי שְׁנָא הָכִי? הֲלֹא אֵין חִילּוּק בֵּין פַּלְגָא לִפְסִיקָא. אֶלָּא, זִימְנִין אָמְרִינַן בְּתַרְוַיְיהוּ פַּלְגָא, בֵּין פַּלְגָא בֵּין פְּסִיקָא — הֵיכָא דְּאָמַר "וְאִלֵּין מַצְרָנָהָא", וְזִימְנִין (א) תִּשְׁעָה קַבִּין — הֵיכָא דְּלֹא אָמַר "וְאִלֵּין מַצְרָנָהָא". פְּשִׁיטָא. שְׁכִיב מְרַע, אוֹ כָּל הַמְחַלֵּק נְכָסָיו עַל פִּיו, שֶׁאָמַר "פְּלוֹנִי יַחֲלוֹק בִּנְכָסַי" — פַּלְגָא שָׁקֵיל. תְּנוּ חֵלֶק לִפְלוֹנִי בִּנְכָסַי מַהוּ. מִי אָמְרִינַן: הַאי "חֵלֶק" — לְשׁוֹן חֲלוּקָה הוּא, וּפַלְגָא קָשָׁקֵיל. אוֹ חֵלֶק הָרָאוּי לִיתֵּן קָאָמַר, וּבְדַעַת ב"ד תָּלוּי הַדָּבָר, לְשַׁעֵר בְּכַמָּה הָוֵי חֵלֶק רָאוּי לִיתֵּן. וְאַע"ג דְּתַנְיָא בַּתּוֹסֶפְתָּא (פרק ז) דְּהַךְ בָּבָא: הָאוֹמֵר "תְּנוּ חֵלֶק לִפְלוֹנִי בִּנְכָסַיי" יִירַשׁ עִם הַבָּנִים, אִיכָּא לְמֵימַר: הָכָא מַיְירֵי כְּגוֹן דְּלֵית לֵיהּ בָּנֵי. וְאַע"ג דְּאִית לֵיהּ יוֹרְשִׁין בְּעָלְמָא — לָא יָהֵב דַּעְתֵּיהּ לְיוֹרְשִׁין אֲחֵרִים, וְחֵלֶק הָרָאוּי לִיתֵּן אוֹ חֲצִי נְכָסִין קָאָמַר. א"נ, הָכָא מַיְירֵי כְּגוֹן דְּאָמַר "תְּנוּ חֵלֶק לִפְלוֹנִי בְּנִי בִּנְכָסַי, וְהַשְּׁאָר נְתוּנִים לִפְלוֹנִי". א"נ אִיכָּא לְמֵימַר, דְּלָא הֲוָה שְׁמִיעַ לְהוּ הַךְ בָּרַיְיתָא, דְּאִי הֲוָה שְׁמִיעַ לְהוּ — הָווּ מַיְיתֵי לָהּ בְּבֵית הַמִּדְרָשׁ. וְאִיכָּא לְמֵימַר: רַבָּנַן הִיא, דִּפְלִיגִי עֲלֵיהּ דְּסוּמָכוֹס. אִי נַמִי: שְׁמִיעָא לְהוּ וְלָא הֲוָה סְבִירָא לְהוּ, מִשּׁוּם דְּפָלֵיג סוּמָכוֹס עֲלָהּ כִּדְלְקַמָּן, וְקַיְימָא לָן כְּסוּמָכוֹס, דְּאָמַר: מָמוֹן הַמּוּטָּל בְּסָפֵק חוֹלְקִין, דִּסְתַם לָן תַּנָּא כְּוָותֵיהּ בְּפֶרֶק "שׁוֹר שֶׁנָּגַח (אַרְבָּעָה" וּבְפֶרֶק "שׁוֹר שֶׁנָּגַח) אֶת הַפָּרָה" (ב"ק דף מו.). בְּבוֹר. שֶׁל מַיִם מְכוּנָּסִים. וְאִית דְּמוֹקְמִי לָהּ בְּבוֹר שֶׁל יַיִן, וְלָא נְהִירָא. סוּמָכוֹס אוֹמֵר אֵין פָּחוֹת מֵרְבִיעַ. סוּמָכוֹס לְטַעֲמֵיהּ, דְּאָמַר בְּפֶרֶק "שׁוֹר שֶׁנָּגַח אֶת הַפָּרָה": חֲצִי נֶזֶק לַפָּרָה וּרְבִיעַ לַוָּלָד, וּמוֹקְמִינַן לָהּ בַּגְּמָרָא אַלִּיבָּא דְּסוּמָכוֹס, דְּאָמַר: מָמוֹן הַמּוּטָּל בְּסָפֵק חוֹלְקִין. וְהָכָא מְסַפְּקִינַן לֵיהּ אִי פַּלְגָא קָאָמַר אוֹ חֵלֶק בְּעָלְמָא מַשֶּׁהוּ קָאָמַר, כְּגוֹן רְבִיעִית הַלּוֹג, הִלְכָּךְ אֵין לוֹ לַמְקַבֵּל מַתָּנָה מִן הַבּוֹר פָּחוֹת מֵרְבִיעַ, (ג) וְשֶׁמָּא יוֹתֵר. מִשּׁוּם דְּאִילּוּ הֲוָה מְסַפְּקָא לָן בְּהַאי נוֹתֵן אִם נָתַן לוֹ פַּלְגָא אוֹ לֹא כְּלוּם — הָיָה לוֹ לִיטּוֹל (ג) מַחֲצִית שֶׁל פַּלְגָא, דְּהַיְינוּ רְבִיעַ הַבּוֹר, מִשּׁוּם מָמוֹן הַמּוּטָּל בְּסָפֵק חוֹלְקִין, דְּהָא פַּלְגָא נַמִי מוּטֶּלֶת בְּסָפֵק אִם יְהָבָהּ לֵיהּ אוֹ לֹא, הִלְכָּךְ יִטּוֹל חֶצְיָהּ שֶׁל פַּלְגָא דְּהַיְינוּ רְבִיעַ. וְכ"שׁ הַשְׁתָּא, דִּמְסַפְּקָא לָן אִי יָהֵיב פַּלְגָא אוֹ רְבִיעִית הַלּוֹג — דְּלֹא יִטּוֹל פָּחוֹת מֵרְבִיעַ. וְרַבֵּינוּ חֲנַנְאֵל פֵּירֵשׁ דְּאָחוּדָא סוּמָכוֹס לְטַעֲמֵיהּ, וְכָל הָנָךְ שִׁיעוּרֵי דִּלְקַמָּן לְחָבִית לִקְדֵירָה לְטָפִיחַ — בְּקִיאִין הָיוּ בְּשִׁיעוּרִין הַלָּלוּ כַּמָּה צָרִיךְ לְכָל אֶחָד, וּפַלְגָא דְּהַהוּא שִׁיעוּרָא קָמְחַיֵּיב סוּמָכוֹס לִיתֵּן, מִשּׁוּם דְּמָמוֹן הַמּוּטָּל בְּסָפֵק חוֹלְקִין. לְחָבִית אֵין פָּחוֹת מִשְּׁמוֹנָה. כְּלוֹמַר, אִם אָמַר: תְּנוּ חֵלֶק לִפְלוֹנִי בַּבּוֹר לְחָבִית — כְּדֵי לְמַלְּאוֹת חָבִית, דְּהַיְינוּ לְהַשְׁקָאַת בְּהֶמְתּוֹ וְלֹא לְהַשְׁקוֹת שְׂדוֹתָיו (ד). אֵין פָּחוֹת מִשְּׁמוֹנָה. בַּבּוֹר, מִשּׁוּם דַּחֲצִי הַבּוֹר צָרִיךְ לְחָבִית. וְכִי קָאָמַר "חֵלֶק" — דִּלְמָא פַּלְגָא דְּחָבִית קָאָמַר, דְּהַיְינוּ רְבִיעַ הַבּוֹר, אוֹ מַשֶּׁהוּ קָאָמַר. הִלְכָּךְ יֵשׁ לוֹ חֲצִי רְבִיעַ, דְּהַיְינוּ אֶחָד מִשְּׁמוֹנָה. וּבְשִׁיטָה זוֹ יֵשׁ לְפָרֵשׁ כּוּלָּם. לִקְדֵירָה. תְּנוּ חֵלֶק לִפְלוֹנִי בַּבּוֹר, לְתַקֵּן מַאֲכָלוֹ. אֵין פָּחוֹת מִי"ב. דְּהַיְינוּ רְבִיעַ, שִׁיעוּר הָרָאוּי לִקְדֵירָה. מִשּׁוּם דִּלְמָא פַּלְגָא קָאָמַר, וּמָמוֹן הַמּוּטָּל בְּסָפֵק חוֹלְקִין. לְטָפִיחַ. כְּלִי קָטָן לִשְׁתּוֹת בּוֹ בְּנֵי אָדָם. וְהַאי שִׁיעוּרָא זוּטַר מִכּוּלְּהוּ. וְהִלְכָּךְ, גַּבֵּי "תְּנוּ חֵלֶק לִפְלוֹנִי בִּנְכָסַי" יִטּוֹל רְבִיעַ — דְּדִלְמָא פַּלְגָא קָאָמַר, אוֹ דִּלְמָא שָׁוֶה פְּרוּטָה קָאָמַר, וּמָמוֹן הַמּוּטָּל בְּסָפֵק חוֹלְקִין. וְאִית דִּמְפָרְשֵׁי כָּל הָנָךְ שִׁיעוּרֵי לְפִי אוֹמֶד הַדַּעַת: אֵין פָּחוֹת מֵרְבִיעַ — דִּסְתָם נוֹתֵן דַּעְתּוֹ לִרְבִיעַ, אֵין פָּחוֹת מִשְּׁמוֹנָה — דְּהָכִי הָוֵי שִׁיעוּר לְמִלּוּי חָבִית לְהַשְׁקָאַת בְּהֵמוֹת, וְכֵן כּוּלָּם. וְלֹא נְהִירָא לִי. בֶּן לֵוִי שֶׁמָּכַר. אוֹרְחָא דְּמִילְּתָא נָקַט, דְּדֶרֶךְ בֶּן לֵוִי הַמּוֹכֵר שָׂדוֹת לְיִשְׂרָאֵל לְהַתְנוֹת כָּךְ, מִשּׁוּם דְּלֹא מוֹזִיל גַּבֵּיהּ מִשּׁוּם הַאי תְּנָאי מִידֵי, דְּזֶה נֶהֱנֶה וְזֶה אֵינוֹ חָסֵר, דִּבְלָאו הָכִי הֲוָה יָהֵיב הַאי לוֹקֵחַ לְהַאי מַעֲשֵׂר לוֹ אוֹ לְאַחֵר, דְּהָא אֵין לוֹ בּוֹ אֶלָּא טוֹבַת הֲנָאָה. וְהוּא הַדִּין לְיִשְׂרָאֵל הַמּוֹכֵר שָׂדֵהוּ לַחֲבֵירוֹ, וְאָמַר לוֹ: עַל מְנָת שֶׁהַמַּעֲשֵׂר שֶׁלִּי הוּא לִיתְּנוֹ לְכָל מִי שֶׁאֶרְצֶה, דְּהָא הַשְׁתָּא נַמִי יֵשׁ לוֹ בּוֹ טוֹבַת הֲנָאָה זוֹ. מַעֲשֵׂר רִאשׁוֹן שֶׁלּוֹ. וּכְדִמְפָרֵשׁ לְקַמָּן, דְּכֵיוָן דְּאֵין אָדָם קוֹנֶה דָּבָר שֶׁלֹּא בָּא לָעוֹלָם — שִׁיּוּרֵי שַׁיֵּיר מְקוֹם מַעֲשֵׂר. הִלְכָּךְ מַעֲשֵׂר רִאשׁוֹן שֶׁלּוֹ, וַאֲפִילּוּ אִם מְכָרָהּ הַלּוֹקֵחַ לְאַחֵר. דִּזְכוּתוֹ שֶׁל לֵוִי אֵינוֹ יָכוֹל לִמְכּוֹר לְאַחֵר, וְהָכִי מוּכָח לְקַמָּן. יִתֵּן לְבָנָיו אַחֲרָיו. אֲבָל אִם לֹא פֵּירֵשׁ כֵּן — אֵינוֹ מוֹרִישׁ בְּדָבָר זֶה זְכוּתוֹ לְבָנָיו. דְּכֵיוָן דְּמִשּׁוּם יִתּוּר לָשׁוֹן הוּא דְּאָמְרִינַן לְקַמָּן דְּשַׁיֵּיר מְקוֹם מַעֲשֵׂר — דַּי לָנוּ אִי אַהֲנֵי יִתּוּרָא לְמַאי שֶׁפֵּירֵשׁ, דְּהַיְינוּ לְעַצְמוֹ. אֵין לוֹ עָלָיו כְּלוּם. דְּמִשֶּׁמְּכָרָהּ לְאַחֵר פָּקַע לֵיהּ מְקוֹם הַמַּעֲשֵׂר שֶׁשִּׁיֵּיר לְעַצְמוֹ, וּכְשֶׁחָזַר וּלְקָחָהּ מַה מָּכַר לוֹ רִאשׁוֹן לַשֵּׁנִי — כָּל זְכוּת שֶׁבָּאָה לְיָדוֹ, דְּכִי הֵיכִי דְּהַהוּא לוֹקֵחַ שֵׁנִי זָכָה אֲפִילּוּ בִּמְקוֹם מַעֲשֵׂר — הוּא הַדִּין לָזֶה הַלּוֹקֵחַ רִאשׁוֹן הַבָּא מִכֹּחוֹ. אַמַּאי. מַעֲשֵׂר רִאשׁוֹן שֶׁלּוֹ? הָא אֵין אָדָם מַקְנֶה כו' (כְּרַבָּנַן דְּר"מ)! מַעֲשֵׂר זֶה עֲדַיִין עָתִיד לִיזָּרַע הַתְּבוּאָה שֶׁיֵּצֵא מִמֶּנּוּ, אַף לֵיחָרֵשׁ הַשָּׂדֶה תְּחִלָּה. כֵּיוָן דְּאָמַר לֵיהּ ע"מ כו'. כְּלוֹמַר, כֵּיוָן דְּעַל תְּנַאי מָכַר — רוֹצֶה הוּא שֶׁיִּתְקַיֵּים הַתְּנַאי, דְּאֵין אָדָם מַתְנֶה עַל חִנָּם, וּלְדַעַת כֵּן מָכַר — שֶׁיִּקְנֶה הַמַּעֲשֵׂר, וְהִלְכָּךְ שִׁיֵּיר בְּיָדוֹ קַרְקַע הָרָאוּי לִיגָּדֵל בָּהּ הַמַּעֲשֵׂר, וּכְמִי שֶׁאָמַר לוֹ: שָׂדֶה שֶׁלִּי אֲנִי מוֹכֵר לְךָ לַאֲרִיסוּת ע"מ שֶׁתִּטּוֹל ט' חֲלָקִים וַאֲנִי אֶטּוֹל חֵלֶק עֲשִׂירִי. וְיֵשׁ סְפָרִים דְּגָרְסִי' בְּהוּ בְּהֶדְיָא: כֵּיוָן דְּא"ל "ע"מ שֶׁמַּעֲשֵׂר רִאשׁוֹן שֶׁלִּי" כו'. וְאִית דִּמְפָרְשִׁים דְּיִיתּוּר לְשׁוֹן דְּע"מ קָא דָּיֵיק, וְכִדְאָמְרִינַן בְּעָלְמָא (קדושין ח.): כָּל הָאוֹמֵר ע"מ — כְּאוֹמֵר "מֵעַכְשָׁיו" דָּמֵי. וְא"א לְהַעֲמִיד שִׁיטַת שְׁמוּעָה זוֹ כֵּן. וּבְפ' "מִי שֶׁמֵּת" (לקמן דף קמח.) אָמְרִי' דְּאִם מָכַר דֶּקֶל וְאָמַר לוֹ "חוּץ מִפֵּירוֹתָיו" — דְּשַׁיֵּיר מְקוֹם פֵּירוֹתָיו. וְה"נ אִם אָמַר "חוּץ מִן הַמַּעֲשֵׂר" — שַׁיֵּיר מְקוֹם מַעֲשֵׂר. הִלְכָּךְ לָאו בִּלְשׁוֹן דְּע"מ תַּלְיָא מִילְּתָא, אֶלָּא כֵּיוָן דְּמַתְנֵי, וְהַתְּנַאי אֵינוֹ מוֹעִיל אֶלָּא ע"י שִׁיּוּר — אָמְרִינַן דְּשַׁיֵּיר מָקוֹם. אָמַר ר"ל זֹאת אוֹמֶרֶת. בָּרַיְיתָא זוֹ, דְּאַשְׁמְעִינַן דְּכָל תְּנַאי שֶׁאֵינוֹ לֹא מַעֲלֶה וְלֹא מוֹרִיד אא"כ שַׁיֵּיר, אָמְרִינַן: שִׁיּוּרֵי שַׁיֵּיר מָקוֹם לְעַצְמוֹ פּוּרְתָּא — מִינָּהּ שָׁמְעִינַן דְּהַמּוֹכֵר בַּיִת לַחֲבֵירוֹ וְאָמַר לוֹ "ע"מ שֶׁהַדְּיוֹטָא הָעֶלְיוֹנָה שֶׁלִּי" — הַדְּיוֹטָא הָעֶלְיוֹנָה שֶׁלּוֹ. הוּא גַּג שֶׁיֵּשׁ לוֹ מַעֲקֶה גָּבוֹהַּ י', דְּאָמְרִינַן בְּמַתְנִיתִין דְּאֵינוֹ מָכוּר עִם הַבַּיִת. וּתְנַאי זֶה אֵינוֹ מוֹעִיל, דִּבְלָאו הָכִי נַמִי הֲרֵי הוּא שֶׁל מוֹכֵר, כִּדְקָתָנֵי בְּמַתְנִיתִין: וְלֹא אֶת הַגַּג כו', וְלֹא הָיָה צָרִיךְ לְהַתְנוֹת, הִלְכָּךְ דְּיוֹטָא הָעֶלְיוֹנָה שֶׁלּוֹ לְהוֹצָאַת זִיזִין כְּנֶגֶד רְשׁוּתוֹ שֶׁל לוֹקֵחַ, כִּדְמְפָרֵשׁ וְאָזֵיל. הוּא הַדִּין אִם אָמַר לוֹ "חוּץ מִדְּיוֹטָא הָעֶלְיוֹנָה" דְּשַׁיֵּיר מָקוֹם בֶּחָצֵר לְהוֹצָאַת זִיזִין, וְאַלִּיבָּא דְּרַב זְבִיד כִּדְאָמְרִינַן בְּפֶרֶק "מִי שֶׁמֵּת".

לְמַאי

אין פחות מרביע. דמספקא לן אי רוצה לומר חצי או כל שהוא. וא"ת: ומה מתנה היא דכל שהוא? וי"ל: דנותן רביעית הלוג או יותר, אבל הגמרא אינו חושש להזכיר זה. פסק רבינו שמואל (ה) בשמעתין דכל דאלים גבר, דהלכה כסומכוס. ונראה דאין הלכה כסומכוס, כמו שפירשתי ב"חזקת הבתים" (לעיל דף לה. ד"ה ומאי).

על מנת שמעשר ראשון שלי כו'. הכא לא הוי כמו כהן המסייע בבית הגרנות (קדושין ו:), דקאמר: מקום המעשר שיורי שייר, והוי מעשר שלו לגמרי, אלא שמכר לו כח זה שיוכל לעשר על חלקו.

ואמאי והא אין אדם מקנה דבר שלא בא לעולם. [לא] הוה מצי לשנויי: ר"מ היא, דכי אמר ר"מ — כגון פירות דקל דעבידי דאתו, שהדקל בעולם והפירות גדלים מאליהן, אבל הכא — מי יימר דחרש וזרע ליה? ואפילו חרש וזרע — שמא לא תגדל התבואה. כדאמרינן בפרק "האומר" בקדושין (דף סב:), אמר רבה: לא אמר ר"א בן יעקב אלא בשחת, שכבר גדלו הזרעים קצת, אבל אגם, שהן עדיין קטנים — לא, *(ורבא) אמר: אפי' באגם, מ"מ תרוייהו מודו דהיכא דאין ניכרים כלל ולא יצאו חוץ לקרקע — דלא קני. ורבינו יצחק פירש דלא מצי מוקי לה כר' מאיר, דאפילו ר"מ מודה דכל דבר שאינו בעולם דלא קנה, כדאמרינן פרק קמא דגיטין (דף יג:), והכא קתני: ואם אמר "לי ולבניי", מת — נותן לבניו. ואין נראה לר"י טעם זה, דשמא לבניו שהן בעולם קאמר.

על מנת שדיוטא עליונה שלי כו'. שאם רוצה להוציא זיזין — מועיל. פי' הקונטרס: להוציא זיזין לחצר. וקשה לר"ת: הא לא איירי הכא במכירת החצר, אלא במכירת בית, והמוכר בית לא מכר חצר! ומפרש ר"ת: להוציא בה זיזין, אם הוא בונה בנין בחצר ורוצה להניח על גבי דיוטא את הזיזין — מניח, אע"פ שמכביד את הכותל.

שאם

יז א מיי' פכ"ח מהל' מכירה הל' כג סמג עשין פב טוש"ע ח"מ סי' ריט סעיף ו:

יח ב ג מיי' פי"א מהל' זכייה ומתנה הל' ז ועי' בהשגות ובכ"מ סמג עשין סב טוש"ע ח"מ סי' רנג סעיף כד:

יט ד מיי' שם הל' ח טוש"ע שם סעיף כה:

כ ה מיי' פ"ז מהלכות מעשר הלכה יט:

כא ו מיי' פכ"ב מהל' מכירה הל' ח סמג עשין פב טוש"ע ח"מ סי' רט סעיף ד:

כב ז מיי' פ"ז מהלכות מעשר הלכה יט:

כג ח מיי' פכ"ד מהל' מכירה הל' יד סמג עשין פב טוש"ע ח"מ סי' ריד סעיף ח:

[שם איתא רב יוסף]

[בערוך ערך בור נכון ומרוות על ברייתא זו]

לקמן [סז.] קמח.

רבינו גרשום

בין א"ל מצר ארעא דמינה פסיקא ובין א"ל מצר ארעא דמינה פלגא. משמע חד לישנא וקנה כל חלקו הואיל וייחד לו מצרים אבל להיכא דלא פירש לו מצרנים בין אמר ליה ארעא דמינה פלגא ובין אמר ליה ארעא דמינה פסיקא הואיל ולא פירש לן שאר מצרנים לא קנה אלא ט' קבין שיעור שדה לחוד דאידי ואידי חדא לישנא הוא: הא פשיטא לי. אם אמר חד שכיב מרע יחלוק פלוני בנכסי ודאי פלגא יהבי' ליה. אבל אי אמר בהאי לישנא תנו חלק לפלוני בנכסי מהו. כמה יהבי' ליה: ת"ש האומר תנו חלק לפלוני בבור. באריתא דדלאי שלו: אין נותנין לו פחות מרביע שבו. משום דלהשקות שדותיו קאמר ליה הכי ושיערו חכמים דברביע די לו. הכי נמי בכולה נכסי יהבי' ליה רביע כי אמר תנו חלק בנכסי. ואם אמר סתם תנו חלק לפלוני בבור בחביות אין לו בה פחות מח' בו. שכך היו רגילין שממלאין חביותיהן מים להסתפק ממנה כל השנה לצורך רחיצת בגדים וכלים: ואם אמר תנו לו בו לקדירה. לספוק מאכלו: לטפיח. כגון כלי חרס כמו כריא א) דפתיא שדולין בו מים לשתות לצורך שתיה: על מנת. שמעשר ראשון של שדה זו שלי יהא שלא תתנו ללוי אחר: ואם אמר מעשר ראשון לי ולבני. אחרי: אין לו עליו כלום. משום דהתנה עמו כל זמן ששדה זו בידך שלא תוציאנה מתחת ידך אבל אם מכרה אע"ג דחזר ולקחה אין לו עליו כלום. אבל היכא דאמר סתם על מנת שמעשר אני נוטל. אע"ג דמכרה הואיל וחזר ולקחה שלו הוא. והיאך יכול להתנות על מעשר והלא דבר שלא בא לעולם הוא: מקום גדולת המעשר שיורי שייר לפניו. דהשתא לא מקני ליה דבר שלא בא לעולם דהא כבר בא דהמקום של מעשר שייר לעצמו שלא מכרו. ואי בעית אימא דקתני דהיכא דאמר ע"מ לטפויא מלתא היא כגון הכא בין מעשר דבלאו ע"מ לית ליה ללוקח מעשר כלום אלא טובת הנאה אקנייה ליה המוכר מהני ע"מ דאינו רשאי ליתנו לאחר אלא לו: זאת אומרת המוכר בית לחבירו ואמר לו ע"מ שדיוטא העליונה. היינו עלייה שעל גבי חבית: ומקשי'

הגהות הב"ח

(א) רשב"ם ד"ה אי אמר וזימנין אמרי' תשעה: (ב) ד"ה סומכוס פחות מרביע ומשום שלא הוה: (ג) בא"ד הוה כו' לה תליא של פלגא וכו': (ד) ד"ה אין וכו' לממון: (ה) תוס' ד"ה אין וכו' שמואל דהלכה כסומכוס וכו' בשמעתין לכל דאלים גבר הס"ד:

עי' בערוך ערך פתח

עין משפט
נר מצוה

כד א ב מיי' פכ"ד מהל' מכירה הל' טז סמג עשין פב טוש"ע ח"מ סי' ריב סעיף ג וסי' ריד סעיף ח:

כה ג מיי' שם הל' טו וסמג שם טוש"ע ח"מ סי' ריד סעיף ג:

לְמַאי הִלְכְתָא? *רַב זְבִיד אָמַר: אשֶׁאִם רָצָה לְהוֹצִיא בָּהּ זִיזִין – מוֹצִיא; רַב פַּפָּא אָמַר: בשֶׁאִם רָצָה לִבְנוֹת עֲלִיָּיה עַל גַּבָּהּ – בּוֹנֶה. בִּשְׁלָמָא לְרַב זְבִיד, הַיְינוּ דְּקָתָנֵי "זֹאת אוֹמֶרֶת", אֶלָּא לְרַב פַּפָּא מַאי "זֹאת אוֹמֶרֶת"? קַשְׁיָא. § אָמַר רַב דִּימִי מִנְּהַרְדְּעָא: גהַאי מַאן דִּמְזַבֵּין לֵיהּ בֵּיתָא לְחַבְרֵיהּ, אַף עַל גַּב דִּכְתַב לֵיהּ "עוּמְקָא וְרוּמָא", צָרִיךְ לְמִכְתַּב לֵיהּ: "קְנֵי לָךְ מִתְּהוֹם אַרְעָא וְעַד רוּם רְקִיעָא"; מַאי טַעְמָא? דְּעוּמְקָא וְרוּמָא בִּסְתָמָא לָא קָנֵי, אַהֲנֵי "עוּמְקָא וְרוּמָא" לְמִיקְנָא עוּמְקָא וְרוּמָא, וְאַהֲנֵי "מִתְּהוֹם אַרְעָא וְעַד רוּם רְקִיעָא" לְמִיקְנָא בּוֹר וְדוּת וּמְחִילוֹת. לֵימָא מְסַיֵּיעַ לֵיהּ: "וְלֹא אֶת הַבּוֹר וְלֹא אֶת הַדּוּת אַף עַל פִּי שֶׁכָּתַב לוֹ "עוּמְקָא וְרוּמָא"; וְאִי סָלְקָא דַּעְתָּךְ בִּסְתָמָא קָנֵי עוּמְקָא וְרוּמָא, לִיהֲנֵי "עוּמְקָא וְרוּמָא" לְמִיקְנָא בּוֹר וְדוּת וּמְחִילוֹת! (א) דְּלָא כְּתַב לֵיהּ. וְהָא "אע"פ שֶׁכָּתַב לוֹ" קָתָנֵי! ה"ק: אע"פ שֶׁלֹּא כָּתַב לוֹ – כְּמִי שֶׁכָּתַב דָּמֵי, לְמִיקְנָא עוּמְקָא וְרוּמָא; לְמִיקְנָא בּוֹר וְדוּת וּמְחִילוֹת, אִי כְּתַב לֵיהּ "עוּמְקָא וְרוּמָא" – קָנֵי, וְאִי לָא כְּתַב – לָא קָנֵי. תָּא שְׁמַע: וְלֹא אֶת הַגָּג בִּזְמַן שֶׁיֵּשׁ לוֹ מַעֲקֶה גָּבוֹהַּ עֲשָׂרָה טְפָחִים; וְאִי

לְמַאי הִלְכְתָא. אָמַר ר"ל דְּאַהֲנֵי תְּנָאֵיהּ לְמֶהֱוֵי דְּיוֹטָא עֶלְיוֹנָה שֶׁלּוֹ? דִּבְלָאו הָכִי הוּא שֶׁלּוֹ, דְּהַמּוֹכֵר הַבַּיִת לֹא מָכַר דְּיוֹטָא הָעֶלְיוֹנָה! שֶׁאִם רָצָה. מוֹכֵר לְהוֹצִיא זִיזִין מִדְּיוֹטָא עֶלְיוֹנָה, כְּנֶגֶד חָצֵר שֶׁל לוֹקֵחַ שֶׁמָּכַר לוֹ זֶה הַבַּיִת וְהֶחָצֵר – מוֹצִיא, דִּלְהָכִי אַהֲנֵי תְּנָאֵיהּ. וְהָכִי קָאָמַר לֵיהּ: עַל מְנָת שֶׁתְּהֵא דְּיוֹטָא הָעֶלְיוֹנָה שֶׁלִּי לְגַמְרֵי לַעֲשׂוֹת בָּהּ חֲפָצַי, אַף לְהוֹצִיא מִמֶּנָּה זִיזִין כְּמִתְּחִילָּה קוֹדֶם שֶׁמָּכַרְתִּי לְךָ הַבַּיִת וְהֶחָצֵר. דְּשַׁיֵּיר בִּתְנַאי מָקוֹם בֶּחָצֵר כְּמוֹ שֶׁשִּׁיֵּיר לְמַעְלָה בַּשָּׂדֶה מְקוֹם מַעֲשֵׂר, דְּכָל תְּנַאי דְּלָא מְהַנֵּי מַאי דְּקָאָמַר – אַהֲנֵי מִיהָא לְשַׁיֵּיר מָקוֹם. וְהַיְינוּ "זֹאת אוֹמֶרֶת" דְּקָאָמַר ר"ל. וְדַוְקָא הוּא, אֲבָל בְּנוֹ – אֵין לוֹ רְשׁוּת לְהוֹצִיא זִיזִין עַד שֶׁיְּפָרֵשׁ "לִי וּלְבָנַיי", כִּדְאָמַר לְעֵיל גַּבֵּי מַעֲשֵׂר. דְּכָל מִילְּתָא דְּדָיְיקִינַן מִיַּתּוּרָא – דַּי לָנוּ אִי אַהֲנֵי יַתּוּרָא לְעַצְמוֹ; כְּמוֹ שֶׁפֵּירֵשׁ "ע"מ שֶׁמַּעֲשֵׂר רִאשׁוֹן שֶׁלִּי" – ה"נ אָמְרִינַן "ע"מ שֶׁהַדְּיוֹטָא הָעֶלְיוֹנָה שֶׁלִּי", אֲבָל לְבָנָיו לָא מְהַנֵּי תְּנַאי הַמְּיוּתָּר. [לקמן סד. קמח:] רַב פַּפָּא אָמַר. כּוּלֵּי הַאי לָא אַהֲנֵי תְּנַאי לְשַׁיֵּיר מָקוֹם מִמַּה שֶּׁמָּכַר. אֶלָּא לְהָכִי אַהֲנֵי תְּנַאי הַמְּיוּתָּר, שֶׁאִם רוֹצֶה לִבְנוֹת דְּיוֹטָא זוֹ אִם תִּפּוֹל, עַל גַּבָּיו שֶׁל הַבַּיִת – בּוֹנֶה. וְהָכִי (ב) הֲוָה מַסִּיק לְקַמָּן: דְּאִי נָפְלָה (ג) הָדַר בָּנֵי לָהּ. דְּאִי הֲוָה שָׁתַק וּמָכַר הַבַּיִת סְתָם – הָיְתָה הַדְּיוֹטָא הָעֶלְיוֹנָה שֶׁלּוֹ כָּל יְמֵי (ד) שֶׁיִּתְקַיֵּים, אֲבָל אִם תִּפּוֹל – לֹא יַחֲזוֹר וְיִבְנֶנָּה ע"ג בַּיִת שֶׁל זֶה, דִּלְהַךְ דְּיוֹטָא הוּא דְּאִשְׁתַּעְבַּד לוֹ בַּיִת, אֲבָל לְדְיוֹטָא אַחֶרֶת לָא מִשְׁתַּעְבֵּד, עַד דְּא"ל בְּהֶדְיָא יַתּוּר לָשׁוֹן. [לקמן סד.] כִּדְאָמְרִינַן נַמִּי בְּפֶרֶק "הַבַּיִת וְהָעֲלִיָּיה" (ב"מ דף קטז:): אִי דְּא"ל "עֲלִיָּיה זוֹ" וְנָפְלָה – אָזְלָא לַהּ, וְאִי דְּא"ל סְתָם – בָּעֵי לְמֵיגַר לֵיהּ אַחֲרִינָא! וּמַסְקָנָא: לָא צְרִיכָא, דְּאָמַר לֵיהּ "עֲלִיָּיה שֶׁעַל גַּבֵּי בַּיִת זֶה אֲנִי מַשְׂכִּיר לָךְ" דְּהָא שִׁעְבֵּד בַּיִת לַעֲלִיָּיה. אֲבָל בְּלֹא יַתּוּר, מִכִּי נָפְלָה – אָזְלָא לַהּ, וְלֹא יִבְנֶה אַחֶרֶת. וְה"ק: ע"מ שֶׁהַדְּיוֹטָא הָעֶלְיוֹנָה שֶׁלִּי לְעוֹלָמִים, וְאַף אִם תִּפּוֹל – אֶחֱזוֹר וְאֶבְנֶנָּה. וְהָא דִּתְנַן (ב"מ דף קיז.): הַבַּיִת וְהָעֲלִיָּיה שֶׁל שְׁנַיִם שֶׁנָּפְלוּ וכו' אִם אָמַר בַּעַל הָעֲלִיָּיה לְבעה"ב לִבְנוֹת כו' – הָתָם בִּדְחָלְקוּ, זֶה נָטַל בַּיִת וְזֶה נָטַל עֲלִיָּיה, וּדְאַתְנוּ בַּהֲדָדֵי לְהִשְׁתַּעְבֵּד בַּיִת לַעֲלִיָּיה כָּל הַיָּמִים, וַאֲפִי' לֹא אַתְנוּ – מִסְתָמָא ע"מ כֵּן חָלְקוּ. וּלְרַב זְבִיד אַהֲנֵי תְּנָאָה לְהוֹצָאַת זִיזִין, וְלָא לַהֲדַר בָּנֵי לַהּ; (ה) הוֹצָאַת זִיזִין – מַסִּיק אַדַּעְתֵּיהּ, שֶׁהֲרֵי צָרִיךְ לוֹ מִיָּד. אֲבָל לַהֲדַר בָּנֵי לַהּ אִם תִּפּוֹל – לָא מַסִּיק אַדַּעְתֵּיהּ לְעִתִּים רְחוֹקוֹת. בִּשְׁלָמָא לְרַב זְבִיד. דְּאוֹקֵי יַתּוּרָא דִּתְנַאי לְהוֹצָאַת זִיזִין, דְּהַיְינוּ שִׁיּוּר מָקוֹם בֶּחָצֵר דּוּמְיָא דְּשִׁיּוּר מָקוֹם בַּשָּׂדֶה – הַיְינוּ דְּקָתָנֵי בְּמִילְּתֵיהּ דְּר"ל "זֹאת אוֹמֶרֶת", שֶׁהוּצְרַךְ ר"ל לִלְמוֹד מִן הַבָּרַיְיתָא דְּלִיהֲנֵי יַתּוּרָא לְשִׁיּוּר מָקוֹם. דְּמִסְּבָרָא לָא הֲוָה אָמְרִינַן דִּמְשַׁיֵּיר אִינִישׁ לְעַצְמוֹ מִמַּה שֶּׁמּוֹכֵר, וְאע"ג דְּקָאָמַר יַתּוּרָא. אֶלָּא לְרַב פַּפָּא מַאי זֹאת אוֹמֶרֶת. לָמָּה לוֹ לר"ל לוֹמַר "זֹאת אוֹמֶרֶת" לְאַשְׁמוּעִינַן דְּאַהֲנֵי יַתּוּר לַחֲזוֹר וְלִבְנוֹת הַדְּיוֹטָא אִם תִּפּוֹל? בְּלָא הַבָּרַיְיתָא נַמִּי הֲוָה יָדְעִינַן דְּאַהֲנֵי יַתּוּר תְּנַאי שֶׁאֵינוֹ צָרִיךְ לְטַפּוּיֵי מִילְּתָא, אוֹ הָא דְּרַב פַּפָּא אוֹ שׁוּם דָּבָר בָּעוֹלָם. כִּדְאָמְרִינַן בְּמַתְנִי' (לקמן סד.): וּמוֹדֶה ר"ע בִּזְמַן שֶׁאָמַר לוֹ "חוּץ מֵאֵלּוּ" שֶׁאֵין צָרִיךְ לִיקַּח לוֹ דֶּרֶךְ – מֵהָתָם שָׁמְעִינַן דְּכָל תְּנַאי בְּלָא צוֹרֶךְ לְטַפּוּיֵי מִילְּתָא קָאָתֵי, וּמִבָּרַיְיתָא לָא שָׁמְעִינַן לֵיהּ טְפֵי מִמַּתְנִי'! וּלְעֵיל נַמִּי אָמְרִינַן: אִי א"ל "אִילֵּין מַלְרָנָהָא" – קָנֵי פַּלְגָּא. וְהָכִי הוה"ל לְמֵימַר: אָמַר ר"ל הַמּוֹכֵר בַּיִת לַחֲבֵירוֹ וְאָמַר לוֹ ע"מ כו'! הַאי מַאן דִּמְזַבֵּין לֵיהּ בֵּיתָא לְחַבְרֵיהּ. וּמָכַר לוֹ גַּם אֶת הַבּוֹר וְאֶת הַדּוּת, וְצָרִיךְ לוֹ לִכְתּוֹב בִּשְׁטַר הַמְּכִירָה כֵּן. אע"ג דְּכָתַב לֵיהּ בִּשְׁטָר "עוּמְקוֹ וְרוּמוֹ שֶׁל בַּיִת אֲנִי מוֹכֵר לָךְ" – לֹא קָנָה בּוֹר וְדוּת, כִּדְמְפָרֵשׁ וְאָזֵיל. דְּלָא אַהֲנֵי מַה שֶּׁכָּתַב "עוּמְקָא וְרוּמָא" אֶלָּא לְמִיקְנֵי עוּמְקוֹ שֶׁל בַּיִת, כְּגוֹן גּוּף הַקַּרְקַע עַצְמוֹ לַחְפּוֹר תַּחַת קַרְקָעִית הַבַּיִת אִם יִרְצֶה. שֶׁאִם לֹא כָּתַב – לָא הֲוֵי קָנֵי לֵיהּ מִסְתָמָא, אֶלָּא הֲרֵי הוּא שֶׁל מוֹכֵר לַחְפּוֹר בּוֹרוֹת שִׁיחִין וּמְעָרוֹת מִתַּחַת קַרְקָעִית הַבַּיִת, אֶלָּא שֶׁלֹּא יַזִּיק לבעה"ב. וְגַם אַהֲנֵי לֵיהּ לְמִיקְנֵי רוּמָא – כְּגוֹן גַּג שֶׁיֵּשׁ לוֹ מַעֲקֶה שֶׁהוּא גָּבוֹהַּ י' שֶׁאֵינוֹ מָכוּר מִסְתָמָא עִם הַבַּיִת, כִּדְקָתָנֵי מַתְנִיתִין. וְגַם לִקְנוֹת כָּל הָאֲוִיר עַד לָרָקִיעַ, שֶׁאִם יִרְצֶה לִבְנוֹת – בּוֹנֶה, דְּמִסְתָמָא לָא הֲוֵי קָנֵי לֵיהּ לוֹקֵחַ, אֶלָּא הֲרֵי הוּא שֶׁל מוֹכֵר לְהוֹצָאַת זִיזִין אוֹ לִבְנוֹת בָּאֲוִיר, וּכְגוֹן שֶׁלֹּא יַכְבִּיד עַל בֵּיתוֹ שֶׁל לוֹקֵחַ. אֲבָל (ו) לְמִיקְנֵי בּוֹר וְדוּת שֶׁאֵין תַּשְׁמִישָׁן שָׁוֶה לַבַּיִת, וְהִלְכָּךְ אֵינוֹ בִּכְלַל עוּמְקוֹ וְרוּמוֹ שֶׁל בַּיִת – וְלָא קָנֵי לֵיהּ עַד דְּכָתַב לֵיהּ: מֵאַרְעִית תְּהוֹמָא, מִשּׁוּלֵי הַתְּהוֹם, עַד לָרָקִיעַ. וְאַהֲנֵי הַאי "מֵאַרְעִית תְּהוֹמָא" לְמִיקְנֵי בּוֹר וְדוּת וּמְחִילוֹת, וְהַאי "עַד רוּם רָקִיעַ" לָא מְהַנֵּי לֵיהּ מִידֵּי, דְּמִשֶּׁכָּתַב לוֹ עוּמְקָא וְרוּמָא – קָנֵי עַד רוּם רָקִיעַ, וְלָא אִיצְטְרִיךְ כְּלָל, אֶלָּא סוֹף דִּיבּוּר הוּא. דְּלָא מָצֵי אָמַר "מֵאַרְעִית תְּהוֹמָא (ז) עַד שִׁיפּוּלֵי בֵּיתָא", דְּמַשְׁמַע דְּלָא זַבֵּין לֵיהּ מִשִּׁיפּוּלֵי הַבַּיִת וּלְמַעְלָה כְּלוּם. ה"ג: מַאי טַעְמָא עוּמְקָא וְרוּמָא בִּסְתָמָא לָא קָנֵי. עַד דִּמְפָרֵשׁ "עוּמְקָא וְרוּמָא". וְהִלְכָּךְ לָא אַהֲנֵי "עוּמְקָא וְרוּמָא" לְמֶהֱוֵי יַתּוּר לָשׁוֹן לְמִקְנֵי בּוֹר וְדוּת, דִּלְגוּפֵיהּ אִיצְטְרִיךְ. אע"פ שֶׁכָּתַב לוֹ עוּמְקָא וְרוּמָא. אַבּוֹר וְדוּת קָאֵי. אֲבָל אַגַּג שֶׁיֵּשׁ לוֹ מַעֲקֶה גָּבוֹהַּ י' – לָא קָאֵי, דְּהָא וַדַּאי אִי כָּתַב לֵיהּ "עוּמְקָא וְרוּמָא" קָנֵי לֵיהּ, כִּדְמוֹכַח לְקַמֵּיהּ. וְאִי ס"ד בִּסְתָמָא. אע"פ שֶׁלֹּא כָּתַב "עוּמְקָא וְרוּמָא" קָנֵי עוּמְקָא וְרוּמָא, א"כ "עוּמְקָא וְרוּמָא" שֶׁכָּתַב מְיוּתָּר הוּא, וְתֵיהֲנֵי לְמִיקְנֵי בּוֹר וְדוּת! אֶלָּא לָאו שְׁמַע מִינָּהּ: "עוּמְקָא וְרוּמָא" לְגוּפֵיהּ אִיצְטְרִיךְ, לְמִיקְנֵי עוּמְקָא וְרוּמָא, וְלֵיכָּא יַתּוּר לָשׁוֹן לְמִיקְנֵי בּוֹר וְדוּת, עַד דְּכָתַב לֵיהּ "מֵאַרְעִית תְּהוֹמָא עַד רוּם רָקִיעַ", כְּרַב דִּימִי. וּמְשַׁנֵּי: דְּלָא כָּתַב לֵיהּ עוּמְקָא וְרוּמָא. הִלְכָּךְ לֹא קָנָה בּוֹר וְדוּת. אֲבָל אִי כָּתַב לֵיהּ – קָנֵי, וְאע"ג דְּלָא כָּתַב "מֵאַרְעִית תְּהוֹמָא", וּדְלָא כְּרַב דִּימִי. ה"ק אע"פ שֶׁלֹּא כָּתַב לוֹ. "עוּמְקָא וְרוּמָא", הֲרֵי הוּא כְּמִי שֶׁכָּתַב לוֹ, כְּדֵי לִקְנוֹת עוּמְקָא וְרוּמָא. אֲבָל לְמִיקְנֵי בּוֹר וְדוּת וּמְחִילוֹת כו' – צָרִיךְ לְכָתְבוֹ בְּפֵירוּשׁ, לִהְיוֹת לוֹ יַתּוּר לָשׁוֹן לְמִיקְנֵי בּוֹר וְדוּת. דְּהָא לְגוּפֵיהּ לָא צָרִיךְ, דְּמִסְתָמָא קָנֵי עוּמְקָא וְרוּמָא. וְהָכִי מַשְׁמַע מַתְנִי': לֹא אֶת הַבּוֹר וְלֹא אֶת הַדּוּת – אע"פ שֶׁכָּתַב בִּשְׁטָר וְנִתְרַבָּה לוֹ בִּשְׁטַר מְכִירָה זוֹ עוּמְקָא וְרוּמָא, שֶׁהֲרֵי כָּתַב לוֹ "בַּיִת זֶה אֲנִי מוֹכֵר לָךְ", וְעוּמְקָא וְרוּמָא בִּכְלַל בַּיִת הוּא – אפ"ה לֹא קָנָה בּוֹר וְדוּת, דְּלָאו בִּכְלַל בַּיִת הוּא כְּעוּמְקָא וְרוּמָא. ת"ש וְלֹא אֶת הַגָּג. קס"ד דְּרֵישָׁא בְּדְלָא כָּתַב לֵיהּ "עוּמְקָא וְרוּמָא" מַיְירֵי, דְּהָא לָא קָתָנֵי בָּהּ "אע"פ שֶׁכָּתַב לוֹ "עוּמְקָא וְרוּמָא", אֶלָּא בִּסְתָמָא מַיְירֵי, (ח) וַאֲפִ"ה לֹא קָנָה גַּג שֶׁיֵּשׁ לוֹ מַעֲקֶה גָּבוֹהַּ עֲשָׂרָה, דְּהַיְינוּ בִּכְלַל "רוּמָא", כִּדְסַלְקָא דַּעְתָּךְ הַשְׁתָּא. וְאִי

שאם רצה לבנות עלייה על גבה. לאו על גבה ממש, (ט) אלא דאי נפלה הדר בני לה, כדמסיק לקמן. אבל אם לא אמר "ע"מ" – לא בני לה, אע"ג דתנן (ב"מ דף קיז.): הבית והעלייה של שנים שנפלו ואמר בעה"ב לבעל העלייה לבנות כו'. ואומר רבינו יצחק: דוקא בעלייה, דעדיפא וחשיבא טפי מדיוטא. אבל דיוטא דלא חשיבא כולי האי – לא יפה כחה כמו עלייה. ובקונט' דחק בחנם לפרש בע"א. אהני מתהום ארעא ועד רום רקיעא למיקני בור ודות ומחילות. פי' בקונט': ד"עד רום רקיעא" לא מהני מידי, דמשכתב לו "עומקא ורומא" – קני עד רום רקיעא, ואפי' גג שיש לו מעקה גבוה י' טפחים. והא דקתני במתני': אע"פ שכתב לו "עומקא ורומא" – אבור ודות קאי, ולא אגג. ולא אצטריך "עד רום רקיעא", אלא סוף דיבור הוא, דלא מצי למימר "עד שיפולי ביתא". וקשה לר"י: דה"מ למימר "רומא ועומקא עד ארעית תהומא"! לכן נראה לר"י: דאגג נמי קאי. דאע"ג דכתב ליה "עומקא ורומא" – לא קני לגג שיש לו מעקה גבוה י"ט. וה"מ למימר: ואהני "עד רום רקיעא" למיקני גג שיש לו מעקה גבוה י' טפחים, אלא דלא חש למינקט אלא גבי בור ודות, וה"ה גג, וכ"ש הוא. ודחק ר"י לקיים פירוש הקונטרס, דמדכתב "עומקא ורומא" – קני גג, ואהני "עד רום רקיעא" – למיקני בור ודות שעל הגג, שהיו רגילין לעשות מקוואות על ראש הגג, כמו שמצינו בפ"ק דיומא (דף יט.): על גג הפרווה ועל גג שער המים. תא שמע ולא את הגג. פי' הקונט': והך דרישא – בלא כתב לו "עומקא ורומא" איירי, דהא לא קתני בה "אע"פ שכתב לו עומקא ורומא". ובחנם פירש כן, דאפילו הוה קאי ארישא – הא אסיק לעיל, למאי דבעי למימר בסתמא קני, דה"ק: אע"פ שלא כתב – כמו שכתב דמי, למיקני עומקא ורומא. ואי

רבינו גרשום

ומקשי' למאי הלכתא. שייר בלא על מנת נמי לא קנה הדיוטא כדקתני מתני' המוכר את הבית סתם לא מכר את היציע והיינו עלייה: רב זביד אמר. להכי אהני על מנת שאם רצה להוציא מן הדיוטא לחצר שמכר עם הבית זיזין וגזוזטראות בחצר מוציא ודלהכי מהני על מנת לטפויי מלתא: ורב פפא אמר. להכי מהני על מנת שאם רצה לבנות עלייה על גבי עלייה בונה: בשלמא לרב זביד היינו דקאמר זאת אומרת. דכי היכי דבן לוי מרויח בהאי דקאמר על מנת האי נמי מוכר מרויח בעל מנת דיכול להוציא זיזין בחצר שאינו שלו: אלא לרב פפא מאי זאת. כלומר מאי קמרויח האי מוכר בעל מנת. בלא על מנת יש לו רשות לבנות עלייה על גבי עלייתו שאין לו לקונה אלא הבית: קשיא: מ"ט. צריך למכתב: משום דעומקא ורומא בסתמא לא קני. אי לא כתב ליה ואהני עומקא ורומא דכתב ליה למיקני עומקא כגון אוצר שתחת הבית. רומא למיקני גג שעל הבית שאין לו מעקה גבוה י' טפח ואהני נמי מתהום ארעא למיקני בור ודות ומחילות דכל הני בתהומא דארעא הן ואהני נמי עד רום רקיעא למיקני א) גג שיש לו מעקה גבוה י' טפח דדבר חשוב הוא בפני עצמו: ליהני עומקא ורומא למיקני בור ודות ומחילות. אלא ש"מ דסתמא לא קני ואמטו להכי צריך תרוייהו דאהני עומקא ורומא למיקני עומקא ורומא ואהני מתהום ארעא עד רום רקיע למיקני בור ודות ומחילות ותסייע לרב דימי: לעולם מהא לא תסייע ליה דודאי בסתמא קני אף על גב דלא כתב עומקא ורומא [עומקא כגון] אוצרות דשייכי בבית ורומא כגון גג שאין לו מעקה גבוה י' טפח ואי כתב עומקא ורומא קני בור ודות וגג שיש לו מעקה גבוה י' טפחים אבל הכא במאי עסקינן דלא קני בור ודות דלא כתב ליה עומקא ורומא ואי כתב ודאי קנה אפי' בור ודות ומחילות. והא אפי' שכתב ליה עומקא ורומא קתני מתני' לא קנה בור ודות והיכי אמרת הא כתב קנה. ומשני הכי קא מפרש למתני' אע"ג דלא כתב ליה עומקא ורומא קני בסתמא מאי דשייך בהדי בית דכמו שכתב דמי למיקני עומקא ורומא אבל למיקני בור ודות ומחילות אי כתב ליה מתהום ארעא ועד רום רקיע תהוא דקני בור ודות ומחילות וגג י' טפח ואי לא לא ומהא לא תסייעה: ת"ש ולא את הגג אי

א) דעת רבינו כזה כדעת ר"י בתוס' כאן ד"ה אהני ע"ש.

הגהות הב"ח

(א) גמ' ומחילות לא כ"ש דלא כתב ליה: (ב) רשב"ם ד"ה רב פפא וכו' והוה מסיק כצ"ל ותיבת נמחק: (ג) בא"ד להדר לה וכו': (ד) בא"ד על שיתקיים אבל (ה) בא"ד דהוצאת (ו) ד"ה האי מאן וכו' לא קני בור ודות שאין (ז) בא"ד עד שיפולי כו' נ"ב לשון זה נעתק הם בפ' ח"ה סוף דף (ח) ד"ה ת"ש ולא וכו' בסתמא מיירי ומש"ה קנה גגו: (ט) תוס' שאם וכו' ממש כדקאמר דלאי:

גמרא

ואי סלקא דעתך בסתמא קני עומקא ורומא, כי גבוה עשרה טפחים מאי הוי? כיון דגבוהה עשרה טפחים — חשיב. א"ל רבינא לרב אשי, תא שמע: א)דאמר ריש לקיש, זאת אומרת: המוכר בית לחבירו, ואמר לו "על מנת שדיוטא העליונה שלי" — דיוטא העליונה שלו; ואמרינן, למאי הלכתא? ב)רב זביד אמר: שאם רצה להוציא בה זיזין — מוציא, רב פפא אמר: שאם רצה לבנות עלייה על גבה — בונה; ואי ס"ד בסתמא לא קני, למה לי "על מנת"? אהני ליה "על מנת", אדאי נפיל הדר בני לה.§

מתני' ג)בלא את הבור ולא את הדות, אע"פ שכתב לו עומקא ורומא. גוצריך ליקח לו דרך, דברי ר' עקיבא; וחכ"א: אינו צריך ליקח לו דרך. דומודה ר"ע, בזמן שאמר לו "חוץ מאלו" — שאין צריך ליקח דרך. מכרן לאחר — ר' עקיבא אומר: האינו צריך ליקח לו דרך, וחכ"א: צריך ליקח לו דרך.§

גמ' יתיב רבינא וקא קשיא ליה: (א) היינו בור היינו דות! א"ל רבא תוספאה לרבינא: ת"ש, דתניא: אחד הבור ואחד הדות בקרקע, אלא שהבור בחפירה והדות בבנין. יתיב רב אשי וקא קשיא ליה: היינו בור היינו דות! א"ל מר קשישא בריה דרב חסדא לרב אשי: ת"ש, דתניא: אחד הבור ואחד הדות בקרקע, אלא שהבור בחפירה והדות בבנין.§ וצריך ליקח לו דרך, דברי ר"ע; וחכ"א: אינו צריך" וכו'.§ (ב) מאי לאו בהא קא מפלגי,

דרבי

רשב"ם

ואי סלקא דעתך בסתמא קני עומקא ורומא. כדקפרכת לעיל. כי גבוה י' טפחים מאי הוי. אמאי לא קנה? אלא לאו ש"מ דרומא מסתמא לא קני, לא גג גבוה עשרה ולא אויר מי' ואילך. והוא הדין דלא קני עומקא מסתמא כלל, כרב דימי. ומיהו, גג שאין לו מעקה גבוה י' — קני מסתמא להשתמש על הגג, דאין זה בכלל רום, אלא בכלל גוף הבית ממש, כעליית הבית. ומדחינן: גבוה עשרה חשיב בית בפני עצמו, ולא מיבטיל לגבי בית בסתמא עד דמפרש עומקא ורומא. אבל אויר הגג עד לרקיע, דהיינו רומא, והוא הדין לעומקא — קני מסתמא. ת"ש דאמר ריש לקיש כו'. מדרב פפא מקשי: אי אמרת בשלמא דמסתמא קני לוקח עומקא ורומא — היינו דאהני תנאה ד"ע"מ" שהוא מיותר, לכדרב פפא, שאם רצה מוכר לבנות על גבי הדיוטא ולהגביה בניינין אחרים ברומו של בית — בונה. דאי לא אתני — הוה קני ליה לוקח לרומא שעל גבי הדיוטא מסתמא, דרומו של בית קונה בכ"מ, ואפי' היכא דאיכא דיוטא עליונה שהיא של מוכר. אלא אי ס"ד דמסתמא לא קני לוקח רומא, אלא של מוכר הוא — ל"ל "ע"מ"? מאי אהני תנאי המיותר? בלא תנאיה נמי הוה קני מוכר לדיוטא העליונה ולרומו של בית, ואם היה רוצה לבנות — בונה! וקס"ד דהאי מקשה דהכי איתיה לפירושה דמילתיה דרב פפא, כדפרישית לה. ה"ג בפירוש רבינו חננאל: דאי נפלה הדר בני לה. לעולם מסתמא לא קני לוקח רומא. ודקאמרת: תנאה ל"ל — להכי אהני, דאי נפלה דיוטא הדר בני לה. וכדפרישית לעיל, דרב פפא לאו בבנין ע"ג דיוטא איירי, אלא בבנין דיוטא עצמה אם תפול. כן נראה שיטת שמועה זאת בעיני, ויש שיטות אחרות ואין בהן ממש.

מתני' אע"פ שכתב לו עומקא ורומא. כדאוקמה רב דימי בגמרא לעיל, דעומקא ורומא בסתמא לא קני, ואהני "עומקא ורומא" למיקני עומקא ורומא, ולא למיקני בור ודות שתשמישן חלוק מן הבית, שאינו עשוי אלא לשאוב ממנו מים. וצריך. המוכר ליקח ממנו דרך מן הלוקח, לילך לבור ודות שלו. דמוכר בעין יפה מוכר, דברי ר"ע. ורבנן סבירא להו דמוכר בעין רעה מוכר, ושייר דרך לעצמו ממה שמכר. בזמן שאמר ליה חוץ מאלו. חוץ מבור ודות. ותנאי שלא לצורך הוא, שהרי אינן בכלל בית, אלא לטפויי מילתא קאתי ושייר לו דרך. ולרבנן לא אתא לטפויי כלל, דבלאו הכי שייר לעצמו דרך, ולרווחא דמילתא אמר כן, שלא יאמר הלוקח: כל הבית מכרת לי ולא עכבת דרך. שאין כל מוכרין בקיאין בדינין, והלכך פירש כל כך. מכרן. לבור ודות לאחר, והבית עיכב לעצמו. רבי עקיבא אומר א"צ הלוקח ליקח לו דרך. לבור ודות שקנה, דמוכר בעין יפה מוכר לו. גמ' היינו בור היינו דות. איזהו בור ואיזהו דות? והלא אין היכר בין זה לזה, ששניהן עמוקין בקרקע, ויש בהן מים מכונסין, ולמה לי למיתני תרתי? בחפירה. בקרקע קשה, שמחזיק מים בלא בנין. בבנין. חופרין בור בעפר תיחוח, ובונין לו כותל אבנים, ומקרי דות. והלכך, אי תנא בור — הוה אמינא: ה"מ בור שהוא בחפירה, אבל דות שהוא בבנין כעין הבית — הרי הוא בכלל בית. ואי תנא דות — משום דבנין בפני עצמו הוא וחשיב, אבל בור לא חשיב, וליבטל גבי בית — צריכא.

דרבי

תוספות

ואי סלקא דעתך בסתמא קני כי גבוה י' טפחים מאי הוי. פי' בקונ': אי בסתמא קני אויר שלמעלה מן הגג שהוא גבוה עשרה מן הגג, וגם הבנין שלמטה ממנה יקנה, והגג שבאמצע לא יקנה, ואין סברא שיהא הפסק בקנינו. וזה דחקו לרבינו שמואל לפרש דלא קאי "אע"פ שכתב לו עומקא ורומא" דמתניתין אגג, דאי קאי אגג — א"כ כי נמי בסתמא לא קני, תקשי ליה הכי, דכשכתב לו עומקא ורומא קני בנין שלמטה מן הגג ואויר שלמעלה, והגג שבאמצע לא קני! ומשני: כיון דגבוה עשרה טפחים — חשיב, ולא קני ליה לגג. אבל אויר שלמעלה — קני. וכן פירש הקונטרס. וכן צריך לפרש, דלא מצי למימר כיון דלא קני גג לא קני נמי אויר, שלא יהא הפסק בקנינו — דהא מוכח בסמוך בהדיא דאי אמר בסתמא קני רומא, אפי' כשהגג גבוה עשרה — קני האויר למעלה הימנו עד לרקיע, אע"ג דלא קני גג. דפריך מדרב פפא דאמר: אם רצה לבנות על גבה בונה, וסלקא דעתך דעל גבה ממש קאמר, באויר שלמעלה מן הגג, ויבנה על גבי עמודים שלא יכביד על הכותל. ואי ס"ד בסתמא לא קני — ל"ל "על מנת"? פי': והלא בלא "ע"מ" נמי יכול לבנות עלייה באויר שלמעלה מן הגג! ואי כי אמר בסתמא נמי קני, כשגג גבוה י' לא קנה לאויר שלמעלה, דא"כ, כי נמי בסתמא קני, תקשי ליה: "ע"מ" ל"ל! וזהו דוחק לפי' רבינו שמואל, שהמקשה הוא מקשה מכח אותה סברא, שאין נראה לו שיהא הפסק בקנינו, והגמ' אינו חושש ממנו. ונראה לר"י לפרש דקאי ארישא "אבל לא את הגג", כדפרי' לעיל. והכי פריך הכא: א"א בשלמא דבסתמא לא קני עומקא ורומא, כיון דבטורח בעי לקני רומא — אתי שפיר, דכיון דגג גבוה עשרה טפחים דלא קנה גג, דבדבר מועט מתבטל הקנין, דלא בטל גג אגב בית. אלא אי אמרת דבסתמא קנה, כיון שנקל כל כך לקנות — א"כ אפי' גג שיש לו מעקה גבוה עשרה יקנה, כיון דבעין יפה כל כך מוכר, דאפי' בסתמא קני רומא! ומשני: לעולם בסתמא קני רומא, ואפ"ה לא מזבין ליה גג גבוה י' בסתמא, אם לא שכתב עומקא ורומא, כיון דחשיב. ורבינו תם אין נראה לו מה שפי' הקונ' ד"דיוטא" — גג שיש לו מעקה גבוה עשרה טפחים, דבמסכת שבת מוכח דלשון דיוטא הוא שורה, דתנן ב"הזורק" (דף צו.): שתי גזוזטראות זו כנגד זו ברה"ר, המושיט והזורק מזו לזו — פטור, היו שתיהם בדיוטא אחת כו'. משמע: בשורה אחת, שאינם זו כנגד זו! ועוד: דמאי דמפרש מילתיה דרב פפא דאי נפלה הדר בני לה — הא לא משמע הכי לישנא דרב פפא, דקאמר: שאם רוצה לבנות עלייה על גבה בונה, דמשמע דעל גבה ממש של דיוטא! ועוד: שצריך לדחוק ולחלק בין הך דיוטא להאיך ד"הבית והעלייה"! ונראה לר"ת: "דיוטא עליונה" היא שורת אבנים עליונה של חומה שהגג עומד עליה. וקאמר: למאי הלכתא קאמר "ע"מ שהדיוטא עליונה שלי"? הלא אינו יכול להסירה אם היה רוצה, שכל הבית מכר לו, ולענין מה היא שלו? ומפרש רב זביד: שאם רוצה להוציא בה זיזין — מוציא. פירוש: על שורה עליונה, אע"פ שמכביד על הבית. ורב פפא אמר: אם רצה לבנות עלייה על גבה — בונה ע"ג עמודים, שלא יכביד על הבית, אבל להכביד אינו רשאי. ופריך: אלא לרב פפא, מאי "זאת אומרת" — דאע"ג דיכול לבנות עלייה על גבה? הא מסקינן דעומקא ורומא מסתמא לא קני, וא"כ כיון דלא מהני דבוריה לשייר בגוף הבית, ואינו יכול להכביד — מאי "זאת אומרת"? דהא פשיטא דמהני דבוריה אם נפלה דהדר בני לה, וממתניתין שמעינן דייתור לשון מהני! אבל לרב זביד אתי שפיר "זאת אומרת", דמשייר בגוף הבית. ולמאי דמסקי' דבסתמא לא קנה עומקא ורומא, (ד) מסיק לרב פפא לענין דאי נפל הדר בני לה — לאו אעלייה קאי, אלא אם נפל הבית ואינו רוצה הלוקח לבנותו — הרי בעל עלייה בונה את הבית והעלייה ע"ג עמודים כאשר בתחלה, ויושב בה עד שיתן לו יציאותיו. וא"ת: ומאי נפקא ליה מינה במה שהבית בנוי תחת העלייה? כיון שהעלייה אינה בנויה ע"ג כתלי הבית, אלא ע"ג עמודים הקבועין בחצר — בלא בית נמי יכול לעשות כן! ואומר ר"ת: שלא יפחד תמיד שלא תפחת העלייה ויפול לארץ. ועוד: דנפקא ליה מינה שלא ינשב הרוח תחת העלייה ויתקרר. וקשיא לפי' ר"ת: דאמר בפרק "זה בורר" (סנהדרין דף לא.): אחד אומר בדיוטא עליונה ואחד אומר בדיוטא תחתונה, מעשה בא לפני רבי וצירף עדותן. ואי "דיוטא" שורת חומה, היאך הלוה חבירו על שורת חומה? אלא משמע דהיינו תקרה. ובשילהי "כיצד משתתפין" (עירובין דף פח.) נמי תנן: שתי דיוטות זו כנגד זו מקצתם עשו עוקה כו' — לא משמע כלל שורת חומה, אלא תקרה.

ממאי

עין משפט נר מצוה

כו א מיי' פכ"ד מהל' מכירה הל' טז סמג עשין פב טוש"ע ח"מ סימן ריד סעיף ח:

כז ב מיי' שם הל' טו ופכ"ה הלכה ב סמג שם טוש"ע שם סעי' ב וסעי' ג:

כח ג ד ה מיי' שם פכ"ה הלכה ג טוש"ע שם סעיף ב:

הגהות הב"ח

(א) גמ' וקא קשיא ליה היינו בור היינו דות כצ"ל ול"ג היינו וכן בפירוש רשב"ם: (ב) שם בפיסקא אינו צריך וכו' במאי קא מיפלגי ר"ע ורבנן בהא קא מיפלגי דר"ע סבר: (ג) רשב"ם ד"ה וצריך המוכר ליקח דרך כצ"ל ותיבת ממנו נמחק: (ד) תום' ד"ה ואי וכו' ומסיק לרב פפא דאהני ליה על מנת לענין דאי נפל הדר בני לה:

מסורת הש"ס

א) לעיל סג. לקמן קמח. ב) [לעיל סג:] ג) ערכין יט. [נזיר ז:]

רבינו גרשום

היכא דמכר הבית ואמר לו ללוקח הכל אני מוכר לך חוץ מאלו בור ודות שאינו צריך ליקח לו דרך משום דבסתם נמי לא מכר הבור והדות וכי אמר הכי ודאי לטפויי מילתא קאתי ולא מכר הדרך: הבור והדות בלבד: ר"ע אומר אינו צריך. הלוקח ליקח דרך מן המוכר דודאי מכר לו את הדרך עם הבור והדות דמוכר בעין יפה מוכר: וחכמים אומרים צריך לקנות לו דרך: המוכר בעין רעה מוכר ולא

עין משפט נר מצוה

כט א מיי' פכ"ה מהל' מכירה הלכה ג סמג עשין פב טוש"ע ח"מ סימן רטז סעיף ז:

מסורת הש"ס

א) [לעיל לז. וש"נ:] ב) [לקמן עא.]

דרבי עקיבא סבר: א)מוכר בעין יפה מוכר, ורבנן סברי: מוכר בעין רעה מוכר. ודקאמר נמי בעלמא: ר' עקיבא לטעמיה, דאמר מוכר בעין יפה מוכר — מהכא? ממאי? דלמא (א) רבי עקיבא סבר: אין אדם רוצה שיתן מעותיו וידרסוהו אחרים, ורבנן סברי: אין אדם רוצה שיטול מעות ויפרח באויר! ואלא מסיפא: מכרן לאחר — ר' עקיבא אומר: אינו צריך ליקח לו דרך, וחכמים אומרים: צריך. (ג) דלמא בהאי פליגי, דרבי עקיבא סבר: בתר דעתא דלוקח אזלינן, ורבנן סברי: בתר דעתא דמוכר אזלינן! ואלא מהא: ב)לא את הבור ולא את הגת ולא את השובך, בין חרבין בין ישובין; וצריך ליקח לו דרך, דברי ר' עקיבא, וחכמים אומרים: אינו צריך; הא תו למה לי? אלא לאו הא קמ"ל, דרבי עקיבא סבר: מוכר בעין יפה מוכר, ורבנן סברי: מוכר בעין רעה מוכר. ודלמא אשמעינן בית, וקא משמע לן שדה. וצריכא; דאי אשמועינן בית — משום דבעי צניעותא, אבל שדה — אימא לא; ואי אשמועינן שדה — משום דקשי ליה דוושא, אבל בית — אימא לא! אלא מסיפא: מכרן לאחר — רבי עקיבא אומר: אינו צריך ליקח לו דרך, וחכמים אומרים: צריך; הא תו למה לי? היינו הך! אלא לאו הא קמ"ל, דרבי עקיבא סבר: מוכר בעין יפה מוכר, ורבנן סברי: מוכר בעין רעה מוכר, שמע מדנה. איתמר, רב הונא אמר רב:

הלכה

תוספות

ממאי דלמא רבי עקיבא סבר בתר דעתא דל"קח אזלינן. פירוש: היכא דאיכא טענה דדריסה ופריחה. אבל היכא דליכא, כמו גבי אילנות — לא.

ה"ג

רשב"ם

דרבי עקיבא סבר מוכר בעין יפה מוכר. בכל דיני מכירות שבעולם. ודאמר נמי בעלמא רבי עקיבא לטעמיה כו'. כלומר, מדמוקמינן בעלמא שאר דיני מכירה דתלו טעמייהו בעין יפה ובעין רעה אליבא דר' עקיבא ורבנן, כגון בפ' "חזקת הבתים" (לעיל דף לז:) דאמרן: מכר אילנות ושייר קרקע לפניו – פלוגתא דר' עקיבא ורבנן, דלר' עקיבא יש לו קרקע לבעל האילן, שאם ימות האילן יטע אחר במקומו, ולרבנן אין לו. מהכא. מתני' הוא דדייקינן לה. ממאי. דלמא דכ"ע התם בעין יפה מוכר ויש לו (ג) קרקע, אי נמי בעין רעה ואין לו. והכא בהא פליגי, דר' עקיבא סבר: אין לוקח רוצה שיתן דמים למוכר, וידרוס על גבי ביתו לילך לבורו ולדותו. ומוכר נמי, יודע הוא שלדעת כן קונה הלוקח – שלא ידרוס מוכר על גבי ביתו, והיה לו למוכר לשייר דרך לעצמו בפירוש, והלכך צריך ליקח לו דרך. אבל גבי מכר אילנות ושייר קרקע – אימא מודי רבי עקיבא דמוכר בעין רעה מוכר, ואין לו קרקע לבעל האילן, דהיינו לוקח. דליכא הכא גבי לוקח טענת ידרסוהו אחרים, דלא דריס מוכר על גבי אילנות של לוקח. ורבנן סברי. לדריסה לא חייש לוקח, דאין כאן חסרון ממון. אבל מוכר יש לו טענה, דאינו רוצה שיקבל דמי ביתו מן הלוקח ע"מ שיצטרך לפרוח באויר אל בורו ודותו שמעכב לעצמו, והלכך ודאי לא מכר דרך בורו, ולא הוצרך לפרש שהוא מעכב גם את הדרך של בורו – דמה הנאה יש לו בבור בלא דרך? (ד) ויד בעל השטר על התחתונה. אבל גבי מכר אילנות ושייר קרקע – מודו רבנן דבעין יפה מכר, דלית ליה למוכר השתא טענת פריסת אויר, ואינו נפסד מקרקע שהוא משייר לעצמו כלום על ידי אילן. אלא מסיפא. דהך בבא, דקתני: מכרן לבור ודות לאחר, והבית עבד לעצמו. רבי עקיבא אומר: א"צ הלוקח ליקח לו דרך, דבעין יפה מכר לו, כדמפרש לקמיה. דהשתא ליכא לפרושי טעמא דרבי עקיבא כדלעיל, אין אדם רוצה שיתן מעותיו וידרסוהו אחרים. וליכא הכא שום טענה ללוקח אלא זאת – דאין רוצה שיתן מעותיו ויפרח באויר, ולהאי טעמא לא חייש רבי עקיבא לעיל. הלכך, טעמיה הכא משום עין יפה הוא. וחכ"א: צריך ללוקח ליקח לו דרך מן המוכר, דבעין רעה מוכר. דליכא הכא לפרושי טעמייהו דרבנן כדלעיל, דאין אדם רוצה שיטול מעותיו ויפרח באויר. ואין למוכר אלא טענת דריסת ביתו נחוד, ולהכיא טענה לא חיישי רבנן לעיל. הלכך משום עין רעה הוא. ולא גרסי' הכא "הא תו למה לי", דהא לפום ריהטא משמע שהחליפו. בכאן טעמייהו, דר' עקיבא אית ליה פריחת אויר ורבנן אית להו טענת דריסה, וקשיא רישא לסיפא. אלא ה"ג: מאי לאו בהא קמיפלגי, דר"ע סבר מוכר בעין יפה מוכר כו'. דאי בתר טעמייהו דלעיל אזלי – איפכא הוה להו למימר הכא: לרבי עקיבא צריך ליקח משום טענת דריסה דמצי למיטען מוכר, ולרבנן א"צ משום טענת פריחת אויר דמצי טעין לוקח. ודלמא בהא פליגי דר"ע סבר בתר דעתא דלוקח אזלינן כו'. כלומר, בין רבנן בין רבי עקיבא חשיבי להו (ה) שתי טענות: דריסה ופריחת אויר, דבתרוייהו אדם מקפיד. אלא דרבי עקיבא מייפה כח לוקח בכ"מ שיש לו טענה כנגד המוכר, ואזיל בתר דעתא דלוקח, משום דלא שדי איניש זוזי בכדי, והיה יודע המוכר שכוונת הלוקח לקנות דבר שלם שלא יהא נפסד במקחו כלום, דאין אדם משליך מעותיו לאבוד. הלכך יד לוקח על העליונה, ולא חיישינן לטענת מוכר נגדו כלל. ורבנן אזיל בתר דעת דמוכר, דיד בעל השטר על התחתונה. אבל גבי מכר אילנות ושייר קרקע, דליכא לא למוכר ולא ללוקח טענת דריסה ופריחת אויר – אימא תרוייהו מודו, או עין יפה או עין רעה. לא את הבור ולא את הגת. מתני' היא (לקמן דף עא.), וקתני רישא: המוכר השדה מכר האבנים כו', אבל לא מכר האבנים שאינם לצרכה, ולא את הבור ולא את הגת כו' – בבור שבתוך השדה מיירי, שהיו כונסין בתוך השדה בור להשקותו. ולא את הגת שבשדה. בין חרבין. שאין מים בבור, ואין כרמים סמוך נגת, ולא יונים בשובך. בין ישובים. מיושבים. ואית דגרסי: יושבים. כל הנך אינן בכלל שדה, וצריך למוכר ליקח לו דרך, דברי ר"ע. אי לאשמועינן טעם דרבי עקיבא, דאין לוקח רוצה שיתן מעותיו וידרסוהו אחרים, וטעמייהו דרבנן דאין מוכר רוצה שיטול מעותיו ויפרח באויר – הא מרישא, דקתני: לא את הבור ולא את הדות וצריך ליקח כו', שמעינן לה! אלא ודאי משנה יתירה היא, לאשמועינן דאפילו בשאר דינין, דליכא הנך טעמי, מייפה רבי עקיבא כח לוקח, משום דמוכר בעין יפה מוכר. ורבנן מייפין כח מוכר, משום דמוכר בעין רעה מוכר. ודלמא. טעמייהו דר"ע ורבנן הכא כדלעיל. ודקאמרת: הא תו למה לי – איצטריך למימר דאשמועינן לעיל בית, כלומר, פלוגתא דרבי עקיבא ורבנן וטעמייהו גבי מכירת בית. והשתא אשמועינן שדה. וצריכא לאפלוגי בתרתי. דאי אשמעינן בית. ולא אשמעינן שדה, הוה אמינא: התם הוא דקאמר ר' עקיבא צריך ליקח לו דרך מן הלוקח – משום טענת דריסה, משום צניעות. כלומר, דהתם ודאי יש לו טענת דריסה, משום דאדם עושה בתוך ביתו מילי דצניעותא ואינו רוצה שידרסוהו אחרים. אבל גבי שדה – מודי להו לרבנן, דאין צריך למוכר ליקח לו דרך, דלא מפסיד לוקח מידי בדריסתו של זה בשדהו, דהא ליכא צניעותא בשדה, שאינו עשוי אלא לפרישה וזריעה. הלכך איצטריך למיתני שדה, לאשמועינן דבשדה נמי פליג רבי עקיבא. משום דקשי ליה דוושא. הלכך יש לו גם בכאן ללוקח טענת דריסה. אבל בית אימא לא. פליג ר' עקיבא. קמ"ל דבבית נמי מזיקא ליה דריסתו, משום צניעותא. ולרבנן נמי, איכא למימר כי האי גוונא: אי אשמעינן בית – משום דליכא דוושא, ואין לו טענה ללוקח, הלכך אזלי בתר טענת מוכר. אבל בשדה, דאיכא דוושא – אימא מודו ליה לר"ע. ואי אשמעינן שדה – משום דליכא צניעות, אבל בית דאיכא צניעות – אימא מודו ליה לר"ע, צריכא. אלא בסיפא. דהמוכר את השדה. מכרן לאחר. בור וגת ושובך, והשדה עכב לעצמו. הא תו ל"ל. לאשמועינן דאזיל רבי עקיבא בתר דעתא דלוקח, ורבנן אזלי בתר דעתא דמוכר, אפי' היכא דמשתנין הטעמים למפרע? היינו הך דקתני בסיפא דרישא דמתניתין: מכרן לבור ודות לאחר! דמהתם שמעינן דאזיל ר' עקיבא בתר דעתא דלוקח, ורבנן אזלי בתר דעתא דמוכר. ומדאשמעינן גבי בית – הוא הדין גבי שדה. דהא תרישא דהך סיפא, דהיינו: לא מכר לא את הבור ולא את הגת, מינה שמעינן דכי היכי דפליגי גבי בית פליגי נמי גבי שדה, דכל טעמי בית: דריסה ופריחה, איכא למימר נמי גבי שדה. וכיון דאשמעינן דהכא נמי גבי שדה אית להו הנך טעמי דלעיל – הוא הדין נמי גבי הך סיפא דמכרן לאחר, שמשתנין הטעמים איפכא, כדלעיל גבי מכרן לבור ודות, אזיל נמי ר"ע בתר דעתא דלוקח ורבנן בתר דעתא דמוכר. אלא לאו. שמע מינה: הך משנה יתירה דקתני – לאשמועינן דאפילו בשאר מקומות דליכא הנך טעמים – מייפה ר"ע כח לוקח משום עין יפה, ורבנן מייפין כח מוכר משום עין רעה. והא ליכא למימר דלרבנן אצטריך למתני הך סיפא, לאשמעינן דאית להו לרבנן דגבי שדה נמי חשיב להו טענת מוכר משום טענת דוושא. דמרישא דקתני: המוכר את השדה לא מכר את הבור – לא שמעינן להו לרבנן גבי שדה טענת דריסה אלא טענת פריחת אויר, (ו) אבל לר"ע הוא דשמעינן ליה דקשי דוושא לשדה, והשתא קא משמע לן דלרבנן נמי אית להו הך סברא, ואי לא תנייה הך סיפא הוה אמרינן דמודו ליה רבנן לר"ע דאין צריך ליקח לו דרך, דלא חיישינן לטענת דריסה דקטעין מוכר. ליכא למימר הכי, דכיון דמרישא דהך סיפא שמעינן לרבי עקיבא דקשי דוושא לשדה – בהך סברא נמי מודו רבנן, דהא לא פליגי בכל הנך בבי אלדרבי עקיבא, אלא דאיהו אזיל בתר דעתא דלוקח, ואינהו אזלי בתר דעת המוכר, ותו לא מידי.

הלכה

רבינו גרשום

ולא מכר הדרך. ודקאמרי' נמי בכל דוכתי בתלמוד מהכא אמרינן. דהכא עיקר מחלוקותן בהכי: ממאי. מציתו למימר דמהכא מייתי ראיה. דלמא לא פליגי לא בעין יפה ולא בעין רעה. אלא בהא פליגי דר' עקיבא סבר משום הכי צריך למוכר לקנות לו דרך מן הלוקח דאין אדם רוצה ליתן מעותיו וידרסהו אחרים ומשום הכי אין לו דרך למוכר אם אינו חוזר וקונה מן הלוקח. ורבנן סברי דאמרי אינו צריך ליקח לו דרך דלא גמר ומקני ליה דרך הבור והדות לפי שאין אדם רוצה שיטול מעות ויפרח באויר לבורו ולדותו. אלמא דבאין אדם רוצה פליגי ולא פליגי בעין יפה דבעלמא אימא לך דאפי' ר' עקיבא מודה דמוכר בעין רעה מוכר כגון אדם שמכר אילנות ושייר קרקע לפניו דכל זמן שהאילנות קיימין יכול להחזיק בהן אבל אי מייבשין אינו רשאי לנטוע אחרים תחתיהן משום דמוכר בעין רעה מוכר ומהא לא תפשוט. אלא מסיפא דמתני' מצינן למימר דפליגי ר' עקיבא ורבנן דר' עקיבא סבר דמוכר בעין יפה מוכר ורבנן סברי בעין רעה מוכר: מכרן לאחר. אותן בור ודות: ר' עקיבא אומר אינו צריך ליקח (ללוקח) דרך וכו'. דהא תו למה לי ר' עקיבא לייפות כחו של לוקח בסיפא הא אשמועינן ברישא דכי אמר צריך ליקח לו דרך למוכר ברישא היינו יפוי כח דלוקח ורבנן מייפים כח דמוכר ברישא ובסיפא הא תו למה לי אלא לאו ש"מ דמסיפא שמעינן דפליגי במוכר בעין יפה וכו'. ממאי דילמא לעולם סיפא אצטריך ופליגי בסיפא כדמיפלגי ברישא באין אדם רוצה. ודקא קשיא לך הא תו למה לי האי אצטריך דר' עקיבא סבר זיל בתר דעת דלוקח ודעתי' דלוקח אין אדם רוצה שיתן מעותיו ויפרח באויר לבורו ולדותו ומשום הכי אין צריך ליקח לו דרך ללוקח. ורבנן סברי זיל בתר דעתיה דמוכר דאינו רוצה שיקבל מעות בסתם וידרסו אחרים בבית לילך לבורו ולדותו ומשום הכי צריך ליקח לו דרך דהא מרישא איפכא שמעינן האי אין אדם ומשום הכי אצטריך נמי למתני בסיפא דלר' עקיבא לעולם בתר דעתיה דלוקח אזלי' בין היכא דמשמע שאין לוקח רוצה שידרסוהו ובין בסיפא דמשמע שאין לוקח רוצה שיפרח. ורבנן סברי בתר דעתא דמוכר וליכא למשמע מהכא דפליגי כלל בעין יפה. אלא מהא דקתני בסיפא דהאי מתני' איכא למשמע דפליגי בעין יפה דתנן מכר את השדה כו' לא מכר את הגת ולא את השובך בין חרבין דליכא בהו יונים בין ישובין דאיכא בהו יונים וצריך ליקח לו דרך וכו' כדפריש' ליה לעיל. כלומר אי משום הכי צריך למיתני דר' עקיבא סבר צריך ליקח לו דרך למוכר כדי שילך לשובכו ולבורו משום דכולה זבין ליה. לפי שאין אדם רוצה שיטול מעות ויפרח באויר לשובכו הא תו למה לי הא כבר שמעינן מרישא דמתני' דהשתא לא מצית לתרוצי כדמתרצת ליה לעיל ולא מייתר לשום דרשא אלא למשמע מיניה דר' עקיבא סבר מוכר בעין יפה מוכר וכו'. ודלמא מהא נמי לא תפשוט אלא אשמועינן הכא כי היכא דפלוגתתן לענין בית דר' עקיבא סבר אין אדם רוצה שיתן מעותיו וידרסוהו אחרים ורבנן סברי דאין אדם רוצה שיטול מעות ויפרח באויר. ה"נ פליגי גבי מוכר את השדה סתם לא מכר לא את הבור ולא את הדות כו'. וצריכא בתרווייהו למתני פלוגתייהו דמהדרא לא מפקי' אידך דאי אשמועינן בית הוה אמינא בהא קאמר ר' עקיבא אין אדם רוצה שיתן מעות וידרסו אחרים משום דבית לצניעותא עביד שמצניע אדם חפצים בביתו. ומשום הכי כולה זבין ליה אבל שדה דלאו לצניעות עביד אימא דלא לימא ר' עקיבא דצריך ליקח לו דרך קמ"ל דאפי' הכי פליג ר' עקיבא. ואי אשמועינן דס"ל לר' עקיבא גבי שדה דאין אדם רוצה שיתן מעותיו וידרסו אחרים הוה אמינא שדה שאני משום דוושא דריסה שדורסין בה בני אדם קשה לזרעים ומש"ה גמר למקני אפי' דרך שדהו ולית ליה בה כלום ומשום הכי צריך לקנות לו דרך אבל בית דמהני ומעליא ליה דישה אימא דלא מקני ליה משום דניחא ליה שידרסוהו אחרים קמ"ל דאפי' הכי אין אדם רוצה שיתן מעות וידרסוהו אחרים הואיל דבית לצניעותא עביד ותרווייהו צריכי. אלא מסיפא דהאי בבא מכר את השדה וכו' מכרן לאחר איכא למשמע מינה דפליגי ר"ע ורבנן בעין יפה ובעין רעה. הא תו ל"ל היינו דקתני בסיפא דרישא דמתני' ותרי זימני ל"ל לאשמועינן דר' עקיבא סבר זיל בתר דעתא דלוקח ורבנן סברי זיל בתר דעתא דמוכר אלא לאו ש"מ וכו': אתמר רב

הגהות הב"ח

(א) גמ' ממאי דלמא בהא פליגי ר' עקיבא סבר: (ב) שם וחכמים אומרים צריך ליקח לו דרך מאי לאו בהא קמיפלגי דר"ע סבר מוכר בעין יפה מוכר ורבנן סברי מוכר בעין רעה מוכר ודלמא בהא פליגי דר"ע סבר בתר דעתא: (ג) רשב"ם ד"ה ממאי וכו' ויש לו בקרקע אי נמי בעין רעה מוכר ואין לו: (ד) ד"ה ורבנן וכו' בלא דרך אבל גבי מוכר אילנות וכו' אילן זה הס"ד ותיבות ויד בעל השטר על התחתונה נמחק: (ה) ד"ה ודלמא וכו' חשיבי להו הנך שתי וכו' ורבנן אזלי בתר: (ו) ד"ה אלא לאו וכו' אלא טענת פריחת אויר אלא לר"ע הוא:

הלכה כדברי חכמים, ורב ירמיה בר אבא אמר שמואל: [א]הלכה כרבי עקיבא. אמר ליה רב ירמיה בר אבא לרב הונא: [ב]והא זמנין סגיאין אמריתה קמיה דרב הלכתא כרבי עקיבא, ולא אמר לי ולא מידי! א"ל: היכי תניתה? א"ל: איפכא תנינא. משום הכי לא אמר לך ולא מידי. א"ל רבינא לרב אשי: לימא אזדו לטעמייהו, [ג]דאמר רב נחמן אמר שמואל: האחין שחלקו — אין להן לא דרך זה על זה, ולא סולמות זה על זה, ולא חלונות זה על זה, ולא אמת המים זה על זה, [ד]והזהרו בהן שהלכות קבועות הן; ורב אמר: יש להן? צריכא, דאי אשמועינן בההיא — בההיא קאמר רב, משום דא"ל: בעינא למידר ביה כי היכי דדרו ביה אבהתי; תדע, דכתיב: °"תחת אבותיך יהיו בניך" (תהלים מה); אבל בהא — אימא מודי ליה לשמואל. ואי איתמר בהא — בהך קאמר שמואל, אבל בהא — אימא מודי ליה לרב, צריכא. אמר ליה רב נחמן לרב הונא: [ה]הלכתא כוותין או הלכתא כוותייכו? אמר ליה: הלכתא כוותייכו, דמקרביתו לבבא דריש גלותא דשכיחי דייני.§ איתמר: [א]שני בתים זה לפנים מזה, שניהם במכר, שניהם במתנה — אין להן דרך זה על זה, (א) כל שכן חיצון במתנה ופנימי במכר. חיצון במכר ופנימי במתנה — סבור מינה: אין להן דרך זה על זה; [ב]ולא היא, מי לא תנן: [ו]במה דברים אמורים — במוכר, אבל בנותן מתנה נותן את כולן? אלמא, [ז]מאן דיהיב מתנה — בעין יפה יהיב, [ג]הכא נמי מאן דיהיב מתנה — בעין יפה יהיב.§

מתני' [י]המוכר את הבית — מכר את הדלת אבל לא את המפתח, מכר את המכתשת קבועה אבל לא את המיטלטלת, מכר את האיצטרוביל אבל לא את הקלת, ולא את התנור ולא את הכירים. [ה]בזמן שאמר לו: "הוא וכל מה שבתוכו" —

הרי

רשב"ם

הלכה כדברי חכמים. דמוכר בעין רעה מוכר. כר' עקיבא. דבעין יפה מוכר (לקמן עא.). והכי הויא מסקנא כר' עקיבא, דאמר ליה רב הונא לרב נחמן: הלכתא כוותייהו, דמקרביתו לבבא דריש גלותא דשכיחי דייני. אמר ליה איפכא. לר' עקיבא בעין רעה, ולרבנן בעין יפה. וגמרא הוא דקמפרש דאיפכא הוה תני רב ירמיה, ומיהו, איהו לא אמר לרב הונא לשון זה "איפכא תנינא". שאם היה יודע שאין רב הונא שונה כמותו — לא היה לו לתמוה, דהיינו הך, דבין לרב הונא בין לרב ירמיה הלכתא דבעין רעה מוכר. משום הכי לא אמר לך ולא מידי. דהא את נמי הוה פסקת הלכתא דבעין רעה מוכר. אזדו לטעמייהו. דלרב בעין רעה, ולשמואל בעין יפה. האחין שחלקו. שניהם מוכרין זה לזה. אין להן דרך זה על זה. אם חלקו שני שדות, אחד נטל חיצון ואחד נטל פנימי, ואין הפנימי יכול ליכנס לשדהו אלא דרך חיצון, בדרך שהיה אביו נכנס — אין לו לפנימי דרך על חיצון. משום דמוכר בעין יפה מוכר, ולא שייר דרך לעצמו, וכיון שמכר לו לאחיו חלקו שבחיצון — בעין יפה מכר לו כל השדה והדרך, ולא שייר לעצמו במכירה זו כלום. והיינו שמואל לטעמיה, דפסק כר' עקיבא דמוכר בעין יפה מוכר. דלגבי פנימי שייך למימר עין יפה, דאע"פ שצריך לפרוח באויר — לא שייר לעצמו את הדרך. אבל גבי חיצון — לא שייך עין רעה במה שאינו נותן לו את הדרך, שהרי אינו מוכר בשדה זו החיצון אלא לוקח, ובלוקח לא שייך עין יפה. אבל בשדה הפנימי הוי הוא מוכר, שמכר לאחיו חלקו, ובההוא שמכר לא שייר לעצמו כלום, וליכא עין רעה גביה כלל. ולא חלונות כו'. כבר מפורשת בפ' ראשון(ב). ולא חלונות כו'. ואם רצה לבנות בחצירו כנגד חלון אחיו — בונה. קבועות. כלומר, שהלכה כן. ורב אמר יש להן. דמוכר בעין רעה מוכר, ומשייר לעצמו במה שמכר לאחיו דבר הצריך לו, כגון דרך ואורה. הכי גרסינן: צריכא. ורב אשי הוא דקמהדר הכי לרבינא, דלא אזדו לטעמייהו לגמרי ואין ללמוד מחלוקת מחבירתה. ומיהו, דרך גמרא הוא לומר "ואזדו לטעמייהו" ו"צריכא", אבל הכא אמוראי הוא דאיירו בה בהדיא, ואמרו: לימא אזדו לטעמייהו — הלכך הוצרך לומר בלשון תירוץ: צריכא. דאי איתמר בהך. דאחין שחלקו. בהך קאמר רב. דיש להן דרך, משום דאמרי אחין: נידור בה כו', וכמו שהיה לאבא דרך בהן — גם לי, שעל מנת כן חלקתי. תדע. דטענה מעלייתא היא גבי חלוקת יורשין, דכתיב: "תחת אבותיך" וגו'. אבל בהך. דר' עקיבא ורבנן — אימא מודי ליה רב לשמואל, דמוכר בעין יפה מוכר. הלכתא כוותין. שמואל, ורב נחמן תלמידו היה. דמקרביתו בי ריש גלותא. רב נחמן חתנא דבי נשיאה הוה, ורגיל במקום הדיינים, דשכיחי דייני ורואה מעשים בכל יום היאך דייני. אי נמי: דיני. כך פירש רבינו חננאל. זה לפנים מזה. ודריסת הפנימי על החיצון לרשות הרבים. שניהם במכר. שמכרן ביחד לשני בני אדם, או שניהם ביחד במתנה לשני בני אדם — אין לו דרך לפנימי על החיצון. דכי היכי דלפנימי זבין ויהב בעין יפה — לחיצון נמי בעין יפה יהב וזבין. ולא מקרי עין רעה אפילו לרבנן אלא היכא דמכר את הפנימי ועיכב לעצמו את החיצון, (ג) כי מתניתין. אבל היכא דלא עיכב לעצמו כלום — דכולי עלמא מודו דלזה מכר כל החיצון, ולזה כל הפנימי, ואין לפנימי על החיצון כלום, דלא תהיה עינו יפה לזה ורעה לזה. וכל שכן חיצון במתנה כו'. דודאי לא תהיה עינו יפה אצל לוקח ורעה אצל מקבל מתנה, דלההוא דיהיב ליה לדידיה רחים ליה. סבור מינה אין לו דרך. דכיון דלשניהם מוכר ונותן, אין רע לזה וטוב לזה. מי לא תנן. בסוף פירקין. במה דברים אמורים. דפליגי רבנן ואמרי דצריך לוקח ליקח דרך, אבל מוכר לא צריך משום דבעין רעה מוכר — הני מילי מוכר, אבל בנותן מתנה מודו דבעין יפה יהיב, ויהיב גם את הדרך. אלמא רבנן דסבירא להו מוכר בעין רעה מוכר, גבי נותן מודו דבעין יפה נותן. והלכך, הכא, לא מיבעיא לרבנן דיש דרך לפנימי על החיצון, דגבי חיצון שמכר לו הוי עין רעה, וגבי פנימי שנתן לו במתנה הוי עין יפה. אלא אפי' לרבי עקיבא דאית ליה עין יפה גבי מוכר, גבי נותן מיהא איכא עין יפה טפי, והלכך יש דרך לו לפנימי על החיצון, דמוכח מילתא דעינו יפה אצלו טפי מחיצון, דקא יהיב ליה מתנה. **מתני'** המוכר את הבית. סתם. מכר כו'. כללא דמילתא: כל תשמישי בית הקבועים — מכורין בכלל בית, והמטלטלין אינם מכורין. את הדלת. דכל המחובר לקרקע הרי הוא כקרקע. אבל לא את המפתח. דמיטלטלא. המכתשת הקבועה. בקרקע. איצטרוביל. עגול שסביב הריחים, לרקיי"א בלע"ז. ודבר קבוע הוא, ואין מזיזין אותו ממקומו. הקלת. האפרכסת, טרמויי"א (ח) בלע"ז, ומיטלטלת היא. הכי גרסינן: לא את התנור ולא את הכיריים. דכל הנך מיטלטלין הן. והכי נמי תניא בתוספתא. ובסדר המשנה גרס: מכר תנור מכר כיריים. ולא נהירא, ואם איתא — צריך לאוקמה במחוברת לקרקע.

הרי

תוספות

הכי גרים רבינו חננאל: ואזדו לטעמייהו וצריכא. והולרך לפרש וצריכא, דלא תקשי: והא איפליגו בה חדא זמנא. וכן היא סוגיית הגמרא בכל מקום.

לא מכר לו את התנור ולא את הכירים ולא את הריחים. להאי גירסא איירי בתלושין, דהא קתני מכר את המכתשת קבועה — אם כן כרבי אליעזר דגמרא אתיא, ואי בתנור וכירים מחוברים — הא רבי אליעזר הוא, דאמר כל המחובר לקרקע הרי הוא כקרקע. אי נמי, אומר רשב"א: דאיירי במחובר, דסתמייהו מחוברים, כדאמרינן (כלים פ"ה מ"ז): וגורר את הטפילה [עד שיהא] בארץ, אבל אין חבורו חשוב חבור. תדע, מדמקבלי טומאה. הלכך, לא מכר אפילו לר' אליעזר תנור וכירים וריחים, אע"ג דלדידיה מכר את המכתשת. ולספרים דגרסי: מכר את התנור וכירים אבל לא את הריחים — צריך לומר דחשיב חיבורן חיבור, ולא דמו לקבלת טומאה. וחיבור הריחים לא חשיב כולי האי כמו של תנור וכירים. ואין להקשות: אמאי נקט בגמרא "ולא את הריחים", כיון דאפילו ר' אליעזר מודה דלא מכר את הריחים! ואומר רשב"א: דנקט להו משום דבעי למיתני: ובזמן שאמר ליה "הוא וכל מה שבתוכו" — כולן מכורים, ואפילו ריחים.

נימא

עין משפט נר מצוה

ל א ב ג מיי' פכ"ה מהל' מכירה הל' ד סמג עשין פב טוש"ע ח"מ סי' ריד סעיף ט:

לא ד ה מיי' שם הל' ה וסמג שם טוש"ע שם סעיף יא:

הגהות הב"ח

(א) גמ' וכל שכן חיצון וכו' ופנימי במתנה מאי סבור: (ב) רשב"ם ד"ה ולא וכו' כפ' ראשון. נ"ב בדף ז' ע"ב: (ג) ד"ה שניהם במכר וכו' כי מתניתין נ"ב פי' כגון מכר לו את הבור ולא את הדות כו':

מסורת הש"ס

א) [לקמן פב:] ב) [ר"ה ... ג) לעיל ז: ד) [לקמן ... ה) [לקמן קמב:] ... [לקמן עא.] ז) [לעיל נג.] ... בחגיגה ג: הוסיף רש"י אפרכסת טרמויי"א שעל הריחים]:

רבינו גרשום

... הונא אמר הלכה ...רי חכמים. דאמרי ...ר בעין רעה מוכר: ...מואל אמר הלכה ...ע. דאמר בעין יפה ...ר: אנא אפכא ...א. דרב הונא דאמר ...כה כחכמים ס"ל ... יפה מוכר ושמואל ... הלכה כר"ע דאמר ...ר בעין רעה מוכר: ...אמר לך מידי. דהיינו ... סבירא ליה: האחין ...לקו. בנכסי אביהן: ... להן דרך זה על זה ... דהואיל דחלקו בעין ... חלקו וצריכין ליקח ... מזה דרך וגם לא ...ת חלונות וגם לא ...ת סולמות להניח זה ...צר זה להעלותו לגגו ... אמת המים של זה ...בור בחלקו של זה: ... אמר יש להן. דס"ל ...שנא קמא כחכמים ...מרי מוכר בעין רעה ...כר: דאי אשמועינן ...א. באחין שחלקו ...הא אמר רב דבעין ...ה חלקו ויש להן. ...שום דכתיב תחת ...ותיך יהיו בניך: אבל ...א. גבי מוכר: קאמר ...מואל. דהמוכר בעין ...ה מוכר אבל בהך ...אחין אימא מודי ליה ...ב קמ"ל דאפי' הכי ...יני: רב נחמן הוה ...למיד דשמואל כדאמרינן ...עיל אמר רב נחמן אמר ...מואל האחין שחלקו ... הונא הוה תלמיד ...יב: הלכתא כוותין. ...אמרינן מוכר בעין יפה ...יבר: או הלכתא ...ותייכו: דאמריתו מוכר ...עין רעה מוכר: שניהם ...כרו במכר או שניהם ...תנו במתנה לשניהם אין ...הם לקוחות ...מקבלין דרך זה על זה. ...שום דהמוכר או הנותן ...עין יפה מוכר ונותן: ...בל שכן דאין להן. ...יבא דחיצון נתן במתנה ...יפה כח מתנה מכח ...מכירה כדאמרינן בגמ' ...סיפא דפרקין ובעין יפה ...תן החיצון ופנימי דמכר ...אין לפנימי דרך על ...חיצון כלום אע"ג ...משועבד חיצון לפנימי: ...חיצון מכר ופנימי נתן ...מהו. מי אמרי' דיפה כח ...מתנה מכח מכירה ובעין ...פה נתן יש לו דרך או לא לטעמיה דר' עקיבא:

מי לא תנן בד"א. דאין צריך ליקח להן דרך לדברי חכמים: במוכר. דבעין רעה מוכר: אבל בנותן מתנה נתן את כולה. דבעין יפה נתן הכי נמי לההוא דיהיב מתנה בעין יפה נתן לו ויש לפנימי דרך על החיצון: **פיסקא** המוכר את הבית מכר את הדלת. דהוי מחובר לבית שהוא מחובר לקרקע וכל מחובר לקרקע הרי הוא כקרקע: אבל לא את המפתח. דלא הוי כלל מחובר דאי בעי מצי לנוטלה ויוצאת ונכנסת היא. המכתשת קבועה. בקרקע: איצטרוביל. היינו מקום שכיבת הרחיים הסדינין שקבוע בקרקע: אבל לא את הקלת. היינו רחיים העליונה שחוזרת דלא הוי מחובר: מכר את התנור ואת הכירים. אם קבועין בקרקע: בזמן שאמר לו הוא

וכל

הֲרֵי כּוּלָּן מְכוּרִין.§ **גמ'** לֵימָא, מַתְנִיתִין דְּלָא כְּר' מֵאִיר, דְּאִי (א) ר"מ, הָא אָמַר: א)מָכַר אֶת הַכֶּרֶם – מָכַר תַּשְׁמִישֵׁי כֶרֶם! אֲפִי' תֵּימָא ר"מ, הָתָם קְבִיעַ, הָכָא לָא קְבִיעַ. וְהָא מַפְתֵּחַ דּוּמְיָא דְּדֶלֶת קָתָנֵי, מַה דֶּלֶת דִּקְבִיעָא, אַף מַפְתֵּחַ דִּקְבִיעַ! אֶלָּא מְחַוַּורְתָּא, מַתְנִי' דְּלָא כְּר"מ. ת"ר: אהַמּוֹכֵר אֶת הַבַּיִת – מָכַר אֶת הַדֶּלֶת וְאֶת הַנֶּגֶר וְאֶת הַמַּנְעוּל, אֲבָל לֹא אֶת הַמַּפְתֵּחַ. מָכַר אֶת הַמַּכְתֶּשֶׁת הַחֲקוּקָה, אֲבָל לֹא אֶת הַקְּבוּעָה. מָכַר הָאִיצְטְרוֹבִיל, אֲבָל לֹא אֶת הַקֶּלֶת, לֹא אֶת הַתַּנּוּר וְלֹא אֶת הַכִּירַיִם וְלֹא אֶת הָרֵיחַיִם; ר' אֱלִיעֶזֶר אוֹמֵר: כָּל הַמְחוּבָּר לַקַּרְקַע הֲרֵי הוּא כַּקַּרְקַע; בבִּזְמַן שֶׁאָמַר לוֹ "הוּא וְכָל מַה שֶּׁבְּתוֹכוֹ" – הֲרֵי כּוּלָּן מְכוּרִין; בֵּין כָּךְ וּבֵין כָּךְ, לֹא מָכַר לֹא אֶת הַבּוֹר וְלֹא אֶת הַדּוּת וְלֹא אֶת הַיָּצִיעַ. ב)ת"ר: גצִינּוֹר שֶׁחֲקָקוֹ וּלְבַסּוֹף קְבָעוֹ – פּוֹסֵל אֶת הַמִּקְוֶה, קְבָעוֹ וּלְבַסּוֹף חֲקָקוֹ – אֵינוֹ פּוֹסֵל אֶת הַמִּקְוֶה. מַנִּי? לָא ר' אֱלִיעֶזֶר וְלָא רַבָּנַן. הֵי ר' אֱלִיעֶזֶר? אִילֵימָא ר"א דְּבַיִת, דִּלְמָא הַיְינוּ טַעֲמָא, דר"א סָבַר: ג)מוֹכֵר בְּעַיִן יָפָה מוֹכֵר, וְרַבָּנַן סָבְרִי: מוֹכֵר בְּעַיִן רָעָה מוֹכֵר! וְאֶלָּא ר"א דְּכַוֶּורֶת דְּבוֹרִים. דִּתְנַן: ד)כַּוֶּורֶת דְּבוֹרִים – רַבִּי אֱלִיעֶזֶר אוֹמֵר: הֲרֵי הִיא כְּקַרְקַע, וְכוֹתְבִין עָלֶיהָ פְּרוֹזְבּוּל, וְאֵינָהּ

רשב"ם

הֲרֵי כּוּלָּן מְכוּרִין. כָּל הָנָךְ תַּשְׁמִישִׁין הַמִּיטַּלְטְלִין. אֲבָל שְׁאָר (ב) מִינֵי תַּשְׁמִישְׁתֵּיהּ לָא מִיזְדַּבְּנִי, וְאַף עַל גַּב דְּאָמַר "כָּל מַה שֶּׁבְּתוֹכוֹ אֲנִי מוֹכֵר לָךְ", שֶׁלֹּא רִיבָּה בְּלָשׁוֹן זֶה אֶלָּא תַּשְׁמִישִׁין הַמְיוּחָדִין לְבַיִת זֶה, שֶׁאֵינָן רְגִילִין לְהַשְׁאִילָן מִפְּנֵי כְּבֵידָן. וּמַפְתֵּחַ נַמִי, עִיקַּר תַּשְׁמִישׁוֹ לַפּוֹתַחַת שֶׁל דֶּלֶת זוֹ, וְאֵין רָאוּי לְאַחֶרֶת. וְהַיְינוּ טַעֲמָא דְּלָא זַבֵּין שְׁאָר מִינֵי תַּשְׁמִישְׁתֵּיהּ – דְּלָא בְּטֵילֵי לְגַבֵּי בַּיִת. אִי נַמִי, אֵינוֹ רוֹצֶה לְהִתְרַחֵק מִן הַשְּׁכוּנָה שֶׁלּוֹ, וְיָדוּר בְּבַיִת אַחֵר, וּצְרִיכִין לוֹ מִטַּלְטְלִין. אֲבָל גַּבֵּי חָצֵר תְּנַן לְקַמָּן דְּאִם אוֹמֵר לוֹ "כָּל מַה שֶּׁבְּתוֹכָהּ" – הֲרֵי כָּל מִטַּלְטְלִין מְכוּרִין, דְּהַיְינוּ כָּל מָאנֵי תַּשְׁמִישְׁתֵּיהּ דְּאִיקְּרוּ מִטַּלְטְלֵי, לְבַד מֵחִיטֵּי וְשַׂעֲרֵי, בְּפֶ' "מִי שֶׁמֵּת" (לקמן דף קנ.), דְּכֵיוָן דְּמִסְתַּלֵּק מִכָּל הַשְּׁכוּנָה – מָכַר אֶת כּוּלָּן, דְּטוֹרַח הוּא לוֹ לְהוֹצִיא כֵּלָיו מִשָּׁם. אִי נַמִי, לְגַבֵּי חָצֵר שֶׁהוּא דָּבָר גָּדוֹל (ג) – בְּטֵילֵי. וְגַבֵּי מוֹכֵר אֶת הָעִיר תְּנַן דְּאִם אָמַר "כָּל מַה שֶּׁבְּתוֹכָהּ" – מָכַר אֶת הַכֹּל, אֲפִילּוּ בְּהֵמָה וַעֲבָדִים דְּהָווּ מִטַּלְטְלֵי דְּנָיְידֵי, וְכ"ש חִיטֵּי וְשַׂעֲרֵי. דְּכֵיוָן דְּמִסְתַּלֵּק מִכָּל הָעִיר – מִכֹּל וָכֹל רוֹצֶה לְהִסְתַּלֵּק, דְּטוֹרַח הוּא לוֹ לְהוֹצִיא מִטַּלְטְלֵי לְעִיר אַחֶרֶת. א"נ, בְּטֵלִין לְגַבֵּי הָעִיר. כְּלָלָא דְּמִילְּתָא: כָּל מֶכֶר הַגָּדוֹל מֵחֲבֵירוֹ – רִיבָּה לִמְכּוֹר יוֹתֵר, הַגָּדוֹל לְפִי גׇּדְלוֹ וְהַקָּטָן לְפִי קׇטְנוֹ. **גמ'** לֵימָא מַתְנִי'. דְּקָתָנֵי: (ד) לֹא מָכַר מַכְתֶּשֶׁת הַמִּיטַּלְטֵל – דְּלָא כְּר"מ, דְּאִי כְּר"מ – הָאָמַר בְּפֶרֶק "הַמּוֹכֵר אֶת הַסְּפִינָה" בְּבָרַיְיתָא בַּגְּמָ': מָכַר כֶּרֶם – מָכַר תַּשְׁמִישֵׁי כֶרֶם, כְּגוֹן קָנִים שֶׁבַּכֶּרֶם שֶׁהֵן לְצׇרְכּוֹ כִּדְתְנַן בְּמַתְנִי'. (ה) וְה"ה לְמוֹכֵר בַּיִת, שֶׁמּוֹכֵר תַּשְׁמִישֵׁי בַּיִת. וּמְשַׁנֵּי: הָתָם קְבִיעַ. כְּלוֹמַר, הָתָם בְּדְר"מ אִיכָּא לְמֵימַר דְּלָא אַיְירֵי ר"מ אֶלָּא בְּתַשְׁמִישִׁין הַקְּבוּעִין לְעוֹלָם בְּתוֹךְ הַכֶּרֶם, שֶׁאֵין מְזִיזִין אוֹתָם מִשָּׁם לְעוֹלָם, וְאַע"ג דְּאֵינָם קְבוּעִין בַּקַּרְקַע. אֲבָל מַכְתֶּשֶׁת שֶׁאֵינָהּ קְבוּעָה בַּקַּרְקַע – זִימְנִין דְּשָׁיְילֵי לַהּ, וְלָא קְבִיעָא בְּבַיִת כׇּל כָּךְ. וְהָא מַפְתֵּחַ דּוּמְיָא דְּדֶלֶת קָתָנֵי מַה דֶּלֶת דִּקְבִיעָא. לְעוֹלָם, שֶׁאֵין מְזִיזִין אוֹתוֹ מִשָּׁם לְהִטַּלְטֵל מִמָּקוֹם לְמָקוֹם, אַף מַפְתֵּחַ – בְּשֶׁל עֵץ מַיְירֵי, דִּקְבִיעָא, שֶׁיֵּשׁ מַפְתְּחוֹת שֶׁאֵין מְזִיזִין אוֹתָן מִן הַפּוֹתַחַת, כְּגוֹן שֶׁל בְּנֵי כְּפָרִים, וְאפ"ה לֹא מָכַר אֶת הַמַּפְתֵּחַ. דְּאִי אִיתָא דְּבְמַפְתֵּחַ שֶׁאֵינוֹ קָבוּעַ מַיְירֵי – לִיפְלוֹג וְלִיתְנֵי בְּדִידֵיהּ: הַמּוֹכֵר אֶת הַבַּיִת מָכַר אֶת הַמַּפְתֵּחַ קָבוּעַ אֲבָל לֹא אֶת הַמִּיטַּלְטֶלֶת, כִּדְקָתָנֵי גַּבֵּי מַכְתֶּשֶׁת, וְכ"ש דֶּלֶת דִּקְבִיעַ טְפֵי. אֶלָּא מִדְּקָתָנֵי דֶּלֶת – שְׁמְעִינַן דְּלֵיכָּא לְאִיפְלוּגֵי אֶלָּא בֵּין דֶּלֶת לְמַפְתֵּחַ, וְאַע"ג דִּקְבִיעַ בְּדֶלֶת אֵינוֹ מָכוּר, שֶׁהֲרֵי תַּשְׁמִישׁ קַל הוּא וְנוֹחַ לְטַלְטְלוֹ, וּפְעָמִים שֶׁמִּיטַּלְטֶלֶת, אֲבָל לֹא תָּדִיר. נֶגֶר. בְּרִיחַ, וְקָבוּעַ בַּכּוֹתֶל. מַנְעוּל. קָבוּעַ בַּדֶּלֶת. הַמַּכְתֶּשֶׁת הַחֲקוּקָה. כְּגוֹן סֶלַע הַיּוֹצֵא מִן הַכּוֹתֶל, וְחָקַק שָׁם מַכְתֶּשֶׁת. אֲבָל לֹא אֶת הַקְּבוּעָה. שֶׁהָיְתָה חֲקוּקָה וַעֲשׂוּיָה, וְאַח"כ קְבָעָהּ בַּקַּרְקַע, וּדְלָא כְּמַתְנִי'. וּמַתְנִיתִין ר' אֱלִיעֶזֶר הִיא, דְּפָלֵיג בְּסֵיפָא, וְאָמַר: כׇּל הַמְחוּבָּר לַקַּרְקַע – הֲרֵי הוּא כְּקַרְקַע. וְכֵן פֵּירֵשׁ ר' חֲנַנְאֵל, וְכֵן עִיקָּר. ר' אֱלִיעֶזֶר כו'. אַמַּכְתֶּשֶׁת קְבוּעָה פָּלֵיג. בֵּין כָּךְ וּבֵין כָּךְ. בֵּין שֶׁאָמַר לוֹ "כׇּל מַה שֶּׁבְּתוֹכוֹ", בֵּין שֶׁלֹּא אָמַר. לֹא מָכַר לֹא אֶת הַבּוֹר כו'. דְּאֵינוֹ בְּתוֹכוֹ שֶׁל בַּיִת, אֶלָּא בִּנְיָינִים בִּפְנֵי עַצְמָן הֵן.

צִינּוֹר. שֶׁל עֵץ אוֹ שֶׁל אֶבֶן, עָשׂוּי כְּמִין סִילּוֹן, וְיוֹרְדִין מִמֶּנּוּ מַיִם לַמִּקְוֶה. קְבָעוֹ בַּקַּרְקַע פּוֹסֵל אֶת הַמִּקְוֶה. דְּמַיִם שְׁאוּבִין פּוֹסְלִין אוֹתוֹ. וְכֵיוָן שֶׁהָיָה תּוֹרַת כְּלִי עָלָיו קוֹדֶם שֶׁקְּבָעוֹ – לָא מִיבְּטִיל תּוּ שֵׁם כְּלִי מִינֵּיהּ, וּמְשַׁוֵּי לְהוּ שְׁאוּבִין לַמַּיִם שֶׁבְּתוֹכוֹ. וּלְבַסּוֹף חֲקָקוֹ. הֲרֵי הוּא כְּעוֹשֶׂה חָרִיץ בַּקַּרְקַע. מַנִּי. הַךְ בָּרַיְיתָא דְּקָתָנֵי דְּמִשּׁוּם קְבִיעוּת בַּקַּרְקַע לָא בָּטֵיל שֵׁם כְּלִי כֵּיוָן דְּמֵעִיקָּרָא? לֹא ר' אֱלִיעֶזֶר וְלֹא רַבָּנַן. דִּפְלִיגִי עֲלֵיהּ. הֵי ר' אֱלִיעֶזֶר. מֵאֵיזֶה דִּבְרֵי ר' אֱלִיעֶזֶר אַתָּה לָמֵד דְּלָא סְבִירָא לֵיהּ הַךְ בָּרַיְיתָא? וְה"ה דה"ל לְמֵימַר "וְהֵי רַבָּנַן", אַךְ אֵין דֶּרֶךְ גְּמָרָא לְהַאֲרִיךְ כׇּל כָּךְ. אִילֵימָא ר' אֱלִיעֶזֶר דְּבַיִת. דְּמַכְתֶּשֶׁת חֲקוּקָה וּלְבַסּוֹף קְבָעוּהָ כְּקַרְקַע מְשַׁוֵּי לַהּ, וּמְכוּרָה בִּכְלַל בַּיִת. וּמִיהוּ, רַבָּנַן דִּפְלִיגֵי עֲלֵיהּ לָא לֶיהֱווּ הָנְהוּ רַבָּנַן דְּקָאָמַר לְעֵיל "לֹא ר' אֱלִיעֶזֶר וְלֹא רַבָּנַן". בְּעַיִן יָפָה מוֹכֵר. וְהִלְכָּךְ, אַע"ג דְּאִיכָּא תּוֹרַת כְּלִי עָלָיו, כֵּיוָן דִּמְחוּבָּר – מְכָרָן הַמּוֹכֵר. אֲבָל גַּבֵּי לִיפּוּר שֶׁחֲקָקוֹ וּלְבַסּוֹף קְבָעוֹ – מוֹדֵי דְּפָסֵיל מִקְוֶה. וְרַבָּנַן סָבְרִי כו'. מִשּׁוּם דְּר' אֱלִיעֶזֶר נְקַט לַהּ, וְאַפְּתֵי כְּדִבְרֵי הַכֹּל אָתְיָא. כַּוֶּורֶת דְּבוֹרִים. מְחוּבֶּרֶת הִיא בַּקַּרְקַע בְּטִיט. הֲרֵי הִיא כְּקַרְקַע. לְכׇל דָּבָר, לִהְיוֹת נִקְנֵית בְּכֶסֶף וּבִשְׁטָר וּבַחֲזָקָה, וְלִקְנוֹת עַל גַּבָּהּ מִטַּלְטְלִין, וְלִכְתּוֹב עָלֶיהָ פְּרוֹזְבּוּל כְּאִילּוּ הִיא קַרְקַע. דִּתְנַן בְּמַסֶּכֶת שְׁבִיעִית פֶּרֶק אַחֲרוֹן (משנה ו): אֵין כּוֹתְבִין פְּרוֹזְבּוּל אֶלָּא עַל הַקַּרְקַע, וְאִם אֵין לוֹ – מְזַכֶּה בְּתוֹךְ שָׂדֵהוּ. וְלָשׁוֹן מְפוֹרָשׁ: לְפִי שֶׁרָאָה הִלֵּל שֶׁנִּמְנְעוּ הָעֲשִׁירִים מִלְּהַלְווֹת לָעֲנִיִּים מִפְּנֵי יִרְאַת שְׁבִיעִית שֶׁמְּשַׁמֶּטֶת, וְהָיוּ עוֹבְרִין עַל מַה שֶּׁכָּתוּב: "פֶּן יִהְיֶה דָבָר עִם לְבָבְךָ בְלִיַּעַל" וגו' – עָמַד הִלֵּל וְהִתְקִין פְּרוֹזְבּוּל. "פְּרוֹז" – רֶיוַח, כְּמוֹ "שֶׁהִפְרִיז עַל מִדּוֹתָיו" דְּבְמַסֶּכֶת נִדָּה (דף ז:), "בּוּל" – עֲשִׁירִים, כְּמוֹ "אֵלּוּ רָאשֵׁי בּוּלָאוֹת שֶׁבִּיהוּדָה" (גיטין דף לז.). כְּלוֹמַר, רֶיוַח לָעֲשִׁירִים שֶׁלֹּא יַפְסִידוּ שֶׁלָּהֶם. וּתְנַן: (ו) גּוּפוֹ שֶׁל פְּרוֹזְבּוּל: מוֹסְרַנִי לָכֶם פְּלוֹנִי וּפְלוֹנִי

תוספות

נימא מתני' דלא כר' מאיר. מדתנן דלא מכר את המפתח דייק, דהא מכח מפתח מדיק דאתיא דלא כר' מאיר. ולא כפ"ה, דפירש דהשתא מדקתני לא מכר את המכתשת המיטלטל קא פריך. **מחוורתא** דלא כר' מאיר. וא"ת: והא קאמר ב"המוכר את הספינה" (לקמן דף עח:) דרבי אליעזר ור"מ קיימי בחדא שיטה, מדתנן בפירקין (דף סז:), רבי אליעזר אומר: המוכר את הבד מכר את הקורה! וי"ל: דלאו ממש בחדא שיטה קאמר. תדע, דהא טעמא דר' אליעזר מפרש בברייתא – שלא נקרא בית הבד אלא על שם קורה. **צינור** שחקקו ולבסוף קבעו פוסל את המקוה. איכא לאוקמי אפילו בפרון משני רוחות כדרך הצינור, וכגון שחטטו באמצע לקבל צרורות. דבהאי בית קבול חשיבי מים שאובים, שעוברים על אותו בית קיבול, כדתנן (מקואות פ"ד מ"ג): החוטט בצינור כדי לקבל צרורות, בשל עץ – בכל שהוא, בשל חרס – רביעית. ר"י אומר: אף בשל חרס בכל שהוא כו'. דאי לא חטטו, אפילו סתום משלשה צדדים – לא חשיב כלי, כדמוכיח רבינו שמואל מהא דתנן (שם מ"ג): המניח את הטבלא תחת הצינור, אם יש לה (ז) לבזבז מארבע רוחות כו'. ואין נראה לאוקמי בצינור שסתום מכל צד. ודוקא שמים נופלין מצינור למקוה, אבל אם נפלו מצינור לקרקע, ומקרקע למקוה – המשכה היא, ואינו פוסל המקוה, אם יש כבר במקום כ"א סאה מי גשמים, כדתנן בפרק קמא דתמורה (דף יב.). **אילימא** רבי אליעזר דבית. התם בהא פליגי. פי' הקונטרס: ומיהו, רבנן דפליגי עליה לא ליהוו הנהו רבנן דאמר לעיל "לא רבי אליעזר ולא רבנן". ונראה לר"י דזה דחקו: לפי מה שמפרש לעיל "מכר את המכתשת חקוקה" היינו קבעה ולבסוף חקקה, "אבל לא את הקבועה" היינו חקקה ולבסוף קבעה – אלמא מיפלגי רבנן בין חקקה ולבסוף קבעה ובין קבעה ולבסוף חקקה, א"כ אתי שפיר כרבנן. ובחנם דחק לפרש, דמצינן לפרש דחקוקה – היינו שלא תלשה מעולם, שנחקקה בסלע היוצא מן ההר, וקבועה – בין קבועה ולבסוף חקוקה בין חקוקה ולבסוף קבועה. **הרי** היא בקרקע. השתא קס"ד דכוורת מחוברת איירי, וצריך לפרש "והרי היא כקרקע" – לקנותה בכסף ושטר וחזקה. אבל לבסוף, דמסקינן טעמא משום דאיתקש ליער – קאי אדבש שבתוך הכוורת, ולא חיישינן בחיבור הכוורת. ואומר רבינו יצחק: דהשתא הוה מצי למיפרך: וליטעמיך, דלא מוקמת טעמא משום היקשא דיער, אלא משום חיבור כוורת בטיט, אמאי חייב חטאת הרודה ממנה בשבת? דה"ל כרודה פת מן התנור, דלא מיחייב, אף על גב דתנור מחובר. ולענין טומאה נמי מקבל הדבש טומאה, אפילו במקומה, כיון דלא בעי מחשבה. ולענין פרוזבול נמי תיפ"ק ליה דהא איכא מקום שסוכבת עליו, כדפריך ב"השולח" (גיטין דף לז.) גבי עציץ נקוב. אלא על כרחך דמנח אסיכי, כדמשני התם. ואם כן אין טעמו של רבי אליעזר משום שמחובר בטיט.

ומקבלת

רבינו גרשום

מה שבתוכו כולם מכורין. אפי' כלים המיטלטלין שיש בו: מכר תשמישי הכרם. משמע תשמישים בין קבועין בין מיטלטלין ומתני' קתני דלא מכר המיטלטלין דהיכי דאמר גבי כרם הוא הדין נמי גבי בית: התם קביע. גבי כרם תשמישין קבועין בקרקע א) אלא קנים המעמידים את הגפנים והצירים שקושרין בהם הגפנים לקנים וכיון דמחובר לקרקע הרי הן כקרקע ומש"ה הרי אלו מכורין אבל הכא לא קביע מפתח ומיטלטל ומשום הכי לא מכור: אף מפתח. נמי קבוע בדלת דאינו נפרד ממנו כלל ואפי' הכי קתני דלא מכרה. אלא מחוורתא מתני' דלא כר' מאיר: ואת הנגר. היינו בריח שקבוע בכותל למעלה מן הדלת וכשנועל הדלת נופל הנגר עד לארץ ונועלו: ואת המנעול. קבוע בדלת: אבל לא את המפתח. דמיטלטל: מכר את המכתשת החקוקה. כמו סלע היוצאת מאליה מקרקע שהיא מחוברת מעיקרא וחוקקין אותה במקומה לצורך מכתשת ומשום הכי הוי כקרקע ומכורה היא: אבל לא את המכתשת קבועה. שהיתה תלושה מעיקרא והדר קבעה וחקקה כלו' דלא מיחבר היא: אבל לא מכר לא את התנור ולא את הכירים ולא את הריחים. משום דכל הני מטלטלין נינהו ולא כקרקע דמי. תנור שהוא עשוי כגיגית רחב מלמטה וצר מלמעלה: ר' אליעזר אומר כל המחובר לקרקע. אפי' מכתשת הקבועה ואת התנור והכי נמי ריחים דמחוברין לקרקע הרי הן כקרקע ומכורין ומסתברא דמתני' ר' אליעזר היא: בין כך ובין כך. אפי' אמר לו הוא וכל מה שבתוכו: לא מכר לא את הבור כו'. דכל הני רשות בפני עצמן הן ולא שייכי כלל עם הבית: ת"ר צינור שחקקו. כדי לקובעו מן המעיין ועד המקוה שילכו המים למקוה דרך הצינור: פוסל את המקוה. משום דהמים דרך הצינור שהוא כלי באין למקוה והוו כמים שאובין דלאו כקרקע הוא: קבעו. מתחלה לארץ: ולבסוף חקקו. כשהוא מחובר: אינו פוסל את המקוה. דבקרקע דמי הואיל ולא הוי ליה תורת כלי בתלוש: לא ר' אליעזר ולא רבנן. אי נימא ר' אליעזר דבית. דאמר לעיל כל המחובר לקרקע הרי הוא כקרקע והכא קתני צינור שחקקו ולבסוף קבעו אע"ג דמחובר לקרקע פוסל את המקוה. ולא רבנן דאמרי לעיל מכר את המכתשת חקוקה אבל לא את הקבועה משום דלא כקרקע דמי הואיל שהיתה תלושה מעיקרא אע"ג דקבעה וחקקה במקומה ב) והכא קתני קבעו ולבסוף חקקו במקומו הרי הוא כקרקע ואינו פוסל את המקוה. ודלמא התם בבית בהא קמיפלגי דר' אליעזר דאמר כל המחובר לקרקע הרי הוא כקרקע סבר מוכר בעין יפה מוכר ורבנן סברי וכו'. אבל הכא לענין מקוה דלמא כברייתא ס"ל: כוורת דבורים. שעשאה וחיבר לקרקע כו' וכותבין עליה פרוזבול. דקאמר מוסר אני לכם שטרותי אגב האי כוורת כדי שלא תהא שביעית משמטת: ואינה

א) נראה דצ"ל דאינו מכור לר"מ אלא קנים המעמידים וכו'. ב) דברי רבינו בכאן הוא כדעת ר"י בתוס' ד"ה אילימא ע"ש.

עין משפט נר מצוה

לב א ב מיי' פכ"ה מהל' מכירה הלכה ה סמג עשין פב טוש"ע ח"מ סי' ריד סעיף יא:

לג ג מיי' פ"ו מהל' מקואות הל' ו סמג עשין רמח טוש"ע י"ד סי' רא סעיף לד וסעיף לו [וברב אלפס עוד בשבועות פ"ב דף רלא:]:

מסורת הש"ס

א) [לקמן עח: ב) ב"מ ...] [תוס' מקוואות ...] ג) [לעיל לז. וש"נ]: ד) ... פ: שביעית פ"י מ"ז ע... פ"ג מ"י:

הגהות הב"ח

(א) גמ' דאי כר ... (ב) רשב"ם ד"ה הרי שאר מאני תשמיש... כצ"ל וכן בסמוך: (ג) בא... שהוא דבר גדול מ... בטילי וכו' אמר לו (ד) ד"ה לימא וכו' ... מכר וכו' המוכר הספינה נ"ב בדף ע... ע"ב: (ה) בא"ד כד... במתני'. נ"ב בסוף ס"ח: (ו) ד"ה הרי ... כקרקע וכו' ותנן זהו ג... וכו': (ז) תוס' ד"ה לי... וכו' לבזבזים מארב... רוחות כו' ואין לנ... לאוקמי:

וְאֵינָהּ מְקַבֶּלֶת טוּמְאָה בִּמְקוֹמָהּ, אוְהָרוֹדֶה מִמֶּנָּה בְּשַׁבָּת — חַיָּיב חַטָּאת; וַחֲכָמִים אוֹמְרִים: אֵינָהּ כְּקַרְקַע, וְאֵין כּוֹתְבִין עָלֶיהָ פְּרוֹזְבּוֹל, וּמְקַבֶּלֶת טוּמְאָה בִּמְקוֹמָהּ, וְהָרוֹדֶה מִמֶּנָּה בְּשַׁבָּת — פָּטוּר. הָתָם כְּדַאֲמַר ר' אֶלְעָזָר טַעֲמָא, א)דַּאֲמַר ר' אֶלְעָזָר: מ"ט דְּר' אֱלִיעֶזֶר? דִּכְתִיב: שמואל א יד °"וַיִּטְבּוֹל אוֹתָהּ בְּיַעְרַת הַדְּבָשׁ", מַה יַּעַר — הַתּוֹלֵשׁ מִמֶּנּוּ בְּשַׁבָּת חַיָּיב חַטָּאת, אַף דְּבַשׁ — הָרוֹדֶה מִמֶּנּוּ בְּשַׁבָּת חַיָּיב חַטָּאת! אֶלָּא ר"א דְּדַף, דִּתְנַן: ב)דַּף שֶׁל נַחְתּוֹמִין שֶׁקְּבָעוֹ בְּכוֹתֶל — ר"א מְטַהֵר, בוַחֲכָמִים מְטַמְּאִין; מַנִּי? אִי רַבִּי אֱלִיעֶזֶר — אֲפִי' חֲקָקוֹ וּלְבַסּוֹף קְבָעוֹ, אִי רַבָּנַן — אֲפִילּוּ קְבָעוֹ וּלְבַסּוֹף חֲקָקוֹ נַמִּי! לְעוֹלָם רַבִּי אֱלִיעֶזֶר הִיא, וְשָׁאנֵי פְּשׁוּטֵי כְלֵי עֵץ, דְּטוּמְאָה דְּרַבָּנַן. מִכְּלָל דְּשְׁאִיבָה דְּאוֹרַיְיתָא? וְהָא

ופְלוֹנִי הַדַּיָּינִין שֶׁבִּמְקוֹם פְּלוֹנִי, שֶׁכָּל חוֹב שֶׁיֵּשׁ לִי אֵצֶל פְּלוֹנִי — שֶׁאֶגְבֶּנּוּ כ"ז שֶׁאֶרְצֶה. וְהַדַּיָּינִין חוֹתְמִין עָלָיו מִלְּמַטָּה, אוֹ הָעֵדִים. וְהִלְכָּךְ מִשֶּׁמָּסַר שְׁטָרוֹתָיו לְב"ד לִגְבּוֹתָן, וְאִיהוּ לָא קָגָבֵי — לָא קָרֵינָא בֵּיהּ "לֹא יִגּוֹשׂ", דְּדַיָּינִין קָמַגְבּוּ לֵיהּ, וְהֶפְקֵר ב"ד הֶפְקֵר. וְה"מ כְּשֶׁיֵּשׁ לוֹ קַרְקַע לַלֹּוֶה, דְּדָמֵי כְּאִילּוּ יֵשׁ לַמַּלְוֶה מַשְׁכּוֹן, דְּבְמַשְׁכּוֹן לֹא שַׁיָּיךְ "לֹא יִגּוֹשׂ". תורה אור

(א) שֶׁכָּל מַה שֶּׁיּוּכְלוּ חֲכָמִים לְתַקֵּן כְּדֵי שֶׁלֹּא יְהוּ נִרְאִין עוֹקְרִין דָּבָר מִן הַתּוֹרָה — הִתְקִינוּ. כֵּן נִרְאֶה הַטַּעַם בְּעֵינַי. וּמֵרַבִּי זְקֵנִי ז"ל שָׁמַעְתִּי דְּהַיְינוּ טַעֲמָא: דִּסְתָם לֹוֶה אֵין רְגִילִין לְהַלְווֹתוֹ אא"כ יֵשׁ לוֹ קַרְקַע לְהִשְׁתַּעְבֵּד לַמַּלְוֶה, וּבְמִילְּתָא דִּשְׁכִיחָא תַּקִּינוּ רַבָּנַן, אֲבָל כְּשֶׁאֵין לוֹ קַרְקַע — מִילְּתָא דְּלָא שְׁכִיחָא הִיא, וְלָא תַּקִּינוּ רַבָּנַן פְּרוֹזְבּוֹל. וַאֲתָא רַבִּי אֱלִיעֶזֶר לְמֵימַר דְּאִם יֵשׁ לַלֹּוֶה כַּוֶּורֶת דְּבוֹרִים — כּוֹתְבִין פְּרוֹזְבּוֹל. דְּסד"א: אע"ג דַּהֲרֵי הִיא כְּקַרְקַע לִשְׁאָר דְּבָרִים, לְגַבֵּי הַךְ תַּקָּנָה לָא חֲשִׁיבָא קַרְקַע, דְּלָא סָמְכָא דַּעְתֵּיהּ דְּמַלְוֶה עִילָּוֵיהּ, הוֹאִיל וִיכוֹלִין לְטַלְטְלָהּ, קמ"ל. וְאֵינָהּ מְקַבֶּלֶת טוּמְאָה. זוֹ הַכַּוֶּורֶת בִּמְקוֹמָהּ, דְּכֵיוָן דִּמְחוּבֶּרֶת הִיא לְקַרְקַע — יָצְתָה מִתּוֹרַת כְּלִי. וְגַם הַדְּבַשׁ שֶׁבְּתוֹכָהּ אֵינוֹ מְקַבֵּל טוּמְאָה, דְּבָטֵל לְגַבֵּי כַּוֶּורֶת. וְדַוְקָא בִּמְקוֹמָהּ, אֲבָל אִם נְטָלָהּ מִשָּׁם — אָז מְקַבֵּל הַדְּבַשׁ טוּמְאָה, כְּמַאן דְּאָמַר (ב) בְּפֶרֶק "הַמּוֹכֵר אֶת הַסְּפִינָה" דְּלָא בָּעֵי מַחֲשָׁבָה. דְּאִיכָּא מַאן דְּמַצְרִיךְ מַחֲשָׁבָה. וְהִלְכָּךְ אִצְטְרִיךְ הָכָא גַּבֵּי טוּמְאָה לְמִיתְנֵי "בִּמְקוֹמָהּ", וְה"ה לְכָל הָנָךְ מִילֵּי. וְהָרוֹדֶה מִמֶּנָּה. כְּשֶׁהִיא בִּמְקוֹמָהּ, דְּהַיְינוּ מְקוֹם גִּידּוּלוֹ שֶׁל דְּבַשׁ — חַיָּיב חַטָּאת, כְּתוֹלֵשׁ מִן הַקַּרְקַע. אַלְמָא לְר' אֱלִיעֶזֶר חֲקָקוֹ וּלְבַסּוֹף קְבָעוֹ — כְּקַרְקַע מְשַׁוֵּי לֵיהּ, וּבָרַיְיתָא דִּלְעֵיל דְּלָא כְּרַבִּי אֱלִיעֶזֶר הִיא. וּמִיהוּ, הָנָךְ רַבָּנַן הִיא. אֵינָהּ כְּקַרְקַע. (ג) מִשּׁוּם דְּחִיבּוּר בְּקַרְקַע לָא בָּטֵיל תּוֹרַת כְּלִי מִינָּהּ, וּמְקַבֶּלֶת טוּמְאָה בִּמְקוֹמָהּ. וְגַם הַדְּבַשׁ דְּלָא בָּעֵי מַחֲשָׁבָה, כִּדְתַנְיָא לְקַמָּן בְּ"הַמּוֹכֵר אֶת הַסְּפִינָה". ה"ג: הָתָם אָמַר רַבִּי אֶלְעָזָר מַאי טַעְמָא דְּר"א. דְּחָשֵׁיב לְכַוֶּורֶת דְּבוֹרִים כִּמְחוּבָּר — דִּכְתִיב: "וַיִּטְבּוֹל אוֹתָהּ בְּיַעְרַת הַדְּבָשׁ". בִּיהוֹנָתָן כְּתִיב, וּבִדְבַשׁ בִּמְקוֹם גִּידּוּלוֹ מַיְירֵי, (ד) וְקָרֵי לֵיהּ יַעַר, וְהִלְכָּךְ חָשֵׁיב לֵיהּ מְחוּבָּר וַאֲפִי' אֵין הַכַּוֶּורֶת מְחוּבֶּרֶת מַמָּשׁ בַּקַּרְקַע. אֲבָל גַּבֵּי כִּיּוֹר שֶׁחֲקָקוֹ וּלְבַסּוֹף קְבָעוֹ — מוֹדֵי ר"א דְּחָשֵׁיב כְּלִי וּפָסֵיל מִקְוֶה, כִּדְקָתָנֵי בָּרַיְיתָא. וְאַכַּתִּי לָא יָדְעִינַן הֵי נִיהוּ ר"א דְּלֵית לֵיהּ הַךְ בָּרַיְיתָא. דַּף שֶׁל נַחְתּוֹמִין. נֶסֶר רָחָב לַעֲרוֹךְ עָלָיו וְלָלוּשׁ אֶת הַפַּת. וְלִי נִרְאֶה: הוּא דַּף שֶׁקָּבוּעַ בַּכּוֹתֶל לִיתֵּן עָלָיו אֶת הַפַּת לִמְכּוֹר, כְּעֵין שֶׁעוֹשִׂין פַּלְטֵרִין שֶׁלָּנוּ בְּכוֹתֶל בָּתֵּיהֶן מִבַּחוּץ. וּלְקַמָּן מוֹקֵי בְּדַף שֶׁל מַתֶּכֶת, דִּפְשׁוּטֵיהֶן טְמֵאִין. רַבִּי אֱלִיעֶזֶר מְטַהֵר. דְּכָל הַמְחוּבָּר לְקַרְקַע הֲרֵי הוּא כְּקַרְקַע. וַחֲכָמִים מְטַמְּאִין. דְּלָא בָּטֵיל לְגַבֵּי קַרְקַע, וְתִיקּוּן הַדַּף שֶׁמַּחֲלִיקִין אוֹתוֹ לְכָךְ הוּא בִּמְקוֹם חֲקִיקַת הַכִּיּוֹר, דְּתִיקּוּן מְשַׁוֵּי לֵיהּ גְּמַר כְּלִי לְקַבֵּל טוּמְאָה. וּמִדְּלָא קָמַפְלִיג בֵּין תִּקְּנוֹ וּלְבַסּוֹף קְבָעוֹ וּבֵין קְבָעוֹ וּלְבַסּוֹף תִּקְּנוֹ — אַלְמָא לְרַבִּי אֱלִיעֶזֶר הַכֹּל טָהוֹר, לָא שְׁנָא חֲקָקוֹ וּלְבַסּוֹף קְבָעוֹ, לָא שְׁנָא קְבָעוֹ וּלְבַסּוֹף חֲקָקוֹ. וּלְרַבָּנַן הַכֹּל טָמֵא. אַלְמָא הַהִיא בָּרַיְיתָא דְּכִיּוֹר דִּלְעֵיל, דְּקָמַפְלִיג בֵּין קְבָעוֹ וּלְבַסּוֹף חֲקָקוֹ, וּבֵין חֲקָקוֹ וּלְבַסּוֹף קְבָעוֹ — לֹא רַבָּנַן וְלֹא רַבִּי אֱלִיעֶזֶר. דְּאִי ר"א אֲפִי' חֲקָקוֹ וּלְבַסּוֹף קְבָעוֹ הָיָה לוֹ לְהַכְשִׁיר, וְאִי רַבָּנַן — אֲפִילּוּ קְבָעוֹ וּלְבַסּוֹף חֲקָקוֹ נַמִּי יִפְסוֹל אֶת הַמִּקְוֶה. לְעוֹלָם רַבִּי אֱלִיעֶזֶר. סְבִירָא לֵיהּ כְּבָרַיְיתָא, דְּכִיּוֹר שֶׁחֲקָקוֹ וּלְבַסּוֹף קְבָעוֹ אַכַּתִּי כְּלִי הוּא, וְלָא בָּטֵיל לְגַבֵּי קַרְקַע, וּפָסֵיל אֶת הַמִּקְוֶה. וְהָכָא גַּבֵּי דַּף — הַיְינוּ טַעְמָא דְּר' אֱלִיעֶזֶר דִּמְטַהֵר לֵיהּ אֲפִילּוּ בְּתִקְּנוֹ וּלְבַסּוֹף קְבָעוֹ, דְּשָׁאנֵי פְּשׁוּטֵי כְּלֵי עֵץ כְּגוֹן הַאי, דַּף דַּאֲפִי' קוֹדֶם שֶׁקְּבָעוֹ אֵין לוֹ טוּמְאָה אֶלָּא מִדְּרַבָּנַן, וְהִלְכָּךְ בִּקְבָעוֹ — מֵיקֵל ר' אֱלִיעֶזֶר. אֲבָל לְעֵיל, גַּבֵּי כִּיּוֹר, שֶׁמַּיִם שְׁאוּבִים פּוֹסְלִין אֶת הַמִּקְוֶה מִן הַתּוֹרָה, כִּדְתַנְיָא בְּת"כ: יָכוֹל מִילֵּא מַיִם עַל כְּתֵפוֹ וְעָשָׂה מִקְוֶה בַּתְּחִלָּה יְהֵא טָהוֹר? ת"ל "מַעְיָן", מַה מַּעְיָן בִּידֵי שָׁמַיִם אַף מִקְוֶה בִּידֵי שָׁמַיִם — הָתָם מוֹדֵי ר"א דְּפָסֵיל מִקְוֶה, דְּמִשּׁוּם קְבִיעוּתוֹ בַּקַּרְקַע לָא בָּטֵיל מִינֵּיהּ תּוֹרַת כְּלִי דְּמֵעִיקָּרָא. וּמִיהוּ, לָא אַשְׁכְּחַן טוּמְאָה לִפְשׁוּטֵי כְּלֵי עֵץ אֲפִי' מִדְּרַבָּנַן חוּץ מֵאוֹתָן הָרְאוּיִן לְמִדְרָס, וּכְדִתְנַן בְּמַסֶּ' נִדָּה (דף מט.): כָּל הַמִּיטַּמֵּא מִדְרָס מִיטַּמֵּא טְמֵא מֵת. וּבְמַסְקָנָא נַמִּי מוֹקְמִינַן לָהּ בְּדַף שֶׁל מַתֶּכֶת. וּמַתְמַהּ גְּמָ': מִכְּלָל דִּשְׁאִיבָה דְּאוֹרַיְיתָא. דְּמִדְּקָא מְשַׁנֵּי הָכִי — שָׁמְעִינַן דְּבָרַיְיתָא דִּלְעֵיל בִּפְסוּל שְׁאִיבָה דְּאוֹרַיְיתָא מַיְירֵי. וַהֲלֹא מִדְּרַבָּנַן הוּא, כִּדְאָמְרִי' בְּמַסֶּכֶת יְבָמוֹת (דף פב:) שֶׁאִם הָיָה מִקְוֶה מ' סְאָה וְנָתַן סְאָה שְׁאוּבִין וְנָטַל סְאָה — כָּשֵׁר. עַד כַּמָּה? רַבִּי יוֹחָנָן אָמַר: עַד רוּבּוֹ. וְהַיְינוּ טַעְמָא, דְּמִדְּאוֹרַיְיתָא הוּא דְּבָעֵינַן מִקְוֶה מִמַּיִם מְכוּנָּסִין לְכַתְּחִלָּה בְּלֹא שְׁאִיבָה, דְּאִיתְקַשׁ לְמַעְיָן, כִּדְפָרֵישִׁית לְעֵיל. וַאֲפִילּוּ נָפְלוּ בָּתַר הָכִי שְׁאוּבִין — בָּטְלוּ בְּרוּבָּא. א"נ, קַמָּא קַמָּא בָּטֵיל. וּלְעֵיל נַמִּי גַּבֵּי כִּיּוֹר — הַמִּקְוֶה הָיָה עָשׂוּי כְּבָר כַּהוֹגֶן, וְאח"כ קְבָעוֹ שָׁם כִּיּוֹר, כִּדְקָתָנֵי: פּוֹסֵל אֶת הַמִּקְוֶה — מִכְּלָל דְּהָיָה שָׁם מִקְוֶה מֵעִיקָּרָא, הִלְכָּךְ פְּסוּלָא מִדְּרַבָּנַן הוּא. [שייך לע"ב] *וְעוֹד. אֲפִילּוּ אִם תִּמְצָא לוֹמַר דְּאַחְמִירוּ בֵּיהּ רַבָּנַן כְּשֶׁל תּוֹרָה, הָכָא גַּבֵּי דַּף נַמִּי בִּדְאוֹרַיְיתָא מַיְירֵי, דִּבְדַף שֶׁל מַתֶּכֶת מַיְירֵי, דְּטוּמְאָתוֹ מִן הַתּוֹרָה. דִּבְשְׁלָמָא עֵץ — אִתְּקַשׁ לְשַׂק, [דִּכְתִיב:] "כְּלִי עֵץ אוֹ בֶגֶד אוֹ עוֹר אוֹ שָׂק" (ויקרא יא), מַה שַּׂק מִיטַּלְטֵל מָלֵא וְרֵיקָן — אַף כְּלִי עֵץ כו'. אֲבָל כְּלֵי מַתֶּכֶת בְּפָרָשַׁת מִדְיָן הוּא [דִּכְתִיב] (במדבר לא): "אַךְ אֶת הַזָּהָב" וגו', וְלָא אִתְקַשׁ לְשַׂק. וְאַכַּתִּי דְּלָא כְּרַבִּי אֱלִיעֶזֶר הִיא הַהִיא דְּכִיּוֹר, דְּרַבִּי אֱלִיעֶזֶר לָא קָמַפְלִיג מִידֵּי בֵּין *חֲקָקוֹ [נ"ל קבעו] מֵעִיקָּרָא לַחֲקָקוֹ וּלְבַסּוֹף קְבָעוֹ. הָאָמַר רַבִּי יוֹסֵי בְּרַבִּי חֲנִינָא כו'. מִשּׁוּם דִּפְשׁוּטֵי כְלֵי עֵץ לֵית לְהוּ טוּמְאָה כְּלָל, הִלְכָּךְ אוֹקְמָהּ בְּדַף שֶׁל מַתֶּכֶת. אֶלָּא

[**וּמְקַבֶּלֶת** טומאה במקומה]. וא"ת: מה טעם נקט גבי טומאה במקומה? דאין חילוק בין במקומה בין שלא במקומה, דהא לאו מחוברת היא! ואומר ר"ת: דשלא במקומה מקבלת טומאה, כיון דמטלטלין אותה ממקום למקום, ודמי לשאר כלים שבבית. וגזרו בה רבנן טומאה, דלמא אתי לאיחלופי.

וְשָׁאנֵי פשוטי כלי עץ דרבנן. וא"ת: דבהנך דחזו למדרסות איכא טומאה דאורייתא, דכל המטמא מדרס מטמא טמא מת, ק"ו מפכין קטנים, כדאמרינן בפרק "כילד הרגל" (ב"ק דף כה:)! ובפרק "על אלו מומין" (בכורות דף לח.) נמי פריך: ואין לו תוך בכלי שטף מדאורייתא בר קבולי טומאה הוא? והא דומיא דשק בעינן! ומשני: בהנך דחזו למדרס. ואי בשאר פשוטי כלי עץ דלא חזו למדרס — הנהו אפי' מדרבנן לא מקבלי טומאה, כדמוכח בריש חולין (דף ג. ושם ד"ה כגון) דאמר: הכל שוחטין — ואפי' טמא במוקדשין. האי טמא דאיטמי במאי כו'. ומשני: כגון שבדק קרומית של קנה ושחט בה. ואי מקבלי טומאה מדרבנן — מאי משני? וכ"ת: התם בדלא עבדה כעין כלי. דעל כרחך איירי בדעבדה כעין כלי, דקדשים טעונים שחיטה בכלי, כדאמרי' ב"התודה" (מנחות דף פב:) מ"ויקח את המאכלת". ועוד, תנן במסכת כלים (פ"ב מ"א) ומייתי לה בפ"ק דשבת (דף טז. ושם): כלי עץ (ה) וכלי עלם וכלי זכוכית — פשוטיהם טהורים, ומקבליהם טמאים, ועל כרחך טהורים אפילו מדרבנן, דכלי זכוכית אפילו מקבליהם ליכא טומאה אלא מדרבנן, כדאמרינן במסכת שבת (שם)! ופירש רבינו שמואל: דודאי אין להם טומאה אפילו מדרבנן, ומסקנא לא קיימא הכי, אלא מוקי לה בדף של מתכת. ויש מפרשים: בדף של נחתומין, אע"פ שהוא פשוטי כלי עץ — מקבל טומאה מדרבנן, כיון שהוא משמש אדם ואת משמשי אדם. דדריש בת"כ בפרשת "ויהי ביום השמיני": "כלי", (ו) יכול אפילו הסולם והקולב כו' — ת"ל "כלי עץ" ולא "כל כלי עץ". יכול שאני מוציא את השולחן ואת הטבלא ואת הדולבקי — ת"ל "כל כלי עץ", ריבה. ומה ראית לרבות את אלו כו' — ת"ל "שק", מה שק שהוא משמש אדם ואת משמשי אדם — אף אני ארבה את השולחן כו'. ועל כרחך כשאין ראוין למדרס — מדלא נקט מטה כסא וספסל, והוה ליה לרבוינהו מקראי דמשכב ומושב. ובאין להם בית קבול (ז) איירי — מדלא קאמר "מה שק מיטלטל מלא וריקם". אלמא מקבלי טומאה. ואע"ג דמפיק להו מקרא — לא הוי אלא אסמכתא, כמו כמה דרשות דת"כ ובספרי דלא הוי אלא אסמכתא. וכן משמע בפרק "שתי הלחם" (מנחות דף נו:), א"ר יוחנן: לדברי האומר מסגרתו למטה היתה, פירוש: למטה ברגלי השולחן ולא בשולחן — טבלא המתהפכת טמאה. פירוש, דדרשינן: "השולחן הטהור" — מכלל שהוא טמא. לדברי האומר מסגרתו למעלה היתה — טבלא המתהפכת תיבעי. דהא דשולחן של מקדש מקבל טומאה, לפי שהיה לו בית קבול. אבל טבלא המתהפכת, שאין לה בית קבול — תיבעי. ואי דרשה גמורה היא (ח) דת"כ — אמאי תיבעי? תיפוק ליה מקרא דהתם! אלא ודאי אסמכתא היא. ובטבלא המתהפכת מספקא ליה אי מקבלא טומאה מדאורייתא, כדפירש הקונט' התם, משום דעדיפא משאר פשוטי כלי עץ, לפי שראוי להשתמש בה משני צדדין. ולמאן דאמר למטה היתה — טמא, מדכתיב "הטהור".

מִכְּלָל דשאיבה דאורייתא. רשב"ם ור"ת מפרשי דכולו שאוב הוי דאורייתא, ומביאים ראיה מדתניא בת"כ, בפרשת "ויהי ביום השמיני": "מקוה מים יהיה טהור", יכול מילא בכתפו ועשה מקוה בתחלה יהא

לד א מיי' פכ"א מהל' שבת הל' ו סמג לאוין סה טוש"ע א"ח סי' שכא סעיף יג:

לה ב מיי' פי"א מהל' כלים הלכה כד:

הגהות הב"ח

(א) רשב"ם ד"ה (בדף הקודם) הרי היא כקרקע וכו' לא שייך לא יגוש דכגבוי ועומד הוא שכל מה שיוכלו: (ב) ד"ה ואינה וכו' בפרק המוכר. נ"ב בדף פ ע"ב: (ג) ד"ה אינה כקרקע דמשום: (ד) ד"ה ה"ג וכו' מיירי וקא קרי ליה: (ה) תום' ד"ה ושאני וכו' כלי עץ וכלי עור וכלי עלם: (ו) בא"ד ביום השמיני כלי עץ יכול וכו' ת"ל מכל כלי עץ: (ז) בא"ד ובאין להם בית קיבול נמי איירי וכו' דא"ר יוחנן: (ח) בא"ד דרשה גמורה היא ההיא דתורת כהנים אמאי קבעי:

אוְהָא קַיְימָא לָן: דְּרַבָּנַן! וְעוֹד, הָאָמַר ר' יוֹסֵי בֶּן ר' חֲנִינָא: בבְּדַ־ף שֶׁל מַתֶּכֶת מַחֲלוֹקֶת! לְעוֹלָם רַבָּנַן הִיא, א)וְשָׁאנֵי שְׁאִיבָה דְּרַבָּנַן. אִי הָכִי, אֲפִי' חֲקָקוֹ וּלְבַסּוֹף קְבָעוֹ נַמִי! שָׁאנֵי הָתָם, דְּאִיכָּא תּוֹרַת כְּלִי עָלָיו בְּתָלוּשׁ. בָּעֵי רַב יוֹסֵף: מֵי גְשָׁמִים שֶׁחָשַׁב עֲלֵיהֶם לְהָדִיחַ אֶת הָאִיצְטְרוֹבְלִין, מַהוּ (א) לְזָרְעִים? אַלִּיבָּא דְּרַבִּי אֱלִיעֶזֶר דְּאָמַר: כָּל הַמְחוּבָּר לְקַרְקַע הֲרֵי הוּא כְּקַרְקַע — לָא תִּיבָּעֵי לָךְ, כִּי תִּיבָּעֵי לָךְ — אַלִּיבָּא דְּרַבָּנַן דְּאָמְרִי: אֵינוֹ כְּקַרְקַע, מַאי? תֵּיקוּ. ב)שְׁלַח לֵיהּ רַב נְחֶמְיָה בְּרֵיהּ דְּרַב יוֹסֵף לְרַבָּה בְּרֵיהּ דְּרַב הוּנָא זוּטִי לִנְהַרְדְּעָא: כִּי אָתְיָא הַךְ אִיתְּתָא לְקַמָּךְ, אַגְבָּהּ

אֶלָּא לְעוֹלָם רַבָּנַן. דְּדַף הוּא. וּדְקַשְׁיָא לָךְ: גַּבֵּי כִּיּוֹר אֲפִילּוּ קְבָעוֹ וּלְבַסּוֹף חֲקָקוֹ נַמִי יִפְסוֹל לְמִקְוֶה, לְרַבָּנַן דִּמְטַמְּאֵי לֵיהּ גַּבֵּי דַּף וַחֲשִׁיבִי לֵיהּ כְּלִי בְּכָל עִנְיָנִים, אֲפִי' בִּקְבָעוֹ וּלְבַסּוֹף חֲקָקוֹ — שָׁאנֵי שְׁאִיבָה דְּרַבָּנַן, כִּדְפָרֵישִׁית לְעֵיל. הִלְכָּךְ, גַּבֵּי כִּיּוֹר הוּא דְּמַקִּילֵי רַבָּנַן וְאָמְרֵי אֵינוֹ פּוֹסֵל בִּקְבָעוֹ וּלְבַסּוֹף חֲקָקוֹ. אֲבָל לְגַבֵּי דַּף, דְּטוּמְאָתוֹ מִן הַתּוֹרָה — לְעוֹלָם טָמֵא, אֲפִי' בִּקְבָעוֹ וּלְבַסּוֹף תִּקְנוֹ. דִּסְבִירָא לְהוּ לְרַבָּנַן דְּכָל הַמְחוּבָּר לְקַרְקַע אֵינוֹ כְּקַרְקַע. א"ה. דִּלְרַבָּנַן הַכֹּל שָׁוֶה, בֵּין קְבָעוֹ וְאַח"כ חֲקָקוֹ בֵּין חֲקָקוֹ וְאַח"כ קְבָעוֹ — לָא בָּטֵיל לְגַבֵּי קַרְקַע, וַחֲשִׁיב כְּלִי גָּמוּר, וְגַבֵּי שְׁאִיבָה הוּא דַּאֲקִילוּ לְבַטְּלוֹ אַגַּב קַרְקַע — אֲפִי' חֲקָקוֹ וּלְבַסּוֹף קְבָעוֹ נַמִי לֹא יִפְסוֹל מִקְוֶה, וְלִבָּטֵיל אַגַּב קַרְקַע! וּמְשַׁנֵּי: הָתָם דְּאִיכָּא תּוֹרַת כְּלִי כו'. וְכָל כָּךְ לֹא רָצוּ לְהָקֵל, דְּאֵין לָךְ שְׁאִיבָה גְּדוֹלָה מִזּוֹ, הוֹאִיל וַהֲוָה שֵׁם כְּלִי עָלָיו קוֹדֶם שֶׁהוּקְבַּע בַּקַּרְקַע, וְאִי לָא חָשְׁבַתְּ לֵיהּ כְּלִי — בָּטְלָה גְּזֵירָתָם לְגַמְרֵי. בָּעֵי רַב יוֹסֵף מֵי גְשָׁמִים. שֶׁהָיוּ יוֹרְדִין, וְחִישֵּׁב עֲלֵיהֶן שֶׁיָּדִיחוּ הָאִיצְטְרוֹבְלִין, מַהוּ שֶׁאוֹתָן גְּשָׁמִים יַכְשִׁירוּ זְרָעִים, אִם נָפְלוּ עֲלֵיהֶן, לְקַבֵּל טוּמְאָה? דִּתְנַן (מכשירין פ"א מ"א): כָּל מַשְׁקֶה שֶׁתְּחִלָּתוֹ לְרָצוֹן, אע"פ שֶׁאֵין סוֹפוֹ לְרָצוֹן — מַכְשִׁיר. וְהָכָא נַמִי, כֵּיוָן דְּנִיחָא לֵיהּ בִּירִידָתָן לְצוֹרֶךְ אִיצְטְרוֹבִּיל, אע"ג דְּלָא נִיחָא לֵיהּ בִּירִידָתָן עַל הַפֵּירוֹת — הָוֵי הֶכְשֵׁר. וּבִלְבַד שֶׁיְּהֵא אִיצְטְרוֹבִּיל חָשׁוּב כְּתָלוּשׁ, דְּלָא מְהַנֵּי מַחְשַׁבְתּוֹ, וְלָא קָרֵינָא בֵּיהּ "וְכִי יֻתַּן", אֶלָּא הֵיכָא דִּמְחַשֵּׁב שֶׁיֵּרְדוּ עַל דָּבָר תָּלוּשׁ. כִּדְאָמְרִינַן בְּפ"ק דִּשְׁחִיטַת חוּלִּין (דף טז.): תָּלוּשׁ וּלְבַסּוֹף חִיבְּרוֹ לְעִנְיַן הֶכְשֵׁר זְרָעִים מַחֲלוֹקֶת, דִּתְנַן: הַכּוֹפֶה קְעָרָה עַל גַּבֵּי הַכּוֹתֶל כו', וּפָרְכִינַן רֵישָׁא לְסֵיפָא, וְדַיְיקִינַן מִינֵּיהּ דְּכוֹתֶל בִּנְיָן חָשׁוּב תָּלוּשׁ, וְאִם חִישֵּׁב שֶׁיּוּדַח — הֲרֵי זֶה בְּ"כִי יוּתַּן", אֲבָל בְּכוֹתֶל מְעָרָה, שֶׁהוּא מְחוּבָּר מֵעִיקָּרוֹ — לָא מְהַנְּיָא מַחְשַׁבְתּוֹ לְהַכְשִׁיר זְרָעִים. וּבְתוֹרַת כֹּהֲנִים יָלֵיף מִקְּרָאֵי דְּבָעֵינַן מַחֲשָׁבָה לְצוֹרֶךְ דָּבָר הַתָּלוּשׁ. וְהַאי אִיצְטְרוֹבִּיל נַמִי, תָּלוּשׁ וּלְבַסּוֹף חִיבְּרוֹ הוּא. וְאַלִּיבָּא דְּרַבָּנַן דִּלְעֵיל דִּפְלִיגֵי בְּמַכְתֶּשֶׁת קְבוּעָה קָמִיבַּעְיָא לֵיהּ, כִּדְמְפָרֵשׁ וְאָזֵיל, אִי סְבִירָא לְהוּ דְּתָלוּשׁ וּלְבַסּוֹף חִיבְּרוֹ לְעִנְיַן הֶכְשֵׁר זְרָעִים הָוֵי תָּלוּשׁ, אוֹ לָא. **אַלִּיבָּא דְּר' אֱלִיעֶזֶר לָא תִּיבָּעֵי לָךְ.** דְּוַדַּאי חָשֵׁיב מְחוּבָּר. וְלָא מִיבַּעְיָא אִיצְטְרוֹבִּיל דְּדָמֵי לְקַרְקַע טְפֵי מִמַּכְתֶּשֶׁת קְבוּעָה, דְּוַדַּאי חָשֵׁיב מְחוּבָּר. אֶלָּא אֲפִילּוּ מַכְתֶּשֶׁת קְבוּעָה דַּחֲשָׁבוּ לָהּ רַבָּנַן תָּלוּשׁ — פָּלֵיג אִיהוּ, וְאָמַר: כָּל הַמְחוּבָּר כו'. וְהָא לֵיכָּא לְמֵימַר דְּטַעְמֵיהּ (ב) הָתָם מִשּׁוּם דִּבְעַיִן יָפָה מוֹכֵר — דְּהָא כְּלָלָא קָאָמַר. וְעוֹד: דְּשָׁמְעִינַן לֵיהּ גַּבֵּי דַּף דִּמְטַהֵר, אֲפִי' בְּתִקְּנוֹ וּלְבַסּוֹף קְבָעוֹ. וְאַלִּיבָּא דְּרַבָּנַן דְּדַף נַמִי לָא קָמִיבַּעְיָא לֵיהּ, דְּוַדַּאי תָּלוּשׁ וּלְבַסּוֹף חִיבְּרוֹ הָוֵי תָּלוּשׁ, כִּדְקָא חֲשִׁיבִי לֵיהּ תָּלוּשׁ גַּבֵּי טוּמְאָה אֲפִי' בִּקְבָעוֹ וּלְבַסּוֹף תִּקְנוֹ, וְהוּא הַדִּין לְהַכְשִׁיר. **כִּי תִּיבָּעֵי לָךְ אַלִּיבָּא.** דְּהָנְהוּ רַבָּנַן דִּלְעֵיל, דִּפְלִיגֵי עֲלֵיהּ דְּרַבִּי אֱלִיעֶזֶר בְּמַכְתֶּשֶׁת קְבוּעָה, מַאי? מִי אָמְרִינַן: הַיְינוּ טַעֲמַיְיהוּ, דִּסְבִירָא לְהוּ דְּכָל תָּלוּשׁ וּלְבַסּוֹף חִיבְּרוֹ חָשֵׁיב תָּלוּשׁ, וְהִלְכָּךְ לֹא מָכַר אֶת הַקְּבוּעָה, וְהוּא הַדִּין לְגַבֵּי הֶכְשֵׁר טוּמְאָה. וְכֵיוָן דְּטַעֲמַיְיהוּ מִשּׁוּם דַּחֲשִׁיבֵי לֵיהּ תָּלוּשׁ — לָא מִבַּעְיָא הֵיכָא (ג) דַּחֲשֵׁיב לְהָדִיחַ מַכְתֶּשֶׁת קְבוּעָה, דְּמַכְשִׁירִין, אֶלָּא אֲפִילּוּ חָשֵׁיב לְהָדִיחַ בָּהֶן אִיצְטְרוֹבִּיל — מַכְשִׁיר אֶת הַזְּרָעִים. דְּעַל כָּרְחָךְ טַעֲמַיְיהוּ גַּבֵּי אִיצְטְרוֹבִּיל

יהא טהור? ת"ל "אך מעין ובור מקוה מים יהיה טהור", מה מעין בידי שמים — אף מקוה בידי שמים. ויש לדחות, דאסמכתא היא, כמו כמה דרשות דתורת כהנים. ועוד מביא ראיה ר"ת, דתנן במס' מקוואות בפ"ב (מ"ד), ר' אליעזר אומר: רביעית בתחלה פוסל את המקוה, ושלשה לוגין על פני המים. ומדמחמיר בתחלה טפי מבסוף — ש"מ דבתחלה פוסלין מדאורייתא. ויש לדחות: דהא דאחמיר רבי אליעזר בתחלה ברביעי' — משום דרביעית הוא שיעור טבילה למחטין ולצינורות, וכבר יש שם פסול מקוה עליהם. ולר"י נראה דאפי' כולו שאוב דרבנן. כדמשמע בתוספתא דמקוואות, דתניא בפרק שני: מקוה שהניחו ריקן, ובא ומצאו מלא — כשר, מפני שזה ספק מים שאובין למקוה. ומדקא מכשר ליה זה מספק — ש"מ דכולו שאוב מדרבנן. וליכא למימר דלאו בכולו שאוב איירי, אלא כשהיה בו מים אך שהיה חסר — דאם כן הוה ליה למימר "שהניחו חסר". ד"ריקן" משמע לגמרי ריקן, שלא היה בו מים כלל. ועוד אמר בפ"ק דפסחים (דף יז: ושם) גבי משקין בית מטבחיא, בכלים — טמאים, בקרקע — טהורים. ומפרש התם דבקרקע טהורים משום דחזי להטביל בהן מחטין וצינורות. אלמא, אפי' כולו שאוב חזי להטביל בו. דבשאוב איירי, מדמפליג בין כלים לקרקע. וסתם משקין בית מטבחיא נמי שאובין הם. ורשב"א דוחה: דהכי קאמר בכלים טמאים — פי': שהיו בכלים, אע"ג דהשתא הן בקרקע. ולפי שהיו שאובים בקרקע, שלא היו מעולם בכלים טהורים. והר"ר משה מפונטויז"א דוחה: דאע"ג דשאיבה דאורייתא היא — בקרקע טהור, משום ג)שאפשר בלא המשכה, דכי נפלו מן הכלי לרצפה שהיא חלקה מימשכי אילך ואילך, והוה ליה כשאיבה שהמשיכה כולה, דכשרה. ובפרק קמא דתמורה (דף יב.) דלא מכשיר המשכה אלא כי איכא כ"א סאה במקוה — אפשר דהיינו מדרבנן. וא"ת: בשלמא אי כולו שאוב מדאורייתא — היינו דגזרו חכמים ג' לוגין מים שאובין פוסלים אטו כולו שאוב, ודוקא בשלשה לוגין גזרו שהן ראוין לרחיצת אדם, כדאמרינן בפרק קמא דשבת (דף יד.): בתחלה היו טובלין במערות סרוחים, ונותנין על גביהן ג' לוגין מים שאובין כו'. אבל אי כולו שאוב דרבנן — אמאי גזרו כלל בשאיבה? וי"ל: גזירה שמא יטבול בכלי. דדומיא דמעין אמר רחמנא, שהן בקרקע. ומההוא מקוה שהניחו ריקן, אר"י: דאדרבה, יש להוכיח דכולו שאוב דאורייתא. דקתני: כשר, מפני שזה ספק מים שאובין וחזקת המקוואות כשרות. שאדם אינו עושה מקוה אלא לטבול בו, ואינו ממלא אותו מסתמא מים שאובים, אלא מים כשרים לטבילה, משמע: דוקא משום חזקה הוא דכשר, הא לאו הכי — פסול, דספיקא דאורייתא נחומרא. תדע, דקתני סיפא: כיור המקלא למקוה והמכתשת נתונה בצדו, ספק מן הכיור למקוה ספק מן המכתשת למקוה — פסול, מפני שהפסול מוכיח. ואם יש בו רוב מקוה — כשר, מפני שיש ספק מים שאובים למקוה. ומדמכשר בשיש בו רוב מקוה מספק, וכשאין רוב פסול — משמע דרובו שאוב דאורייתא. ועוד, תניא התם: שני מקוואות, אחד שאוב ואחד כשר, וטבל באחד מהן מטומאה חמורה, ועשה טהרות — הרי הן תלויות. ומדלא מטהרין מספק — אלמא כולו שאוב דאורייתא. והראיות לא נראו לר"י. עוד האריך רשב"א. ועוד אומר ר"ת: דדוקא במקוה חסר פוסלים מים שאובין, אבל במקוה שלם — כל מים שאובין שבעולם אין פוסלין אותו. ושמה כתב ראיות ממסכת מקוואות, ואין להאריך. ואכתוב ראיה אחת, דתנן התם פרק ששי (מ"ח): היה בעליון מ' סאה ובתחתון אין כלום — ממלא בכתף ונותן בעליון, עד שירדו בתחתון מ' סאה. משמע, אע"פ שרוב מים שאובין — אין נפסל, כיון שהיה שלם. דהא אי אפשר אם לא נתן בעליון יותר מארבעים סאה. **בעי** רב יוסף מי גשמים שחישב עליהם להדיח בהן את האיצטרובלין מהו להכשיר בהן את הזרעים. פירש הקונטרס: דבכל תלוש ובסוף חיברו מיבעיא ליה לענין הכשר זרעים, ואליבא דרבנן דמכתשת. ואין נראה לר"י, דאם כן לימא סתמא: תלוש ולבסוף חיברו לענין הכשר זרעים לרבנן, מהו? כדנקיט בפרק קמא דחולין (דף טז. ושם), ולא הוה ליה למינקט אילטרוביל טפי משאר מילי. ועוד: דאין סברא לדמות הכשר זרעים למכר, שתהא מכתשת חשובה כתלוש לענין הכשר זרעים כמו שחשובה לענין מכר. ועוד: דלענין שחיטה נמי תיבעי: לרבנן תלוש ולבסוף חיברו, מהו? אי הוי כתלוש או לא. ועוד: דפירש דלרבנן דדף לא מיבעיא ליה, דלדידהו ודאי הוי כתלוש, א"כ, אדמיבעיא ליה לרבנן דמכתשת אי סבירא ליה כר' אליעזר או כרבנן דדף, לענין הכשר זרעים — תיבעי ליה לענין טומאת דף גופיה, דאיפליגו בה רבי אליעזר ורבנן! ועוד: כיון דלרבנן דדף פשיטא ליה דהוה כתלוש — ה"נ לרבנן דמכתשת, דאמאי אית לן למימר דפליגי הני רבנן דרבי אליעזר אהנך רבנן דר"א? ועוד: דאינו מחלק בין דף למכתשת לכותל ואילטרוביל. ובפרק קמא דחולין (דף טז:) מחלק בין סכין הקבועה לגור היוצא מן הכותל, דקאמר: שאני סכין דלא מבטל ליה. ונראה לר"י: דלרבנן דדף מיבעיא ליה, דחשבי ליה לדף תלוש לענין טומאה, והוא הדין לענין הכשר זרעים, דהכשר וטומאה דמו אהדדי. ואליבא דמאן דאמר בפ"ק דחולין (דף טז. ושם) דתלוש ולבסוף חיברו דכותל בנין, לענין הכשר זרעים הוי כמחובר. והשתא מיבעיא ליה לרבנן דדף ומכתשת, דכולהו רבנן דרבי אליעזר מסתמא חדא נינהו, באילטרוביל מהו? ובאילטרוביל דוקא מיבעיא ליה, והכי קמבעיא ליה: אילטרוביל דבטל לגבי קרקע גבי מכר לרבנן דמכתשת, אי הוי בטל לגמרי כמו כותל, וחשיב נמי מחובר לענין הכשר זרעים. או דלמא לענין הכשר זרעים לא חשיב מחובר כמו כותל, אלא דוקא לענין מכר, משום עין יפה. אע"ג דלא מהני עין יפה לענין מכתשת — היינו משום שאין סופה כל כך להתעכב בבית כמו האילטרוביל. ומיהו, לענין הכשר זרעים לא חשיב האילטרוביל מחובר, לפי שעשוי לינטל יותר מכותל. ואליבא דרבי אליעזר לא מיבעיא ליה, דהא חשיב דף מחובר לענין טומאה, והוא הדין לענין הכשר זרעים, וכ"ש אילטרוביל. והא דקאמר "אליבא דרבי אליעזר לא תיבעי לך, דאמר כל המחובר לקרקע הרי הוא כקרקע" — לאו דוקא נקט ההוא לישנא, דהא ממכר אין להוכיח אהכשר זרעים, אלא אמאי דמטהר בדף קא סמיך.

מעמלא

עין משפט נר מצוה

לו א מיי' פ"ד מהל' מקוואות הל' א סמג עשין רמח:

לז ב מיי' פי"א מהל' כלים הלכה כז:

רבינו גרשום

מדאורייתא היא: והא קי"ל. דמים שאובין האי דפסלי מדרבנן היא כדאמרי' במס' יבמות [דף פב:] היו עושין מקוה של מ' סאה ונטל סאה ונתן סאה כשר עד כמה אמר ר' יוחנן עד רובה יותר מרובה פסיל ליה. ל"א שאיבה לטבילה מדרבנן פסול ולא מדאוריתא דמן התורה כשר דלא מצינו בתורה שצריך מים חיים אלא זב דכתיב וכי יטהר הזב וגו': ועוד. קושיא אחריני הא אמר ר' יוסי בר חנינא בדף של מתכת מחלוקת. ר' אליעזר ורבנן דפשוטי כלי מתכת דאורייתא מיטמו ואפי' הכי קאמר ר' אליעזר כי קבעו בכותל טהור ולטעמיה אמאי חקקו ולבסוף קבעו פוסל את המקוה: אלא לעולם רבנן היא. דמטמאי גבי דף של מתכת דאפי' קבעו בכותל לא קמבטל ליה: אי הכי. לטעמייהו בקבעו ולבסוף חקקו אמאי אינו פוסל את המקוה. היינו טעמא דשאיבה דרבנן היא ולאו מדאורייתא. אי הכי אפי' חקקו ולבסוף קבעו אמאי פוסל את המקוה: שאני התם דאיכא תורת כלי עליו בתלוש. משום הכי לא קמבטל אפי' בדרבנן: בעי רב יוסף מי גשמים שחישב להדיח בהן את האיצטרוביל. שהוא מחובר לקרקע מי הוו חשיבי הני מים להכשיר הזרעים אי לא. מי אמרינן דאין מכשירין כי היכי דגרסינן בשחיטת חולין הכופה קערה על הכותל אם בשביל שיודח הכותל אינו בכי יותן משום דחשיב דבר המחובר לקרקע וכל המחובר לקרקע הרי הוא כקרקע ולא חשיב כלום ואם בשביל שיודח הקערה הרי זה בכי יותן. הא גופא קשיא. הא בכותל מערה דהוה מחובר מעיקרו אינו בכי יותן דכקרקע דמי. בכותל בנין הרי זה בכי יותן משום דהוי תלוש ולבסוף חיברו דתורת כלי עליו הכא נמי לגבי אצטרוביל המחובר לקרקע מכשירין מי גשמים אי לא: אליבא דר' אליעזר דאמר כל המחובר לקרקע הרי הוא כקרקע לא תיבעי לך. דודאי אפי' בכותל בנין סבירא ליה דבקרקע דמי ואין מכשירין: כי תיבעי לך אליבא דרבנן דאמרי כל המחובר לקרקע אינו כקרקע. מאי מי אמרינן דהאי דקאמרי כל המחובר לקרקע אינו בקרקע לכל מילי קאמרי אפי' לגבי איצטרוביל ומכשיר או דלמא בעלמא כגון כותל בנין אמרי' דאינו בקרקע דזימנין משנהו אבל גבי איצטרוביל דקביע הוא כקרקע דמי ואין מכשירין תיקו:

מסורת הש"ס

א) [ב"ק סז.]: ב) כ' סט.: ג) [נ"ל משום אפשר וכ"ה בס"

הגהות הב"ח

(א) גמ' מהו להכשיר את הזרעים אליבא אליעזר: (ב) רשב"ם אליבא וכו' דטעמיה אליעזר התם כדקחשבי ליה (ג) ד"ה כי תיבעי היכא דחישב ל המכתשת וכו' אפילו להדיח:

אַגְבָּהּ עִישּׂוּר נִכְסֵי אֲפִי' מֵאִצְטְרוּבְּלֵי דְּרֵיחַיִים. א"ר אַשִׁי: כִּי הֲוֵינַן בֵּי רַב כָּהֲנָא, אמַגְבִּינַן אֲפִי' מֵעֲמָלָא דְּבָתֵּי.§ **מתני'** בהַמּוֹכֵר אֶת הֶחָצֵר — מָכַר בָּתִּים, בּוֹרוֹת שִׁיחִין וּמְעָרוֹת, גאֲבָל לֹא אֶת הַמִּטַּלְטְלִין; דבִּזְמַן שֶׁאָמַר לוֹ: "הוּא וְכָל מַה שֶּׁבְּתוֹכוֹ" — הֲרֵי כּוּלָּן מְכוּרִין. הבֵּין כָּךְ וּבֵין כָּךְ, לֹא מָכַר לֹא אֶת הַמֶּרְחָץ וְלֹא אֶת בֵּית הַבַּד שֶׁבְּתוֹכָהּ. ר"א אוֹמֵר: הַמּוֹכֵר אֶת הֶחָצֵר — לֹא מָכַר אֶלָּא אֲוִירָהּ שֶׁל חָצֵר.§ **גמ'** ת"ר: והַמּוֹכֵר אֶת הֶחָצֵר — מָכַר בָּתִּים הַחִיצוֹנִים וּבָתִּים הַפְּנִימִים וּבֵית הַחוּלְסָאוֹת; חֲנוּיוֹת פְּתוּחוֹת לְתוֹכָהּ — נִמְכָּרוֹת עִמָּהּ, וְשֶׁאֵין פְּתוּחוֹת לְתוֹכָהּ — אֵין נִמְכָּרוֹת עִמָּהּ; פְּתוּחוֹת לְכָאן וּלְכָאן (א) — א)[אֵלּוּ] וָאֵלּוּ נִמְכָּרוֹת עִמָּהּ. ר"א אוֹמֵר: הַמּוֹכֵר אֶת הֶחָצֵר — לֹא מָכַר אֶלָּא מִילוֹסָא שֶׁל חָצֵר. אָמַר מָר: פְּתוּחוֹת לְכָאן וּלְכָאן — נִמְכָּרוֹת עִמָּהּ. וְהָא תָּנֵי ר' חִיָּיא: אֵין נִמְכָּרוֹת עִמָּהּ! לָא קַשְׁיָא: זהָא דְּרוֹב תַּשְׁמִישְׁתַּיְיהוּ לְגוֹ, הָא דְּרוֹב תַּשְׁמִישְׁתַּיְיהוּ לְבַר.§ ר"א אוֹמֵר: הַמּוֹכֵר אֶת הֶחָצֵר — לֹא מָכַר אֶלָּא אֲוִירָהּ שֶׁל חָצֵר.§ אֲמַר ב)(רַבָּה:) אִי דַּאֲמַר לֵיהּ "דִּירְתָּא" — דְּכוּלֵּי עָלְמָא לָא פְּלִיגֵי דְּבָתֵּי מַשְׁמַע, כִּי פְּלִיגֵי — דַּא"ל "דַּרְתָּא", מָר סָבַר: תַּרְבִּיצָא מַשְׁמַע, וּמָר סָבַר: בָּתֵּי מַשְׁמַע. אִיכָּא דְּאָמְרִי, אֲמַר ב)(רַבָּה:) אִי דַּאֲמַר לֵיהּ "דַּרְתָּא" — דְּכוּלֵּי עָלְמָא לָא פְּלִיגֵי דְּבָתֵּי מַשְׁמַע, כִּי פְּלִיגֵי — דַּא"ל "חָצֵר", מָר סָבַר: חָצֵר — אֲוִירָא מַשְׁמַע, וּמָר סָבַר: כַּחֲצַר הַמִּשְׁכָּן. וְאָמַר ב)(רַבָּה) אָמַר רַב נַחְמָן: מָכַר לוֹ גחוּלְסִית וּמְצוּלָה, הֶחֱזִיק בַּחוּלְסִית — לֹא קָנָה מְצוּלָה, הֶחֱזִיק בִּמְצוּלָה — לֹא קָנָה חוּלְסִית. אִינִי? וְהָא דאָמַר שְׁמוּאֵל: מָכַר לוֹ עֶשֶׂר שָׂדוֹת בְּעֶשֶׂר מְדִינוֹת, כֵּיוָן שֶׁהֶחֱזִיק בְּאַחַת מֵהֶן — קָנָה כּוּלָּן! (ב) הָתָם הוּא דְּסַדְנָא דְּאַרְעָא חַד הוּא, וְכוּלָּהּ חֲדָא תַּשְׁמִישְׁתָּא הוּא, אֲבָל הָכָא — הָא תַּשְׁמִישְׁתָּא לְחוּד, וְהָא תַּשְׁמִישְׁתָּא לְחוּד. וְאִיכָּא דְּאָמְרִי, אָמַר

אַלְטְרוּבִּיל דְּאָמְרִי מָכוּר — לָאו מִשּׁוּם דַּחֲשִׁיב מְחוּבָּר, דְּהָא גַּבֵּי מָכַר מַכְתֶּשֶׁת חָשְׁבֵי לֵיהּ לְתָלוּשׁ וּלְבַסּוֹף חִיבְּרוֹ כְּתָלוּשׁ, וְאַלְטְרוּבִּיל נַמִּי תָּלוּשׁ וּלְבַסּוֹף חִיבְּרוֹ הוּא, דְּקוֹדֶם שֶׁיִּקְבָּעֶנּוּ בַּקַּרְקַע הָוֵי בָּנוּי וְעוֹמֵד. וְאֶלָּא הַיְינוּ טַעֲמַיְיהוּ: מִשּׁוּם דְּעִיקַּר עֲשִׂיָּיתוֹ לִקְבִיעוּת בַּקַּרְקַע טְפֵי מִמַּכְתֶּשֶׁת, חֲשִׁיב כְּבַיִת לְעִנְיַן מְכִירַת בַּיִת. דּוּמְיָא דְּכוֹתְלֵי הַבַּיִת, דַּחֲשִׁיבִי תָּלוּשׁ לְעִנְיַן הֶכְשֵׁר זְרָעִים, וּלְגַבֵּי מֶכֶר הֲרֵי הֵן בִּכְלַל בַּיִת וַחֲשִׁיבִי כְּקַרְקַע. אוֹ דִּלְמָא טַעֲמַיְיהוּ גַּבֵּי מַכְתֶּשֶׁת מִשּׁוּם דִּבְעֵין רָעָה מוֹכֵר, אֲבָל לְגַבֵּי הֶכְשֵׁר — כְּקַרְקַע מְשַׁוּוּ לֵיהּ, וּכְר"א סְבִירָא לְהוּ. תֵּיקוּ. הַאי דְּנָקַט "לְהָדִיחַ בָּהֶן אֶת הָאַלְטְרוּבִּיל" וְלָא נָקַט מַכְתֶּשֶׁת — אוֹרְחָא דְּמִילְּתָא נָקַט, שֶׁהָיוּ רְגִילִין לְהָדִיחוֹ. אִי נַמִּי רְבוּתָא הוּא דְּנָקַט, כְּדְפָרִישִׁי', דְּאַע"ג דְּאָמְרִי רַבָּנַן מָכַר אֶת הָאַלְטְרוּבִּיל — אִיכָּא לְמֵימַר דְּחָשְׁבֵי לֵיהּ תָּלוּשׁ לְעִנְיַן הֶכְשֵׁר זְרָעִים, כְּדְפָרִישִׁית. **עִישּׂוּר נִכְסֵי.** שֶׁהַבַּת נוֹטֶלֶת בְּנִכְסֵי אָבִיהָ בִּשְׁבִיל פַּרְנָסַת הַבַּעַל לְהִינָּשֵׂא בּוֹ. וְקיי"ל בִּכְתוּבּוֹת (דף סח.): לְפַרְנָסָה שָׁמִין בָּאָב, וְהֵיכָא דְּאֵין יוֹדְעִין דַּעְתּוֹ — נוֹטֶלֶת עִישּׂוּר נְכָסִים, וּמִמְּקַרְקְעֵי וְלָא מִמִּטַּלְטְלֵי, כְּדְאָמַר בִּכְתוּבּוֹת. **אֲפִי' מֵאִצְטְרוּבְּלֵי.** כְּר"א, דְּכָל הַמְחוּבָּר לַקַּרְקַע הֲרֵי הוּא כְּקַרְקַע. וּפֵירֵשׁ רַבֵּינוּ חֲנַנְאֵל: וְקיי"ל הָכִי, דְּהָא לֵית מַאן דְּפָלֵיג עֲלָהּ. וּלְדִבְרֵי הַכֹּל פַּרְנָסָה דְּהִיא עִישּׂוּר נִכְסֵי — מִמְּקַרְקְעֵי וְלָא מִמִּטַּלְטְלֵי הִיא, וַאֲפִילּוּ בַּזְּמַן הַזֶּה, דְּהָא בְּהֶדְיָא פָּסַק רָבָא בְּפֶרֶק "מְצִיאַת הָאִשָּׁה" הִלְכְתָא מִמְּקַרְקְעֵי וְלָא מִמִּטַּלְטְלֵי, בֵּין לִכְתוּבָּה בֵּין לִמְזוֹנֵי בֵּין לְפַרְנָסָה. וְאַף עַל גַּב דְּרַבּוֹתֵינוּ הַגְּאוֹנִים תִּקְנוּ לִגְבּוֹת כְּתוּבָּה אֲפִי' מִמִּטַּלְטְלֵי, גּוֹבִים גַּם מְזוֹנֵי אֲפִי' מִמִּטַּלְטְלֵי, דְּהָא קיי"ל (כתובות דף נד:): תְּנָאֵי כְתוּבָּה כִּכְתוּבָּה דָּמֵי — הָנֵי מִילֵּי בִּכְתוּבָּה וּמְזוֹנֵי, אֲבָל הַפַּרְנָסָה אֵינָהּ מִתְּנָאֵי כְתוּבָּה — הִלְכָּךְ בִּמְקוֹמָהּ עוֹמֶדֶת, וּמִמְּקַרְקְעֵי גָּבְיָא וְלָא מִמִּטַּלְטְלֵי (ג). **אַגְבָּהּ מֵאִצְטְרוּבְּלֵי.** דְּאִינּוּן מִטַּלְטְלֵי קְבוּעִין בַּקַּרְקַע. שָׁמְעִינַן מִינָּהּ, דְּסוּגְיָא דִּשְׁמַעְתָּא כְּר"א סַלְקָא, דְּסָבַר: כָּל הַמְחוּבָּר לַקַּרְקַע — הֲרֵי הוּא כְּקַרְקַע. כֵּן פֵּי' ר' חֲנַנְאֵל, וְהָכִי פָּסַק' הֲלָכָה דְּהִלְכְתָא, וְכֵן עִיקָּר. **מֵעֲמָלָא דְּבָתֵּי.** מִשְּׂכִירוּת הַבָּתִּים. דִּכְמִקַּרְקְעֵי חָשֵׁיב לֵיהּ, דִּשְׂכַר מִקַּרְקְעֵי חֲשִׁיב מִקַּרְקְעֵי. **מתני'** הַמּוֹכֵר אֶת הֶחָצֵר. סְתָם, מָכַר בָּתִּים הַפְּתוּחִים לֶחָצֵר, וּבוֹרוֹת שִׁיחִין וּמְעָרוֹת שֶׁבְּתוֹךְ הַבַּיִת. אַע"ג דְּהַמּוֹכֵר אֶת הַבַּיִת לֹא מָכַר בּוֹרוֹת שִׁיחִין וּמְעָרוֹת — לְגַבֵּי חָצֵר מִיהָא בְּטֵלִים, וְנִמְכָּרִין בִּכְלַל חָצֵר. **אֲבָל לֹא אֶת הַמִּטַּלְטְלִין.** תַּשְׁמִישֵׁי הַבַּיִת שֶׁאֵינָן קְבוּעִין (ד) כָּל כָּךְ: הָנָךְ דַּאֲמָרַן לְעֵיל דְּאֵינָן מְכוּרִין בִּכְלַל בַּיִת, וְכ"ש שְׁאָר מִטַּלְטְלִין שֶׁאֵינָן בִּכְלַל תַּשְׁמִישֵׁי בַּיִת. **הֲרֵי כּוּלָּן מְכוּרִין.** הַמִּטַּלְטְלִין — תַּשְׁמִישֵׁי בַּיִת כּוּלָּן, דְּאִיקְרוּ מִטַּלְטְלֵי, כִּדְאָמְרִי' לְקַמָּן בְּ"מִי שֶׁמֵּת" (דף קנ.): מָאנֵי תַּשְׁמִישְׁתֵּיהּ אִיקְרוּ מִטַּלְטְלֵי, וְלָא חִיטֵּי וְשַׂעֲרֵי. **בֵּין כָּךְ וּבֵין כָּךְ.** בֵּין שֶׁאָמַר לוֹ "כָּל מַה שֶּׁבְּתוֹכָהּ" בֵּין לֹא אָמַר. **לֹא אֶת הַמֶּרְחָץ.** דְּאֵינוֹ בִּכְלַל חָצֵר. **אֶלָּא אֲוִירָהּ.** אֲבָל בָּתִּים וּבוֹרוֹת לֹא מָכַר כְּלָל. וְדָמִים מוֹדִיעִים לֵיכָּא לְמֵימַר, דְּאֵין אוֹנָאָה לְקַרְקָעוֹת. **גמ'** הַחִיצוֹנִים. הַפְּתוּחִין לֶחָצֵר. **חוּלְסָאוֹת.** פר"ח: קַרְקַע שֶׁעֲפָרוֹ חוֹל, שֶׁמּוֹצִיאִין מִמֶּנּוּ זְכוּכִית. וּבְפ"ק דְּשַׁבָּת (דף טו:) אָמְרִינַן בִּזְכוּכִית שֶׁתְּחִלַּת בְּרִיָּיתוֹ מִן הַחוֹל, וְהִלְכָּךְ מָקוֹם חָשׁוּב (ה) בִּפְנֵי עַצְמוֹ. **חֲנוּיוֹת הַפְּתוּחוֹת לְתוֹכָהּ.** שֶׁאֵין מוֹכְרִין (ו) אֶלָּא לִבְנֵי חָצֵר זוֹ. **שֶׁאֵין פְּתוּחוֹת לְתוֹכָהּ.** אֶלָּא לִרְשׁוּת הָרַבִּים. **מִילוֹסָא.** אֲוִירָא. **וְהָתָנֵי ר' חִיָּיא.** דִּפְתוּחוֹת לְכָאן וּלְכָאן אֵין נִמְכָּרוֹת עִמָּהּ! **הָא.** דְּר' חִיָּיא — דְּרוֹב תַּשְׁמִישַׁיְיהוּ לְבַר, פֶּתַח שֶׁל צַד הַחוּץ פָּתוּחַ יוֹתֵר לְהִשְׁתַּמֵּשׁ בּוֹ מִפֶּתַח הַפְּנִימִי. **אָמַר רָבָא כָּל הֵיכָא דְּא"ל דִּירְתָּא.** שֶׁאָמַר לוֹ מוֹכֵר לַלּוֹקֵחַ "דִּירָה זוֹ אֲנִי מוֹכֵר לְךָ", וּבְלָשׁוֹן זֶה מָכַר לוֹ אֶת הֶחָצֵר, שֶׁלֹּא אָמַר "חָצֵר זוֹ אֲנִי מוֹכֵר לְךָ" אֶלָּא "מָדוֹר זֶה" — דְּכוּלֵּי עָלְמָא לָא פְּלִיגֵי דְּבָתִּים מַשְׁמַע, דְּבֶחָצֵר אֵין דָּרִין, אֶלָּא בְּבָתִּים. וְהִלְכָּךְ הָכָא מוֹדֵי ר"א דְּחָצֵר וּבָתִּים מָכַר לוֹ, שֶׁהַכֹּל בְּיַחַד קָרוּי דִּירָה. **כִּי פְּלִיגֵי דְּא"ל דַּרְתָּא.** חָצֵר מְתַרְגְּמִינַן: דַּרְתָּא. **ר"א סָבַר תַּרְבִּיצָא** מַשְׁמַע. אֲוִיר מַשְׁמַע, כְּאִילּוּ אָמַר לוֹ "חָצֵר זוֹ אֲנִי מוֹכֵר", (ז) דַּאֲוִיר לְבַד קָרוּי "חָצֵר". וְרַבָּנַן סָבְרִי בָּתֵּי מַשְׁמַע. דְּדַרְתָּא וְדִירְתָּא אַחַת הֵם, שְׁנֵיהֶם לְשׁוֹן דִּירָה הֵם. וּלְהַךְ לִישָּׁנָא קַמָּא דְּרָבָה מַשְׁמַע דְּהֵיכָא דְּא"ל "חָצֵר זוֹ אֲנִי מוֹכֵר לְךָ" — הַכֹּל מוֹדִין דְּלֹא מָכַר אֶלָּא אֲוִירָהּ שֶׁל חָצֵר. וּמַתְנִי' הָכִי קָתָנֵי: הַמּוֹכֵר (ח) חָצֵר בְּאוֹתוֹ לָשׁוֹן שֶׁרְגִילִין לְקָרוֹתוֹ, דְּהַיְינוּ "דַּרְתָּא" — מָכַר אֶת הַבָּתִּים כו'. ר"א אוֹמֵר: הַמּוֹכֵר אֶת הֶחָצֵר, אֲפִי' בְּלָשׁוֹן "דַּרְתָּא" — לֹא מָכַר אֶלָּא אֲוִירָהּ שֶׁל חָצֵר. הָכִי גָּרְסִינַן: **אִיכָּא דְּאָמְרִי אָמַר רָבָא כָּל הֵיכָא דְּא"ל דַּרְתָּא כּוּלֵּי עָלְמָא לָא פְּלִיגֵי דְּבָתֵּי מַשְׁמַע.** דְּגַם הוּא לְשׁוֹן דִּירָה, דְּעַל שֵׁם דִּירָה נִקְרֵאת הֶחָצֵר דַּרְתָּא. הָכִי גָּרְסִינַן: **כִּי פְּלִיגֵי דְּא"ל חָצֵר.** כִּדְקָתָנֵי מַתְנִי' "הַמּוֹכֵר אֶת הֶחָצֵר". מָר סָבַר: "חָצֵר" אֲוִירָא מַשְׁמַע. וּמָר סָבַר כַּחֲצַר הַמִּשְׁכָּן. חֲכָמִים סָבְרִי: "חָצֵר" כַּחֲצַר הַמִּשְׁכָּן, כִּדְכְתִיב: "אוֹרֶךְ הֶחָצֵר מֵאָה בָאַמָּה וְרוֹחַב חֲמִשִּׁים בַּחֲמִשִּׁים" (שמות כז), וּבִכְלַל אֵלּוּ ק' אַמָּה קֹדֶשׁ הַקֳּדָשִׁים וְאֹהֶל מוֹעֵד שֶׁהֵם כְּמוֹ בָּתִּים וּקְרָאָן הַכָּתוּב חָצֵר, מִכָּאן שֶׁהַבָּתִּים נִמְכָּרִין בִּכְלַל חָצֵר. כֵּן פר"ח, וְעִיקָּר. וּמִסְתַּבְּרָא כְּהַאי לִישָּׁנָא בַּתְרָא, דִּבְדַאֲמַר לֵיהּ "חָצֵר" פְּלִיגֵי, דְּהָכִי תְּנַן מַתְנִי'. וְהִלְכָּךְ, לֹא שְׁנָא א"ל "דִּירְתָּא" וְלֹא שְׁנָא א"ל "דַּרְתָּא" וְלָא שְׁנָא א"ל "חָצֵר" — מָכַר אֶת הַבָּתִּים. **מְצוּלָה.** קַרְקָעִית הַנָּהָר (ט) שֶׁמּוֹצִיאִין בּוֹ כֶּסֶף וְזָהָב. כֵּן פֵּירֵשׁ ר' חֲנַנְאֵל. וְיֵשׁ מְפָרְשִׁים: לְדָגִים. **הֶחֱזִיק בְּחוּלְסִית.** לָאו בְּחֶזְקַת שָׁלֹשׁ שָׁנִים מַיְירֵי, אֶלָּא בַּחֲזָקָה כְּדֵי לִקְנוֹת, שֶׁלֹּא יוּכַל מוֹכֵר לַחֲזוֹר בּוֹ. דְּקַיְימָא לָן: קַרְקַע נִקְנֵית בְּכֶסֶף בִּשְׁטָר וּבַחֲזָקָה. **לֹא קָנָה מְצוּלָה.** שֶׁהֲרֵי שְׁנֵי תַּשְׁמִישִׁין הֵן, זֶה לְחוֹל וְזֶה לְכֶסֶף וְזָהָב, וּשְׁנֵי שֵׁמוֹת הֵן, וְאע"פ שֶׁסְּמוּכִין זֶה לָזֶה לָא מְהַנְּיָא חֶזְקַת חוּלְסִית לִקְנוֹת מְצוּלָה. וְהַיְינוּ טַעְמָא: דְּמֵהַאי קְרָא נָפְקָא לָן חֶזְקַת הַקּוֹנֶה קַרְקַע בְּמַסֶּכֶת קִדּוּשִׁין (דף כו.): "וּשְׁבוּ בְּעָרֵיכֶם אֲשֶׁר תְּפַשְׂתֶּם" (בָּהּ) בַּמֶּה תְּפַשְׂתֶּם — בִּישִׁיבָה, וְעוֹד קְרָא אַחֲרִינָא: "וִירִשְׁתֶּם אוֹתָהּ וִישַׁבְתֶּם בָּהּ" בַּמֶּה יְרִשְׁתֶּם — בִּישִׁיבָה — מִשָּׁם לָמַדְנוּ שֶׁאוֹתוֹ קַרְקַע שֶׁהוּא יוֹשֵׁב בּוֹ אוֹ אוֹתָהּ הָעִיר שֶׁהוּא יוֹשֵׁב בָּהּ, הוּא קוֹנֶה בְּחֶזְקַת יְשִׁיבָה, אֲבָל עִיר אַחֶרֶת אֵינוֹ קוֹנֶה בִּישִׁיבַת חֲבֵירְתָּהּ. הִלְכָּךְ חוּלְסִית וּמְצוּלָה שֶׁהֵן שְׁנֵי דְבָרִים חֲלוּקִין זֶה מִזֶּה, בְּאוֹתוֹ שֶׁהוּא מַחֲזִיק הוּא זוֹכֶה וְלֹא בַּחֲבֵירוֹ. **כֵּיוָן שֶׁהֶחֱזִיק בְּאַחַת מֵהֶן קָנָה כּוּלָּן.** וּכְדִמְפָרֵשׁ בפ"ק דְּקִדּוּשִׁין (דף כז:): שֶׁנָּתַן לוֹ דְּמֵי כּוּלָּן. דְּכֵיוָן דְּקִיבֵּל הַמּוֹכֵר כָּל הַדָּמִים שֶׁל עֶשֶׂר הַשָּׂדוֹת, הֲרֵי אִשְׁתַּעְבּוּד כּוּלְּהוּ לַלּוֹקֵחַ בִּשְׁבִיל מְעוֹתָיו שֶׁנָּתַן לוֹ, וְדַי לָן בְּחֶזְקַת אַחַת מֵהֶן. וּכְדִמְפָרֵשׁ טַעְמָא בב"ק: דְּסַדְנָא דְּאַרְעָא חַד הוּא — כָּל הַשָּׂדוֹת אֲדוּקִין בְּגוּף קַרְקַע שֶׁל עוֹלָם שֶׁהוּא אֶחָד, וּכְמוֹ שֶׁהֶחֱזִיק בְּכוּלְּהוּ דָּמֵי. וְהָא דְּאָמְרִינַן בְּ"חֶזְקַת הַבָּתִּים" (לעיל דף נג.): שְׁנֵי שָׂדוֹת וּמֶצֶר אֶחָד בֵּינֵיהֶן, הֶחֱזִיק בְּאַחַת מֵהֶן לֹא קָנָה חֲבֵירְתָּהּ — לָא תִּקְשֵׁי לִשְׁמוּאֵל, דְּהָתָם בְּנִכְסֵי הַגֵּר קָאֵי, דְּמִמֵּילָא קָא קָנֵי בְּלָא מַתָּן

מעמלא דבתי. וא"ת: היכי דמי? אי כבר בא השכירות ליד האחין — אם כן מטלטלי נינהו, ולא גביא מנייהו. ואי אתא לאשמועינן שיכולה להשכיר לצורך נדונייתה — פשיטא, דאפילו למכור יכולה! וי"ל: כגון שהשכירו הבית לשנה, וכבר עבר חצי הזמן. וקא משמע לן דאפילו שכירות מזמן שעבר תטול, דאין השכירות משתלמת אלא לבסוף, ולא דמי למטלטלין.

לח א מיי' פ"כ מהל' אישות הל' ה סמג עשין מח טוש"ע אה"ע סי' קיג סעי' ב:

לט ב ג ד ה ו ז מיי' פכ"ה מהל' מכירה הלכה ו סמג עשין פב טוש"ע ח"מ סי' רטו סעיף א:

הגהות הב"ח

(א) גמ' פתוחות לכאן ולכאן נמכרות עמה כצ"ל ותיבות אלו ואלו נמחק: (ב) שם קנה כולן הכי השתא התם הוא דסדנא: (ג) רשב"ם ד"ה אפילו וכו' ולא ממטלטלי ומדלא ליה אגבה כצ"ל והד"א: (ד) ד"ה אבל וכו' שאינן קבועין והיינו כל הנך לאמרן: (ה) ד"ה חולסאות וכו' חשוב הוא בפני עצמו: (ו) ד"ה חנויות וכו' שאין מוכרין מהן אלא: (ז) ד"ה ר"א סבר וכו' מוכר לך לאויר: (ח) ד"ה ורבנן וכו' המוכר את החצר בלשון שרגילין לקרותה חצר להיינו: (ט) ד"ה מצולה וכו' שמוצאין בו:

[נ"א הרי]: ב) [נ"ל ...]. ג) [עי' תוס' ערכין ... ועי' ערוך ערך חלס]: ... קדושין כז. ב"ק יב. ... עי' כתובות פ"ב ... תוספתא ב"ב פ"ב]:

רבינו גרשום

...ור נכסים. דיש לה ...ת בנכסי אביה ...שת ממקרקעי: אפילו ...צטרוביל. דכקרקע ...: מעמלא דבתי. ...כירות הבתים. ויש ...מרים מעמלא דבתי ...נו זבל שמוציאין לפני ...תחים גובה מהן ...שור נכסים: **פים'** ...וכר את החצר מכר ... הבתים. שפתוחין ...צר: בורות שיחין ...ערות. שתחת הבית ...תוחין לחצר דכל הני ...שעבדי לחצר: לא מכר ...ת בית המרחץ ולא את ...ת הבד שבתוכה. ...ום דלא שייכי לחצר ...שות בפני עצמו הוא: ...לא אוירה של חצר. ...

אָמַר א)(רַבָּה) אָמַר רַב נַחְמָן: אהֶחֱזִיק בַּחוּלְסִית קָנָה מְצוּלָה. (א) פְּשִׁיטָא, דְּהָא אָמַר שְׁמוּאֵל: מָכַר לוֹ עֶשֶׂר שָׂדוֹת וכו'! מַהוּ דְּתֵימָא: הָתָם הוּא דְּסַדְנָא דְּאַרְעָא חַד הוּא, אֲבָל הָכָא הָא תַּשְׁמִישְׁתָּא לְחוּד וְהָא תַּשְׁמִישְׁתָּא לְחוּד, קָא מַשְׁמַע לָן.§ **מתני'** בהַמּוֹכֵר בֵּית הַבַּד – מָכַר אֶת הַיָּם וְאֶת הַמְּמָל וְאֶת הַבְּתוּלוֹת, גאֲבָל לֹא מָכַר אֶת ב)הָעֲבִירִים וְאֶת הַגַּלְגַּל וְאֶת הַקּוֹרָה, דוּבִזְמַן שֶׁאָמַר לוֹ: "הוּא וְכָל מַה שֶּׁבְּתוֹכוֹ" – הֲרֵי כּוּלָּן מְכוּרִין; ג)ר"א אוֹמֵר: הַמּוֹכֵר בֵּית הַבַּד – מָכַר אֶת הַקּוֹרָה.§ **גמ'** יָם – טְלָפְחָא. מְמָל – א"ר אַבָּא בַּר מְמָל: מַפְרַכְתָּא. בְּתוּלוֹת – א"ר יוֹחָנָן: כְּלוֹנְסוֹת שֶׁל אֶרֶז שֶׁמַּעֲמִידִין בָּהֶן אֶת הַקּוֹרָה. עֲבִירִים – כִּבְשֵׁי. גַּלְגַּל – חוּמְרְתָא. קוֹרָה – קוֹרָה. ת"ר: ההַמּוֹכֵר בֵּית הַבַּד – מָכַר אֶת נְסָרִים וְאֶת הַיְּקָבִים וְאֶת הַמַּפְרֵכוֹת, וְאֶת הָרֵיחַיִם (ב) הַתַּחְתּוֹנוֹת אֲבָל לֹא הָעֶלְיוֹנָה, וּבִזְמַן שֶׁאָמַר לוֹ: "הוּא וְכָל מַה שֶּׁבְּתוֹכוֹ" – הֲרֵי כּוּלָּן מְכוּרִין; בֵּין כָּךְ וּבֵין כָּךְ, ולֹא מָכַר לֹא אֶת הָעֲבִירִים וְלֹא אֶת הַשַּׂקִּין וְלֹא אֶת הַמַּרְצוּפִין; רַבִּי אֱלִיעֶזֶר אוֹמֵר: הַמּוֹכֵר בֵּית הַבַּד – מָכַר אֶת הַקּוֹרָה, שֶׁלֹּא נִקְרָא בֵּית הַבַּד אֶלָּא עַל שׁוּם קוֹרָה.§ **מתני'** זהַמּוֹכֵר אֶת (ג) הַמֶּרְחָץ – לֹא מָכַר אֶת הַנְּסָרִין וְאֶת הַסַּפְלִין וְאֶת ד)הַבַּלָּנִיּוֹת; בִּזְמַן שֶׁאָמַר לוֹ: "הִיא וְכָל מַה שֶּׁבְּתוֹכָהּ" – הֲרֵי כּוּלָּן מְכוּרִין; בֵּין כָּךְ וּבֵין כָּךְ, לֹא מָכַר לֹא אֶת הַמְּגוּרוֹת שֶׁל מַיִם וְלֹא אֶת אוֹצָרוֹת שֶׁל עֵצִים.§ **גמ'** ת"ר: חהַמּוֹכֵר אֶת הַמֶּרְחָץ – מָכַר אֶת בֵּית הַנְּסָרִין וְאֶת בֵּית הַיְּקָמִין, וְאֶת בֵּית הַסַּפָּלִים וְאֶת בֵּית הַוִּילָאוֹת, אֲבָל לֹא אֶת (ד) נְסָרִין עַצְמָן וְלֹא יְקָמִין עַצְמָן, וְלֹא סְפָלִים עַצְמָן וְלֹא וִילָאוֹת עַצְמָן, וּבִזְמַן שֶׁאָמַר לוֹ: "הִיא וְכָל מַה שֶּׁבְּתוֹכָהּ" – הֲרֵי כּוּלָּן מְכוּרִין; טבֵּין כָּךְ וּבֵין כָּךְ, לֹא מָכַר לוֹ אֶת הַבְּרֵיכוֹת הַמְּסַפְּקוֹת לוֹ מַיִם, בֵּין

בימות

מַתַּן מָעוֹת, הִלְכָּךְ לֹא קָנָה אֶלָּא אוֹתוֹ שֶׁהֶחֱזִיק. (ה) דְּהָא הַךְ דִּשְׁמוּאֵל נַמִּי, אִילּוּ לֹא נָתַן מָעוֹת – לֹא קָנָה אֶלָּא מַה שֶּׁהֶחֱזִיק, וְאִם נָתַן דְּמֵי חֶלְיָין – לֹא קָנָה בְּחֶזְקַת אַחַת מֵהֶן אֶלָּא כְּנֶגֶד מְעוֹתָיו. וא"ת: כֵּיוָן דִּבְנָתַן דְּמֵי כּוּלָּן מַיְירֵי שְׁמוּאֵל, מַה לָּנוּ לְחֶזְקַת אַחַת מֵהֶן? וַהֲלֹא קַרְקַע נִקְנֶה בְּכֶסֶף, וְלֹא צְרִיכָה תּוּ חֲזָקָה! אִיכָּא לְמֵימַר דִּבְמָקוֹם שֶׁכּוֹתְבִין הַשְּׁטָר מַיְירֵי, דְּהָתָם לָא קָנֵי קַרְקַע בְּמָעוֹת, אֶלָּא בִּשְׁטָר אוֹ בַּחֲזָקָה, כִּדְאָמְרִי' בְּפ"ק דְּקִדּוּשִׁין (דף כו.) עֲלָהּ דְּהַךְ מִשְׁנָה "נְכָסִים שֶׁיֵּשׁ לָהֶן אַחֲרָיוּת נִקְנִין בְּכֶסֶף" כו', אָמַר רַבָּא: לֹא שָׁנוּ אֶלָּא בְּמָקוֹם שֶׁאֵין כּוֹתְבִין אֶת הַשְּׁטָר, אֲבָל בְּמָקוֹם שֶׁכּוֹתְבִין אֶת הַשְּׁטָר – לֹא קָנָה עַד שֶׁיִּכְתּוֹב אֶת הַשְּׁטָר, א"נ עַד שֶׁיַּחֲזִיק. חֲדָא תַּשְׁמִישְׁתָּא. (ו) כָּל הָעֶשֶׂר שָׂדוֹת עוֹמְדִין לִזְרִיעָה, וְהִלְכָּךְ כְּשָׂדֶה אַחַת חֲשׁוּבִין עַל יְדֵי סַדְנָא דְּאַרְעָא שֶׁמְּחַבֵּר אוֹתָן. **מתני'** הַמּוֹכֵר אֶת בֵּית הַבַּד. בַּיִת שֶׁהַבַּד בּוֹ, וְאוֹתוֹ בַּיִת לְתַשְׁמִישׁ בַּד לְבַדּוֹ עָשׂוּי. מָכַר אֶת הַיָּם. בַּגְּמָ' מְפָרֵשׁ דְּהַיְינוּ בַּד עַצְמוֹ, כִּדְקָמְפָרֵשׁ וְאָזֵיל. וְנִרְאֶה בְּעֵינַי דְּכָל הָנָךְ דְּקָתָנֵי דְּהוּ מָכַר – קְבוּעִין הֵן שָׁם, וְאִינָךְ דְּאֵינָן מְכוּרִים בִּכְלַל בֵּית הַבַּד – מִיטַּלְטְלֵי הֵן, כִּדְאָמְרַן נַמִּי (לעיל ד' סה.) גַּבֵּי בַּיִת, שֶׁמָּכַר מַכְתֶּשֶׁת קְבוּעָה וְלֹא הַמִּיטַּלְטֶלֶת. הַמְּמָל (ז) הַבְּתוּלוֹת. בַּגְּמָ' מְפָרֵשׁ, וּקְבוּעִין הֵן. עֲבִירִים וְגַלְגַּל וְקוֹרָה. מִיטַּלְטְלֵי הֵן. וּבַגְּמָ' מִיפָרְשֵׁי כּוּלְּהוּ. וּבִזְמַן שֶׁאָמַר לוֹ הוּא. הַבַּיִת שֶׁל בַּד, וְכָל מַה שֶּׁבְּתוֹכוֹ אֲנִי מוֹכֵר לְךָ – כּוּלָּן מְכוּרִין. וְדַוְקָא הָנֵי הַצְּרִיכִין לְבֵית הַבַּד, אֲבָל שְׁאָר תַּשְׁמִישִׁין שֶׁמּוּנָּחִין בְּתוֹכוֹ לְהִשָּׁמֵר – אֵינָן מְכוּרִין. מָכַר אֶת הַקּוֹרָה. כִּדְמְפָרֵשׁ טַעֲמָא בַּגְּמָרָא, דְּהַיְינוּ עִיקַּר בֵּית הַבַּד. **גמ'** טְלָפְחָא. הִיא עֲרֵיבָה שֶׁקּוֹרִין מיי"ט, עֲגוּלָּה כַּעֲדָשָׁה. וַעֲדָשָׁה קָרֵי לָהּ בַּבָּרַיְיתָא בְּמַסֶּכֶת ע"ז (דף עה.). "עֲדָשִׁים" – מְתַרְגְּמִינַן טְלוֹפְחִין. מְמָל אָמַר רַבִּי אַבָּא בַּר מְמָל מַפְרַכְתָּא. אֶבֶן נְקוּבָה שֶׁמַּכְנִיסִין בָּהּ עֵץ וּמְפָרְכִין בָּהּ הַזֵּיתִים בְּבֵית הַבַּד. דְּהַיְינוּ דּוּמְיָא דְּמַכְתֶּשֶׁת. וְיֵשׁ מְפָרְשִׁים דְּהַיְינוּ עֵץ עַצְמוֹ שֶׁמְּפָרְכִין בּוֹ אֶת הַזֵּיתִים, וּלְפִי שֶׁהוּא (ח) תַּשְׁמִישֵׁי בֵּית הַבַּד הוּא מָכוּר בִּכְלַל בֵּית הַבַּד, וְאַעֲ"ג דְּמִיטַּלְטֵל. וְלָשׁוֹן רִאשׁוֹן מִפֵּירוּשֵׁי ר' חֲנַנְאֵל, וְעִיקָּר. כְּלוֹנְסוֹת. אוֹתָן שֶׁנּוֹעֲצִין ה) בְּרֹאשׁ הַגַּת מִכָּאן וּמִכָּאן (ט) וְנוֹקְבִים זֶה כְּנֶגֶד זֶה, וְנוֹתְנִים בְּרִיחִים מִזֶּה לָזֶה, וּמַעֲמִידִין הַקּוֹרָה עַל הַבְּרִיחַ. וּבְלַעַ"ז קוֹרִין לָהֶן יזמייל"ן = תְּאוֹמִים. וְיֵשׁ מְקוֹמוֹת שֶׁקּוֹרִין שרור"ש = אֲחָיוֹת. כִּבְשֵׁי. נְסָרִים שֶׁנּוֹתְנִין עַל הַזֵּיתִים בְּבֵית הַבַּד כְּשֶׁמּוֹרִידִין הַקּוֹרָה עֲלֵיהֶן לְכָבְשָׁן, וּמִשּׁוּם דְּמִיטַּלְטְלֵי לָא מִזְדַּבְּנֵי. חוּמְרְתָא. ויי"ן בְּלַעַ"ז, שֶׁמְּגַלְגְּלִין בָּהּ אֶת הַקּוֹרָה לְהַעֲלוֹתָהּ וּלְהוֹרִידָהּ. קוֹרָה. דְּמַתְנִי' הַיְינוּ קוֹרָה כְּמַשְׁמָעָהּ, שֶׁגַּם בְּבָבֶל קוֹרִין לָהּ כֵּן. מָכַר אֶת הַנְּסָרִים. אֵינָם כִּיבְשֵׁי, דְּא"כ תִּקְשֵׁי לְמַתְנִי', דְּהָתָם קָתָנֵי לֹא מָכַר וְהָכָא קָתָנֵי מָכַר. אֶלָּא הֵן כְּעֵין נְסָרִים נְתוּנִים סָבִיב הַזֵּיתִים בְּבֵית הַבַּד כְּדֵי שֶׁלֹּא יִתְפַּזְּרוּ אָנֶה וָאָנָה בְּהַכְבִּיד הַקּוֹרָה עֲלֵיהֶם. וְנִרְאֶה בְּעֵינַי שֶׁמְּחוּבָּרִים שָׁם וּקְבוּעִים הֵם שָׁם לְעוֹלָם. וּבַתּוֹסֶפְתָּא גָּרֵס: מָכַר אֶת הַיְּלָרִים. וְנִרְאֶה דִּגְלָרִים גָּרֵס, וְהַיְינוּ עֶגֶל בֵּית הַבַּד, שֶׁקּוֹשְׁרִין בָּהֶם הַזֵּיתִים כְּדֵי שֶׁלֹּא יִתְפַּזְּרוּ(י). יְקָבִים. הַיְינוּ יָם, הַחֲקוּקָה וַעֲשׂוּיָה כְּעֵין יֶקֶב, וּכְדִכְתִיב (יואל ב): "וְהֵשִׁיקוּ הַיְקָבִים תִּירוֹשׁ וְיִצְהָר", וְהֵשִׁיקוּ – לְשׁוֹן הוֹמֶה וְרַעַשׁ שֶׁהַיַּיִן עוֹשֶׂה כְּשֶׁנּוֹפֵל מִן הַיֶּקֶב. הַמַּפְרֵכוֹת. הַיְינוּ מְמָל דְּמַתְנִי' דְּפָרֵישְׁנָא לְעֵיל: מַפְרַכְתָּא הָרֵיחַיִם הַתַּחְתּוֹנָה. קְבוּעָה הִיא, וְטוֹחֲנִין בָּהּ זֵיתִים. שֶׁבַּתְּחִלָּה מְפָרְכִין אוֹתָן בַּמַּפְרֵכוֹת, וְאַחַ"כ טוֹחֲנִין בָּרֵיחַיִם, וְאַחַ"כ עוֹצְרִין אוֹתָן בְּבֵית הַבַּד. וְהָכִי אָמְרִינַן בִּמְנָחוֹת (דף פו.). וְשַׂקִּין וּמַרְצוּפִין. לָשֵׂאת בָּהֶן זֵיתִים בְּבֵית הַבַּד. אֶלָּא שֶׁהַמַּרְצוּפִין הֵן שֶׁל עוֹר, וְהַשַּׂקִּין מְנוֹצָה שֶׁל עִזִּים. וְכָל דְּמִטַּלְטֵל לָא מִזְדַּבַּן. **מתני'** הָכִי גָּרְסִינַן בְּסֵדֶר הַמִּשְׁנָה: הַמּוֹכֵר אֶת בֵּית הַמֶּרְחָץ. בַּיִת שֶׁעָשׂוּי לִרְחוֹץ בּוֹ. וְג' בָּתִּים הֵן, זֶה לִפְנִים מִזֶּה, כִּדְאָמְרִינַן בְּ"יְצִיאוֹת הַשַּׁבָּת" (שבת דף י.): פְּנִימִי – לִרְחִיצָה, חִיצוֹן – שֶׁעוֹמְדִין שָׁם מְלוּבָּשִׁין, בֵּינוֹנִי – שֶׁפּוֹשְׁטִין שָׁם בִּגְדֵיהֶם. וּבַתּוֹסֶפְתָּא קָתָנֵי בְּהֶדְיָא: הַמּוֹכֵר אֶת הַמֶּרְחָץ מָכַר בָּתִּים הַפְּנִימִים וּבָתִּים הַחִיצוֹנִים. הַנְּסָרִים. שֶׁנּוֹתְנִין עַל גַּבֵּי קַרְקַע הַמֶּרְחָץ, וְעוֹמְדִין עֲלֵיהֶם הָרוֹחֲצִים שֶׁלֹּא יִכָּווּ רַגְלֵיהֶם מֵחוֹם הַקַּרְקַע, אִי נַמִּי – שֶׁלֹּא יִטַּנְּפוּ רַגְלֵיהֶן. וּמִשּׁוּם דְּמִטַּלְטְלֵי לָא מִיזְדַּבְּנֵי. סְפָלִים. לָתֵת בָּהֶן מַיִם לִרְחוֹץ, וּמִיטַּלְטְלִין. ווילאוֹת. מָסָךְ כְּנֶגֶד הַפֶּתַח. וְלִי נִרְאֶה: בֶּגֶד שֶׁמִּסְתַּפְּגִין בּוֹ, דְּהַיְינוּ אֲלוּנְטִית. לֹא מָכַר מְגוּרוֹת שֶׁל מַיִם. בְּרֵיכוֹת מַיִם שֶׁשּׁוֹפְכוֹת מַיִם לַמֶּרְחָץ. וְלֹא אוֹצָרוֹת שֶׁל עֵצִים. שֶׁהָיוּ לְחַמֵּם בָּהֶן הַמֶּרְחָץ. וְהַיְינוּ טַעֲמָא, דְּאֵין אֵלּוּ תַּשְׁמִישִׁין הַמְיוּחָדִין לַמֶּרְחָץ כִּי הָנָךְ דִּלְעֵיל, וְאֵין אֵלּוּ מֵאֵלֵי תַּשְׁמִישְׁתֵּיהּ, אֶלָּא מָמוֹנוֹ הֵן לֵיהָנוֹת בָּהֶם אֲפִי' בְּתוֹךְ בֵּיתוֹ. דִּכְשֶׁקּוֹנֶה אוֹתָם קוֹנֶה לְהַסְפִּיק בְּבֵיתוֹ וְלַאֲפוֹת וּלְבַשֵּׁל בָּהֶן, כְּמוֹ חִיטֵּי וְשַׂעֲרֵי. מְגוּרוֹת – כְּמוֹ "נֶהֶרְסוּ מַמְּגוּרוֹת" (יואל א), כַּיּוֹצֵא בּוֹ – "מְגוּרָה שֶׁהִיא מְלֵאָה פֵּירוֹת" (פסחים דף ט.). **גמ'** בֵּית הַנְּסָרִין. בַּיִת (כ) שֶׁמַּכְנִיסִין בּוֹ הַנְּסָרִים לְאַחַר רְחִיצָה. אֶת בֵּית הַיְּקָמִים. גָּרְסִי' בַּתּוֹסֶפְתָּא. יֵשׁ מְפָרְשִׁים: חֶדֶר שֶׁמַּצְנִיעִין בּוֹ הַגִּיגִיּוֹת שֶׁמְּשִׂימִין בּוֹ מַיִם חַמִּין. וְלָא נְהִירָא לִי, דְּהַיְינוּ נַמִּי בֵּית הַיּוֹרוֹת דְּקָתָנֵי בַּתּוֹסֶפְתָּא. וְיֵשׁ מְפָרְשִׁים ו) יְקָמִים – סוּדָר שֶׁמְּעַטְּפִין בָּהֶן רֹאשָׁן מִפְּנֵי סוֹס הַמֶּרְחָץ. וְכָל הָנֵי בָּתִּים מִיחַבְּרֵי לְבֵית הַמֶּרְחָץ. אֲבָל לֹא אֶת הַנְּסָרִים. דְּמִיטַּלְטְלֵי. וְלֹא (ל) הַסַּפָּלִים. גָּרְסִינַן. וְאִית דְּגָרְסִי: סַפְסָלִין, שֶׁיּוֹשְׁבִין עֲלֵיהֶן בְּבֵית הַמֶּרְחָץ. וְרִאשׁוֹן עִיקָּר, דְּהָא בְּמַתְנִיתִין נַמִּי סְפָלִים גָּרְסִינַן.

בין

ים טלפחא. היינו עדשים דסוף מסכת ע"ז (דף עה.) דאמר: בעו מיניה מרב הונא הני ז)(גודגא) דארמאי מאי? א"ל: תניתוה: מי שהיו גיתיו ובית בדיו טמאים – הדפין והלולבין והעדשים מדיחן. ופירש נמי הקונטרס התם דעדשה היינו גת עצמה. וקשה: דהתם תנן דגת צריכה ניגוב! ואומר (מ) בקונטרס: דאברייתא סמכינן דלא נהיגין למעבד ניגוב בגת. ח)(ורש"י) מגיה התם בברייתא "מנגבן", ע"פ התוספת', ומצריך ניגוב לגת. ט)(ור"ת) אומר דאכילו אי גרסינן "מדיחן" לא פליג אמתניתין, דעדשים לאו היינו גת, י)אלא כמו שפי' בערוך בערך "טלפח": מביאין טיט ומערבין בו תבן ונעורת של פשתן ועושים כמין ריחים גדולים, ונותנין על הזיתים שילא שומנן. וההוא סגי ליה בהדחה. וא"ת: לר"ת, אמאי לא חשיב במתניתין בד עצמו דמכר? וי"ל: דפשיטא הוא, שהוא עיקרו של מכר, ולא נקרא בית הבד אלא על שם בד. ויקבים נמי דקתני בגמ' – אינו בד עצמו, אלא כמו שפירש בערוך: יקבים – סלים שמביאים בו זיתים. והתם נמי גבי מי שהיו גיתיו ובית בדיו טמאים, הא דלא חשיב גת עצמו – מפני שאין רגילות שיטמא, לפי ששומרים אותו מליטמא מפני חשיבותו, שלא ימלאו אחר מזומן אם יטמא זה. וגם אין כל היד ממשמשין בו, שהוא כבד, ואי אפשר לטלטל. ועוד, שכבר פי' דין גת לענין יין נסך דבעי ניגוב, והוא הדין לענין טהרות. כ)וא"ת: בשלמא לפ"ה דכל הנהו(נ) דמכר הן מחוברין, אלא לר"ת שמפרש טלפחא עיגול של טיט שאינו מחובר, ויקבים סלים – אמאי מכר, כיון שאינן מחוברין? וי"ל: מפני שאינן חשובין כ"כ, ובטלים אגב בד גופיה. א"נ, לפי שאין עובדין אלא לכך.

לא מכר את הנסרים. נראה לר"י דהיינו נסרים שמכסין בהן את החמין, כדאשכחן בפרק "כירה" (שבת דף מ.): אלא א"כ היו חמין שלו מחופים בנסרים.

מ א מיי' פ"א מהל' מכירה הל' יט סמג עשין פב טוש"ע ח"מ סימן קלב סעיף יב:

מא ב ג ד ה ו מיי' שם פכ"ה הלכה ז סמג שם טוש"ע ח"מ סימן רטו סעיף ב:

מב ז ח ט מיי' שם הל' ט טוש"ע שם סעיף ג:

רבינו גרשום

קמ"ל. דאפי' הכי קנה דסדנא דארעא כלומר כל הקרקע חד הוא: **פיסקא** ים טלפחא. לועזין מיי"ש שאוצרין בהו: ממל. מפרכתא. זה כמו קורנס שמפרכין בו א) הענבים שהן עיקר תשמישי הבד: כלונסאות. אלו עצים שעומדים מיכן ומיכן לקירה ונקובין ומשימין בריח מזה לזה ומעמידי' הקורה על הבריח. עבירין כבשי אותן קצעין שמשימין על הקרשים (דין): קורה קורה ממש: הנסרים. הם הקרשים שמשכיבין על גבי התמד ויש אומרי' אלו אותם שמקיפין אותן סביב לתמד וקושרין שלא יתפזרו הענבים אילך ואילך: היקבים. הם הסלים שמביאין בהם הזיתים מן השדה לבית הבד: ריחים התחתונים. שהיו טוחנים בהן הזיתים ואחר כך משימין הזיתים ביקב כדי להוציא השמן יפה וכל הני שייכי לבית הבד לפיכך נמכרין הם: העליונה. דהיינו הרכב אינה נמכרת דלא שייכא היא בהדי בד בלבד: השקין. אלו השקין עצמן שהיו מביאין הענבים או הזיתים בהם לאותו כלי שהוא חוץ לכרם שהוא הולך ובא מכרם לבד ומבד לכרם והוא עשוי מן עור מרצופין שלועזין מאל"ש: **פים'** הנסרים. בית המרחץ שלהן היה עשוי מאבני שיש וכשהאש בוער מתחתיו מתחמם השיש מאד ומשימין נסרים על גבי הרצפה של שיש כדי שיעמדו עליהן הרוחצין: ספלים. גביעין שמזריקין מהן המים עליהן: הוילאות. אלו הבגדים שפורשין כנגדן לפתח המרחץ כעין וילון. כל הני לא שייכי למרחץ: מגורות המים. מקוואות המים שמכניסין אותן דרך סילון למרחץ: מכר את בית הנסרים. שמצניעין שם הנסרים כן הכי נמי בית היקמין: יקמין. אלו בגדים שמעטפין ראשיהם במרחץ מפני החום שלא יזיק להם בראשם וכל הני בנינים שייכי למרחץ ולא הוי מטלטלין דה"נ קתני מתני' לקמן:

א) נראה דל"ל הזיתים:

א) [ל"ל רבא]: ב) הערוך ערך עבר העבירים וכן הגי' בכ... שבמשניות וכתב הת... שכן גירסת הר... ג) [לקמן עת: ע"ש]: ד) ... הוילאות: ה) [בנ"י ... בארץ בגת]: ו) [וזהו פ... הערוך ערך יקמין]: ז) ... גורגי]: ח) [ל"ל ו... ט) [ל"ל ור"י]: י) [ועי' ב... סוף טהר']: כ) תוספות נדה סה. הדפין וכו']:

הגהות הב"ח

(א) גמ' קנה מצולה הר... במצולה קנה חול... פשיטא דהא: (ב) שם ... הריחים התחתונה אבל העליונה (ובזמן שאמר וכו' את המרצופין) תא... ונ"ב ס"א לא מכר לא העבירים ולא את הש... ולא את המרצופין וב... שאמר לו הוא וכל שבתוכו הרי כולן מכו... כו': (ג) שם במ... המוכר את בית המר... (ד) גמ' אבל לא ... הנסרין עצמן ולא ... היקמין עצמן ולא ... הספלים עצמן ו... את הוילאות עצ... (ה) רשב"ם ד"ה (בע"... כיון וכו' אלא אותו שהח... הואיל ואין מי שמוס... ואומר לו לך חזק וקני ד... הך דשמואל: (ו) ד"ה ח... תשמישתא כל שדות עומ... לזריעה והלכך העש... כשדה אחת כל"ל: (ז) ד"... הממל ואת הבתול... בגמרא מפרש דקבועין ... (ח) ד"ה ממל וכו' ול... שהוא עיקר תשמישי ב... הבד: (ט) ד"ה כלונס... וכו' מכאן ומכאן לקור... ונוקבים: (י) ד"ה מכר א... הנסרים וכו' שלא יתפז... אנה ואנה הס"ד: (כ) ד"... בית הנסרין בית שמצניע... בו את הנסרים: (ל) ד"... ולא את הספלים: (מ) תוס' ד"ה ים וכו' ואומר ש... בקונטרס וכו' ניגוב בג... ורשב"ם מגיה ... דפסיטא הוא שהוא עיקר ... (נ) בא"ד דכל הנהו מכר שהרי הן מחוברין:

אלא מאי עבדא כמטלטלא דמי, (ג) מאי אפי'? אלא מאי אית לך למימר, שאני בין מטלטלא דנייד ממטלטלא דלא נייד? אפילו תימא: עבדא כמקרקע דמי, שאני בין מקרקע דנייד למקרקע דלא נייד.

בימות החמה (א) ובימות הגשמים, ולא בית כינוס העצים; אואם אמר לו: "בית המרחץ וכל תשמישיו אני מוכר לך" — כולן מכורין. ההוא דאמר ליה לחבריה: "בית הבד וכל תשמישיו אני מוכר לך", (ב) הויא הנהו חנואתא אבראי דהוו שטחו בהו שומשמי, אתא לקמיה דרב יוסף, א"ל: תנינא, אם אמר: א)"בית המרחץ וכל תשמישיו אני מוכר לך" — הרי כולן מכורין. אמר ליה אביי, והא תני רבי חייא: אין כולן מכורין! אלא אמר רב אשי: בחזינן, אי א"ל: "בית הבד וכל תשמישיו ואלין מצרנהא" — קני, ואי לא — לא קני.§ **מתני'** ב)גהמוכר את העיר — מכר בתים, בורות שיחין ומערות, מרחצאות ושובכות, בית הבדין ובית השלחין, אבל לא את המטלטלין; ובזמן שאמר לו: "היא וכל מה שבתוכה", אפילו היו בה בהמה ועבדים — הרי כולן מכורין. רשב"ג אומר: גהמוכר את העיר — מכר את הסנטר.§ **גמ'** אמר ליה רב אחא בריה דרב אויא לרב אשי, שמעת מינה: ד)עבדא כמטלטלא דמי, דאי כמקרקע דמי, ניזדבן אגב מתא. ואלא מאי? עבדא כמטלטלא דמי, (ג) מאי אפי'? אלא מאי אית לך למימר, שאני בין מטלטלא דנייד ממטלטלא דלא נייד? אפילו תימא: עבדא כמקרקע דמי, שאני בין מקרקע דנייד למקרקע דלא נייד.§ "רבן שמעון בן גמליאל אומר: המוכר את העיר — מכר את הסנטר".§ מאי סנטר? הכא תרגימו: בר מחווניתא; שמעון בן אבטולמוס אומר: באגי. מאן דאמר בר מחווניתא, כל שכן באגי; מ"ד באגי, אבל בר מחווניתא לא מיזדבן. תנן: בית הבדים ובית השלחין; סברוה: מאי "שלחין" — באגי, דכתיב: °"ושולח מים על פני חוצות"; בשלמא למאן דאמר בר מחווניתא, אמר תנא קמא: באגי מיזדבני, בר מחווניתא לא מיזדבן, ואתא רבן שמעון בן גמליאל למימר: אפי' בר מחווניתא נמי מיזדבן; אלא למ"ד באגי, ת"ק נמי הכי קאמר! מי סברת מאי "שלחין" — באגי? לא, מאי "שלחין" — גינונייתא, שנאמר: °"שלחיך פרדס רמונים", אבל באגי לא מיזדבני; ואתא רבן שמעון בן גמליאל למימר: אפי' באגי נמי מיזדבני. איכא דאמרי: סברוה מאי "שלחין" — גינונייאתא; בשלמא למאן דאמר באגי, אמר תנא קמא: גינונייתא מיזדבן, באגי לא מיזדבני, ואתא רשב"ג למימר: אפילו באגי מיזדבני; אלא

רשב"ם

בין בימות החמה. שהן מועטין, וסד"א ליבטלו גבי המרחץ. ולא בית כניסת העצים. גרסינן בתוספתא: לא מכר לא את הבית ולא את העלים. דכי היכי דעלים לאו תשמישין (ד) נינהו — גם הבית שעשוי לערכו לא מיקרי תשמיש מרחץ כל כך. וכל תשמישיו. לטפויי אתא בריכות ואוצרות של עלים, דהוו תשמיש למרחץ פורתא. וכדמפרש לקמן: שכתב לו מצרים החיצונים, והכס בתוך המצר. חנואתא. חנויות למכור בו פת ויין. שטחו בה שומשמי. לייבשן, כדי לעשות מהן שמן בבית הבד זה, כדתנן (שבת דף כד:): בשמן שומשמין. אבל עיקר תשמישן למכור פת ויין הוא. הרי כולן מכורין. ואפילו אוצרות של עלים, וה"ה לחנות זה. אין כולן מכורין. שהרי אין מיוחדין לבית הבד. הכי כתוב בפירושי רבינו חננאל וכן עיקר: אמר רב אשי: חזינן אי א"ל "בית הבד וכל תשמישיו ואלין מצרנוהי", והני בכלל הנהו מצרי — קנה להו, ואי לא — לא קנה. וסוגיא דשמעתא (ה) דאמר הכי סלקא, וקיימא לן כרב אשי דהוא בתרא. ושמעינן מינה: בזמן שא"ל "בית המרחץ וכל מה שבתוכו אני מוכר" אע"פ שמכר לו מצרים החיצונים — לא קנה בריכות של מים, ולא בית כינוס עלים, דקיימא לן מצרים הרחיב. (ו) אבל אם א"ל "מרחץ וכל תשמישיו" ומכר לו מצריו, והכס בתוך המצר — הרי הן מכורין, הואיל וחזו פורתא לתשמיש בית הבד. ואע"ג דאמרן לעיל בריש פירקין: מצרים הרחיב לו — הכא לא אמרינן הכי, דכיון דחזי להך בית קלת לתשמיש בית הבד, והוא בתוך המצר — ודאי מכרו לו, דלכך תיחם את המיצר חוצה לו. לשון אחר כתוב בספרים: אי אמר לי' "בית הבד וכל תשמישיו ואלין מצרנהא" — לא קני. דהשתא לא קאי "ואלין מצרנהא" אתשמישין, אלא אבית הבד קאי, הלכך לגבי תשמישין נאמר מצרים הרחיב לו. אבל אי אמר "אלין מצרי בית הבד וכל תשמישיו" — קני, דהשתא אתרווייהו קאי, וכמאן דאמר "אלו מצרי בית הבד ואלו מצרי כל תשמישיו" דמי. ולא נהירא, דלא שנא הכי ולא שנא הכי, אתרווייהו קאי. ולשון ראשון עיקר.

מתני' מכר את הבתים. דבתים בכלל עיר. ומכר את המגרות לא איצטריך למיתני, דהיינו עיקר עיר, דעיר משמע אויר העיר. בית השלחין. שחוץ לעיר וסמוכין לעיר. ובגמרא מפרש מאי שלחין. אבל לא את המטלטלין. מאני תשמישתיה, כגון תנור וכירים וכל הנך מטלטלין דלעיל דאמרן בהו לא מכר, וכ"ש חיטי ושערי. ואפילו היו בה כו'. בגמ' מפרש מאי "אפילו", ממה חמורין יותר משאר מטלטלין לימכר בכלל העיר. בהמה ועבדים. אין נקראין מאני תשמישתיה, ומאחר שהן מכורין כ"ש חיטי ושערי וכסף וזהב דהוו מטלטלי דלא ניידי, כדמוכח בגמ'. הסנטר. בגמ' מפרש. **גמ'** ש"מ. ממתני' דקתני ברישא: לא מכר את המטלטלין, וקאמר בסיפא: אבל אם אמר לו "כל מה שבתוכה" אף העבדים מכורין. מכלל דמעיקרא לא הוו מזדבני אגב מתא, משום דמטלטלי נינהו? בתמיה: והא מיבעיא לן בפרק "מי שמת" אי כמטלטלי (ז) אי כמקרקעי דמי! כלומר, הא מיבעיא ליה אם לפי לשון בני אדם קרוי מטלטלי או מקרקעי. דמדאורייתא ודאי כמקרקעי דמי לקנות בכסף בשטר ובחזקה, כדתנן בקידושין (דף כב:) משום דאיתקוש לקרקעות, דכתיב: "והתנחלתם אותם". אבל לגבי לשון בני אדם, לגבי מאן דאמר "מטלטלי לפלניא" מיבעיא לן התם אי דעתו של אדם ליתן עבדו בלשון זה או לא. ולא איפשוט התם, ואמאי? הא איכא למפשטה ממתני' דהכא, דלפי דעת בני אדם חשוב מטלטלי, שהרי המוכר את העיר סתמא דעתו אמקרקעי, ואפי' הכי לא מכר את העבדים! מאי אפילו. דמשמע: אפי' עבדים, שאין להם דין מטלטלי! אלא מאי אית לך למימר. אמאי קתני אפי' — משום דשאני מטלטלי דנייד, שיש בו רוח חיים ויכול להוליכו לעיר אחרת, ממטלטלי דלא ניידי. סד"א אפי' כי אמר "כל מה שבתוכה" ונמכרו מטלטלי דלא ניידי, אלו העבדים והבהמות אינן מכורין, דלא מבטלו אגב מתא, קמ"ל דמכורין הן. ואפי' תימא נמי דעבדא לגבי שאר דיני כמקרקעי דמו, ואמאי לא קני להו הכא גבי מקרקעי — משום דשאני כו', דאין דעתו של מוכר עיר אלא לדברים הקבועים בעיר, ונקראין על שם העיר, אבל זה שיכול לצאת מן העיר — אינו בכלל עיר. בר מחווניתא. עבד הממונה להגיד ולאחוויי תחומי השדות של מי זה ושל מי זה, והוא עבד לשר העיר, ואי אפשר לעיר בלא אותו. (ח) ורבינו חננאל פירש: סנטר — הוא שומר העיר, לשון "נוטרה את הכרמים" (שיר א). שמעון בן אבטולמוס. כפר"ח. באגי. שדות שסביב המדינה. כל שכן באגי. דלא ניידי. לא מזדבן. משום דנייד. דכתיב ושולח מים. כלומר, להכי נקראין שלחין — שצריכין לגשמים. הכא לא גרסינן "אבל בר מחווניתא לא", אלא הכי גרסינן: (ט) ושולח מים וגו'. בשלמא למאן דאמר בר מחווניתא כו'. אלא למאן דאמר סנטר דרבי שמעון היינו באגי — מה בא להוסיף על תנא קמא? היינו שלחין דקאמר תנא קמא! גינונייתא. גנות הסמוכין לעיר ושבתוך העיר, דשייכי לעיר טפי מבאגי, שהרי גן ראוי לטייל בו כמו בבית. שלחיך. גנות, המשלחין פירות בכל שנה. בשלמא למאן דאמר. דסנטר היינו באגי — היינו דקאמר תנא קמא: גינונייתא, דהיינו שלחין — מזדבני, אבל באגי — לא. ואתא רבן שמעון בן גמליאל למימר: אפילו באגי מזדבני.

תוספות

אלא מאי עבדא כמטלטלי דמי מאי אפילו. לאו משום דלאו כמקרקעי דמי אתי שפיר, דהא מ"מ מנהמה איכא לאקשויי: מאי "אפי'". אלא לומר דלא מפלגינן בין מטלטלי דניידי למטלטלי דלא ניידי פריך, וה"ה דהוי מצי למיפרך: אי כמטלטלי דמי — אפי' גבי חצר יהו מכורין. מי סברת מאי שלחין כו'. ואם תאמר: דכולי גמרא הוו בית השלחין — באגי, שדות שמשקין אותן, ומאי שנא הכא דמשנינן להו מכל בית השלחין שבגמרא? ויש לומר: דפשיטא ליה לגמרא דאין חילוק בין שדה בית השלחין ושדה בית הבעל לענין מכר, ויש חילוק בין באגי לגינוניתא, לכך לא ניחא לפרש שלחין כמו בעלמא, דהוה משמע דאתא למעוטי שדה בית הבעל. שלחיך פרדס וגו'. על שם האילן שעושה בדים ושולח פארות, כדכתיב "ותעש בדים ותשלח פארות" וגו' (יחזקאל יז). אמר תנא קמא ה)באגי לא מזדבני ומהדר ליה רבן שמעון בן גמליאל בר מחווניתא מזדבן. ואף על גב דשמעינן מק"ו דבאגי מזדבני, מ"מ כיון דתנא קמא אית ליה דאפילו באגי לא מזדבני — הוה ליה לרשב"ג לפרושי שפיר, ולמימר דבאגי ובר מחווניתא מזדבן.

עין משפט נר מצוה

מג א מיי' פכ"ה מהל' מכירה הלכה ט סמג עשין פב טוש"ע ח"מ סי' רטו ס"ג:
מד ב מיי' שם הל' ח טוש"ע שם סעי' ב:
מה ג מיי' שם פכ"ו הלכה א סמג שם טוש"ע שם סעיף ז:

הגהות הב"ח

(א) גמ' בימות החמה ובין בימות הגשמים ולא את בית כינוס: (ב) שם הויין הנהו חנואתא: (ג) שם כמטלטלא דמי אי הכי מאי אפילו: (ד) רשב"ם ד"ה ולא בית כניסת וכו' לאו תשמישין המיוחדין למרחץ נינהו: (ה) ד"ה הכי כתב וכו' וסוגיא דשמעתא הכי כל"ל ותיבת דאמר נמחק: (ו) בא"ד דהרחיב לו אבל וכו' לחזי הך בית קלת וכו' לא קאי אהאי ואלין: (ז) ד"ה ש"מ וכו' כמטלטלי דמי או כמקרקעי דמי כדפרשינן בלשון זה: (ח) ד"ה בר וכו' בלא אותו עבד וכו' ורבינו: (ט) ד"ה דכתיב וכו' אלא ה"ג דכתיב ושולח:

מו א ב ג ד מיי' פכ"ו מהל' מכירה הל' א סמג עשין פב טוש"ע ח"מ סי' רטו סעיף ז:
מז ה מיי' שם הל' ב טוש"ע שם סעי' ה:

תורה אור

אלא למאן דאמר בר מחווניתא, אמר תנא קמא גינונייתא, ומהדר ליה רבן שמעון בן גמליאל בר מחוניתא?! מי סברת מאי "שלחין" – גינונייתא? לא, מאי "שלחין" – בגי, דכתיב: °"ושולח מים על פני חוצות" (איוב ה), אבל בר מחווניתא לא מזדבן, ואתא רבן שמעון בן גמליאל למימר דאפי' בר מחווניתא נמי מזדבן. תא שמע, ר' יהודה אומר: סנטר אינו מכור, אנקולמוס מכור; מאי לאו מדאנקולמוס גברא, סנטר נמי גברא! מידי איריא? הא כדאיתא והא כדאיתא. ומי מצית אמרת הכי? והא קתני סיפא: א אבל לא שייריה ולא בנותיה, ולא חורשין המוקצין לה, ולא ביברין של חיה ושל עופות ושל דגים; ואמרינן, מאי שייריה? ביזלי, מאי ביזלי? א"ר אבא: פיסקי בגי. פיסקי בגי הוא דלא מזדבני, הא בגי עצמן מזדבני! איפוך, ר' יהודה אומר: סנטר מכור, אנקולמוס אינו מכור. ב ומי מצית אמרת: רבי יהודה כרשב"ג סבירא ליה? והא רבי יהודה כרבנן סבירא ליה! דקתני סיפא: אבל לא שייריה ולא בנותיה, ואילו רשב"ג האמר: מכר את העיר – מכר בנותיה, דתניא: המוכר את העיר – לא מכר את בנותיה, רשב"ג אומר: המוכר את העיר – מכר בנותיה! רבי יהודה סבר ליה כוותיה בחדא, ופליג עליה בחדא. § "ולא ביברין של חיה ושל עופות ושל דגים". § ורמינהי: היו לה בנות – אין נמכרות עמה; ג היה לה חלק אחד בים וחלק אחד ביבשה, ביברים של חיה ושל עופות ושל דגים – הרי אלו נמכרים עמה! לא קשיא: ג הא דנגיח קאיהי לגו, והא דנגיח קאיהי לבר. והא קא תני: ולא את חורשין המוקצין לה! אימא: ד המוקצין הימנה. §

מתני' ה המוכר את השדה – מכר את האבנים שהם לצרכה, ואת הקנים שבכרם שהם לצרכו, ואת התבואה שהיא מחוברת לקרקע, ואת חיצת הקנים שהיא פחותה מבית רובע, ואת השומירה שאינה עשויה בטיט, ואת החרוב שאינו מורכב, ואת בתולת השקמה; אבל לא מכר לא את האבנים שאינן לצרכה, ולא את הקנים שבכרם שאינן לצרכו, ולא את התבואה שהיא תלושה מן הקרקע; בזמן שאמר לו: "היא וכל מה שבתוכה" – הרי כולן מכורין; בין כך ובין כך, לא מכר לא את חיצת הקנים שהיא בית רובע, ולא את השומירה שהיא עשויה בטיט, ולא את החרוב המורכב, ולא את סדן השקמה. §

גמ'

אלא למאן דאמר. סנטר היינו בר מחווניתא, מה ענין תוספת זו על דברי ת"ק? דת"ק אמר גינונייתא מזדבני אבל באגי לא מזדבני, וקמהדר (א) רשב"ג בר מחווניתא נמי מזדבן?! בתמיה. הכי הוה ליה למיתני: רשב"ג אומר המוכר את העיר מכר את הבאגי ואת הסנטר. אבל מדנקט סנטר לחוד – מכלל דשמעינהו לרבנן דבסנטר לחוד אמרי אינו מכור, ואתא איהו למימר דמזדבן. ובע"כ כיון דשלחין גינונייתא – בבאגי הוא דאמור רבנן לא מזדבני, ואתא איהו למימר דמזדבני. ה"ג: תא שמע ר' יהודה אומר סנטר אינו מכור אנקולמוס מכור. דהא לקמן מפכינן לה ואמרי: סנטר מכור אנקולמוס אינו מכור, וכך היא שנויה בתוספת' (פרק ג) כדמפכינן לה בסמוך. ואית דגרסי הכא בתרוייהו אינו מכור, ולקמן לא גרסי' "איפוך", אלא הכי גרסינן: אימא רבי יהודה אומר סנטר מכור אנקולמוס אינו מכור. אנקולמוס. הוא סופר המלך, לכתוב מספר השדות והבתים והאנשים, לתת מס של כל אחד לשר העיר. מידי איריא כו'. בתמיה. (ב) אלא לעולם סנטר היינו באגי. ומי מצית אמרת הכי. דסנטר דרבי יהודה היינו באגי. והקתני סיפא. דהך ברייתא, דפיסקי באגי לא מזדבני, דמשמע: הא באגי – מזדבני. והיכי קתני רישא סנטר אינו מכור, כלומר באגי לא מזדבני? א"כ קשיא רישא לסיפא. שיריה. ואית גרס: שיריה, ולקמן מפרש. ולא בנותיה. כפרים הסמוכים לה. ולא החורשים. יערים. כדכתיב: "חרש מצל" ביחזקאל (לא), "ביער" – מתרגמינן: בחורשא. המוקצים לה. הסמוכין לעיר ופתוחין לה. ולקמן מוקמינן לה בשאין פתוחין לעיר, ומתרלין: המוקצין ממנה. המוקצין – מזומנין. ה"ג בתוספתא: ולא ביברין של חיה ושל עופות ושל דגים. ולקמיה מוקמינן לה בדנגיח קמייהו לבר. ביזלי פיסקי באגי. חתיכות בקעה הגדולה הסמוכה לעיר, אלא שמופלגת ממנה קצת, שיש הפסק לונמא בינתיים. ושיריה – לשון שיריים הוא. פיסקי באגי הוא דלא מזדבני. שהרי רחוקין ומופלגים מן העיר, הא באגי עצמן, הסמוכין לעיר – מזדבני. ה"ג: איפוך ר' יהודה אומר סנטר מכור אנקולמוס אינו מכור. ולעולם סנטר – באגי. והיינו דקאמר סנטר מכור, דהיינו באגי, אבל שיריה, דהיינו פיסקי באגי – לא מזדבני. והשתא סבירא ליה לר' יהודה בסנטר כרשב"ג. והיינו דקפריך: ומי מצית אמרת ר' יהודה כרשב"ג סבירא ליה? הקתני בסיפא דמילתיה דר' יהודה: ואם אמר לו "כל מה שבתוכה" הרי כולן מכורין, בין כך ובין כך לא מכר לא את שיריה ולא את בנותיה. ואילו כו'. ומשני: סבר ליה כוותיה בחדא ופליג עליה בחדא. ר' יהודה בסנטר סבר לה כרשב"ג, ובבנותיה פליג עליה. הכי נמי מסתברא. לא גרסינן בכולה סוגיא. ה"ג: ולא ביברין של חיה ועופות ודגים. כעין "אמר מר". ורמינהי כו'. בהך ברייתא גרסינן: הרי אלו נמכרין עמה. הכי גרסינן: היה לה חלק אחד בים וחלק אחד ביבשה וביברין של חיה ועופות ודגים הרי אלו נמכרין עמה. וחלק אחד בים נמי אעיר קאי. דכיון דקתני רישא: היו לה בנות אין נמכרות עמה, משמע: בנות הוא דלא מזדבנן, דמופלגין מן העיר ואינם מאותה העיר ממש, שהרי שם אחר יש להם. אבל אם יש לעיר חלק אחד בים, ונקרא בשם העיר – נמכר עמה, דהא עיר אחת היא בין הכל. א"נ, חלק אחד ביבשה כמו שאר העיר, אלא שמופלג מן העיר, ומיהו על שם העיר נקרא. דנגיח קיידו לגאו. פתיחתן לצד העיר – נמכרין עמה. אבל הך קמייתא – בדנגיח קייהו לבר. והקתני. בהך קמייתא: ולא את החורשין המוקצין לה, דמשמע דנגיח קייהו לגאו, ואפי' הכי לא מכר! אימא המוקצין הימנה. ופתוחין לחוץ. **מתני'** האבנים שהן לצרכה. בגמרא מפרש. ואף על גב דתשמישין המטלטלין הן, כיון דקביעי להאי תשמיש, ואין מזיזין *אותה [נ"ל אותם] מהאי שדה לעולם – כמחובר חשיב להו. את הקנים שבכרם שהן לצרכו. בגמרא מפרש. ומתוך שמעינן דהמוכר את השדה מכר את הכרם, שכל אילנות בכלל שדה, אחד גפנים ואחד כל האילן, חוץ מחרוב המורכב וסדן השקמה, כדמוכח במתניתין ובגמרא. דאמרי' בגמרא: אי אית ליה גופני – לבר מגופני. כלומר, אדם שאומר לחבירו "שדה אני מוכר לך חוץ מן האילנות", ויש בו גפנים – חוץ מן הגפנים אמר לו, מכלל דאילו שתק היו מכורין בכלל שדה. חיצת הקנים. טרו"ק בלע"ז, קנים הרבה גדילים בקלח אחד. שהיא פחותה. בטילה לגבי שדה. שומירה. סוכת נוצרים. שאינה עשויה בטיט. טוחה בטיט. דהיינו בבחרותו. ואת החרוב שאינו מורכב. אבל כשמזקין ומתגבר מרכיבין אותו, ויש לו שם בפני עצמו, ולא בטיל לגבי שדה. בתולת השקמה. בבחרותה, קודם שנחתכו ענפיה. אבל כשמזקין וגדל הרבה – קוצצין הענפים, ובאים אחרים במקומן, ונקרא סדן השקמה = טרונ"ק בלע"ז. לא את חיצת הקנים כו'. שכל אלו חשובין שדה בפני עצמן, והרי הוא כמו שמוכר לחבירו שתי שדות ויש לו שדה אחרת בתוך השתים, ואם אמר לו "שתי השדות וכל מה שבתוכן אני מוכר לך" – דאין שדה השלישית שביניהן מכור. אף כאן, שדה אחת מכר לו ולא שתי שדות, וחיצת קנים וחרוב המורכב וסדן השקמה חשובין שדה בפני עצמן.

גמ'

הכי גרים רבינו חננאל, וכן בתוספתא (פ"ג): תא שמע, רבי יהודה אומר: סנטר מכור אנקולמוס אינו מכור. מאי לאו מדאנקולמוס גברא, סנטר נמי גברא. הא כדאיתא והא כדאיתא. ה"נ מסתברא דקתני סיפא כו', מאי ביזלי פיסקי באגי, פיסקי באגי הוא דלא מזדבני, אבל באגי עצמם מזדבני. פירוש: ומדקאמר "אבל לא את שיריה", דהיינו פיסקי באגי – מכלל דאיירי לעיל בבאגי. וקאמר: מי סברת רבי יהודה כר"ש סבירא ליה, וקאי כוותיה? והא לא מצית אמרת הכי, דהא פליג עליה בבנותיה, והוא הדין דפליג עליה בסנטר. אלמא דסנטר דרשב"ג בר מחווניתא, וקשיא למ"ד באגי והא לא תקשי למ"ד בר מחווניתא, וא"כ תרי גווני סנטר נינהו, דסנטר דרשב"ג גברא הוא, ודרבי יהודה באגי. דבלאו הכי צריכין אנו לומר דתרי גווני סנטר נינהו, כדאמרינן ב"הזורק" בגיטין (דף פ:): אפי' לא כתב לה אלא לשם סנטר שבעיר – הרי זו מגורשת. ובבראשית רבה (פט"ז): אתנסיבת לסנטירא (*יקירא.) [נ"ל דקרקא] ובתוספתא דבבא מציעא: גוי שעשה לישראל אפוטרופוס או סנטר. משמע מכל הני דסנטר גברא, ודרבי יהודה הוי באגי.

ואת

רבינו גרשום

ת"ק וכו' ומהדר ליה רשב"ג [בר] מחווניתא. והא תנא קמא בר מחווניתא לא דכר שמיה בלשון קושיא גרסי': מאי שלחין דקאמר ת"ק באגי מיזדבנא. אבל בר מחווניתא לא מזדבן ואתא רשב"ג למימר אפי' בר מחווניתא מזדבן: ת"ש. אם סנטר בר מחווניתא הוא אי לא: אנקולמוס מכור. וזהו סופר העיר שכותב כמה יוצאין ופורעין מס למלך מבתים ושדות: סנטר נמי גברא. דהיינו בר מחווניתא ולא בגי: והא כדאיתא. דסנטר בגי. ה"ג ומי מצית אמרת הכי. דסנטר בגי: והא מדקתני סיפא. דהא ברייתא דר' יהודה: שייריה. מפרש לקמן: חורשין. יערין: המוקצין לעיר. כלומר שהן פתוחין לעיר וקוצצין ממנו בני העיר לצרכן: פיסקי באגי. קטנות שמסתפקות מהן בהמות: הא בגי. שהן גדולות מזדבני ואי אמרת דסנטר היינו בגי דמזדבני א"כ קשיא לר' יהודה דאמר ברישא דברייתא סנטר אינו מכור: לעולם סנטר באגי ומזדבן ודקא קשיא לך רישא. איפוך רישא ר' יהודה אומר סנטר מכור דהיינו כר' שמעון דאמר מכר את העיר מכר את הסנטר: והא ר' יהודה כרבנן ס"ל. בברייתא והכי מסתברא דהכי קתני ר' יהודה לא את שיריה ולא את בנותיה ותניא המוכר את העיר לא מכר את בנותיה דהיינו רבנן ור' יהודה נמי הכי קאמר. ומשני ר' יהודה סבר לה כוותי' דרשב"ג בחדא דבגי מזדבנא. ופליג עליה בחדא דלא מכר את בנותיה משום דלא שייכי לעיר הוי: והבנות. כפרים אין נמכרות. עמה עם העיר: חלק אחד בים. מצד זה של עיר: וחלק אחד ביבשה מאידך צד של עיר: הא דנגיח קייהו לגאו. בברין שמחוץ לעיר ופתוחין לעיר נמכרין עמה דשייכי עם העיר. אבל אם פתוחות לבר חוץ לעיר אין נמכרין עמה: והא קתני ולא הורשין המוקצין לה אין נמכרין עמה. אלמא אע"ג דנגיח קייהו לגיו אין נמכרין. ומשני אימא המוקצין הימנה דלאו פתוחין לה משום הכי אין נמכרין הא אי הוי מוקצין לה נמכרין: שהם לצרכה. מפר' בגמ': פיס' ואת חיצת הקנים שהוא פחות. שאם יש בסוף השדה חיצת הקנים. והן קנים הדוקרנין שעולין הרבה בנגע אחד. ואותו מקצת הוא פחות מבית זרעת רובע קב אינו חשוב ולא אמרי' דשיירו אלא נמכר עמה: ואת השומירה. בית קטן שבשדה שיושב בה השומר: ואת החרוב שאינו מורכב. בו ענף ממין אחר ולא השיב ונמכר עמה: ואת בתולת השקמה. היינו ארז שעדיין לא קצצו נופה התחתונים שישביח ויגדל לצורך קורה להיות סדן גדול לא חשיב ונמכר עמה אבני

(א) רשב"ם ד"ה אלא וקמהדר ליה רשב"ג דמזדבן (ובע"כ כיון דמזדבני) תא"מ ונ"ב אין זה: (ב) ד"ה איריא כו' בתמיה ו כנ"ל ותיבת אלא נ

גמ' מאי אבנים שהן לצרכה? הכא תרגימו: [א]אבני דאכפא. עולא אמר: [ב]אבנים הסדורות לגדר. והא תני ר' חייא: אבנים צבורות לגדר! תני: סדורות. הכא תרגימו: אבני דאכפא; לר"מ — דמתקנן אע"ג דלא מחתן, לרבנן — [ג]הוא דמחתן. ולעולא דאמר: אבנים הסדורות לגדר; לר"מ — דמתקנן אע"ג דלא סדרן, לרבנן — [ד]הוא דסדרן.§ "ואת הקנים שבכרם שהן לצרכו".§ קנים מאי עבידתייהו? אמרי דבי רבי ינאי: [ה]הקנים המחולקין שמעמידים תחת הגפנים; לר"מ — דמשפיין אע"ג דלא מוקמן, לרבנן — הוא דמוקמן.§ "ואת התבואה המחוברת לקרקע" וכו'.§ ואע"ג דמטאי למיחצד.§ "ואת חיצת הקנים שפחותה מבית רובע".§ ואע"ג דאלימי.§ "ואת השומירה שאינה עשויה בטיט".§ אע"ג דלא קביעא בארעא.§ "ואת החרוב שאינו מורכב, ואת בתולת השקמה".§ אע"ג דאלימי.§ "אבל לא מכר (א) את האבנים שאינן לצרכה".§ לר"מ — דלא מתקנן, לרבנן — דלא מחתן. ולעולא דאמר: אבנים הסדורות לגדר; לר' מאיר — דלא מתקנן, לרבנן — דלא סדרן.§ "ולא את הקנים שבכרם שאינן לצרכו".§ לר' מאיר — דלא משפיין, לרבנן — דלא מוקמן.§ "ולא את התבואה התלושה מן הקרקע".§ ואע"ג דצריכא לארעא.§ "ולא את חיצת הקנים שהיא בית רובע".§ ואע"ג דקטיני. א"ר חייא בר אבא א"ר יוחנן: לא חיצת הקנים בלבד, אלא אפילו ערוגה קטנה של בשמים ויש לה שם בפני עצמה — אינה נמכרת עמה. אמר רב פפא: והוא דקרו לה וורדא דפלניא.§ "ולא השומירה העשויה בטיט".§ ואע"ג (ב) דמחברא בארעא.§ ("ולא את חרוב המורכב ולא סדן השקמה".§ ואע"ג דקטיני.) בעי רבי אלעזר: מלבנות של פתחים, מהו? היכא דמחברי בטינא לא תיבעי לך — דהא מחבר, כי תיבעי לך — דנקיטי בסיכי, מאי? תיקו. בעי רבי זירא: מלבנות של חלונות, מהו? מי אמרינן: לנוי בעלמא הוא דעבידי, או דלמא כיון דמחברי — מחברי? תיקו. בעי רבי ירמיה: מלבנות של כרעי המטה, מהו? כל היכא דמיטלטלי בהדה לא תיבעי לך — דהא מיטלטלי, כי תיבעי לך — היכא דלא מיטלטלי, מאי? תיקו.§ "ולא את חרוב המורכב ולא סדן השקמה" (ג) וכו'.§
מנא

גמ' אבני דאכפא. לאחר שקצרו העומרים מניחין אותן לייבשן, ומניחין עליהם אבנים כדי שלא יפזרם הרוח. **הסדורות.** בתוך השדה, לעשות גדר לשדה. **צבורות.** ואע"ג דאינן סדורות חשיב להו תשמיש קבוע דשדה לימכר עמו. **הכא תרגימו אבני דאכפא.** כעין "אמר מר", הדר למילתיה לפרושי אליבא דר"מ ואליבא דרבנן. **לר"מ.** דאמר פרק "המוכר את הספינה" (לקמן דף עח.) מכר כרם — מכר תשמישי כרם. ושמעינן דאתא לאיפלוגי אדרבנן, ולמימר דאפי' אותן תשמישין שאינן נמכרין לרבנן עם הכרם, דלא קביעי כל כך — לר"מ מכורין הן. והלכך, בכל תשמישי כרם ושדה השנוין במשנתינו בעינן לפרושי היכי דמי דלר"מ מכור ולרבנן אינו מכור. והלכך, לר"מ הני אבני דאכפא מכורין הן בכלל שדה, כיון דמתוקנות ומזומנות לצורך העומרים. **ואע"ג דלא מחתן.** שאינן מונחות בתוך השדה אלא חוץ לשדה, דלהכי אהני מאי דאמר ר"מ מכר כל תשמישי כרם — לטפויי במכירת השדה אפילו הנהו תשמישין שאינן מונחין בתוכו, הואיל ולצורך השדה נתקנו. והא דאמרן לעיל (דף סח:): אפילו תימא ר"מ התם קביע כו' — הני אבני דאכפא דמיתקני קרי קביעי; אף על פי שאין מחוברין בקרקע הרי קבועין לתשמיש שדה זו, ואין דרך לטלטלן לשדה אחר, ולא להשאילן. **לרבנן.** דאמרי: לא מכר כל תשמישי כרם אלא המיוחדין הרבה לתשמיש — אין נמכרין אלא א"כ מחתן לתוך השדה. **ולעולא דאמר אבנים הסדורות לגדר.** ובעל כרחך סתמא כרבנן נקט למילתיה. דלר"מ לא בעינן סדורות, אלא דמתקנן לצורך גדר שדה זו. **אע"ג דלא סידרם.** זו על גב זו, דבכלל כל תשמישי כרם הוא. לרבנן לא מזדבני עד דסידרן לכך, דהיינו מעשה גדול (ד) ותשמיש קבוע. **קנים מאי עבידתייהו.** מה צריכין לכרם קנים הגדלים בקרקע? דקנים סתמא משמע ליה במקום גידולן, כמו חיצת הקנים. **קנים המחולקין.** (ה) מפוצלין, שמעמידים תחת הגפנים כדי שיהו הגפנים זקופין, והאשכולות תולין באויר ולא יתקלקלו בקרקע, וקורין להו פאשיל"ש. **דמשפיין.** משופין ומתוקנין לכך. **אע"ג דלא מוקמן.** שאינן זקופין ונעוצים עדיין בקרקע. **ואע"ג דמטאי למיחצד.** הגיע זמן קצירתה, וסד"א: כל העומד לקצור כקצור דמי — אפ"ה לגבי מכירה מכורים בכלל שדה. ובדלא מטאי לא איצטריך למיתני מכר, דפשיטא היא, שהרי השדה מוכר עכשיו לגמרי, וזה הלוקח לא יניח למוכר לבשל כאן פירותיו, וללקיטה השתא לא חזו, הלכך פשיטא דודאי מכר. **אע"ג דאלימי.** דבתר תפיסת הקרקע אזלינן. ופרושי הוא דקמפרש גמ' למתני' ואזיל. **דלא קביעא.** בקרקע. **לר' מאיר דלא מתקנן.** דהשתא אינן תשמיש (ו) כלל. ולרבנן — דלא מחתן, דלא הוי תשמיש קבוע וחשוב. **דצריכא לארעא.** לשהות בשדה לאחר קצירה, להפסק התבואה מריח הקרקע וליבש. **דקטיני.** קנים דקים. נראה בעיני לפי שטת המשנה דקתני: בין כך ובין כך לא מכר את חיצת הקנים שהיא בית רובע ולא את השומירה שהיא עשויה בטיט ולא את חרוב כו', ובסיפא דרישא לא תנינן להו במתניתין — שכן סדר שמועה זו, והכי גרסינן לה: ולא את התבואה התלושה מן הקרקע ואע"ג דצריכא לארעא, ולא את חיצת הקנים שהיא בית רובע ואע"ג דקטיני. אמר ר' חייא בר אבא אמר ר' יוחנן לא את חיצת הקנין בלבד כו' עד אמר רב פפא והוא דקרו לה וורדא דפלניא. ולא את השומירה העשויה בטיט ואע"ג דקביעא. בעי ר' אלעזר מלבנות של פתחים כו'. בעי ר' זירא כו'. בעי ר' ירמיה כו' עד היכא דלא מיטלטלי מאי תיקו. ולא את חרוב המורכב ולא את סדן השקמה אע"ג דקטיני. מנהני מילי אמר רב יהודה דאמר קרא ויקם כו'. ולפי שיש דברים קצרים בשמועה זו טעו הסופרים ונשתבשו הספרים, ולפי סדר שסדרתי אפרשנה. **לא את חיצת הקנים בלבד.** שהוא דבר חשוב ומחזיק בית רובע בקרקע, אמרו דאינו (ז) מוכר עם השדה. אלא אפי' ערוגה קטנה דלא הוי בית רובע. ואורחא דמילתא נקט של בשמים, לפי שדרך לקרות לה שם בפני עצמה, והוא הדין לכל דבר שיש לו שם בפני עצמו. ובחיצת קנים בלבד פירש לך שיעורא, דמילתא דפסיקא היא, דאי הוי בית רובע — יש לו שם בפני עצמו, ואי לא — לא. **אמר רב פפא והוא דקרו כו'.** לפרושי אתא, היכי דמי "יש לה שם בפני עצמה" דקאמר רבי יוחנן. **וורדא דפלניא.** ערוגת בושם של פלוני. **אע"ג דקביעא.** השומירה בקרקע, כיון דטוחה בטיט — אינה מיטלטלת עוד, וחשיבא, ויש לה שם בפני עצמה. והרי הוא כמוכר את השדה שלא מכר את הבית, דאין בית בכלל שדה אלא בכלל חצר. **בעי רבי אלעזר כו'.** משום מתני' דקמיפלגא בשומירה בין עשויה בטיט לשאינה עשויה בטיט נקט לה הכא להך בעיא, דקמיפלגא נמי בין עשויה בטיט לנקיטי בסיכי. ובמוכר את הבית לחבירו קבעי, אם מכר בכלל הבית מלבנות של פתחים אם לאו. והוא תיקון שעושין סביב המזוזות ומלמעלה ומלמטה, שהדלת שוקף עליהן. מחוברין בכותל אבנים בטיט. **דהא מחבר.** והוי מן הבית עצמו. **בסיכי.** יתידות, קביל"ש, ונוח לפרקן. **מאי.** מי אמרינן אינן צריכין לפתח כל כך, ולא מכרן, או לא? תיקו. **בעי ר' זירא.** אם תמצי לומר מלבנות של פתחים דנקיטי בסיכי מכורין בכלל הבית — היינו משום דלחיזוק עבידן. אבל מלבנות של חלונות דנקיטי בסיכי מהו? לנוי עבידן ולא מזדבני, או דלמא כיון דמחברי בסיכי הא מיחברי, ונמכרין, כדאמרן גבי מלבנות פתחים? אבל (ח) מחברי בטיט — לא מיבעיא לן. כן נראה בעיני. **מלבנות של כרעי המטה.** חתיכות עץ היו נותנים תחת כרעי המטה כדי שלא ירקבו בקרקע. ואם תמצי לומר גבי פתחים וחלונות דמזדבני — היינו משום דמחברי מיהא בסיכי, אבל הכא דלא מיחברי למטה כלל, כדמפרש ואזיל, קמיבעיא ליה אם הוא מכור עם המטה, או לא. **דמיטלטלי בהדה.** שמחוברין במסמרות או בסיכי.
מנהני

רס"ל מ"ז

ואת השומירה. רשב"ם גריס ברישא "שאין עשויה בטיט", ובסיפא גבי לא מכר, גריס "העשויה". ורבינו חננאל גריס איפכא.

והוא דמחתן. אין נראה לפרש לר"י דמחתי על העומרי'. דמה אנו צריכין שיהו מונחים על העומרים, הואיל והעומרים שהן תלושין אינן מכורין! ונראה לר"י דלא מחתן — היינו שמעולם לא הניחו על העומרים, ומחתן — היינו שכבר הונחו, ולאו דמחתי השתא.

מחולקין. בערוך* פירש: שהסירו הקליפות כדי שלא יתליעו. **ולא** את חיצת הקנים כו'. אע"ג דקטיני. עוד יארך לקמן על משנה זו, ובההיא דשומירה וחרוב. אלא כן דרך הגמרא שמתחלה מפרש המשנה ואח"כ מאריך.

בעי ר' אלעזר מלבנות פתחים. לא כפי' הקונטרס דאפתח הבית קאי, דהא לא איירי כלל במכר בית. אלא נראה לר"י דאפתח שומירה קאי, ואשומירה דרישא קאי, דקתני דמכר את השומירה.

ארעא

מח א ב ג ד ה מיי' פכ"ו מהל' מכירה הל' ב סמג עשין פב טוש"ע ח"מ סימן רטו סעיף ה:

[ערך חלק א']

הגהות הב"ח

(א) גמ' אבל לא מכר לא את האבנים שאינן לצרכה למ"ד אבני דאכפא לר"מ דלא מתקנן: (ב) שם בטיט ואע"ג דקביעא בארעא: (ג) שם ולא סדן השקמה ואע"ג דקטיני מנא הני מילי כצ"ל ותיבת וכו' נמחק: (ד) רשב"ם ד"ה אע"ג וכו' מעשה גדול לתשמיש קבוע דומה הס"ד: (ה) ד"ה קנים המחולקין מפוצלין הס"ד ואח"כ מ"ה שמעמידים וכו' והאשכולות תלויין באויר: (ו) ד"ה לרבי מאיר וכו' תשמיש שדה כלל: (ז) ד"ה לא את חיצת וכו' דאינו מכור עם השדה: (ח) ד"ה בעי ר' זירא וכו' אבל אי מחברי:

דאכפא. אותן ... שמשימין על ... רין כדי שלא ... ו אילך ואילך: לר' ... דאמר מכר את ... מכר כל תשמישי ... כיון דמתקנן. ... ופין אע"ג דלא ... על העומרין עדיין ... על הבנין מכורות. ... אין נמכרות עד ... ן בבנין משום דלאו ... של קרקע דמי ... מא עד דמנחן ... תני סדורות. ... קנים המחולקין ... מידין הגפנים. שלאותן ... עמידי' בהם הגפנים ... ין הן הקליפות ... יהן כדי שלא יכנסו ... ם בין הקליפה ובין ... ומתליע שלא יהיו ... תולעין יוצאין ... ליען הכרם: לר"מ ... דמשפיין. שמקולעין ... ודין הוו שימושי ... ם. לרבנן לא הוו ... ושי הכרם עד דמנחן ... קמי בכרם ואין נמכר: ... ג דמטאי למיחצד. ... יל דמחובר לקרקע ... קע דמי: ואע"ג ... לימי. הקנים נמכרין ... ה הואיל דפחותה: ... ינה עשויה בטיט ... ג דלא קביעא יפה ... קע. סד"א כיון דלא ... ע לאו כגופה של ... קע דמי אפי' הכי ... רה: ואת חיצת ... ים. אלו קנים ... קרנין ושיוצאין כמה ... ם בגזע אחד אע"ג ... לימי. דמהו דתימ' ... ה בפני עצמה דמי ... ' הכי מכורה: ואת ... רוב שאינו מורכב. ... כתי כל זמן דלא צריך ... בא לא דבר חשוב ... א. חרוב מורכב. כעין ... רכיבין בין האילנות ... ים כדי להחזירם ... יחן הואיל שאינו ... רכב לאו שדה בפ"ע ... יא: ואת בתולת ... שקמה. שלא הגדיל כל ... שהוא בחור. שקמה ... הוא שם האילן: ... ע"ג דצריכא לארעא. ... תהא מונחת שם עד ... תייבש: אף על גב ... קביעי בשדה לא ... כרה. [כיון] שהיא ... שויה בטיט ורשות ... פ"ע הוי: סדן השקמה. ... ור אילן חשוב ... קוצצין הענפים שלו ... י להגדילן לצורך ... רות וזהו סדן: מלבנות ... ל פתחים. אותן אבנים ... עומדין במזוזות הפתח ... לועזין אושריי"ש. אותן ... חות שבפתח הבית ... מחובר בקרקע מהו. ... כרן או לא מכרן: כי ... יבעי לך היכא דנקיטי ... סיכי. שאין מחוברות ... קרקע כי אם כעין ... עושין ציר לדלת ... זימנא) שכל אחת ... נכנסת בחברתה ובכך ... חוברין: לנוי עבידן. ... מלבנות ולא מזדבני. או ... למא (לא) אינהו ... מזדבני: מלבנות של ... רעי המטה. אלו לבנים ... משימין תחת כרעי ... מטה שלא יתליעו ... לחלוחית של קרקע. ... והיא בית רובע רשות ... פ"ע הוי ולא מזדבני:

עין משפט נר מצוה

מט א מיי' פכ"ד מהל' מכירה הל' יד סמג עשין פב טוש"ע ח"מ סי' רטו סעיף ח:
נ ב ג ד מיי' שם הל' יג ועיין בהשגות ובמ"מ טוש"ע שם ס"ה:
נא ה מיי' שם הל' יח טוש"ע שם סעי' ג:
נב ו ז מיי' שם הל' יב טוש"ע שם סעי' ד:

ופי' דיקלין תמרים גבוהין תאלין שאר אילנות גדולים הוצין שאר אילנות קטנים צינין דקלים קטנים. ערוך ערך צנין

מְנָא הָנֵי מִילֵּי? אֲמַר רַב יְהוּדָה אֲמַר רַב, דְּאָמַר קְרָא: °"וַיָּקָם שְׂדֵה עֶפְרוֹן אֲשֶׁר בַּמַּכְפֵּלָה" וגו', (א) מִי שֶׁצָּרִיךְ לִגְבוּל סָבִיב, יָצְאוּ אֵלּוּ שֶׁאֵין צְרִיכִין לִגְבוּל סָבִיב. אָמַר רַב מְשַׁרְשְׁיָא: מִכָּאן לְמִצְרִים מִן הַתּוֹרָה.§ אָמַר רַב יְהוּדָה: אהַאי מַאן דִּמְזַבֵּן אַרְעָא לְחַבְרֵיהּ, צָרִיךְ לְמִכְתַּב לֵיהּ: "קְנֵי לָךְ *דִּיקְלִין וְתָאלִין וְהוּצִין *וְצִיצִין". וְאַע"ג דְּכִי לָא כְּתַב לֵיהּ הָכִי קָנֵי, אפ"ה – שׁוּפְרָא דִּשְׁטָרָא הוּא. באָמַר לֵיהּ: "אַרְעָא וְדִיקְלֵי"; חָזֵינַן, אִי אִית לֵיהּ דִּיקְלֵי – יָהֵיב לֵיהּ תְּרֵי דִּיקְלֵי, וְאִי לֵית לֵיהּ – זָבֵין לֵיהּ תְּרֵי דִּיקְלֵי, וְאִי מְשַׁעְבְּדִי – פָּרֵיק לֵיהּ תְּרֵי דִּיקְלֵי. ג"אַרְעָא בְּדִיקְלֵי" – חָזֵינַן, אִי אִית בָּהּ דִּיקְלֵי – (ב) יָהֵיב לֵיהּ, וְאִי לָאו – מִקַּח טָעוּת הוּא. ד"אַרְעָא בֵּי דִיקְלֵי" – לֵית לֵיהּ דִּיקְלֵי, (ג) דְּחַזְיָא לְדִיקְלֵי קָאָמַר לֵיהּ. אָמַר לֵיהּ: "לְבַר מִדִּיקְלָא פְּלָנְיָא" – החָזֵינַן, אִי דִּיקְלָא טָבָא הוּא – שִׁיּוּרֵי שַׁיְירֵיהּ, אִי דִּיקְלָא בִּישָׁא הוּא – כָּל שֶׁכֵּן הָנָךְ. ואָמַר לֵיהּ: "לְבַר מֵאִילָנֵי", אִי אִית לֵיהּ אִילָנֵי – לְבַר מֵאִילָנֵי, אִי אִית לֵיהּ דִּיקְלֵי – לְבַר מִדִּיקְלֵי, אִי אִית לֵיהּ גּוּפְנֵי – לְבַר מִגּוּפְנֵי, אִילָנֵי וְגוּפְנֵי – לְבַר מֵאִילָנֵי, אִילָנֵי וְדִיקְלֵי – לְבַר מֵאִילָנֵי. גּוּפְנֵי וְדִיקְלֵי – לְבַר מִגּוּפְנֵי. אָמַר רַב: זכָּל שֶׁעוֹלִין לוֹ בְּחֶבֶל – הָוֵי שִׁיּוּר, כָּל שֶׁאֵין עוֹלִין לוֹ בְּחֶבֶל – לָא הָוֵי שִׁיּוּר;

וְדַיָּינֵי

תוספות

ארעא ודיקלי אי אית בה דיקלי כו'. אע"ג דאם לא אמר דיקלי – בסתמא היו כולן מכורין, מיהו השתא גרע, (ל) כדבעי למימ' לקמן: "חוץ מחרוב פלוני" – דקני שאר חרובין, אע"ג דבסתמא לא קני. ד"דיקלי" משמע תרי. ולא שייך הכא שופרא דשטרא אלא דוקא כשכותב בשטר, אבל הכא דבעל פה – לא. ועוד, דהתם כתיב "דיקלין ותאלין" כו', והכא דלא קאמר אלא דיקלין – לא שייך למימר הכי.

חוץ

רשב"ם

מִנְּהָנֵי מִילֵּי. דְּחָרוּב הַמּוּרְכָּב וְסַדַּן הַשִּׁקְמָה אֵין נִמְכָּרִין בִּכְלַל שָׂדֶה? (ד) וְכֵיוָן דְּמַשְׁכְּחִינַן דְּאֵינָן בִּכְלַל שָׂדֶה – מִמֵּילָא יָדְעִינַן דַּאֲפִי' אִם אָמַר "כָּל מַה שֶּׁבְּתוֹכָהּ" – אֵינָן נִמְכָּרִין, כִּדְקָתָנֵי מַתְנִי': אֵין כָּךְ וְאֵין כָּךְ לֹא מָכַר כו'. ד"כָּל מַה שֶּׁבְּתוֹכָהּ" לָא מְהַנֵּי אֶלָּא לְטַפּוּיֵי תַּשְׁמִישֵׁי דְּשָׂדֶה שֶׁאֵינָן קְבוּעִין כָּל כָּךְ, כְּגוֹן קָנִים וַאֲבָנִים שֶׁאֵינָן מְתוּקָּנִין לְצָרְכָּהּ, וּמִיהוּ, לְהָכִי קָיְימִי. אֲבָל חָרוּב הַמּוּרְכָּב וְסַדַּן הַשִּׁקְמָה – אַשְׁמְעִינַן קְרָא דַּחֲשִׁיבִי שָׂדֶה בִּפְנֵי עַצְמָן. וּמִי שֶׁיֵּשׁ לוֹ ג' שָׂדוֹת וּמָכַר שְׁנַיִם הַחִיצוֹנִים, וְאָמַר לוֹ "כָּל מַה שֶּׁבְּתוֹכָן אֲנִי מוֹכֵר לָךְ" דְּלֹא מָכַר שָׂדֶה הַשְּׁלִישִׁי שֶׁבֵּינֵיהֶן, אַף כָּאן לֹא מָכַר חָרוּב הַמּוּרְכָּב וְסַדַּן הַשִּׁקְמָה. דִּכְתִיב וַיָּקָם שְׂדֵה עֶפְרוֹן וגו'. עֶפְרוֹן מָכַר לוֹ הַשָּׂדֶה לְאַבְרָהָם בִּסְתָמָא, כִּדְכְתִיב: "נָתַתִּי כֶּסֶף הַשָּׂדֶה" וגו', וְקָמְהַדַּר לֵיהּ עֶפְרוֹן: "אֶרֶץ אַרְבַּע מֵאוֹת" וגו', וַאפ"ה קָנָה אַבְרָהָם כָּל הָאִילָנוֹת, כִּדְכְתִיב: "וַיָּקָם שְׂדֵה עֶפְרוֹן וגו' וְכָל הָעֵץ אֲשֶׁר בְּכָל גְּבוּלוֹ סָבִיב", ע"י קְנִיַּית הַשָּׂדֶה סְתָם קָנָה גַּם אֶת כָּל הָאִילָנוֹת. וְהַאי "אֲשֶׁר בְּכָל גְּבוּלוֹ" קְרָא יְתֵירָא הוּא, דְּמָצֵי לְמִיכְתַּב "וְכָל הָעֵץ אֲשֶׁר בַּשָּׂדֶה" דְּהַיְינוּ בְּתוֹךְ גְּבוּלֵי הַשָּׂדֶה, וּלְמִידְרַשׁ אֲתָא: מִי שֶׁצָּרִיךְ לִגְבוּל – אוֹתָן אִילָנוֹת קָנָה, שֶׁצְּרִיכִין לִהְיוֹת (ה) לְהוּ גְּבוּל סָבִיב, שֶׁלֹּא יְעַרְעֵר אָדָם עֲלֵיהֶם לוֹמַר: בְּתוֹךְ שֶׁלִּי נְטוּעִים וְשֶׁלִּי הֵם, דְּהַיְינוּ כְּגוֹן אִילָנוֹת דַּקִּין שֶׁאֵין לָהֶם שֵׁם, וְהַדָּבָר שָׁכוּחַ מִי נְטָעָם, לְפִיכָךְ צָרִיךְ לַעֲשׂוֹת לָהֶם גְּבוּל סָבִיב. אֲבָל כָּל חָרוּב הַמּוּרְכָּב וְסַדַּן הַשִּׁקְמָה – גְּדוֹלִים וַחֲשׁוּבִים, וְאַוְושָׁא מִילְּתַיְיהוּ, וְיָדוּעַ שֶׁל מִי הֵן וּבְקַרְקַע מִי הֵן נְטוּעִין, וְאֵין צְרִיכִין גְּבוּל. הִלְכָּךְ, אֵינָן בִּכְלַל הַשָּׂדֶה סָבִיב. אָמַר רַב מְשַׁרְשְׁיָא מִכָּאן לְמִצְרִים מה"ת. שֶׁהַקּוֹנֶה אֶת הַשָּׂדֶה קָנָה אֶת הַמְּצָרִים עַצְמָן, וְכָל הָאִילָנוֹת הַנְּטוּעִין בַּמֵּצֶר, דְּמְצָרִים בִּכְלַל שָׂדֶה, דְּהָכִי מַשְׁמַע "סָבִיב" – כָּל הָאִילָנוֹת הַנְּטוּעִין בְּקַרְקַע הַמֵּצֶר שֶׁהוּא סְבִיב הַשָּׂדֶה קָנָה אַבְרָהָם. כֵּן נִרְאֶה בְּעֵינַי. דִּיקְלֵי. שֶׁגְּדֵלוּ כָּל צָרְכָּן. תָּאלִין. שְׁתִילִין, נְטָעִים בַּחוּרִים. הוּצִין וְצִיצִין. גַּם הֵם מִינֵי דְקָלִים, כִּדְתְנַן (סוכה דף כט:): לִינֵי הַר הַבַּרְזֶל כְּשֵׁרִין. וְיֵשׁ מְפָרְשִׁים: שֶׁאֵין אֵלּוּ טוֹעֲנִין פֵּירוֹת. וְאַע"ג דְּכִי לָא כְּתַב לֵיהּ הָכִי קָנֵי. כִּדְתְנַן: הַמּוֹכֵר אֶת הַשָּׂדֶה סְתָם – מָכַר חָרוּב שֶׁאֵינוֹ מוּרְכָּב, וּבְתוּלַת הַשִּׁקְמָה, וכ"ש שְׁאָר אִילָנוֹת, דְּהָא לֹא מְשַׁיֵּיר בְּמַתְנִי' אֶלָּא חָרוּב הַמּוּרְכָּב וְסַדַּן הַשִּׁקְמָה. שׁוּפְרָא דִּשְׁטָרָא. יִיפּוּי כֹּחַ הַשְּׁטָר. דַּאֲפִי' אִי אָתוּ לִפְנֵי ב"ד טוֹעֵין – יָהֵיב לֵיהּ, שֶׁהֲרֵי מְפוֹרָשִׁין בְּתוֹךְ הַשְּׁטָר. א"ל לְבַר מִדִּיקְלָא פְּלָנְיָא כו'. הָכָא לָא גָּרְסִינַן, אֶלָּא לְקַמָּן בְּסָמוּךְ, אַחַר "דְּחַזְיָא לְדִיקְלֵי קא"ל". קְפָסֵיק גְּמָרָא: א"ל. מוֹכֵר לַלּוֹקֵחַ "אַרְעָא וְדִיקְלֵי מְזַבֵּינָא לָךְ" – שְׁנֵי מְכִירוֹת הֵן: שָׂדֶה זוֹ אֲנִי מוֹכֵר לָךְ, וְקָנָה אֶת הַשָּׂדֶה וְאֶת הַדְּקָלִים שֶׁבְּתוֹכוֹ. וְדִיקְלֵי נַמִּי מְזַבֵּינָא לָךְ בְּמָקוֹם אַחֵר, דְּהָא לָא קָאָמַר "אַרְעָא בְּדִיקְלֵי" כִּדְלְקַמָּן, דַּהֲוֵי מַשְׁמַע דְּקָלִים שֶׁבְּתוֹכָהּ. הָכִי גָּרְסִינַן: אִי אִית לֵיהּ דִּיקְלֵי יָהֵיב לֵיהּ תְּרֵי דִּיקְלֵי. לְבַד אוֹתָן שֶׁבַּשָּׂדֶה, הַמְּכוּרִין בִּכְלַל שָׂדֶה. דִּמְכִירָה אַחֶרֶת הִיא זוֹ, וּמִיעוּט דִּיקְלֵי שְׁנַיִם. וְיֵשׁ סְפָרִים שֶׁכָּתוּב בָּהֶן: אִי אִית בֵּיהּ דִּיקְלֵי – יָהֵיב לֵיהּ תְּרֵי דִּיקְלֵי. דְּמַשְׁמַע דְּאִם יֵשׁ שָׁם דְּקָלִים הַרְבֵּה בְּאוֹתוֹ שָׂדֶה שֶׁמָּכַר לוֹ – יִתֵּן לוֹ מֵהֶן שְׁנַיִם וְלֹא יוֹתֵר, וְהַשְּׁאָר יְעַכֵּב לְעַצְמוֹ. וְלָא נִהְיְרָא כְּלָל, דְּאִילּוּ א"ל "הַאי אַרְעָא מְזַבֵּינָא לָךְ" – קָנָה הַכֹּל, אֲפִילּוּ הַדְּקָלִים, וּכְשֶׁהוֹסִיף לְפָרֵשׁ אַרְעָא וְדִיקְלֵי יַפְסִיד הַלּוֹקֵחַ? כ"ש שֶׁיִּיפָּה כֹּחוֹ, כִּדְאָמְרַן לְעֵיל: צָרִיךְ לְמִכְתַּב לֵיהּ קְנֵי לָךְ דִּיקְלִין וְתָאלִין כו', דַּהֲוֵי שׁוּפְרָא דִּשְׁטָרָא. וְלָא אָמְרִינַן שְׁנֵי דְקָלִים מָכַר לוֹ וְהַשְּׁאָר עִיכֵּב לְעַצְמוֹ! וְעוֹד, הָכִי אִיבְּעֵי לֵיהּ לְמֵימַר: חָזֵינַן, אִי אִית בֵּיהּ דִּיקְלֵי – לָא יָהֵיב לֵיהּ אֶלָּא תְּרֵי דִּיקְלֵי. שֶׁהֲרֵי כּוּלָּן הָיוּ מְכוּרִין מִסְּתָמָא, וְהַאי יִתּוּר לָשׁוֹן זֶה לְשַׁיֵּיר לְעַצְמוֹ. וּמִדְּלָא קָאָמַר הָכִי, אֶלָּא קָאָמַר "יָהֵב לֵיהּ תְּרֵי דִּיקְלֵי" ש"מ דה"ק: אִם יֵשׁ לוֹ דִּיקְלֵי, לְבַד אוֹתָן שֶׁמָּכַר עִם הַשָּׂדֶה, שֶׁהֵן בְּתוֹךְ הַשָּׂדֶה – יָהֵיב לֵיהּ תְּרֵי דִּיקְלֵי. (ו)זָבֵין לֵיהּ תְּרֵי דִּיקְלֵי. יִקְנֶה לְצָרְכּוֹ שֶׁל זֶה שְׁנֵי דְקָלִים. שֶׁלֹּא יְהֵא מְחוּסַּר אֲמָנָה, שֶׁכָּךְ הִתְנָה לוֹ: אֲנִי מוֹכֵר לָךְ אִילָנוֹת שֶׁאֶקְנֶה לְצָרְכָּךְ. אוֹ יַחֲזִיר לוֹ מִן הַמָּעוֹת כְּנֶגֶד דְּמֵי שְׁנֵי דְקָלִים. וְאִי מְשַׁעְבְּדֵי. לְמַלְוֶה. אַרְעָא בְּדִיקְלֵי. שָׂדֶה עִם דְּקָלִים שֶׁבְּתוֹכוֹ אֲנִי מוֹכֵר לָךְ. ה"ג: אִי אִית בָּהּ. מִקַּח טָעוּת הוּא. שֶׁשִּׁיקֵּר בּוֹ, וְהָדְרֵי מָעוֹת. וְנִהִי דְּאֵין אוֹנָאָה לְקַרְקָעוֹת הֵיכָא דְּמוֹכֵר בְּיוֹקֶר, אֲפִי' יוֹתֵר מִשְּׁתוּת (ז) – מִקַּח טָעוּת מִיהָא הָוֵי, דְּלְדַעַת כֵּן לֹא לָקַח, אֶלָּא הָיָה סָבוּר שֶׁיֵּשׁ בָּהּ דְּקָלִים כְּמוֹ שֶׁאָמַר לֵיהּ. אַרְעָא (ח) בֵּיהּ דִּיקְלֵי. מָקוֹם הָרָאוּי לִדְקָלִים – לֵית לֵיהּ לַלּוֹקֵחַ דִּיקְלֵי. שֶׁאִם אֵין דְּקָלִים בַּשָּׂדֶה – אֵין זֶה מִקַּח טָעוּת; מ"ט – דְּחַזְיָא לְדִיקְלֵי קא"ל, קַרְקַע יָפָה לְגַדֵּל דְּקָלִים. וּמִיהוּ, אִי אִית בֵּיהּ דִּיקְלֵי – ה"ז שֶׁל לוֹקֵחַ, דְּכ"ש דה"ק: אַרְעָא דְּחַזְיָא לְדִיקְלֵי מְזַבֵּינָא לָךְ, כְּלוֹמַר שֶׁהַדְּקָלִים שֶׁבָּהּ טְעוּנִין פֵּירוֹת הַרְבֵּה. א"ל. מוֹכֵר: (ט) שָׂדֶה אֲנִי מוֹכֵר לָךְ, לְבַר מִדִּיקְלָא פְּלָנְיָא. חָזֵינַן אִי דִּיקְלָא טָבָא הוּא. כְּלוֹמַר, מִן הַבֵּינוֹנִים שֶׁטְּעוּנִין פֵּירוֹת קְצָת – לְחוּדֵיהּ שַׁיְירֵיהּ, דְּדַעְתּוֹ לֵיהָנוֹת מִפֵּירוֹת שֶׁלּוֹ פּוּרְתָּא, וְקָנָה הַלּוֹקֵחַ כָּל הַשְּׁאָר בִּכְלַל הַשָּׂדֶה. וְאִי דִּיקְלָא בִּישָׁא הוּא. אע"פ שֶׁיֵּשׁ עֲדַיִין רָעִים מִמֶּנּוּ, אֶלָּא דְּקָרוּ לֵיהּ אֱינָשֵׁי לְהַאי "דִּיקְלָא בִּישָׁא". כְּגוֹן דְּלָא טָעִין קַבָּא, דְּאִילּוּ רָעִין קַבָּא – לָאו דִּיקְלָא בִּישָׁא הוּא, כִּדְאָמְרִינַן בְּעָלְמָא (לעיל דף כו.): דִּיקְלָא דְּטָעִין קַבָּא – אָסוּר לְמִקְצְיֵיהּ. כ"ש הָנָךְ. הַמְּעוּלִּים מִמֶּנּוּ, שֶׁשִּׁיְּירָן לְעַצְמוֹ. דְּהָכִי קָאָמַר: אֲפִי' הַהוּא דִּיקְלָא בִּישָׁא אֲנִי מְשַׁיֵּיר לְעַצְמִי. וּמִיהוּ, אִם יֵשׁ בַּשָּׂדֶה דִּיקְלֵי בִּישָׁא טְפֵי מֵהַאי – אִינְהוּ מִזְדַּבְּנֵי בִּכְלָל. (י) דְּהָא דְּאָמְרִי' "כ"ש הָנָךְ" – אַדִּיקְלֵי דְּטָבֵי טְפֵי מֵהַאי קָאֵי. ה"ג: לְבַר מֵאִילָנֵי אִי אִית לֵיהּ אִילָנֵי לְבַר מֵאִילָנֵי. כְּלוֹמַר, אִם אָמַר מוֹכֵר לַלּוֹקֵחַ: שָׂדֶה (כ) אֲנִי מוֹכֵר לָךְ לְבַר מֵאִילָנֵי. חָזֵינַן אִי אִית בָּהּ שְׁאָר אִילָנוֹת, כְּגוֹן זֵיתִים וּתְאֵנִים וְתַפּוּחִים וְכָל שְׁאָר אִילָנוֹת, חוּץ מִדְּקָלִים וּגְפָנִים שֶׁאֵין נִקְרָאִין אִילָנֵי. לְבַר מֵאִילָנֵי. מָכַר לוֹ אֶת הַשָּׂדֶה, אֲבָל הָאִילָנוֹת אֵינָן מְכוּרִין, שֶׁהֲרֵי הוֹצִיאָן מִכְּלַל שָׂדֶה וְשִׁיְּירָן לְעַצְמוֹ. וְהַאי מִילְּתָא דִּפְשִׁיטָא הוּא, אֲבָל מִשּׁוּם דְּבָעֵי לְמֵימַר לְקַמָּן: אִילָנֵי וְגוּפְנֵי לְבַר מֵאִילָנֵי, נָקַט לָהּ. אִי אִית בֵּיהּ דִּיקְלֵי. בְּהַהוּא שָׂדֶה, וְאֵין בּוֹ שְׁאָר אִילָנוֹת, וְאִיהוּ אָמַר לֵיהּ "לְבַר מֵאִילָנֵי" – וַדַּאי לְבַר מִסִּילָנֵי מָכַר הַשָּׂדֶה, וְהָנְהוּ דְּקָלִין שַׁיֵּיר לְעַצְמוֹ. וְאע"ג דְּאֵין סְתָמָן קְרוּיִין אִילָנוֹת, אֶלָּא רְגִילִין הָיוּ לְקָרוֹתָן דְּקָלִין מִתּוֹךְ חֲשִׁיבוּתָן. וּמִתּוֹךְ שֶׁהָיוּ רוֹב אִילָנוֹת שֶׁלָּהֶן דְּקָלִים, כֵּיוָן דְּאֵין כָּאן שְׁאָר אִילָנוֹת אֶלָּא דְּקָלִים, הַאי דְּקָאָמַר "לְבַר מֵאִילָנֵי" – אַדְּקָלִים קָאֵי. אִי אִית בֵּיהּ גּוּפְנֵי. בְּהַהוּא שָׂדֶה, וְהַמּוֹכֵר אֶת הַשָּׂדֶה מָכַר אֶת הַגְּפָנִים, וְכֵיוָן דְּאָמַר "לְבַר מֵאִילָנֵי", וּבְשָׂדֶה זוֹ אֵין בּוֹ אֶלָּא גְּפָנִים – לְבַר מִגּוּפְנֵי קָאָמַר. וְאִם יֵשׁ בַּשָּׂדֶה אִילָנֵי וְגוּפְנֵי, וְאִיהוּ אָמַר "לְבַר מֵאִילָנֵי" – הַכֹּל מָכַר, וַאֲפִי' הַגְּפָנִים, לְבַר מֵאִילָנֵי. דִּגְפָנִים אֵין קוֹרִין לָהֶן אִילָנוֹת, וַעֲלֵיהּ דְּמוֹכֵר רָמְיָא לְגַלּוּיֵי דְּגַם הַגְּפָנִים שַׁיֵּיר לְעַצְמוֹ, הִלְכָּךְ יַד הַלּוֹקֵחַ עַל הָעֶלְיוֹנָה. אִילָנֵי וְדִיקְלֵי לְבַר מֵאִילָנֵי. הַכֹּל מָכַר לְבַר מֵאִילָנֵי, שֶׁהַדְּקָלִים אֵין קוֹרִין לָהֶם אִילָנֵי. גּוּפְנֵי וְדִיקְלֵי לְבַר מִגּוּפְנֵי. אִי א"ל "לְבַר מֵאִילָנֵי" וְאֵין בַּשָּׂדֶה אֶלָּא דְּקָלִים וּגְפָנִים – הַדְּקָלִים מָכַר, וְהַגְּפָנִים שַׁיֵּיר. דִּגְפָנִים לְגַבֵּי דְּקָלִים נִקְרָאִין אִילָנֵי, וּבִכְלַל אִילָנֵי הֵן טְפֵי מִדִּיקְלֵי. כֵּן נִרְאֶה בְּעֵינַי. וי"מ: דְּאֵין זֶה וָזֶה בִּכְלַל אִילָנֵי, וְאֵין זֶה נִקְרָא אִילָן יוֹתֵר מִזֶּה, וְהִלְכָּךְ הַמּוּטָב דְּהַיְינוּ גְּפָנִים שַׁיֵּיר לְעַצְמוֹ. וְלָא נְהִירָא, דְּאִם אִיתָא דִּשְׁנֵיהֶן שָׁוִין, וְאֵין זֶה נִקְרָא אִילָן יוֹתֵר מִזֶּה, וְאִיהוּ אָמַר "לְבַר מֵאִילָנֵי" – הֲוָה לָן לְמֵימַר דִּתְרְוַיְיהוּ שַׁיֵּיר לְעַצְמוֹ, שֶׁהֲרֵי גִּילָּה דַּעְתּוֹ שֶׁהַכֹּל קָרָא אִילָנֵי, מֵאַחַר שֶׁאֵין כָּאן שׁוּם אִילָן אַחֵר שֶׁיִּקָּרֵא אִילָן אֶלָּא אֵלּוּ. ה"ג: אָמַר רַב כָּל שֶׁעוֹלִין כו'. וּלְעֵיל קָאֵי, הֵיכָא דְּא"ל "לְבַר מֵאִילָנֵי". וְקָמְפָרֵשׁ רַב אֵלּוּ הֵן אִילָנוֹת שֶׁשִּׁיֵּיר, שֶׁאִם קְטַנִּים הֵן הַרְבֵּה – לָא מִיקְרֵי אִילָנֵי. וְלָא גָּרְסִינַן: לְבַר מִדִּיקְלֵי, וְאִילָנֵי א"ר כו'. וּפֵירוּשׁ בְּעָלְמָא הוּא. כָּל שֶׁעוֹלִין לוֹ בְּחֶבֶל. לְלַקֵּט פֵּירוֹתָיו – חָשִׁיב אִילָן. וּבְדֶקֶל מַיְירֵי, כִּדְמְפָרֵשׁ לְקַמֵּיהּ, שֶׁגָּבוֹהַּ הַרְבֵּה וּפֵירוֹתָיו בְּרֹאשׁוֹ.

דַּיָּינֵי

רבינו גרשום

וכל העץ אשר בשדה אשר בכל גבולו סביב. אותו אילן שצריך גבול סביביו שאין משתמר אלא על ידי גבול כעין שמקיפין גדר סביב השדה כדי שיהא משומר על ידי גבול מפני שנמוך האילן ויכלי אינשי ליטול פירות אותו אילן נקנה אגב קרקע. אבל אילן שגבוה הוא כגון חרוב מורכב וסדן השקמה שאינו צריך לשומר ואינו צריך גבול דמחמת גבהותו משומר הוא שאין ידו של אדם יכולה להגיע לפירותיהן והענפים והפירות שלו בגבהות עומדין ואין עולין לו אלא בחבל אינו נקנה אגב קרקע דדבר חשוב בפני עצמו הוא: אשר בכל גבולו סביב מיכן למצרים מן התורה. שהראה לו המצרים שסביבותיה מצר פלוני כך וכך מצר פלוני כך וכך. ואית דמפרשי מיכן ללוקחין שקונין המצרים שסביבות השדה דהיינו גבולי: דיקלי. אילנות תמרים גבוהים: תאלין אלו שאר אילני בחורין קטנים: הוצין. אילנות קטנים: וציצין. דקלים קטנים כעין ציניתא דבבל: ואע"ג דכי לא כתב ליה הכי ודאי קני. דאי אתי לפני בית דין פקח יהבי ליה והאי דלא כתב ליה הכי משום דטעות סופר הוא. אפילו הכי צריך למכתב ליה הכי דשופרא דשטרא הוא דאפי' אתי לפני בית דין טועין דיהבין ליה דאי לא כתב הכי ואתי לפני בית דין הדיוטות לא יהבי ליה אבל השתא ליכא למיחש: אמר ליה. המוכר ללוקח: ארעא ודיקלי. מזבינא לך: אי אית בה דיקלי יהיב לי' תרי דיקלי. דדיקלי לא פחות מתרתי. ואי אית בה דיקלי משעבדי לבעל חוב של מוכר פריק להו מיניה ויהיב ליה ללוקח: ואי אמר ליה ארעתא ודיקלי מזבינא לך ולית בארעא תרי דיקלי זבין ויהיב ליה: אי אמר ליה ארעא בדיקלי. אי איכא דיקלי זביניה זביני ואי לא מקח טעות הוא ולא קני כלום: בי דיקלא. משמע ארעא דראויה לדקלים. ואי בישא הוא ושיירה כל שכן דהנך דמעלו ממנו לא זבין ושיירינהו: אי אמר ליה ארעא מזבין לך בר מאילני. אי אית ביה אילני זבין ליה הקרקע לבר מאילני כדמתני ליה. ואי בההיא קרקע אית בה גופני ואמר ארעא מזבינא לך לבר מאילני ודאי גופני בכלל אילני ניהו ולא זבין ליה אפי' גופני אי אית ביה דיקלי קרי להו אילני ולא זבין ליה. ואי אית בה אילני וגופני ואמר מזבינא לך בר מאילני ודאי גופני זבין ליה דלאו אילני נינהו לגבי שאר אילנות: ואי אמר ליה לבר באילני. ואית בה אילני ודיקלי ודאי אילני לא זבין ליה דיקלי זבין ליה דלגבי אילני לאו אילני נינהו הדיקלי: גופני ודיקלי. ודאי גבי דיקלי גופני אילנות נינהו ולא שייר אלא הגפנים: ואי אמר ליה ארעא מזבינא לך לבר מדיקלי. מר שייר: אמר רב כל שגבוה כל כך שעולין עליו בחבל הוי שיור. ואידך אילני לא הוי שיור חבין ליה כל

נ"א וצינין

הגהות הב"ח

(א) גמ' אשר במכפלה וכל העץ אשר בשדה בכל גבולו סביב מי ש[צריך] לגבול יצאו אלו כצ"ל ו[תיבת] סביב נמחק: (ב) שם בה דיקלי (יהיב) תא"מ ונ"ב ס"א זב[ין] זביני: (ג) שם לית דיקלי מ"ט דחזיא לדי[קלי]: (ד) רשב"ם ד"ה מ[נהני] מילי וכו' בכלל שדה דכ[תיב] ויקם וגו' וכיון דמשכ[חינן]: (ה) ד"ה דכתיב ויקם להיות להם גבול וכו' הם נטועים וכו' [...] השדה הס"ד ואח"כ [...] סביב אמר רב: (ו) [...] ואי לא זבין ליה תרי די[קלי]: (ז) ד"ה מקח טעות יותר משתות אבל מ[...]: (ח) ד"ה ארעא בי לדקלים הס"ד ואח"כ [...] לית ליה וכו' הרי הן [של] לוקח: (ט) ד"ה א"ל מ[וכר] ללוקח שדה זו אני מוכר הס"ד: (י) ד"ה כ"ש [...] וכו' בכלל שדה [...] דאמרינן: (כ) ד"ה [...] גרסינן וכו' שדה זו וכו' אילני לבר הד[...]: (ל) תוס' ד"ה ארעא ו[כו'] השתא גרע לדיקלי מש[מע] תרי כדבעי למימר לו[קמן] וכו' לא קני ולא שייך כל[ל]

ודייני גולה אמרי: א כל שהעול כובשו – לא הוי שיור, כל שאין העול כובשו – הוי שיור. ב ולא פליגי: הא בדיקלי, הא באילני. בעא מיניה רב אחא בר הונא מרב ששת: "חוץ מחרוב פלוני", "חוץ מסדן פלוני", מהו? אותו חרוב הוא דלא קני, הא שאר חרובים קני, או דלמא שאר חרובין נמי לא קני? אמר ליה: ג לא קנה. איתיביה: "חוץ מחרוב פלוני", "חוץ מסדן פלוני" – לא קנה; מאי לאו, אותו חרוב הוא דלא קנה, הא שאר חרובין קנה? א"ל: לא, אפילו שאר חרובין נמי לא קנה. תדע, דאילו א"ל: "שדי מכורה לך חוץ משדה פלונית" – ההיא הוא דלא קני, הא אחרנייתא קני? אלא לא קנה, ה"נ לא קנה. ואיכא דאמרי, בעא מיניה רב אחא בר הונא מרב ששת: "חוץ מחצי חרוב פלוני", "חוץ מחצי סדן פלוני", מהו? שאר חרובין ודאי לא קני, הא מה ששייר באותו חרוב קני, או דלמא אפילו מה ששייר באותו חרוב נמי לא קני? א"ל: ד לא קני. איתיביה: "חוץ מחצי חרוב פלוני", "חוץ מחצי סדן פלוני" – שאר חרובין לא קנה; מאי לאו, שאר חרובין הוא דלא קנה, הא מה ששייר באותו חרוב קנה? א"ל: לא, אפי' מה ששייר באותו חרוב נמי לא קנה. תדע, דאילו א"ל: "שדי מכורה לך חוץ מחצי שדה פלוני" – ההוא הוא דלא קנה, הא אידך קנה? אלא לא קני, ה"נ לא קני. בעא מיניה רב עמרם מרב חסדא: המפקיד אצל חבירו בשטר, ואמר לו "החזרתים לך", מהו? מי אמרינן: מיגו דאי בעי אמר "נאנסו" מהימן – השתא נמי מהימן, או דלמא (א) אמר ליה "שטרך בידי מאי בעי"? א"ל: ה מהימן. ולימא ליה "שטרך בידי מאי בעי"! א"ל: וליטעמיך, וכי א"ל "נאנסו", מי מצי א"ל "שטרך בידי מאי בעי"? אמר ליה:

סוף

רשב"ם

דייני גולה. שמואל וקרנא, בפ"ק דסנהדרין (דף יז: ע"ש). כל שהעול כובשו. חורשין היו בבקר סביב האילנות, ואם העול כופף את האילן ועובר השור לדרכו, ואין האילן מעכב השור – לא חשיב. ומיהו, אם אין אילנות גדולים בשדה אלא אלו – הוו שיור, כדאמרן גבי דיקלי. הא בדיקלי. מילתיה דרב. הא באילני. שהעול כובשו. דשיעור דעליית חבל לא שייך בהו, דבלא חבל עולין בכל שאר אילנות על ידי ענפים המתפללים לכל צד. ושיעורא דכבישת עול נמי איכא למימר דלא שייך בדיקלי, דאפי' היכא דכביש ליה עול חשיב הוא אם עולין לו בחבל. חוץ מחרוב. המורכב פלוני, חוץ מסדן השקמה פלוני, והיו בה הרבה חרובין וסדנא, מהו? דאם הוה שתיק – לא היו מכורין בכלל שדה, אבל עכשיו ששייר אחד איכא למימר דשאר חרובין מכר לו. או דלמא שיורי לא יגרע כחו, אלא אפילו שאר חרובין נמי לא קני הלוקח. דבשביל שייפה המוכר את כח שלו, שפירש בפירוש "אינני מוכר לך ההוא חרוב" אין לנו לגרע כחו בשאר. אלא אי איכא מילתא לטפויי בהאי "חוץ", כגון דרך – מטפינן ליה. כדאמר במתניתין: ומודי ר"ע בזמן שאמר לו "חוץ מאלו" שאינו צריך ליקח לו דרך. והאי "חוץ מחרוב פלוני" דקאמר – לשייר דרך להאי (ב) דקל נתכוין, ולא למעט השאר. ואפי' לרבנן נמי איכא למימר: לפיכך אמר "חוץ מחרוב פלוני" – דבההוא חרוב היה חפץ יותר, ולא היה רוצה שיתבענו לוקח לדין. ולחרוב זה איכוין, לשופרא דשטרא. אבל על שאר חרובין – לא חשיש לכתוב שופרא דשטרא, דמ"מ בוטח הוא במאי דקי"ל שאין חרוב המורכב נמכר בכלל שדה. כן נראה בעיני, ועיקר. (הג"ה. א"ל לא קנה. לא הוא ולא זולתו. דכיון שאפי' לא פירש ליה "חוץ", כגון אלו אינן נמכרין בכלל שדה – ה"נ לא קנה, ולא פירש הללו אלא להודיעו שכל אילן שבאותה שדה הרי הן כמו אלו ולא נמכרו. ע"כ). ה"ג: איתיביה חוץ מחרוב פלוני חוץ מסדן פלוני לא קנה. ולא גרסינן "אותו חרוב לא קנה". דא"כ קשיא מעלייתא היא, ולא מצי לתרוצי לקמיה: שאר חרובין נמי לא קנה. לא שאר חרובין נמי לא קנה. דהאי דקתני "לא קנה" – אשאר חרובין קאי, וכל שכן האי דקמשייר. ולאשמועינן אתא, דלא הפסיד שאר חרובין בשביל ההוא ששייר יחידי. תדע. דלא קני. חוץ משדה פלוני. הסמוך (ג) לו חוץ למיצר. הא אחריני קני. בתמיה, והלא שדה אחת מכר לו ולא השאר! ה"ג: אלא לא קני ה"נ לא קני. כלומר, אלא פשיטא לן דלא קני הלוקח שאר שדות, דהא המוכר שדה אחת לא מכר כל שדותיו בכלל. ובשביל שאמר שטות זה "חוץ משדה פלוני" אין לנו לומר שמכר מה שלא רצה למכור, דשדה אחת נתכוין למכור ולא שתי שדות. ה"נ, המוכר את השדה – לא מכר חרוב וסדן, דחשיבי שדה בפני עצמן, והלכך, בשביל ששייר אחת מהן בלא צורך – אין לנו לומר שמכר השאר. ואית דגרס: אלא לדמי ה"נ לדמי. כלומר, באותו שדה שמכר שייר לעצמו דמי ההוא שדה דקאמר "חוץ משדה פלוני", ה"נ ה"ק: שדה מכור לך חוץ מדמי חרוב פלוני. ויש עוד פירושים אחרים. ולא נהירא כלל גירסא זו, ופירושה (ד) משובש היה בספרים ליתן טעם בדבר, כיון דלא קני אמאי קאמר "חוץ משדה פלוני". ומיהו הטעם כדפרישית, לשייר ליה דרך להאי חרוב או להאי שדה ששייר נתכוין, וכדאמרינן נמי (לעיל דף סג:) גבי "על מנת שהדיוטא העליונה שלי" – ששייר מקום זיזין. ומיהו, היכא דליכא לטפויי שום דבר – אין לנו לומר: כיון דליכא לטפויי, לגרועי נתכוין. דדי לנו אם אינו מטפי ומרויח בשיורו, אלא שיפסיד? בתמיה. חוץ מחצי סדן פלוני מהו. ולהאי לישנא פשיטא ליה ד"חוץ מסדן פלוני" לא קנה נמי שאר סדנין. שאר חרובין פשיטא הוא דלא קני. כדאמרן טעם לעיל: תדע דאי א"ל כו'. ומשני: לא מה ששייר באותו חרוב נמי לא קנה. והא דקתני "שאר חרובין לא קנה" – הכל קורא שאר חרובין, אפילו חצי חרוב הנשאר. וה"נ גרסי': אלא לא קני ה"נ לא קני. בעא מיניה רב עמרם כו'. משום דדייני גולה נקט לה הכא. בשטר. שכתב כמה הפקיד לו וחתמו בעדים, ואהני ליה האי שטרא דלא מצי טעין נפקד להד"מ. וא"ל. נפקד: היום ולמחר החזרתיו לך, מהו? דהא קי"ל ב"חזקת הבתים" (לעיל דף מה:) דהמפקיד את חבירו בעדים א"צ להחזיר בעדים. אבל הכא, דאיכא שטר ביד המפקיד – מי אמרינן דה"נ מהימן; מיגו דאי בעי אמר נאנסו והוה מהימן, ובשבועה כדלקמן, וכדכתיב: "שבועת ה' תהיה בין שניהם" (שמות כב) שהתורה האמינתו לנפקד – השתא נמי מהימן, ובשבועה כדלקמן, דמה לו לשקר, אי בעי הוה פטר נפשיה בטענת שקר דנאנסו. ומשום דלא רצה לשקר ואמר החזרתיו – נאמן. או דלמא אמר ליה. מפקיד: שטרך בידי מאי בעי? לא היה לך להניח השטר בידי אילו החזרת לי פקדוני, כדי שלא אחזור ואתבענו. וכמו "מה לי לשקר" במקום עדים דמי, ולא אמרינן מה לו לשקר. וליטעמיך אילו אמר ליה נאנסו כו'. הלכך לא מצי למיטען מפקיד "שטרך בידי מאי בעי". ו"למה לי לשקר" במקום עדים לא דמי, דהא עביד איניש למידחי ואמר "אבדתי את שטרי". ונפקד נמי לא הוה חייש לשטרא, משום דהוה מצי למיפטר נפשיה בטענת אונס. אבל מלוה את חבירו בשטר – לא מצי טעין לוה "פרעתי", דא"ל אידך "שטרך בידי מאי בעי"? וגבי לוה ליכא שום מיגו, דאפי' טעין נאנסו צריך לשלם, דמלוה להוצאה ניתנה.

לאו

תוספות

חוץ מחרוב פלוני אותו לא קני. לא גרסי' "אותו חרוב". דהא מסיק דשאר חרובין נמי לא קנה. ומיהו, לפי הספרים דגרסי בתר הכי "אלא לדמי ה"נ לדמי" — גרסי' ליה שפיר, ודמי חרוב לא קנה בקרקע. או דלמא מצי א"ל שטרך בידי מאי בעי. אפילו למ"ד (כתובות יט.) מודה בשטר שכתבו צריך לקיימו, ומהימן לוה לומר דפרוע הוא, ולא אמר "א"כ שטרך בידי מאי בעי" — התם משום דזימנין אפשיטי דספרא זייר ליה, דעל הלוה ליתן שכר כתיבת השטר, ופעמים כשאין לו ללוה נותן המלוה בשבילו. אבל הכא — אין על הנפקד ליתן שכר. ועוד: דהתם לוה מאמין למלוה להניח שטר בידו, משום דכתיב ביה "תומת ישרים תנחם" כדאמרי' ב"המפקיד" (ב"מ דף לה.). אבל הנפקד אינו מאמין את המפקיד, ולעולם אינו מחזיר את הפקדון עד שיחזיר לו השטר. ועוד: דאין מדקדק כל כך לוה אחר המלוה, לפי שעשה לו טובה. ולימא ליה שטרך בידי מאי בעי. לאו משום דליהוי מיגו במקום עדים קפריך. דא"כ מאי משני: וליטעמיך כי א"ל נאנסו מי מצי אמר ליה "שטרך בידי מאי בעי"? הא כי אמר נאנסו לא מוכחא מילתא דלאו קושטא קאמר, דאע"פ שהשטר בידו — יכול להיות שנאנסו. אלא אור"י: דס"ד דמקשה, דהא דקאמר דנאמן — נאמן לגמרי קאמר, אפי' בלא שבועה. ולכך היה סבור דבלאו מיגו דנאנסו מצי למימר "החזרתי לך", דאי ע"י מיגו דנאנסו — אמאי נאמן בלא שבועה? ולהכי פריך: ולימא ליה "שטרך בידי מאי בעי"! ומשני: דמטעם מיגו נאמן. ופריך: כי אמר נאנסו, לאו שבועה בעי?

סוף

רבינו גרשום

כל שהעול כובשו. שהיו רגילין לחרוש אילנות במחרישה כשדה זרעים ומשימין עול בראשי השורים כעין שאנו רגילין ואם מכה העול באילן כשהוא חורש והעול כופף את האילן ודאי מכרו דלא הוי דבר חשוב. ואידך שיש בהן כח דאין העול יכול לכובשן הוי שיור: הא בדיקלי. בעינן כל שעולין לו בחבל: בעא מיניה רב אחא מרב ששת. אם אמר לו קרקע אני מוכר לך חוץ מחרוב זה וחוץ מסדן פלוני ואיכא חרובין אחריני מורכבין וסדן שקמה מהו. מי אמרי' הואיל דבלא תנאי נמי לא מכר שום חרוב מורכב ולא שום סדן שקמה דקתני מתני' לא מכר לא חרוב המורכב ולא סדן שקמה והאי הואיל דקא מתני ליה הכי חוץ מסדן פלוני לטפויי ללוקח קאתי דמשמע הכי האי הוא דלא יקנה הא שאר חרובין קני. או דלמא אפי' שאר חרובין נמי לא קני והאי דקאמר הכי משום האי טעמא דאמרי' לקמן לדמי: א"ל לא קני. אפי' שאר חרובין: תדע. דאפי' שאר חרובין נמי לא קנה: דאילו אמר ליה מוכר ללוקח שדי אני מוכר לך חוץ משדה פלוני. כלומר חוץ מן אותה שדה. וכי מי אמרי' ההיא דלא קני הא אחרנייתא דיליה קני בתמיה. והא לא אמר ליה שדותי מכורין לך. אלא לדמי דאמר ליה שדי אני מוכר לך חוץ משדה פלוני שאיני נותן לך באותן דמים שנתתי לך זו. אבל איזו מן האחרות שתרצה אתן לך באותן דמים שנתתי לך זו. הכא נמי להיכא דאמר ליה חוץ מחרוב פלוני וחוץ מסדן פלוני אפי' בלאו הכי לא קני ליה. לדמי קאמר ליה. כלומר שאותן איני נותן לך אלא בדמים יקרים אבל האחרים אתנם לך בדמי שאר אילנות. ואמר לן המור"ה האי לישנא דלדמי לאו דוקא כל כך. אלא האי לישנא מסתבר שפיר דכתב אלא לא קני הכא נמי לא קני: חוץ מחצי חרוב מחצי סדן שקמה [פלו]ני מהו. מי אמרי' הואיל דבלאו הכי לא קני שאר חרובין מורכבין והאי דקאמר הכי לגרועי לנפשיה קאתי ושאר חרובין ודאי לא קני. והאי חצי חרוב דשייר קני הלוקח או לא. אלא לדמי שאמר לו שדי אני מוכר לך חוץ מחצי שדה פלוני שאיני נותן לך באותן דמי שקנית זו. הכא נמי להיכא דאמר ליה שדי אני מוכר לך חוץ מחצי חרוב פלוני שאיני מוכר בדמים של שאר חרובין דעלמא אלא בדמים יקרים ולא קנה [ש]ום מן החרוב. והכא נמי מוגה בספר לישנא אחרינא אלא דלא קני הכא נמי לא קני: בשטר. שכתב בשטר והעיד עדים כמה הפקיד לו: מגו דאי בעי א"ל נאנסתי מהימן. האי דקאמר נפקד זה נאנסתי הוא הדין נמי [ש]ה טוען נגנבה לו או נאבדה היה פטור דש"ח הוא וש"ח פטור מגנבה ואבדה. אלא מש"ה אמר נאנסתי דאפי' (א) שואל דחייב על הכל פטור אי טוען נאנסתי. או דלמא מצי אמר ליה המפקיד אם איתא דהחזרת לי [ש]טרך בידי שיש לך משלי כך וכך מאי בעי: א"ל. אפי' הכי נאמן: אמר ליה ולטעמיך כי אמר ליה נאנסתי מי מצי א"ל שטרך בידי מאי בעי. אלא לא מצי א"ל הכי נמי בהחזרתי לך לא מצי א"ל שטרך בידי כו':

(א) נראה דט"ס וצ"ל דאפי' ש"ש דחייב כו'

סוף

עין משפט נר מצוה

נג א ב מיי' פכ"ד מהל' מכירה הל' יב סמג עשין פב טוש"ע ח"מ סי' רטז סעיף ד:
נד ג טוש"ע שם סעיף ד בהג"ה:
נה ד טור שם ועי' בב"י:
נו ה מיי' פ"ב מהל' שכירות הל' יב סמג עשין פט טוש"ע ח"מ סי' רצו סעיף ב:

הגהות הב"ח

(א) גמ' או דלמא מצי א"ל: (ב) רשב"ם ד"ה חוץ מחרוב וכו' דרך להאי נתכוין ולא: (ג) ד"ה משדה פלוני הסמוך כצ"ל ותיבות לו חוץ נמחק: (ד) ד"ה א"נ אלא זו ופירושה ופירוש משובש:

סוֹף סוֹף כִּי אֲמַר לֵיהּ "נֶאֱנְסוּ" לָאו שְׁבוּעָה בָּעֵי? ה"נ מַאי נֶאֱמָן? אנֶאֱמָן בִּשְׁבוּעָה. לֵימָא, בִּפְלוּגְתָּא דְהָנֵי תַּנָּאֵי; דְּתַנְיָא: שְׁטַר כִּיס הַיּוֹצֵא עַל הַיְתוֹמִים — דַּיָּינֵי גוֹלָה אָמְרִי: נִשְׁבָּע וְגוֹבֶה כּוּלּוֹ, וְדַיָּינֵי א"י אָמְרִי: בנִשְׁבָּע וְגוֹבֶה מֶחֱצָה. וּדְכוּלֵּי עָלְמָא אִית לְהוּ דִּנְהַרְדְּעֵי, *דְּאָמְרִי נְהַרְדְּעֵי: גהַאי עִיסְקָא — פַּלְגָא מִלְוָה וּפַלְגָא פִּקָּדוֹן; מַאי לָאו בְּהָא קָא מִיפַּלְגִי, דְּמָר סָבַר: מָצֵי א"ל "שְׁטָרָךְ בְּיָדִי מַאי בָּעֵי", וּמָר סָבַר: לָא? (א) אָמְרִי: לָא, דְּכוּלֵּי עָלְמָא אִית לְהוּ דְּרַב חִסְדָּא, וְהָכָא בְּהָא קָמִיפַּלְגִי, דְּמָר סָבַר: אִם אִיתָא דִּפְרָעֵיהּ מֵימַר הֲוָה אָמַר, וּמָר סָבַר: אֵימוּר מַלְאַךְ הַמָּוֶת הוּא דְּאַנְסֵיהּ. שְׁלַח רַב הוּנָא בַּר אָבִין: הַמַּפְקִיד אֵצֶל חֲבֵירוֹ בִּשְׁטָר, וְאָמַר לוֹ "הֶחֱזַרְתִּיו לְךָ" — נֶאֱמָן, וּשְׁטַר כִּיס הַיּוֹצֵא עַל הַיְתוֹמִין — נִשְׁבָּע וְגוֹבֶה כּוּלּוֹ. תַּרְתֵּי? שָׁאנֵי הָתָם, דְּאִם אִיתָא דִּפְרָעֵיהּ מֵימַר הֲוָה אָמַר. רָבָא אֲמַר, הִלְכְתָא: נִשְׁבָּע וְגוֹבֶה מֶחֱצָה. אֲמַר מָר זוּטְרָא: הִלְכְתָא כְּדַיָּינֵי גוֹלָה. א"ל רָבִינָא לְמָר זוּטְרָא, הָא אֲמַר רָבָא: נִשְׁבָּע וְגוֹבֶה מֶחֱצָה! אֲמַר לֵיהּ: אֲנַן דְּדַיָּינֵי גוֹלָה

אִיפְּכָא

סוף סוף כי א"ל נאנסו לאו שבועה בעי. תימה: למ"ד דמפרש ר"ת ב"הגוזל קמא" (ב"ק דף קו. ושם) בשמעתא דהטוען טענת גנב בפקדון, דלא מיחייב שבועת שומרין אלא היכא דאיכא הודאה במקצת, היכי קאמר: לאו שבועה בעי? אין ה"נ דלא מיחייב שבועה דאורייתא! ואין לומר: לאו שבועה בעי — שבועת היסת קאמר. דהיכי תיסק אדעתיה דרב עמרם דנאמן דקאמר רב חסדא ליפטר אפילו משבועת היסת? ועוד: דאמר בפרק "כל הנשבעין" (שבועות דף מה:) גבי רמי בר חמא ורבא: מכלל דתרווייהו סברי המפקיד אצל חבירו בעדים אין צריך להחזיר לו בעדים, בשטר — צריך להחזיר לו בשטר. וצריך לפרש: וצריך להחזיר לו בשטר — אם אין רוצה לישבע. אבל בשבועה — נאמן, כי היכי דלא תיקשי דרבא אדרבא. דרבא אמר לקמן דמהימן לומר "החזרתי לך" במיגו דנאנסו, דקאמר רבא: הלכתא דנשבע וגובה מחצה. ואי בשבועת היסת איירי — היכי קאמר: בעדים א"צ להחזיר לו בעדים, ומהימן לומר "החזרתיו לך" בלא שבועה? הא לעולם בעי שבועת היסת! ואומר ר"ת: דהך שבועה דהכא מדרבנן, ונתקנה קודם שבועת היסת. כמו ההיא ד"הכותב" (כתובות דף פז:) דהפוגמת כתובתה ועד אחד מעידה שהיא פרועה, דקאמר התם דהויא שבועה דרבנן. **מ"ד** נשבע וגובה כולו לית ליה דרב חסדא. וא"ת: אכתי, אמאי גובה כולו? דניטעון ליתמי נאנסו! וי"ל: דמלתא דלא שכיח היא לא טענינן ליתמי, דנאנסו קלא אית ליה. ואע"ג דאבוהון הוי מהימן לומר שנאנסו, מיהו לא טענינן להו. ומאן דאמר נשבע וגובה מחצה — סבר דלא מצי אמר ליה "שטרך בידי מאי בעי". וטענינן להו "החזרתיו לך" אף על גב דלא טענינן להו נאנסו, כיון דאבוהון היה מהימן בטענה זו מיגו דאי בעי אמר נאנסו. ואין להקשות: לרבי אבא, דאית ליה מתוך שאינו יכול לישבע משלם, אמאי פטרינן להו? הא מחויבין הן שבועה ואין יכולין לישבע! דלגבי יורשין לא אמרינן מתוך שאינו יכול לישבע משלם, כדדרשינן בפ' "כל הנשבעין" (שבועות דף מז. ושם): "שבועת ה' תהיה בין שניהם" — ולא בין היורשין. ואם תאמר: לרב ושמואל דקאמרי התם: אין אדם מוריש שבועה לבניו, פי': אין אדם מוריש ממון שיש בו שבועה לבניו, אמאי פטורין מלשלם? וי"ל: דהא דאין אדם מוריש — היינו דאין נזקקין לא לשבועה ולא לפרעון, כדפירש הקונט' התם, ואם באין לגבות בשטר — אין גובין. אבל אם מוחזקין הן ובאין לגבות מהן, כי הכא — אין מוציאין מהן, ופטורין. וכן מוכח בהדיא בפ' "כל הנשבעין" (שם דף מח:) דמשני: הא מני ב"ש היא, דאמרי: שטר העומד לגבות כגבוי דמי. אלמא בדבר הגבוי אדם מוריש שבועה לבניו. **נשבע** וגובה מחצה. נראה דאינו נשבע על הכל, דלמה ישבע בחנם, כיון דאין משלמין לו אלא החצי? הלכך ישבע שבועה "שיש לי בידם, ואין לי בידם פחות מחצי", דלא ליהוי מרע ליה לדיבוריה, כי ההיא ד"שנים אוחזין בטלית" (ב"מ דף ה:). **דאם** איתא דפרע מימר הוה אמר. דוקא הכא שיש שטר על בניו היה לו להודיעם דפרוע הוא. אבל מלוה על פה אמרינן דאין גובה מן היורשין ואפילו הניח קרקעות, ואפי' מגדולים, אלא כשהודה ומת, א"נ דשמתוהו ומית בשמתא. דהתם לא אמרינן אם איתא דפרע מימר הוה אמר, דאין לו להודיעו כל מה שלוה ופרע כל ימי חייו, אלא דוקא הכא שיש שטר, כדפרישית. **אמר** רבא הלכתא נשבע וגובה מחצה. ומה שקשה דרבא אדרבא בשבועות, פירשתי לעיל. וריב"ם מפרש: דלא קשיא מידי, דהכי איתא התם: א"ל רבא: מאי מעלייתא, א"כ שבועת שומרין דחייב רחמנא היכי משכחת לה? מתוך שיכול לומר לא היו דברים מעולם — יכול לומר נאנסו! דאפקיד ליה בעדים. דאפקיד ליה בעדים נמי, מתוך שיכול לומר החזרתי לך יכול לומר נאנסו! דאפקיד ליה בשטר. פירוש, כיון דאפקיד ליה בשטר — איכא שבועה בנאנסו, דאז אין לומר מתוך שיכול לומר החזרתיו לך והיה נאמן בלא שבועה, דהא המפקיד אצל חבירו בשטר צריך להחזיר לו בעדים. ומן הדין אפילו בשבועה לא היה נאמן, אי לאו משום דמהימן במיגו דנאנסו בשבועה. והשתא אין להקשות כלום משם.

האחין

לָאו שְׁבוּעָה בָּעֵי. בִּתְמִיָּה. וְהַשְׁתָּא אָמְרַתְּ נֶאֱמָן בְּלֹא שְׁבוּעָה? וְע"י מִיגּוֹ לָא מָצֵית לְמִיפְטְרֵיהּ מִשְּׁבוּעָה ע"י טַעֲנָתוֹ לְקַיְּימָהּ בְּלֹא שְׁבוּעָה, כִּדְכְתִיב: "שְׁבוּעַת ה' תִּהְיֶה בֵּין שְׁנֵיהֶם". לֵימָא **בִּפְלוּגְתָּא**. הָא דְּרַב חִסְדָּא. שְׁטַר כִּיס הַיּוֹצֵא עַל הַיְתוֹמִים. רְאוּבֵן שֶׁנָּתַן מָעוֹת לְשִׁמְעוֹן לְמַחֲצִית שָׂכָר, וְכָתַב לוֹ שְׁטָר כַּמָּה הִפְקִיד לוֹ. וּמֵת שִׁמְעוֹן, וְהוֹצִיא רְאוּבֵן אוֹתוֹ שְׁטָר עַל הַיְתוֹמִים לִתְבּוֹעַ מֵהֶם פִּקְדוֹנוֹ. וְהַיְתוֹמִים טוֹעֲנִין: שֶׁמָּא אָבִינוּ הֶחֱזִירוֹ לְךָ. א"נ טַעֲנַת בָּרִי טְעָנוּ. וְאִילּוּ הָיָה מִלְוֶה בְּעָלְמָא, שֶׁהִלְוָה רְאוּבֵן לְשִׁמְעוֹן וּמֵת שִׁמְעוֹן — כּוּלֵּי עָלְמָא מוֹדוּ דְּנִשְׁבָּע רְאוּבֵן וְגוֹבֶה כָּל הַשְּׁטָר מִן הַיְתוֹמִים, דְּלֵית לַאֲבוּהוֹן שׁוּם טַעֲנָה גַּבֵּי מִלְוֶה, וְלָא (ב) מָצֵי טָעֵין נֶאֶנְסוּ, אֶלָּא הָיָה נִשְׁבָּע שֶׁלֹּא הִתְקַבֵּל מִן הַלֹּוֶה כְּלוּם, וּכְגוֹן שֶׁהָיָה טוֹעֲנוֹ הַלֹּוֶה: אִשְׁתַּבַּע לִי דְּלָא פְּרַעְתִּיךְ, כִּדְאָמְרִינַן בִּשְׁבוּעוֹת (דף מא.). וְגַבֵּי יַתְמֵי דִּידֵיהּ דְּלָא יָדְעִי לְמִיטְעַן — טָעֲנִינַן לְהוּ, וְנִשְׁבָּע וְגוֹבֶה חוֹבוֹ (ג) וכו'. אֲבָל הַשְׁתָּא דְּלָא הָוֵי כּוּלּוֹ מִלְוֶה, אֶלָּא פַּלְגָא מִלְוֶה וּפַלְגָא פִּקָּדוֹן, כְּדִין כָּל מָעוֹת הַנִּתּוּנוֹת לְמַחֲצִית שָׂכָר, כִּדְמְפָרֵשׁ וְאָזֵיל — הוּא דִּפְלִיגִי דַּיָּינֵי גוֹלָה, דְּהַיְינוּ שְׁמוּאֵל וְקַרְנָא, וְדַיָּינֵי א"י, דְּהַיְינוּ ר' אַמִי וְר' אַסִי, בְּפ"ק דְּסַנְהֶדְרִין (דף יז: ע"ש). נִרְאֶה בְּעֵינַי דְּה"ג: וּדְכ"ע אִית לְהוּ דִּנְהַרְדְּעֵי. וְכ"פ רַבֵּינוּ חֲנַנְאֵל. וְלָא גָּרַס: סַבְרוּהָ, דְּמַסְקָנָא נַמִי הָכִי ס"ל. דְּאָמְרִי נְהַרְדְּעֵי. בְּבָבָא מְלִיעָא, בְּפֶרֶק "הַמְקַבֵּל": הַאי עִיסְקָא דְּיָהֵיב אִינִישׁ לְחַבְרֵיהּ לְמַחֲצִית שָׂכָר — פַּלְגָא הָוֵי מִלְוֶה לְהִתְחַיֵּיב בְּאַחֲרָיוּת הַמְקַבֵּל, דְּהַיְינוּ אוֹתוֹ חֵצִי שֶׁנּוֹטֵל מִמֶּנּוּ הָרֶיוַח, וּפַלְגָא הָוֵי פִּקָּדוֹן גַּבֵּיהּ, וְאֵינוֹ חַיָּיב בְּאַחֲרָיוּתוֹ דְּהַךְ פַּלְגָא דְּקָשָׁקֵיל מִמֶּנָּה מַפְקִיד רַוְוחָא. וְהָתָם מְפָרֵשׁ טַעֲמָא: עֲבוּד רַבָּנַן מִילְּתָא דְּנִיחָא לֵיהּ לַלֹּוֶה וְנִיחָא לֵיהּ לַמַּלְוֶה, דְּאִיכָּא קְצָת אַחֲרָיוּת עַל זֶה וּקְצָת עַל זֶה, וְאִם נִגְנַב אוֹ אָבַד הַכֹּל — אֵין הָאֶחָד מַפְסִיד הַכֹּל, אֶלָּא בֵּין שְׁנֵיהֶן. וְהִלְכָּךְ, כֵּיוָן דִּסְתָמָא דְּמִילְּתָא כֵּן הוּא, דְּפַלְגָא הָוֵי מִלְוֶה גַּבֵּיהּ — צָרִיךְ הַנּוֹתֵן לְקַבֵּל עָלָיו תְּרֵי תִּילְתֵּי בְּהֶפְסֵד, הוֹאִיל וְשָׁקֵיל פַּלְגָא בְּאַגָּר, כִּי הֵיכִי דְּלָא לֶהֱוֵי רִבִּית מַאי דְּטָרַח מְקַבֵּל בְּפַלְגָא דְּפִקָּדוֹן מִשּׁוּם פַּלְגָא דְּמִלְוֶה שֶׁהִלְוָהוּ. דְּמַאי דִּמְקַבֵּל נוֹתֵן אַחֲרָיוּת עֲלֵיהּ טְפֵי מִפַּלְגָא — הָוֵי שָׂכָר לַמְקַבֵּל, בִּשְׁבִיל טִירְחָא דְּקָטָרַח בְּפַלְגָא פִּקָּדוֹן. אוֹ פַּלְגָא יְקַבֵּל הַנּוֹתֵן בְּהֶפְסֵד וְתִילְתָּא בְּאַגָּר, וּמְקַבֵּל יִטּוֹל תְּרֵי תִּילְתֵּי. דְּהַאי דְּקָשָׁקֵיל מְקַבֵּל רַוְוחָא טְפֵי מִפַּלְגָא — זֶהוּ שְׂכַר טִירְחָא, וְאֵין כָּאן רִבִּית. וְהָכִי מְפָרֵשׁ בְּ"אֵיזֶהוּ נֶשֶׁךְ" (ב"מ דף סח:). **מַאי לָאו**. בְּפַלְגָא דְּפִקָּדוֹן קָמִפַּלְגִי, בִּדְרַב חִסְדָּא, דְּאָמַר לְעֵיל: נֶאֱמָן? דִּבְפַלְגָא דְּמִלְוֶה הַכֹּל מוֹדִין דְּנִשְׁבָּע וְגוֹבֶה אוֹתוֹ, דַּאֲפִילּוּ אִי הֲוָה אֲבוּהוֹן קַיָּים לָא מָצֵי טָעֵין "הֶחֱזַרְתִּי", דְּאָמַר לֵיהּ "שְׁטָרָךְ בְּיָדִי מַאי בָּעֵי", וְטַעֲנַת מִיגּוֹ לֵיכָּא, דַּאֲפִילּוּ אִם נֶאֶנְסוּ צָרִיךְ לְהַחֲזִיר, דְּהָא מִלְוֶה הִיא גַּבֵּיהּ. הִלְכָּךְ נִשְׁבָּע וְגוֹבֶה, כְּדִין הַבָּא לִיפָּרַע מִנִּכְסֵי יְתוֹמִים. אֶלָּא בְּפַלְגָא דְּהָוֵי פִּקָּדוֹן קָמִיפַּלְגִי, וּבִדְרַב חִסְדָּא. דְּדַיָּינֵי גוֹלָה דְּאָמְרִי נִשְׁבָּע וְגוֹבֶה כּוּלּוֹ — לָא סְבִירָא לְהוּ כְּרַב חִסְדָּא דְּאָמַר נֶאֱמָן, אֶלָּא אִי הֲוָה אֲבוּהוֹן קַיָּים לָא הָוָה נֶאֱמָן לוֹמַר "הֶחֱזַרְתִּיו לְךָ", וְאַף עַל גַּב דְּאִיכָּא מִיגּוֹ דְּטַעֲנַת אוֹנֶס, מִשּׁוּם דְּא"ל אִידָךְ "שְׁטָרָךְ בְּיָדִי מַאי בָּעֵי". הִלְכָּךְ נִשְׁבָּע וְגוֹבֶה כּוּלּוֹ מִן הַיְתוֹמִים, אֲפִילּוּ פַּלְגָא דְּפִקָּדוֹן. וְדַיָּינֵי א"י סָבְרִי לָהּ כְּרַב חִסְדָּא, דְּאִילּוּ הָיָה אֲבוּהוֹן קַיָּים הֲוָה מָצֵי לְמִיטְעַן "הֶחֱזַרְתִּיו לְךָ", בְּמִיגּוֹ דַּהֲוָה מָצֵי לְמֵימַר נֶאֶנְסוּ, וְלָא הָוֵי אִידָךְ מָצֵי לְמֵימַר "שְׁטָרָךְ בְּיָדִי מַאי בָּעֵי". וְטָעֲנִינַן נַמִי הָכִי בִּשְׁבִיל יַתְמֵי. וּמִשְׁתַּבְּעֵי יַתְמֵי שְׁבוּעַת יוֹרְשִׁין, כִּדְמְפָרֵשׁ בִּשְׁבוּעוֹת: שְׁבוּעָה שֶׁלֹּא פְּקָדָנוּ אַבָּא כו' כִּדְמְפָרֵשׁ הָתָם. הִלְכָּךְ נִשְׁבָּע וְגוֹבֶה מֶחֱצָה מִלְוֶה, אֲבָל פַּלְגָא פִּקָּדוֹן לֵית לֵיהּ. ה"ג: **לָא דְּכ"ע אִית לְהוּ דְּרַב חִסְדָּא וְהָכָא** כו'. דַּיָּינֵי גוֹלָה סָבְרִי: בְּעָלְמָא סְבִירָא לָן כְּרַב חִסְדָּא, דְּנֶאֱמָן לוֹמַר "הֶחֱזַרְתִּיו לְךָ". אֲבָל גַּבֵּי יַתְמֵי לֵיכָּא לְמֵימַר הָכִי, דְּכֵיוָן דְּאִיכָּא שְׁטָרָא בְּיַד נוֹתֵן, וְאִיהוּ לָא קָטָעֵין "פְּרַעְתִּיךְ" — אֲנַן לָא טָעֲנִינַן לְיַתְמֵי. דְּאִם אִיתָא דִּפְרָעֵיהּ — מֵימַר הֲוָה אָמַר בִּשְׁעַת צַוָּאַת מִיתָה. וְהַשְׁתָּא דְּאִיכָּא תַּרְתֵּי: שְׁטָר בְּיַד הַנּוֹתֵן, וְגַם לֹא צִוָּה בִּשְׁעַת מִיתָה — הִלְכָּךְ נִשְׁבָּע וְגוֹבֶה כו'. **דְּאַנְסֵיהּ**. וְלֹא הִסְפִּיק לְצַוּוֹת. תַּרְתֵּי. בִּתְמִיָּה, דְּסָתְרָן אַהֲדָדֵי. דְּכֵיוָן דְּנֶאֱמָן — אַמַּאי נִשְׁבָּע וְגוֹבֶה כּוּלּוֹ? וְהָא מָצֵי אֲבוּהוֹן לְמִיטְעַן: הֶחֱזַרְתִּי לְךָ פַּלְגָא פִּקָּדוֹן,

וְנִטְעוֹן

ב"מ קד.

רבינו גרשום

סוף סוף כי אמר ליה נאנסתי מי לא צריך שבועה. אנא נמי הכי אמינא מאי נאמן בשבועה: שטר כים היוצא על היתומים. כגון מי שנתן לחבירו ממון שירויח לצורך שניהן והקרן של נותן וכתב לו שטר שכך וכך נתן לו ממון למחצית שכר ומת המקבל והוציא הנותן אותו שטר כים על היתומין: דייני גולה. דגרסי' בכל התלמוד היינו שמואל וקרנא: אמרו נשבע. הנותן וגובה כל הקרן שלו אע"ג דיש שטר בידו דהבא ליפרע מן היתומים לא יפרע אלא בשבועה: האי עיסקא. דיהיב חד ממון לחבירו להרויח לשניהן איהו לא הוי כולה פקדון ביד המקבל אלא שויוה רבנן פלגא מלוה ופלגא פקדון ועבדו מלתא דניחא ליה למלוה וניחא ליה ללוה. דאי אמרי' דכולה מלוה ביד המקבל ונגנבה או אבדה משלם המקבל כולה כדין מלוה שנגנבית כולה ואי אמרי' דכולה פקדון משתבע המקבל דנגנבה או אבדה וקא מפסיד הנותן הכל. ומש"ה פלגא מלוה כיון דאית ליה למקבל הנאה מיניה משלם פלגא ופלגא פקדון הואיל דהנותן אית ליה רווחא מיניה: מאי לאו בדרב חסדא קמיפלגי. דבעא מיניה רב עמרם מרב חסדא לעיל המפקיד אצל חבירו בשטר וכו' ואמר ליה רב חסדא נאמן ודייני גולה לית להו דרב חסדא דאם איתא דאית להו דרב חסדא לא הוו משלמי היתומין אלא פלגא דהיינו מלוה ולא הפקדון דמגו דאי בעו מצו למימר היתומין נאנסו בידי אבא ואמרי החזירו לך מהימני ולית להו לשלם אלא פלגא דמלוה דאההוא פלגא דמלוה לא מצי פטרי גופייהו בנאנס משום דחייב באחריות החצי. ודייני א"י אית להו דרב חסדא: לא דכ"ע אית להו דרב חסדא. ושאני התם אמאי אמרו דייני גולה הגובה כולה משום דליכא למימר מיגו ולא מצו לטעון אבא החזירו דאם איתא דפרעיה אבוהון מימר הוה אמר קודם מיתתו פרעתי. ודייני ארעא דישראל סברי לא יהיבנא ליה אלא פלגא דאכתי איכא למימר מגו. ודאמרת הוה ליה לאבוהון למימר. דאימר מלאך המות אנסיה בפתאום ולא מצי אמר: תרתי. ליכא למימר דסתרא דא ל[illegible] דאי אמרי' המפקיד אצל חבירו בשטר ואמר לו החזרתי לך נאמן לא אמרי' דשטר כים היוצא על היתומין דגבי כולה משום דהאי עסקא פלגא פקדון ואמרי' מגו. ומשני אמאי גובה כולו דאי איתא וכו': אנן דדייני גו[illegible]
איפכא

נז א מיי' פ"ב מהל' שכירות הל' יב סמג עשין פט טוש"ע ח"מ סי' רצו סעיף ב [וברב אלפס ב"מ פ"ג דף פז. ובכתובות פ"ט דף קיב.]:
נח ב מיי' פ"ז מהלכות שלוחין ושותפין הל' א ועי' בהשגות ובמ"מ סמג עשין סט טוש"ע ח"מ סי' קח סעיף ד [וברב אלפס ב"מ פ"ט דף קכח.]:
נט ג מיי' שם וסמג שם טוש"ע שם וטוש"ע י"ד סי' קעז סעיף ב:

הגהות הב"ח

(א) גמ' ומר סבר לא אמר ליה שטרך בידי בעי לא דכולי ע
(ב) רשב"ם ד"ה שטר וכו' ולא הוה מצי וכו': (ג) בא"ד וגובה כולו אבל השתא:

אִיפְּכָא מַתְנִינַן לָהּ.§ **מתני'** *אלֹא אֶת הַבּוֹר וְלֹא אֶת הַגַּת וְלֹא אֶת הַשּׁוֹבָךְ, בֵּין חֲרֵבִין בֵּין יְשׁוּבִין. בוְצָרִיךְ לִיקַּח לוֹ דֶּרֶךְ, דִּבְרֵי ר"ע; וַחכ"א: אֵינוֹ צָרִיךְ. (א) גוּמוֹדֶה ר"ע, בִּזְמַן שֶׁאָמַר לוֹ "חוּץ מֵאֵלּוּ" – שֶׁאֵינוֹ צָרִיךְ לִיקַּח לוֹ דֶּרֶךְ. מְכָרָן לְאַחֵר – ר"ע אוֹמֵר: אֵינוֹ צָרִיךְ לִיקַּח לוֹ דֶּרֶךְ, וַחכ"א: צָרִיךְ לִיקַּח לוֹ דֶּרֶךְ. *דבד"א – בְּמוֹכֵר, אֲבָל בְּנוֹתֵן מַתָּנָה – נוֹתֵן אֶת כּוּלָּהּ. ההָאַחִין שֶׁחָלְקוּ, זָכוּ בְּשָׂדֶה – זָכוּ בְּכוּלָּהּ. והַמַּחֲזִיק בְּנִכְסֵי הַגֵּר, הֶחֱזִיק בְּשָׂדֶה – הֶחֱזִיק בְּכוּלָּהּ. *זהַמַּקְדִּישׁ אֶת הַשָּׂדֶה – הִקְדִּישׁ אֶת כּוּלָּהּ; ר"ש אוֹמֵר: הַמַּקְדִּישׁ אֶת הַשָּׂדֶה – לֹא הִקְדִּישׁ אֶלָּא אֶת הֶחָרוּב הַמּוּרְכָּב וְאֶת סַדַּן הַשִּׁקְמָה.§ **גמ'** מַאי שְׁנָא מֶכֶר וּמַאי שְׁנָא מַתָּנָה? פֵּירֵשׁ יְהוּדָה בֶּן נְקוֹסָא לִפְנֵי רַבִּי: זֶה פֵּירֵשׁ וְזֶה לֹא פֵּירֵשׁ. הַאי זֶה פֵּירֵשׁ וְזֶה לֹא פֵּירֵשׁ, זֶה לֹא פֵּירֵשׁ וְזֶה לֹא פֵּירֵשׁ הוּא! חאֶלָּא, זֶה הָיָה לוֹ לְפָרֵשׁ, וְזֶה לֹא הָיָה לוֹ לְפָרֵשׁ. טהַהוּא דַּאֲמַר לְהוּ: הֲבוּ לֵיהּ לִפְלָנְיָא בֵּיתָא דְּמַחֲזִיק מְאָה גּוּלְפֵי, אִשְׁתַּכַּח דַּהֲוָה מַחֲזִיק מְאָה וְעֶשְׂרִין. אֲמַר מָר זוּטְרָא: מְאָה אֲמַר לֵיהּ, מְאָה וְעֶשְׂרִין לָא אֲמַר לֵיהּ. רַב אַשִׁי אֲמַר, מִי לָא תְּנַן: בַּמֶּה דְּבָרִים אֲמוּרִים – בְּמוֹכֵר, אֲבָל בְּנוֹתֵן מַתָּנָה – נוֹתֵן אֶת כּוּלָּן? אַלְמָא *מַאן דְּיָהֵיב מַתָּנָה – בְּעַיִן יָפָה יָהֵיב, יה"נ, מַאן דְּיָהֵיב מַתָּנָה – בְּעַיִן יָפָה יָהֵיב.§ "הַמַּקְדִּישׁ אֶת הַשָּׂדֶה – הִקְדִּישׁ" וכו'.§ אֲמַר רַב הוּנָא, אע"ג דַּאֲמוּר רַבָּנַן: *כהַקּוֹנֶה שְׁנֵי אִילָנוֹת בְּתוֹךְ שֶׁל חֲבֵירוֹ – הֲרֵי זֶה לֹא קָנָה קַרְקַע, למָכַר קַרְקַע וְשִׁיֵּיר שְׁנֵי אִילָנוֹת לְפָנָיו – יֵשׁ לוֹ קַרְקַע; וַאֲפִי' לר"ע דְּאָמַר: מוֹכֵר בְּעַיִן יָפָה מוֹכֵר, הָנֵי מִילֵּי *גַּבֵּי בּוֹר וְדוּת דְּלָא קָא מַכְחֲשֵׁי בְּאַרְעָא, אֲבָל אִילָנוֹת דְּקָא מַכְחֲשֵׁי בְּאַרְעָא, (ב)

אִם

שייך לדף ע: וְנִטְעוֹן נַמִּי לְיַתְמֵי! *אָמַר רָבָא הִלְכְתָא נִשְׁבָּע וְגוֹבֶה מֶחֱצָה. פַּלְגָא מִלְוֶה. אֲבָל פַּלְגָא פִּקָּדוֹן – לָא גָּבֵי, דְּטָעֲנִינַן לְהוּ לְיַתְמֵי: אֲבִיהֶם הֶחֱזִיר לָךְ. וּמִשְׁתַּבְּעִין שְׁבוּעַת יוֹרְשִׁין, וּפְטוּרִין. וְהַךְ דְּאָמְרִינַן בְּפֶ' "כָּל הַנִּשְׁבָּעִין" (שבועות דף מה:) אָמַר רָמִי בַּר חָמָא: כַּמָּה מַעַלְיָא הָא שְׁמַעְתָּא, א"ל רָבָא: מַאי מַעַלְיוּתָא כו', עַד: מִכְּלָל דְּתַרְוַיְיהוּ סְבִירָא לְהוּ הַמַּפְקִיד אֵצֶל חֲבֵירוֹ בְּעֵדִים א"צ לְהַחֲזִיר לוֹ בְּעֵדִים, [לעיל סד.] בִּשְׁטָר מִיהָא צָרִיךְ לְהַחֲזִיר לוֹ בִּשְׁטָר – פר"ח: וא"נ בְּעֵדִים. וְהָכָא קָפָסֵיק רָבָא נִשְׁבָּע וְגוֹבֶה מֶחֱצָה, דְּמַשְׁמַע דְּאֵין צָרִיךְ לְהַחֲזִיר לוֹ בְּעֵדִים, כְּרַב חִסְדָּא! אִיכָּא לְמֵימַר, דְּהַאי דְּקָאָמַר הָתָם: מִכְּלָל דְּתַרְוַיְיהוּ סְבִירָא לְהוּ – לָא קָאֵי [לעיל סה.] אֶלָּא אַהַמַּפְקִיד אֶת חֲבֵירוֹ בְּעֵדִים, אֲבָל אַהַמַּפְקִיד בִּשְׁטָר – לָא קָאֵי. וא"נ קָאֵי – לָאו דַּוְקָא, דְּהָא מִדְּרָמִי בַּר חָמָא [ערכין יד.] דְּשַׁנֵּי לְרָבָא דְּאַפְקִיד לֵיהּ בִּשְׁטָר, אִיכָּא לְמֵידַק דְּס"ל לְרָמִי בַּר חָמָא הָכִי. אֲבָל מִדְּשָׁתֵיק רָבָא לֵיכָּא לְמֵידַק, דְּהַאי דִּשְׁתֵיק – מִשּׁוּם דִּלְפִי סְבָרַת רָמִי בַּר חָמָא, דְּס"ל דְּמַפְקִיד בִּשְׁטָר צָרִיךְ לְהַחֲזִיר לוֹ בְּעֵדִים – לֵיכָּא לְאַקְשׁוּיֵי תּוּ. וּמִיהוּ, רָבָא אַכַּתִּי בְּקוּשְׁיָא קָאֵי, דְּלָא מַעַלְיָא הַהִיא שְׁמַעְתָּא כִּדְפָסֵיק הִלְכְתָא הָכָא: נִשְׁבָּע וְגוֹבֶה מֶחֱצָה וְאֵין צָרִיךְ לְהַחֲזִיר לוֹ בְּעֵדִים. **אִיפְּכָא** מַתְנִינַן. דַּיָּינֵי גוֹלָה אָמְרִי: נִשְׁבָּע וְגוֹבֶה מֶחֱצָה, דְּהַיְינוּ נַמִּי כְּרָבָא. **מתני' לֹא אֶת הַבּוֹר.** שֶׁבַּשָּׂדֶה, אע"פ שֶׁאָמַר לוֹ [לעיל נג. סה.] "כָּל מַה שֶּׁבְּתוֹכָהּ". **מְכָרָן לְאַחֵר.** [לקמן פא.] וְהַשָּׂדֶה עִיכֵּב לְעַצְמוֹ. **בַּמֶּה דְּבָרִים אֲמוּרִים.** כָּל הָנֵי לָא מָכַר דְּמַתְנִי' (ג). **בְּמוֹכֵר.** דַּאֲפִי' לְמ"ד מוֹכֵר בְּעַיִן יָפָה [לעיל לז. לקמן פב:] מוֹכֵר, ה"מ דְּמַה שֶּׁמְּפָרֵשׁ בִּמְכִירָתוֹ מָכַר הַכֹּל, וְלֹא עִיכֵּב לְעַצְמוֹ כְּלוּם מִמַּה שֶּׁמָּכַר לַחֲבֵירוֹ, כְּגוֹן הַמּוֹכֵר בַּיִת וְשָׂדֶה, שֶׁלֹּא עִיכֵּב דֶּרֶךְ לֵילֵךְ לְבוֹרוֹ וּלְדוּתוֹ וּלְגִתּוֹ. אֲבָל לִמְכּוֹר יוֹתֵר מִמַּה שֶּׁפֵּירֵשׁ – לְגַבֵּי הָכִי לָא הָוֵי עַיִן יָפָה לִמְכּוֹר בִּכְלַל שָׂדֶה דְּבָרִים אֲחֵרִים שֶׁאֵינָן בִּכְלַל שָׂדֶה. **אֲבָל בְּנוֹתֵן מַתָּנָה נוֹתֵן אֶת כּוּלָּהּ.** כָּל הָנֵי (ד) דְּאָמְרוּ לָא מָכַר, וַאֲפִילּוּ הָנֵי דְּאֵינָן בִּכְלַל מַה שֶּׁבְּתוֹכָהּ, כְּגוֹן חָרוּב הַמּוּרְכָּב וְסַדַּן הַשִּׁקְמָה, וּבוֹר וְגַת וְשׁוֹבָךְ. וְהָכִי מוֹכַח גַּבֵּי הֶקְדֵּשׁ, וה"ה לְכָל הָנָךְ. וְטַעֲמָא, מִשּׁוּם דְּנוֹתֵן בְּעַיִן יָפָה נוֹתֵן יוֹתֵר מִדַּאי, וַאֲפִילּוּ מַאי דְּלָא הָוֵי בִּכְלַל שָׂדֶה, הוֹאִיל וְקָבוּעַ בְּתוֹךְ הַשָּׂדֶה. וּמִיהוּ, אִם יֵשׁ מָעוֹת בַּשָּׂדֶה, אוֹ תְּבוּאָה תְּלוּשָׁה שֶׁאֵינָהּ צְרִיכָה לְקַרְקַע, אוֹ כָּל דָּבָר שֶׁלֹּא הוּצְרַךְ לַתַּנָּא דְּמַתְנִי' לְהַזְכִּיר וְלוֹמַר לָא מָכַר, מִשּׁוּם דְּמִילְּתָא דִּפְשִׁיטָא הוּא דְּאֵינוֹ בִּכְלַל שָׂדֶה כְּלָל – הַהִיא וַדַּאי לָא קָנָה לָהּ מְקַבֵּל מַתָּנָה. **זָכָה בְּכוּלָּהּ.** אֲפִילּוּ בּוֹר וְגַת וְשׁוֹבָךְ שֶׁבַּשָּׂדֶה קָנָה. שֶׁכֵּיוָן שֶׁזֶּה נוֹטֵל שָׂדֶה אַחַת וְזֶה אַחַת כְּנֶגְדּוֹ – לְהִסְתַּלֵּק זֶה מִשֶּׁל זֶה נִתְכַּוְּונוּ. וּמִיהוּ, לִהְיוֹת לוֹ דֶּרֶךְ לִפְנִימִי עַל הַחִיצוֹן אִיכָּא לְמֵימַר דְּאִית לֵיהּ, כְּרַב, כִּדְפָרִישְׁנָא טַעַם לְעֵיל (דף סה.) דְּא"ל: אָדוּר בַּשָּׂדֶה שֶׁלִּי כִּי הֵיכִי דְּדָרוּ בָּהּ אֲבָהָתַי, כִּדְכְתִיב: "תַּחַת אֲבוֹתֶיךָ יִהְיוּ בָנֶיךָ". **הֶחֱזִיק בְּכוּלָּהּ.** אֲפִילּוּ בְּחָרוּב וְסַדָּן, וְאע"ג דְּחָשֵׁיבְנָא לֵיהּ בַּגְּמָ' כִּשְׁתֵּי שָׂדוֹת, וְגַבֵּי ב' שָׂדוֹת וּמֶצֶר אֶחָד בֵּינֵיהוּ וְהֶחֱזִיק בְּאַחַת מֵהֶן ע"מ לִקְנוֹת אוֹתָהּ וְאֶת חֲבֶירְתָּהּ, אָמְרִינַן בְּ"חֶזְקַת הַבָּתִּים" (לעיל דף נג:): אוֹתָהּ קָנָה חֲבֶירְתָּהּ לֹא קָנָה – אפ"ה הָכָא קָנָה. דְּהָנֵי נַמִּי דְּב' שָׂדוֹת חָשְׁבִינַן לְשָׂדֶה וּלְחָרוּב הַמּוּרְכָּב, מִיהוּ לֵיכָּא מֶצֶר בֵּינֵיהֶן, דְּכִב' שָׂדוֹת וְאֵין מֶצֶר אַחֵר בֵּינֵיהֶן דָּמוּ. **הִקְדִּישׁ אֶת כּוּלָּן.** דִּבְעַיִן יָפָה מַקְדִּישׁ כְּמוֹ נוֹתֵן. **ר"ש אוֹמֵר הַמַּקְדִּישׁ אֶת הַשָּׂדֶה לֹא הִקְדִּישׁ** כְּלוּם. מִכָּל אוֹתָן דְּבָרִים שֶׁאָמַרְנוּ גַּבֵּי מוֹכֵר דְּלָא מָכַר. דְּהַמַּקְדִּישׁ דַּעְתּוֹ כְּדַעַת מוֹכֵר, שֶׁלֹּא הִקְדִּישׁ אֶלָּא מַה שֶּׁפֵּירֵשׁ. **אֶלָּא אֶת חָרוּב הַמּוּרְכָּב כו'.** דְּאע"ג דְּגַבֵּי מְכִירַת הַשָּׂדֶה אֵינָן מְכוּרִין, הָכָא מוּקְדָּשִׁין. וְטַעֲמָא מְפָרֵשׁ בַּגְּמָ'. **גמ' מַאי שְׁנָא מֶכֶר וּמ"ש מַתָּנָה.** נְהִי נַמִּי דְּנוֹתֵן בְּעַיִן יָפָה נוֹתֵן טְפֵי מִמּוֹכֵר, אפ"ה, זִימְנִין שֶׁאֵינוֹ נוֹתֵן אֶלָּא מַה שֶּׁמְּפָרֵשׁ בְּפִיו. אֲבָל מִידֵּי שֶׁאֵינוֹ בִּכְלָל – לָא קָיָהֵיב. כְּגוֹן הָנָךְ דִּתְנַן בְּהוּ: לֹא מָכַר. **זֶה פֵּירֵשׁ.** נוֹתֵן פֵּירֵשׁ לוֹ אֶת הַכֹּל, וְהִלְכָּךְ קָנָה הַכֹּל. וּלְקַמֵּיהּ פָּרֵיךְ עֲלָהּ. וּמִתְמַהּ: הַאי כו' וַהֲרֵי זֶה **לֹא פֵּירֵשׁ** (ה). דְּהַמּוֹכֵר וְהַנּוֹתֵן סְתָמָא קָתָנֵי! **זֶה הָיָה לוֹ לְפָרֵשׁ.** נוֹתֵן מַתָּנָה, כֵּיוָן דְּרָגִיל לִיתֵּן בְּעַיִן יָפָה, אִם אִיתָא דְּהַאי לָאו בְּעַיִן יָפָה יָהֵיב – הָיָה לוֹ לְפָרֵשׁ וּלְשַׁיֵּיר בּוֹר וָגַת וְשׁוֹבָךְ וְכָל הָנָךְ דְּמַתְנִי' וּמִדְּלָא (ו) שִׁיֵּיר – הִפְסִיד. אֲבָל מוֹכֵר – זוּזֵי אֲנָסוּהוּ, וְלֹא מָכַר אֶלָּא מַה שֶּׁפֵּירֵשׁ. וַאֲפִילּוּ אִם יֵשׁ שֶׁרָגִיל לִמְכּוֹר בְּעַיִן יָפָה – מִסְּתָמָא אֵין לוֹמַר כֵּן, דְּיַד לוֹקֵחַ עַל הַתַּחְתּוֹנָה, דְּלָא הָיָה לוֹ לְפָרֵשׁ. וְרַבֵּינוּ חֲנַנְאֵל פֵּירֵשׁ: הַקּוֹנֶה הָיָה לוֹ לְפָרֵשׁ. דְּכֵיוָן שֶׁנּוֹתֵן דָּמִים אֵינוֹ מִתְפַּיֵּיס מִן הַמּוֹכֵר, וּמִדְּלָא הִזְקִיק לַמּוֹכֵר לְפָרֵשׁ לוֹ הַכֹּל – הִפְסִיד. אֲבָל מְקַבֵּל מַתָּנָה – בּוֹשֶׁת יֵשׁ לוֹ מִן הַנּוֹתֵן, וְאֵין לוֹ לְפָרֵשׁ וְלִשְׁאוֹל לוֹ בּוֹר וָגַת וְשׁוֹבָךְ. הִלְכָּךְ עֲלֵיהּ דְּנוֹתֵן רָמְיָא לְגַלּוּיֵי, וְאִם לֹא פֵּירֵשׁ – קָנָה הַכֹּל. **דְּמַחֲזִיק מְאָה גּוּלְפֵי.** בְּקַרְקַע, רוֹחַב וְאוֹרֶךְ הַבַּיִת יְכוֹלִין לְסַדֵּר מֵאָה חָבִיּוֹת, דְּהַיְינוּ י' חָבִיּוֹת אוֹרֶךְ עַל י' חָבִיּוֹת רוֹחַב. **דַּהֲוָה מַחֲזִיק מֵאָה וְעֶשְׂרִים.** וְלֹא הָיָה לוֹ בַּיִת אַחֵר שֶׁל מֵאָה. **מֵאָה וְעֶשְׂרִים לֹא א"ל.** וְיִטּוֹל בַּבַּיִת ה' חֲלָקִים, וְחֵלֶק ו' דְּהַיְינוּ כ' חָבִיּוֹת, יַפְסִיד. **בְּעַיִן יָפָה יָהֵיב.** כָּל הַבַּיִת כּוּלּוֹ. וְהַאי דְּקָאָמַר מַחֲזִיק מְאָה גּוּלְפֵי – סָבוּר הָיָה שֶׁלֹּא הָיָה מַחֲזִיק יוֹתֵר, וּלְשֵׁם חֲשִׁיבוּת אָמַר כֵּן, דְּמַתָּנָה גְּדוֹלָה כָּזוֹאת נוֹתֵן לוֹ. **דַּאֲמוּר רַבָּנַן.** בְּמַתְנִי' דְּ"הַמּוֹכֵר אֶת הַסְּפִינָה" (לקמן דף פא.). **שְׁנֵי אִילָנוֹת.** אֲבָל ג' חֲשִׁיבִי שְׂדֵה אִילָן, וְקָנָה קַרְקַע בֵּינֵיהֶן וְחוּצָה לָהֶן כִּמְלֹא אוֹרֶה וְסַלּוֹ, וְאִם מֵתוּ יֵשׁ לוֹ קַרְקַע. (ז) כִּדְתְנַן לְקַמָּן בְּ"הַמּוֹכֵר אֶת הַסְּפִינָה". **ה"ז לֹא קָנָה קַרְקַע.** בֵּינֵיהֶן וְחוּצָה לָהֶן. וְגַם אִם מֵתוּ – אֵין לוֹ קַרְקַע לִיטַּע אֲחֵרִים בִּמְקוֹמָן, כִּדְתְנַן לְקַמָּן בְּאִידָךְ פִּירְקִין. וְלֹא קָנָה אֶלָּא לְפֵירוֹתָיו, כָּל זְמַן שֶׁיִּתְקַיֵּים הָאִילָן. וְאַלִּיבָּא דְּרַבָּנַן קָאֵי, דְּאָמְרִי (ח) בְּעַיִן רָעָה מוֹכֵר, אֲבָל אַלִּיבָּא דר"ע יֵשׁ לוֹ קַרְקַע לִיטַּע אֲחֵרִים בִּמְקוֹמָן אִם יָמוּתוּ אֵלּוּ. כִּדְמוֹכַח לְקַמָּן בִּשְׁמַעְתִּין גַּבֵּי מַקְדִּישׁ ג' אִילָנוֹת בָּזֶה אַחַר זֶה, דְּאָמְרִינַן דְּלֹא הִקְדִּישׁ קַרְקַע, אָמְרִי' אֲפִי' ר"ע – הָא מוֹכֵר בְּעַיִן יָפָה מוֹכֵר, וכ"ש מַקְדִּישׁ. אַלְמָא, בְּמוֹכֵר ב' אִילָנוֹת לַחֲבֵירוֹ, דְּהַיְינוּ דּוּמְיָא דְּג' אִילָנוֹת בָּזֶה אַחַר זֶה – דְּקָנָה קַרְקַע עִם הָאִילָן. וְה"נ אָמְרִינַן בְּ"חֶזְקַת הַבָּתִּים" (לעיל דף לז:): מָכַר אִילָנוֹת וְשִׁיֵּיר קַרְקַע לְפָנָיו – פְּלוּגְתָּא דר"ע וְרַבָּנַן. וְאע"ג דְּסֵיפָא דְּמַיְירֵי בְּג' אִילָנוֹת מוֹקְמִינַן לְקַמָּן בְּאִידָךְ פִּירְקִין אֲפִילּוּ כְּר"ע מִיהוּ רֵישָׁא לָאו ר"ע הִיא. **יֵשׁ לוֹ קַרְקַע.** לִיטַּע אַחֵר בִּמְקוֹמוֹ, דִּבְעַיִן רָעָה מָכַר לוֹ הַקַּרְקַע. **וַאֲפִי' לר"ע.** גְּמָרָא קָאָמַר לֵיהּ, דַּאֲפִילּוּ לר"ע אֲמָרָהּ רַב הוּנָא. דְּאִי לְרַבָּנַן – פְּשִׁיטָא, כִּדְפָרֵיךְ לְקַמָּן. **הָנֵי מִילֵּי.** גַּבֵּי מָכַר אֶת הַבַּיִת וְשִׁיֵּיר בּוֹר וָדוּת, דְּלֵית לֵיהּ שׁוּם הֶיזֵּק לַלּוֹקֵחַ, דְּהָא לָא מַכְחֲשֵׁי בְּאַרְעָא, וְהִלְכָּךְ לֹא חָשַׁשׁ לְשַׁיֵּיר כְּלוּם מִן הַקַּרְקַע סְבִיב הַבּוֹר, וְלֹא הַדֶּרֶךְ. אֲבָל אִילָנוֹת שֶׁמְּקַלְקְלִין אֶת הַקַּרְקַע – שִׁיֵּיר מִן הַקַּרְקַע עִם הָאִילָנוֹת אַף לַחֲזוֹר וְלִיטַּע בִּמְקוֹמָן אִם יַזְקִינוּ אֵלּוּ, מִשּׁוּם דְּלָא נֵימָא לֵיהּ לוֹקֵחַ: עֲקוֹר אִילָנָךְ כְּשֶׁיָּמוּת, וְהִיפָּטֵר מִכָּאן.

דְּאִם

האחין שחלקו זכו בשדה זכו בכולה. וא"ת: לרב דאמר לעיל (דף סה.): יש להן דרך זה על זה משום דמוכר בעין רעה מוכר, היכי אמר הכא זכו בכולה כמו גבי מתנה? וי"ל: הכא לאו משום עין יפה הוא, אלא משום דרוצין להסתלק זה מזה, ואין משיירין לכל אחד אלא הצריך לחלקו, כגון דרך. **אמר** רב הונא אע"ג דאמור רבנן הקונה שני אילנות כו'. וא"ת: לפי' רבינו שמואל, דלר"ע דאמר בעין יפה מוכר, קנה אילן אחד יש לו קרקע, מאי קאמר רב הונא: אף על גב דאמרי רבנן הקונה ב' אילנות אין לו קרקע כו', משמע דאי הוה אמר דקנה קרקע — אז לא היה חידוש במשייר ב' אילנות, דיש לו קרקע. א"כ מאי קאמר: ואפילו לר"ע וכו', מה אפילו? הא לדידיה קנה אילן אחד יש לו קרקע! וי"ל דה"ק: דאע"ג דאמור רבנן דב' אילנות לא קנה קרקע ובשלשה קנה — משום דלא אזיל קרקע בתר אילנות אלא כשיש ג' ולא בב', ולא מטעם עין יפה, אפ"ה, בשייר — אזיל קרקע בתר שני. והשתא ודאי אי לאו טעמא דעין יפה, ה"א (ט) דבשנים קנה קרקע — כל שכן בשייר שני אילנות לפניו דיש לו קרקע.

לימא

ם א ב ג מיי' פכ"ו מהל' מכירה הל' ג ד סמג עשין פב טוש"ע ח"מ סי' רטו סעיף ה:

סא ד מיי' שם הל' ה טוש"ע שם סעיף ו:

סב ה ו ז מיי' שם הל' ו טוש"ע שם סעיף ז:

סג ח מיי' שם הל' ה טוש"ע שם סעיף ו:

סד ט י מיי' פי"א מהל' זכיה ומתנה הל' כב סמג שם טוש"ע ח"מ סי' רנג סעיף יד:

סה כ מיי' פכ"ד מהל' מכירה הל' ו סמג שם טוש"ע ח"מ סי' רטז סעיף ט:

סו ל מיי' שם הל' ח טוש"ע שם סעיף יח:

רבינו גרשום

איפכא מתנינן. דהכי אמרו דאינו גובה אלא מחצה: זה פירש. שהוא קונה השדה מן המוכר. וכיון דלא פירש כל הדבר שבה הלכך לא קנה הני דמפיק מתני' וזה המקבל מתנה אין דרכו לפרש מהמקבל הלכך יש לו הכל. ומקשה רבי האי זה לא פירש וזה לא פירש הוא. דאין דרכו של קונה לכתוב כך אני קונה אלא המוכר דרכו לכתוב כך וכך אני מוכר: אלא זה היה לו לפרש. ללוקח שנותן דמים היה לו לדקדק שיכתוב לו המוכר בשטר כל מה שיש בשדה וכיון דלא דקדק שיפרוש לו הוא הוא דאפסיד אנפשיה ואין לו כל הני דמפיק מתני'. אבל המקבל מתנה לא היה לו לפרש לדקדק שיתן לו הכל אלא כיון שנתן לו סתם ולא אמר חוץ מזה קנה הכל: מאה גולפי. מאה חביות: **פיסקא** האחין שחלקו. זכו בשדה: בכולה. שחלקו עם הבור ועם הדות דכל אחד מקנה לחבירו חלקו בעין יפה: המקדיש את השדה הקדיש את כולה. דכל המקדיש בעין יפה מקדיש אפי' הבור והדות: ר"ש אומר המקדיש את השדה לא הקדיש. מכל הני דקתני מתני' טפי ממוכר אלא חרוב ושקמה דהמוכר לא מכר והמקדיש הקדיש כדמפרש בגמ': הרי זה לא קנה קרקע. דג' אילנות יש להן קרקע ולא לשנים: דלא מכחשי בארעא. לא לניר ולא לזריעה הלכך לא קפיד בעל השדה הלוקח בהן והן של מוכר השדה וצריך ליקח לו דרך אבל הכא היכא דמשייר אילנות דהנהו אילנות שרשייהו מכחשי בהקרקע ולא אמר ליה הלוקח כלום ש"מ דודאי שיורי משייר המוכר קרקע מקום האילנות לפניו להכי לא קאמר ליה מידי:

הגהות הב"ח

(א) במשנה וחכ"א אינו ...ך ליקח לו דרך ומודה: (ב) גמ' דקא מכחשי ...עא שיוריה שייר דאם ...את: (ג) רשב"ם ד"ה ...ה דברים וכו' דמתני' ...רקין הס"ד: (ד) ד"ה ...ל וכו' כל הני דאמרן לא ...ר ואפי' הנהו דאינן ...לל: (ה) ד"ה ומתמה ...' לא פירש הוא ...מוכר: (ו) ד"ה זה היה ...' ומדלא פירש הפסיד: ... ד"ה שני אילנות וכו' ... לו קרקע ליטע אחרים ...קומן כדתנן לקמן: ...) ד"ה ה"ז וכו' דאמרי ...כר בעין: (ט) תום' ד"ה ...מר וכו' ה"א דכיון דבשנים קנה.

אִם אִיתָא דְּלָא שַׁיֵּיר, לֵימָא לֵיהּ: "עֲקוֹר אִילָנָךְ שְׁקוֹל וְזִיל". תְּנַן, ר' שִׁמְעוֹן אוֹמֵר: הַמַּקְדִּישׁ אֶת הַשָּׂדֶה — לֹא הִקְדִּישׁ אֶלָּא חָרוּב הַמּוּרְכָּב וְסַדַּן הַשִּׁקְמָה; וְתָנֵי עֲלָהּ, אָמַר ר"ש: מַה טַּעַם? הוֹאִיל וְיוֹנְקִין מִשְּׂדֵה הֶקְדֵּשׁ; וְאִי סָלְקָא דַּעְתָּךְ שִׁיּוּרֵי שַׁיֵּיר, כִּי קָא יָנְקִי — מִדְּנַפְשֵׁיהּ קָא יָנְקִי! ר"ש דְּאָמַר — כְּר"ע. וְרַב הוּנָא דְּאָמַר — כְּרַבָּנַן. כְּרַבָּנַן, פְּשִׁיטָא! נָפְקָא מִינָּהּ, דְּאִי נָפְלֵי הָדַר שָׁתֵיל לְהוּ. וּמִי

דְּאִם אִיתָא דְּלָא שַׁיֵּיר כו'. וַהֲנַן סָהֲדֵי דִּלְדַעַת כֵּן עִיכֵּב אֶת הָאִילָנוֹת לְעַצְמוֹ – שֶׁיִּהְיוּ כָּאן לְעוֹלָם, אַף לַחֲזוֹר וְלִיטַּע אֲחֵרִים בִּמְקוֹמָן, כְּדֶרֶךְ שֶׁהָיָה לוֹ כֹּחַ זֶה בָּאִילָנוֹת הַלָּלוּ עַד עַכְשָׁיו. אֲבָל לוֹקֵחַ אִילָנוֹת – אֵין לוֹמַר לְצוֹרֶךְ כָּל הַיָּמִים לְקָחוֹ וְלִיטַּע אֲחֵרִים בִּמְקוֹמָן, דַּעֲבִיד אִינִישׁ דְּזָבֵין אַרְעָא לְיוֹמֵיהּ, וּלְפֵירוֹת קְנָאוֹ. לֹא הִקְדִּישׁ. מִכָּל הָנָךְ דַּאֲמָרַן: לֹא מָכַר. אֶלָּא חָרוּב הַמּוּרְכָּב כו'. אֲבָל שְׁאָר אִילָנוֹת מֵאֵילָא קְדוֹשִׁים הֵם בִּכְלַל שָׂדֶה, כְּמוֹ שֶׁמְּכוּרִין מִסְתָּמָא בִּכְלַל שָׂדֶה. אָמַר ר"ש מַה טַּעַם. הָווּ מוּקְדָּשִׁין חָרוּב וְסַדָּן טְפֵי מִכָּל הָנָךְ דִּלְעֵיל? דְּס"ל מַקְדִּישׁ כְּמוֹכֵר, שֶׁלֹּא הִקְדִּישׁ אֶלָּא דְּבָרִים דְּשַׁיְּיכִי לַשָּׂדֶה טוּבָא, דְּהָווּ נַמִי מְכוּרִין לְעִנְיַן מֶכֶר, וְהִלְכָּךְ חָרוּב הַמּוּרְכָּב אֵינוֹ מוּקְדָּשׁ בִּכְלַל שָׂדֶה. הוֹאִיל וְיוֹנְקִין מִשְּׂדֵה הֶקְדֵּשׁ. הוּא הִקְדִּישׁ אֶת הַשָּׂדֶה בְּעַיִן יָפָה, אֲפִילּוּ מְקוֹם הֶחָרוּב וְהַסַּדָּן, וּכְשֶׁשִּׁיְּירוֹ לְעַצְמוֹ – לֹא שִׁיֵּיר עִמָּהֶן קַרְקַע. נִמְצְאוּ גְּדֵלִים מִקַּרְקַע הֶקְדֵּשׁ, וְגִידּוּלֵי הֶקְדֵּשׁ הֶקְדֵּשׁ נִינְהוּ. אַלְמָא: הַמְשַׁיֵּיר אִילָנוֹת לְעַצְמוֹ – אֵינוֹ מְשַׁיֵּיר קַרְקַע, אֶלָּא בְּעַיִן יָפָה מוֹכֵר וּמַקְדִּישׁ כָּל הַקַּרְקַע. וְאִי אָמְרַתְּ. דְּמַאן דְּמְזַבֵּין קַרְקַע לְאַחֵר וּמְשַׁיֵּיר אִילָנוֹת לְעַצְמוֹ – מְשַׁיֵּיר כְּמוֹ כֵן קַרְקַע יְנִיקַת הָאִילָנוֹת, וְה"ה לְמַקְדִּישׁ אַלִּיבָּא דְּר"ש דְּהָא כִּי הֲדָדֵי נִינְהוּ – א"כ אַמַּאי קָדְשֵׁי חָרוּב וְסַדָּן מִשּׁוּם שֶׁיּוֹנְקִין מִשְּׂדֵה הֶקְדֵּשׁ? הָא כִּי יָנְקִי – מִדְּנַפְשַׁיְיהוּ קָא יָנְקִי, מִמַּה שֶׁשִּׁיֵּיר לְעַצְמוֹ, וְלֹא מִקַּרְקַע הֶקְדֵּשׁ! וּמְשַׁנֵּי: ר"ש דְּאָמַר כְּר"ע. רְצוֹ, דְּמוֹכֵר בְּעַיִן יָפָה מוֹכֵר הַכֹּל, וְלֹא שִׁיֵּיר מִן הַקַּרְקַע כְּלוּם, בֵּין לְצוֹרֶךְ דֶּרֶךְ בּוֹר וְדוּת שֶׁעִיכֵּב, בֵּין לִינִיקַת הָאִילָנוֹת שֶׁשִּׁיֵּיר לְפָנָיו. וּמָצֵי לוֹקֵחַ לְמֵימַר לֵיהּ: הַיּוֹם וּלְמָחָר כְּשֶׁיִּיבַשׁ הָאִילָן – עֲקוֹר אִילָנָךְ שְׁקוֹל וְזִיל. וְה"ה לְהֶקְדֵּשׁ. וּמִיהוּ, לְגַבֵּי מוֹכֵר בִּכְלַל שָׂדֶה דְּבָרִים שֶׁאֵינָן בִּכְלָלוֹ – לֹא שַׁיָּיךְ לְמֵימַר עַיִן יָפָה וְעַיִן רָעָה, דְּמַה שֶּׁלֹּא פֵּירֵשׁ – לֹא מָכַר. וְהַשְׁתָּא הָדַר בֵּיהּ הַגְּמָרָא מִמַּאי דְּקָאמַר לְעֵיל: וַאֲפִילּוּ לְרַבִּי עֲקִיבָא כו'. וְרַב הוּנָא. דִּמְשַׁיֵּיר קַרְקַע עִם הָאִילָנוֹת, דְּקָאמַר כְּרַבָּנַן, דִּבְעַיִן רָעָה מוֹכֵר, וְשִׁיֵּיר לְעַצְמוֹ מִמַּה שֶּׁמָּכַר אֶת הַצָּרִיךְ לִינִיקַת אִילָנוֹתָיו, דּוּמְיָא דְּדֶרֶךְ בּוֹרוֹ וְדוּתוֹ שֶׁשִּׁיֵּיר עִם הַבּוֹר וְהַדּוּת. וּמִיהוּ, בְּמַסְקָנָא דִּשְׁמַעְתָּא מִיתּוֹקְמָא הָא דְּרַב הוּנָא אֲפִילּוּ לְר"ע. וְה"נ אָמְרִינַן בְּ"חֶזְקַת הַבָּתִּים" (לעיל דף לז.): פְּשִׁיטָא, מָכַר קַרְקַע וְשִׁיֵּיר הָאִילָנוֹת לְפָנָיו – יֵשׁ לוֹ קַרְקַע, וַאֲפִילּוּ לְר' עֲקִיבָא כו'. וְהָא דִּמְשַׁנֵּי גְּמָרָא: ר"ש דְּאָמַר כְּר"ע וְלָא קָמְשַׁנֵּי: ר"ש ס"ל הַמַּקְדִּישׁ בְּעַיִן יָפָה מַקְדִּישׁ טְפֵי מִמּוֹכֵר, דְּאִילּוּ מוֹכֵר וְשִׁיֵּיר אִילָנוֹת לְפָנָיו כְּמוֹ כֵן שִׁיֵּיר קַרְקַע לְעַצְמוֹ כִּדְרַב הוּנָא, אֲבָל מַקְדִּישׁ בְּעַיִן יָפָה הִקְדִּישׁ הַכֹּל וְלֹא שִׁיֵּיר אֶלָּא הֶחָרוּב לְבַדּוֹ בְּלֹא קַרְקַע. לֵיכָּא לְמֵימַר הָכִי, דְּאִם כֵּן לָאו לַמּוֹכֵר מְדַמֵּי לֵיהּ מִכֹּל וָכֹל, וְלֹא לְנוֹתֵן מַתָּנָה מְדַמֵּי לֵיהּ מִכֹּל וָכֹל, אֶלָּא קְצָת מְדַמֵּי לֵיהּ לַמּוֹכֵר – דְּלֹא הִקְדִּישׁ אֶלָּא דְּבָרִים שֶׁבִּכְלַל שָׂדֶה, וּלְנוֹתֵן מַתָּנָה מְדַמֵּי לֵיהּ – שֶׁלֹּא שִׁיֵּיר כְּלוּם לְעַצְמוֹ בַּמֶּה שֶׁפֵּירֵשׁ וְהִקְדִּישׁ, דְּכָל הַקַּרְקַע הִקְדִּישׁ וְלֹא שִׁיֵּיר מְקוֹם יְנִיקַת חָרוּב. וְהָא לָאו סְבָרָא הוּא, אֶלָּא אוֹ לְנוֹתֵן מַתָּנָה מְדַמֵּי לֵיהּ לְגַמְרֵי, כְּרַבָּנַן דְּאָמְרֵי הִקְדִּישׁ אֶת כּוּלָּן, אוֹ לְמוֹכֵר מְדַמִּינָא לֵיהּ מִכֹּל וָכֹל, דְּכִי הֵיכִי דְּמוֹכֵר שָׂדֶה לֹא מָכַר בּוֹר וְגַת וְשׁוֹבָךְ – הוּא הַדִּין לְמַקְדִּישׁ. וְכִי הֵיכִי דְּמוֹכֵר בְּעַיִן יָפָה מוֹכֵר, כָּל מַה שֶּׁפֵּירֵשׁ בִּמְכִירָתוֹ וְלֹא שִׁיֵּיר מִן הַקַּרְקַע כְּלוּם, אֲפִילּוּ לִינִיקַת אִילָנוֹתָיו ה"ה לְמַקְדִּישׁ. וְקָמַתְמַהּ: כְּרַבָּנַן פְּשִׁיטָא. כֵּיוָן דִּבְעַיִן רָעָה מוֹכֵר. וְעוֹד, דְּמָצֵי לוֹקֵחַ לְמֵימַר לֵיהּ: עֲקוֹר אִילָנָךְ, שְׁקוֹל וְזִיל, מִשּׁוּם דְּמַכְחֲשֵׁי בְּאַרְעָא – קַל וָחוֹמֶר הוּא: לְגַבֵּי בּוֹר וְדוּת דְּלָא מַכְחֲשֵׁי בְּאַרְעָא, וַאפ"ה אָמְרֵי רַבָּנַן דְּשִׁיֵּיר דֶּרֶךְ לְעַצְמוֹ לְבוֹרוֹ וּלְדוּתוֹ – כָּל שֶׁכֵּן גַּבֵּי אִילָן! נָפְקָא מִינָּהּ. הָא דְּרַב הוּנָא, דַּאֲתָא לְאַשְׁמְעִינַן אַלִּיבָּא דְּרַבָּנַן דְּשִׁיֵּיר קַרְקַע לְעַצְמוֹ, דְּאִי נָפְלֵי – הָדַר שָׁתֵיל לְהוּ. דְּאִי לָאו דְּרַב הוּנָא הֲוָה אָמֵינָא: שִׁיֵּיר אִילָנוֹת לְפָנָיו – יֵשׁ לוֹ קַרְקַע כָּל יְמֵי קִיּוּם הָאִילָנוֹת

לימא ליה עקור אילנך שקול וזיל. פ"ה: עקור אילנך לכשייבש. ותימה: דמה כח הוא זה? דמנא ליה שאינו רוצה לעולם להסתלק מן הקרקע? ואין ה"נ, דמצי א"ל: עקור אילנך לכשייבש! ועוד, מדמסיק בתר הכי: דאי נפלי הדר שתיל להו, משמע דעד השתא הא דקאמר יש לו קרקע — היינו לזרוע תחת האילן, ועל זה אינו מפרש שום טעם! ועוד קשה: דהשתא משמע דטפי אית ליה בקרקע (א) דמשייר לפניו ב' אילנות ממאי דאית ליה דרך כשמשייר בור ודות לר"ע. ובלוקח הוי איפכא, דקנה ב' — לא קנה קרקע, לפי מה דפרישית בפרק "חזקת הבתים" (לעיל דף לז.), וקנה בור ודות — יש לו דרך לר"ע! על כן נראה לר"י לפרש: דאי (ב) לאו דלא שייר כלל קרקע, לימא ליה "עקור אילנך לאלתר", ולכך זקוק הוא לשייר הקרקע ליניקת האילן, ומיגו דנחת לשיורא — משייר נמי קרקע לזרוע סביב האילן וליטע אחר במקומו לכשייבש, כדמסיק. אבל גבי לוקח — לא שייך למימר הכי: מגו דזבין קרקע ליניקת האילן זבין נמי לזרוע סביב וליטע אחר במקומו. שהמוכר, מה שהוא רוצה מוכר ומה שרוצה משייר, אבל הלוקח אינו קונה מה שרוצה, אלא מה שהמוכר רוצה למכור לו. וא"ת: דהשתא משמע דטפי משייר קרקע עם האילן ממה שמשייר דרך לבור ודות, ולעיל משמע דאי לאו דרב הונא הוה אמינא: מכר קרקע ושייר (ג) אילנות שנים — אין לו קרקע אפילו לרבנן, כדמסיק דאי נפלי הדר שתיל להו, ואמאי? הא *לרב' [נ"ל לרבנן] כששייר בור ודות יש לו דרך, א"כ כ"ש שיש לו קרקע עם האילנות ששייר, כדפי'! וי"ל: דה"מ מעיקרא, דלא ידעינן טעמא דמיגו דנחת לשיורא משייר טפי דרך לבור ודות, לפי שהוא צריך יותר דרך לבור ודות ממה שצריך לקרקע בשביל האילן. אבל השתא, דאשמועינן רב הונא טעמא מיגו דנחת לשיורא — שייר טפי קרקע עם האילן מדמשייר דרך עם בור ודות, דהא ודאי ביניקת האילן משייר טפי מדרך, לכולי עלמא, שאינו רוצה לקוצו לאלתר.

ואי סלקא דעתך שיורי משייר כו'. תימה לר"י ולר"ת: דמ"מ לאו מדנפשייהו ינקי, דלא שייר אלא חוצה לו כמלא אורה וסלו, כדאמרינן בפרק "הספינה" (לקמן דף פב.), והאילן יונק ט"ז אמה! וי"ל: דלא מפליג ר"ש ואמר אפילו חרוב ושקמה שענפיו יוצאים חוץ לט"ז אמה קאמר דהקדיש, ואמאי? הא לא ינקי משדה הקדש, שקנה כל הקרקע שתחת ענפיו וחוצה להן כמלא אורה וסלו. א"כ כשהוא מוכר לאחרים לא קנה הלוקח אלא חוצה להן כמלא אורה וסלו. אבל הכא, כשמשייר לעצמו — משייר כל צורך יניקת האילן. **מדנפשייהו** קא ינקי. תימה: מאי קשיא ליה? נהי דגבי מכר אמר דמשייר קרקע בהדי אילן, גבי הקדש לא משייר, דמקדיש טפי בעין יפה מקדיש ממוכר! וכי האי גוונא פריך לקמן לר"ש, אליבא דמ"ד מקדיש אילן אחד לא הקדיש קרקע: אי אליבא דר"ע — האמר מוכר בעין יפה מוכר לענין דרך, כל שכן מקדיש, דמקדיש טפי בעין יפה הוא מקדיש להיות קרקע קדושה לגבי אילן, אע"ג דבמכר אין הקרקע מכורה עם האילן. דכן צריך לפרש, כדפרישית ב"חזקת הבתים" (לעיל דף לו: ד"ה ממטע). והיה ר"י מתרץ: דהכא לא בעי לשנויי הכי, משום דאית לן לדמויי הקדש או למכר או למתנה, וא"כ לא הוה דמי לחד מינייהו, דבמכר משייר בהדי אילן קרקע, ולמתנה נמי לא דמי, דבמתנה נתן את כולן. אבל לקמן פריך שפיר, דכיון דסבר ר"ע דמוכר בעין יפה מוכר — א"כ מקדיש בעין יפה מקדיש כמו במתנה, דבמתנה נמי הוי דינא דכי יהיב ג' אילנות בזה אחר זה — יהיב נמי קרקע. וחזר בו ר"י, דא"כ מגופה דמתניתין תפשוט דר"ש דלא כר"ע, דבמתנה לכולי עלמא נתן את כולן, ובהקדש קאמר ר"ש דלא הקדיש את כולן. ובמסקנא נמי מפרש דר"ש לדבריהם דרבנן קאמר. פירוש: די לכם אם תעשו עין יפה דהקדש מעט יותר ממכר, והקדיש כל הקרקע, ולא תאמרו בהקדש בעין יפה כמו במתנה. ואומר ר"י: (ד) לר"ש, דודאי דלא עביד בהקדש כחו כמתנה — אין נראה לגמרא שיהא בהקדש עין יפה טפי ממכר, אלא פורתא, דהיינו, לענין שאם הקדיש אילן הקדיש נמי קרקע, אף על גב דבמכר לא מכר קרקע עם האילן. אבל עין יפה כולי האי, שיהא קרקע של החרוב קדוש בהדי שדה — כולי האי אין לנו לעשות עין יפה לר"ש. והשתא, לפירוש זה, משמע דאית לן למימר טפי כשמוכר אילן שיהא קרקע הצריך לאילן מכור עם האילן, מדנימא כשמכר שדה שיהא הקרקע הצריך לאילן המשויר מכור עם השדה. ותימה: דמשמע דאי לאו מילתא דרב הונא הוה אמינא מוכר קרקע ושייר אילנות לפניו — אין לו קרקע, אלא מכר הקרקע הצריך לאילן בהדי שדה, אע"ג דכשמכר אילן — לא מכר קרקע הצריכה לאילן! וי"ל: דהיינו משום דאי לאו דרב הונא, הוה ס"ד דכשמכר שדה ושייר אילן — מכר כל השדה, אף הצריך לאילן, ששם שדה על הקרקע יותר ממה ששם אילן על הקרקע הצריכה לו. אבל השתא דאשמעינן רב הונא דשם שדה לא מהני ליה לאזדווני בהדי שדה, משום דנחת לשיורא — סברא היא למשדייה בתר אילן המשויר, לפי שהיא צריכה לאילן, מבתר שדה המשויר. וא"ת: אכתי, והא במסקנא דשמעתין אמר: לדבריהם דרבנן קאמר, דאודו לי מיהא דלא ליהוי הקדש כמו מתנה, אלא לכל היותר לא הקדיש אלא חרוב וסדן. ובהכי הוי מקדיש בעין יפה טפי ממכר, ואע"ג דבמכר לא מכר חרוב ולא קרקע הצריך לו, כשהקדיש — הקדיש כל הקרקע, ולכך הקדיש גם החרוב. וכמו שאמר ר"ש לרבנן כן נאמר עתה אליבא דר"ש, כל זמן שלא ידע הברייתא דמייתי מינה דלא הקדיש טפי ממכר! ואומר ר"י: דאע"ג דקאמר הכי ר"ש לרבנן במסקנא, מכל מקום נראה לגמרא דוחק לר"ש לומר שיסבור דכולי האי מקדיש בעין יפה טפי ממכר. ר"י.

רב הונא כרבנן פשיטא. תימה לרשב"א: מנין פשיטא לו זהו? ע"כ היינו משום דלרבנן יש לו דרך במשייר בור ודות, וכל שכן כשמשייר אילן

רבינו גרשום

דאי לא שייר. מצי למימר ליה הלוקח דקא מכחשי לארעאי עקור אילנך שקול וזיל. ומה טעם מקדיש החרוב המורכב וסדן השקמה משום דקא ינקי משדה הקדש ומשתכח דקא מתהני משל הקדש. אבל חרוב שאין מורכב ושקמה לא הוי מוקדש. ולדבריך דאמרת מכר הקרקע ושייר אילנות לפניו יש לו קרקע מקום האילנות משיפולא עד תהום. אי הכי אמאי הקדיש חרוב וסדן השקמה. והא כי ינקי מדנפשייהו קא ינקי. דאיכא למימר דשייר המקדיש מקום האילנות ומדחול קא ינקי. אלא ש"מ מדהקדיש חרוב וסדן דלא שייר כלום בקרקע הכי נמי להיכא דמכר קרקע ושייר אילנות לפניו אין לו קרקע וקשיא לרב הונא. אלא ש"מ מדאמר רב הונא לעיל מכר את השדה ושייר אילנות לפניו יש לו קרקע כדרבנן ס"ל דאמרי בעין רעה מוכר ושייר מקום אילנות: ור"ש דאמר. המקדיש את השדה הקדיש חרוב וסדן שקמה ומשום דמשדה הקדש קא ינקי כר"ע ס"ל דאמר מוכר בעין יפה מוכר כ"ש מקדיש. ואי קשיא לך ר"ש נמי אליבא דרבנן מצי למימר א) אין הכי נמי אלא מפרש לקמן מה הפרש יש: פשיטא. דהכי הוא דרב הונא כרבנן ס"ל. להכי נפקא מינה. ויש לו מקום האילנות לעולם דאי מתעקרו דיבשי הדר מצי שתיל במקומן:

א) אינו מובן כוונתו ואולי צ"ל ר"ש אליבא דרבנן נמי מצי לאוקמא וכמו שמפרש לקמן (דף עב ע"ב) אלא א"כ לאכתי לא ידע דמה הפרש יש בין מוכר למקדיש כצ"ל ועי' בתוס' כאן סד"ה מדנפשייהו.

הגהות הב"ח

(א) תום' ד"ה לימא ו... דטפי אית ליה בקר... היכא דמשייר: (ב) בא... לר"י לפרש דאי איתא ד... שייר: (ג) בא"ד ה"א מ... קרקע ושייר לפניו ... אילנות אין לו קרק... (ד) ד"ה מדנפשייהו ו... ואומר ר"י דודאי לר... דלא עביד:

א) ערכין יד. ב) [מנחות קז: ערכין יד.] ג) [לעיל לז. וש"נ:]

סז א ב מיי' פ"ד מהל' ערכין וחרמין הל' ח סמג עשין קלו וטוש"ע כל"מ:
סח ג מיי' שם הל' יח:
סט ד מיי' שם הל' טו:

וּמִי מָצֵית מוֹקְמַתְּ לָהּ לְר' שִׁמְעוֹן כְּר' עֲקִיבָא? וְהָא א)תַּנְיָא: אהִקְדִּישׁ שְׁלֹשָׁה אִילָנוֹת מִמַּטַּע עֲשָׂרָה לְבֵית סְאָה — הֲרֵי הִקְדִּישׁ אֶת הַקַּרְקַע וְאֶת הָאִילָנוֹת שֶׁבֵּינֵיהֶם, לְפִיכָךְ כְּשֶׁהוּא פּוֹדֶה — פּוֹדֶה בֵּית זֶרַע חוֹמֶר שְׂעוֹרִים בַּחֲמִשִּׁים שֶׁקֶל כֶּסֶף; בפָּחוֹת מִכָּאן אוֹ יוֹתֵר עַל כֵּן, אוֹ שֶׁהִקְדִּישָׁן בָּזֶה אַחַר זֶה — הֲרֵי זֶה לֹא הִקְדִּישׁ לֹא הַקַּרְקַע וְלֹא אֶת הָאִילָנוֹת שֶׁבֵּינֵיהֶם, גלְפִיכָךְ כְּשֶׁהוּא פּוֹדֶה — פּוֹדֶה אֶת הָאִילָנוֹת בְּשָׁוְויֵהֶן; וְלֹא עוֹד, אֶלָּא אֲפִילּוּ הִקְדִּישׁ אֶת הָאִילָנוֹת וְחָזַר וְהִקְדִּישׁ אֶת הַקַּרְקַע, כְּשֶׁהוּא פּוֹדֶה — פּוֹדֶה אֶת הָאִילָנוֹת בְּשָׁוְויֵהֶן, וְחוֹזֵר וּפוֹדֶה בֵּית זֶרַע חוֹמֶר שְׂעוֹרִים בַּחֲמִשִּׁים שֶׁקֶל כֶּסֶף; מַנִּי? אִי (א) רַבִּי עֲקִיבָא — הָא אָמַר: מוֹכֵר בְּעַיִן יָפָה מוֹכֵר, וְכָל שֶׁכֵּן מַקְדִּישׁ! (ב) אִי רַבָּנַן — הָא אָמְרִי: מוֹכֵר הוּא דִּבְעַיִן רָעָה מוֹכֵר, אֲבָל ב)מַקְדִּישׁ דבְּעַיִן יָפָה מַקְדִּישׁ! אֶלָּא פְּשִׁיטָא רַבִּי שִׁמְעוֹן הִיא; וְרַבִּי שִׁמְעוֹן אַלִּיבָּא דְּמַאן? אִי אַלִּיבָּא דְּר"ע, הָא אָמַר: ג)מוֹכֵר בְּעַיִן יָפָה מוֹכֵר, וְכָל שֶׁכֵּן מַקְדִּישׁ! אֶלָּא פְּשִׁיטָא אַלִּיבָּא דְּרַבָּנַן, וְקָא סָבַר ר"ש: (ג) כִּי הֵיכִי דְּמוֹכֵר בְּעַיִן רָעָה מוֹכֵר, מַקְדִּישׁ נַמִּי בְּעַיִן רָעָה מַקְדִּישׁ, וּמְשַׁיֵּיר אַרְעָא; וְאֶלָּא

רשב"ם

הָאִילָנוֹת, אֲבָל הִזְקִינוּ — אֵין לוֹ קַרְקַע, דּוּמְיָא דְּבוֹר וְדוּת, דְּאִי נָפֵיל הַבּוֹר וְהַדּוּת וְאִי אֶפְשָׁר לְתַקְּנוֹ — אֵין לוֹ עוֹד דֶּרֶךְ. וּמֵעִיקָּרָא נַמִּי הֲוָה יָדְעִינַן דַּאֲתָא רַב הוּנָא לְאַשְׁמוּעִינַן דְּאִי נָפְלֵי הָדַר שָׁתֵיל לְהוּ. אֲבָל גְּמָרָא לָא הֲוָה מַסִּיק אַדַּעְתֵּיהּ שֶׁיֵּשׁ שׁוּם חִידּוּשׁ בְּדִבְרֵי רַב הוּנָא אֶלָּא הַאי, וַאֲפִילּוּ לְר"ע כו'. וְהִלְכָּךְ, כֵּיוָן דְּלֵיתָא לְהַאי אֲפִי' הֲוָה פָּרֵיךְ פְּשִׁיטָא. וּמִי מָצֵית מוֹקְמַתְּ לֵיהּ ר"ש כְּר"ע. וּלְמֵימַר דִּבְעַיִן יָפֶה מַקְדִּישׁ. ג' אִילָנוֹת. חֲשִׁיבִי שְׂדֵה הָאִילָן, וְהִקְדִּישׁ קַרְקַע עִמָּהֶן כָּל הַצָּרִיךְ לִינִיקָתָם. וּבִנְטִיעוֹת מַיְירֵי, דְּאִילּוּ בְּאִילָנוֹת זְקֵנִים אָמְרוּ בְּ"לֹא יַחְפּוֹר" דְּבֵית סְאָה צָרִיךְ לִשְׁלֹשָׁה. מִמַּטַּע י' לְבֵית סְאָה. דְּהַיְינוּ מָאתָן וַחֲמִשִּׁין לְכָל חַד, כְּדַאֲמַרַן בְּ"לֹא יַחְפּוֹר" (לעיל דף כו:). וְאַע"ג דִּלְגַבֵּי מוֹכֵר שְׁלֹשָׁה אִילָנוֹת אָמְרִינַן שִׁיעוּרָא לְקַמָּן בְּ"הַמּוֹכֵר אֶת הַסְּפִינָה" (דף פב:): וְהוּא שֶׁנְּטוּעִין מִד' אַמּוֹת וְעַד ט"ז — הָתָם בְּדַעַת מוֹכֵר תַּלְיָא מִילְּתָא, וְזֶהוּ דַּעְתּוֹ לְהַקְנוֹת לוֹ הַצָּרִיךְ לוֹ לִלְקִיטַת פֵּירוֹתָיו, בֵּינֵיהֶן וְחוּצָה לָהֶן כִּמְלֹא אוֹרֶה וְסַלּוֹ, כִּדְאָמְרִי' הָתָם. אֲבָל הָכָא — בִּינִיקָה תַּלְיָא מִילְּתָא. וְאֶת הָאִילָנוֹת. קְטַנִּים, שֶׁבֵּינֵיהֶן. וּכְשֶׁהוּא פּוֹדֶה. אֵינוֹ צָרִיךְ לִפְדּוֹת הָאִילָנוֹת בְּשָׁוְויֵהֶן, וְהַקַּרְקַע כְּפִי חֶשְׁבּוֹן הַכָּתוּב בַּפָּרָשָׁה (ויקרא כז): "וְאִם מִשְּׂדֵה אֲחֻזָּתוֹ יַקְדִּישׁ אִישׁ לַה' וְהָיָה עֶרְכְּךָ לְפִי זַרְעוֹ זֶרַע חוֹמֶר שְׂעוֹרִים בַּחֲמִשִּׁים שֶׁקֶל כָּסֶף". אֶלָּא הַכֹּל פּוֹדֶה בְּיַחַד לְפִי חֶשְׁבּוֹן בֵּית זֶרַע חוֹמֶר שְׂעוֹרִים בְּנ' שֶׁקֶל כֶּסֶף, דְּהַיְינוּ לְבֵית כּוֹר סֶלַע וּפוּנְדְּיוֹן לְשָׁנָה, שֶׁזֶּהוּ חֶשְׁבּוֹן נ' שֶׁקֶל כֶּסֶף לְמ"ט שְׁנֵי יוֹבֵל. אֶלָּא שֶׁיֵּשׁ פוּנְדְּיוֹן יוֹתֵר בִּשְׁבִיל הַקֶּרַע, כִּדְמִפָרֵשׁ בַּעֲרָכִין, דְּהַסֶּלַע לָא הָוֵי אֶלָּא מ"ח פּוּנְדְּיוֹנִין. פּוֹדֶה בֵּית זֶרַע כו'. דִּכְתִיב בִּקְרָא: "וְאִם מִשְּׂדֵה אֲחֻזָּתוֹ" וגו', וְאִילָנוֹת בִּכְלַל שָׂדֶה, כִּדְנָפְקָא לְעֵיל (דף סט:) מִ"וַּיָּקָם שְׂדֵה עֶפְרוֹן". פָּחוֹת מִיכָּן. חָשִׁיב יַעַר, וְסוֹפוֹ לִיתָּלֵשׁ (ד). אוֹ יוֹתֵר מִיכָּן. אֵין הַקַּרְקַע צָרִיךְ לָהֶן, וַהֲוֵי כְּמַקְדִּישׁ אִילָן אֶחָד, שֶׁאֵינוֹ מַקְדִּישׁ קַרְקַע. וְכִי הַאי גַּוְונָא נַמִּי תַּנְיָא גַּבֵּי מוֹכֵר ג' אִילָנוֹת בְּפֶרֶק "הַמּוֹכֵר אֶת הַסְּפִינָה". בָּזֶה אַחַר זֶה. לֹא הָיָה דַּעְתּוֹ לְהַקְדִּישׁ קַרְקַע. פּוֹדֶן בְּשָׁוְויֵהֶן. כְּדִין כָּל הֶקְדֵּשׁ. שֶׁלֹּא נֶאֱמַר חֶשְׁבּוֹן חֲמִשִּׁים שֶׁקֶל כֶּסֶף אֶלָּא בְּמַקְדִּישׁ שְׂדֵה אֲחוּזָּה, אֲבָל בְּאִילָן בְּלֹא קַרְקַע — לֹא נֶאֱמַר. ה"ג: וְלֹא עוֹד אֶלָּא אֲפִילּוּ הִקְדִּישׁ אֶת הָאִילָנוֹת וְחָזַר וְהִקְדִּישׁ אֶת הַקַּרְקַע כו'. לָא מִיבַּעְיָא הֵיכָא דְּהִקְדִּישׁ אֶת הָאִילָנוֹת בָּזֶה אַחַר זֶה וְשׁוּב לֹא הִקְדִּישׁ אֶת הַקַּרְקַע, דְּפוֹדָן בְּשָׁוְויֵהֶן, אֶלָּא אֲפִילּוּ חָזַר וְהִקְדִּישׁ אֶת הַקַּרְקַע אַחַר שֶׁהִקְדִּישׁ הָאִילָנוֹת בָּזֶה אַחַר זֶה, שֶׁאֵינוֹ פּוֹדֵם עִם הַקַּרְקַע, דְּהָא מֵעִיקָּרָא קָדְשׁוּ לִדְמֵיהֶן, וּכְשֶׁהִקְדִּישׁ שׁוּב אֶת הַקַּרְקַע צָרִיךְ לִפְדּוֹת גַּם אֶת הַקַּרְקַע, סֶלַע וּפוּנְדְּיוֹן לְשָׁנָה, לְבַד פִּדְיוֹן הָאִילָנוֹת בְּשָׁוְויֵהֶן. דִּשְׁנֵי הֶקְדֵּשׁוֹת הֵן — זֶה הוּקְדַּשׁ לְדָמָיו וְזֶה לְפִי חֶשְׁבּוֹן חֲמִשִּׁים, וְאֵין לָנוּ לְהַפְסִיד הֶקְדֵּשׁ דְּמֵי הָאִילָנוֹת, דַּאֲמִירָתוֹ לַגָּבוֹהַּ כִּמְסִירָתוֹ לַהֶדְיוֹט, וּמִשָּׁעָה שֶׁהוּקְדְּשׁוּ רְאוּיִין לִפְדּוֹת בִּדְמֵיהֶן בְּלֹא קַרְקַע. מַנִּי. הַךְ בָּרַיְיתָא, דְּקָתָנֵי: פּוֹדָן בְּשָׁוְויֵהֶן, דְּמַשְׁמַע דַּאֲפִילּוּ מְקוֹם הָאִילָנוֹת לֹא הִקְדִּישׁ, אֶלָּא בְּעַיִן רָעָה הִקְדִּישׁ אִילָנוֹת בְּלֹא קַרְקַע, הֵיכָא דְּלֹא הִקְדִּישׁ ג' בְּיַחַד. אִילֵימָא ר"ע הָאָמַר בְּעַיִן יָפֶה מוֹכֵר. וּסְבִירָא לֵיהּ דְּמוֹכֵר שְׁנֵי אִילָנוֹת יֵשׁ לוֹ קַרְקַע לַלּוֹקֵחַ. דְּלֵית לֵיהּ מַתְנִי' דְּ"הַמּוֹכֵר אֶת הַסְּפִינָה" דְּהַלּוֹקֵחַ שְׁנֵי אִילָנוֹת בְּתוֹךְ שֶׁל חֲבֵירוֹ אֵין לוֹ קַרְקַע, אֶלָּא רַבָּנַן הִיא, כִּדְפָרִישִׁית לְעֵיל. וְכָל שֶׁכֵּן לְר"ע מַקְדִּישׁ ב' אִילָנוֹת אוֹ ג' בָּזֶה אַחַר זֶה, דְּיֵשׁ לוֹ מִיהָא לְהֶקְדֵּשׁ מְקוֹם הָאִילָנוֹת, וְיִפְדּוּ אַגַּב קַרְקַע לְפִי חֶשְׁבּוֹן בֵּית זֶרַע חוֹמֶר שְׂעוֹרִים. וְאִי רַבָּנַן. דִּפְלִיגִי עֲלֵיהּ דְּר"ע הִיא — הָאָמְרִי: מוֹכֵר בְּעַיִן רָעָה מוֹכֵר. אֲבָל מַקְדִּישׁ כו'. כִּדְקָתָנֵי סֵיפָא: בד"א בְּמוֹכֵר כו'. אֶלָּא פְּשִׁיטָא ר"ש הִיא. דְּשָׁמְעִינַן לֵיהּ בְּמַתְנִי' דִּמְשַׁוֵּי דִּין מוֹכֵר כְּמַקְדִּישׁ, שֶׁלֹּא הִקְדִּישׁ בּוֹר וְדוּת וְגַת וְשׁוֹבָךְ בִּכְלַל שָׂדֶה. וְאַשְׁמוּעִינַן הָכָא דִּס"ל נַמִּי דְּמִכֹּל וָכֹל הָוֵי מַקְדִּישׁ בְּעַיִן רָעָה, דְּהֵיכָא דְּמַקְדִּישׁ אִילָן — לֹא הִקְדִּישׁ מְקוֹמוֹ. וְר"ש אַלִּיבָּא דְּמַאן. מֵרַבּוֹתָיו? שֶׁהֲרֵי מִתַּלְמִידֵי ר"ע הָיָה, כִּדְאָמְרִינַן (יבמות דף סב: ע"ש): עַד שֶׁבָּא רַבִּי עֲקִיבָא אֵצֶל רַבּוֹתֵינוּ שֶׁבַּדָּרוֹם וּשְׁנָאָהּ לָהֶם; רַבִּי יְהוּדָה וְרַבִּי מֵאִיר וְרַבִּי יוֹסֵי וְרַבִּי שִׁמְעוֹן וְרַבִּי נְחֶמְיָה כו'. אֶלָּא פְּשִׁיטָא אַלִּיבָּא דְּרַבָּנַן דְּר"ע הִיא. וְהַאי "בד"א בְּמוֹכֵר" כו' — רַבָּנַן דְּר"ש קָאָמְרִי לֵיהּ. אֲבָל לְר"ש, כִּי הֵיכִי דִּפְלִיגִי רַבָּנַן וְר"ע בְּמוֹכֵר, פְּלִיגִי נַמִּי בְּמַקְדִּישׁ, וְקָסָבַר ר"ש דִּין גָּבוֹהַּ לְרַבָּנַן דְּר"ע כְּדִין הֶדְיוֹט (ה). אַף מַקְדִּישׁ נַמִּי בְּעַיִן רָעָה מַקְדִּישׁ. אַלְמָא לָא מָצֵית לְתָרוּצֵי לְעֵיל ר"ש אַלִּיבָּא דְּר"ע. וְהָדְרָן קוּשְׁיָין קַמַּיְיתָא לְדוּכְתָּהּ, דְּשָׁמְעִינַן לֵיהּ לְר"ש דְּהַמַּקְדִּישׁ אֶת הַשָּׂדֶה הִקְדִּישׁ חָרוּב מִשּׁוּם יְנִיקַת שְׂדֵה הֶקְדֵּשׁ, דְּלֹא שַׁיֵּיר אַרְעָא לְעַצְמוֹ לְצוֹרֶךְ הֶחָרוּב, אֶלָּא בְּעַיִן יָפֶה הִקְדִּישׁ — וְה"ה לַמּוֹכֵר דְּשַׁיֵּיר אִילָנוֹת לְפָנָיו, וְקַשְׁיָא לְרַב הוּנָא. וּמִיהוּ, לְר"ש נַמִּי קַשְׁיָא דִּידֵיהּ אַדִּידֵיהּ כִּדְקָפָרֵיךְ לְקַמָּן, דִּלְעֵיל אָמַר עַיִן יָפֶה גַּבֵּי הֶקְדֵּשׁ, וְהָכָא אִית לֵיהּ עַיִן רָעָה. אַךְ שִׁיטַת הַגְּמָרָא עַתָּה לְהַקְשׁוֹת לְרַב הוּנָא, וּמִתְכַּוֵּין לְהַעֲמִיד קוּשְׁיָא רִאשׁוֹנָה שֶׁתֵּירֵץ (ו) רַב הוּנָא וְאָמַר ר"ש כְּר"ע, וְאָנוּ הֶעֱמַדְנוּ דְּלֵית לֵיהּ הָא דְּר"ע וְתִיהְדַּר קוּשְׁיָא לְדוּכְתָּהּ. "וּמְשַׁיֵּיר אַרְעָא" לֹא גָּרַס, דְּמַשְׁמַע שֶׁמִּתְכַּוֵּין הַגְּמָרָא לְהַקְשׁוֹת דְּר"ש אַדְּר"ש, דְּהָכָא שָׁמְעִינַן לֵיהּ עַיִן רָעָה וְהִלְכָּךְ מְשַׁיֵּיר אַרְעָא גַּבֵּי מַקְדִּישׁ (ז) קַרְקַע וְשַׁיֵּיר אִילָנוֹת לְפָנָיו, וּלְעֵיל שָׁמְעִינַן דְּלֹא שַׁיֵּיר כִּדְדָיְיקִינַן מִדְּקָאָמַר הוֹאִיל וְיוֹנְקִין כו'. דְּא"כ, מַאי הַאי דְּקָאָמַר תּוּ: וְאֶלָּא קַשְׁיָא כו'? אֶלָּא לְרַב הוּנָא מַקְשִׁינַן, כִּדְפָרִישִׁית. וְהַיְינוּ

תוספות

אילן, ומשום הכי פשיטא ליה. אלמא מסתברא דמשייר טפי קרקע בהדי אילן, מדמשייר דרך בהדי בור ודות. והא בלוקח הוי איפכא לרבי עקיבא, דיש לו דרך כשקנה בור ודות, וקנה אילן אין לו קרקע! וא"ר"י: דפשיטא ליה טעם דנחית לשיורא אליבא דרבנן, אפילו בלא רב הונא ידעינן דטעם דנחית לשיורא מהני לרבנן לשייר קרקע בהדי אילן, כמו דרך בהדי בור. **ואת** האילנות שביניהם. כגון אילנות סרק. ומשום אותן אילנות לא חשבינן להו רצופין, דכיון שאין טוענים פירות עומדים ליעקר טפי מן השאר, כדאמרינן ב"המוכר את הספינה": (ח) היה אריס בינייהם מהו כו'. א"ל: קני. פי': דלא חשיב רצופין. **אלא** פשיטא אליבא דרבנן וקסבר כי היכי דמוכר כו'. אבל כר"ע לא מצית לאוקמה, דהא דכיון דנחית לעין יפה במוכר, אית לן למימר דמקדיש בעין יפה טפי מקדיש. אבל השתא דסבר כרבנן, דלא נחתי כלל במכר לעין יפה — אתי שפיר, דלית ליה בהקדש נמי עין יפה.

מדמוכר בעין רעה מוכר מקדיש נמי בעין רעה מקדיש. פירש רבינו שמואל: דפריך לרב הונא, דאמר לרבנן דמשייר קרקע בהדי אילן, דהכא אשכח דר"ש סבר כרבנן, ואפילו הכי לא משייר קרקע כשמשייר חרוב, דקאמר דינקי משדה הקדש. והא דקאמר "אלא קשיא", פירוש: אדקשיא לך מר"ש לרב הונא, תקשי לך דר"ש אדר"ש גופיה, היכי מצי למימר כרבנן. ותימה: דהו"ל למימר "וליטעמיך". ועוד: דמעיקרא פריך: אי כרבנן — פשיטא דמשייר קרקע בהדי אילנות לזרוע. והשתא פריך דלרבנן נמי לא משייר קרקע, דהא ר"ש כרבנן סבירא ליה! ונראה לרבינו יצחק: דלא פריך לרב הונא כלל, אלא אדרבה בא לקיים דבריו הראשונים, הא דאמרינן: אפילו לרבי עקיבא כו'. והכי קאמר: ומי מצית מוקמת ר"ש כר"ע? והא ע"כ ר"ש כרבנן, ולרבנן פשיטא דמשייר ארעא, כדקאמר לעיל. וא"כ תקשי דר"ש אדר"ש, דהיכי קאמר ר"ש דינקי משדה הקדש? אלא ע"כ ר"ש לדבריהם דרבנן קאמר. וא"כ אתי שפיר נמי הא (ט) רב הונא, דקאמר: ואפילו לר"ע כו', דאתיא מילתיה דרב הונא אפילו כר"ע, דלדידיה נמי — לדבריהם דרבנן קאמר. והא דאמר "ואלא קשיא", ה"פ: ואלא קשיא דר"ש אדר"ש, ומאי משני? ורשב"א פירש: דלא פריך אלא לרב הונא. דאי לאו דרב הונא — לא קשיא מידי דר"ש אדר"ש. אלא משום דאמר רב הונא דאי נפלי הדר שתיל להו, הוא דקשיא לן דר"ש אדר"ש, דכיון דסבר ר"ש כרבנן — א"כ לא ינקי משדה הקדש. אבל אי אמרת דאי נפלי לא הדר שתיל להו, אע"ג דר"ש כרבנן — מ"מ ינקי משדה הקדש, דכיון דאי נפלי חל ההקדש מאליו — סתמא דמלתא דעתיה שיקדשו חרוב וסדן בהדי קרקע. והיינו דקאמר "ואלא קשיא", כלומר, לרב הונא דאמר אי נפלי הדר שתיל להו, הדרא קושיא לדוכתה: אמאי קאמר ר"ש הואיל וינקי משדה הקדש? **ומשייר** ארעא. פירש רבינו שמואל דלא גרסינן ליה. ועל חנם פירש כן, דמנא ליה דסבר דבעין רעה מקדיש, אי לאו מהאי דקתני: בזה אחר זה לא הקדיש קרקע, והיינו דמשייר ארעא. ולמאי דפרישית נמי ב"חזקת הבתים" (לעיל דף לז:) דמוכיח דבעין רעה מקדיש, מדלא קתני ברישא דפודה וחוזר ופודה — יש לפרש נמי ומשייר ארעא, כלומר דהא פשיטא לך דלרבנן דמשייר, והיכי קאמר ר"ש לעיל דלא משייר?

הכי

הגהות הב"ח

(א) גמ' מני אי נימא ר"ע וכו': (ב) שם ואי רבנן: (ג) שם וקא סבר ר"ש דין גבוה כדין הדיוט מה דין הדיוט מוכר בעין רעה מוכר: (ד) רשב"ם ד"ה פחות מיכן וכו' וסופו ליתלש כדי שתתן יפה הס"ד: (ה) ד"ה אלא פשיטא וכו' כדין הדיוט מה דין הדיוט מוכר בעין רעה מוכר אף מקדיש נמי כצ"ל והד"א: (ו) בא"ד שתירץ לרב הונא וכו': (ז) בא"ד גבי מקדיש ולעיל שמעינן כצ"ל ותיבות קרקע ושייר אילנות לפניו נמחק: (ח) תוס' ד"ה ואת וכו' בהמוכר את הספינה דף פ"ע היה אריס בינייהם מהו כו' א"ל קנה וקנה פי' דלא חשיב רצופין: (ט) ד"ה מדמוכר וכו' אתי שפיר נמי הא דרב הונא:

רבינו גרשום

והא תניא הקדיש שלשה אילנות שהן ממטע עשרה לבית סאה. כלומר שכך שיעור יש בין אלו ג' אילנות שאם היו עוד שבעה סמוכין לאלו בשטה אחת והיה הפרש בין כל אחת ואחת כמו שיש הפרש בין אלו ג' בין כאו"א היו תופשין הני י' מקום בית סאה וי' אילנות בתוך בית סאה מקרי שדה אילן: ה"ז הקדיש את הקרקע. כשיעור שמגיע לאלו אילנות מההוא בית סאה ואת האילנות קטנים שביניהן ואם הם שדה אחוזה והוא רוצה לפדותן קודם היובל פודה כשיעור זרע חומר וכו' ולפי השנים של יובל סלע ופונדיון לכל שנה: פחות מיכן. כלומר אם נטועין הן הני ג' בסמוך משיעור י' (אמות) לבית סאה או ביותר ריוח כשיעור ט' לבית סאה: או שהקדישן בזה אחר זה. הני ג' אילנות לא הקדיש הקרקע ולא האילנות שביניהן דבפחות מכאן יער מקרי ולא שדה אילן וביותר על כן שדה לבן מיקרי ולא שדה אילן: וכשהוא פודן. האילנות אינו פודן אגב קרקע כשיעור זרע חומר שעורים אלא בשווייהן פודה האילנות בלבד: ולא עוד. כלומר לא מיבעיא היכא דהקדיש בזה אחר זה דלא הקדיש לא את הקרקע ולא את האילנות שביניהן וכשהוא פודה אינו פודה אלא האילנות שהקדיש לתחילה אלא אפי' הקדיש את האילנו' ואח"כ הקדיש הקרקע כו' בשווייהן. כשהן שוין ולא יותר: מני. הא ברייתא דערכין: אילימא ר"ע. דמתני' הא קאמר מוכר וכו' וכ"ש מקדיש. והבא קתני להיכא דהקדיש האילנו' לא הקדיש קרקע אלמא דהמקדיש בעין רעה מקדיש: והא אמרי. רבנן במתני' אבל מקדיש בעין יפה מקדיש בדקתני במתני' המקדיש את השדה הקדיש את כולה משום דבעין יפה מקדיש: אלא פשיטא. הא מתני' ר"ש דקתני במתני' המקדיש את השדה לא הקדיש אלא חרוב וסדן שקמה אבל בור ודות לא הקדיש משום דמקדיש בעין רעה מקדיש וקסבר ר"ש המקדיש חרוב וסדן שקמה לא הקדיש קרקע. והאי דקאמר לעיל הואיל ויונק משדה הקדש היינו כשהקדיש השדה: ור"ש אליבא דמאן. דעתו נוטה: אילימא אליבא דר"ע וכו' אלא פשטא אליבא דרבנן. דאמרי מוכר בעין רעה מוכר והכי ס"ל לר' שמעון מדמוכר בעין רעה מוכר מקדיש נמי בעין רעה מקדיש ומשייר קרקע משום הכי להיכא דהקדיש את האילנות לא הקדיש את הקרקע דהמקדיש בעין רעה מקדיש ומתני' דערכין ר' שמעון היא:
אלא

עין משפט
נר מצוה

ע א ב מיי' פ"ד מהל' ערכין וחרמין הל' כח סמג עשין קלה:
עא ג מיי' שם הל' יז:
עב ד מיי' פ"ג מהל' מכירה הל' ג סמג עשין פב טוש"ע ח"מ סי' רטו סעיף ה:
ענ ה מיי' פ"ה מהל' מתנות ענים הל' יד:
עד ו מיי' שם הל' יח:

וְאֶלָּא קַשְׁיָא: הוֹאִיל וְיוֹנְקִין מִשְּׂדֵה הֶקְדֵּשׁ! אֶלָּא, רַבִּי שִׁמְעוֹן לְדִבְרֵיהֶם דְּרַבָּנַן קָאָמַר לְהוּ: לְדִידִי, כִּי הֵיכִי דְּמוֹכֵר בְּעַיִן רָעָה מוֹכֵר, מַקְדִּישׁ נַמִי בְּעַיִן רָעָה מַקְדִּישׁ, וְשִׁיּוּרֵי מְשַׁיֵּיר. לְדִידְכוּ, אוֹדוּ לִי מִיהָא דְּלֹא הִקְדִּישׁ אֶלָּא חָרוּב הַמּוּרְכָּב וְסַדַּן הַשִּׁקְמָה. וְאָמְרִי לֵיהּ רַבָּנַן: לָא שְׁנָא. בְּמַאי אוֹקִימְתָּא לָהּ? כְּרַבִּי שִׁמְעוֹן; אֵימָא סֵיפָא: וְלֹא עוֹד, אֶלָּא אֲפִילּוּ הִקְדִּישׁ אֶת הָאִילָנוֹת וְחָזַר וְהִקְדִּישׁ אֶת הַקַּרְקַע, כְּשֶׁהוּא פּוֹדֶה – פּוֹדֶה אֶת הָאִילָנוֹת בְּשָׁוְויֵיהֶן, וְחוֹזֵר וּפוֹדֶה בֵּית זֶרַע חוֹמֶר שְׂעוֹרִים בַּחֲמִשִּׁים שֶׁקֶל כֶּסֶף; וְאִי ר' שִׁמְעוֹן, לֵיזִיל בָּתַר פִּדְיוֹן וְנִיפָּרְקוּ אַגַּב אַרְעַיְיהוּ, דְּהָא שָׁמְעִינַן לֵיהּ לְר"ש דְּאָזֵיל בָּתַר פִּדְיוֹן! דְּתַנְיָא:* אמִנַּיִן לַלּוֹקֵחַ שָׂדֶה מֵאָבִיו וְהִקְדִּישָׁהּ וְאַחַר כָּךְ מֵת אָבִיו, מִנַּיִן שֶׁתְּהֵא לְפָנָיו כִּשְׂדֵה אֲחוּזָּה? ת"ל: °"וְאִם אֶת שְׂדֵה מִקְנָתוֹ אֲשֶׁר לֹא מִשְּׂדֵה אֲחוּזָּתוֹ" (ויקרא כז), שָׂדֶה שֶׁאֵין רְאוּיָה לִהְיוֹת שְׂדֵה אֲחוּזָּה, יָצְתָה זוֹ שֶׁרְאוּיָה לִהְיוֹת שְׂדֵה אֲחוּזָּה, דִּבְרֵי רַבִּי יְהוּדָה וְרַבִּי שִׁמְעוֹן. רַבִּי מֵאִיר אוֹמֵר: מִנַּיִן

הדרן עלך המוכר את הבית

לַלּוֹקֵחַ שָׂדֶה מֵאָבִיו וּמֵת אָבִיו וְאח"כ הִקְדִּישׁ, מִנַּיִן שֶׁתְּהֵא לְפָנָיו כִּשְׂדֵה אֲחוּזָּה? תַּלְמוּד לוֹמַר: "וְאִם אֶת שְׂדֵה מִקְנָתוֹ אֲשֶׁר לֹא מִשְּׂדֵה אֲחוּזָּתוֹ", שָׂדֶה שֶׁאֵינָהּ שְׂדֵה אֲחוּזָּה, יָצְתָה זוֹ שֶׁהִיא שְׂדֵה אֲחוּזָּה; וְאִילּוּ רַבִּי יְהוּדָה וְרַבִּי שִׁמְעוֹן, (א) הֵיכָא דְּמֵת אָבִיו וְאַחַר כָּךְ הִקְדִּישָׁהּ בלָא צְרִיכִי קְרָא, כִּי אִצְטְרִיךְ קְרָא – הֵיכָא דְּהִקְדִּישָׁהּ וְאַחַר כָּךְ מֵת אָבִיו; מְנָא לְהוּ? אִי מֵהַאי קְרָא, אֵימָא: לְכִדְרַבִּי מֵאִיר הוּא דְּאָתָא! אֶלָּא, לָאו מִשּׁוּם דְּאָזְלִי בָּתַר פִּדְיוֹן? אָמַר רַב נַחְמָן בַּר יִצְחָק: לְעוֹלָם בְּעָלְמָא רַבִּי יְהוּדָה וְרַבִּי שִׁמְעוֹן לָא אָזְלִי בָּתַר פִּדְיוֹן, וְהָכָא קְרָא אַשְׁכְּחוּ וּדְרוּשׁ: א"כ, לִכְתּוֹב קְרָא: "וְאִם אֶת שְׂדֵה מִקְנָתוֹ אֲשֶׁר לֹא אֲחוּזָּתוֹ", אִי נַמִי: "שְׂדֵה אֲחוּזָּתוֹ", מַאי "אֲשֶׁר לֹא מִשְּׂדֵה אֲחוּזָּתוֹ"? אֶת שֶׁאֵינָהּ רְאוּיָה לִהְיוֹת שְׂדֵה אֲחוּזָּה, יָצְתָה זוֹ שֶׁרְאוּיָה לִהְיוֹת שְׂדֵה אֲחוּזָּה. אָמַר רַב הוּנָא: חָרוּב הַמּוּרְכָּב וְסַדַּן הַשִּׁקְמָה – תּוֹרַת אִילָן עָלָיו וְתוֹרַת קַרְקַע עָלָיו; תּוֹרַת אִילָן עָלָיו, גדְּהֵיכָא דְּאַקְדֵּישׁ אוֹ דבֵּין שְׁנֵי אִילָנוֹת וְהַאי – יֵשׁ לוֹ קַרְקַע; תּוֹרַת קַרְקַע עָלָיו, הדְּלָא מִזְדַּבַּן אַגַּב אַרְעָא. וְאָמַר רַב הוּנָא: עוֹמֶר שֶׁיֵּשׁ בּוֹ סָאתַיִם – תּוֹרַת עוֹמֶר עָלָיו וְתוֹרַת גָּדִישׁ עָלָיו; תּוֹרַת עוֹמֶר עָלָיו, ודִּשְׁנֵי עֳמָרִים שִׁכְחָה, שְׁנַיִם וְהוּא – אֵינָן שִׁכְחָה; תּוֹרַת גָּדִישׁ עָלָיו, דִּתְנַן:* זעוֹמֶר שֶׁיֵּשׁ בּוֹ סָאתַיִם, (ב) שְׁכָחוֹ – אֵין שִׁכְחָה. אָמַר רַבָּה בַּר בַּר חָנָה אָמַר רֵישׁ לָקִישׁ: חָרוּב הַמּוּרְכָּב וְסַדַּן הַשִּׁקְמָה – בָּאנוּ לְמַחֲלוֹקֶת רַבִּי מְנַחֵם (*בַּר) יוֹסֵי וְרַבָּנַן. וְלֵימָא

ערכין יז. כו: גיטין מח.
פאה פ"ו מ"ה
[נ"ל ברבן]

רשב"ם

וְהַיְינוּ דְּקָפְרִיךְ: וְאֶלָּא קַשְׁיָא הוֹאִיל וְיוֹנְקִין כו'. כְּמוֹ וְלִיטַעֲמִיךְ, אַדְּמַקְשֵׁי' לְרַב הוּנָא – תִּקְשֵׁי לְר' שִׁמְעוֹן אַדְּרַבִּי שִׁמְעוֹן, דְּהָכָא שָׁמְעִינַן לֵיהּ בְּעַיִן רָעָה מַקְדִּישׁ, וּלְעֵיל קָאָמַר הוֹאִיל וְיוֹנְקִין כו', דְּמַשְׁמַע: הַכֹּל הִקְדִּישׁ בְּעַיִן יָפָה וְלֹא שִׁייֵּר קַרְקַע לְחָרוּב שֶׁלּוֹ! ה"ג: אֶלָּא ר"ש לְדִבְרֵיהֶם דְּרַבָּנַן כו'. וְשִׁינּוּיָא הוּא דְּקָא מְשַׁנֵּי, דְּלָא תִּקְשֵׁי לְמַאי דְּאָמַר רַב הוּנָא וַאֲפִילּוּ לְרַבִּי עֲקִיבָא כו', וְלָא תִּקְשֵׁי נַמִי דְּר"ש אַדְּר' שִׁמְעוֹן כו'. מַקְדִּישׁ נַמִי בְּעַיִן רָעָה מַקְדִּישׁ. דַּאֲפִי' בַּמֶּה שֶׁהִקְדִּישׁ מְשַׁיֵּיר לְעַצְמוֹ, וְכֵיוָן דְּלֹא הִקְדִּישׁ חָרוּב וְשִׁקְמָה – לֹא הִקְדִּישׁ נַמִי קַרְקַע הַצָּרִיךְ לוֹ. כְּמוֹ גַּבֵּי מוֹכֵר וְשִׁייֵּר אִילָנוֹת לְפָנָיו יֵשׁ לוֹ קַרְקַע אֲפִי' לְר"ע, כְּמוֹ שֶׁאָמַר רַב הוּנָא, וְכָל שֶׁכֵּן לְרַבָּנַן. אֶלָּא לְדִידְכוּ. דְּאִית לְכוּ בְּעַיִן יָפָה יוֹתֵר מִדַּאי גַּבֵּי הֶקְדֵּשׁ, אֲפִי' לְהַקְדִּישׁ בּוֹר וְגַת שֶׁאֵינָם בִּכְלַל שָׂדֶה – דַּי הָיָה לָכֶם אִילּוּ עֲשִׂיתֶם מַקְדִּישׁ כְּמוֹכֵר לְר"ע, לְמֵימַר בֵּיהּ עַיִן יָפָה לְגַבֵּי מַאי דְּמַקְדִּישׁ בְּהֶדְיָא, כְּגוֹן הַמַּקְדִּישׁ אֶת הַשָּׂדֶה הִקְדִּישׁ כָּל הַקַּרְקַע כּוּלּוֹ בְּעַיִן יָפָה, וְלֹא שִׁייֵּר מִן הַקַּרְקַע כְּלוּם לְצוֹרֶךְ חָרוּב שֶׁלּוֹ – נִמְצָא יוֹנֵק מִן הַהֶקְדֵּשׁ, וְקָדוֹשׁ. אֲבָל בּוֹר וְדוּת וְשׁוֹבָךְ וְכָל הָנָךְ דַּאֲמָרַן לְעֵיל דְּאֵינָן בִּכְלַל שָׂדֶה – לָא לִיקְדְּשׁוּ, שֶׁהֲרֵי אֵין דַּעְתּוֹ לְהַקְדִּישׁ יוֹתֵר מִמַּה שֶּׁהוּא מְפָרֵשׁ! וְאָמְרִי לֵיהּ רַבָּנַן לָא שְׁנָא. כְּלוֹמַר, לֹא חָשׁוּ לִדְבָרָיו. דְּהָא קָאָמְרִי "הִקְדִּישׁ אֶת כּוּלָּן", דִּמְדַמּוּ לֵיהּ לְנוֹתֵן מַתָּנָה שֶׁנּוֹתֵן וּמַקְדִּישׁ בְּעַיִן יָפָה כָּל מַה שֶּׁבַּשָּׂדֶה, הוֹאִיל וְשַׁיָּיךְ גַּבֵּיהּ דְּשָׂדֶה פּוּרְתָּא. וּמֵהָשְׁתָּא מִיתּוֹקְמָא מִילְּתֵיהּ דְּרַב הוּנָא אֲפִילּוּ כְּרַבִּי עֲקִיבָא, כְּדַאֲמָרַן מֵעִיקָּרָא. לֵיזִיל בָּתַר שְׁעַת פִּדְיוֹן. דְּהָא עַכְשָׁיו הַכֹּל קָדוֹשׁ, אִילָנוֹת בַּהֲדֵי קַרְקַע, וְהַכֹּל קְרוּי שָׂדֶה. דְּהָא שָׁמְעִינַן לֵיהּ כו'. וּסְבָרָא בְּעָלְמָא הִיא (ג). וְהָכִי מַשְׁמַע לֵיהּ קְרָא: "וְאִם מִשְּׂדֵה אֲחוּזָּתוֹ יַקְדִּישׁ אִישׁ לַה' וְהָיָה עֶרְכְּךָ" – עַכְשָׁיו, בִּשְׁעַת פִּדְיוֹן – "בֵּית זֶרַע חוֹמֶר שְׂעוֹרִים" וגו'. הַמַּקְדִּישׁ. שְׂדֵה מִקְנֶה פּוֹדֵהוּ בְּשָׁוְויוֹ, כִּדְכְתִיב בְּהֶדְיָא בַּפָּרָשָׁה. אֲבָל בִּשְׂדֵה אֲחוּזָּה קָצַב הַכָּתוּב: זֶרַע חוֹמֶר שְׂעוֹרִים בַּחֲמִשִּׁים שֶׁקֶל כֶּסֶף. וְאַחַר כָּךְ מֵת אָבִיו. וְכ"ש אִם מֵת אָבִיו תְּחִלָּה וְאַחַר כָּךְ הִקְדִּישָׁהּ, דְּבִשְׁעַת הַקְדָּשָׁה כְּבָר הָיְתָה שְׂדֵה אֲחוּזָּה מַמָּשׁ. כִּשְׂדֵה אֲחוּזָּה. לְפָדוֹתָהּ בְּסֶלַע וּפוּנְדְּיוֹן לְשָׁנָה. וְאִם אֶת שְׂדֵה מִקְנָתוֹ וגו'. וְסֵיפֵיהּ דִּקְרָא: "וְנָתַן אֶת הָעֶרְכְּךָ". שָׂדֶה שֶׁאֵינָהּ רְאוּיָה. בִּשְׁעַת הֶקְדֵּשׁ לִהְיוֹת שְׂדֵה אֲחוּזָּה הַיּוֹם וּלְמָחָר, כְּגוֹן שֶׁלְּקָחוֹ מֵאַחֵר. אִי נַמִי, מֵאָבִיו וְלֹא מֵת קוֹדֶם הַיּוֹבֵל. וְקָא ס"ד הָשְׁתָּא דִּקְרָא לָא כְּמָר דָּיֵיק וְלָא כְּמָר דָּיֵיק, אֶלָּא לְפִי סְבָרַת דִּבְרֵיהֶן מְפָרְשִׁים הַפָּסוּק. דְּס"ל לְרַבִּי שִׁמְעוֹן דְּאָזְלִינַן בְּכָל הֶקְדֵּשׁוֹת בָּתַר שְׁעַת פִּדְיוֹן כְּקִנְיַן כָּל דָּבָר, שֶׁאֵין לוֹקְחִין אֶת הַחֵפֶץ אֶלָּא לְפִי שָׁוְויוֹ בִּשְׁעַת מִקָּח. שֶׁהִיא שְׂדֵה אֲחוּזָּה. בְּשָׁעָה שֶׁהִקְדִּישָׁהּ. דְּאִילּוּ לֹא מֵת אָבִיו – הָיְתָה חוֹזֶרֶת בַּיּוֹבֵל לְאָבִיו, כִּדְכְתִיב: "בִּשְׁנַת הַיּוֹבֵל יָשׁוּב הַשָּׂדֶה לַאֲשֶׁר קָנָהוּ מֵאִתּוֹ". וְעַתָּה כְּשֶׁמֵּת אָבִיו – הֲרֵי הִיא לוֹ שְׂדֵה אֲחוּזָּה (ד) וְיַחֲזוֹר לוֹ בַּיּוֹבֵל. אֲבָל הִקְדִּישָׁהּ וְאח"כ מֵת אָבִיו – ס"ל לְר"מ דְּאֵינָהּ כִּשְׂדֵה אֲחוּזָּה. לְכִדְר"מ הוּא דְּאָתָא. דְּמִרְבּוּי אֶחָד אֵין לְךָ לְרַבּוֹת אֶלָּא הַהוּא דְּדָמֵי טְפֵי לְרַבּוּיֵי. אֶלָּא [לָאו] מִשּׁוּם דְּאָזְלֵי מִסְּבָרָא בִּשְׁעַת פִּדְיוֹן, וּמְפָרְשֵׁי לֵיהּ לִקְרָא לְפִי דַּעְתָּם. קְרָא אַשְׁכְּחוּ. דְּמְרַבֵּי לֵיהּ בְּהֶדְיָא. אֲבָל בְּעָלְמָא נֵיזִיל גַּבֵּי שְׁעַת הֶקְדֵּשׁ לְחוּמְרָא, דְּכֵיוָן דְּקָדְשׁוּ אִילָנוֹת לְדָמֵיהֶן – אֵין לָנוּ לְהַפְסִיד הֶקְדֵּשׁ. א"כ. כְּדְר' מֵאִיר, דְּלֹא רִיבָּה הַכָּתוּב בְּדִין שְׂדֵה אֲחוּזָּה, אֶלָּא מֵת וְאח"כ הִקְדִּישׁ. ה"ג: לִכְתּוֹב קְרָא אֲשֶׁר לֹא שְׂדֵה אֲחוּזָּתוֹ מַאי מִשְּׂדֵה. דְּהָכִי מַשְׁמַע קְרָא: וְאִם אֶת (ה) הַשָּׂדֶה מִקְנֶה שֶׁאֵינָהּ מִקְנַת שְׂדֵה אֲחוּזָּה. אֲבָל אִם הִיא שְׂדֵה אֲחוּזָּה מִקְנַת, דְּהַיְינוּ הִקְדִּישָׁהּ וְאח"כ מֵת אָבִיו, דִּכְמַשְׁמַע (ו) קְנוּי הִיא בִּכְלַל שְׂדֵה אֲחוּזָּה בִּשְׁעַת הֶקְדֵּשׁ, שֶׁהֲרֵי יְכוֹלָה לִהְיוֹת שְׂדֵה אֲחוּזָּה אִם יָמוּת קוֹדֶם הַיּוֹבֵל. וּלְעוֹלָם בָּתַר שְׁעַת הֶקְדֵּשׁ אָזִיל. יֵשׁ לוֹ קַרְקַע. כְּדִין הַקּוֹנֶה שְׁלֹשָׁה אִילָנוֹת בְּתוֹךְ שֶׁל חֲבֵירוֹ, דַּחֲשִׁיבוּתוֹ לֹא תִּגְרַע כֹּחוֹ. דְּלָא מִיזְדַּבַּן אַגַּב אַרְעָא. כִּדְתְנַן בְּמַתְנִי', וְאִם הָיוּ שְׁנֵי אִילָנוֹת וְהַאי חָרוּב – הָאִילָנוֹת מְכוּרִין, וְהַאי אֵינוֹ מָכוּר. וּמִשּׁוּם רֵישָׁא נָקֵט סֵיפָא. תּוֹרַת עוֹמֶר עָלָיו. כְּשֶׁיֵּשׁ עִמּוֹ שְׁנַיִם מִצְטָרְפִין לִשְׁלֹשָׁה עֳמָרִים, וְלָא הָווּ שִׁכְחָה. שְׁנֵי עוֹמָרִים שִׁכְחָה שְׁלֹשָׁה אֵינָן שִׁכְחָה. בְּסִפְרֵי מַפִּיק לֵיהּ מֵהַאי קְרָא "וְשָׁכַחְתָּ עוֹמֶר בַּשָּׂדֶה" (דברים כד) – וְלֹא גָּדִישׁ. וְגַם עוֹמֶר שֶׁיֵּשׁ בּוֹ סָאתַיִם מַפִּיק לֵיהּ הָתָם מִדִּכְתִיב "לְקַחְתּוֹ" – לְמַעוּטֵי הַאי דְּאֵינוֹ נִיקָּח בְּפַעַם אַחַת יָפֶה. תּוֹרַת גָּדִישׁ עָלָיו. דַּאֲפִילּוּ כְּשֶׁהוּא לְבַדּוֹ אֵינוֹ שִׁכְחָה, כִּדְדָרְשִׁינַן בְּסִפְרֵי: "עוֹמֶר" – וְלֹא הַגָּדִישׁ. חָרוּב הַמּוּרְכָּב וְסַדַּן הַשִּׁקְמָה. אִם קָדוֹשׁ בִּכְלַל שָׂדֶה אִם לָאו – בָּאנוּ לְמַחֲלוֹקֶת ר' מְנַחֵם בַּר' יוֹסֵי וְרַבָּנַן. דְּלְרַבָּנַן קָדְשֵׁי, דִּבְעַיִן יָפָה מַקְדִּישׁ, כִּדְתְנַן בְּמַתְנִיתִין. וְרַבִּי מְנַחֵם בַּר' יוֹסֵי כְּרַבִּי שִׁמְעוֹן, דִּבְעַיִן רָעָה מַקְדִּישׁ. וַאֲפִי' חָרוּב שֶׁיּוֹנֵק מִן הַשָּׂדֶה לֹא קָדֵישׁ, דִּבְעַיִן רָעָה כָּל כָּךְ הִקְדִּישׁ אֶת הַשָּׂדֶה, שֶׁשִּׁיֵּיר מִן הַשָּׂדֶה לְצוֹרֶךְ יְנִיקַת חָרוּב שֶׁלּוֹ, וּכְדְפָרֵישִׁית לְעֵיל רַבִּי שִׁמְעוֹן לְדִבְרֵיהֶם דְּרַבָּנַן קָאָמַר לְהוּ כו'. וְהָכִי הֲוָה שְׁמִיעַ לֵיהּ רֵישׁ לָקִישׁ מֵרַבּוֹתָיו, דְּרַבִּי מְנַחֵם בְּרַבִּי יוֹסֵי סְבִירָא לֵיהּ כְּרַבִּי שִׁמְעוֹן.
וְלֵימָא

תוספות

הכי גרסינן: ואילו רבי יהודה ור"ש הקדיש ואח"כ מת אביו כשדה אחוזה דמיא. ולא גרסינן "היכא דמת אביו ואח"כ הקדישה לא צריך קרא", דשפיר צריך קרא לכך. אלא ר' יהודה ור"ש דידעי מסברא דהוא הדין הקדישה ואח"כ מת אביו – משום דאזלי בתר פדיון. אלא ב"השולח" (גיטין דף מח.) גרסינן ליה, והסופרים טעו וכתבו גם כאן. **קרא** אשכחו ודרוש. ה"נ הוה מצי למדחי דבהא פליגי: רבי יהודה ור"ש סברי: קנין פירות לאו כקנין הגוף דמי, ולא איצטריך קרא למת אביו ואחר כך הקדישה, דהא לגמרי הוה שדה אחוזה, דהא בחיי האב לא היה לו כי אם פירות. ולא איצטריך קרא אלא להקדישה ואח"כ מת אביו, ולא משום דאזלי בתר פדיון. ורבי מאיר סבר כקנין הגוף דמי, ואיצטריך קרא למת אביו ואחר כך הקדישה, שלא ירש כלום, דמעיקרא נמי היתה שלו. והכי הוה בעי לאוקמי פלוגתא בסוף "השולח" (שם). **לדבריהם** דרבנן. ולא מצי למימר דסברא דנפשיה קאמר, דהא לדידיה אפילו הקדיש אילן לא הקדיש קרקע, כדקתני בברייתא, כ"ש דלא הקדיש עם השדה קרקע הצריך לאילן, כדפרישית לעיל.

רבינו גרשום

אלא קשיא. הך דקתני מתני' ר' שמעון אומר המקדיש את השדה הקדיש חרוב וסדן שקמה וקתני הכא מ"ט הואיל וינקי משדה הקדש אלמא דס"ל לר"ש מקדיש בעין יפה מקדיש והקדיש כל השדה ה"נ מקדיש אילנות בעין יפה הקדיש והקדיש הקרקע ומקומן. ומשני לעולם ס"ל לר"ש מקדיש בעין רעה מקדיש ושייר הקרקע והאי דקאמר הואיל וינקי משדה הקדש דמשמע בעין יפה מקדיש לדבריהן דרבנן קאמר להו וכו': מקדיש נמי בעין רעה מקדיש ושיורי משייר אפי' חרוב ושקמה והקרקע של מקומן: הואיל ויונקין משדה הקדש אבל בור ודות דלא מכחשי בארעא לא. ורבנן אמרו ליה ל"ש. דכי היכי דהקדיש חרוב וסדן שקמה ה"נ הקדיש בור ודות אע"ג דלא מכחשי בארעא ולעולם ברייתא דערכין ר"ש היא: במאי אוקימתא להך ברייתא דערכין כר"ש. אי ר"ש אימא סיפא וכו' וניזיל בתר שעת הפדיון. דכי קא פודה הני אילנות בההיא שעתא הקרקע נתקדשה. ואמאי פודה את האילנות לבדן בשווייהן. ליפרקינהו אגב קרקע כשיעור בית זרע חומר שעורים כו': ללוקח שדה מאביו. שקנאה ממנו: מנין שתהא לפניו כשדה אחוזה. אע"ג דקנאה מאביו ופריק ליה בדין שדה אחוזה זרע חומר שעורים בחמשים שקל כסף: ת"ל אם את שדה מקנתו אשר לא משדה אחוזתו יקדיש וחשב לו הכהן את מכס' ופודה אותה בשוויה: שדה מקנה. דעלמא שאינה ראויה להיות שדה אחוזה שאינה של אבותיו יפדה בשוויה: יצאה זו. שקנאה מאביו שאם לא קנאה היתה ראויה להיות לו שדה אחוזה שיורשה מאביו להכי פודה אותה כדין שדה אחוזה דברי ר' יהודה ור"ש. אלמא אע"ג דהקדישה קודם שמת אביו דאכתי בשעת הקדש לא הוה שדה אחוזה כיון דבשעת פדייה הוה שדה אחוזה אזלי בתר שעת פדיון. וה"נ אם איתא דמוקמת כר"ש ליזל בתר שעת פדיון: לא צריך קרא. היכא דכי הקדישה היה שדה אחוזה כי איצטריך קרא וכו': ומנא להו. לר' יהודה ור"ש דהיכא דהקדישה ואח"כ מת אביו דכשדה אחוזה ממש דמיא: אי מהאי קרא. דכתיב ואם משדה אחוזתו וגו': אימא קרא לדרשה דר"מ קאתי. דהכי מסתבר קרא כר"מ: אלא לאו משום דאזלי בתר פדיון. אלא לאו ש"מ דלאו ר"ש היא ואכתי קא מיבעי לך מני: אמר רב נחמן. לעולם ברייתא ר"ש. ודקא קשיא ליזל בתר פדיון דבההוא שעתא שדה אחוזה היא. ואי ברייתא דערכין [אליבא דר'] שמעון היא ליזל לבתר שעת פדיון. הכא לאו משום ההוא טעמא דאזלי בתר פדיון אלא מש"ד אמרי ר"ש ור' יהודה דכשדה אחוזה דמיא אע"ג דהקדישה קודם שמת אביו משום דקרא אשכח ודרוש: א"כ. הוא כדאמר ר"מ ניכתוב קרא אם את שדה מקנתו אשר לא אחוזתו דאי כתב הכי הוה משמע אותה אינה נפדית כי אם בשוויה אבל אותה שדה שלקחה מאביו ומת אביו ואח"כ הקדישה ודאי הויא לפניו כש"ה אחוזה ונפדית בבית זרע חומר שעורים: אי נמי. הכי מיבעי לקרא למימר אשר לא שדה אחוזתו מאי כתיב משדה אחוזתו ש"מ ראויה וכו': תורת אילן עליו. דהיכא דזבין ב' אילנות והאי חרוב מורכב או סדן שקמה בהדי שני אילנות וקנה קרקע דחשיב שדה אילן: תורת קרקע עליו. דלא מזדבן אגב ארעא דכי היכי כי מכר קרקע לא מכר לו בור ודות הכי לא מכר נמי האי חרוב וסדן דדבר חשוב בפ"ע הוא: תורת שמר עליו. דהכי קי"ל דשני עומרין שכחה ג' אינן שכחה. ואם השנים הם כל אחד כשיעור עומר והאי עומר של סאתים הוה ביניהם השלישי לא לימא דהוי השנים שכחה והאי עומר גדול כמאן דליתא אלא מצטרף האי עומר גדול לשנים והוי ג' ולא הוי שכחה: ותורת גדיש עליו. דאם שכחו לבדו לא הוי שכחה דאינו עומר אלא גדיש:
ונימא

הגהות הב"ח

(א) גמ' ואילו ר' יהודה ור"ש היכא דמת אביו ואח"כ הקדישה לא צריכי קרא כי אצטריך קרא היכא דהקדישה ואח"כ מת אביו הוי שדה אחוזה מנא להו כצ"ל ותיבות היכא דמת אביו ואח"כ הקדישה לא צריכי קרא כי אצטריך קרא נמחק: (ב) שם שיש בו סאתים ושכחו אינו שכחה: (ג) רשב"ם ד"ה דהא שמעינן וכו' בעלמא היא דניזיל בתר פדיון וכבר משמע ליה: (ד) ד"ה שהיא שדה וכו' שדה אחוזה אבל הקדישה ואח"כ מת אביו ויחזור לו ביובל נמחק: (ה) ד"ה וכו' ואם את שדה מקנתו שאינה מקנת: (ו) בא"ד דכמשמע קנוי היא בכלל:

וְלֵימָא מַחֲלוֹקֶת ר"ש וְרַבָּנַן. וַהֲוָה מַשְׁמַע לָן דר"ש לְדִבְרֵיהֶם דְּרַבָּנַן קָאָמַר לְהוּ, כִּדְאָמְרָן לְעֵיל. דְּאִי מַתְנִי' הֲוָה מַשְׁמַע דִּבְחָרוּב וְשִׁקְמָה מוֹדֵי לְהוּ כִּדְקָתָנֵי בְּהֶדְיָא: אֶלָּא חָרוּב הַמּוּרְכָּב כו', מַשְׁמַע דִּבְחָרוּב וְסַדָּן מוֹדֵי לְהוּ ר"ש לְרַבָּנַן. **הָא קמ"ל כו'.** הָא עֲדִיפָא לַאֲשְׁמוּעִינַן, דְּהַשְׁתָּא דר"ש מִמֵּילָא שָׁמְעִינַן לֵיהּ דִּלְדִבְרֵיהֶם דְּרַבָּנַן קָאָמַר לְהוּ, כִּדְדַיְיקִינַן מִבָּרַיְיתָא לְעֵיל. **הדרן עלך המוכר את הבית**

וְלֵימָא: מַחֲלוֹקֶת רַבִּי שִׁמְעוֹן וְרַבָּנַן! הָא קמ"ל, דְּרַבִּי מְנַחֵם בְּר' יוֹסֵי כְּר' שִׁמְעוֹן סְבִירָא לֵיהּ.§

הדרן עלך המוכר את הבית

הַמּוֹכֵר אֶת הַסְּפִינָה — [א]מָכַר אֶת הַתּוֹרֶן וְאֶת הַנֵּס וְאֶת הָעוֹגִין, וְאֶת כָּל הַמַּנְהִיגִין אוֹתָהּ. אֲבָל לֹא מָכַר לֹא אֶת הָעֲבָדִים וְלֹא אֶת הַמַּרְצוּפִין וְלֹא אֶת הָאַנְתִּיקִי; וּבִזְמַן שֶׁאָמַר לוֹ "הִיא וְכָל מַה שֶּׁבְּתוֹכָהּ" — הֲרֵי כּוּלָּן מְכוּרִין.§ **גמ'** תּוֹרֶן — אִיסְקַרְיָא, וְכֵן הוּא אוֹמֵר: (יחזקאל כז) "אֶרֶז מִלְּבָנוֹן לָקָחוּ לַעֲשׂוֹת תֹּרֶן עָלָיִךְ".§ נֵס — אַדְרָא, וְכֵן הוּא אוֹמֵר: (שם) "שֵׁשׁ בְּרִקְמָה מִמִּצְרַיִם הָיָה מִפְרָשֵׂךְ לִהְיוֹת לָךְ לְנֵס".§ עוֹגִין — תָּנֵי רַבִּי חִיָּיא: אֵלּוּ עוֹגִינִין שֶׁלָּהּ, וְכֵן הוּא אוֹמֵר: (רות א) "הֲלָהֵן תְּשַׂבֵּרְנָה עַד אֲשֶׁר יִגְדָּלוּ הֲלָהֵן [א]תֵּעָגֵנָה לְבִלְתִּי הֱיוֹת לְאִישׁ".§ מַנְהִיגִין — א"ר אַבָּא: אֵלּוּ הַמְשׁוֹטִין שֶׁלָּהּ, וְכֵן הוּא אוֹמֵר: (יחזקאל כז) "אַלּוֹנִים מִבָּשָׁן עָשׂוּ מְשׁוֹטָיִךְ". וְאִבָּעֵית אֵימָא, מֵהָכָא: (שם) "וְיָרְדוּ מֵאֳנִיּוֹתֵיהֶם כֹּל תֹּפְשֵׂי מָשׁוֹט". ת"ר: הַמּוֹכֵר אֶת הַסְּפִינָה — מָכַר אֶת הָאִיסְכָּלָה וְאֶת בּוֹר הַמַּיִם שֶׁבְּתוֹכָהּ. [ב]רַבִּי נָתָן אוֹמֵר: הַמּוֹכֵר אֶת הַסְּפִינָה — מָכַר אֶת הַבִּיצִית. סוּמְכוֹס אוֹמֵר: [ג]הַמּוֹכֵר אֶת הַסְּפִינָה — מָכַר אֶת הַדּוּגִית. אָמַר רָבָא: בִּיצִית הַיְינוּ דּוּגִית, [ד]רַבִּי נָתָן בַּבְלָאָה הֲוָה, קָארֵי לָהּ בּוּצִית, כִּדְאָמְרִי אֱינָשֵׁי: [ה]בּוּצִיאָתָא דְּמֵיאשָׁן; סוּמְכוֹס, דְּבַר אֶרֶץ יִשְׂרָאֵל, קָארֵי לָהּ דּוּגִית, כְּדִכְתִיב: (עמוס ד) "וְאַחֲרִיתְכֶן בְּסִירוֹת דּוּגָה".§ אָמַר רַבָּה, אִשְׁתַּעוּ לִי נָחוֹתֵי יַמָּא: הַאי גַּלָּא דְּמַטְבַּע לִסְפִינָה, מִיתַחֲזֵי כִּי צוּצִיתָא דְּנוּרָא חִיוָּורְתָּא בְּרֵישָׁא, וּמָחֵינַן לֵיהּ בְּאַלְוָותָא דַּחֲקִיק עֲלֵיהּ "אֶהְיֶה אֲשֶׁר אֶהְיֶה יָהּ ה' צְבָאוֹת אָמֵן אָמֵן סֶלָה", וְנָיֵיח. אָמַר רַבָּה, אִשְׁתַּעוּ לִי נָחוֹתֵי יַמָּא: בֵּין גַּלָּא לְגַלָּא תְּלָת מְאָה פַּרְסֵי, וְרוּמָא דְּגַלָּא תְּלָת מְאָה פַּרְסֵי. זִימְנָא חֲדָא הֲוָה אָזְלִינַן בְּאוֹרְחָא, וְדַלְיַן גַּלָּא עַד דַּחֲזֵינַן בֵּי מַרְבַּעְתֵּיהּ דְּכוֹכְבָא זוּטָא, וַהֲוָיָא לִי כְּמִבְזַר אַרְבְּעִין גְּרִיוֵי בִּזְרָא דְּחַרְדְּלָא, וְאִי דַּלְיַן טְפֵי — הֲוָה מִקְלִינַן מֵהַבְלֵיהּ. וְרָמֵי לָהּ גַּלָּא קָלָא לַחֲבֶרְתָּהּ: חֲבִירְתִּי, שָׁבַקְתְּ מִידֵּי בְּעָלְמָא דְּלָא שְׁטַפְתֵּיהּ, דְּנֵיתֵי אֲנָא (א) וְנַאַבְדֵיהּ? א"ל: פּוּק חֲזִי גְּבוּרְתָּא דְּמָרִיךְ, (ב) מְלֹא חוּטָא חָלָא וְלָא עֲבַרִי, שֶׁנֶּאֱמַר: (ירמיה ה) "הַאוֹתִי לֹא תִירָאוּ נְאֻם ה' אִם מִפָּנַי לֹא תָחִילוּ אֲשֶׁר שַׂמְתִּי חוֹל גְּבוּל לַיָּם חָק עוֹלָם וְלֹא יַעַבְרֶנְהוּ". אָמַר [ו]רַבָּה: לְדִידִי חֲזֵי לִי [ז]הוּרְמִין בַּר לִילִית, כִּי קָא רָהֵיט אַקּוּפְיָא דְּשׁוּרָא דְּמָחוֹזָא, וְרָהֵיט פָּרָשָׁא כִּי רָכֵיב [ח]חֵיוָתָא מִתַּתָּאֵיהּ, וְלָא יָכֵיל לֵיהּ. זִמְנָא חֲדָא הֲוָה מְסָרְגָאן לֵיהּ תַּרְתֵּי כּוּדַנְיָיתֵי וְקַיְימָן אַתְּרֵי

הַמּוֹכֵר אֶת הַסְּפִינָה. סְתָם. **תּוֹרֶן** וְנֵס וְעוֹגִין וְכָל הַמַּנְהִיגִין. בַּגְּמָ' מְפָרְשִׁי. **עֲבָדִים.** שֶׁיֵּשׁ לוֹ לְבַעַל הַסְּפִינָה לְהַנְהִיגָהּ וְלִשְׁמוֹר פְּרַקְמַטְיָא שֶׁלּוֹ שֶׁבְּתוֹכָהּ. **מַרְצוּפִין.** לָתֵת בְּתוֹכָן הָאַנְתִּיקִי, דְּהַיְינוּ פְּרַקְמַטְיָא שֶׁל סְפִינָה, כִּדְמְפָרֵשׁ בַּגְּמָ'. וְכָל הָנֵי נַמִּי לֵיתְנְהוּ בִּכְלַל הֶקְדֵּשׁ, שֶׁאִם הִקְדִּישׁ אֶת הַסְּפִינָה – לֹא הִקְדִּישׁ אֶת אֵלּוּ, מִדְּלָא קָתָנֵי לָהּ בְּפִירְקִין דִּלְעֵיל. וְהַיְינוּ טַעַם, דְּכָל הָנֵי דַּחֲשִׁיבְנָא בְּפִרְקִין דִּלְעֵיל – בֵּית הַמֶּרְחָץ בֵּית הַבַּד וְעִיר וְשָׂדֶה – כּוּלְּהוּ מְקַרְקְעֵי נִינְהוּ, וְכָל הָנֵי דַּחֲשִׁיב לֹא מָכַר בְּטֵלִים קְצָת אַגַּבָּן לְגַבֵּי הֶקְדֵּשׁ וּמַתָּנָה וַחֲלוּקַת אַחִין, אֲבָל הָנֵי דְּהַאי פִּירְקָא – מִטַּלְטְלֵי נִינְהוּ, לָא שְׁנָא מֶכֶר וְלָא שְׁנָא מַתָּנָה וְהֶקְדֵּשׁ – כּוּלָּן שָׁוִין בְּקִנְיָינוּ דְּלֹא מָכַר, שֶׁכְּשֵׁם שֶׁלֹּא מָכַר כְּמוֹ כֵן לֹא הִקְדִּישׁ וְלֹא נָתַן. **גְּמָ' אִסְקַרְיָא.** מס"ט, שֶׁפּוֹרְשִׂין עָלָיו אֶת הַוִּילוֹן בְּרֹאשׁ הַסְּפִינָה. **וְכֵן הוּא אוֹמֵר אֶרֶז מִלְּבָנוֹן כו'.** רְאָיָה לַדָּבָר דְּתוֹרֶן דְּמַתְנִיתִין הַיְינוּ אִסְקַרְיָא. שֶׁהָאִסְקַרְיָא מֵאֶרֶז אוֹ מֵאִילָן גָּבוֹהַּ עוֹשִׂין אוֹתָהּ. **אַדְרָא.** הוּא הַוִּילוֹן שֶׁפּוֹרְסִים עַל הַתּוֹרֶן לְהוֹלִיךְ אֶת הַסְּפִינָה בָּרוּחַ, ווייל"א בְּלַעַ"ז. **וְכֵן הוּא אוֹמֵר.** דְּהַיְינוּ אַדְרָא, שֶׁעָשׂוּי מִפִּשְׁתִּים וְקַנְבּוֹס, מִין בֶּגֶד. **עוֹגִינִין.** אנקר"ש שֶׁל בַּרְזֶל, וּמַשְׁלִיכִין בַּמַּיִם לְהַעֲמִיד הַסְּפִינָה בְּמָקוֹם אֶחָד. **וְכֵן הוּא אוֹמֵר.** דְּעִיגּוּן דְּמַתְנִיתִין לְשׁוֹן עִכּוּב הוּא, כְּדִכְתִיב "הֲלָהֵן תֵּעָגֵנָה" כְּמוֹ תֵּעָגֵנָה, תִּתְעַכְּבוּ מִלְּהִנָּשֵׂא לְבַעַל. אַלְמָא, עוֹגִין דְּמַתְנִי' הַיְינוּ עִיגּוּן. **מְשׁוֹטוֹת.** שֶׁקּוֹרִין רִימ"א, שֶׁמְּשׁוֹטְטִין בָּהֶן אֶת הַסְּפִינָה. **וְכֵן הוּא אוֹמֵר אַלּוֹנִים מִבָּשָׁן עָשׂוּ מְשׁוֹטָיִךְ.** בִּסְפִינָה מַיְירֵי, בִּיחֶזְקֵאל. וְקָחָשִׁיב תַּשְׁמִישֵׁי הַסְּפִינָה וְכֵלֶיהָ, וּמִדְּקָחָשִׁיב הַמְּשׁוֹטוֹת – ש"מ דְּעִיקַּר תַּשְׁמִישֵׁי הַסְּפִינָה הֵן, וְנִמְכָּרִין בִּכְלַל הַסְּפִינָה. וְהִלְכָּךְ אָמְרִי' דְּכָל הַמַּנְהִיגִין דְּמַתְנִי' אָתָא לְרַבּוּיֵינְהוּ. **כָּל תּוֹפְשֵׂי מָשׁוֹט.** אַלְמָא עִיקַּר (ג) הַסְּפִינָה עַל יְדֵי שֶׁתּוֹפְסִין מְשׁוֹטוֹת. דְּסַד"א חֲבָלִים הַמּוֹשְׁכִין הַסְּפִינָה לֶיהֱווּ עִיקַּר מַנְהִיגִין, אֲבָל מְשׁוֹטוֹת לָא מִיזְדַּבְּנֵי, קמ"ל. **אִסְכָּלָה.** כֶּבֶשׁ שֶׁל הַסְּפִינָה שֶׁעוֹלִין בּוֹ, וּלְשׁוֹן יָוָן הוּא. וְכֵן פר"ח וְרַב הַאי. **בּוֹר הַמַּיִם שֶׁבְּתוֹכָהּ.** נוֹתְנִין בּוֹ מַיִם הַמְּתוּקִין, לְפִי שֶׁמֵּי הַיָּם מְלוּחִין. **בִּיצִית וְדוּגִית.** הַיְינוּ סְפִינָה קְטַנָּה שֶׁקּוֹשְׁרִין לִסְפִינָה גְּדוֹלָה, וּכְשֶׁרוֹצִין לַעֲלוֹת לַיַּבָּשָׁה נִכְנָסִין בְּאוֹתָהּ קְטַנָּה מֵהַגְּדוֹלָה. שֶׁהַגְּדוֹלָה אֵינָהּ יְכוֹלָה לְהִתְקָרֵב אֶל שְׂפַת הַיָּם מִפְּנֵי עוּמְקָהּ, קוקיי"ט בְּלַעַ"ז. וְיֵשׁ לוֹעֲזִים בּוּצָא, קָרוֹב לִלְשׁוֹן הָעִבְרִי. **בִּיצְיָיתָא דְּמֵישָׁן.** מֵישָׁן נָהָר קָטָן, וְאֵין מְהַלְּכִין בּוֹ אֶלָּא בִּסְפִינוֹת קְטַנּוֹת, וּבְמַסֶּ' שַׁבָּת אָמְרִי' בְּפֶ' "הַזּוֹרֵק" (דף קא.): הָנֵי בִּילְיָיתָא דְּמֵישָׁן כו'. **רַבִּי נָתָן.** מִבָּבֶל עָלָה. **דּוּגִית.** עַל שֵׁם שֶׁצָּדִין בָּהּ דָּגִים, דְּקַלָּה הִיא עַל פְּנֵי הַמַּיִם. **וְאַחֲרִיתְכֶן בְּסִירוֹת דּוּגָה.** בִּסְפִינוֹת קְטַנּוֹת כִּקְדֵרוֹת הַקְּרוּיוֹת דּוּגָה, וְקַלִּים עַל פְּנֵי מַיִם, יוֹלִיכוּ אֶתְכֶם מְהֵרָה בַּגָּלוּת. **אָמַר רַבָּה אִשְׁתַּעוּ לִי כו'.** כָּל הָנֵי עוּבְדֵי דְּקָא חָשֵׁיב מִשּׁוּם "מָה רַבּוּ מַעֲשֶׂיךָ ה'", (ד) וּמֵהֶן לְהוֹדִיעַ מַתַּן שְׂכָרָן שֶׁל צַדִּיקִים לֶעָתִיד לָבֹא, אוֹ לְפָרֵשׁ מִקְרָאוֹת הָאֲמוּרִים בְּסֵפֶר אִיּוֹב הַמְדַבְּרִים בְּעוֹפוֹת גְּדוֹלִים וּבְהֵמוֹת וְדָגִים גְּדוֹלִים. שֶׁכָּל שִׂיחַת תַּלְמִידֵי חֲכָמִים צְרִיכָה תַּלְמוּד. **דְּמַטְבַּע.** שֶׁרוֹצָה לְטַבְּעָהּ. **אִית לֵיהּ בְּרֵישָׁא.** שֶׁהוֹלֵךְ לְפָנֶיהָ. **צוּצִיתָא דְּנוּרָא חִיוָּרְתָּא.** אֵשׁ לְבָנָה, וּמַלְאָךְ מַזִּיק הוּא. **אַלְוָותָא.** מַקְלוֹת, כְּמוֹ: לֹא בְּקַלָּה וְלֹא בְּרוֹמַח, בְּמַסֶּכֶת שַׁבָּת (דף סג.). **אָמֵן אָמֵן סֶלָה.** גָּרְסִינַן. **וְנָיֵיח.** מִזַּעְפּוֹ. **בֵּין גַּלָּא לְגַלָּא תְּלָתָא מְאָה פַּרְסֵי.** וּמִשּׁוּם דְּקָאָמַר בְּסָמוּךְ: וְרָמְיָא לֵיהּ גַּלָּא קָלָא לַחֲבֶרְיָהּ, אִיצְטְרִיךְ לְאַשְׁמוּעִינַן דְּמִשְּׁלֹשׁ מֵאוֹת פַּרְסֵי (ה) שׁוֹמְעִין קוֹלוֹת לַחֲבֵירוֹ. **דַּלְיַן גַּלָּא.** יוֹתֵר מִשִּׁיעוּר גָּבְהוֹ הִשְׁלִיכוּ לְמַעְלָה, עַד לָרָקִיעַ. אִי נַמִּי, הַגַּלָּא דְּרָקִיעַ נָפִישׁ עַד מַהֲלָךְ קָרוֹב לַחֲמֵשׁ מֵאוֹת שָׁנָה שֶׁיֵּשׁ מִן הָרָקִיעַ עַד לָאָרֶץ. **מַרְבַּעְתֵּיהּ.** (ט) שִׁכְבוֹ. **דְּכוֹכְבָא זוּטָא.** כּוֹכָב קָטָן שֶׁבַּקְּטַנִּים. **בִּזְרָא.** בֵּית זֶרַע אַרְבָּעִים כּוֹר שֶׁל חַרְדָּל, דְּנָפִישׁ מִשֶּׁל שְׁאָר זְרָעִים. **מִקְלִינַן מֵהַבְלֵיהּ.** נִשְׂרָפִים מֵחוֹם כּוֹכָב. **וְרָמְיָא לֵיהּ גַּלָּא.** נָתַן קוֹלוֹ, כְּלוֹמַר צָעַק, כְּדוּגְמַת "תְּהוֹם אֶל תְּהוֹם קוֹרֵא". וְשֶׁמָּא מַלְאָכִים הַמְּמוּנִּים עֲלֵיהֶם הֵם. **שָׁבַקְתְּ מִידֵּי בְּעָלְמָא כו'.** מִפְּנֵי שֶׁהִגְבִּיהַּ כָּל כָּךְ הָיָה סָבוּר שֶׁיָּצָא חוּץ לִשְׂפַת הַיָּם וְשָׁטַף אֶת הָעוֹלָם. **וְנַחֲרְבֵיהּ.** מִפְּנֵי עֲוֹן הַדּוֹר. **א"ל.** גַּלָּא לַחֲבֶרְיָהּ. **פּוּק חֲזִי גְּבוּרְתָּא דְּמָרָךְ כו'.** כְּלוֹמַר אֵין (ו) לִי רְשׁוּת לָצֵאת. **בִּמְלֹא חוּטָא חָלָא.** מְלֹא רוֹחַב חוּט אֵינִי יָכוֹל לָצֵאת מִן הַחוֹל. **שֶׁנֶּאֱמַר הַאוֹתִי וגו'.** גְּמָרָא קָאָמַר לֵיהּ. **הוּרְמִין.** בְּנו"ן גָּרְסִי', כָּךְ שָׁמַעְתִּי מֵאַבָּא מָרִי. וַאֲנִי שָׁמַעְתִּי: "הוּרְמִיז" בְּזַיי"ן = שֵׁד, כִּדְאָמְרִי' בְּסַנְהֶדְרִין (דף לט.): מִפַּלְגָא דְּתַתָּא דְּהוּרְמִיז. **אַקּוּפֵי דְּשׁוּרָא.** עַל שִׁינֵּי הַחוֹמָה. וְהַאי עוּבְדָּא, לְהוֹדִיעַ צִדְקוֹתָיו שֶׁל הקב"ה, שֶׁמְּרַחֵם עַל בְּרִיּוֹתָיו וְאֵינוֹ נוֹתֵן רְשׁוּת לְאֵלּוּ לְהַזִּיקָן, וְגַם שֶׁלֹּא לָצֵאת בַּדֶּרֶךְ יָחִיד. **וְרָהֵיט פָּרָשָׁא.** לְפִי תּוּמּוֹ. **וְלָא יָכֵיל לֵיהּ.** (ז) שֶׁהָיָה הַשֵּׁד רָץ בְּיוֹתֵר. וּמִיהוּ, הַפָּרָשׁ לֹא הָיָה מִתְכַּוֵּין לְכָךְ. **כּוּדְנָ'.** שֶׁהָיָה אוּכָּף וְסַרְגָּא נְתוּנִין עַל הַפְּרָדוֹת.

אַתְּרֵי

הַמּוֹכֵר אֶת הַסְּפִינָה. וְלֹא אֶת הָאַנְתִּיקִי. מִשּׁוּם סֵיפָא דְקָתָנֵי: בִּזְמַן שֶׁאָמַר לוֹ הִיא וְכָל מַה שֶּׁבְּתוֹכָהּ — כּוּלָּן מְכוּרִין, נָקַט לָהּ. אֲבָל מִשּׁוּם רֵישָׁא לָא אִיצְטְרִיךְ, דְּכֵיוָן דְּאַשְׁמוּעִינַן דְּמַרְצוּפִין, דְּכָל שָׁעָה נִשְׁאָרִים בַּסְּפִינָה עַצְמָהּ, לֹא מָכַר — כָּל שֶׁכֵּן סְחוֹרָה עַצְמָהּ.

הָכִי

רבינו גרשום

ונימא באנו למחלוקת ר"ש ורבנן. במתני' וכדאוקימנ' לפלוגתייהו לעיל. מש"ה נקיט דר' מנחם בר' יוסי ורבנן דהא קמ"ל דר' מנחם כר' יוסי כר"ש ס"ל:

הדרן עלך המוכר את הבית

המוכר את הספינה: איסקריא. זהו משוט: נס אדרא. אותו בגד שתולין בראש התורן להוליך הספינה ברוח: ואת העוגין. אלו שקורין אנקר"ש בלע"ז שמעמידין הספינה שלא תזוז לכאן ולכאן: הלהן תעגנה. אמרה להן וכי תעכבו עצמכן מלהנשא לבעל: אלו המשוטות. שלועזין ריימ"ש: משוט. שמשוטטין הספינה לכאן ולכאן: האיסכלה. היינו הכירה שמתקנין בספינה כדי לבשל עליו צרכיהן. ואית דאמרי סולם שיורדין בו מן הספינה: ואת בור המים. שמתקנין שם בספינה כעין בור ומשימין שם מים מתוקין לשתות: ואת הדוגית. היינו ספינה קטנה ומנהיגין אותה לספינה הגדולה וכשרוצין לצאת ליבשה הולכין ובאין באותו ביצית. והיינו ביציתא דמישן. נהרא הוא ששמו מישן קטן הוא ואין יכולין לבוא בנהר כי אם בהני בוציאתא: ואחריתכן בסירות דוגה. כך הנביא אמר לישראל סוף שיוליכו אתכם בשבי באותן ספינות קטנות: גלא. גל של ים: כי צוציתא דנורא חיוורתא. כמו ציצית הראש: אלוותא. מקלות: עד דחזינן לבי מרבעתא דכוכבא. שהיינו רואין בית רביצת הכוכב ויהי מקומו כשיעור שיכולין לזרוע בו מ' מדות של חרדל: ואי דלינן טפי. האי גלא הוי מקלינן מהבלא דההוא כוכב. וג"ם תמ"ה המור"ה וכמה הולכת הבלא דכוכבא. דמבדי קים לן כמה מהלך אדם בינוני ביום י' פרסאות נמצא מהלך תלת מאה פרסי ההיינו מהלך ל' יום וקתני הכא ואי דלינן טפי כלומר מעט יותר נמצא דהאי הבלא מהלך חמש מאות שנה פחות ל' יום שיעור תלת מאה פרסי דהלי הני לעיל דהא מן הארץ ועד לרקיע מהלך חמש מאות שנה אבל בין ארעא לעובא ליכא אלא תלת פרס: שבקת מידי בעלמא דלא אחריבת. לפי שראה אותו מגביה על כך נדמה לו לגל שפנימי לו כי זה הרצון היה שוטף כל העולם: אמר ליה החוצין תא חזי גבורתא. כאומר אל תחשוב בדעתך שאוכל אני להגביה עצמי כלום יותר משיעורי שאפי' כמלא חוט השערה איני רשאי עבור חוץ מן החול שלי חוץ מתחומי: הורמין בר לילתא. אותו שד: אקופיא דשורא. על שיני החומה: ולא יכיל. פרשא למימטייה לההוא שד: מסרגאן ליה. שמו לו שני אוכפין על שתי פרדות:

א א מיי' פכ"ו מהל' מכירה הל' ח סמג עשין פב טוש"ע ח"מ סי' רכ סעיף ח:

הגהות הב"ח

תלמוד בבלי

הוצאת קורן ירושלים

— מהדורת נאה —

מסכת בבא בתרא

דף סא. עד דף עג.

COMMENTARY BY

Rabbi Adin Even-Israel Steinsaltz

EDITOR-IN-CHIEF

Rabbi Dr Tzvi Hersh Weinreb

EXECUTIVE EDITOR

Rabbi Joshua Schreier

•

STEINSALTZ CENTER
KOREN PUBLISHERS JERUSALEM

Please note that the number ranges that appear at the bottom of each daf of the Vilna pages indicate the corresponding pages of the Koren Talmud Bavli translation and commentary.

תלמוד בבלי

— מהדורת נאה —

בבא בתרא חלק ג

Steinsaltz Center

ירושלים

KOREN